D0224444

New Venture Creation

ENTREPRENEURSHIP FOR THE 21st CENTURY

TENTH EDITION

New Venture Creation

ENTREPRENEURSHIP FOR THE 21st CENTURY

Stephen Spinelli, Jr., BA, MBA, PhD
President
Philadelphia University
Philadelphia, Pennsylvania

Robert J. Adams, Jr., BS, MBA, PhD
Director of Venture Labs, IC^2 Fellow, Senior Lecturer
The University of Texas at Austin
Austin, Texas

NEW VENTURE CREATION: ENTREPRENEURSHIP FOR THE 21st CENTURY, TENTH EDITION

Published by McGraw-Hill Education, 2 Penn Plaza, New York, NY 10121. Copyright © 2016 by McGraw-Hill Education. All rights reserved. Printed in the United States of America. Previous editions © 2012, 2009, and 2007. No part of this publication may be reproduced or distributed in any form or by any means, or stored in a database or retrieval system, without the prior written consent of McGraw-Hill Education, including, but not limited to, in any network or other electronic storage or transmission, or broadcast for distance learning.

Some ancillaries, including electronic and print components, may not be available to customers outside the United States.

This book is printed on acid-free paper.

3 4 5 6 7 8 QVS/QVS 21 20 19 18 17

ISBN 978-0-07-786248-0
MHID 0-07-786248-1

Senior Vice President, Products & Markets: *Kurt L. Strand*
Vice President, General Manager, Products & Markets: *Michael Ryan*
Vice President, Content Design & Delivery: *Kimberly Meriwether David*
Director: *Michael Ablassmeir*
Director, Product Development: *Meghan Campbell*
Product Developer: *Kelly Pekelder*
Marketing Manager: *Michael Gedatus*
Director of Development: *Ann Torbert*
Digital Product Analyst: *Kerry Shannahan*
Director, Content Design & Delivery: *Terri Schiesl*
Content Project Manager: *Lisa Bruflodt*
Buyer: *Laura M. Fuller*
Content Licensing Specialists: *Leonard Behnke*
Cover Image: *Glenn Coombridge/Getty Images*
Compositor: *Aptara®, Inc.*
Printer: *Quad/Graphics*

All credits appearing on page or at the end of the book are considered to be an extension of the copyright page.

Library of Congress Control Number

2014958004

The Internet addresses listed in the text were accurate at the time of publication. The inclusion of a website does not indicate an endorsement by the authors or McGraw-Hill Education, and McGraw-Hill Education does not guarantee the accuracy of the information presented at these sites.

DEDICATION

Jeff Timmons—Professor, Scholar, Mentor, Friend

Jeff Timmons is the original author of this textbook. He passed away a few years ago, just after completing the final edits on the eighth edition. His presence remains a powerful influence in this edition.

Jeff's commitment to higher education and to entrepreneurship was a statement of his belief in humanity. He believed goodness and achievement were inherent in everyone. And he believed that entrepreneurship classes were a perfect vehicle to refine and amplify purposeful study and action that would lead to a better life and a better world.

Always striving for the betterment of the human condition, Jeff's contributions to entrepreneurship in the classroom and in practice changed the playing field. He embraced both the academic and the entrepreneur and made both better through collaboration. Thousands of students and teachers have been affected by his work and the world continues to be a better place because of him.

ABOUT THE AUTHORS

Jeffry A. Timmons (December 7, 1941–April 8, 2008): **In Memoriam**

Director, Price-Babson College Fellows Program at Babson College; AB, Colgate University; MBA, DBA, Harvard University Graduate School of Business

Success magazine (September 1995), in a feature article, called him "one of the two most powerful minds in entrepreneurship in the nation." Michie P. Slaughter, former president of the Kauffman Center for Entrepreneurial Leadership at the Ewing Marion Kauffman Foundation, calls him "the premier entrepreneurship educator in America." In 2007, *Forbes Small Business* called Dr. Timmons one of the country's best entrepreneurship educators.

In 1985, he designed and launched the Price-Babson College Symposium for Entrepreneurship Educators (SEE), aimed at improving teaching and research by teaming highly successful entrepreneurs with "an itch to teach" with experienced faculty. This unique initiative was in response to a need to create a mechanism enabling colleges and universities to attract and support entrepreneurship educators and entrepreneurs and help them create lasting collaborations that would enhance the classroom experience for their students. There is now a core group of over 2,000 entrepreneurship educators and entrepreneurs from over 350 colleges and universities in the United States and 38 foreign countries who are alumni of the Price-Babson College Fellows Program. *INC.* magazine's "Who's Who" special edition on entrepreneurship called Jeff Timmons "the Johnny Appleseed of entrepreneurship education" and concluded that this program had "changed the terrain of entrepreneurship education."

In 2003 Dr. Timmons worked with Professor Steve Spinelli to conceive a sister program to the SEE program which would be available for engineering schools with an interest in entrepreneurship. They partnered with colleagues at the new Olin College of Engineering on the Babson campus, President Rick Miller, Provost David Kerns, Dean Michael Moody and Professors John Bourne, Ben Linder, Heidi Neck, and Stephen Schiffman to win a 3-year National Science Foundation grant to design, develop, and deliver such a program.

During the past decades, Dr. Timmons helped launch several new initiatives including the Babson-Kauffman Entrepreneurship Research Conference, the Kauffman Foundation/CEL Challenge Grant, the Price Challenge Grant, business plan competitions, and a president's seminar. He provided leadership in developing and teaching in initiatives that assist Native Americans seeking economic self-determination and community development, most notably through, entrepreneurship education programs at the nation's several Tribal Colleges. In April 2001, Professor Timmons was recognized for these efforts in a citation voted by the legislature of the State of Oklahoma naming him Ambassador for Entrepreneurship.

A prolific researcher and writer, he wrote nine books, including this textbook first published in 1974. *New Venture Creation* has been rated by *INC.*, *Success*, and *The Wall Street Journal* as a "classic" in entrepreneurship, and has been translated into Japanese, Portuguese, and Chinese.

Stephen Spinelli, Jr.

President, Philadelphia University

The majority of Dr. Spinelli's professional experience has been in entrepreneurship. He was a founding shareholder, director, and executive of Jiffy Lube International. He was also founder, chairman, and CEO of American Oil Change Corporation. In 1991, he completed a sale of Jiffy Lube to Pennzoil Company. Dr. Spinelli has led the Entrepreneurship Division at Babson and taught full-time. He has not

abandoned his business roots. He continues to consult with regional, national, and international companies; serves as a Director at several corporations; and participates as an angel investor with investments in more than a dozen startups.

Dr. Spinelli is the quintessential "pracademic"–a business practitioner turned academic. Having successfully harvested Jiffy Lube, Dr. Spinelli enrolled in the Imperial College of Science Technology and Medicine (London, UK), receiving his PhD in Economics in 1995. Dr. Spinelli's expertise is in startup and growth management. His research has focused on an understanding of strategic entrepreneurial relationships. He is the author of more than two dozen journal articles, book chapters, academic papers, and teaching case studies. He is also the author of seven books including *Franchising: Pathway to Entrepreneurship* (Prentice-Hall, 2003). His latest book, *Disrupt Together: How Teams Consistently Innovate* (co-edited with Heather McGowan) was on Amazon's "Hottest New Releases" list in December 2013. A superb educator, he served as a key member of the faculty of the Price-Babson College Fellows Program's Symposium for Entrepreneurship Educators (SEE) for 12 years, in addition to his teaching in the undergraduate, graduate, and executive education programs. In 2007 Forbes named him one of USA's best entrepreneurship professors. Dr. Spinelli is a shining example of the many contributions that entrepreneurs can make to an academic institution. He has led the internationalization of SEE to Chile, Argentina, Costa Rica, China, and Europe. In 2003 Dr. Spinelli founded the Babson Historically Black Colleges and Universities case writing consortium. This group is dedicated to writing entrepreneurship teaching cases focused on African American entrepreneurs.

He has been a leading force in curriculum innovation at Babson and, with his colleagues in Entrepreneurship Division, continually defines and delivers new initiatives. In 1999, he led the design and implementation of an Entrepreneurship Intensity Track for MBAs seeking to launch new business ventures upon graduation. Building on this highly successful initiative, he led the design and development of ACE—an accelerated honors curriculum for aspiring entrepreneurs in Babson's undergraduate program. Dr. Spinelli's presentation to the United States Association for Small Business and Entrepreneurship (USASBE) resulted in the naming of the F.W. Olin Graduate School of Business as the 2002 National Model MBA program.

As Philadelphia University's President since 2007, DR. Spinelli led the transformation of the University around the theme of innovation. In 2010 Philadelphia University's new Design, Engineering, and Commerce transdisciplinary curriculum won the Core77 award for the most innovative new curriculum in the United States.

Dr. Spinelli has been a strong voice for entrepreneurship. He has been a keynote speaker for Advent International's CEO Conference, the MCAA National Convention and Allied Domecq International's Retailing Conference, the Entrepreneur's Organization at MIT and many others; he has been called to testify before the US Senate Subcommittee on Small Business and Entrepreneurship. He is often quoted as an expert in the field in such leading publications as *The Wall Street Journal, Forbes, The Financial Times, Success* magazine, and INC. He also serves as a director for several regional and national not-for-profits and community-based associations.

President Stephen Spinelli was touted as a new model of college president in a front page story on May 17, 2008, in the *Philadelphia Inquirer*. He calls Philadelphia University a 126-year-old startup, a university with the entrepreneurial zeal that drives an innovative curriculum and applied research.

Robert J. Adams, Jr.

Rob Adams is on the faculty of The University of Texas at Austin where he teaches entrepreneurship in the MBA and MSTC programs and is the Director of Texas Venture Labs. He is a former software executive, entrepreneur, and institutional fund manager. He has served on many corporate boards and has founded or financed more than 40 companies, which have launched more than 100 products and raised significant amounts of capital in both private and public markets.

Prior to his appointment at The University of Texas, he was in the venture capital industry, ultimately founding AV Labs, a fund affiliated with Austin Ventures. Prior to the venture business, he was a software operating executive for two decades. This career included positions in sales, marketing, and general management. He was with Lotus (NYSE: IBM), joining the company shortly after its public offering. Adams was their first corporate sales representative and went on to be instrumental in the development and launch of both 1-2-3 for Macintosh and Lotus Notes. He founded and was CEO of Business Matters, a venture backed developer of financial modeling products that was acquired. He was an executive with Pervasive Software (NASDAQ: PVSW), a company he helped take public.

Dr. Adams holds a Bachelor of Science degree in Industrial Engineering from Purdue University, where he received their Outstanding Engineer Award, a Masters of Business Administration from Babson College's Olin School of Management, and a PhD in Management from Capella University. He has taught in the MBA programs of The Acton

School of Business, Babson College, and The University of Texas at Austin and is the recipient of numerous teaching awards.

He is an internationally recognized speaker on innovation, commercialization, and entrepreneurship. He speaks frequently on his pioneering work in Market Validation and has keynoted the *Inc. 500* business conference, international venture conferences, and consults for numerous global 500 companies. His work has been covered in *Business Week, Forbes, Fortune, Money, The New York Times, The Wall Street Journal, Washington Post,* on Bloomberg Radio, Public Television and public radio's nationally syndicated "Marketplace" program.

He is the author of *A Good Hard Kick in the Ass: Basic Training for Entrepreneurs* (Random House/Crown, 2002), and *If You Build It Will They Come? Three Steps to Test and Validate Any Market Opportunity* (Wiley, 2010).

He provides expert testimony on technology related business issues and has consulted on economic development and early stage company investment and its impact on economies for governments including Canada, Chile, Costa Rica, India, Malaysia, New Zealand and Thailand. In the United States he has advised the White House and the Department of Commerce.

Adams is a Fellow at the IC^2 Institute; a University of Texas based foundation that runs the Austin Technology Incubator and has held visiting professor positions at the University of Auckland, Thammasat University and the University of Manitoba. He is an avid downhill skier and runner and lives in Austin, Texas.

PREFACE

A Book for a New Generation of Entrepreneurial Leaders—Worldwide

The entrepreneurship revolution in America over the past 50 years has had an extraordinary impact on the cultural and economic landscape in the United States. While there will always be opportunities for improvement and innovation, America's opportunity-driven style of entrepreneurship has sparked an entrepreneurial revolution around the globe.

Technology has certainly played a major role in this global phenomenon. In 2001 there were almost 500 million Internet users; in 2007 that number more than doubled to 1.1 billion. Four years later Internet users in the world total over 2 billion. In the United States an iPod is sold *every 8 seconds*. Entrepreneurship and the Internet continue to flatten the world at a staggering pace, spawning fertile fields of opportunities.

In our roles as students, teachers, researchers, observers, and participants in this stunning revolution, we see that global adoption of the entrepreneurial mind-set is growing exponentially. That new venture mind-set, which increasingly places a premium on sustainable models, is now affecting strategies at global corporations and in the not-for-profit world as well. The golden age of entrepreneurial reasoning, value creation and capture, and philanthropy has arrived.

An Edition for an Era of Uncertainty and Extraordinary Opportunity

The new millennium is being defined as much by worldwide challenges and uncertainty as it is by the enormous opportunities afforded by technology, global communications, and the increasing drive to develop socially, economically, and environmentally sane and sensible new ventures. As with past generations, entrepreneurs in this arena face the ultimate and most demanding juggling act: how to simultaneously balance the insatiable requirements of marriage, family, community, and new ventures.

A Book about the Entrepreneurial Process: The Basis for a Curriculum as Well as a Course!

New Venture Creation is about the actual process of getting a new venture started, growing the venture, successfully harvesting it, and starting again.

There is a substantial body of knowledge, concepts, and tools that entrepreneurs need to know—before, during, and after taking the startup plunge—if they are to get the odds in their favor. Accompanying the explosion in entrepreneurship has been a significant increase in research and knowledge about the entrepreneurial process. Much of what was known previously has been reinforced and refined, whereas some traditional knowledge has been challenged. Numerous new insights have emerged. *New Venture Creation* continues to be the product of experience and considerable research in this field—rooted in real-world application and refined in the classroom.

The design and flow of this book are aimed at creating knowledge, skills, and awareness. In a pragmatic way—through text, case studies, and hands-on exercises—students are drawn in to discover critical aspects of entrepreneurship, and what levels of competencies, know-how, experience, attitudes, resources, and networks are required to pursue different entrepreneurial opportunities. There is no substitute for the real thing–actually starting a company. But short of that, it is possible to expose students to many of the vital issues and immerse them in key learning experiences, such as critical self-assessment and the development of a business plan.

The exciting news is that you can learn from other people's experiences, know-how, and wisdom; you do not have to learn it all by doing it yourself. By fully engaging the material in this book–the required analysis, thinking, and practice with the cases, exercises, assignments, and discussions both in and out of the classroom–you can significantly compress your learning curve, reduce your ultimate risk and pain, and gain a lot more from your subsequent hands-on experiences.

This book is divided into five parts. Parts I through IV detail the driving forces of entrepreneurship: opportunity recognition, the business plan, the founder and the team, and resource requirements. Part I describes the global entrepreneurial revolution and addresses the mind-set required to tackle this tremendously challenging and rewarding pursuit. Part II lays out the process by which real opportunities–not just ideas–can be discovered and selected. The chapters in Part II examine the type of opportunity around which higher-potential ventures can be built (with acceptable risks and trade-offs), sustainable enterprising, and opportunities for social entrepreneurship. Part III concerns entrepreneurial leadership, team creation, and personal ethics. Part IV addresses franchising as an entrepreneurial vehicle, marshalling resources, entrepreneurial finance, and fund-raising. In Part V, the book concludes with a discussion of strategies for success, managing rapid growth, and harvest issues.

Once you understand how winning entrepreneurs think, act, and perform, you can establish goals to emulate those actions, attitudes, habits, and strategies. The book addresses practical issues such as the following:

> What are my real talents, strengths, and weaknesses? How can I exploit my talents and strengths and minimize my weaknesses? How can I recognize when an opportunity is more than just another good idea, and whether it is one that fits with my personal mind-set, capabilities, and life goals? Why do some firms grow quickly to several million dollars in sales but then stumble, never growing beyond a single product? What are the critical tasks and hurdles in seizing an opportunity and building the business? How much money do I need, and when, where, and how can I get it on acceptable terms? What financing sources, strategies, and

mechanisms can I bring to bear throughout the process–from pre-start, through the early growth stage, to the harvest of my venture?

What are the minimum resources I need to gain control over the opportunity, and how can I do this? Is a business plan needed? If so, what kind is required, and how and when should I develop one? For what constituents must I create or add value to achieve a positive cash flow and to develop harvest options? What is my venture worth, and how do I negotiate what to give up? What are the critical transitions in entrepreneurial management as a firm grows from $1 million, to $5 million, to over $25 million in sales?

What are some of the pitfalls, minefields, and hazards I need to anticipate, prepare for, and respond to? What contacts and networks do I need to access and develop?

Do I know what I do and do not know, and do I know what to do about this? How can I develop a personal entrepreneurial game plan to acquire the experience I need to succeed? How critical and sensitive is the timing in each of these areas? Why do entrepreneurship and entrepreneurial leadership seem surrounded by paradoxes, well-known to entrepreneurs, such as these:

- Ambiguity and uncertainty versus planning and rigor.
- Creativity versus disciplined analysis.
- Patience and perseverance versus urgency.
- Organization and management versus flexibility.
- Innovation and responsiveness versus systemization.
- Risk avoidance versus risk management.
- Current profits versus long-term equity.

The *New Venture Creation* models are useful not only as a comprehensive textbook for a course in entrepreneurship, but also as a road map for a curriculum or departmental major in entrepreneurship.

The Tenth Edition: An Additional Offer, New Data, and More Succinct Presentation

This new edition of *New Venture Creation* is a significant update from the ninth edition. Rob Adams continues from the last edition as a co-author.

Professor Adams is another classic "pracademic" but with a twist. After being a successful entrepreneur Rob became a successful venture investor before becoming a professor. He continues to balance his life through involvement in the practice, finance, and teaching of entrepreneurship. He has also brought special attention to the impact and exploitation of technology in entrepreneurship.

A special effort has been made to include cases that capture the dynamic ups and downs new firms experience over an extended time. By grappling with decisions faced by entrepreneurs–from startup to harvest–this text offers a broad and rich perspective on the often turbulent and unpredictable nature of the entrepreneurial process.

We have continued to edit for conciseness in this new edition, continuing to streamline your reading experience and reducing the total volume of the text by another 20 percent since the last edition. This improves the flow of the discussion, which now has a greater emphasis on the practical application of entrepreneurship.

The new tenth edition of *New Venture Creation* contains the latest updates, including examples of entrepreneurs in action coping with the post-Internet bubble era, the mortgage loan crisis of 2007, and the recession of 2008.

We have also added resources to the publishers' website for this text. This includes additional cases and a concise Venture Opportunity Quick Screen in Excel form. We have found students use this more readily than paper and pencil. They tend to iterate and share among their team more dynamically.

As we head into the second decade of the 21st century, entrepreneurship has established itself as a form of strategy for companies of all sizes competing in the global economy. We are confident that a study of *New Venture Creation* will help you in your pursuit of success as a student, as an entrepreneur, and as a player on the stage of worldwide commerce!

Stephen Spinelli, Jr.
e-mail: SpinelliS@PhilaU.edu
website: www.philau.edu

Robert J. Adams, Jr.
e-mail: rob.adams@mccombs.utexas.edu
website: www.drrobadams.com

BRIEF CONTENTS

TABLE OF CONTENTS

PART II

The Opportunity 75

I

The Founder

At the heart of the entrepreneurial process is the founder: the energy, the soul, and the driving force behind the start-up. The founder is the passion behind finding an innovative solution to a compelling market problem.

So what does an entrepreneur need to know to beat the odds and be successful? What pattern recognition can we garner from successful endeavors to improve the odds of success? This tenth edition focuses on you—the entrepreneur. We will examine the mind-sets, attitudes, and habits that lead to entrepreneurial success and failure.

It is impossible develop a rout checklist to build a successful company or discern the attributes of an entrepreneur. In this book we will examine how successful entrepreneurs think, feel, respond, and use these attributes as pattern recognition for successful entrepreneurs and companies.

Take, for example, Rick Adam, who by the late 1990s had made his fortune as a software entrepreneur. He had also spotted a compelling opportunity in the general aviation industry. As an avid pilot, Adam knew firsthand how few new aircraft designs were available—at any price. The reason was that the cost to design, engineer, and bring to market an FAA-certified general aviation product was estimated by industry veterans to be in the neighborhood of $250 million and a time frame of 10 years. Despite having no previous experience in manufacturing, Adam put up tens of millions of his own money to start up Adam Aircraft. Using sophisticated model fabrication technology, and by applying design and engineering practices Adam had mastered in software development, his company spent under $60 million to develop the A-500—a sleek, pressurized twin-engine design that achieved FAA certification in just 5 years. Their A-700 prototype—a personal jet that utilized the same airframe structure—was flying for another $20 million. By the fall of 2007, the A-700 was nearing FAA certification, and the company was reporting an order backlog for the jet of just under $800 million. Rick Adam commented on the endeavor:

> I've done a lot of entrepreneurial things, and when you think there is a big opportunity, you look at it thoughtfully and you say, well, if this is such a big opportunity, why isn't anybody taking it? What do I know, or what do I see that nobody else is seeing? So, very often, entrepreneurial opportunities occur because a series of events come together—particularly with technology—and you suddenly

have all the ingredients you need to be successful at something that just moments ago was impossible. Then, assuming you are a good business person and a good executer, you can get there if you focus, and keep at it.

It makes a lot of sense for entrepreneurs to pay particular attention to picking partners, key business associates, and managers with an eye for complementing the entrepreneurs' own weaknesses and strengths and the needs of the venture. As will be seen, they seek people who fit. Not only can an entrepreneur's weakness be an Achilles' heel for new ventures, but also the whole is almost always greater than the sum of its parts.

Finally, ethics are terribly important in entrepreneurship. In highly unpredictable and fragile situations, ethical issues cannot be handled according to such simplistic notions as "always tell the truth." It is critical that an entrepreneur understand, develop, and implement an effective integrity strategy for the business.

Chapter One

The Global Entrepreneurial Revolution for a Flatter World

LEARNING OUTCOMES: After reading this chapter you will be able to understand:

I-I The company founder, their role and examples

I-2 The global entrepreneurial revolution

I-3 Nobel Prizes in entrepreneurship

I-4 Entrepreneurship's effect on management, education, not-for-profit and philanthropy paradigms

I-5 How innovation and entrepreneurship leads to prosperity and philanthropy

I-6 Entrepreneurial job creation and the impact on economies

I-7 New venture formation

I-8 Famous young entrepreneurs

I-9 Formation of new industries

I-10 The role of innovation

I-11 Venture and growth capital

I-12 Philanthropy and entrepreneurship

I-13 Self-made millionaires

I-14 Private equity

I-15 Building an entrepreneurial society

I-16 The equal opportunities, economic and social mobility created by entrepreneurship

Entrepreneurship Flattens the World

In 2011 there were 2.1 billion Internet users in the world and only 13 percent of the total was in the United States.[1] In the United States an iPod was sold every 8 seconds. Entrepreneurship and the Internet continue to flatten the world at a staggering pace and in the process are spawning fertile fields of opportunities that are being tilled and seized on every continent. How is this global revolution manifesting itself?

For starters, Exhibit 1.1 shows just how far international Web entrepreneurs have penetrated the world. This remarkable array of 39 Web clone knockoffs of leading Web sites represents just a tiny tip of the worldwide iceberg. While the Internet alone is reshaping the world in staggering ways, the spread of global entrepreneurship reaches far beyond. Consider, for example:

- In 2010, immigrants working in the United States sent over $50 billion back to their families.[2] Sahara House Care, a firm in India, has tapped into that market by providing 60 products and services immigrants can buy for their families. These include such services as delivering flowers, finding buyers for real estate, offering exhaustive online catalogs of just about anything, and even accompanying loved ones to a hospital.

- Consider a new supersize RV built on an 18-wheeler chassis turned into a mobile hotel facility that can accommodate as many as 44 people. A 36-year-old Spaniard, Fernando Saenz de Tejada, has created Hotelmovil. The first five units will roll out of a factory in Italy and will sell for $500,000 a unit or rent for $8,000 per week.

- In Norway, entrepreneur Jan-Olaf Willums, already wealthy from his investment in REC, a solar energy company, is leading the development of a Web-enabled, carbon-free electric car he calls Think. He has teamed with Segway creator Dean Kamen, Google founders Larry Page and Sergey Brin, and Silicon Valley and European investors to raise $78 million. His

---

[1] http://www.internetworldstats.com/stats.htm.
[2] http://www.internetworldstats.com/stats.htm/01/payback-time/.

EXHIBIT I.I

Send in the Clones

	digg	Facebook	LinkedIn	YouTube
Brazil	Linkk *linkk.com.br*	—	—	Videolog *videolog.uol.com.br*
China	Verydig *verydig.com*	Xiaoneiwang *xiaonei.com*	Wealink *wealink.com*	56.com *56.com*
France	Scoopeo *scoopeo.com*	Skyrock *skyrock.com*	Viadeo *viadeo.com*	Dailymotion *dailymotion.com*
Germany	Yigg *yigg.de*	StudiVZ *Studivz.net*	Xing *xing.com*	MyVideo *myvideo.de*
India	Best of Indya *bestofindya.com*	Minglebox *minglebox.com*	Rediff Connexions *connexions.rediff.com*	Rajshri *rajshri.com*
Israel	Hadash Hot *hadash-hot.co.il*	Mekusharim *mekusharim.co.il*	Hook *hook.co.il*	Flix *flix.co.il*
Mexico	Enchilame *enchilame.com*	Vostu *vostu.com*	InfoJobs *infoJobs.com.mx*	BuscaTube *buscatube.com*
Netherlands	eKudos *ekudos.nl*	Hyves *hyves.net*	—	Skoeps *skoeps.nl*
Russia	News2 *news2.ru*	V Kontakte *vkontakte.ru*	MoiKrug *moiKrug.ru*	Rutube *rutube.ru*
South Africa	Muti *muti.co.za*	—	—	MyVideo *myvideo.co.za*
Turkey	Nooluyo *nooluyo.com*	Qiraz *qiraz.com*	Cember *cember.net*	Resim ve Video *resimvideo.org*

Source: *Business 2.0.* ©2007 Time Inc. All rights reserved.

vision: Upend the century-old fossil fuel–based automotive paradigm by changing how cars are made, sold, owned, and driven.

- "Anything seems possible in Rwanda," asserts former San Francisco resident Josh Ruxin, who, with his wife Alissa, has invested life savings of $100,000 to build the Heaven Café in the capital city of Kigali. The African nation of 8 million–ravaged by the genocide of 1 million people in 1994–is now attracting foreign entrepreneurs in tourism, telecom, mining, farming, and real estate.

- Everyone is now aware of just how dynamic and entrepreneurial the Chinese economy has become in recent years. Consider the following examples of explosive growth. In 2004 the authors of this text wrote, "Computer usage increased from 2.1 million in 1999 to 68 million in 2004–a 34-fold increase!" Seven years later we can report usage is nearing 1 billion.[3] According to Volkswagen, Chinese automotive production in 2003 was 4.44 million and grew to over 13 million by 2010. From 1998 to 2004, mobile phones exploded from around 10 million to over 350 million. In 2011 there are almost 900 million mobile phones in China.

Two Nobel Prizes Recognize Entrepreneurship

The front page of *The Wall Street Journal* on October 10, 2006, had the following headline: "The New Nobel Prize Winner Makes a Case for Entrepreneurship." The accompanying article by Professor Edmund S. Phelps of Columbia University, New York, the prize recipient, was full of wonderful commentary and arguments for entrepreneurship. The awarding of this prize in economics to Professor Phelps is the most important academic recognition of the field and subject in our lifetime.

The ink was barely dry on this announcement when the Nobel Peace Prize was announced for another economist championing microenterprise. Farid Hossain of the Associated Press wrote the story in the Manchester, New Hampshire, *Union Leader* on October 14, 2006: "A simple yet revolutionary idea–in the form of a $90 loan–changed her life, putting the Bangladeshi villager out of a devastating cycle of poverty. Yesterday, that idea–lending tiny sums to poor people looking to escape poverty by starting a business–won the Nobel Peace Prize for economist Muhammad Yunus and the Grameen Bank he founded."

[3]http://www.washingtontimes.com/news/2009/jul/01/payback-time.html; http://www.inc.com/news/articles/200707/computers.html.

In just 4 days these two Nobel Prizes changed forever the academic and practical significance of entrepreneurship as a fertile ground for education and research. This should stimulate even more and wider interest in entrepreneurship as a field of study and research.

A Macro Phenomenon

The work of Phelps and Yunus, along with our earlier examples, illustrates how dynamic entrepreneurs and their firms are altering the landscape of global business. In his contribution to the Praeger Perspectives series, *Going Global*, Pat Dickson reviews research that shows just how prevalent this global phenomenon is. Eighty percent of all small- to medium-sized enterprises are affected by or involved with international trade, and advances in technology, manufacturing, and logistics have created opportunities where firms of all sizes can compete internationally. Dickson notes that this view of an emerging world market accessible to even the most resource-constrained and remote nations and organizations is described by Thomas Friedman in *The World Is Flat*, which traces the convergence of technology and world events and its role in bringing about significant changes in traditional value chains.

America's entrepreneurial revolution has become a model for business people, educators, and policy makers around the globe. For example, as part of a goal to "make the EU the most competitive economy," an action plan was derived with the following broad objectives:

1. Fueling entrepreneurial mind-sets.
2. Encouraging more people to become entrepreneurs.
3. Gearing entrepreneurs for growth and competitiveness.
4. Improving the flow of finance.
5. Creating a more entrepreneurial-friendly regulatory and administrative framework.

These goals mirror the factors that have been critical in advancing entrepreneurship in the United States. An EU commission followed up on these goals with recommendations for fostering entrepreneurial mind-sets through school education. These too reflect the American experience:

- Introduce entrepreneurship into the national (or regional) curriculum at all levels of formal education (from primary school to university), either as a horizontal aspect or as a specific topic.
- Train and motivate teachers to engage in entrepreneurial education.
- Promote the application of programs based on "learning by doing," such as by means of project work, virtual firms, and minicompanies.
- Involve entrepreneurs and local companies in the design and running of entrepreneurship courses and activities.
- Increase the teaching of entrepreneurship within higher education outside economic and business courses, notably at scientific and technical universities, and place emphasis on setting up companies in the curricula of business-type studies at universities.

Four Entrepreneurial Transformations That Are Changing the World

Evidence and trends point to at least four entrepreneurial transformations that profoundly impact how the world lives, works, learns, and enjoys leisure. Consider the following:

1. Entrepreneurship is the new management paradigm: Entrepreneurial thinking and reasoning—so common in dynamic, higher-potential, and robust new and emerging firms—are now becoming infused and embedded into the strategies and practices of corporate America.
2. Entrepreneurship has spawned a new education paradigm for learning and teaching.
3. Entrepreneurship is becoming a dominant management model for running nonprofit businesses and in the emerging field of social ventures.
4. Entrepreneurship is rapidly transcending business schools: Engineering, life sciences, architecture, medicine, music, liberal arts, and K-12 are new academic grounds that are exploring and embracing entrepreneurship in their curricula.

Entrepreneurship as the New Management Paradigm

Virtually every management model in vogue today can find its roots in great entrepreneurial companies and organizations founded within the past 40 years. Progressive researchers of new and different ways of conceptualizing and practicing management found those dynamic and creative founders and leaders at new ventures and at high-growth businesses—and rarely at large, established firms.

Nevertheless, virtually all research and case development until the 1970s dwelled on large companies; new and smaller ventures were mostly ignored. New research is uncovering refreshing, at times radically different, modes: flat organizations, innovation, comfort with change, chaos, team-driven efforts, significant performance-based equity incentives, and consensual decision making. Researchers also found cultures and value systems where people, integrity, honesty and ethics, a sense of responsibility to one's environment and community, and fair play were common. Much of what is sought after and emulated by companies trying to reinvent themselves and to compete globally today embodies many of these principles, characteristics, and concepts of entrepreneurship.

Business schools are including more topics and issues relating to entrepreneurship including new start-up focus for traditional accounting, finance, marketing, and information technology courses. As a unit of analysis, few things are more exciting to study than the birth, growth, and adaptation of new companies and the complex issues they face as they grow.

Entrepreneurship as a New Education Paradigm

Entrepreneurship programs have quickly become successful, attracting large enrollments, fueled by the use of seasoned entrepreneurs in the classroom. These are highly successful founders and builders of companies with a real itch and talent for teaching. Students have raved about their exciting classes and quality of teaching.

Transformation of What and How Business Leaders Learn

Entrepreneurship education has created a new teaching paradigm that can transform what and how students learn. The fundamental philosophies and beliefs about learning and teaching, attitudes toward teachers and views of the role of the student versus instructor all differ radically from traditional academic approaches.

Some prime examples are worth noting. For one thing, most entrepreneurship educators are not faculty centric; they are student and opportunity centric. They do not believe that expertise, wisdom, and knowledge are housed solely in the faculty brain, or in the library, or accessed through Google.

They reject the traditional lecture model: Students sit with pens ready, open craniums, pour in facts, memorize facts, regurgitate facts to achieve top grades, and begin again. Rather, there is a more student-centered, work-in-progress philosophy that is more hands-on and treats the learning process as not occurring solely in the classroom but as more of an apprenticeship, much like the medical model of "see one–do one–teach one." Entrepreneurship faculties are more likely to see their role as mentors, coaches, and advocates for students. We are notoriously inaccurate in predicting who will be the next Bill Gates, Steve Jobs, or Tom Stemberg, so we do not even try. It is impossible to say in advance that here are the students who will be the best entrepreneurs, and here are the ideas that will win. Getting students to see that they often start with an unanswerable and thus irrelevant question: Will I be a good entrepreneur? This leads to a critical learning transformation for them. They mature and grow to ask more relevant questions: Is this a good business worth pursuing or just another feature? How do I know, and who does know? What are the risks and rewards here, and what can I do to improve them?

A third dimension that is a central part of the new paradigm is the richness and creativity of many entrepreneurship faculty, courses, and curricula. The classroom as a place for the intellectual and practical collisions of theory, practice, ideas, and strategies has been a major anchor at many schools for the last decade.

Entrepreneurship as the New Not-for-Profit and Philanthropy Management Paradigm

Over the last several decades there has been a focus on new philanthropic foundations and not-for-profit organizations have been created from scratch using the entrepreneurship and new venture development model. From the beginning they have employed many of the concepts and principles for conceptualizing an idea, transforming it into an opportunity, building a brain trust, raising funds, and growing the management team and organization as if it were a new entrepreneurial venture.

The Energy Creation Effect

The energizing process for faculty and students alike is also driving the rapid explosion of entrepreneurship education worldwide: China, India, Japan, Russia, South America, the old Eastern bloc, and developing countries.

First, the field seems to attract, by its substance and nature, highly entrepreneurial people. Historically entrepreneurial thinkers and doers have been few and far between in the vast majority of schools in the United States and abroad. These creative, can-do, resilient, and passionate people bring their entrepreneurial ways of thinking, acting, doing, and building to their courses, their research, and their institutions. They are the change agents–the movers and shakers.

Second, their entrepreneurial bent brings a new mind-set to universities and schools: They think and act like owners. They are creative, courageous, and determined to make it work and happen; they build teams, practice what they preach, are institution builders, and do not let myopic allegiance to their disciplines impede becoming better educators. Students, deans, and colleagues can be energized by the leading-by-example pace they establish.

Third, entrepreneurship faculties constantly think in terms of opportunity. Entrepreneurial faculty realize that money follows superior teams and superior opportunities, so they create them. They find ways to innovate, raise money, and implement curricula in resource-strapped universities. They match innovative ideas with wealthy entrepreneurs and their foundations to raise money and launch programs.

Fourth, they create powerful strategic alliances with others–colleagues, alumni, and entrepreneurs by practicing the teamwork principles of entrepreneurship they teach. There is something exciting and compelling about being around highly intelligent and creative entrepreneurs as the centerpiece of your subject matter. They invariably inspire other faculty and students as well.

The Road Ahead

In this book we will urge you to think big. You will see failure as part of the learning process that leads to success. Businesses fail; strategies may not work; a product may be flawed, but the entrepreneurial spirit persists. The key for beginners is to keep the investment low and learning experience high.

It is increasingly clear that beyond learning the knowledge-based nuts and bolts of accounting, finance, cash flow, and business plans there are teachable and learnable ways of skills, concepts, and principles that when translated into strategies, tactics, and practices can significantly improve

the odds of success. These are at the heart of the content and process you will engage in with *New Venture Creation.* Among the most important things you can learn are how to think about the difference between a good idea and a good opportunity; the development and molding of the idea into an opportunity; the minimizing and control of resources; and resource parsimony and bootstrapping.

For the entrepreneur, the mind-set when 1,000 experiments fail is just like that of Thomas Edison: "Those weren't 1,000 failures; those were just 1,000 ways that didn't work!" The new venture is nothing more than a huge, perpetual learning puzzle.

Entrepreneurship: Innovation + Entrepreneurship = Prosperity and Philanthropy

The relevance and economic importance of the entrepreneurial phenomenon have legitimized entrepreneurship as vital to any debate about our social economic policies. The creation of the National Commission on Entrepreneurship in 1999 launched an awareness building educational initiative to help legislators, governors, and policy makers understand the contributions and potential of the entrepreneurial economy.

In June 2001 the long-standing U.S. Senate Committee on Small Business changed its name to Small Business and Entrepreneurship, sending a significant message. The National Governor's Association is also including entrepreneurship in its meetings and policy discussions.

Job Creation

Twenty years ago, MIT researcher David Birch began to report his landmark findings that defied all previous notions that large established businesses were the backbone of the economy and the generator of new jobs. In fact, one Nobel Prize-winning economist gained his award by "proving" that any enterprise with fewer than 100 employees was irrelevant to the study of economics and policy making. Birch stunned researchers, politicians, and the business world with just the opposite conclusion: New and growing smaller firms created 81.5 percent of the net new jobs in the economy from 1969 to 1976.[4] This general pattern has been repeated ever since.

---

[4]D.L. Birch, 1979, The Job Creation Process, unpublished report, MIT Program on Neighborhood and Regional Change; prepared for the Economic Development Administration, U.S. Department of Commerce, Washington, DC.

Entrepreneurial firms account for a significant amount of employment growth (defined by at least 20 percent a year for 4 years, from a base of at least $100,000 in revenues). These "gazelles," as David Birch calls them, made up only 3 percent of all firms but added 5 million jobs from 1994 to 1998. According to the U.S. Small Business Administration's Office of Advocacy, in 2004 small firms with fewer than 500 employees represented 99.9 percent of the 26.8 million businesses in the United States. Over the past decade, small businesses created 60–80 percent of the net new jobs. In the most recent year with data (2010), small firms accounted for *all* of the net new jobs. When one considers the history of Microsoft, a start-up in the late 1970s, these job creation findings are not so surprising. In 1980, for instance, Microsoft had just $8 million in revenue and 38 employees. By the end of 2010, its sales were nearly $90 billion, it had over 88,000 employees, and the total market value of its stock was over $255 billion.

We can readily see the far-reaching change in employment patterns caused by this explosion of new companies. In the 1960s about one in four persons worked for a Fortune 500 company. As recently as 1980, the Fortune 500 employed 20 percent of the workforce. By 2010 that figure had dropped to less than 9 percent.

New Venture Formation

Classical entrepreneurship means new venture creation. But it is much more, as you will discover throughout this chapter and book. It is arguably the single most powerful force to create economic and social mobility. It is results oriented and rewards only and performs without regard to religion, gender, skin color, social class, and national origin, it enables people to pursue and realize their dreams.

The role of women in entrepreneurship is particularly noteworthy. Consider what has happened in just a single generation. In 1970 women-owned businesses were limited mainly to small service businesses and employed fewer than 1 million people nationwide. They represented only 4 percent of all businesses. A 2010 published report by The Guardian Life Small Business Research Institute projects that female-owned small businesses, now 16 percent of total U.S. employment, will be responsible for creating one-third of the 15.3 million new jobs anticipated by the Bureau of Labor Statistics by 2018.

A similar pattern can be seen for a variety of ethnic and racial groups (Exhibit 1.2). The U.S. Census Bureau says blacks owned nearly 2 million businesses in 2007, the year of the last survey of business owners. That was up by more than 60 percent from the previous survey in 2002. The jump was more than triple the growth rate for all U.S. businesses, and the highest rate of increase of any minority.

Hispanics owned 2.3 million nonfarm U.S. businesses operating in the 50 states and the District of Columbia in 2007, an increase of 43.7 percent from 2002. These Hispanic-owned firms accounted for 8.3 percent of all nonfarm businesses in the United States, 1.6 percent of total employment and 1.1 percent of total receipts. In addition, 242,766 nonfarm U.S. businesses were equally (50 percent/50 percent) owned by both Hispanics and non-Hispanics.[5]

The American Dream Aspiring to work for oneself is deeply embedded in American culture as recent data bears out. In a 2004 Gallup Poll, 90 percent of American parents said they would approve if one or more of their children pursued entrepreneurship. In a 2006 poll of 1,474 middle

---

EXHIBIT 1.2

Growth of Entrepreneurship among Ethnic and Racial Groups

Ownership	Number of Firms Owned			Sales and Receipts ($ billion)			Number of Employees (Millions)		
	1997	2002	% Change	1997	2002	% Change	1997	2002	% Change
African American	780,770	1,197,567	53	42.7	88.6	107	0.7	0.8	14
Hispanic	1,120,000	1,573,600	41	114.0	221.9	95	1.3	1.5	15
Asian/Pacific Islander	785,480	1,133,137	44	161.0	331.0	106	2.2	2.24	1
Native American	187,921	201,387	7	22.0	26.8	22	0.3	0.19	37

---

[5]http://www.census.gov/econ/sbo/get07sof.html?11.

and high school students, the youth entrepreneurship organization Junior Achievement found that 70.9 percent would like to be self-employed at some point in their lives. That is up from 68.6 percent in 2005 and 64 percent in 2004. The National Association for the Self-Employed projected that its ranks would increase to about 250,000 members by the end of 2006, up from 100,000 in 1988. In 2004 *USA Today* asked a national sample of men and women if for 1 year they could take any job they wanted, what would that job be? The results reveal how ingrained the entrepreneurial persona has become in society: 47 percent of the women and 38 percent of the men said they would want to run their own companies. Surprisingly, for the men, this was a higher percentage than those who responded with professional athlete.

A 2006 study showed that young people with entrepreneurs as role models were more likely to achieve a broad range of success in business, school, and in life.[6] Uniformly, the self-employed report the highest levels of personal satisfaction, challenge, pride, and remuneration.

Sir Winston Churchill probably was not thinking about the coming entrepreneurial generation when he wrote in his epic book *While England Slept*, "The world was meant to be wooed and won by youth." Yet this could describe perfectly what has transpired over the past 30 years as young entrepreneurs in their 20s conceived, launched, and grew new companies that spawned entirely new industries. Consider just a few of these 20-something entrepreneurs in Exhibit 1.3.

There are many lesser known players in the entrepreneurial revolution, and you will come to know and appreciate some of them in this book. For example, Martin Migoya, founder of Globant, an IT outsourcing company based in Buenos Aires, Argentina. In 4 years he and his team built a company with more than 240 employees, sales approaching $12 million, and clients in Europe and the Americas. Their goal: Build an offshore IT services business that can go head to head with major players such as Infosys, IBM, and Accenture.

Roxanne Quimby is a very different but extraordinary entrepreneur. Enjoying basic subsistence living on a small farm in the woods of Maine, she conceived of an idea to develop natural products from beeswax and other natural components. Her new business began slowly and was fragile. She thrived, relocated the business to North Carolina, and eventually sold her company for nearly

EXHIBIT 1.3

Mega-Entrepreneurs who Started in their 20s

Entrepreneurial Company	Founder(s)
Microsoft	Bill Gates and Paul Allen
Netscape	Marc Andreessen
Dell Computer	Michael Dell
Gateway 2000	Ted Waitt
McCaw Cellular	Craig McCaw
Apple Computer	Steve Jobs and Steve Wozniak
Digital Equipment Corporation	Ken and Stan Olsen
Federal Express	Fred Smith
Google	Larry Page and Sergey Brin
Genentech	Robert Swanson
Polaroid	Edward Land
Nike	Phil Knight
Lotus Development Corporation	Mitch Kapor
Ipix.com	Kevin McCurdy
Yahoo!	David Filo and Jerry Yang
PayPal	Max Levchin
Skype	Janus Friis
Facebook	Mark Zuckerberg (at 19)
YouTube	Chad Hurley
MySpace	Tom Anderson

$200 million. Roxanne returned to Maine and is using a significant portion of her fortune to buy up huge parcels of undeveloped land in northern Maine—over 28,000 acres so far—that she hopes will one day be part of a federal preserve.

Jack Stack had worked his way up, after dropping out of school, to the mailroom and the factory floor at an International Harvester Plant in Springfield, Missouri, in the early 1980s, when it was announced that the plant would likely close. He and a handful of colleagues pooled $100,000 of their own money and borrowed $8.9 million from a local bank (note the 89 to 1 leverage) and bought the plant for 10 cents a share to try to save the business and their jobs. The plant was failing with only $10 million in revenues. Starting as a rebuilder of engines shipped to the United States by Mercedes, the business expanded to include over 20 businesses. The outcome is an organization that moved from near death to revenues of $200 million. Stack's book, *The Great Game of Business*, is a business classic.

Brian Scudamore started his company 1-800-GOT-JUNK? in 1989 straight out of high

---

[6]H. Van Auken; F.L. Fry; and P. Stephens, "The Influence of Role Models on Entrepreneurial Intentions," *Journal of Developmental Entrepreneurship*, June 2006.

school with $700 and a beat-up old pickup truck. In 2006 the company posted sales of more than $112 million, up from just $2 million in 2000. Over 2 years its corporate staff burgeoned from 43 to 116 employees. Their plan to double again by 2008 would be partly fueled by their first international offices in Australia (2005) and in England (2006). With 330 locations and 250 franchisees, 1-800-GOT-JUNK? is the world's largest junk removal service.

Wayne Postoak, a Native American, was a young professor and a highly successful basketball coach at Haskell Indian Nations University, in Lawrence, Kansas, in the 1970s. Haskell is the only national 4-year university for Native Americans, enrolling students from nearly 200 tribes throughout North America. Haskell also launched the first Center for Tribal Entrepreneurial Studies in 1995. Postoak's children had aspirations for a college education and medical school, which he knew he could not afford on his coaching and teaching salary. He decided to launch his own construction firm, which at its peak employed 100 people and had sales exceeding $10 million.

In 2001, at age 14, Sean Belnick invested $500 to start up a direct shipping company for office furniture–out of his bedroom. The Georgia-based company, which had 2006 revenues of $24 million, has branched out into home furniture, medical equipment, and school furniture. Notable clients include Microsoft, the *American Idol* television show, and the Pentagon.

Matt Coffin founded LowerMyBills.com in 1999 while still in his 20s. The company partnered with service providers across more than 20 categories, including home mortgage, home equity loans, purchase loans, debt consolidation loans, credit cards, auto loans, insurance, and cell phones. The company devised a wide range of creative online advertising to attract customers to the free service that matched them with the companies that best met their needs, making money on referral fees. In 2007 LowerMyBills.com was one of the top five Internet advertisers, and ranked number one among financial advertisers. Matt, a high-energy motivational leader, bootstrapped, scrimped, and managed by the numbers to such an extent that he was able to raise $13 million in venture capital while retaining over 25 percent ownership–quite a feat. In May 2005 he sold the company to Experian for approximately $400 million.

Formation of New Industries This generation of economic revolutionaries has become the creators and leaders of entire new industries, not just a few outstanding new companies. From among the staggering raw number of start-ups emerge the lead innovators and creators that often become the dominant firms in new industries. This is evident from the 20-something list in Exhibit 1.3. Exhibit 1.4 is a partial list of entirely new industries, not in existence a generation ago, that are major sectors in the economy.

These new industries have transformed the economy. In the true creative birth and destruction processes first articulated by Joseph Schumpeter, these new industries replace and displace older ones. David Birch has reported how this pace has accelerated from the 1960s to the 1990s; it took 20 years to replace 35 percent of the companies then on the list of Fortune 500 companies. By the late 1980s, that replacement took place every 5 years; and in the 1990s, it occurred in 3 to 4 years.

Consider the following example of a new industry in the making. Skype began as a software program in the early 2000s. Developed by Swedish entrepreneurs Niklas Zennström and Janus Friis, Skype allowed users to make telephone calls from their computers to other Skype users free of charge, or to landlines and cell phones for a fee. The main difference between Skype and voice over Internet protocol (VoIP) clients was that Skype was devised as a peer-to-peer model rather than the more traditional server–client model. As a decentralized system, the Skype user directory was able to scale easily without a complex and costly infrastructure.

This unique concept was quickly embraced by consumers around the world. In late 2005 the Skype Group was acquired by eBay for $2.6 billion, plus a performance earn-out of another $1.5 billion. In 2007 the company introduced SkypeOut, a system to allow Skype users to call traditional telephone numbers, including mobile telephones, for a fee. By the second quarter of that year, Skype reported that nearly 220 million active user accounts had logged

EXHIBIT 1.4

New Industries Launched by the E-Generation

Personal computers	Cellular phone services
Biotechnology	CD-ROM
Wireless cable TV	Internet publishing and shopping
Fast oil changes	Desktop computing
PC software	Virtual imaging
Desktop information	Convenience foods superstores
Wireless communications/ handheld devices/PDAs	Digital media and entertainment
	Pet care services
Healthful living products	Voice over Internet applications
Electronic paging	Green buildings
CAD/CAM	Large, scalable wind and solar
Voice mail information	power systems
Technology services	Biofuels and biomaterials

7.1 billion Skype-to-Skype minutes and 1.3 billion minutes using SkypeOut—for total Q2 revenues of $90 million. In May 2011 Microsoft announced their acquisition of Skype for over $8 billion.

Time and again, in industry after industry, the vision, drive, and innovations of entrepreneurial ventures demolish the old Fortune 500 group. The capital markets note the future value of these up-and-comers, compared to the old giants. Take, for instance, the Big Three automakers, giants of the prior generation of the 1950s and 1960s. By year-end 2006 they had combined sales of $568 billion, employed 923,000, but had a year-ending market capitalization of $92.9 billion, or just 16 cents per dollar of revenue. Intel, Microsoft, and Google had 2006 total sales of $96.2 billion, employed just 215,000, but enjoyed a market capitalization of $517.7 billion. That is 5.6 times the value of the Big Three, and $5.38 per dollar of revenue or 34 times the Big Three.

This pattern of high market value characterizes virtually every new industry that has been created, and is also the case when entrepreneurs directly take on industry stalwarts. In 2006 American, Continental, and Delta airlines employed 181,600 employees, had combined sales in 2006 of $54.1 billion, and a combined market capitalization of $15.4 billion, about 28 cents per dollar of revenue. In contrast, with a total of 45,400 employees, JetBlue, Southwest, and Frontier had 2006 sales of $13.1 billion and a combined market capitalization of $14.8 billion, almost four times their stalwarts of more than $1 per dollar of revenue. Exhibit 1.5 shows these relationships.

Innovation   At the heart of the entrepreneurial process is the innovative spirit. After all, from Ben Franklin to Thomas Edison to Steve Jobs and Bill Gates, the history of the country shows a steady stream of brilliant entrepreneurs and innovators. For years it was believed by the press, the public, and policy makers that research and development occurring in large companies after World War II and driven by the birth of the space age after Sputnik in 1957 were the main drivers of innovation in the nation.

This belief was shown to be a myth—similar to the earlier beliefs about job creation—as the National Science Foundation, U.S. Department of Commerce, and others began to report research in the 1980s and 1990s that surprised many. They found that since World War II, small entrepreneurial firms have been responsible for half of all innovation and 95 percent of all radical innovation in the United States. Other studies showed that research and development at smaller entrepreneurial firms were more productive and robust than at large firms: Smaller firms generated twice as many innovations per R&D dollar

EXHIBIT 1.5

The Impact of Entrepreneurship on American Giants Old and New

Firm	Sales in 2006 ($ billion)	Employees in 2006 (000s)	Market Capitalization in Late December 2006 ($ billion)
Ford	162.4	283.0	14.0
GM	198.9	280.0	17.1
DaimlerChrysler	206.7	360.4	61.7
Total	**568.0**	**923.4**	**92.9**
Intel	36.0	94.1	116.4
Microsoft	49.6	71.0	255.1
Google	10.6	10.7	146.1
Total	**96.2**	**175.8**	**517.7**
Delta	17.9	51.3	4.1
American	22.6	86.6	7.3
Continental	13.6	43.7	4.0
Total	**54.1**	**181.6**	**15.4**
JetBlue	2.5	8.4	2.5
Southwest	9.4	32.7	12.0
Frontier	1.2	4.3	0.3
Total	**13.1**	**45.4**	**14.8**

EXHIBIT I.6

Major Inventions by U.S. Small Firms

Acoustical suspension speakers	Aerosol can	Air conditioning
Airplane	Artificial skin	Assembly line
Audiotape recorder	Automatic fabric cutting	Automatic transfer equipment
Bakelite	Biosynthetic insulin	Catalytic petroleum cracking
Continuous casting	Cotton picker	Fluid flow meter
Fosin fire extinguisher	Geodesic dome	Gyrocompass
Heart valve	Heat sensor	Helicopter
Heterodyne radio	High-capacity computer	Hydraulic brake
Leaning machine	Link trainer	Nuclear magnetic resonance
Pacemaker	Personal computer	Prefabricated housing
Piezoelectrical devices	Polaroid camera	Cellophane
Quick-frozen foods	Rotary oil drilling bit	Safety razor
Six-axis robot arm	Soft contact lens	Sonar fish monitoring
Spectrographic grid	Stereographic image sensing	Zipper

Source: Office of Advocacy of the U.S. Small Business Administration.

spent as the giants; twice as many innovations per R&D scientist as the giants; and 24 times as many innovations per R&D dollar versus those large firms with more than 10,000 employees.

This innovation cylinder of the entrepreneurial engine of America's economy has led to the creation of major new inventions and technologies. Exhibit 1.6 summarizes some of these major innovations.

Today the fast pace of innovation is actually accelerating. New scientific breakthroughs in biotechnology and nanotechnology are driving the next great waves of innovation. *Nano* means one-billionth, so a nanometer is one-billionth of a meter or 1/80,000 the diameter of a human hair. A new class of nano-size products in drugs, optical network devices, and bulk materials is attracting substantial research funding and private equity.[7]

Venture and Growth Capital Venture capital has deep roots in our history, and the evolution to today's industry is uniquely American. This private risk capital is the rocket fuel of America's entrepreneurial engine. Classic venture capitalists work as coaches and partners with entrepreneurs and innovators at a very early stage to help shape and accelerate the development of the company.[8] The fast-growth, highly successful companies backed by venture capital investors read like a "Who's Who of the Economy": Apple Computer, Intuit, Compaq Computer, Staples, Intel, Federal Express, Cisco, e-Bay, Starbucks Coffee, Nextel Communication, Juniper Networks, Yahoo!, Sun Microsystems, Amazon.com, Genentech, Google, Blackberry, Microsoft, and

thousands of others. Typical of these legendary investments that both created companies and lead their new industry are the following:

- In 1957 General George Doriot, father of modern American venture capital, and his young associate Bill Congelton at American Research & Development (ARD) invested $70,000 for 77 percent of the founding stock of a new company created by four MIT graduate students, led by Kenneth Olsen. By the time their investment was sold in 1971, it was worth $355 million. The company was Digital Equipment Corporation and became the world leader in microcomputers by the 1980s.

- In 1968 Gordon Moore and Robert Noyce teamed with Arthur Rock to launch Intel Corporation with $2.5 million, and $25,000 from each of the founders. Intel is the leader in semiconductors today.

- In 1975 Arthur Rock, in search of concepts "that change the way people live and work," invested $1.5 million in the start-up of Apple Computer. The investment was valued at $100 million at Apple's first public stock offering in 1978.

- After monthly losses of $1 million and more for 29 consecutive months, a new company that launched the overnight delivery of small packages turned the corner. The $25 million invested in Federal Express was worth $1.2 billion when the company issued stock to the public.

---

[7]"Nanotech Grows Up," *Red Herring,* June 15 and July 1, 2001, pp. 47-58.
[8]W.D. Bygrave and J.A. Timmons, Venture Capital at the Crossroads (Boston, MA: *Harvard Business School,* 1992), Chapter 1.

EXHIBIT 1.7

Solar Investments Soar

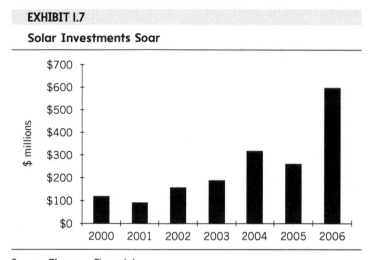

Source: Thomson Financial.

Note: Data are for totals invested by U.S.-based venture capitalists in solar and/or photovoltaic companies.

For a century and a half, innovation in solar energy sources has never managed to yield a cost-competitive model to rival fossil fuels. Venture capitalists have been placing modest bets on solar for years, but in 2006 things changed (see Exhibit 1.7), when venture capitalists invested $590 million into 49 solar technologies, up from $254 million in 41 solar-related ventures a year earlier. As of 2010, solar technologies generate electricity in more than 100 countries and, while yet comprising a tiny fraction of the 4.8 TW total global power-generating capacity from all sources, is the fastest growing power-generation technology in the world.

The recent surge in venture capital interest in biofuels also reflects this investment profile. Biofuel ventures, business models focused on creating cheap alternatives to fossil fuels using plant and waste materials are capital intensive investments, requiring about 10 times the average for a software start-up. Biofuel businesses typically require up to another $100 million in follow-on money in the form of debt and project financing.[9] The upside is sooner or later an Exxon/Mobil of biofuels will emerge to change the entire energy use and production landscape.

Studies suggest that more than one out of three Americans will use a medical product or service generated by a venture-backed life sciences company.[10] According to Global Insight (www.globalinsight.com), U.S.-based, venture-backed companies accounted for more than 10.4 million jobs and generated over $2.3 trillion in revenue. Nearly 1 out of every 10 private sector jobs is at a company that was originally venture backed. Almost 18 percent

of U.S. GDP comes from venture-backed companies. What is particularly important is that these are new jobs and, in fact, often new industries, as depicted in Exhibit 1.6.

The angel investor market in 2010, following a considerable contraction in investment dollars in 2008 and 2009, exhibited a rise in investment dollars and in the number of investments. Total investments in 2010 were $20.1 billion, an increase of 14 percent over 2009, according to the Center for Venture Research at the University of New Hampshire. A total of 61,900 entrepreneurial ventures received angel funding in 2010, for an increase of 8.2 percent over 2009. The number of active investors in 2010 was 265,400 individuals showing growth of 2.3 percent from 2009.

Similar to the venture capitalists, these angels bring far more than money to the entrepreneurial process. As successful entrepreneurs themselves, they bring experience, networks, wisdom, and maturity to the companies they fund. As directors and advisors, they function as coaches, confidants, mentors, and cheerleaders.

Philanthropy and Leadership: Giving Back to the Community   Another lesser known and largely ignored role of American entrepreneurs is that of philanthropists and creative community leaders. A majority of new buildings, classrooms, athletic facilities, and universities have been funded by an entrepreneur who wanted to give back.

As we might imagine, when a successful entrepreneur gets involved in the nonprofit sector the

---

[9]*Thomson Venture Capital Journal,* June 2007, pp. 24, 25.

[10]House of Representatives Committee on Ways and Means, September 6, 2007, "Hearing on Fair and Equitable Tax Policy for America's Working Families." Testimony of Jonathan Silver, founder and managing director, Core Capital Partners.

engagement involves strategic business skills like long-term planning, board and executive recruitment, coaching, and leveraging relationships. These high-engagement philanthropists have a stronger focus and deeper investments in a smaller, more select number of investment partners, and a healthy ambition for the long-term reach of their efforts.[11]

These sentiments are mirrored time and again by highly successful entrepreneurs who have created America's leading foundations like Carnegie, Olin, Ford, Kellogg, Lilly, Gates, and Buffett. One cannot find a building, stadium, science or arts center at universities in America that has not come from the wealth creation and gift of a highly successful entrepreneur.

Entrepreneurs: America's Self-Made Millionaires

The founders of great companies such as Apple Computer, Federal Express, Staples, Intuit, and Lotus Development Corporation become millionaires when their companies became publicly traded. But the majority of these founders are invisible to most Americans and do not fit the media stereotype. The authors of *The Millionaire Next Door*, Thomas J. Stanley and William D. Danko, share some new insights into this group:

> *[T]he television image of wealthy Americans is false: The truly wealthy are not by and large ostentatious but, rather, are very persistent and disciplined people running ordinary businesses.[12]*

The profile of these 3.1 million—out of 100 million households in the nation—millionaires is revealing: They accumulated their wealth through hard work, self-discipline, planning, and frugality, all entrepreneurial virtues. Two-thirds of them still working are self-employed and are self-made: More than 80 percent are ordinary people who have accumulated their wealth in one generation, live below their means, and prefer financial independence to social status. They get rich slowly, with the average millionaire being 57 years old. Their businesses are ordinary ones they started and built like ambulance services, citrus farming, cafeteria services, diesel engine rebuilding, consulting, janitorial services, job training schools, meat processors, mobile home parks, pest controllers, newsletter publishers, rice farmers, and sandblasting contractors.[13]

Private Equity—A New Era of Equity Creation

Value creation is not a linear process as it requires a long-term perspective. While the U.S. investment and capital markets have fueled the revolution in entrepreneurship, it is more important to recognize the long-term resilience of the system.

U.S. private equity (PE) funds raised a total of $1.5 trillion through 1,674 funds from 2001 to 2010. For a sense of scale, PE raised $325 billion in 2007, the same amount as the GDP of Denmark that year. PE fundraising crossed the $100 billion mark for the first time in 2005. One year later it crossed $200 billion and 1 year after that it crossed the $300 billion mark; capital raised increased by 6.7 times from 2003 to 2007, but the number of funds only increased by 2.4 times.[14]

Building an Enterprising Society

The Poor Get Richer   Many traditional sociologists and economists support this notion by talking about socioeconomic classes in America as if they are permanent castes. Although moving up from an impoverished urban existence requires persistence, self-direction, and a strong work ethic, it is by no means a rare occurrence in the United States. In her book *Chutes and Ladders*, Katherine Newman describes the economic and personal trajectories of a number of black and Latino workers from Harlem, a New York neighborhood with high poverty rates and low expectations.[15] Nevertheless, over 20 percent of the workers she tracked over a decade are no longer poor. Their persistence paid off in the form of educational degrees, better living standards, and well-paying jobs with benefits and pensions. In doing so, they were able to break free and move themselves and their families up and out of a seemingly hopeless social and economic environment. Here are three that made that journey.

Adam: The Union Path.   Adam is the classic embodiment of a character from Horatio Alger. He grew up black and poor in Brooklyn, and his mother went on welfare after his father left her. His mom took low-paying jobs and put in long hours to work her way up and out of welfare. Adam has applied the same work ethic in his own life. He dropped out of high school in the 10th grade, and at age 27 he was rejected for an entry-level position at a local Burger Barn. He

[11]Venture Philanthropy Partners (www.vppartners.org), "High-Engagement Philanthropy: The Bridge to a More Effective Social Sector," 2004.
[12]"The Millionaire Next Door," *Success Magazine*, March 1997, pp. 45–51.
[13]Ibid., pp. 46–48.
[14]PitchBook Data is a private equity research firm that publishes extensive data regarding small, medium, and large companies involved in private equity.
[15]K.S. Newman, *Chutes and Ladders* (Cambridge, MA: Harvard University Press, 2006).

persisted, survived on meager wages, and eventually landed an entry-level job with a unionized express delivery firm in New York City. He took whatever shifts they offered, secured his commercial driver's license, and worked his way up the union ladder.

At 36 Adam is now a well-respected and reliable driver for the firm, earning $70,000 a year with full benefits. Over the years he has turned down opportunities to move into management: "Supervisors are often fired, and I prefer the protection of the union." Inspired by a delivery client with a screenprinting business, Adam created a second job for himself running a T-shirt printing company out of his home. He and his wife are bringing in another $30,000 a year with that venture. The extra money is critical because he now has custody of his two children from previous marriages–a 13-year-old girl and a 6-year-old boy. They rent in the Bronx, but they are in the process of building a home of their own in North Carolina, near where Adam's family lives, and where the schools are superior to the ones his children attend in the city. Although transferring to a new post down south with the same delivery firm is proving to be a challenge (comparable wage rates but no benefits), Adam is confident that he can figure out a way to make it work.[16]

Helena: The Corporate Ladder.

Ten years ago Helena, a 21 year old of Dominican descent, was married and the mother of a 2-year-old son. Her first experience in the corporate sector had been in high school as an intern at a large insurance company. Although she interspersed her unpaid internship time with stints at a Burger Barn in her Harlem neighborhood, she was able to land a "real job" as an entry-level administrative assistant at the insurance firm. Helena immediately understood that she had grabbed onto the lower rung of an internal ladder that promised increasing wages and more responsibility on the job.

While racking up seniority, security, and skills, she took full advantage of the educational allowances and programs offered by the firm. While raising two young boys and creatively juggling parenting duties and schedules with her husband and extended family members, she completed her associate's degree at a City University of New York junior college, and then advanced to the City College of New York for her bachelor's in public administration. The arrangement worked for both parties; her employer got a more skilled and educated worker who could be promoted, and Helena ended up with a much better résumé than she could ever have hoped for if

she had had to cover the educational costs herself. She is married with two children, and her full-time job at the insurance company as the call center manager pays more than $60,000 a year with benefits.[17]

Lanice: The Enterprising Route.

As a teen African American in Harlem, Lanice struggled to find steady employment. Burger Barn would not hire her, and the few companies she had worked for had gone out of business or moved away. Lanice was not picky: She said she would work for any kind of company, so long as she had an opportunity to advance. She finished high school and took some adult education classes. In 1 year she applied for more than 20 jobs, mostly at retail stores. When she did find work, the pay was paltry and the job never seemed to last very long.

With almost reckless confidence in herself, Lanice landed a job in the entertainment industry. Her boss, a demanding taskmaster, had cycled through 17 administrative assistants in the previous year. He took an immediate liking to Lanice, who was personable, a quick learner, and a tolerant subordinate–someone who did not take offense at the stream of Post-it notes left on her desk, with things not done written in big letters and underlined. She has been there for 2 years, makes a $42,000 salary, and is loving every minute of it.

Experience and success have made Lanice more ambitious. At the age of 26, she has found a job she likes, but she is clear that she does not want to stay there for the rest of her life. Now she has bigger plans. Lanice is starting her own business: a consulting firm that will help individuals, schools, and small businesses with fundraising and networking. She has already hooked up with an accounting firm and a legal service and is intent on working (and networking) her way into the big leagues.[18]

Create Equal Opportunities, Not Equal Incomes

What has been lost historically in this debate is that equal incomes are neither desirable nor possible. Most important is that opportunities are available for anyone who wants to prepare and to compete. The entrepreneurial process will take over and result in economic expansion and accompanying social mobility. A recent study at the Federal Reserve Bank of Dallas sheds valuable insight.[19] In one experiment in the 1970s, for instance, three groups of Canadians, all in their 20s, all with at least 12 years of schooling, volunteered to work in a simulated economy where the only employment was making woolen belts on

---

[16]Ibid., pp. 95, 184, 218.
[17]Ibid., pp. 91–92.
[18]Ibid., pp. 245–46.
[19]W.M. Cox and R. Aim, *By Our Own Bootstraps: Economic Opportunity and the Dynamics of Income Distribution, 1995 Annual Report.* (Dallas, TX: Federal Reserve Bank), pp. 2–23.

small hand looms. They could work as much or as little as they liked, earning $2.50 for each belt. After 98 days, the results were anything but equal: 37.2 percent of the economy's income went to the 20 percent with the highest earnings. The bottom 20 percent received only 6.6 percent.[20]

Entrepreneurship = Economic and Social Mobility

The authors of the Federal Reserve study would agree with the earlier case presented here showing the radical transformation of the American economy as a result of the entrepreneurial revolution. Their data also show that this is still the land of opportunity. Income mobility in America from 1975 to 1991 shows that a significant portion of those in the lowest quintile in 1975 had moved up, including 29 percent all the way to the top quintile (see Exhibit 1.8). In terms of absolute gain, the data, adjusted for inflation, showed that the poor are getting richer faster (see Exhibit 1.9). The study concluded with this important summation:

Striving to better oneself is not just private virtue. It sows the seeds of economic growth and technical advancement. There's no denying that the system allows some Americans to become richer than others. We must accept that. Equality of income is not what

EXHIBIT 1.8

Moving Up

Income Quintile in 1975	Percentage in Each Quintile in 1991				
	1st	2nd	3rd	4th	5th
5th (highest)	0.9	2.8	10.2	23.6	62.5
4th	1.9	9.3	18.8	32.6	37.4
3rd (middle)	3.3	19.3	28.3	30.1	19.0
2nd	4.2	23.5	20.3	25.2	26.8
1st (lowest)	5.1	14.6	21.0	30.0	29.0

has made the U.S. economy grow and prosper. "It's opportunity. . . Our proper cultural icon is not the common man. It's the *self-made* man or woman."[21]

In another comparison, the standard of living of the bottom 10 percent of American families in 1995 was actually higher than the average family in 1970. It is clear that America's success is becoming a global success story. Just as this nation has created and encouraged policies and priorities to support the entrepreneurial process, countries around the world are following that lead, and in doing so, they are fostering and ensuring the mobility of opportunity just described.

EXHIBIT 1.9

The Poor are Getting Richer Faster

Income Quintile in 1975	Average Income in 1975[a] ($)	Average Income in 1991[a] ($)	Absolute Gain ($)
5th (highest)	45,704	49,678	3,974
4th	22,423	31,292	8,869
3rd (middle)	13,030	22,304	9,274
2 nd	6,291	28,373	22,082
1st (lowest)	1,153	26,475	25,322

[a]Figures are in 1993 dollars.

---

[20]Ibid., p. 5.
[21]Ibid., p. 18.

Chapter Summary

- Entrepreneurship is a truly global phenomenon, and, coupled with the Internet, is flattening and democratizing the world.

- Entrepreneurs are the creators, the innovators, and the leaders who give back to society as philanthropists, directors, and trustees, and who, more than any others, change how people live, work, learn, play, and lead.

- Entrepreneurs create new technologies, products, processes, and services that become the next wave

of new industries, and these in turn drive the economy.

- Entrepreneurs create value with high-potential, high-growth companies, which are the job creation engines of the U.S. economy.

- Venture capital provides the fuel for high-potential, high-growth companies.

- America and the world are at the dawn of a new age of equity creation as evidenced by a 10- to 30-fold increase in our capital markets in just 20 years.

- Entrepreneurs are realizing the value they have created; more than 95 percent of the wealth America has today has been created since 1980.
- North America's 3.1 million millionaires are mostly self-made entrepreneurs.

- In America, the poor get richer as a result of the entrepreneurial process.
- Building an entrepreneurial society for the 21st century and beyond is the highest priority for the new and global e-generation.

Study Questions

1. How has the economy changed in your region and country over the past generation?
2. How has the number of new venture formations in the United States changed in the past 30 years? Why has this happened? Why will this pattern continue?
3. Where do the new jobs in America come from? Why?
4. Which contribute more to all innovations and to radical innovations–large companies or new and emerging companies? Why?
5. When and by whom was the vast majority of wealth created in America? *(a)* The Carnegies, Vanderbilts, and Rockefellers before 1990.

(b) Automobile, food, and real estate magnates between 1900 and 1970. *(c)* Founders of companies since 1970.
6. Who are the millionaires today?
7. Name some exceptional companies founded by people in their 20s.
8. What role has venture capital played in this economic transformation?
9. It is often argued that "the rich get richer and the poor get poorer." How and why has the entrepreneurial revolution affected this stereotype? What are its implications?
10. What has happened to large and established companies as a result of this surge by entrepreneurial upstarts?

Internet Resources

www.gemconsortium.org. *The Global Entrepreneurship Monitor (GEM) project is an annual assessment of entrepreneurial activity performed by a nonprofit academic research consortium. GEM is the largest single study of entrepreneurial activity in the world.*

www.babson.edu/Academics/centers/blank-center/Pages/home.aspx. *The Arthur M. Blank Center for Entrepreneurship, Babson College.*

www.olin.edu. *Olin College of Engineering.*

www.ncaied.org. *The National Center for American Indian Enterprise Development (NCAIED) is a nonprofit*

organization dedicated to developing Native Americans' economic self-sufficiency through business ownership.

www.venturesource.com. *A Dow Jones company database of research focused on the venture capital industry.*

www.nfte.com. *The Network for Teaching Entrepreneurship describes its mission as providing programs that inspire young people from low-income communities to stay in school, to recognize business opportunities, and to plan for successful futures.*

www.nvca.org. *The National Venture Capital Association is the US venture capital industry's trade group.*

Exercise I

Create a Lifelong Learning Log and Visit with an Entrepreneur

Create a Lifelong Learning Log

Create a computer file or acquire a notebook or binder in which you record your entrepreneurial goals, triumphs, disappointments, and lessons learned. You can make entries after major events and/or on a regular basis. For

example, you might make entries during a crisis about what you are experiencing, and at the end of a year to sum up your accomplishments for the year and your goals for the next year. The record of personal insights, observations, and lessons learned can help you with difficult decisions and make interesting reading—for you at least.

A Visit with an Entrepreneur

Interviewing entrepreneurs who have, within the past 5 to 10 years, started profitable firms with more than $2 million in annual sales can provide insight into an entrepreneur's reasons, strategies, approaches, and motivations for starting and owning a business. Gathering information with interviews is a valuable skill. You can learn a great deal in a short time through interviewing if you prepare thoughtfully and thoroughly.

Interview at least two entrepreneurs with differing experiences, such as the founder of a company with rapid and large growth potential and the founder of a lifestyle business, which enables him or her to make a comfortable living but will not change the world.

STEP 1

Contact the Person You Have Selected and Make an Appointment.
Explain why you want the appointment and how much time you will need.

STEP 2

Identify Specific Questions You Want Answered and the General Areas about Which You Want Information. (See the Interview In Step 3.)
Use a combination of open-ended questions, such as, "How did you get started?" and "What happened next?" and more specific questions, such as "What were your goals?" and "Did you have to find partners?" That will help keep the interview focused while allowing for unexpected comments and insights.

STEP 3

Conduct the Interview.
Record the interview unless your subject objects. Remember that you will learn more if you are an interested listener.

The Interview

Questions for Gathering Information

- Tell me about yourself before you started your first venture.

  Did you know anyone who had started or owned a business while you were growing up? If so, how did they influence you? How about after you were 21 years old?

  Were your parents, relatives, or close friends entrepreneurial? How so?

  Did you have role models?

  What was your education and/or military experience? In hindsight, was it helpful? In what specific ways?

  Did you have a business while growing up?

Did you have any sales or marketing experience before you started your company? How important was it, or your lack of it, in starting your company?

When, under what circumstances, and with whose help did you become interested in entrepreneurship and learned some of the critical lessons about it?

- Describe how you decided to create a job by starting your venture instead of taking a job with someone else.

  How did you spot the opportunity? How did it surface?

  What were your goals? What were your lifestyle needs or other personal requirements? How did you fit these together?

  How did you evaluate the opportunity in terms of the critical elements for success? The competition? The market? Did you have specific criteria you wanted to meet?

  Did you find or have partners? What kind of planning did you do? What kind of financing did you have?

  Did you have a business plan? If so, please tell me about it.

  How long did you need to turn your company from an idea to an operational business? How many hours a day did you work on it?

  How much capital did you need to get your business up and running? How long did your business take to attain positive cash flow and break-even sales volume? If you did not have the capital you needed, how did you bootstrap the venture (bartering, borrowing, etc.)? Tell me about the pressures and crises during that early survival period.

  What outside help did you get? Did you have experienced advisors? Lawyers? Accountants? Tax experts? Patent experts? How did you find them and how long did it take?

  How did any outside advisors make a difference in your company?

  What was your family situation when you started your company?

  What did you perceive to be your venture's strengths? Weaknesses?

  What was your most triumphant moment? Your worst moment?

  Did you want to have partners? Why or why not?

- Once you got going:

  What were the most difficult gaps to fill and problems to solve as you began to grow rapidly?

  Did you look for any personal attributes or attitudes in your key partners, advisors, or managers because you thought they would enable the people to fit with you and help your company succeed? How did you find people with those attributes?

Are there attributes you try to avoid in partners and advisors?

Have things at your business become more predictable? Or less?

Do you spend more time, the same amount of time, or less time with your business now than in the early years?

Do you feel more managerial and less entrepreneurial now? Why or why not?

Do you plan to maintain, expand, or harvest your business?

Ideally, how many days a year would you want to work? Please explain.

Do you ever plan to retire? Why or why not?

Have your goals changed? Have you met them?

Has your family situation changed? How?

What do you learn from success? From failure?

What were/are the most demanding conflicts or trade-offs you face (the business versus personal hobbies or a family, etc.)?

Did you ever run out of cash? If so, what pressures did this create for you, the business, and your family? What you did about it? What lessons did you learn?

Can you describe a venture that did not work out for you and how this prepared you for your next venture?

Questions for Concluding

- What do you consider to be your most valuable asset, the thing that enabled you to make it?

- If you had it to do over again, would you do it again? In the same way?

- What were the most critical concepts, skills, attitudes, and know-how you needed to get your company started and grown to where it is today? What will be the most critical concepts, skills, attitudes, and know-how you will need in the next 5 years? To what extent can they be learned?

- Is being an entrepreneur very stressful? How does it compare with other "hot seat" jobs, such as the head of a big company, or a partner in a large law or accounting firm?

- What things about being an entrepreneur do you find personally rewarding and satisfying? What have been the rewards, risks, and trade-offs?

- Who should try to be an entrepreneur? Who should not?

- What advice would you give an aspiring entrepreneur? What are the three most important lessons you have learned? How can I learn them while minimizing the tuition?

- Could you suggest another entrepreneur I should talk to? Who?

- Are there questions I didn't ask that could provide me with valuable lessons?

STEP 4

Evaluate What You Have Learned.
Summarize the most important observations and insights from your interviews, especially noting the differences and similarities between lifestyle and high-potential entrepreneurs. Who can be an entrepreneur? What surprised you the most? What did you have confirmed about entrepreneurship? What new insights emerged? What are the implications for your personal and career goals and aspirations?

STEP 5

Write a Thank-You Note.
In addition to being polite, this will help the entrepreneur remember you favorably should you want to follow up on the interview.

Exercise 2

The Venturekipedia Exercise—Time Is Everything!

Doing Frugal and Parsimonious Research and Due Diligence College overloads you with course work, sports, and other extracurricular activities, not

to mention social opportunities. As a result, it teaches you to prioritize and triage: the *must dos*, the *should dos*, and the *can waits*. Couple this with the "80 to 20 rule" (you get 80 percent of the creative work done in the first 20 percent of the effort; 20 percent of your sales force will account for 80 percent of your sales, etc.) and you can develop some effective ways of setting goals, establishing priorities, and managing your time. Here is a tool to help you use your time while doing research, due diligence, and other similar tasks.

Create Your Own "Venturekipedia"

STEP I

Think Keywords and Phrases.
Throughout your entrepreneurship education, you will face different tasks, problems, and opportunities requiring research. In all cases, you can start by focusing on key words. These can be both generic, such as creativity or new ventures, or more specific, such as entrepreneurial mind, opportunity identification, opportunity assessment, bootstrapping, team formation, sustainable business opportunities, mentors, business plan, spreadsheet cash flow templates, and social ventures. Be especially sensitive to the words that inspire and excite you.

STEP 2

Deepen the Search.
For illustration, let us say you have an offer to join a family business after college—yours or someone else's. Once you have identified the key words related to family business and the business' industry, search for

them and closely related words and phrases in Wikipedia (https://www.wikipedia.org).

STEP 3

Share and Discuss.
Read at least one article in Wikipedia about family business and share what you learn with classmates and colleagues interested in its topic. The article will contain a list of links to additional information on the subject. Use the links to find, read, and share insights from at least two additional sources about family business. Identify and discuss the critical issues and challenges associated with family businesses. Would you start or join one? Why, and under what conditions? Why not? What did you discover that reinforced what you already knew or raised questions you had not considered before?

STEP 4

Create an Insites Log.
You will use this log to record the insights you gain from the Web sites you discover—hence its name. Also include insights and Web sites your classmates discover.

Limitless Applications

It is easy to imagine other applications for this exercise. Think, for instance, about the new venture opportunity you are working on this semester or quarter. By using this method to do your research and due diligence for it, you will save time and do better research and due diligence.

Case

ImageCafé

Preparation Questions

1. Evaluate Clarence Wooten's strengths and weaknesses.

2. What do you think about Wooten's product versus service conclusion? What are the strengths and weaknesses of his argument?

3. Analyze and assess the ImageCafé opportunity.

4. What do you think of Wooten's fund-raising strategy?

5. Should he have taken Dwayne Walker's offer?

6. Does he need to raise $3 million?

7. How would you respond to the Network Solutions offer?

8. How would you go about valuing ImageCafé?

9. What are the personal implications for Wooten if he sells or not?

Staying Afloat

With his company, ImageCafé, struggling with financial uncertainty, Clarence Wooten, Jr., faced some difficult decisions. With a burn rate[1] of nearly $50,000 per month, the bridge loans[2] and angel investments[3] of $710,000 would not carry the company to break even. While he was struggling to close a $3 million financing round, a Virginia-based Internet services company, Network Solutions Inc., approached Wooten about selling.

Should he sell ImageCafé to Network Solutions, or risk losing it all for the potential of a greater gain, if and when the financing materialized? And if he did decide to sell, what was the right price? Time was clearly not on his side.

Clarence Wooten, Jr.

Clarence Wooten, Jr., had a typical childhood dream: to get rich. His early childhood, however, was less typical. Wooten was fascinated by television-based video games; one Christmas, he convinced his parents to buy

Source: This case was written by Kathryn F. Spinelli under the direction of Professor Stephen Spinelli, Jr. © Copyright Babson College, 2004. Funding provided by the HBCU Consortium. All rights reserved.

[1]*Burn rate* is the amount of cash consumed by a new venture. It's usually stated in months.

[2]A *bridge loan* is a short-term financing that is expected to be paid off quickly by another financing.

[3]*Angel investors* are wealthy individuals who invest in startups.

him an Atari game system. Wooten soon discovered its game cartridges were too expensive for him to purchase. One day, a friend told him that home computers such as the Commodore 64 used program diskettes instead of cartridges. Multiple diskettes could be copied from the original, eliminating having to pay for game cartridges. Wooten also learned that with a computer, games could be transferred between computers through conventional telephone lines using a modem and bulletin board software (BBS). (A bulletin board was a computer that ran 24 hours a day so people could log in and download files from it.) The following Christmas, Wooten persuaded his parents to buy him a Commodore 64 home computer equipped with a modem.

From the age of 12, Wooten was on his computer from the minute he came home from school until well after midnight, when his parents would make him go to sleep. He became so immersed in this computer-based world, so obsessed with downloading the latest games, that by age 14 his parents decided it was necessary to intervene. They banned him from using the computer; it spent more than 3 months on a shelf locked in a closet. He remembers, "It was like going cold turkey, like sending a hacker to jail. But I was always computer savvy because of that background."

Growing Up

Wooten saw good times and bad during his childhood, moving between Baltimore and its suburbs. Wooten was an only child; by the time he was a teenager, both of his parents had become self-employed. As such, the family's income fluctuated depending on the success of his parents' businesses. His father, Clarence Wooten, Sr., formerly a steel mill laborer, gradually accumulated rental properties in Baltimore. His mother, Cecilia, formerly a seamstress, ran a 24-bed assisted living home with her sisters. The Wootens owned a house in the city, and when times were good, they would rent that out while renting a house in the suburbs for themselves. When times were not as good, they would move back into the city.

These frequent moves meant that Wooten had to transfer in and out of different school systems—eight times in all. The constant transitioning between homes, school systems, and friends was difficult for Wooten; however, this lifestyle enabled him to become comfortable adapting quickly to different situations. Wooten also credits his tumultuous lifestyle as his motivation to create wealth. He did not want his adult life to be dictated by small fluctuations in income, as his parents' lives had.

An Underworld Introduction to Entrepreneurship

In suburban Baltimore, Wooten became a member of a "cracking group."[4] Under the alias of "King Kaoz," Wooten and fellow group members used their computers to crack electronic games' anti-copying features so they could be duplicated. Unknown to his parents, Wooten had become well known as part of a competitive and elite computer underworld. The term "elite" referred to someone who, within 24 hours of a new game's release, had either cracked it or gotten access to a cracked version. Wooten said he "was more interested in getting the games than actually playing them; it was the competition." With his computer and his intellect, he began to feel nothing was out of his reach.

Wooten's days as a software pirate started with his love of video games. Diskettes could easily be copied, but the software companies started writing code onto the disks for copyright protection. This is where Wooten and his cracking group came in. The group was a team: Each had a task to perform in the duplication process. The rich kid bought the software as soon as it was released; the cracker removed the copy protection and added the group's intro screen to the game; and then Wooten, the distributor, posted the games on virtual bulletin boards. The software was distributed to pirates and crackers around the world. The bulletin board distribution method also involved getting around the phone bill incurred from the dial-up connection necessary to distribute and download software. One of the "entry exams" to becoming "elite" was learning all this on your own. Crackers never divulged their dodging techniques. Wooten explained,

> I eventually ran my own bulletin board, Kastle Kaoz, with my computer, which went all day and night, connected to the phone line so that people could log in, and if you were "elite," I would give you access so you could download all the latest games. There were only about 15 to 20 people in the world that had access to my bulletin board; if you had access, you were like a "made" guy. Our group was the biggest in the world on the Commodore 64 for 6 to 7 months. So it's like being an entrepreneur, it's like being part of the Fortune 500, when you think of it.

College Years: From Architecture to Computer Graphics

In 1990 Wooten, then 18, wanted to attend college to study architecture. A few schools that were offering him a basketball scholarship also had well-known architectural programs. Wooten thought the study of architecture would satisfy his creative drive, but had to limit his choice of academic programs to those offering him money. After Wooten's best scholarship offer fell through, he decided to attend Catonsville Community College in Maryland. There, he balanced his time between basketball and architecture classes while deciding which college he would eventually transfer to.

The recession of the late 1980s and early 1990s left many professionals out of work; many returned to school to gain more marketable skills. Wooten met many professional architects who had returned to the classroom to learn the newest computer-aided design, or CAD programs. Wooten learned that architects generally did not have large incomes until they reached their 40s and started their own firms. That raised doubts about architecture as his career choice—Wooten wanted to achieve above-average financial success in a less-than-average amount of time. He remembered an event from his childhood when he attended a catered party at a friend's house. The reality of what "catered" meant came to him as a shock; he had not previously known such things existed. In that seemingly wealthy neighborhood everyone's father was an entrepreneur of sorts, and no one's mother had to work.[5]

While still enrolled in architecture classes, Wooten submitted a prototype of one of his computer programs to a competition held by *CADalyst* magazine. He came in first, winning an AutoDesk Caddie Image Award for his production of 3-D architectural walk-through animation[6]. Wooten's skill with CAD and animation began to surpass that of his professors. As a result, the college asked him to teach a course in animation while still a student. He accepted.

Startup #1: Envision Design

At 20, while still a Catonsville Community College student, Wooten started his first company—Envision Design, which used his CAD and animation prowess. Wooten's idea was to produce 3-D walk-through animation for architects using software similar to that which won Wooten the *CADalyst* magazine contest.

Wooten identified his competition as the scale model business; architects still made elaborate scale models of proposed buildings out of foam and cardboard. Some architectural companies were willing to pay between $10,000 and $50,000 for such scale models. He decided to price his service in line with scale models and charged between $10,000 and $20,000 for a complete walk-through animation sequence. He attempted to attract clients by sending

---

[4] *Crackers* are individuals who crack the copy-protection codes on software so they can duplicate it.

[5] http://research.aarp.org/econ/dd44_wealth.html. This link appears to be dead.
[6] *Fast Company*, July 2000.

letters to every small architectural firm in the telephone directory from Baltimore to Washington, D.C. Envision Design was ultimately unsuccessful. After one paying contract with a small firm, Envision fizzled.

Failure and Restart: Lessons Learned Despite Envision's failure, Wooten wanted to continue working with animation. To do that, he sought to learn more about special effects and film animation and discovered he would need to learn how to use the latest high-end computer animation software that ran on Silicon Graphics Computers (SGI). Wooten found that the University of Maryland–Baltimore County was building a state-of-the-art computer science building equipped with SGI computers and transferred there. At UMBC, Peggy Southerland, a three-time Emmy-winning computer animator, ran the university's imaging researching center. Wooten was constantly talking to Peggy, asking her countless questions and soliciting career advice. Eventually she offered him an internship.

Startup #2: Metamorphosis Studios

Wooten used his knowledge of SGI animation software to start his second company, Metamorphosis Studios, with Andre Forde. Wooten and Forde had met at a party when Wooten overheard a group of college students (including Forde) talking about SGI software.

Metamorphosis Studios focused on special effects and multimedia presentations, which it made using PC-based animation and authoring software packages because its founders could not afford high-end Silicon Graphics Computers. The company developed presentations and electronic brochures for any medium, including diskettes, CD-ROMs, and touch screens. The first Metamorphosis customer, Bingwa, was an educational software company that offered it a year-long contract. The contract required Metamorphosis to develop one software product per month for a year, a total of 12 products, one for each grade (1 to 12). Metamorphosis was to be paid $30,000 per product, a total of $360,000 by the year's end. But after paying $60,000 for the software programs for grades 1 and 2, Bingwa asked Wooten and Forte to relocate to Princeton, New Jersey, and to become employees of Bingwa. Although they were offered annual salaries of $80,000, they rejected the offer. They knew they were headed for bigger things.

Shifting Gears

After the experience with Bingwa, Wooten decided to shift from a service-oriented focus to a product-oriented focus. He wanted to bypass the payment and commitment problems that had arisen in dealing with customers such as Bingwa. Wooten saw service customers as unreliable.

As Wooten and Forde contemplated their next move, they concluded that one of their largest failings was their lack of focus and dedication to a specific task or goal. Their multimedia skills gave them too many options to pursue. To succeed, they would have to pick the "most" right product idea and develop it from start to finish without distraction.

Another problem Wooten and Forde encountered was that Metamorphosis Studios was not generating revenue during its new product development cycle. There seemed to be a dearth of capital available for the right deal, especially for young African American entrepreneurs[7]. Traditionally, African American entrepreneurs tended to be trapped in small-scale ventures more often than their Caucasian counterparts because they had more difficulty obtaining growth capital. Wooten believed that social, cultural, and racial hierarchies and biases were to blame for the disproportionately large number of Caucasian investors—and for the disproportionately small amount of growth capital available to the African American business community. Although he could empathize with the risk perspective of such investors, he felt the result to be unfortunate. (See Notes 1 and 2 at the end of this case.) Despite this belief, Wooten remained undeterred. Once they had identified the idea and target market for their next venture, ImageCafé, Wooten and Forde sold the assets of Metamorphosis Studios for $20,000.

Back to School Again

Fascinated by entrepreneurs and their roads to success, Wooten read everything he could about their lives and experiences. He found the stories of Fred Smith, Reginald Lewis, and Bill Gates particularly inspirational. Wooten realized that the common thread connecting these entrepreneurs was that they all understood finance. Based on this, he changed his major to business administration and finance and enrolled at Johns Hopkins University. Wooten knew he needed a much deeper understanding of finance to be a successful entrepreneur, regardless of how creative he was with a computer. In addition to finance, Wooten wanted to know how to scale and grow a business—the two kernels essential for success as Wooten envisioned it. Wooten received his business degree in 1998.

In 1995, the Internet began to grow with exponential speed. Even small companies that lacked the resources to hire professional Web design firms needed an online presence. Creating websites

---

[7]"Small Business, The Racial Ravine: Minority Entrepreneurs Who Want A Piece of the Internet Gold Rush Face a Formidable Barrier: The Clubby, White-Male Universe of Venture Capitalists," *The Wall Street Journal*, May 22, 2000.

seemed natural for Wooten and Forde. In fact, it was what they did best. And Wooten knew how they could make creating websites for companies a product, not a service. This time, he believed they had the knowledge and the focus to succeed.

Launching ImageCafé　Wooten became obsessed with websites. Online observers forecast that in 1996 there would be nearly 80,000 websites worldwide, and in 2001 approximately 50 million.[8]

Netcraft's March 2014 Web Server Survey found there were 919.5 million active websites.[9]

Wooten saw that a company could obtain a website in two ways: Hire a dedicated, full-time Web design firm, which cost from $3,000 to $6,000[10]; or use a relatively inexpensive software program to design its own site. Wooten perceived problems with both options. His experience with Metamorphosis Studios had shown him that small businesses could not afford to hire a full-service Web design company. And the software had a steep learning curve and required creativity to use. Without technical skill and artistic ability, the results were often websites that seemed cheap and unprofessional. Wooten saw a clear demand from small businesses for his innovative product. He knew he could meet some of it, and in early 1998 ImageCafé was founded.

Wooten wanted to create the world's first online superstore of prefabricated websites for small businesses. Using its extensive software knowledge and artistic ability, ImageCafé would design website templates that imitated the custom sites designed by fully dedicated Web design firms. Wooten referred to the templates as "customizable Web site masters," a term he felt was marketable. By prefabricating the "Web site masters," ImageCafé lowered its costs without sacrificing the websites' appearance. The template business model also took the service aspect out of the business by providing a product that was ready to be deployed quickly. ImageCafé would offer the website templates through its online superstore. Customers would create an account, log in, and shop for a website, which could then be customized easily using ImageCafé's online website manager tools. Wooten remarked,

> Small businesses are tough clients because they want the world, but they are not willing to pay for it. Business owners started to see a website like they did their telephones. They couldn't imagine not having a telephone, and they started to think the same about a website.

By prefabricating the templates, ImageCafé could charge under $500 for websites that would have cost much more had they been built individually. This seemed like an incredible value for small businesses. Wooten's slogan was "look like the Fortune 500 for under $500." ImageCafé addressed and solved the pitfalls that had been the downfall of his two previous companies. Wooten knew this market, he focused on what he knew he could do best, and he transitioned from the service industry to the product industry as planned.

The Search for Capital

Once Wooten had thoroughly thought through the concept and model of ImageCafé, the next step was to secure enough capital for its launch. Wooten had recently read *The Burn Rate*[11], which mentioned the Silicon Valley law firm of Wilson, Sonsini, Goodrich & Rosati (WSGR). Wooten thought becoming a WSGR client would help give him the credibility to raise capital.

Wooten read the attorney profile section of WSGR's website and picked out four associates close to his age who he hoped could relate to him and his goals. He sent them e-mail messages saying he had founded an East Coast–based e-commerce startup and was looking for not only Silicon Valley–based legal representation but also venture capital funding.

Wooten caught the attention of attorney Mike Arrington. After reading ImageCafé's executive summary and viewing the Web-based prototype, Arrington thought Wooten and Forde would be able to obtain funding. Within a few days, Wooten and Forde had WSGR representation. Wooten had negotiated a package of legal services totaling $40,000, which would be written off if ImageCafé couldn't get funding.

The Relentless Pursuit of Capital

Now began ImageCafé's quest for capital. Wooten decided he needed to meet other entrepreneurs or individuals who might be interested in supporting his vision. One was Dwayne Walker, a well-known ex-Microsoft employee who left with stock options, great technical knowledge, and a thirst to start his own company—Techwave. As Wooten put it, "He was a black man who raised $10 million. That qualified him as a man I needed to meet." After calling Walker daily, Wooten eventually set up a meeting in Seattle, where Walker was based. As the meeting ended, Walker declared that he wanted to be ImageCafé's first angel investor.

There were two catches. First, Walker wanted to incubate[12] ImageCafé in the Seattle area. Wooten

---

[8]"Computer Industry Forecasts: Communications," Third Quarter 1996, p. 81.

[9]"March 2014 Web Server Survey" http://news.netcraft.com/archives/2014/ 03/03/march-2014-web-server-survey.html.

[10]*Fast Company*, July 2000.

[11]M. Wolff, *The Burn Rate: How I Survived the Gold Rush Years on the Internet* (New York: Simon & Schuster, 1998.)

[12]An incubator is a program or facility designed to foster entrepreneurship and help startup companies, usually technology ones, grow.

and Forde had two people working part-time on the back-end programming, who had agreed to be paid $30,000 in stock or cash once capital had been raised. When Walker made his offer, the ImageCafé superstore was 60 percent finished; Wooten couldn't relocate his whole team at the crucial last hour. After hearing the second catch—that the half million dollars would be paid to ImageCafé in $20,000 increments based on milestones—Wooten and Forde said no thank you and goodbye to Walker.

Still Going

WSGR set up several meetings for Wooten with venture capital firms in Silicon Valley. While waiting for a flight to the West Coast, Wooten remembered reading about an African American, Earl Graves (see Note 3 at the end of this case), who had obtained his Pepsi bottling franchise in part by sitting next to one of the Pepsi executives on a plane in first class. Wooten convinced a flight attendant friend to move him up from coach and found himself seated next to Bill Daniels, a principal at Bank Boston Robertson Stevenson. Wooten recalled, "I had a captive audience for literally 6 hours. I talked about why I was going to Silicon Valley and whom I was going to see. I showed him the business plan." By the end of the flight, Daniels had become Wooten's first realistically interested angel investor.

Shortly after returning from Silicon Valley, Wooten decided to speak to his family and friends to raise a few hundred thousand dollars. Closing the "friends and family round" proved to be challenging. However, his girlfriend (now wife) passed his business plan to her cousin, who worked for Sonny Stern, a New Jersey doctor who had been involved with venture capital for many years. Stern turned out to be a client of the same Bill Daniels that Wooten had met on his trip to Silicon Valley. After conferring with Daniels and sending Wooten to meet with other potential investors in New York. He decided to lead an angel round with Daniels. Wooten also got WSGR to participate.

Wooten wanted $300,000 in capital, based on a $3,000,000 valuation, meaning he would give up 10 percent of the company. Instead, ImageCafé received $110,000 from 10 angel investors, for 11 percent of its equity. Wooten was disappointed—he had expected more.

It was December 1998, the software was 70 percent finished, and the $110,000 would not be nearly enough. With a touch of sour grapes, Wooten remembered, "During that time, everybody was throwing out $5,000,000 valuations before they had anything. I had a functional prototype, as well as a plan. I went from Silicon Valley to Silicon Alley,

raising money. I thought a $3,000,000 valuation was fair, but I couldn't get a bite."

In April 1999, ImageCafé's website was finished and ready for launch—but Wooten and Forde were out of cash. Upon launch, ImageCafé received enough press attention to attract new potential investors, which enabled Wooten to negotiate an additional $150,000 in the form of a bridge loan from the company's existing investors. The loan would be convertible to equity at a small discount at the close of the first venture capital round. Wooten expected to raise $3,000,000 at a $10,000,000 valuation from one or more venture capitalist firms.

Just before the $150,000 came through, Wooten secured a big customer. Mindspring, one of the largest Internet service providers (ISPs) agreed to commit to ImageCafé's products before Wooten and Forde had even finished them! They had only a prototype and knew they would need millions of dollars to execute their plan. Wooten recalls,

> We wanted to leverage the existing channel, and that was the Internet service providers. They had a lot of small business customers. We basically would allow them to co-brand and create their own, what I call, virtual franchise, their own ImageCafé superstore—ImageCafé at Mindspring, ImageCafé at Earthlink, ImageCafé at AOL . . . and it was good for them because it allowed them to pick up more hosting business. They wanted to host the website; we wanted to sell the website as well as subscriptions to our Web site manager tool. I made sure we didn't go into the hosting business because I didn't want to cannibalize our channel. It was a beautiful business model.

Still, this required cash that ImageCafé did not have. Although Wooten and Forde had burned through the $260,000 (the initial $110,000 equity investment plus the $150,000 bridge loan), they had managed to launch the product and attract a large customer.

At the same time as the Mindspring deal, Wooten was also courting Network Solutions, Inc., which nearly had a monopoly on dot-com domain names. Wooten thought Network Solutions would be a perfect channel for ImageCafé. Millions of people went to Network Solutions "credit card in hand" to buy a domain name; the next natural step was to build (or buy) a website. Because ImageCafé was a shopping experience and not a building experience, Network Solutions could attach ImageCafé to its purchase flow. As soon as a small business customer bought a domain name, the new company could also buy an ImageCafé website. Wooten recalls, "It didn't hurt their channel because most of their resellers of domain names were ISPs. So here we could help them to reward their top resellers, by sending them hosting business from customers who had purchased ImageCafé websites."

Wooten met with Network Solutions's new CEO, Jim Rutt. He loved ImageCafé and believed it was the perfect product extension for Network Solutions' business.

Product on Track, But Out of Cash ("OOC")

By June 1999, ImageCafé was again out of cash. Wooten had been working to arrange what he perceived as the perfect financing round for several months and had three major investors lined up—two venture capital firms, and Network Solutions. Wooten wanted a total investment of $3,000,000–$1,000,000 from each investor, on a $10,000,000 valuation. One investor felt the valuation was too high. As the negotiations dragged on, another agreed to lend ImageCafé $150,000. Negotiations continued to drag because of the valuation, even though Wooten was willing to sweeten the deal with $500,000 in warrants, split three ways.

During the valuation discussions, Network Solutions made a buyout offer that was potentially worth $21 million: one-third in cash, one-third in Network Solutions stock, and one-third in an earn-out.[13] Wooten owned a majority of ImageCafé, and this offer would clearly mean a big payday. But there was a hitch. The last bridge loan Wooten had received from the venture capitalists had a 90-day "no shop" clause attached. Running out of cash, and unable to sell the company until September, Wooten went to a company called Mid-Atlantic Venture Association, which had been interested in investing all along.

With more than 20 employees and a burn rate of $50,000 per month, the cash was going fast. Although interested, Mid Atlantic Ventures (MAV) couldn't invest until it had performed its due diligence. In the meantime, understanding Wooten's immediate cash needs, MAV referred him to two new angel investors who agreed to extend him a $300,000 bridge loan with warrant coverage on a $6,000,000 valuation; this would at least hold ImageCafé over through the summer. Wooten remembered intensely, "I had worked so long and hard to put together the perfect financing round that never went through because I wanted a $10,000,000 valuation—and on a Sunday afternoon, I ended up giving that away out of necessity."

It was September, and again out of cash, Wooten had a difficult decision to make. ImageCafé hung in the balance. Should he sell now or secure more capital to continue the fight?

Additional Case Information

Note 1

Research suggests that African American applicants for small business financing are denied more often than Caucasians with similar creditworthiness, and that the percentage of Small Business Association loans going to African Americans has dropped since the 2008 financial crisis. A 2002 study by the National Bureau of Economic Research found raw loan denial rates of 27 percent for Caucasians and 66 percent for African Americans.[14] An analysis of Small Business Association loans by The Wall Street Journal found that 1.7 percent of the $23.09 billion in SBA loans made during the agency's 2013 fiscal year went to African Americans, down from 8.2 percent in fiscal 2008.[15]

Note 2

A study from the Ewing Marion Kauffman Foundation provides a detailed look at the connections between minority entrepreneurs and the venture capital industry. The report examines funds operated by members of the National Association of Investment Companies (NAIC), an association of investment firms with interest in backing minority business enterprises (MBEs). A few interesting findings stand out. First, the growth in minority enterprise venture financing was rapid. In the early 1990s, only several million dollars had been invested in MBEs. By 2001, the industry had more than $1 billion under management. The researchers, Wayne State's Timothy Bates and University of Washington's William Bradford, also found that this sector was quite profitable. The average investment per firm was $562,000; the average net return on this investment exceeded $1 million. The average rate of return exceeded 20 percent—compared to a 17 percent return for the S&P 500 over the same period. These funds also tend to invest in a wider mix of industrial sectors, thus cushioning the industry from some effects of the technology downturn. Overall, the authors concluded that the minority venture capital investment sector was poised for further expansion.[16]

---

[13]An earn-out is an agreement that gives sellers of a business future payments contingent upon how well the business performs under its new owners.

[14]"Discrimination in the Small Business Credit Market," David Blanchflower, Phillip Levine, David Zimmerman, August 2002 http://www.dartmouth.edu/~blnchflr/papers/finalrestat.pdf.

[15]Ruth Simon and Tom McGinty, "Loan Rebound Misses Black Businesses," *The Wall Street Journal,* March 14, 2014.

[16]See the following for more information: "Minorities and Venture Capital: A New Wave in American Business" by Timothy Bates and William Bradford, http://sites.kauffman.org/pdf/minorities_vc_report.pdf.

Note 3

Earl G. Graves[17] has long been considered the pre-eminent authority on African American business. The locus of that authority is *Black Enterprise*, the magazine he founded in 1970, which now has a circulation of 500,000 and revenues of $24 million. Graves is the magazine's publisher as well as the chairman of its parent company, Earl G. Graves Ltd. He previously was chairman and CEO of Pepsi Cola of Washington, D.C. L.P., which was the largest minority-controlled Pepsi franchise in the nation before Pepsico Inc. purchased it in 1997. Graves is a leading spokesperson on issues that affect the well-being and economic success of African Americans and uses his expertise to educate others about trends and opportunities in African American entrepreneurship.

[17]http://www.blackenterprise.com/management/earl-graves/. When I rewrote the section, I used a different source than originally referenced. The original source was Biography Resource Center, Gale Group Inc., 2001.

Chapter Two

The Entrepreneurial Mind: Crafting a Personal Entrepreneurial Strategy

LEARNING OUTCOMES: After reading this chapter you will be able to understand:

2-1 Entrepreneurial characteristics

2-2 Desirable and acquirable attitudes, habits, and behaviors of entrepreneurs

2-3 Tolerance of risk, ambiguity, and uncertainty

2-4 Creativity, self-reliance, and adaptability

2-5 The entrepreneurial mind in action

2-6 Who is the entrepreneur?

2-7 The concept of apprenticeship

2-8 Role models

2-9 Myths and realities

2-10 What can be learned?

Entrepreneurs Are Good Business People

The entrepreneur of the 21st century is just as likely to be inside a Southwest Airlines, a Google, or a General Electric as in a startup. Today entrepreneurship is indicative of a form of strategy rather than a size of company.

In either environment effective entrepreneurs are intrinsically motivated, high-energy leaders who can tolerate ambiguity, mitigate risk, effectively commercialize technologies, and innovate. These leaders identify and pursue opportunities by marshalling the diverse resources required to develop new markets and engage the inevitable competition.

Three Characteristics of Entrepreneurship

Numerous ways of analyzing human behavior have implications in the study of entrepreneurship.[1] The psychological motivation of entrepreneurial behavior is a generally accepted part of the literature. The theory states that people are motivated by three principal needs: (1) the need for achievement, (2) the need for power, and (3) the need for affiliation.

- The *need for achievement* is the need to excel and the need for measurable personal accomplishment.
- The *need for power* is the need to influence others to achieve a goal.
- The *need for affiliation* is the need to build a relationship with others.

The key issue here is the visionary who participates in the day-to-day routine has these attributes in successful startups. Entrepreneurs motivated purely by monetary reward typically do not build companies of substantial value.

Academics continue to research the characteristics of entrepreneurs as outlined in Exhibit 2.1. Our own research and experience indicate that successful entrepreneurs concentrate on certain fundamentals: responsiveness, resiliency, and adaptability in seizing new opportunities. Entrepreneurs have the ability "to make things happen" and a willingness to invest in new techniques

The authors would like to thank Frederic M. Alper, a long-time friend and colleague for his insights and contributions to this chapter, in particular the graphic representation of entrepreneurial attributes and the development of the QuickLook exercise to develop a personal entrepreneurial strategy.

[1]See J.W. Atkinson, *An Introduction to Motivation* (Princeton, NJ: Van Nostrand, 1964); J.W. Atkinson, *Motives in Fantasy, Action and Society* (Princeton, NJ: Van Nostrand, 1958); D.C. McClelland, *The Achieving Society* (Princeton, NJ: Van Nostrand, 1961); J.W. Atkinson and N.T. Feather, eds., *A Theory of Achievement Motivation* (New York: John Wiley & Sons, 1966); and D.C. McClelland and D.G. Winter, *Motivating Economic Achievement* (New York: Free Press, 1969).

EXHIBIT 2.1

Characteristics of Entrepreneurs

Date	Authors	Characteristics
1848	Mill	Risk bearing
1917	Weber	Source of formal authority
1934	Schumpeter	Innovation; initiative
1954	Sutton	Desire for responsibility
1959	Hartman	Source of formal authority
1961	McClelland	Risk taking; need for achievement
1963	Davids	Ambition; desire for independence, responsibility, self-confidence
1964	Pickle	Drive/mental; human relations; communication ability; technical knowledge
1971	Palmer	Risk measurement
1971	Hornaday and Aboud	Need for achievement; autonomy; aggression; power; recognition; innovative/independent
1973	Winter	Need for power
1974	Borland	Internal locus of power
1982	Casson	Risk; innovation; power; authority
1985	Gartner	Change and ambiguity
1987	Begley and Boyd	Risk taking; tolerance of ambiguity
1988	Caird	Drive
1998	Roper	Power and authority
2000	Thomas and Mueller	Risk; power; internal locus of control; innovation
2001	Lee and Tsang	Internal locus of control

while maintaining a professional attitude and being patient. Research reveals the importance of fundamentally enjoying and being interested in business as well as treating entrepreneurship as a way of life. A consulting study by McKinsey & Co. of medium-sized growth companies (with sales between $25 million and $1 billion and with sales or profit growth of more than 15 percent annually over 5 years) confirms that the chief executive officers of winning companies were notable for three common traits: perseverance, a builder's mentality, and a strong propensity for taking calculated risks.[2]

Converging on the Entrepreneurial Mind

Desirable and Acquirable Attitudes, Habits, and Behaviors

All successful business people share characteristics of raw energy and intelligence. There is increasing evidence that entrepreneurs have certain innate characteristics and that certain successful attitudes and behaviors can be developed through experience and study.[3] Research shows three entrepreneurial attributes for success in new ventures: (1) positive response to challenges and mistakes, (2) personal initiative, and (3) perseverance.[4]

New Research   The Praeger Perspectives is a three volume series from 2007 that researched entrepreneurship from three perspectives: people, process, and place. This study brings together insights into the field of entrepreneurship by some of the leading scholars in the world. We have drawn on this work liberally in this edition of *New Venture Creation*.

The first volume, *people*, takes a broad view of entrepreneurship as a form of human action, pulling together the current research with respect to cognitive, economic, social, and institutional factors that influence entrepreneurial behavior. Why do people start new businesses? How do people make entrepreneurial decisions? What is the role played by the social and economic environment in individuals' decisions about entrepreneurship? Do institutions matter? Do some groups of people such as immigrants and women face particular issues when deciding to start a business?

The second volume, *process*, proceeds through the life cycle of a new venture startup by tackling

---

[2]D.K. Clifford, Jr., and R.E. Cavanagh, *The Winning Performance* (New York: Bantam Books, 1985), p. 3.

[3]D.C. McClelland, "Achievement Motivation Can Be Developed," *Harvard Business Review*, November–December 1965; D.C. McClelland and D.G. Winter, *Motivating Economic Achievement* (New York: Free Press, 1969); and J.A. Timmons, "Black Is Beautiful–Is It Bountiful?" *Harvard Business Review*, November–December 1971, p. 81.

[4]J.A. Hornaday and N.B. Tieken, "Capturing Twenty-One Heffalumps." In *Frontiers of Entrepreneurship Research: 1983*, ed. J.A. Hornaday et al. (Babson Park, MA: Babson College, 1983), pp. 23–50.

several key steps in the process: idea, opportunity, team building, resource acquisition, growth management, and entering global markets. It is clear from this volume that much progress has been made in understanding the entrepreneurial process.

The third volume in the series examines *place*, which refers to a wide and diverse range of contextual factors that influence the entrepreneur and the entrepreneurial process. The research examines the impact of public policy and entrepreneurship support systems at the country and community level and from an economic and social perspective.

We will also be referring to the work of Professors Stefan Kwiatkowski and Nawaz Sharif, editors of the *Knowledge Café* series on "Intellectual Entrepreneurship and Courage to Act." This text, the fifth in Kwiatkowski's series, provides further insight into the entrepreneurial mind-set involved in creating new intellectual property and knowledge creation ventures.

Seven Dominant Themes

A consensus has emerged around seven dominant themes, shown in Exhibits 2.2 and 2.3.

EXHIBIT 2.2

Seven Themes of Desirable and Acquirable Attitudes and Behaviors

Theme	Attitude or Behavior
Commitment and determination	Tenacious and decisive, able to re-commit/commit quickly
	Persistent in solving problems, disciplined
	Willing to undertake personal sacrifice
	Immersed in the mission
Courage	Moral strength
	Fearless experimentation
	Not afraid of conflicts, failure
	Intense curiosity in the face of risk
Leadership	Self-starter; high standards but not perfectionist
	Team builder and hero maker; inspires others
	Treats others as you want to be treated
	Shares the wealth with all the people who helped create it
	Honest and reliable; builds trust; practices fairness
	Not a lone wolf
	Superior learner and teacher; courage
	Patient and urgent
Opportunity obsession	Leadership in shaping the opportunity
	Has intimate knowledge of customers' needs and wants
	Market driven
	Obsessed with value creation and enhancement
Tolerance of risk, ambiguity, and uncertainty	Calculated risk taker
	Risk minimizer
	Risk sharer
	Manages paradoxes and contradictions
	Tolerates uncertainty and lack of structure
	Tolerates stress and conflict
	Able to resolve problems and integrate solutions
Creativity, self-reliance, and adaptability	Nonconventional, open-minded, lateral thinker (helicopter mind)
	Restless with status quo
	Able to adapt and change; creative problem solver
	Quick learner
	No fear of failure
	Able to conceptualize and "sweat details"
Motivation to excel	Goal and results oriented; high but realistic goals
	Drive to achieve and grow
	Low need for status and power
	Interpersonally supporting (vs. competitive)
	Aware of weaknesses and strengths
	Has perspective and sense of humor

EXHIBIT 2.3

Core and Desirable Entrepreneurial Attributes

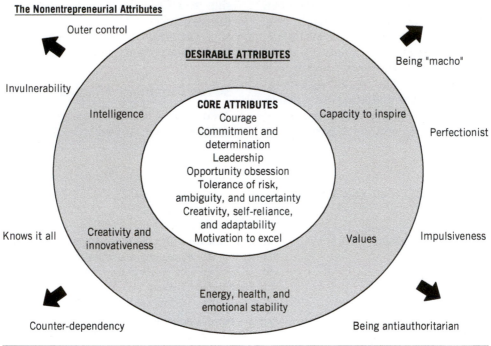

Commitment and Determination Commitment and determination are seen as more important than any other factor. With commitment and determination, an entrepreneur can overcome incredible obstacles and also compensate enormously for other weaknesses.

For 16 long years following his graduation from college, Mario Ricciardelli worked to create a travel agency that catered to students. He endured lean personal finances and countless setbacks, including several near bankruptcies, the sudden failure of a charter airline that left his young clients stranded in Mexico, and a stock swap deal with a high-profile Internet venture that fell to earth after 2 difficult years. Mario and Jacqui Lewis, his partner from a subsequent acquisition, convinced the troubled parent company to let them turn in their shares in exchange for their cash-strapped online travel portal. Having no money to expand into other markets, in 2003 the team refocused its efforts on building the most comprehensive and exciting online spring break travel program anywhere. By pouring all of its attention into that narrow space, the company was able to dramatically increase bookings and profitability. In its first season as a newly independent venture, it generated just under $1 million in free cash flow. In early 2004, with year-over-year growth in bookings of 100 percent, the partners

decided to look for a buyer. Ninety days later, Mario and Jacqui joined the ranks of American millionaires when their company, StudentCity.com, was acquired by First Choice Holidays, a $5 billion tour operator in Europe. Today Mario operates a division of the acquiring company that generates nine figures in revenue.

Total commitment is required in nearly all entrepreneurial ventures. Almost without exception, entrepreneurs live under huge, constant pressures—first for their firms to survive startup, then for them to stay alive, and finally for them to grow. A new venture demands top priority for the entrepreneur's time, emotions, and loyalty. Thus commitment and determination usually require personal sacrifice. An entrepreneur's commitment can be measured in several ways—through a willingness to invest a substantial portion of his or her net worth in the venture, through a willingness to take a cut in pay because he or she will own a major piece of the venture, and through other major sacrifices in lifestyle and family circumstances.

Courage As we noted earlier, we are indebted to Stefan Kwiatkowski and Nawaz Sharif for their insightful and thoughtful work on *courage* as an important dimension of the entrepreneurial mind-set.

EXHIBIT 2.4

Online Search for Desirable Attributes of Entrepreneurship

Timmons/Spinelli Theme	Google	EBSCO	ProQuest
Commitment	534,000	151	7,042
Leadership	1,200,000	377	7,230
Opportunity obsession	9,010	1	0
Opportunity immersion[a]	14,000	0	0
Risk tolerance	57,600	4	53
Adaptability	50,400	21	688
Achievement	370,000	192	4,169
Courage	81,000	10	647

[a]A non-Timmons/Spinelli theme.

Source: S. Kwiatkowski and N.M.Sharif. *Knowledge Café for Intellectual Entrepreneurship and Courage to Act.* (Warsaw, Poland: Publishing house of Leon Kozminsky Academy of Entrepreneurship and Management, 2005), p. 231.

In his paper "What the Hell, Let's Give It a Try," Kwiatkowski asserts that courage is not simply bravery resulting from deficient information about a given situation, nor pluck anchored in feelings of invulnerability. Courage rather has its source in broadly understood knowledge, experience, and integrity of the courageous individual. To prove his point, Kwiatkowski googled "core and desirable entrepreneurial attributes" combined with "entrepreneurship." Results of that search, and two other searches also conducted in March 2005, are depicted in Exhibit 2.4.

Hence, as we continue to converge on the entrepreneurial mind, we have included and elevated courage to the second of what are now seven themes. We see courage having at least three important aspects: first, *moral strength and principles.* This means the character and the personal integrity to know right from wrong, and the will and commitment to act accordingly. The second is *being a fearless experimenter.* Fearless experimentation suggests restlessness with convention and a rejection of the status quo. This relentless experimentation is enhanced by a third aspect of courage: *a lack of fear of failing at the experiment*—and most undertakings for that matter—*and a lack of fear of conflicts that may arise.* In other words, there is a mental toughness that is quite impervious to fears but is not ignorant or oblivious to possible consequences.

Leadership   Successful entrepreneurs are usually experienced, with considerable domain knowledge of the marketplace in which they will compete, sound general management skills, and a proven track record.

Three clear areas are at the foundation of a successful new venture: the lead entrepreneur, the venture team, and the external environmental influences, which are outlined in further detail in Exhibit 2.5. These three attributes are "metaphorically associated with a *troika,* a Russian vehicle pulled by three horses of *equal* strength. Each horse represents a cluster of the success factors. The troika was driven toward success by the visions and *dreams* of the founding entrepreneurs."[5]

Successful entrepreneurs possess a well-developed capacity to exert influence *without* formal power and are adept at conflict resolution. To run a successful venture, an entrepreneur learns to get along with many different constituencies, the customer, the supplier, the financial backer, and the creditor, as well as the partners and others on the inside. In a corporate setting, this critical attribute is "hero-making" for successful entrepreneurial managers.[6] These managers have a capacity for objective interpersonal relationships which enables them to smooth out individual differences of opinion by keeping attention focused on the common goal to be achieved.[7]

Opportunity Obsession   Successful entrepreneurs consistently focus on the market-based opportunity rather than the money, resources, contacts, and appearances.

The entrepreneur's credo is to think opportunity first and cash last. Time and again, even after harvesting a highly successful venture, lead entrepreneurs will start another company. They possess all the money and material wealth anyone would ever hope for, yet like the artist, scientist, athlete, or musician who strives for another discovery.

An excellent example of this pattern is David Neeleman, founder of discount airline JetBlue, who created the first electronic airline ticket a few years earlier while at Morris Air, which sold to Southwest Airlines. In 1998 he developed a unique vision for a new airline, and was having dinner with financial backer Michael Lazarus of Weston-Presidio Capital Partners. Lazarus asked, "Why do you want to start a new airline—what is the big

[5]A. Grant, "The Development of an Entrepreneurial Leadership Paradigm for Enhancing New Venture Success." In *Frontiers of Entrepreneurship Research: 1992*, ed. J.A. Hornaday et al. (Babson Park, MA: Babson College, 1992).

[6]D.L. Bradford and A.R. Cohen, *Managing for Excellence: The Guide to Developing High Performance in Contemporary Organizations* (New York: John Wiley & Sons, 1984).

[7]N. Churchill, "Entrepreneurs and Their Enterprises: A Stage Model." In *Frontiers of Entrepreneurship Research: 1983*, ed. J.A. Hornaday et al. (Babson Park, MA: Babson College, 1983), pp. 1–22.

EXHIBIT 2.5

The Entrepreneurial Leadership Paradigm

The Lead Entrepreneur

Self-concept	Has a realist's attitude rather than one of invincibility.
Intellectually honest	Trustworthy: his/her word is his/her contract.
	Admits what and when he/she does not know.
Pacemaker	Displays a high energy level and a sense of urgency.
Courage	Capable of making hard decisions: setting and beating high goals.
Communication skills	Maintains an effective dialogue with the venture team, in the marketplace, and with other venture constituents.
Team player	Competent in people management and team-building skills.

The Venture Team

Organizational style	The lead entrepreneur and the venture team blend their skills to operate in a participative environment.
Ethical behavior	Practices strong adherence to ethical business practices.
Faithfulness	Stretched commitments are consistently met or bettered.
Focus	Long-term venture strategies are kept in focus, but tactics are varied to achieve them.
Performance/reward	High standards of performance are created, and superior performance is rewarded fairly and equitably.
Adaptability	Responsive to rapid changes in product/technological cycles.

External Environmental Influences

Constituent needs	Organization needs are satisfied, in parallel with those of the other publics the enterprise serves.
Prior experience	Extensive prior experiences are effectively applied.
Mentoring	The competencies of others are sought and used.
Problem resolution	New problems are immediately solved or prioritized.
Value creation	High commitment is placed on long-term value creation for backers, customers, employees, and other stakeholders.
Skill emphasis	Marketing skills are stressed over technical ones.

Source: Adapted from A.J. Grant. "The Development of an Entrepreneurial Leadership Paradigm for Enhancing Venture Capital Success," *Frontiers of Entrepreneurship Research: 1992*, ed. J.A. Hornaday et al. Babson Park, MA: Babson College, 1992.

opportunity you see?" Neeleman replied, "I'm going to fly people where they want to go!" This simple but brilliant concept saw an opportunity in what all other would-be airline entrepreneurs saw as a barrier to entry: the entrenched, massive hub system of large, established airlines.

Tolerance of Risk, Ambiguity, and Uncertainty

Successful entrepreneurs are not gamblers; they take calculated risks. One study[8] found that while entrepreneurs shunned risk, they sustained their courage by the clarity and optimism with which they saw the future. Successful entrepreneurs maximize the good "higher-performance" results of stress and minimize the negative reactions of exhaustion and frustration. Two surveys have suggested that very high levels of both satisfaction and stress characterize founders, to a greater degree than managers, regardless of the success of their ventures.[9]

Creativity, Self-Reliance, and Adaptability High levels of uncertainty and rapid change characterizing new ventures require organizations that can respond quickly. The most successful entrepreneurial teams have the ability to focus on a goal with outstanding execution, while being flexible enough to shift when the market and circumstances require it. At the same time, entrepreneurs are not afraid of failing; rather, they are more intent on succeeding.

Motivation to Excel Entrepreneurs are self-starters who are internally driven by a strong desire to compete and attain challenging goals. This need to achieve has been well established in the literature on entrepreneurs since the pioneering work of McClelland and Atkinson. The best entrepreneurs have a keen awareness of their own strengths and weaknesses and those of their partners and of the competitive environment surrounding and influencing them.

---

[8]D. Mitton, "No Money, Know-How, Know-Who: Formula for Managing Venture Success and Personal Wealth." In *Frontiers of Entrepreneurship Research: 1984*, ed. J.A. Hornaday et al. (Babson Park, MA: Babson College, 1984), p. 427.

[9]E.A. Fagonson, "Personal Value Systems of Men and Women Entrepreneurs versus Managers," *Journal of Business Venturing*, 1993.

The Entrepreneurial Mind in Action

How do successful entrepreneurs think, what actions do they take, and how do they start and build businesses? By understanding the attitudes, behaviors, management competencies, experience, and know-how that contribute to entrepreneurial success, one has some useful benchmarks for gauging what to do. Exhibit 2.6 examines the role of opportunity in entrepreneurship.

Successful entrepreneurs have a wide range of personality types, and research about entrepreneurs has focused on the influences of genes, family, education, and career experience with no repeatable model being supported. Studies have shown that an entrepreneur does not need specific inherent traits, but rather a set of acquired skills.[10] A Price-Babson College fellow phrased it best when he said, "One does not want to overdo the personality stuff, but there is a certain ring to it."[11]

"There is no evidence of an ideal entrepreneurial personality. Great entrepreneurs can be gregarious or low-key, analytical or intuitive, charismatic or boring, good with details or terrible, delegators or control freaks. What you need is a capacity to execute in certain key ways."[12] Those who have succeeded speak of this capacity time and again.[13] For example, two famous entrepreneurs have captured the intense commitment and perseverance of entrepreneurs. Wally Amos, famous for his chocolate chip cookies, said, "You can do anything you want to do."[14] John Johnson of Johnson Publishing Company (publisher of *Ebony*) expressed it this way: "You need to think yourself out of a corner, meet needs, and never, never accept no for an answer."[15]

Although the skills of the manager and the entrepreneur overlap in the area of solid management skills, the manager is more driven by conservation of resources and the entrepreneur more opportunity-driven[16] as outlined in Exhibit 2.7.

EXHIBIT 2.6

Opportunity Knocks—Or Does It Hide? An Examination of the Role of Opportunity Recognition in Entrepreneurship

Number (and Proportion) of Opportunities of Various Sources and Types		
Sources of Opportunities	**Entrepreneurs**	**Nonentrepreneurs**
Prior work	67 (58.3%)	13 (48.2%)
Prior employment	36	6
Prior consulting work	11	4
Prior business	20	2
Network	25 (21.7%)	8 (29.6%)
Social contact	7	6
Business contact	18	2
Thinking by analogy	13 (11.3%)	6 (22.2%)
Partner	10 (8.7%)	—
Types of Opportunities	**Entrepreneurs**	**Nonentrepreneurs**
Niche expansion/underserved niche	29 (25.2%)	7 (29.2%)
Customer need	34 (29.6%)	6 (25.0%)
Own firm's need	6 (5.2%)	1 (4.2%)
Better technology	46 (40.0%)	10 (41.7%)

Source: Zietsma, Charlene, "Opportunity Knocks—Or Does it Hide? An Examination of the Role of Opportunity Recognition in Entrepreneurship." In *Frontiers of Entrepreneurship Research: 1999*, eds. P.D.Reynolds et al. Babson Park, MA: Babson College. Used by permission of the author.

Note: Numbers equal total people in the sample allocated to each category. Numbers in parentheses equal percentage of total surveyed.

---

[10]W. Lee, "What Successful Entrepreneurs Really Do," *Lee Communications*, 2001.

[11]Comment made during a presentation at the June 1987 Price-Babson College Fellows Program by Jerry W. Gustafson, Coleman-Fannie May Candies Professor of Entrepreneurship, Beloit College, at Babson College.

[12]Lee, "What Successful Entrepreneurs Really Do."

[13]See the excellent summary of a study of the first 21 inductees into Babson College's Academy of Distinguished Entrepreneurs by J.A. Hornaday and N. Tieken, "Capturing Twenty-One Heffalumps." In *Frontiers of Entrepreneurship Research: 1983*, pp. 23, 50.

[14]Made during a speech at his induction in 1982 into the Academy of Distinguished Entrepreneurs, Babson College.

[15]Made during a speech at his induction in 1979 into the Academy of Distinguished Entrepreneurs, Babson College.

[16]J.A. Timmons, D.F. Muzyka, H.H. Stevenson, and W.D. Bygrave, "Opportunity Recognition: The Core of Entrepreneurship." In *Frontiers of Entrepreneurship Research* (Babson Park, MA: Babson College, 1987), pp. 42–49.

EXHIBIT 2.7

Who Is the Entrepreneur?

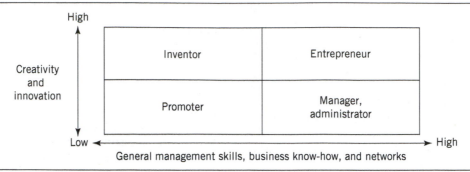

The Concept of Apprenticeship

Shaping and Managing an Apprenticeship

When one looks at successful entrepreneurs, you see 10 years of relevant domain knowledge. The more successful ones have made money for their employer before doing it for themselves. Consider the following examples.

- Apple Computer founders Steve Jobs and Steve Wozniak were computer enthusiasts as preteens and had accumulated significant experience when they started Apple in their 20s.
- Paul Tobin had no prior cellular phone experience when he was picked up by John Kluge to launch Cellular One, but he had had 6 years of experience at Satellite Business Systems in marketing and had previously spent over 5 years launching and building his own company.
- Jeff Parker worked for 10 years in the bond-trading business at three major investment banks and acquired computer skills that enabled him to write programs for bond traders. He launched Technical Data Corporation with $100,000 using his bond-trading and computer experience, selling his company to Telerate for more than $20 million[17] a few years later.

The Concept of Apprenticeship: Acquiring the 50,000 Chunks

Increasingly, research studies on the career paths of entrepreneurs and the self-employed show that the role of experience and know-how is central in successful venture creation. Also critical to the entrepreneur is the ability to gain information and act on it.[18] Evidence also suggests that success is linked to preparation and planning.[19] This is what getting 50,000 chunks of experience is about.

In another study supporting 50,000 chunks of experience, a study found that entrepreneurs' view believing in the idea and experimenting with new ones that result in both failures and successes are the most important components of opportunity recognition.[20]

Role Models

Studies show a strong connection between the presence of role models and the emergence of entrepreneurs. For instance, an early study showed that more than half of those starting new businesses had parents who owned businesses.[21] Likewise, 70 percent of MIT graduates who started technology businesses had entrepreneurial parents.[22]

Myths and Realities

Exhibit 2.8 lists myths about entrepreneurs that have persisted and realities that are supported by research. Studies have indicated that 90 percent of founders start their companies in the same marketplace, technology, or industry they have been working in.[23] Others have found that entrepreneurs are likely to have role models, 8 to 10 years of

[17]This example is drawn from "Technical Data Corporation," HBS Cases 283-072, 283-073, Harvard Business School, 198-1.
[18]K.H. Vesper, "New Venture Ideas: Don't Overlook the Experience Factor," *Harvard Business Review*, reprinted in *Growing Concerns: Building and Managing the Smaller Business*, ed. D.E. Gumpert (New York: John Wiley & Sons, 1984), pp. 28–55.
[19]See R. Ronstadt's and H. Stevenson's studies reported in *Frontiers of Entrepreneurship Research: 1983*.
[20]"Successful Entrepreneurs' Insights into Opportunity Recognition," G. Hills and R. Shrader, University of Illinois, Chicago, 2000.
[21]A. Cooper and W. Dunkelberg, *A New Look at Business Entry* (San Mateo, CA: National Federation of Independent Businesses, March 1984).
[22]*Fortune*, June 7, 1999.
[23]A good summary of some of these studies is provided by R. H. Brockhaus, "The Psychology of the Entrepreneur." In *Encyclopedia of Entrepreneurship*, ed. C. Kent, D. Sexton, and K. Vesper (Englewood Cliffs, NJ: Prentice-Hall, 1982), pp. 50, 55.

EXHIBIT 2.8

Myths and Realities about Entrepreneurs

Myth 1—Entrepreneurs are born, not made.

Reality—While entrepreneurs are born with certain native intelligence, a flair for creating, and energy, these talents by themselves are like unmolded clay or an unpainted canvas. The making of an entrepreneur occurs by accumulating the relevant skills, know-how, experiences, and contacts over a period of years and includes large doses of self-development. The creative capacity to envision and then pursue an opportunity is a direct descendant of at least 10 or more years of experience that lead to pattern recognition.

Myth 2—Anyone can start a business.

Reality—Entrepreneurs who recognize the difference between an idea and an opportunity, and who think big enough, start businesses that have a better chance of succeeding. Luck, to the extent it is involved, requires good preparation. And the easiest part is starting. What is hardest is surviving, sustaining, and building a venture so its founders can realize a harvest. Perhaps only one in 10 to 20 new businesses that survive 5 years or more results in a capital gain for the founders.

Myth 3—Entrepreneurs are gamblers.

Reality—Successful entrepreneurs take very careful, calculated risks. They try to influence the odds, often by getting others to share risk with them and by avoiding or minimizing risks if they have the choice. Often they slice up the risk into smaller, quite digestible pieces; only then do they commit the time or resources to determine if that piece will work. They do not deliberately seek to take more risk or to take unnecessary risk, nor do they shy away from unavoidable risk.

Myth 4—Entrepreneurs want the whole show to themselves.

Reality—Owning and running the whole show effectively puts a ceiling on growth. Solo entrepreneurs usually make a living. It is extremely difficult to grow a higher-potential venture by working single-handedly. Higher potential entrepreneurs build a team, an organization, and a company. Besides, 100 percent of nothing is nothing, so rather than taking a large piece of the pie, they work to make the pie bigger.

Myth 5—Entrepreneurs are their own bosses and completely independent.

Reality—Entrepreneurs are far from independent and have to serve many masters and constituencies, including partners, investors, customers, suppliers, creditors, employees, families, and those involved in social and community obligations. Entrepreneurs, however, can make free choices of whether, when, and what they care to respond to. Moreover, it is extremely difficult, and rare, to build a business beyond $1 million to $2 million in sales single-handedly.

Myth 6—Entrepreneurs work longer and harder than managers in big companies.

Reality—There is no evidence that all entrepreneurs work more than their corporate counterparts. Some do, some do not. Some actually report that they work less.

Myth 7—Entrepreneurs experience a great deal of stress and pay a high price.

Reality—Being an entrepreneur is stressful and demanding. But there is no evidence that it is any more stressful than numerous other highly demanding professional roles, and entrepreneurs find their jobs very satisfying. They have a high sense of accomplishment, are healthier, and are much less likely to retire than those who work for others. Three times as many entrepreneurs as corporate managers say they plan to never retire.

Myth 8—Start a business and fail and you will never raise money again.

Reality—Talented and experienced entrepreneurs—because they pursue attractive opportunities and are able to attract the right people and necessary financial and other resources to make the venture work—often head successful ventures. Further, businesses fail, but entrepreneurs do not. Failure is often the fire that tempers the steel of an entrepreneur's learning experience and street savvy.

Myth 9—Money is the most important startup ingredient.

Reality—If the other pieces and talents are there, the money will follow, but it does not follow that an entrepreneur will succeed if he or she has enough money. Money is one of the least important ingredients in new venture success. Money is to the entrepreneur what the paint and brush are to the artist—an inert tool that in the right hands can create marvels.

Myth 10—Entrepreneurs should be young and energetic.

Reality—While these qualities may help, age is no barrier. The average age of entrepreneurs starting high-potential businesses is in the mid-30s, and there are numerous examples of entrepreneurs starting businesses in their 60s. What is critical is possessing the relevant know-how, experience, and contacts that greatly facilitate recognizing and pursuing an opportunity.

Myth 11—Entrepreneurs are motivated solely by the quest for the almighty dollar.

Reality—Entrepreneurs seeking high-potential ventures are more driven by building enterprises and realizing long-term capital gains than by instant gratification through high salaries and perks. A sense of personal achievement and accomplishment, feeling in control of their own destinies, and realizing their vision and dreams are also powerful motivators. Money is viewed as a tool and a way of keeping score, rather than an end in itself. Entrepreneurs thrive on the thrill of the chase; and, time and again, even after an entrepreneur has made a few million dollars or more, he or she will work on a new vision to build another company.

(continued)

EXHIBIT 2.8   (concluded)

Myths and Realities about Entrepreneurs

Myth 12—Entrepreneurs seek power and control over others.

Reality—Successful entrepreneurs are driven by the quest for responsibility, achievement, and results, rather than for power for its own sake. They thrive on a sense of accomplishment and of outperforming the competition, rather than a personal need for power expressed by dominating and controlling others. By virtue of their accomplishments, they may be powerful and influential, but these are more the by-products of the entrepreneurial process than a driving force behind it.

Myth 13—If an entrepreneur is talented, success will happen in a year or two.

Reality—An old maxim among venture capitalists says it all: The lemons ripen in two and a half years, but the pearls take seven or eight. Rarely is a new business established solidly in less than 3 or 4 years.

Myth 14—Any entrepreneur with a good idea can raise venture capital.

Reality—Of the ventures of entrepreneurs with good ideas who seek out venture capital, only 1 to 3 out of 100 are funded.

Myth 15—If an entrepreneur has enough startup capital, he or she cannot miss.

Reality—The opposite is often true; that is, too much money at the outset often creates euphoria and a spoiled-child syndrome. The accompanying lack of discipline and impulsive spending usually lead to serious problems and failure.

Myth 16—Entrepreneurs are lone wolves and cannot work with others.

Reality—The most successful entrepreneurs are leaders who build great teams and effective relationships working with peers, directors, investors, key customers, key suppliers, and the like.

Myth 17—Unless you attained 600! on your SATs or GMATs, you will never be a successful entrepreneur.

Reality—Entrepreneurial IQ is a unique combination of creativity, motivation, integrity, leadership, team building, analytical ability, and ability to deal with ambiguity and adversity.

experience, and be well educated. It also appears that successful entrepreneurs have a wide range of experiences in products, markets, and across functional areas.[24] Studies also have shown that most successful entrepreneurs start companies in their 30s, with one study of founders of high-tech companies on Route 128 in Boston showing the average age of the founders was 40.

What Can Be Learned?

Throughout the text are cases about real, young entrepreneurs, including some of our former students. You will face the same situations these aspiring entrepreneurs faced as they sought to turn dreams into reality. The cases and text, combined with other online resources, will enable you to grapple with the conceptual, practical, financial, and personal issues entrepreneurs encounter. This book will help you tilt the odds of success in your favor. It will focus your attention on developing answers for the most important of these questions, including these:

- What does an entrepreneurial career take?
- What is the difference between a good opportunity and just another idea?
- Is the opportunity I am considering the right opportunity for me now?
- Why do some firms grow quickly to several million dollars in sales but then stumble, never growing beyond a single-product firm?
- What are the critical tasks and hurdles in seizing an opportunity and building the business?
- How much money do I need and when, where, and how can I get it?
- What financing sources, strategies, and mechanisms can I use?
- What are the minimum resources I need?
- What is my venture worth and how do I negotiate what to give up?
- What are the critical transitions in entrepreneurial management as a firm grows from $1 million to $5 million to $25 million in sales?
- How has the business landscape shifted for 21st century entrepreneurs and the Internet, clean technology, and nano-sciences industries?
- What are the contacts and networks I need to access and to develop?

---

[24]Over 80 studies in this area have been reported in *Frontiers of Entrepreneurship Research* (Babson Park, MA: Babson College) for the years 1981 through 1997.

We believe that we can significantly improve the quality of decisions students make about entrepreneurship and also improve the fit between what they aspire to do and the requirements of the particular opportunity. These choices often lead to self-employment or careers in new and growing firms, including large corporations that realize entrepreneurial strategy is critical to 21st century success. Others seek careers in the financial institutions and professional services firms that are part of the entrepreneurial ecosystem: venture capital, private equity, investment banks, commercial banks, and consulting.

Chapter Summary

- Entrepreneurs are men and women of all sizes, ages, shapes, religions, colors, and backgrounds. There is no single profile or psychological template.
- Successful entrepreneurs share seven common themes that describe their attitudes and ways of thinking and acting.
- Rather than being inborn, the behaviors inherent in these seven attributes can be nurtured, learned, and encouraged, which successful entrepreneurs model for themselves and those with whom they work.
- Entrepreneurs love competition and actually avoid risks when they can, preferring carefully calculated risks.
- Entrepreneurship can be learned; it requires an apprenticeship.
- Most entrepreneurs gain the apprenticeship over 10 years or more after the age of 21 and acquire networks, skills, and the ability to recognize business patterns.

- The entrepreneurial mind-set can benefit large, established companies today just as much as smaller firms.
- Many myths and realities about entrepreneurship provide insights for aspiring entrepreneurs.
- A word of caution: IQ tests, SATs, GMATs, LSATs, and others do not measure some of the most important entrepreneurial abilities and aptitudes.
- Most successful entrepreneurs have had a personal strategy to help them achieve their dreams and goals, both implicitly and explicitly.
- The principal task for the entrepreneur is to determine what kind of entrepreneur he or she wants to become based on his or her attitudes, behaviors, management competencies, experience, and so forth.
- Self-assessment is the hardest thing for entrepreneurs to do, but if you do not do it, you will really get into trouble. If you do not do it, who will?

Study Questions

1. Define entrepreneurial leadership.
2. How does a manager differ from a leader?
3. Define the seven major themes that characterize the mind-sets, attitudes, and actions of successful entrepreneurs. Which are most important? Why? How can they be encouraged and developed?
4. Do you agree with the saying, "Entrepreneurs are made, not born?" Why or why not?
5. Explain the meaning of the apprenticeship concept. Why is it so important to young entrepreneurs?
6. What is your personal entrepreneurial strategy? How should it change?
7. "One person's ham is another person's poison." What does this mean?
8. Evaluate thoroughly your attraction to entrepreneurship.
9. Who should be an entrepreneur and who should not?

Crafting a Personal Entrepreneurial Strategy

If you do not know where you are going, any path will take you there.
From *The Wizard of Oz*

Crafting a personal entrepreneurial strategy is the personal equivalent of developing a business plan. The keys to doing it are the process and discipline that enable an individual to evaluate choices, make decisions and initiate actions, rather than just let things happen. A longer-term sense of direction can be highly motivating. It also can help an entrepreneur determine when to say no (which is much harder than saying yes) and how to temper impulsive hunches with strategic purpose. Those things are important because today's choices become tomorrow's track record.

While a personal strategy can be invaluable, it need not be a prison sentence. It can and will change over time. The process of developing a personal strategy for an entrepreneurial career is a very individual one and, in a sense, one of self-selection.

The reasons for crafting a personal entrepreneurial strategy are similar to the reasons for developing a business plan (see Chapter 7). Among other things, planning helps an entrepreneur manage the risks and uncertainties of the future; helps him or her work smarter, not just harder; keeps him or her future-oriented; helps him or her develop and update a keener strategy by testing his or her ideas and approaches with others; helps him or her motivate himself or herself; makes him or her "results oriented"; and helps make him or her effective in managing and coping with what is by nature a stressful role.

Rationalizations and reasons given for not planning, like those that will be covered in Chapter 7, include that plans are out of date as soon as they are finished; and no one knows what tomorrow will bring so committing to uncertainty is dangerous. Further, the cautious, anxious person may find that setting personal goals creates additional pressure and a heightened fear of failure. In addition, planning may lead to the exclusion of future or yet unknown options that might be more attractive than the ones chosen.

Committing to a career-oriented goal, particularly for a young entrepreneur without much real-world experience, can be premature. For compulsive and obsessive competitors and achievers, setting such a goal may add gasoline to the fire. And some events and environmental factors beyond one's control may boost or sink the best-laid plans.

Personal plans fail for the same reasons as business plans. People may get frustrated when they do not work immediately or have trouble changing from activity-oriented to goal-oriented behavior. Other problems include developing plans based on missions, such as improving performance, rather than goals; plans that do not anticipate obstacles, and plans without milestones or reviews.

A Conceptual Scheme for Self-Assessment

Exhibit 2.9 shows a conceptual scheme for thinking about the self-assessment process called the Johari Window. According to it, there are two sources of information about the self—the individual and others—and three areas in which individuals can learn about themselves.

Self-assessment efforts are hard because obtaining feedback, let alone receiving and benefiting from it, is difficult. Since everyone has a personal frame of reference, values, and so forth that influence first impressions

EXHIBIT 2.9

Peeling the Onion

	Known to Entrepreneur and Team	Not Known to Entrepreneur and Team
Known to Prospective Investors and Stakeholders	Area 1, *Known area:* (what you see is what you get)	Area 2, *Blind area:* (we do not know what we do not know, but you do)
Not Known to Prospective Investors and Stakeholders	Area 3, *Hidden area:* (unshared—you do not know what we do, but the deal does not get done until we find out)	Area 4, *Unknown area:* (no venture is certain or risk free)

Source: J.McIntyre, I.M.Rubin, and D.A.Kolb, *Organizational Psychology: Experiential Approach*, 2nd ed., © 1974.

it is almost impossible for people to obtain unbiased views of themselves from others. Further, in most social situations, people present self-images that they want to preserve and protect, and behavioral norms prohibit others from challenging those images, even if they are not accurate.

The first step of self-assessment for an individual is to generate data by observing his or her own thoughts and actions and by getting feedback from others to (1) become aware of his or her blind spots; and (2) reinforce or change his or her existing perceptions of his or her strengths and weaknesses.

Once an individual has generated the data, the next steps are to study it, develop insights, and then establish apprenticeship goals to gain learning, experience, and so forth.

Finally, the individual can choose goals and opportunities to be created or seized.

Crafting an Entrepreneurial Strategy

Profiling the Past

A useful way for an individual to begin the process of self-assessment and planning is to think about his or her entrepreneurial roots (what he or she has done, his or her preferences in terms of lifestyle and work style, etc.), what he or she would like to do, and how he or she would like to live. Unless an entrepreneur enjoys what he or she is doing for work, having a great deal of money will be a very hollow success.

Profiling the Present

It is useful to profile the present. Having certain personal entrepreneurial attitudes and behaviors (i.e., an "entrepreneurial mind") has been linked to success in entrepreneurship. These attitudes and behaviors deal with such factors as commitment, determination, and perseverance; the drive to achieve and grow; an orientation toward goals; the taking of initiative and personal responsibility; and so forth.

In addition, pursuing opportunities forces entrepreneurs to play various roles. As will be discussed in Chapter 6, the external business environment is given, the demands of a higher-potential business are given, and the ethical values and integrity of key actors are given. Starting, owning, and operating a substantial business requires such factors as accommodation to the venture, toleration of stress, and so forth. Realistically appraising entrepreneurial attitudes and behaviors in light of the requirements of successful entrepreneurship is a useful part of self-assessment.

Another part of self-assessment is an assessment of management competencies and the experience, know-how, and contacts an individual needs to develop.

Getting Constructive Feedback

A Scottish proverb says, "The greatest gift that God hath given us is to see ourselves as others see us." One common denominator among successful entrepreneurs is a desire to know how they are doing and where they stand.

Receiving feedback from others can be very demanding. The following guidelines can help:

- The individual should solicit feedback from those he or she knows well and trusts. How he or she knows the person should be considered. For example, an individual can probably get better feedback about his or her managerial skills from a business colleague than from a friend. A personal friend, however may be able to better comment on the individual's motivation or how a decision could affect his or her family situation. It is helpful to chat with the person before asking him or her to provide any written impressions and to indicate the areas he or she can best comment upon.

- The individual should solicit comments in areas that are particularly important either personally or to the success of his or her venture and ask for more detail if the feedback is unclear. A good way to check if a statement is being understood is to paraphrase it. The person giving feedback needs to be encouraged to describe and give examples of specific situations or behaviors that have influenced his or her impressions.

- Feedback should be actionable and is most helpful if it is neither all positive nor all negative.

- Feedback should be obtained in writing so the person can take some time to think about the issues and pull together feedback from various sources.

- The person asking for feedback should be honest and straightforward with himself or herself and others.

- The person receiving feedback should avoid becoming defensive and taking negative comments personally.

- It is important to listen carefully to what is being said and think about it. Answering, debating, or rationalizing should be avoided.

- The person soliciting feedback should assess whether he or she has considered all important information and been realistic in his or her inferences and conclusions.

- Help should be requested in identifying common threads or patterns, the possible implications of self-assessment data and certain weaknesses (including alternative inferences or conclusions), and relevant information that is missing.

- Additional feedback from others should be sought to verify feedback and to supplement the data.

- Reaching final conclusions or decisions should be left until later.

EXHIBIT 2.10

Fit of the Entrepreneur and the Venture Opportunity

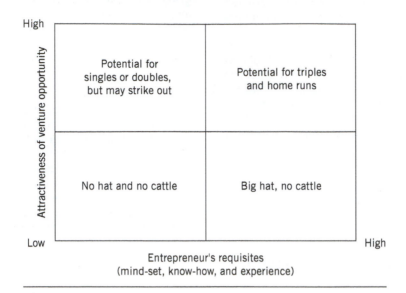

Putting It All Together

Exhibit 2.10 shows the relative fit of an entrepreneur with a venture opportunity, given (1) his or her relevant attitudes and behaviors; (2) his or her relevant management skills, experience, know-how, and contacts; and (3) the role demands of the venture opportunity. A clean appraisal is almost impossible. Self-assessment just is not that simple. The process is cumulative, and what an entrepreneur does about weaknesses, for example, is far more important than what the particular weaknesses might be.

Thinking Ahead

Goal setting is as important in personal planning as it is in developing business plans. Goal setting is a process, a way of dealing with the world. Effective goal setting demands time, self-discipline, commitment and dedication, and practice. Goals, once set, do not become static targets.
A number of distinct steps are involved in goal setting, steps that are repeated over and over as conditions change:

- Establishment of goals that are specific and concrete (rather than abstract and out of focus), measurable, related to time (i.e., specific about what will be accomplished over a certain time period), realistic, and attainable.

- Establishment of priorities, including the identification of conflicts and trade-offs and how these can be resolved.

- Identification of problems and obstacles that could prevent goals from being attained.

- Specification of action steps to accomplish the goal.

- Indication of how results will be measured.

- Establishment of milestones for reviewing progress tied to specific dates on a calendar.

- Identification of risks involved in meeting the goals.

- Identification of help and other resources that may be needed to obtain goals.

- Periodic review of progress and revision of goals.

Exercise 2

Personal Entrepreneurial Strategy

The following exercise will help you gather data, both from yourself and from others, evaluate it, and craft a personal entrepreneurial strategy.

The exercise takes one-and-a-half to three hours to complete. Issues addressed will require a great deal of thought, and there are no wrong answers.

Although this is a self-assessment exercise, it is useful to receive feedback. Whether you choose to solicit feedback and how much of the data you choose to share with others is your decision. The value of this exercise depends on how honestly and realistically you approach it.

A complex set of factors goes into making someone a successful entrepreneur. No one has all the personal qualities, managerial skills, and other qualities included in the exercise. And even if someone did, his or her values, preferences, and such might still make him or her unlikely to succeed as an entrepreneur.

The presence or absence of any single factor does not guarantee success or failure as an entrepreneur. Before proceeding, remember, it is no embarrassment to reach for the stars and fail to reach them. It is a failure not to reach for the stars.

Part I: Profile of the Past: Tear Out and Complete.

Name:

Date:

STEP I

Examine Your Personal Preferences.
What gives you energy, and why? These can be things from work, leisure, or both.

Activities/Situations That Give You Energy	Reasons for Your Joy and Satisfaction

What takes away your energy, and why?

Activities/Situations That Sap Your Energy	Reasons for This

Rank the items you have just listed:

Gives Energy	Takes Energy

In 20 to 30 years, how would you like to spend an ideal month? Describe your desired lifestyle, work style, income, friends, and so forth, and say what attracts you to, and what repels you about, this ideal existence.

Complete the idea generation guide in Chapter 5 and list the common attributes of the 10 businesses you wanted to enter and the 10 businesses you did not:

Attributes—Would Energize	Attributes—Would Turn Off

Which of these attributes would give you energy and which would take it away, and why?

Attribute	Give or Take Energy	Reason

Complete this sentence: "I would/would not like to start/acquire my own business someday because . . ."

Discuss any patterns, issues, insights, and conclusions that have emerged:

Rank the following in terms of importance to you:

	Important	←	_____	→	Irrelevant
Location	5	4	3	2	1
Geography (particular area)	5	4	3	2	1
Community size and nature	5	4	3	2	1
Community involvement	5	4	3	2	1
Commuting distance (one way):					
20 minutes or less	5	4	3	2	1
30 minutes or less	5	4	3	2	1
60 minutes or less	5	4	3	2	1
More than 60 minutes	5	4	3	2	1
Lifestyle and Work Style					
Size of business:					
Less than $2 million sales or under 5–10 employees	5	4	3	2	1
More than $2 million sales or 5–10 employees	5	4	3	2	1
More than $10 million sales and 40–50 employees	5	4	3	2	1
Rate of real growth:					
Fast (over 25%/year)	5	4	3	2	1
Moderate (10–15%/year)	5	4	3	2	1
Slow (less than 5%/year)	5	4	3	2	1
Workload (weekly):					
Over 70 hours	5	4	3	2	1
55–60 hours	5	4	3	2	1
40 hours or less	5	4	3	2	1
Marriage	5	4	3	2	1
Family	5	4	3	2	1
Travel away from home:					
More than 60%	5	4	3	2	1
30–60%	5	4	3	2	1
Less than 30%	5	4	3	2	1
None	5	4	3	2	1
Standard of Living					
Tight belt/later capital gains	5	4	3	2	1
Average/limited capital gains	5	4	3	2	1
High/no capital gains	5	4	3	2	1
Become very rich	5	4	3	2	1
Personal Development					
Utilization of skill and education	5	4	3	2	1
Opportunity for personal growth	5	4	3	2	1
Contribution to society	5	4	3	2	1
Positioning for opportunities	5	4	3	2	1
Generation of significant contacts, experience, and know-how	5	4	3	2	1
Status and prestige	5	4	3	2	1
Impact on ecology and environment: sustainability	5	4	3	2	1
Capital Required					
From you	5	4	3	2	1
From others	5	4	3	2	1
Other Considerations	5	4	3	2	1

Imagine you had $1,000 to spend on the items you ranked on the previous page. Indicate below how you would allocate the money with the most important item receiving the greatest amount, the second-most important item receiving the second largest amount, and so forth. You can give more than one item the same allocation and allocate nothing to items. Once you have allocated the $1,000, rank the items in order of importance, with the most important being number 1.

Item	Share of $1,000	Rank
Location		
Lifestyle and work style		
Standard of living		
Personal development		
Status and prestige		
Ecology and environment		
Capital required		
Other considerations		

What are the implications of these rankings?

STEP 2

Examine Your Personal History.
List activities that (1) have provided you financial support in the past (e.g., jobs you had or businesses you owned), (2) have contributed to your well-being (e.g., financing your education or hobbies), and (3) you have done on your own (e.g., building something).

Discuss why you became involved in each activity and what influenced your decisions to get involved. Which decisions were driven by financial necessity and which were driven by opportunity?

Discuss what you learned about yourself, about self-employment, about managing people, and about working for money and someone else as opposed to creating or seizing an opportunity and building something from scratch.

List and discuss your full-time work experience, including descriptions of specific instances in which you innovated and led something, how many people you led, whether you were successful, and so forth.

Discuss why you became involved in each employment situation and what influenced your decisions to become involved.

Discuss what you learned about yourself; about creating, innovating, or originating a project, club, or business; and about making money.

List and discuss other activities, such as sports, in which you have participated; indicate whether each activity was individual (e.g., chess or tennis) or team (e.g., football). If it was the latter, did you have a leadership role?

What lessons and insights emerged from your activities, and how do these apply to entrepreneurship?

If you have been fired from or quit a job, indicate the job, why you were fired or quit, the circumstances, and what you learned and what difference this has made regarding working for yourself or someone else.

If you changed jobs or relocated, indicate the job, why the change occurred, the circumstances, and what you learned from those experiences.

Among those individuals who have mentored and influenced you most, do any have their own businesses or engage independently in a profession (e.g., certified public accountant)? How have these people influenced you? How do you view them and their roles? What have you learned from them about self-employment? Include a discussion of the things that attract or repel you, the trade-offs they have had to consider, the risks they have faced and rewards they have enjoyed, and entry strategies that have worked for them.

If you have ever started a business of any kind or worked in a small company, list the things you liked most and those you liked least, and why:

Like Most	Reason	Like Least	Reason

If you have ever worked for a larger company (over 500 employees or over $50 million in sales), list the things you liked most about it and those you liked least about it, and why.

Like Most	Reason	Like Least	Reason

Part II: Profile of the Present: Where You Are

STEP I

Examine Your "Entrepreneurial Mind."
Examine your attitudes, behaviors, and know-how. Rank yourself (on a scale of 5 to I).

	Strongest	←	_____	→	Weakest
Commitment and Determination					
Decisiveness	5	4	3	2	I
Tenacity	5	4	3	2	I
Discipline	5	4	3	2	I
Persistence in solving problems	5	4	3	2	I
Willingness to sacrifice	5	4	3	2	I
Total immersion in the mission	5	4	3	2	I
Courage					
Moral strength	5	4	3	2	I
Fearless experimentation	5	4	3	2	I
Unafraid of conflicts, failure	5	4	3	2	I
Intense curiosity in the face of risk	5	4	3	2	I
Opportunity Obsession					
Leadership in shaping the opportunity					
Having knowledge of customers' needs	5	4	3	2	I
Being market driven	5	4	3	2	I
Obsession with value creation and enhancement	5	4	3	2	I
Tolerance of Risk, Ambiguity, and Uncertainty					
Calculated risk taker	5	4	3	2	I
Risk minimizer	5	4	3	2	I
Risk sharer					
Tolerance of uncertainty and lack of structure	5	4	3	2	I
Tolerance of stress and conflict	5	4	3	2	I
Ability to resolve problems and integrate solutions	5	4	3	2	I
Creativity, Self-Reliance, and Ability to Adapt					
Nonconventional, open-minded, lateral thinker (helicopter mind)	5	4	3	2	I
Restlessness with status quo	5	4	3	2	I
Ability to adapt	5	4	3	2	I
Lack of fear of failure	5	4	3	2	I
Ability to conceptualize and to "sweat details"	5	4	3	2	I
Motivation to Excel					
Goal and results orientation	5	4	3	2	I
Drive to achieve and grow (self-imposed)	5	4	3	2	I
Low need for status and power	5	4	3	2	I
Ability to be interpersonally supporting (vs. competitive)	5	4	3	2	I
Awareness of weaknesses (and strengths)	5	4	3	2	I
Having perspective and sense of humor	5	4	3	2	I
Leadership					
Being self-starter	5	4	3	2	I
Having internal locus of control	5	4	3	2	I
Having integrity and reliability	5	4	3	2	I
Having patience	5	4	3	2	I
Being team builder and hero maker	5	4	3	2	I

Summarize your entrepreneurial strengths.

Summarize your entrepreneurial weaknesses.

STEP 2

Examine Entrepreneurial Role Requirements.

Rank where you fit in the following roles:

	Strongest	←	_____	→	Weakest
Accommodation to Venture					
Extent to which career and venture are no. I priority	5	4	3	2	I
Stress					
The cost of accommodation	5	4	3	2	I
Values					
Extent to which conventional values are held	5	4	3	2	I
Ethics and Integrity	5	4	3	2	I

Summarize your strengths and weaknesses.

STEP 3
Examine Your Management Competencies.
Rank your skills and competencies below:

	Strongest	←	_____	→	Weakest
Marketing					
Market research and evaluation	5	4	3	2	1
Marketing planning	5	4	3	2	1
Product pricing	5	4	3	2	1
Sales management	5	4	3	2	1
Direct mail/catalog selling	5	4	3	2	1
Telemarketing	5	4	3	2	1
Search engine optimization	5	4	3	2	1
Customer service	5	4	3	2	1
Distribution management	5	4	3	2	1
Product management	5	4	3	2	1
New product planning	5	4	3	2	1
Operations/Production					
Manufacturing management	5	4	3	2	1
Inventory control	5	4	3	2	1
Cost analysis and control	5	4	3	2	1
Quality control	5	4	3	2	1
Production scheduling and flow	5	4	3	2	1
Purchasing	5	4	3	2	1
Job evaluation	5	4	3	2	1
Finance					
Accounting	5	4	3	2	1
Capital budgeting	5	4	3	2	1
Cash flow management	5	4	3	2	1
Credit and collection management	5	4	3	2	1
Managing relations with financial sources	5	4	3	2	1
Short-term financing	5	4	3	2	1
Public and private offerings	5	4	3	2	1
Administration					
Problem solving	5	4	3	2	1
Communications	5	4	3	2	1
Planning	5	4	3	2	1
Decision making	5	4	3	2	1
Project management	5	4	3	2	1
Negotiating	5	4	3	2	1
Personnel administration	5	4	3	2	1
Management information systems	5	4	3	2	1
Computer/IT/Internet	5	4	3	2	1
Interpersonal/Team					
Leadership/vision/influence	5	4	3	2	1
Helping and coaching	5	4	3	2	1
Feedback	5	4	3	2	1
Conflict management	5	4	3	2	1
Teamwork and people management	5	4	3	2	1

(continued)

	Strongest	←	_____	→	Weakest
Law					
Corporations and LLCs	5	4	3	2	1
Contracts	5	4	3	2	1
Taxes	5	4	3	2	1
Securities and private placements	5	4	3	2	1
Intellectual property rights and patents	5	4	3	2	1
Real estate law	5	4	3	2	1
Bankruptcy	5	4	3	2	1
Unique Skills	5	4	3	2	1

STEP 4

Based on an Analysis of the Information Given in Steps 1–3, Indicate the Items You Would Add to a "Do" List, Including (1) Need for External Brain Trust Advisors; (2) Board Composition; (3) Additional Team Members; and (4) Additional Knowledge/Skills/Experience.

Part III: Getting Constructive Feedback

STEP 1

(Optional) Give a Copy of Your Answers to Parts I and II to the Person Designated to Evaluate Your Responses. Ask Him or Her to Answer the Following:
Have you been honest, objective, hard-nosed, and complete in evaluating your skills?

Have you incorrectly inventoried any strengths and weaknesses? If so, which ones.

Are there other events or past actions that might affect this analysis? What are they?

STEP 2

Solicit Feedback.
Give one copy of the feedback form that begins on the next page to each person you have asked to evaluate your responses.

Feedback Form

Feedback for:

Prepared by:

STEP I

Please Check the Appropriate Column Next to the Statements about the Entrepreneurial Attributes, and Add Any Additional Comments You May Have.

	Strong	Adequate	Weak	No Comment
Commitment and Determination				
Decisiveness	S	A	W	NC
Tenacity	S	A	W	NC
Discipline	S	A	W	NC
Persistence in solving problems	S	A	W	NC
Willingness to sacrifice	S	A	W	NC
Total immersion in the mission	S	A	W	NC

(continued)

	Strong	Adequate	Weak	No Comment
Courage				
Moral strength	S	A	W	NC
Fearless experimentation	S	A	W	NC
Not afraid of conflicts, failure	S	A	W	NC
Intense curiosity in the face of risk	S	A	W	NC
Opportunity Obsession				
Leadership in shaping the opportunity				
Having knowledge of customers' needs	S	A	W	NC
Being market driven	S	A	W	NC
Obsession with value creation and enhancement	S	A	W	NC
Tolerance of Risk, Ambiguity, and Uncertainty				
Calculated risk taker	S	A	W	NC
Risk minimizer	S	A	W	NC
Risk sharer	S	A	W	NC
Tolerance of uncertainty and lack of structure	S	A	W	NC
Tolerance of stress and conflict	S	A	W	NC
Ability to resolve problems and integrate solutions	S	A	W	NC
Creativity, Self-Reliance, and Ability to Adapt				
Nonconventional, open-minded, lateral thinker (helicopter mind)	S	A	W	NC
Restlessness with status quo	S	A	W	NC
Ability to adapt	S	A	W	NC
Lack of fear of failure	S	A	W	NC
Ability to conceptualize and to "sweat details"	S	A	W	NC
Motivation to Excel				
Goal and results orientation	S	A	W	NC
Drive to achieve and grow (self-imposed standards)	S	A	W	NC
Low need for status and power	S	A	W	NC
Ability to be interpersonally supportive (vs. competitive)	S	A	W	NC
Awareness of weaknesses (and strengths)	S	A	W	NC
Having perspective and sense of humor	S	A	W	NC
Leadership				
Being self-starter	S	A	W	NC
Having internal locus of control	S	A	W	NC
Having integrity and reliability	S	A	W	NC
Having patience	S	A	W	NC
Being team builder and hero maker	S	A	W	NC

Please make any comments you can on such additional matters as my energy, health, and emotional stability; my creativity and innovativeness; my intelligence; my capacity to inspire; my values; and so forth.

STEP 2

Please Check the Appropriate Column Next to the Statements about Entrepreneurial Role Requirements to Indicate My Fit and Add Any Additional Comments You May Have.

	Strong	Adequate	Weak	No Comment
Accommodation to venture	S	A	W	NC
Stress (cost of accommodation)	S	A	W	NC
Values (conventional economic and professional values of free enterprise system)	S	A	W	NC
Ethics and integrity	S	A	W	NC

Additional Comments:

STEP 3
Please Check the Appropriate Column Next to the Statements about Management Competencies, and Add Any Additional Comments You May Have.

	Strong	Adequate	Weak	No Comment
Marketing				
Market research and evaluation	S	A	W	NC
Marketing planning	S	A	W	NC
Product pricing	S	A	W	NC
Sales management	S	A	W	NC
Direct mail/catalog selling	S	A	W	NC
Telemarketing	S	A	W	NC
Search engine optimization				
Customer service	S	A	W	NC
Distribution management	S	A	W	NC
Product management	S	A	W	NC
New product planning	S	A	W	NC
Operations/Production				
Manufacturing management	S	A	W	NC
Inventory control	S	A	W	NC
Cost analysis and control	S	A	W	NC
Quality control	S	A	W	NC
Production scheduling and flow	S	A	W	NC
Purchasing	S	A	W	NC
Job evaluation	S	A	W	NC
Finance				
Accounting	S	A	W	NC
Capital budgeting	S	A	W	NC
Cash flow management	S	A	W	NC
Credit and collection management	S	A	W	NC
Managing relations with financial sources	S	A	W	NC
Short-term financing	S	A	W	NC
Public and private offerings	S	A	W	NC
Administration				
Problem solving	S	A	W	NC
Communications	S	A	W	NC
Planning	S	A	W	NC
Marketing				
Decision making	S	A	W	NC
Project management	S	A	W	NC
Negotiating	S	A	W	NC
Personnel administration	S	A	W	NC
Management information systems	S	A	W	NC
Computer/IT/Internet	S	A	W	NC
Interpersonal/Team				
Leadership/vision/influence	S	A	W	NC
Helping and coaching	S	A	W	NC
Feedback	S	A	W	NC
Conflict management	S	A	W	NC
Teamwork and people management	S	A	W	NC

(continued)

	Strong	Adequate	Weak	No Comment
Law				
Corporations and LLCs	S	A	W	NC
Contracts	S	A	W	NC
Taxes	S	A	W	NC
Securities and private placements	S	A	W	NC
Intellectual property rights and patents	S	A	W	NC
Real estate law	S	A	W	NC
Bankruptcy	S	A	W	NC
Unique Skills	S	A	W	NC

Additional Comments:

STEP 4

Please Evaluate My Strengths and Weaknesses.
In what area or areas do you see my greatest potential or existing strengths in terms of the venture opportunity we have discussed, and why?

Area of Strength	Reason

In what area or areas do you see my greatest potential or existing weaknesses in terms of the venture opportunity we have discussed, and why?

Area of Strength	Reason

If you know my partners and the venture opportunity, what is your evaluation of their fit with me and the fit among them?

Given the venture opportunity, what you know of my partners, and your evaluation of my weaknesses, should I consider any additional members for my management team, board, and brain trust of advisors? If so, what should be their strengths and relevant experience? Can you suggest anyone?

Please make any other suggestions that would be helpful for me to consider (e.g., comments about what you see that I like to do, my lifestyle, work style, patterns evident in my skills inventory, the implications of my particular constellation of management strengths and weaknesses and background, the time implications of an apprenticeship, or key people you think I should meet.)

Part IV: Putting It All Together

STEP 1
Reflect on Your Previous Responses and the Feedback You Have Solicited or Have Received Informally (from Class Discussion or from Discussions with Friends, Parents, etc.).

STEP 2
Assess Your Entrepreneurial Strategy.
What have you concluded at this point about entrepreneurship and yourself?

How do the requirements of entrepreneurship—especially the sacrifices, total immersion, heavy workload, and long-term commitment—fit with your own aims, values, and motivations?

What conflicts do you anticipate between your aims and values, and the demands of entrepreneurship?

How would you compare your entrepreneurial mind, your fit with entrepreneurial role demands, your management competencies, and so forth, with those of other people you know who have pursued or are pursuing an entrepreneurial career?

Think ahead 5 to 10 years or more, and assume that you would want to launch or acquire a higher-potential venture. What "chunks" of experience and know-how do you need to accumulate?

What does this assessment of your entrepreneurial strategy say about whether you should proceed with your current venture opportunity?

What is it about the specific opportunity you want to pursue that will provide you with sustained energy and motivation? How do you know this?

At this time, given your major entrepreneurial strengths and weaknesses and your specific venture opportunity, are there other "chunks" of experience and know-how you need to acquire or attract to your team? (Be specific!)

Who are the people you need to get involved with you?

What other issues or questions have been raised for you at this point that you would like answered?

What opportunities would you most want to be in a position to create/pursue in 5 to 10 years? What new skills, know-how, mentors, team members, and resources would you need to create/pursue them?

Part V: Thinking Ahead

Part V considers the crafting of your personal entrepreneurial strategy. Remember, goals should be specific and concrete, measurable, and, except where indicated, realistic and attainable.

STEP 1

List, in 3 Minutes, Your Goals to Be Accomplished by the Time You Are 70.

STEP 2

List, in 3 Minutes, Your Goals to Be Accomplished over the Next 7 Years. (If You Are an Undergraduate, Use the Next 4 Years.)

STEP 3

List, in 3 Minutes, the Goals You Would Like to Accomplish If You Have Exactly 1 Year to Live. Assume You Would Enjoy Good Health but Would Not Be Able to Acquire Any More Life Insurance or Borrow an Additional Large Sum of Money for a "Final Fling." Assume Further That You Could Spend That Last Year of Your Life Doing Whatever You Want to Do.

STEP 4

List, in 6 Minutes, Your Real Goals and the Goals You Would Like to Accomplish over Your Lifetime.

STEP 5

Discuss the List from Step 4 with Another Person and Then Refine and Clarify Your Goal Statements.

STEP 6

Rank Your Goals According to Priority.

STEP 7

Concentrate on the Top Three Goals and Make a List of Problems, Obstacles, Inconsistencies, and So Forth That You Will Encounter in Trying to Reach Each of These Goals.

STEP 8

Decide and State How You Will Eliminate Any Important Problems, Obstacles, Inconsistencies, and So Forth.

STEP 9

For Your Top Three Goals, Write Down All the Tasks or Action Steps You Need to Take to Help You Attain Each Goal and Indicate How Results Will Be Measured.
Organize the goals by priority.

Goal	Task/Action Step	Measurement	Rank

STEP 10

Rank Tasks/Action Steps in Terms of Priority.
To identify high-priority items, make a copy of your list and cross off any activities or task that cannot be completed, or at least begun, in the next 7 days, and then identify the single most important goal, the next most important, and so forth.

STEP 11

Establish Dates and Durations (and, If Possible, a Place) for Tasks/Action Steps to Begin.
Organize tasks/action steps according to priority. If possible, the date should be during the next 7 days.

Goal	Task/Action Step	Measurement	Rank

STEP 12
Make a List of Problems, Obstacles, Inconsistencies, and So Forth.

STEP 13
Decide How You Will Eliminate Any Important Problems, Obstacles, Inconsistencies, and So Forth, and Adjust the List in Step 12.

STEP 14
Identify Risks Involved and Resources and Other Help Needed.

Note on setting goals: Tear out Part V, keep a copy, and repeat the exercise at least once a year, or after a critical event (job change, marriage, etc.).

Case

Lakota Hills

Preparation Questions

1. Discuss the challenges and advantages of developing a specialty food business.
2. Is their current strategy the best way to build Lakota Hills?
3. How might they integrate other channels into their overall selling model?
4. How will Lakota Hills make money?
5. As an angel investor, would you participate in the round this venture is seeking?

In August 2007, Laura Ryan and her son Michael were flying home to Wyoming following a specialty food trade show in Houston, Texas. The event had generated a lot of interest for their growing enterprise, Lakota Hills. Their flagship product, a retail bag of traditional Native American fry bread, was currently on the shelves in over 350 Midwestern supermarkets.

While they had made encouraging progress, they were nowhere near the critical mass they would need to spark buyer momentum. Buyers and brokers were not eager to commit time and shelf space to new brands. So until more stores said, "Yes," most would continue to smile, nod, and say, "Maybe."

Getting to profitability in the hypercompetitive retail channel was going to require many more expense-laden trips, and hundreds of more in-store demonstrations. Entering other sales channels was possible, but gaining a foothold in this marketplace was their first priority. Their investors agreed, but with the need for a follow-on round of funding in the near term, everyone wanted to be sure that Lakota Hills was on the best path to profits.

An Early Start

The daughter of a successful hog farmer and an enterprising elementary school teacher, Laura Ryan was an industrious adolescent:

I was entrepreneurial ever since I was very young. I raised and sold little pigs, and my mother—who had always had sideline businesses like Avon and Mary Kay—taught me how to sew and bead. I was always

making things, and being a member of 4-H[1] gave me the ability to talk to people, make presentations, and work with basic business concepts.

At 16, Laura married Jim Cooper, the 18-year-old son of a local cattle rancher. Laura recalled the inevitable clash of cultures:

My father was German and Russian and my mother was almost full-blood Lakota[2] with a little bit of French. So I'm actually 7/16th Native American. That was very hard for Jim's family—the idea that he would marry an Indian. Family gatherings were civil but very strained. Still, we knew we could make it work.

Within 3 years they were in college and raising two sons, Michael and Matt. Jim had started a cattle ranch, and Laura did double duty as a mother and part-time college student. She had planned to pursue a business degree, but found business classes boring and chose to major in psychology. Her view of business began to change in 1987 when, at the age of 21, she met an enterprising uncle:

For a class project, I had to interview a family member about our personal history. I found an uncle I had never met, and he was quite a character. He had never worked for anyone his entire life—lots of great dreams and great ideas, but he'd never had a successful venture. He was living in a motel and writing business plans for a living. He was the most fascinating person I'd ever met, and we talked for several hours about all sorts of business ideas.

Quilting for the Stars

Laura's uncle suggested that because Laura and her mother had a talent for sewing, materials, and color, they could produce traditional Native American star quilts. After handcrafting a couple of samples, they decided to produce a range of sizes priced from $500 to over $5,000. Her uncle guided them through the process of writing a business plan that qualified for a Small Business Administration (SBA) loan of just over $27,000.[3] Laura recalled that their early momentum had obscured a few important details:

[1] 4-H is a youth organization in the United States that originated in rural communities but has since expanded to urban areas. The pledge: I pledge my Head to clearer thinking, my Heart to greater loyalty, my Hands to better service, and my Health to better living for my club, my community, my country, and my world.

[2] The Lakota form one of a group of seven Native American tribes (the Great Sioux Nation) and speak Lakota, one of the three major dialects of the Sioux language.

[3] Details of the SBA loan: rate and terms.

We got the money and thought, "Now we're big-time entrepreneurs in the quilting business!" This was 1987, before the Internet was widely available for research. We didn't think much about cash flow, margins, or costs, and we had a hard time trying to figure out the demographics; like, who was really going to buy a $5,000 quilt? We went through the funding in about 8 months, so it quickly became a word-of-mouth business.

They found a couple of galleries in Santa Fe, New Mexico, that catered to quilt collectors. A prominent U.S. state senator bought two, and the Smithsonian Institute put one on display and offered smaller versions through its catalog.

Their efforts got a boost in summer 1992 when Laura became an assistant wardrobe designer for a movie shooting on location:

I worked on the movie *Thunderheart*, which featured Val Kilmer, Sam Shepard, and singer David Crosby. After two weeks, I was promoted to work as Val Kilmer's personal wardrobe assistant. They all purchased our quilts, and that opened up a really neat market for us.

While they made enough to pay off the SBA loan, Laura said the business was not scalable:

It took forever to make these handmade quilts. My mom, myself, some local artists, and a couple of other ladies in the community just couldn't make them fast enough to make much money at it.

Fry Bread Feeds

Motherhood and the quilting business had limited Laura to a few classes per semester. In 1993, during her final year in college, she became vice president of a Native American club. She organized fund-raising events, and one hinted at a new venture opportunity:

Every Friday at lunchtime we sold Indian tacos—deep-fried dough we call fry bread. It was a huge event. The students loved it, and we would sell between 350 and 500 in 2 hours. Our bread is very soft, and what makes it so popular is that you can actually cut it with a plastic fork. The students were all saying, "Wow, this is the best fry bread ever."

We decided to go a step further and try a couple of county fairs that summer. We attended a festival with 6,000 people. We were the only Indian taco vendor, and we sold around 5,000 in one day. Once again, everyone was commenting that our bread was the best they'd ever tasted.

That summer, Laura's husband Jim had an idea:

I figured that if festival-goers like the product, why not try selling it to tourists? Government annuities[4] include bulk flour sacks that are simply stamped *FLOUR* with the net weight at the bottom. Why not create hand-tied muslin-lined burlap bags that would look like a mini-version of a flour sack—stamped in the same printing?

Laura called various bag makers, but found no one willing to produce less than 5,000 per run:

We couldn't buy that many—this was just a concept—we didn't know how well the product would sell. As I've said, my mother is a really good seamstress. We bought some burlap and muslin, used rubber stamps, and made the bags ourselves. They were stamped "Lakota Hills Fry Bread Mix" and "Net Wt. 24 oz."

Laura got the bread mix into two tourist centers. The product sold so well that they spent many hours in their ranch kitchen sewing, stamping, hand-mixing ingredients, and filling bags. By the time tourist season ended in October, Laura and her family were confident they had found a reasonably simple seasonal enterprise. Meanwhile, 23 and fresh out of college, Laura was thinking about her career.

Entrepreneurship Educator

Laura wanted to pursue a PhD in clinical psychology, but she did not get into either program she had applied to. In early 1994 she got an unexpected call from Gene Taylor, the tribal college president at a nearby university:

Gene had heard that I'd finished up my undergrad degree, and he knew that my mom and I were pretty entrepreneurial. The chair of his entrepreneurship department was leaving to start her own business, so he asked me if I would like to be the new department chair and a business teacher. I reminded him my degree was in psychology, and that I had only taken a couple of business courses. But he said, "You're an entrepreneur, and that's awesome; I think you can teach." So I accepted.

[4]For centuries the Indians of the Plains had lived a far-ranging nomadic existence. By the late 1800s the Western Expansion had decimated wild game populations and annexed most of the land. Reservation lands were established in the area of the Black Hills and the Badlands of South Dakota. To prevent starvation while the tribes of the Sioux Nation transitioned to an agricultural lifestyle, the U.S. government agreed to deliver monthly rations—also known as annuities. The treaty of 1877 provided the head of each separate household with "a pound and a half of beef (or in lieu thereof, one half pound of bacon), one-half pound of flour, and one-half pound of corn; and for every one hundred rations, four pounds of coffee, eight pounds of sugar, and three pounds of beans, or in lieu of said articles the equivalent thereof, in the discretion of the Commissioner of Indian Affairs."

The university sent her to the Symposium for Entrepreneurship Educators (SEE) at Babson College in Wellesley, Massachusetts. SEE's mission was to further entrepreneurship education by teaching motivated entrepreneurs how to teach at their respective institutions. Laura's predecessor had already been accepted as a faculty sponsor, so Laura had only about a month to locate an entrepreneur with an interest in spending time in the classroom. She found a woman who made a living as an independent seamstress and quilter. When Laura began the four-day seminar, she felt overwhelmed:

> I'll never forget the fear I had when I walked into a room filled with experienced instructors and successful entrepreneurs who were speaking in a language of business that I'd never heard. The businesses these people were talking about were huge—as big as some of the egos in the room. I felt totally lost and out of place. I wanted to just sneak away and sit in the back so I'd never get called on.
>
> But there were a couple of other Native American colleagues there, and slowly I became more comfortable with the group. I discovered that they did care about what we had to say—about our culture, our values, and the tiny businesses we were working on. By the end of the week, I was certain I needed to take some more classes so that I could follow through.

Laura enrolled in an 18-month distance-learning program in New Hampshire for a degree in community economic development. That summer, her studies had to be balanced with the fry bread business when their sales got a boost from an appearance she made on QVC:

> As a one-time event, QVC had selected 20 specialty companies from around the country. It was a bit of a risk to go on, since the way they operate is they place their order based on their estimate of what will sell. You ship them the product, and then whatever doesn't sell they ship back at our expense. Anyway, that wasn't a concern, since we sold out in 3 minutes—twice.

Laura received her degree in the spring of 1998. In 2000, she decided to pursue a PhD in education—a decision concurrent with the arrival of her third child:

> Our boys were teenagers by this time. We had never had the intention of having another child, but the neat thing was, our daughter changed my entire outlook on life. I was gearing up to be entirely focused on my career, and now I was taking a step back. It was a good balance. Lisa was 6 months old when I started the [PhD] program. I took her with me to class; everyone called her the PhD baby.

For the next 4 years, Laura worked on her dissertation, taught entrepreneurship, and spent time with her daughter. All the while, the family fry bread business supported itself as a seasonal operation.

New Opportunities

In the early 2000s, actor Kevin Costner developed Tatanka, a tourist destination near Deadwood, South Dakota, that told the story of the bison in relation to the Plains Indians.[5] In 2004, when Costner and his local investor group decided to bring in a Native American to run the operations, Laura got a call:

> I was still teaching entrepreneurship at a university not far from Tatanka. I went down there and was really intrigued. This was an interpretive center built around an authentic mid-1800s Native American camp. It was a living museum with everyone in period dress and in character—much like Plimoth Plantation in Massachusetts. I decided to take the job, and set up a leave of absence from my teaching duties.

The gift shop, of course, sold bags of their fry bread mix, and the restaurant offered Lakota Hills luncheon tacos.[6]

In the summer of 2004, fry bread sales topped $58,000—a somewhat modest figure that Laura knew reflected their in-home manufacturing setup and their limited market reach.[7] In early 2005, Laura decided it was time to move out of the kitchen and turned to Mark Wills, the Tatanka investor who had recommended her for the job:

> Mark had founded Greenhill, a small venture capital firm in Spearfish [South Dakota] that works with Native American entrepreneurs.

Although Laura worked up a three-page outline of the business, Mark's decision to invest was largely based on what he saw in her:

> I was familiar with Laura's long-time involvement with entrepreneurship, and I knew how popular their fry bread mix was becoming. As manager at Tatanka, she had done a great job building on our vision. We gave her a credit line of $80,000 to cover raw materials and rent a more appropriate manufacturing space. We wanted to see how she'd do, and we left the door open for more funding down the road.

That season was encouraging to the point where Laura was sure they could scale the business into a year-round operation. At the end of the summer, she resigned from Tatanka to find the best path for

---

[5] *Tatanka*: Lakota for a bull bison.

[6] The restaurant staff prepared a batch of measured dough balls. These were fried on order in the same oil used to fry the onion rings and French fries. A tent card was displayed on every table describing the history of fry bread and the story of the Lakota Hills family business.

[7] In 2005 the Lakota Hills mix was sold in eight tourist destination gift shops in Wyoming and in South Dakota.

Lakota Hills. Her first iteration proved to be more trouble than it was worth:

> Our rented manufacturing space in Spearfish had a real rustic look, so in October we set up a small shop in front and started selling gift baskets for the holidays. Our baskets featured 100 percent Native American specialty foods: teas, jams, sweets, and our fry bread mix.
>
> We actually did really well with the business through the holiday season, but I knew at that point I was not going to stay in the gift basket industry. We spent hours upon hours designing and setting up elaborate baskets—only to have them arrive in terrible condition after being shipped across the country.

Laura had also begun making contact with specialty food stores in the hope of expanding their retail distribution. Those efforts came up short as well:

> I approached chain stores like Cabella's and Cracker Barrel because they sell lots of specialty food products. They seemed interested in the concept, but said our muslin bags were just not very professional. They also felt it was too specific of a product, and that there was not enough consumer awareness. They said, "We don't know what fry bread is, so how are our consumers going to know?"
>
> At that point I thought that it was time to raise enough money to cover the design of some proper packaging, find a professional co-packer, and really go for it.

A Plan to Expand

Although her PhD had opened up a number of academic career options, Laura decided to focus on developing the fry bread business. In January 2006, she presented her plan to Greenhill Venture (Exhibit A). Mark Wills said it agreed to invest $470,000 for 15 percent of the business:

> We suggested that she target grocery chains. To do that, she was going to need a new package, supermarket floor displays, sell sheets, and other marketing collateral. When that was ready to go, she was going to need to find a co-packer with the machinery and capacity to serve that channel.

Laura spent the spring and summer designing a new look and feel for Lakota Hills. The retail unit weight was trimmed by a third to 16 ounces, and the package—now a full-color poly bag designed to work on a high-volume heat-crimp production line—featured recipe suggestions and a history lesson (Exhibit B). Sell sheets, a basic website, and other collateral were color and concept coordinated. Laura said they also found a co-packer with a willingness to invest:

> John Gower has a pretty big kosher-certified dry mix operation in Laramie. He has lots of equipment like huge rotary mixers, augers, and bulk storage systems. He believed in our company and believed that we were going to have enough volume to justify

EXHIBIT A

Excerpts from the Lakota Hills Executive Summary

The Opportunity

This business promises to be successful because of the increased demand for specialty food products, and the interest in Native American products in particular. Based on current market trends and statistical data, bread and dessert mixes have been on a steady growth curve since 2004. Lakota Hills has been selling its fry bread since 1993, and positive consumer, distributor, and food broker feedback demonstrates that it has a quality product in the marketplace.

Competitive Advantage

Our primary competitors are Wooden Knife Fry Bread Mix, Crow Fry Bread Mix, and the Oklahoma Fry Bread Company. Wooden Knife Fry Bread has been in operation for over 15 years, while the other two companies were started less than 2 years ago. None of the three companies have improved their packaging design or have been aggressive in their marketing approach to meet the

consumer's needs. Wooden Knife Fry Bread is the only company selling their product outside of their local area.

Lakota Hills has a competitive advantage in the taste of our product.

Pricing

Wooden Knife Fry Bread Mix sells their 1.5-pound box of fry bread mix on the retail shelf in the range of $3.50–$7.00. The Oklahoma Fry Bread is priced for an 8-ounce bag of fry bread mix for approximately $3.20 retail. A 1-pound bag of the Crow Fry Bread Mix is priced at $6.00–$7.50. The key to success for Lakota Hills is to keep our pricing consistent in the marketplace. Our 16-ounce retail package will have a suggested retail price of $3.69.

Wooden Knife Fry Bread Mix is our only competitor in food service. They have frozen fry bread patties: 25 per case. They also have a 5-pound bulk dry fry bread mix. Both products are priced at $1.90–$2.25 per pound. Lakota Hills offers a 25-pound bulk pack at $1.40 per pound.

EXHIBIT B

Selected Copy from the Retail Poly Bag

Directions

Fry Bread is incredibly easy to prepare. First, place the entire contents of the bag into a large mixing bowl. Add 3/4 cups of warm water and stir until the dough becomes sticky. Then add all-purpose flour a little at a time until the dough is no longer sticky.

Heat 3 cups of oil or shortening in a skillet or deep fryer to 375 degrees. Form your dough into the desired shape on a well-floured surface and roll or pat to about 1/2 inch in thickness. Lower the fry bread carefully into the hot oil and cook approximately 2 minutes on each side until golden in color. If you have made the fry bread into balls, no turning is required; just remove them from the oil when they are golden brown in color.

Place the hot fry bread on a paper towel and allow it to cool slightly before handling. Any leftover dough can be covered and held in a refrigerator for up to 24 hours.

Fry Bread History

At the turn of the century the Lakota people were given the ingredients to make bread. In their creative nature, the women developed a fry bread recipe from those ingredients. These recipes became closely guarded secrets passed from one generation to the next.

Laura Ryan was given this recipe by her great-grandmother to share with future generations. Please enjoy this traditional Native American family recipe. We hope it becomes a tradition for your family too!

Fry Bread Nuggets

Prepare fry bread mix as directed. Drop teaspoon-size balls into 375 degree oil until fry bread is golden brown on each side. Serve with whipped honey butter, maple syrup, or your favorite jelly. For a donutlike treat, roll the hot bread in powdered sugar and cinnamon or plain sugar.

---

his purchase of automatic bagging machinery that he tweaked into his system.[8]

We talked a lot about where we had to be with our pricing, and his delivered price was based on our ramping up sales pretty quickly. The minimum order run for our poly bags was 500,000, and we also ordered printed shipping boxes to match that inventory at 6 units per box.

To introduce their product to major grocers, Laura participated in a trade show in Atlanta, Georgia:

I had found some info about a show called Efficient Collaborative Retail Marketing (ECRM). They facilitate sourcing reviews called Efficient Program Planning Sessions for retailers all over the country.[9] We were in their specialty/Hispanic/ethnic food show in August.

It was very expensive—over $13,000 for the event. It starts with an evening reception where you mingle with the buyers. Over the next 2 days—from eight in the morning to six at night—you have 20-minute appointments with major supermarkets. It was very rigorous. They loved our packaging, our story, and our fry bread.

Hearing how well the show had gone, Laura said their co-packer took it upon himself to see what the new equipment could do:

John's a really nice guy, and I think he just wants to see our business make it. In late August he filled 300,000 bags, boxed them all up, palletized them, and then said, "I hope you can sell these". . . *Oh my gosh!*

Knowing they were not going to move close to 2,600 pallets of product quickly, they shipped it to a dry storage warehouse in Chicago. With their date stamp giving them just 18 months to sell it, the clock was ticking.

Buyer Education and Re-education

The ECRM event generated a long list of intrigued buyers and a performance-based agreement with a food broker in the Chicago area.[10] By the late fall of 2006, Laura's eldest son Michael had come on full-time as general manager. As he began to follow up on leads from the show, he could see that "getting to yes" with the supermarket buyers was going to be a real challenge:

In school, and in football, there was always a clear and concise learning environment. The professor or coach would lay out their expectations, and let you know what you can expect in return.

Working with buyers is a very different experience. They don't call back, they aren't there to take your call when they say they will be, samples get lost, samples get eaten . . . After many calls to people who seem almost ready to buy, suddenly they're not even sure if they can use the product.

---

[8]The cost of the fill and heat-sealing additions to the plant equipment was approximately $42,000.

[9]In 2007 ECRM held more than 45 EPPS events. Planning sessions included every major supermarket category: hair care; pharmacy; personal care; cosmetics, fragrance, and bath; cough and cold/analgesics; private-label health and beauty care and food; general merchandise; sun care; grocery; snack, and beverage; cosmetics; vitamin, nutrition, and diet; school and office products; household products; health care; candy; photo; frozen foods; and international.

[10]Food brokers typically received between 10 and 15 percent of sales on the grocery chain accounts they sold and managed.

I have an undergraduate business degree, and I've just enrolled in a 1-year MBA program—and I can tell you, nowhere in all of that education is there anything about the food industry—and more importantly, the grocery industry. There is a lot of terminology you have to learn, and it takes experience to know how to work with buyers and brokers.

For example, you don't hear "No," very much in this business. Instead you get a lot of "I'll get back to you" and "We're getting close." In some ways that's harder to deal with than straight rejection because there is a lot of running around chasing leads that ultimately won't pan out.

Laura, who was still working leads as well, offered her assessment of the challenge:

At the food shows, you get a lot of interest when they try the product, and you collect tons of cards. They get home to their regular work where they are sampling dozens of products a week, and they push it off and push it off until they forget how good it was and what it tasted like.

Lines of Entry

The Lakota Hills team and their investors agreed that because the product's story was so compelling, grocery retailing represented their best entry into high-volume sales. Laura said they were working on line extensions to gain strength in the channel:

It's hard for the supermarkets to justify bringing in one product to see if it will sell—especially since for many chains fry bread represents a whole new subcategory under bread mixes. Creating a line of products will give us more credibility, and those additional SKUs[II] will translate into better visibility and more sales.

Steve Foster, a partner at Greenhill Ventures, said that once Lakota Hills built up a reputation in retail, the company would be ready to branch into other channels:

As a minority-certified business, they are exempt from upfront slotting fees—which at a top-tier supermarket chain can run $25,000 per SKU. That advantage can also be carried over into packaging mixes for volume government contracts. They have a 25-pound bag ready to go for wholesale food service accounts, but it is harder to leverage the product and family story in those channels.

Another wholesale possibility would be setting up a national program with restaurant chains like Denny's or Pizza Hut, although it's not clearly the best way to enter that market. Retailing is where they ought to start out because that's a more straightforward effort involving advertising, promotion, and building a consumer connection.

[II]Pronounced "skews": stock keeping units.

Michael described the various channels for their fry bread mix:

Specialty food outlets like the gift shop at Mt. Rushmore represent the best margins because they will pay the most and still double the price on the shelf. The grocery store chains will want a lower delivered price, and their markup will be around 50 percent. Food service has the highest volume and the easiest pack, ship, and support profile, but they are going to want it as cheap as they can get it because they would be ordering truckloads.

We are a little cautious about the food service segment. In terms of volume, I think bulk wholesale has far more potential, but the margins are very small (Exhibit C). Our current production setup, and having a large amount of date-stamped retail packs in inventory, sort of forces us to pursue specialty food chains and supermarkets right now.

Laura said they were targeting the retail segment with a consumer education plan:

To draw people in, we are going to build on our human interest themes: a Native American woman entrepreneur and her family going national with a traditional family favorite. We are looking for all the free publicity we can get, like having newspapers we advertise in write up stories about what we're doing. We will also be sending our press clippings and information to a few major East Coast newspapers like the *Washington Post* and *The New York Times*, and samples to food critics in New York, and to celebrity hosts like Martha Stewart, Oprah, and Letterman.

At the local level, we'll be running coupons in the Sunday papers and in the store flyers. We need to make sure that wherever we do run coupons, we're in the area that week to put on in-store demos. We could also build awareness by selling tacos and handing out store coupons at motorcycle rallies, state fairs, and festivals.

On the Road

In late November, a 280-store chain in the Midwest agreed to carry the product. But selling the buyer in corporate did not mean the individual stores would be given a heads-up on the incoming SKU. Laura explained:

This was what they call a force-out, meaning they required all of their stores to take a case of our product, and some of the busier locations would receive our floor display that holds 24 bags. Well, that was great, but the downside was we didn't have the people out there to go to every store that week to educate the managers about what exactly it was that they had just received.

EXHIBIT C

Channel Costs and Pricing Snapshot

Retail units: 16-ounce bags

Unit cost: $1.17
Delivered cost per pallet (115 cases per pallet/6 bags
per case): $807.30

Distributors
Price per case/unit: $9.60/1.60
Pop-up floor display (36 units): $57.60/$1.60

Supermarkets
Price per case/unit: $10.80/1.80
Pop-up floor display (36 units): $64.80/$1.80
Estimated retail price per unit: $3.59

Specialty food stores
Price per case/unit: $13.50/$2.25
Estimated retail price per unit: $4.29

Tourist destination shops
Price per case/unit: $18.00/$3.00
Estimated retail price per unit: $6.49

Wholesale bulk: 25-pound bags

Delivered cost per pallet (50 bulk bags): $600
Distributors: $30.00 per bag
Wholesale (food service): $35.00 per bag

Terms: Minimum order: 1 pallet

Payment: 2% 10, net 30

NOTE: Unit cost includes the following: ingredients, packaging, utilities, labor, and delivery.

When Michael went to a few stores to see how the product was being handled, visiting the rest became a top priority:

> We put a very specific store placement sheet in every case, and a trifold brochure is attached to every bag explaining the product. But the teenagers working in the stockroom don't care about that stuff. A few hadn't even bothered to bring it out from the receiving area. When it did get put out, it was all over the stores. I found it in the Oriental section, the breakfast food aisle, and the Hispanic section. A couple of managers thought it looked like a fish coating and put it in the meat department.

Their in-store tastings—conducted at various times by Laura, Michael, his brother Matt, and their grandmother—put a personal face on the business for store workers and enticed shoppers to try a bag. Michael noted that customer feedback suggested that loyal users would be regular, as opposed to frequent, buyers:

> This is not like macaroni and cheese, where every time you go grocery shopping you get several boxes. Kids love to eat fry bread too, but it's a matter of the parents being willing to mix the dough, heat the oil, cook the bread, and then clean everything up.
>
> A typical family would not prepare this a few times a week. More likely once a month, or even once every 2 or 3 months in place of taco shells. That said, we feel that if we can get our product into enough stores and get consumers using it at that level of regularity, we can do very well.

Fortunately, when the bags were on the right shelf (with the bread mixes), and customers got a chance to try warm samples at an in-store tasting, the product moved. In July 2007, they landed an even larger grocery chain with nearly 800 stores from South Dakota to Colorado. Unlike the previous force-out, the team would be required to personally introduce the buyer-approved product to each store manager. Laura said they were making excellent progress:

> We are able to visit about 20 stores a day, and we have gotten into about 100 stores so far. We're hardly ever turned down when we make our presentation. So that's great, but it's a lot of expense up front to get out to every one of those stores. Michael is doing most of that work right now until we can bring on a food broker to represent us in that territory. But of course, selling a broker is just as difficult as selling a [supermarket] buyer.

Buy One, Get One Free

With over 1,300 pallets of retail product still on hand and barely 6 months left before its expiration date, the team was offering a free pallet with every pallet sold. Laura said the promotion was helping to clear the backlog, but the increase in sales was bringing a new concern:

> Right now we have a small enough number of accounts that if we see that the product isn't moving, we can go in and do damage control like tastings and making sure the product is displayed correctly. As we add new large accounts, we are going to have to find ways to educate consumers and in-store workers about our fry bread without having to visit each and every store personally.
>
> Right now we are working with our investors to lay out how much we're spending in advertising, demo expenses, and store visits. Our costs are so crazy because when Michael is on the road selling, he has hotels, meals, mileage . . . that adds up. We've set up some projections (see Exhibits D(i)–(iii)) and estimate we are going to need an additional $500,000 to fund another year of this type of direct selling while we can build up a broker network.

EXHIBIT D(i)

Income Statement and Projections

	Actuals					Projected						
Sales Made	Q1 2007	Q2 2007	Q3 2007	Q4 2007	2007 Total	Q1 2008	Q2 2008	Q3 2008	Q4 2008	2008 Total	2009 Total	2010 Total
1.5-lb cases muslin	560	10,560	1,440	1,440	14,000	480	480	480	480	1,920	2,208	2,517
1.5-lb cases—world link	0	720	1,200	1,200	3,120	1,200	1,200	1,200	1,200	4,800	5,520	6,293
25-lb bags	375	2,910	6,480	12,960	22,725	12,960	12,960	25,920	25,920	77,760	89,424	101,943
Online sales	12	75	150	150	387	150	150	150	150	600	690	787
Future product line	0	0	0	0	0	0	0	0	0	0	0	0
Future product line	0	0	0	0	0	0	0	0	0	0	0	0
1-lb cases paper	0	8,400	39,200	50,400	98,000	67,200	84,000	100,800	117,600	369,600	425,040	484,546
Revenue												
1.5-lb cases muslin	16,800	316,800	43,200	43,200	420,000	14,400	14,400	14,400	14,400	57,600	66,240	75,514
1.5-lb cases—world link	0	22,810	38,016	38,016	98,842	38,016	38,016	38,016	38,016	152,064	174,874	199,356
5-lb cases	8,438	65,475	145,800	291,600	511,313	291,600	291,600	583,200	583,200	1,749,600	2,012,040	2,293,726
Online sales	216	1,350	2,700	2,700	6,966	2,700	2,700	2,700	2,700	10,800	12,420	14,159
Future product line	0	0	0	0	0	0	0	0	0	0	0	0
Future product line	0	0	0	0	0	0	0	0	0	0	0	0
Shipping charges	1,621	25,111	10,747	17,357	54,836	15,398	15,398	28,618	28,618	88,032	101,237	115,410
Discounts	0	(1,140)	(1,901)	(1,901)	(4,942)	0	0	0	0	0	0	0
1-lb cases paper	0	151,200	705,600	907,200	1,764,000	1,209,600	1,512,600	1,814,400	2,116,800	6,652,800	12,902,400	14,708,736
Total Revenue	27,074	581,605	944,162	1,298,172	2,851,014	1,571,714	1,874,114	2,481,334	2,783,734	8,710,896	15,269,210	17,406,900
Cost of Goods Sold												
Raw material	8,196	166,780	237,831	331,963	744,770	393,302	464,030	628,718	699,446	2,185,498	2,513,322	2,865,187
Labor	1,348	32,135	29,901	36,621	100,004	44,397	54,477	64,557	74,637	238,068	273,778	312,107
Total COGS	9,543	198,914	267,732	368,584	844,774	437,699	518,507	693,275	774,083	2,423,566	2,787,100	3,177,295
Gross Profit	17,531	382,690	676,430	929,588	2,006,240	1,134,015	1,355,607	1,788,058	2,009,650	6,287,330	12,482,110	14,229,605
Operating Expenses												
Sales and marketing	56,010	26,202	26,034	26,432	134,678	58,779	23,728	33,348	49,612	165,467	904,127	1,030,705
Production/distribution	3,153	47,659	34,181	44,968	129,961	46,086	50,385	69,225	73,374	239,070	279,809	318,982
Administration	45,388	69,501	77,291	80,517	272,698	122,010	121,969	111,897	111,766	467,642	502,678	573,053
Total Operating Expense	104,551	143,362	137,507	151,917	537,336	226,875	196,083	214,470	234,752	872,179	1,686,614	1,922,739
Net Income	(87,019)	239,329	538,923	777,671	1,468,904	907,140	1,159,524	1,573,588	1,774,899	5,415,151	10,795,496	12,306,866

EXHIBIT D(ii)

Cash Flow Actuals and Projections 2007

| | Actuals | | | | | | Projected | | | | | | 2007 |
	Jan-07	Feb-07	Mar-07	Apr-07	May-07	Jun-07	Jul-07	Aug-07	Sep-07	Oct-07	Nov-07	Dec-07	Total
Revenue collected	2,190	6,582	11,348	164,984	175,442	132,774	255,921	281,121	331,521	407,322	432,724	432,724	2,634,652
Increase in debt	12,500	25,000	25,000	25,000									87,500
Total cash sources	14,690	31,582	36,348	189,984	175,442	132,774	255,921	281,121	331,521	407,322	432,724	432,724	2,722,152
Purchase raw materials	2,652	4,217	96,540	10,609	59,630	71,418	71,418	94,994	110,654	110,654	110,564	131,101	874,545
Production labor	193	386	770	23,426	1,542	7,167	8,847	8,847	12,207	12,207	12,207	12,207	100,004
Operating expenses	14,930	22,835	64,381	55,578	37,380	47,270	48,829	47,104	38,787	48,530	47,805	54,953	528,383
Less non cash items:													
Depreciation	0	0	0	0	0	0	0	0	0	0	0	0	0
Debt payments:								0					
Principal				0	3,000	3,000	3,000	3,000	53,000	53,000	53,000	53,000	224,000
Interest				75	75	75	75	75	3,075	3,075	3,075	3,075	12,675
Capital investments													0
Total cash uses	17,775	27,438	161,691	89,688	101,627	128,931	132,170	154,021	217,723	227,467	226,742	254,336	1,739,607
Net cash increase/decrease	(3,085)	4,144	(125,344)	100,296	73,815	3,843	123,751	127,100	113,797	179,856	205,982	178,388	982,545
Cash beginning of month	0	(3,085)	1,059	(124,284)	(23,988)	49,827	53,670	177,421	304,522	418,319	598,174	804,157	982,545
Cash end of month	(3,085)	1,059	(124,284)	(23,988)	49,827	53,670	177,421	304,522	418,319	598,174	804,157	982,545	982,545

72

EXHIBIT D(iii)

Cash Flow Projections 2008–2010

	Projected						
	QI 2008	Q2 2008	Q3 2008	Q4 2008	2008 Total	2009 Total	2010 Total
Revenue collected	1,526,124	1,823,714	2,380,130	2,733,334	8,463,302	15,096,949	17,361,491
Increase in debt					0	0	0
Total cash sources	1,526,124	1,823,714	2,380,130	2,733,334	8,463,302	15,096,949	17,361,491
Purchase raw materials	416,878	518,926	652,294	675,741	2,263,840	2,303,879	2,649,461
Production labor	44,391	54,477	64,557	74,637	238,068	273,778	314,845
Operating expenses	227,134	196,479	215,036	235,545	874,194	1,690,063	1,943,572
Less noncash items:							
Depreciation	0	0	0	0	0	0	0
Debt payments:							
Principal	9,000	9,000	13,000	15,000	46,000	0	0
Interest	225	225	375	450	1,275	0	0
Capital investments					0	0	0
Total cash uses	697,634	779,107	945,262	1,001,374	3,423,377	4,267,720	4,907,878
Net cash increase/decrease	828,490	1,044,607	1,434,868	1,731,960	5,039,925	10,829,229	12,453,613
Cash beginning of period	982,545	1,811,034	2,855,642	4,290,510		6,022,470	16,851,699
Cash end of period	1,811,034	2,855,642	4,290,510	6,022,470	6,022,470	16,851,699	29,305,312

Michael added that the moment the 2006 inventory was out the door, they would begin to consider expanding into other areas:

My mom and I are always trying to think about what market channels we should be in. At the food shows you get lots of advice, but there is no consensus. Right now we are geared up for and focused on the supermarket industry. That may change once we get a chance to think this through and get a bit deeper into the trade-offs, the logistics, and the numbers.

PART TWO

The Opportunity

First time entrepreneurs frequently have a haphazard "Go for it!" attitude. This reflects a commendable approach as there can be no substitute for doing, but the reality is successful entrepreneurs work hard to mitigate risk before launching their venture. Risk mitigation also reflects the attitude of investors, who want to maximize their risk-adjusted return by minimizing risk. Experience shows most entrepreneurial endeavors fail by running out of cash, and this cash flow shortfall is usually based on an overly optimistic revenue forecast.

Successful entrepreneurs also know it is important to think on a big enough, which means go beyond good ideas, beyond new features and products and think about a scalable company, pointing to the need to screen opportunities with great care.

As important as it is to find a good opportunity, even good opportunities have risks. The perfect deal has yet to be seen. Identifying risks and problems before the launch while steps can be taken to eliminate or reduce them is another dimension of opportunity screening.

Chapter Three

The Entrepreneurial Process

LEARNING OUTCOMES: After reading this chapter you will be able to understand:

3-1   Demystifying entrepreneurship

3-2   The classic entrepreneurial startup

3-3   Entrepreneurship and large corporations

3-4   Startups as the new corporations

3-5   Entrepreneurship and paradoxes

3-6   The odds are against you if you stay small

3-7   Getting the odds in your favor

3-8   The Timmons model

Demystifying Entrepreneurship

Entrepreneurship is a way of thinking, reasoning, and acting that is opportunity obsessed, holistic in approach, and leadership balanced for the purpose of value creation and capture.[1] Entrepreneurship results in the creation, enhancement, realization, and renewal of value, not just for owners, but for all participants and stakeholders. At the heart of the process is the creation and recognition of opportunities,[2] followed by the will and initiative to seize these opportunities.

Classic Entrepreneurship: The Startup

The classic expression of entrepreneurship is the raw startup company, an innovative idea that develops into a high-growth company. The best of these become entrepreneurial legends: Microsoft, Netscape, Amazon, Sun Microsystems, Home Depot, McDonald's, Intuit, Staples, and countless other household names. Entrepreneurship also requires the skill and ingenuity to find and control resources, often owned by others, in order to pursue the opportunity. Successful entrepreneurs assemble and hold together a team and acquire financial backing to chase an opportunity others may not recognize.

Entrepreneurship and Large Corporations

As we have seen, the upstart companies of the 1970s and 1980s have had a profound impact on the competitive structure of the United States and world industries. Apple and Microsoft have forever changed the face of IBM and put Digital Equipment Corporation out of business. Walmart has decimated Sears and Kmart. MCI and Verizon have forever changed the original AT&T. On the flipside, classic corporations like *The New York Times* have reinvented themselves to become one of the most popular news sources in the country.[3] Between 2006 and 2008 large companies shrank payrolls while, despite the recession[4], venture-backed companies accounted for 11 percent of U.S. employment. Venture investment is particularly important in the software and computer segment of the technology sector where nearly 90 percent of all jobs are within venture-backed companies.[5]

---

[1]This definition of entrepreneurship has evolved over the past three decades from research by Jeffry A. Timmons, Babson College and the Harvard Business School, and has recently been enhanced by Stephen Spinelli, Jr., former vice provost for entrepreneurship and global management at Babson College, and current president of Philadelphia University.

[2]J.A. Timmons, D.F. Muzyka, H.H. Stevenson, and W.D. Bygrave, "Opportunity Recognition: The Core of Entrepreneurship." In *Frontiers of Entrepreneurship Research* (Babson Park, MA: Babson College, 1987), p. 409.

[3]"Newspapers Going Digital," http://www.nytimes.com/2010/01/21/business/media/21times.html.

[4]http://www.ssti.org/Digest/2009/092309.htm#story4.

[5]National Venture Capital Association, Venture Impact: The Economic Importance of Venture Capital-Backed Companies to the U.S. Economy, 2007.

Startups as the New Corporations

Fortunately, for many giant firms, the entrepreneurial revolution continues to be a source for growth. Researchers document how large firms are applying entrepreneurial thinking to enhance their futures in companies like GE, Corning, and Motorola,[6] Harley-Davidson ($4.29 billion in revenue in 2009), Marshall Industries ($2.2 billion), and Science Applications International Corporation (SAIC).

Entrepreneurship Means Paradoxes

One of the most confounding aspects of the entrepreneurial process is its contradictions as outlined in the following examples. Can you think of other paradoxes that you have observed or heard about?

- *An opportunity with no or very low perceived value can be an enormously big opportunity.* Steve Jobs and Steve Wozniak originally approached their employer, Hewlett-Packard, with their idea for a personal computer. In one of the most famous rejections of all time, they were told this was not an opportunity for HP, and went on to start Apple Computer. Scott Cook, the founder of Intuit and maker of Quicken, was rejected by 20 venture capitalists before funding.
- *It takes money to make money.* To grow companies of significant value founders need to sell portions of their company for investment capital. This requires entrepreneurs to carefully measure their dilution against the increased value of their company.
- *Entrepreneurship requires considerable thought, preparation, and planning, yet is basically an unpredictable phenomenon.* The highly dynamic changing character of high-growth markets makes planning a necessary but fluid exercise.
- *For creativity and innovativeness to prosper, rigor and discipline must accompany the process.* Thousands of patents for new products and technologies currently exist in corporate, government, and university research labs awaiting commercialization by innovators who can apply them to compelling market problems.
- *The greater the organization, orderliness, discipline, and control, the less you will control your ultimate destiny.* Entrepreneurship requires great flexibility and nimbleness in strategy

and tactics. Too much control and an obsession with orderliness are impediments to the entrepreneurial approach. As the great race car driver Mario Andretti said, "If I am in total control, I know I am going too slow!"
- *To realize long-term value, you have to forgo the temptations of short-term profitability.*

Building long-term equity requires large, continuous reinvestment in people, products, and services in advance of revenues. The classic paradox is high growth, highly profitable companies in rapidly growing markets frequently are cash-flow negative, requiring ongoing investment to fund this shortfall.

The world of entrepreneurship is not neat, tidy, linear, consistent, nor predictable and is fraught with paradoxes.[7] It is from these paradoxes that value is created, as illustrated in Exhibit 3.1. To thrive in this environment, one needs to be very adept at coping with ambiguity, chaos, and uncertainty, while having management skills that mitigate risk in the face of all this uncertainty.

The Higher-Potential Venture: Think Big

One of the biggest mistakes aspiring entrepreneurs make is strategic in thinking too small. Sensible as it may be to think in terms of a very small, simple business as being more affordable, more manageable, less demanding, and less risky, the chances of survival and success are lower. As one founder of numerous businesses put it, unless this business can pay you at least five times your present salary, the risk and wear and tear will not be worth it.

EXHIBIT 3.1

Entrepreneurship is a Contact Sport

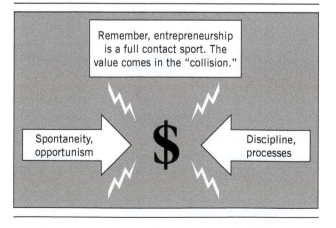

[6]Fast Company, June–July 1997, pp. 32, 79, 104; and U.S. Rangan, "Alliances Power Corporate Renewal," Babson College, 2001.
[7]See H.H. Stevenson, *Do Lunch or Be Lunch* (Boston, MA: Harvard Business School Press, 1998) for a provocative argument for predictability as one of the most powerful of management tools.

Nearly 8 percent of the U.S. population is actively working toward starting a new venture.[8] More than 90 percent of startups have revenues of less than $1 million annually, while 863,505 reported revenues of $1 million to $25 million–just over 9 percent of the total. Of these, only 296,695 grew at a compounded annual growth rate of 30 percent or more for the prior 3 years, or about 3 percent. Similarly, just 3 percent–1 in 33–exceeded $10 million in revenues, and only 0.3 percent exceeded $100 million in revenues.

Not only can nearly anyone start a business, but also a great many can succeed. While it certainly might help, a person does not have to be a genius to create a successful business. As Nolan Bushnell, founder of Atari, one of the first desktop computer games in the early 1980s, and Pizza Time Theater, said, "If you are not a millionaire or bankrupt by the time you are 30, you are not really trying!"[9] It is an entrepreneur's preparedness for the entrepreneurial process that is important. Being an entrepreneur has moved from cult status in the 1980s to rock star infamy in the 1990s to become de rigueur in the 21st century. Amateur entrepreneurship is over. The professionals have arrived.

A stunning number of mega-entrepreneurs launched their ventures during their 20s. While the rigors of new ventures may favor the "young at start," age is *not* a barrier to entry. One study showed that nearly 35 percent of founders were over 40 when they embarked on their entrepreneurial careers, many were in their 30s, and just over one-fourth did so by the time they were 25. Further, numerous examples exist of founders who were over 60 at the time of launch, including one of the most famous seniors, Colonel Harland Sanders, who started Kentucky Fried Chicken with his first Social Security check.

Smaller Means Higher Failure Odds

Unfortunately, the record of survival is not good among all firms started. One of the most optimistic research firms estimates the failure rate for startups is 46.4 percent. While government data, research, and business mortality statisticians may not agree on the precise failure and survival figures for new businesses, they do agree that failure is the rule, not the exception.

Complicating efforts to obtain precise figures is the fact that it is not easy to define and identify failures, and reliable statistics and databases are not available. However, the Small Business Administration determined that in 2008 there were 627,200 startups, while 595,600 firms closed their doors.[10]

The following discussion provides a distillation of a number of failure rate studies over the past 50 years.[11] These studies illustrate that (1) failure rates are high, and (2) although the majority of the failures occur in the first 2 to 5 years, it may take considerably longer for some to fail.[12]

Government data, research, and business mortality statisticians agree that startups run a high risk of failure. Research has shown that two-thirds of new employer establishments survive at least 2 years, and 44 percent survive at least 4 years. (Exhibit 3.2.)

EXHIBIT 3.2

Starts and Closures of Employer Firms, 2002–2006

Category	2002	2003	2004	2005	2006
New Firms	569,750	612,296	628,917	653,100[a]	649,700[a]
Closures	586,890	540,658	541,047	543,700[a]	564,900[a]
Bankruptcies	38,540	35,037	39,317	39,201	19,695

[a]Estimate.

Sources: U.S. Dept. of Commerce, Bureau of the Census; Administrative Office of the U.S. Courts; U.S. Dept. of Labor, Employment and Training Administration.

[8]The Global Entrepreneurship Monitor Babson College and the London Business School, 2009.

[9]In response to a student question at Founder's Day, Babson College, April 1983.

[10]http://www.score.org/small_biz_stats.html, 2008.

[11]Information has been culled from the following studies: D.L. Birch, MIT Studies, 1979-1980; M.B. Teitz et al., "Small Business and Employment Growth in California." Working Paper No. 348, University of California at Berkeley, March 1981, table 5, p. 22; U.S. Small Business Administration, August 29, 1988; B.D. Phillips and B.A. Kirchhoff, "An Analysis of New Firm Survival and Growth." In *Frontiers in Entrepreneurship Research: 1988*, ed. B.A. Kirchhoff et al. (Babson Park, MA: Babson College, 1988), pp. 266-267; and BizMiner 2002. *Startup Business Risk Index: Major Industry Report.* Brandow Co., Inc., 2002.

[12]Summaries of these are reported by A.N. Shapero and J. Gigherano, "Exits and Entries: A Study in Yellow Pages Journalism." In *Frontiers of Entrepreneurship Research: 1982*, ed. K. Vesper et al. (Babson Park, MA: Babson College, 1982), pp. 113-141; and A.C. Cooper and C.Y. Woo, "Survival and Failure: A Longitudinal Study." In *Frontiers of Entrepreneurship Research: 1988*, ed. B.A. Kirchhoff et al. (Babson Park, MA: Babson College, 1988), pp. 225-237.

To make matters worse, most people think the failure rates are actually much higher. Since actions often are governed by perceptions rather than facts, this perception of failure, in addition to the dismal record, can be a serious obstacle to aspiring entrepreneurs.

In 2009, the highest bankruptcy rate fell into the manufacturing industry and business services, trade, and repairs representing over 1.6 thousand failures.[13] One study calculates a risk factor or index for startups by industry, which sends a clear warning signal to the would-be entrepreneur.[14] At the high end of risk is tobacco products, and at the low end you find the affinity and membership organizations such as AAA or Welcome Wagon. "The fishing is better in some streams versus others," is a favorite saying of the authors. Further, 99 percent of these failed companies had fewer than 100 employees. Through observation and practical experience one would not be surprised by such reports. The implications for would-be entrepreneurs are important: knowing the difference between a good idea and a real opportunity is vital, and this will be addressed in detail in Chapter 5.

Getting the Odds in Your Favor

Fortunately there is a pattern to overcome the failure rate of small, marginal firms created each year.

Threshold Concept

Who are the survivors? The odds for survival and a higher level of success change dramatically if the venture reaches a critical mass of 10 to 20 people with $2 million to $3 million in revenues and is currently pursuing opportunities with growth potential. Looking at a cross-section of all new firms, 1-year survival rates increase steadily as the firm size increases as outlined in Exhibit 3.3, with the rates jump from 54 percent for firms having up to 24 employees to 73 percent for firms with between 100 and 249 employees.

One study found that empirical evidence supports the liability of newness and smallness make

EXHIBIT 3.3

One-Year Survival Rates by Firm Size

Firm Size (Employees)	Survival Percentage
1–24	53.6
25–49	68.0
50–99	69.0
100–249	73.2

Source: *BizMiner 2002 Startup Business Risk Index: Major Industry Report,* © 2002 BizMiner. Reprinted by permission.

survival problematic. The authors inferred, "Perceived satisfaction, cooperation, and trust between the customer and the organization [are] important for the continuation of the relationship. High levels of satisfaction, cooperation, and trust represent a stock of goodwill and positive beliefs which are critical assets that influence the commitment of the two parties to the relationship."[15] The authors noted, "Smaller organizations are found to be more responsive, while larger organizations are found to provide greater depth of service. . . . The entrepreneurial task is to find a way to either direct the arena of competition away from the areas where you are at a competitive disadvantage, or find some creative way to develop the required competency."[16]

After 4 years, the survival rate jumps from 35 to 40 percent for firms with fewer than 19 employees to about 55 percent for firms with 20 to 49 employees. Although any estimates based on sales per employee vary considerably from industry to industry, this minimum translates roughly to a threshold of $50,000 to $100,000 of sales per employee annually.

Promise of Growth

It takes a long time for companies to become established and grow. Historically, two of every five small firms founded survive six or more years, but few achieve growth during the first 4 years.[17] Studies also found that survival rates more than double for firms that grow, and the earlier in the life of the business that growth occurs, the higher the chance of survival.[18] The 2007 INC. 500 exemplify this, with a 3-year growth rate of 939 percent.[19]

[13]http://www.cbs.nl/en-GB/menu/themas/veiligheid-recht/publicaties/artikelen/archief/2010/2010-012-pb.htm.
[14]BizMiner 2002 Startup Business Risk Index.
[15]S. Venkataraman and M.B. Low, "On the Nature of Critical Relationships: A Test of the Liabilities and Size Hypothesis." In *Frontiers in Entrepreneurship Research: 1991* (Babson Park, MA: Babson College, 1991), p. 97.
[16]Ibid., pp. 105–106.
[17]B.D. Phillips and B.A. Kirchhoff, "An Analysis of New Firm Survival and Growth." In *Frontiers in Entrepreneurship Research: 1988* (Babson Park, MA: Babson College, 1988), pp. 266–267.
[18]This reaffirms the exception to the failure rule noted above and in the original edition of this book in 1977.
[19]S. Greco, "The INC. 500 Almanac," *INC,* October 2001, p. 80.

Venture Capital Backing

Another exception to the failure rule is for businesses that attract startup financing from institutional venture capital funds. While venture-backed firms account for a very small percentage of new firms each year, in 2009, 12 out of 41 (29 percent) had venture backing.[20] Venture capital is not essential to a startup, nor is it a guarantee of success. Of the companies making the 2007 INC. 500, about 18 percent raised venture capital and only 3 percent had venture funding at startup.[21]

Private Investors Join Venture Capitalists

As noted previously, harvested entrepreneurs have become "angel investors" or "angels" as private investors in the next generation of entrepreneurs. Many of the more successful entrepreneurs have created their own investment pools and are competing directly with venture capitalists for deals. Their operating experiences and successful track records provide a compelling case for adding value to an upstart company.

Angel investors have similar selection criteria as venture capitalists, looking for high-potential, higher-growth ventures. Unlike the venture capitalists, however, they are not constrained by having to invest so much money in a relatively short period that they must invest in large chunks. These angels are funding more and more early stage companies, enabling risk mitigation before larger, institutional venture funds invest.

Find Investors Who Add Value

One of the most distinguishing disciplines of these higher-potential ventures is how the founders identify financial partners and key team members. They insist on backers and partners who do more than bring just money, commitment, and motivation to the venture. They surround themselves with backers who can add value to the venture through their experience, know-how, networks, and wisdom.

Option: The Lifestyle Venture

For many aspiring entrepreneurs, issues of family roots and location take precedence. Accessibility to a preferred way of life can be more important than how large a business one has or the size of one's net worth. Take Jake and Diana Bishop, for instance, both have advanced degrees in accounting and gave up six-figure jobs to return to their home state of Michigan for several important life-style reasons. They wanted to work together again in a business, which they had done successfully earlier in their marriage, and it was important to be much closer than the 14-hour drive to Diana's aging parents. They report never to have worked harder in their 50 years, nor have they been any happier. They are growing their rental business more than 20 percent a year, making an excellent living, and creating equity value. If done right, one can have a lifestyle business and actually realize higher potential.

Paradoxically, some couples who give up successful careers in New York City to buy an inn in Vermont to avoid the rat race generally last only 6 to 7 years. They discover the joys of self-employment, including 7-day, 70- to 90-hour workweeks, chefs and day help that do not show up, roofs that leak when least expected, and the dealing with the general public.

The Timmons Model: Where Theory and Practice Meet in the Real World

How can aspiring entrepreneurs and their investors increase the odds of success? What do these talented and successful high-potential entrepreneurs and their venture capitalists do differently?

These are the central questions of our lifetime work. We have been immersed as students, researchers, teachers, and practitioners of the *entrepreneurial process*. As founding shareholders and investors of multiple ventures, some of which are now public, venture investors, directors and advisors and as director of the Arthur M. Blank Center for Entrepreneurship at Babson College, we have each applied, tested, refined, and tempered academic theory across multiple industries.

Value Creation: The Driving Forces

A core, fundamental entrepreneurial process accounts for the substantially greater success pattern among higher-potential ventures. Despite the great variety of businesses, entrepreneurs, geographies,

---

[20]IPO Reporter, http://bear.warrington.ufl.edu/ritter/IPOs2009VC.pdf.
[21]www.inc.com/inc5000.

and technologies, central themes or driving forces dominate this highly dynamic entrepreneurial process.

- It is *opportunity driven.*
- It is driven by a *lead entrepreneur* and an *entrepreneurial team.*
- It is *resource parsimonious* and *creative.*
- It depends on the *fit* and *balance* among these.
- It is *integrated* and *holistic.*
- It is *sustainable.*

These are the controllable components of the entrepreneurial process that can be assessed, influenced, and altered. Founders and investors focus on these forces during their careful due diligence to analyze the risks and determine what changes can be made to improve a venture's chances of success.

First, we will elaborate on each of these forces to provide a blueprint and a definition of what each means. Then using Google as an example, we will illustrate how the holistic, balance, and fit concepts pertain to a startup.

Change the Odds: Fix It, Shape It, Mold It, Make It

The driving forces underlying successful new venture creation are illustrated in Exhibit 3.4. The process starts with opportunity, not money, strategy, networks, team, or the business plan. Most genuine opportunities are much bigger than the talent and capacity of the team or the initial resources available to the team. The business plan provides the language and code for communicating the quality of the three driving forces of the Timmons Model and of their fit and balance.

In the entrepreneurial process depicted in the Timmons Model, the shape, size, and depth of the opportunity establish the required shape, size, and depth of both the resources and the team. We have found that many people are a bit uncomfortable viewing the opportunity and resources somewhat precariously balanced by the team. It is especially disconcerting to some because we show the three key elements of the entrepreneurial process as circles, and thus the balance appears tenuous. These reactions are justified, accurate, and realistic as the entrepreneurial process is dynamic.

The lead entrepreneur's job is simple enough. He or she must carry the deal by *taking charge of the success equation.* In this dynamic context, ambiguity and risk are actually your friends. Central to the homework, creative problem solving and strategizing, and due diligence that lie ahead is analyzing the fits and gaps that exist in the venture. What is wrong with this opportunity? What is missing? What good news and favorable events can happen, as well as the adverse? What has to happen to make it attractive and a fit for me? What market, technology, competitive, management, and financial risks can be reduced or eliminated? What can be changed

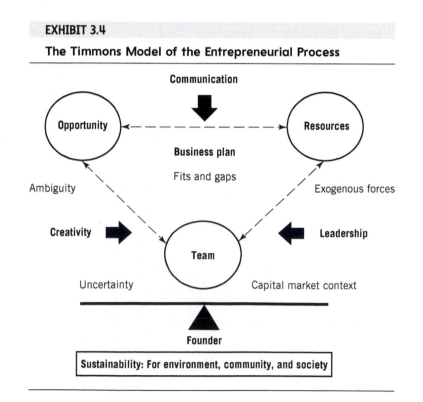

EXHIBIT 3.4

The Timmons Model of the Entrepreneurial Process

to make this happen? Who can change it? What are the least resources necessary to grow the business the farthest? Is this the right team? By implication, if you can determine these answers and make the necessary changes by figuring out how to fill the gaps and improve the fit and attract key players who can add such value, then the odds for success rise significantly. In essence, the entrepreneur's role is to manage and redefine the risk–reward equation— all with an eye toward *sustainability*. Because part of the entrepreneur's legacy is to create positive impact without harming the environment, the community, or society, the concept of sustainability appears as the underlying foundation in the model.

The Opportunity   At the heart of the process is the opportunity. Successful entrepreneurs and investors know that a good idea is not necessarily a good opportunity. For every 100 ideas presented to investors in the form of a business plan or proposal, usually fewer than four get funded. More than 80 percent of those rejections occur in the first few hours; another 10 to 15 percent are rejected after investors have read the business plan carefully. Fewer than 10 percent attract enough interest to merit a more due diligence thorough review that can take several weeks or months. An important skill for an entrepreneur or an investor is to be able to quickly evaluate whether serious potential exists, and to decide how much time and effort to invest.

John Doerr is a senior partner at one of the most famous and successful venture capital funds ever, Kleiner, Perkins, Caulfield & Byers, and is considered by some to be the most influential venture capitalist of his generation. During his career, he has been the epitome of the revolutionaries described earlier, who have created new industries as lead investors in such legends as Sun Microsystems, Compaq Computer, Lotus Development Corporation, Intuit, Genentech, Millennium, Netscape, and Amazon.com. Regardless of these past home runs, Doerr insists, "There's never been a better time than now to start a company. In the past, entrepreneurs started businesses. Today they invent new business models. That's a big difference, and it creates huge opportunities."[22]

Another venture capitalist recently stated, "Cycles of irrational exuberance are not new in venture investing. The Internet bubble burst, we came back to earth, and then we began another period of excessive valuation that is subsiding in late 2007 with a credit squeeze."[23]

Exhibit 3.5 summarizes the most important characteristics of good opportunities. Underlying market demand—because of the value-added properties of the product or service, the market's size and 20-plus percent growth potential, the economics of the business, particularly robust margins (40 percent or more), and free cash flow characteristics— drives the value creation potential.

We build our understanding of opportunity by first focusing on market readiness: the consumer trends and behaviors that seek new products or services. Once these emerging patterns are identified, the aspiring entrepreneur develops a service or product concept, and finally the service or product delivery system is conceived. We then ask the questions articulated in the exhibit.

These criteria will be described in great detail in Chapter 5 and can be applied to the search and evaluation of any opportunity. In short, the greater the growth, size, durability, and robustness of the gross and net margins and free cash flow, the greater the opportunity. The greater the inconsistencies in existing service and quality, in lead times

---

EXHIBIT 3.5

The Entrepreneurial Process Is Opportunity Driven[a]

Market demand is a key ingredient to measuring an opportunity:
- Is customer payback less than one year?
- Do market share and growth potential equal 20 percent annual growth and is it durable?
- Is the customer reachable?

Market structure and size help define an opportunity:
- Emerging and/or fragmented?
- $50 million or more, with a $1 billion potential?
- Proprietary barriers to entry?

Margin analysis helps differentiate an opportunity from an idea:
- Low-cost provider (40 percent gross margin)?
- Low capital requirement versus the competition?
- Break even in 1–2 years?
- Value added increase of overall corporate P/E ratio?

---

[a]Durability of an opportunity is a widely misunderstood concept. In entrepreneurship, durability exists when the investor gets her money back plus a market or better return on investment.

---

[22]"John Doerr's Start-Up Manual," *Fast Company*, February–March 1997, pp. 82–84.
[23]Ernie Parizeau, Partner, Norwest Venture Partners, June 2007.

and lag times, and the greater the vacuums and gaps in information and knowledge, the greater is the opportunity.

Resources: Creative and Parsimonious   One of the most common misconceptions among untried entrepreneurs is that you first need to have all the resources in place, especially the money, to succeed with a venture. Money follows high-potential opportunities conceived of and led by a strong management team as there is a shortage of quality entrepreneurs and opportunities, not money. Successful entrepreneurs devise ingeniously creative and stingy strategies to marshal and gain control of resources (Exhibit 3.6). Surprising as it may sound, investors and successful entrepreneurs often say one of the worst things that can happen to an entrepreneur is to have too much money too early.

Howard Head is a wonderful, classic example of succeeding with few resources. He developed the first metal ski, which became the market leader, and then the oversize Prince tennis racket; developing two totally unrelated technologies is a rare feat. Head left his job at a large aircraft manufacturer during World War II and worked in his garage on a shoestring budget to create his metal ski. It took more than 40 versions before he developed a ski that worked and could be marketed. He insisted that one of the biggest reasons he finally succeeded is that he had so little money. He argued that if he had financing he would have blown it all long before he evolved the workable metal ski.

Bootstrapping is a way of life in entrepreneurial companies and can create a significant competitive advantage. Doing more with less is a powerful competitive weapon. Effective new ventures strive to minimize and control the resources, but not necessarily own them. Whether it is assets for the business, key people, the business plan, or startup and growth capital, successful entrepreneurs think investment last. Such strategies encourage a discipline of leanness, where everyone knows that every dollar counts, and the principle "conserve your equity" becomes a way of maximizing shareholder value.

The Entrepreneurial Team   There is little disputing today that the entrepreneurial team is a key ingredient in the higher-potential venture. Investors are captivated "by the creative brilliance of a company's head entrepreneur: a Mitch Kapor, a Steve Jobs, a Fred Smith…and bet on the superb track records of the management team working as a group."[24] Venture capitalist John Doerr reaffirms General George Doriot's dictum: I prefer a Grade A entrepreneur and team with a Grade B idea, over a Grade B team with a Grade A idea. Doerr stated, "In the world today, there's plenty of technology, plenty of entrepreneurs, plenty of money, plenty of venture capital. What's in short supply is great teams. Your biggest challenge will be building a great team."[25]

Exhibit 3.7 summarizes the important aspects of the team. These teams invariably are formed and led by a very capable entrepreneurial leader whose

---

EXHIBIT 3.6

Understand and Marshall Resources, Do not Be Driven by Them

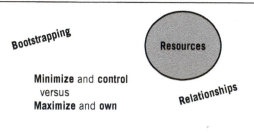

Bootstrapping

Minimize and control
versus
Maximize and own

Relationships

Unleashing creativity

Financial resources
Assets
People
Your business plan

Think cash last!

EXHIBIT 3.7

An Entrepreneurial Team Is a Critical Ingredient for Success

An entrepreneurial leader
- Learns and teaches—faster, better
- Deals with adversity, is resilient
- Exhibits integrity, dependability, honesty
- Builds entrepreneurial culture and organization

Team

Quality of the team

Passion
- Relevant experience and track record
- Motivation to excel
- Commitment, determination, and persistence
- Tolerance of risk, ambiguity, and uncertainty
- Creativity
- Team locus of control
- Adaptability
- Opportunity obsession
- Leadership and courage
- Communication

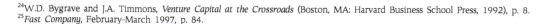

[24]W.D. Bygrave and J.A. Timmons, *Venture Capital at the Crossroads* (Boston, MA: Harvard Business School Press, 1992), p. 8.
[25]*Fast Company*, February–March 1997, p. 84.

track record exhibits both accomplishments and several qualities that the team must possess. The ability and skill in attracting other key management members and then building the team is one of the most valued capabilities investors look for. The founder who becomes the leader does so by building heroes in the team. A leader adopts a philosophy that rewards success and supports honest failure, shares the wealth with those who help create it, and sets high standards for both performance and conduct. We will examine in detail the entrepreneurial leader and the new venture team in Chapter 7.

Importance of Fit and Balance   Rounding out the model of the three driving forces is the concept of fit and balance between and among these forces. Note that the team is positioned at the bottom of the triangle in the Timmons Model (Exhibit 3.4). Imagine the founder, the entrepreneurial leader of the venture, standing on a large ball, balancing the triangle over her head. This imagery is helpful in appreciating the constant balancing act because opportunity, team, and resources rarely match. Vivid examples of the failure to maintain a balance are everywhere, such as when large companies throw too many resources at a weak, poorly defined opportunity.

Sustainability as a Base   Building a sustainable venture means achieving economic, environmental, and social goals without compromising the same opportunity for future generations. The sea change

in entrepreneurship regarding environment, community, and society is driven by many factors. We are seeing an elevated social awareness concerning a wide range of sustainability-related issues, including human rights, food quality, energy resources, pollution, global warming, and the like. By understanding these factors, the entrepreneur builds a firmer base, girding the venture for the long term.

While the drawings oversimplify these incredibly complex events, they help us to think conceptually—an important entrepreneurial talent—about the company-building process, including the strategic and management implications of striving to achieve balance, and the inevitable fragility of the process. Visually, the process can be appreciated as a constant balancing act, requiring continual assessment, revised strategies and tactics, and an experimental approach. By addressing the types of questions necessary to shape the opportunity, the resources, and the team, the founder begins to mold the idea into an opportunity, and the opportunity into a business, just as you would mold clay from a shapeless form into a piece of art.

Exhibit 3.8 a–c shows how this balancing act evolved for Google from inception through its initial public and secondary offerings. Back in 1996, online search was a huge, rapidly growing, but elusive opportunity. There were plenty of early entrants in the search space, but none had yet broken out of the pack. Stanford graduate students Larry Page and Sergey Brin began to collaborate on a search engine called BackRub, named for its

EXHIBIT 3.8(a)

Google—Classic Resource Parsimony, Bootstrapping—Journey through the Entrepreneurial Process: At Startup, a Huge Imbalance

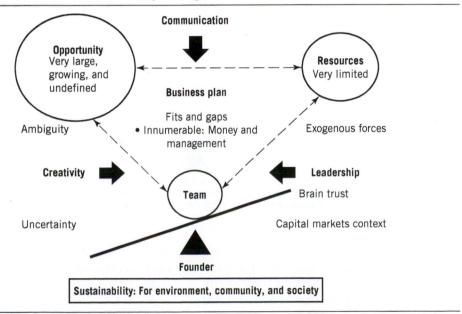

EXHIBIT 3.8(b)

Google—Marshaling of Team and Resources to Pursue Opportunity—Journey through the Entrepreneurial Process: At Venture Capital Funding, toward New Balance

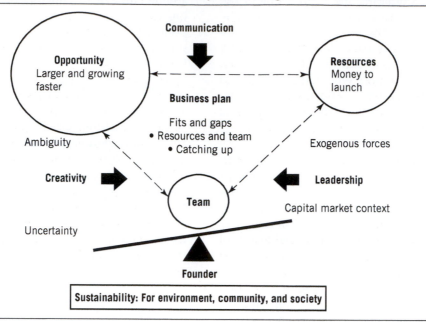

EXHIBIT 3.8(c)

Google—Building and Sustaining the Enterprise; Rebalancing—Journey through the Entrepreneurial Process: At IPO, a New Balance

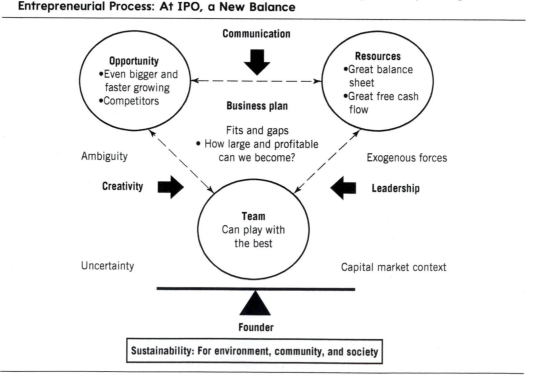

unique ability to analyze the "back links" pointing to a given website. Within a year, their unique approach to link analysis was earning their dorm-room search engine a growing reputation as word spread around campus. Still, they had no team and no capital, and their server architecture was running on computers they borrowed from their computer science department.

Such a mismatch of ideas, resources, and talent could quickly topple out of the founders' control and fall into the hands of someone who could turn it into a real opportunity. At this tenuous point, the founders would have seen something like the first figure, Exhibit 3.9(a), with the huge search engine opportunity far outweighing the team and resources. The gaps were major.

Enter entrepreneur and angel investor Andy Bechtolsheim, one of the founders of Sun Microsystems. The partners of the search engine (now named Google, a variant of *googol*, an immense number) met Bechtolsheim very early one morning on the porch of a Stanford faculty member's home in Palo Alto. Impressed, but without the time to hear the details, Bechtolsheim wrote them a check for $100,000. From there, Page and Brin went on to raise a first round of $1 million. The partners were now in a position to fill the resource gaps and build the team.

In September 1998 they set up shop in a garage in Menlo Park, California, and hired their first employee: technology expert Craig Silverstein. Less than a year later, they moved to a new location, which quickly became a crush of desks and servers. In June 1999 the firm secured a round of funding that included $25 million from Sequoia Capital and Kleiner, Perkins, Caufield & Byers—two of the leading venture capital firms in Silicon Valley. The terrible office gridlock was alleviated with a move to Google's current headquarters in Mountain View, California.

This new balance in Exhibit 3.8(b) created a justifiable investment. The opportunity was still huge and growing, and some competitors were gaining market acceptance as well. To fully exploit this opportunity, attract a large and highly talented group of managers and professionals, and create even greater financial strength than competitors like Yahoo!, the company had to complete an initial public stock offering (IPO). Following the close of that IPO in the summer of 2004, Google was worth more than $25 billion, giving it a first-day market capitalization greater than that of Amazon.com, Lockheed Martin, or General Motors. Within a year the company had raised another $4 billion in a secondary public offering.

By 2010 Google (see Exhibit 3.8(c)) had a share price in the range of $500 and was larger and stronger in people and resources than any direct competitor. The company was the place to work and employed over 20,000 of the best and brightest in the industry.[26]

This iterative entrepreneurial process is based on both logic and trial and error. It is both intuitive and consciously planned. It is a process not unlike what the Wright brothers originally engaged in while creating the first self-propelled airplane. They conducted more than 1,000 glider flights before succeeding. These trial-and-error experiments led to the new knowledge, skills, and insights needed to actually fly. Entrepreneurs have similar learning curves.

The fit issue can be appreciated in terms of a question: This is a fabulous opportunity, but for whom? Some of the most successful investments ever were turned down by numerous investors before the founders received backing. Intuit received 20 rejections for startup funding by sophisticated investors. One former student, Ann Southworth, was turned down by 24 banks and investors before receiving funding for an elderly extended care facility. Ten years later, the company was sold for an eight-figure profit. Time and again, there can be a mismatch between the type of business and investors, the chemistry between founders and backers, or a multitude of other factors that can cause a rejection. Thus how the unique combination of people, opportunity, and resources come together at a particular time may determine a venture's ultimate chance for success.

The potential for attracting outside funding for a proposed venture depends on this overall fit and how the investor believes he or she can add value to this fit and improve the fit, risk–reward ratio, and odds for success. Exhibit 2.10 in the previous chapter shows the possible outcome.

Importance of Timing   Equally important is the timing of the entrepreneurial process. Each of these unique combinations occurs in real time, where the hourglass drains continually and may be friend, foe, or both. Decisiveness in recognizing and seizing the opportunity can make all the difference. Do not wait for the perfect time to take advantage of an opportunity: There is no perfect time. Most new businesses run out of money before they can find enough customers and the right teams for their great ideas. Opportunity is a moving target.

Recent Research Supports the Model   The Timmons Model originally evolved from doctoral dissertation research at the Harvard Business School about new and growing ventures. Over nearly three decades, the model has evolved and been enhanced by ongoing research, case development, teaching, and experience in high-potential ventures and venture capital funds. The fundamental components of the model have not changed, but their richness and the relationships of each to the whole have been steadily enhanced as they have become better understood. Numerous other researchers have examined a

---

[26]Google, 2010.

EXHIBIT 3.9

Leading Practices

Leading marketing practices of fast-growth firms

- Deliver products and services that are perceived as highest quality to expanding segments.
- Cultivate pacesetting new products and services that stand out in the market as best of the breed.
- Deliver product and service benefits that demand average or higher market pricing.
- Generate revenue flows from existing products and services that typically sustain approximately 90% of the present revenue base, while achieving flows from new products and services that typically expand revenue approximately 20% annually.
- Generate revenue flows from existing customers that typically sustain approximately 80% of the ongoing revenue base, while achieving flows from new customers that typically expand revenue flows by about 30% annually.
- Create high-impact, new product and service improvements with development expenditures that typically account for no more than approximately 6% of revenues.
- Utilize a high-yield sales force that typically accounts for approximately 60% of marketing expenditures.
- Rapidly develop broad product and service platforms with complementary channels to help expand a firm's geographic marketing area.

Leading financial practices of fast-growth firms

- Anticipate multiple rounds of financing (on average every 2.5 years).
- Secure funding sources capable of significantly expanding their participation amounts.
- Utilize financing vehicles that retain the entrepreneur's voting control.
- Maintain control of the firm by selectively granting employee stock ownership.
- Link the entrepreneur's long-term objectives to a defined exit strategy in the business plan.

Leading management practices of fast-growth firms

- Use a collaborative decision-making style with the top management team.
- Accelerate organizational development by assembling a balanced top management team with or without prior experience of working together.
- Develop a top management team of three to six individuals with the capacity to become the entrepreneur's entrepreneurs. Align the number of management levels with the number of individuals in top management.
- Establish entrepreneurial competency first in the functional areas of finance, marketing, and operations. Assemble a balanced board of directors composed of both internal and external directors.
- Repeatedly calibrate strategies with regular board of directors meetings.
- Involve the board of directors heavily at strategic inflection points.

Leading planning practices of fast-growth firms

- Prepare detailed written monthly plans for each of the next 12 to 24 months and annual plans for three or more years.
- Establish functional planning and control systems that tie planned achievements to actual performance and adjust management compensation accordingly.
- Periodically share with employees the planned versus actual performance data directly linked to the business plan.
- Link job performance standards that have been jointly set by management and employees to the business plan.
- Prospectively model the firm based on benchmarks that exceed industry norms, competitors, and the industry leader.

---

wide range of topics in entrepreneurship and new venture creation. The bottom line is that the model, in its simple elegance and dynamic richness, harnesses what you need to know about the entrepreneurial process to get the odds in your favor. As each of the chapters and accompanying cases, exercises, and issues expand on the process, addressing individual dimensions, a detailed framework with explicit criteria will emerge. If you engage this material fully, you cannot help but improve your chances of success.

Similar to the INC. 500 companies mentioned earlier, the Ernst & Young LLP Entrepreneur of the Year winners were the basis of a major research effort conducted by the National Center for Entrepreneurship Research at the Kauffman Center for Entrepreneurial Leadership, with a specific focus on 906 high-growth companies.[27] These findings provide important benchmarks of the practices in a diverse group of industries among a high-performing group of companies.

Exhibit 3.9 summarizes the 26 leading practices identified in four key areas: marketing, finances, management, and planning. (A complete version of the study is available from the National Center for Entrepreneurship Research, http://www.kauffman.org.)

---

[27]D.L. Sexton and F.I. Seale, *Leading Practices of Fast Growth Entrepreneurs: Pathways to High Performance* (Kansas City, MO: Kauffman Center for Entrepreneurial Leadership, 1997).

Chapter Summary

- We began to demystify entrepreneurship by examining its classic startup definition and a broader, holistic way of thinking, reasoning, and acting that is opportunity obsessed and leadership balanced.
- Entrepreneurship has many metaphors and poses many paradoxes.
- Getting the odds in your favor is the entrepreneur's perpetual challenge, and the smaller the business, the poorer are the odds of survival.

- Thinking big enough can improve the odds significantly. Higher-potential ventures are sought by successful entrepreneurs, venture capitalists, and private investors.
- The Timmons Model is at the heart of spotting and building the higher-potential venture and understanding its three driving forces: opportunity, the team, and resources. The concept of fit and balance is crucial.

Study Questions

1. What is meant by classic entrepreneurship and the high-potential venture? Why and how are threshold concepts, covering your equity, bootstrapping of resources, fit, and balance important?
2. How many additional metaphors and paradoxes about entrepreneurship can you write down?
3. "People don't want to be managed, they want to be led." Explain what this means and its importance and implications for developing your own style and leadership philosophy.
4. What are the most important determinants of success and failure in new businesses? Who has the best and worst chances for success, and why?

5. What are the most important things you can do to get the odds in your favor?
6. What criteria and characteristics do high-growth entrepreneurs, venture capitalists, and private investors seek in evaluating business opportunities? How can these make a difference?
7. Define and explain the Timmons Model. Apply it and graphically depict, as in the Google example, the first 5 years or so of a new company you are familiar with.
8. What are the most important skills, values, talents, abilities, and mind-sets one needs to cultivate as an entrepreneur?

Internet Resources

http://archive.sba.gov/advo/research/ *The Office of Advocacy of the U.S. Small Business Administration (SBA) describes itself as the voice for small business in the federal government and the source for small business statistics.*
www.ypo.org/ *The Young Presidents' Organization is a network of 20,000 leaders in more than 120 countries.*

Its mission is "Better Leaders Through Education and Idea Exchange."
www.inc.com/inc5000/ *Inc. magazine's list of the nation's 5,000 fastest-growing private companies and related articles.*

Case

Roxanne Quimby

Preparation Questions

1. Who can be an entrepreneur?
2. What are the risks, rewards, and trade-offs of a lifestyle business versus a high-potential business—one that will exceed $5 million in sales and grow substantially?
3. What is the difference between an idea and an opportunity? For whom? What can be learned from Exhibits C and D?
4. Why has the company succeeded so far?
5. What should Roxanne and Burt do, and why?

> *Our goal for the first year was $10,000 in total sales. I figured if I could take home half of that, it would be more money than I'd ever seen.*
>
> Roxanne Quimby

Introduction

Roxanne Quimby sat in the president's office of Burt's Bees' newly relocated manufacturing facility in Raleigh, North Carolina. She missed Maine, the company's previous home. Quimby had founded and built Burt's Bees, a manufacturer of beeswax-based personal care products and handmade crafts, in central Maine and wondered if she should move it back there. She explained,

> When we got to North Carolina, we were totally alone. I realized how much of the business existed in the minds of the Maine employees. There, everyone had their mark on the process. That was all lost when we left Maine in 1994. I just kept thinking, "Why did I move Burt's Bees?" I thought I would pick the company up and move it and everything would be the same. Nothing was the same except that I was still working 20-hour days.

Quimby needed to make a decision quickly because Burt's Bees was hiring employees and purchasing equipment. If she pulled out now, she could minimize her losses and rehire the 44 employees she had left back in Maine, since none had new jobs yet. On the other hand, she couldn't ignore the reasons she had decided to leave Maine. In Maine, Burt's Bees would probably never grow over $3 million in sales, and Quimby felt it had potential for much more.

Roxanne Quimby

The Black Sheep

"I was a real black sheep in my family," Quimby said. One sister worked for AMEX, another worked for Charles Schwab, and her father worked for Merrill Lynch, but she was not interested in business. Quimby attended the San Francisco Art Institute in the late 1960s and "got radicalized out there," she explained. "I studied, oil painted, and graduated without any job prospects. I basically dropped out of life. I moved to central Maine where land was really cheap—$100 an acre—and I could live removed from society."

While Quimby was in college, her father discovered she was living with her boyfriend and disowned her. Her father, a Harvard Business School graduate and failed entrepreneur, did give her one gift—an early entrepreneurial education. At the age of five, he told her he wouldn't give her a cent for college but would match every dollar she earned herself. By her high school graduation Quimby had banked $5,000 by working on her father's entrepreneurial projects and selling handmade crafts.

In 1975, Quimby and her boyfriend married and moved to Guilford, Maine—an hour northwest of Bangor. They bought 30 acres at $100 an acre and built a two room house with no electricity, running water, or phone. In 1977, Quimby had twins, and her lifestyle became a burden. She washed diapers in pots of boiling water on a wood-burning stove and struggled to make ends meet with minimum wage jobs. Her marriage broke apart when the twins were four. Quimby put her belongings on a toboggan and pulled it across the snow to a friend's house.

The money-making skills her father forced her to develop allowed Quimby to survive. She and her children lived in a small tent, and Quimby made almost $150 a week by working local flea markets, buying low and selling high. She also held jobs waitressing. Quimby said, "I always felt I had an entrepreneurial spirit. Even as a waitress I felt entrepreneurial because I had control. I couldn't stand it when other people controlled my destiny or performance. Other jobs didn't inspire me to do my best, but waitressing did because I was accountable to myself. Eventually I got fired from these jobs because I didn't hesitate to tell the owners what I thought."

© Copyright Jeffry A. Timmons, 1997. This case was written by Rebecca Voorheis, under the direction of Jeffry A. Timmons, Franklin W. Olin Distinguished Professor of Entrepreneurship, Babson College. Funding provided by the Ewing Marion Kauffman Foundation. All rights reserved.

In 1984, Quimby began to question her lifestyle: "I decided I had to make a real income. I started to feel the responsibility of having kids. I had waitressing jobs but there were only three restaurants in town and I had been fired from all three. That's when I hooked up with Burt."

A Kindred Spirit

Like Quimby, Burt Shavitz had dropped out in the early 1970s. A New York native and ex-photographer for *Life* and *New York* magazines, Shavitz lived in an 8-foot by 8-foot former turkey coop on a 20 acre farm in Dexter, Maine. A beekeeper with 30 hives, he earned maybe $3,000 a year selling honey during hunting season, which allowed him to pay property taxes and buy gas for his pickup truck.

When Roxanne first saw Burt, whom she described as a "good-looker," she knew she had to meet him. In an article in *Lear's* magazine Quimby said, "I pretended I was interested in the bees, but I was really interested in Burt. Here was this lone beekeeper. I wanted to fix him, to tame the wild man."[1] When they met in 1984, the bond was immediate. Quimby talked about Shavitz's role at Burt's Bees:

> I convinced Burt into this enterprise. He has always believed in my vision, but unlike me he's emotionally detached and uninvolved. Therefore, he has some great ideas and is more likely to take risks. He's my main sounding board and gives me a lot of moral and psychological support. I never could have done this without him. In all this time, there's never been a conflict between us. The chemistry has always been there. We're just really on the same wavelength. We've been through a lot together that would have broken other relationships. I've always been the motivator and the one involved in day-to-day operations, but very rarely does he disagree with me. He's kind of my guru.

Shavitz taught Quimby about beekeeping and Quimby discovered Shavitz's large stockpile of beeswax. She made candles with the beeswax, took them to a local crafts fair and brought home $200. She remembers, "I had never held that much money in my hand." Burt's Bees was born.

Quimby and Shavitz pooled $400 to launch a honey and beeswax business. They purchased some kitchen appliances for mixing, pouring, and dipping. A friend rented them an abandoned one-room schoolhouse with no heat, running water, windows, or electricity for $150 a year—the cost of the fire insurance. Neither had a phone, so they convinced the local health food store to take messages for Burt's Bees. Quimby traveled to fair after fair, sleeping in the back of a pickup truck and

making a few hundred dollars a day. She set what seemed like an impossible goal for the first year's sales—$10,000. That year, 1987, sales were $81,000.

Burt's Bees' Early Success

Burt's Bees' big break came in 1989 at a wholesale show in Springfield, Massachusetts. The owner of an upscale Manhattan boutique bought a teddy bear candle and put it in his store's window. The candle was a hit, and the boutique owner barraged the health food store with messages asking for new shipments. Quimby began hiring employees to help with production and expanded the product line to include other handmade crafts and beeswax-based products like lip balm. In 1993, Burt's Bees employed 44.

Quimby explained her transformation into a businessperson:

> After a while, I realized I just liked it. I liked buying and selling things well, adding value. I had no security issues because I'd been living at the bottom for so many years. I knew if worse came to worse and the business failed, I could survive. I'd seen the worst and knew I could handle it. I'd never been trapped by the need for security or a regular paycheck. I loved the freedom of starting a business, of not knowing how it would turn out. It was this big experiment and whether it succeeded or failed totally depended on me. I realized the goal was not the most interesting part; the problems along the way were. I found business was the most incredibly liberating thing. I never would have thought that before. The only rule is that you have to make a little bit more than you spend. As long as you can do that, anything else you do is OK. There are no other opportunities that have as few rules.

Quimby not only liked business, she was good at it. Burt's Bees had been profitable and seen its profits increase (Exhibit A) every year since its founding. National retailers that stocked its products included L.L. Bean, Macy's, and Whole Foods, and it had sales representatives across the country and sold its

[1] J. Bentham, "Enterprise," *Lear's*, March 1994, pp. 20–21.

EXHIBIT A

Burt's Bees Sales, 1987–1993

Year	Sales
1987	$ 81,000
1988	$ 137,779
1989	$ 180,000
1990	$ 500,000
1991	$ 1,500,000
1992	$2,500,000
1993	$3,000,000

products in every state. Quimby explained its products' appeal:

> We sell really well in urban areas. People in urban areas need us more because they can't step out the front door and get freshness or simplicity. Our products aren't sophisticated or sleek. They're down-home and basic. Everyone has an unconscious desire for more simplicity and our products speak to that need.

The company was debt-free and had never taken out a loan. Quimby didn't even have a credit card. When she applied for one in 1993, by then a millionaire, her sister had to cosign because she had no credit history. She explained:

> I've never taken on debt because I don't ever want to feel like I can't walk away from it this afternoon. That's important to me. A monthly payment would trap me into having to explain my actions. I love being on the edge with no predictability, no one to report to.

Quimby was so debt-averse and cash-aware, she refused to sell products to any retailer that didn't pay its bill within 30 days. That meant refusing orders from retailing powerhouses like I. Magnin and Dean & Deluca. In 1993, with about $3 million in sales, the company wrote off only $2,500 in uncollected debts. That year, Burt's Bees had $800,000 in the bank, and pretax profits of 35 percent of sales.

The Move

The Costs of Doing Business in Maine

Despite its success, Burt's Bees faced three problems due to its northern Maine location:

1. *High transport costs:* Since it wasn't near any metropolitan areas, Burt's Bees paid a fortune to ship products and receive materials.

2. *High payroll taxes:* Burt's Bees was being taxed about 10 percent of its payroll by the state of Maine.

3. *Lack of expertise:* In 1993 Burt's Bees had 44 employees, who Quimby said "brought a set of hands and a good attitude to work, but no skills." As a result, the company made everything by hand. "When we received a shipment of containers or labels, we had to break down the pallets inside the truck because no one knew how to operate a forklift," Quimby said. "There weren't any people with expertise in Maine."

Additionally, Burt's Bees had struggled to keep up with demand since its start. Quimby couldn't focus on broad management issues because she spent most of her time pouring beeswax alongside Burt's Bees' other workers. She explained,

> The business had developed a life of its own and it was telling me it wanted to grow. But it was growing beyond me, my expertise, my goals, and definitely beyond Maine. If I kept it in northern Maine, I would have stunted its growth. But the business was my child in a way, and as its mother I wanted to enable it to grow. The business provided a great income and I could have gone on like that for a while. But I knew it had a lot more potential than $3 million. At the same time, I knew $3 million was the most I could do on my own. I was working all of the time and there was no one to lean on or delegate to.

Why North Carolina?

Quimby felt she had to move the company away from Maine. But to where? She didn't want to live in a big city, but the new location had to be central. Quimby explained how she finally chose North Carolina:

> I had a map of the United States in my office with pins where all of our sales reps were. I used to always look at that map—when I was on the phone, doing paperwork, or just sitting at my desk—until one day I noticed North Carolina. It just seemed central, well placed. And, it turned out, a large percentage of the country's population lives within a 12-hour drive of North Carolina. One of my biggest worries about moving was telling Burt. I said to Burt one day, "We need to move and it looks like North Carolina is the place to go." Burt said, "OK, Roxy," and I thought to myself, "Thank God Burt is always on my wavelength."

Shavitz called the North Carolina Department of Commerce and told him about Burt's Bees. North Carolina was aggressively recruiting companies and was eager to attract Burt's Bees, even though it was much smaller than other companies locating in the "Triangle."[2] The North Carolina Department of Commerce sent Burt's Bees a software program that Quimby used to calculate the taxes Burt's Bees would pay in North Carolina. They were significantly less than the taxes it paid in Maine.

Even better was the large supply of skilled labor in North Carolina. If Burt's Bees moved, it could hire an ex-Revlon plant engineer to establish and operate its manufacturing facility. Quimby also had a lead on a marketing manager in North Carolina with experience at Lancome, Vogue, and Victoria's Secret's personal care products division.

The North Carolina Department of Commerce invited Quimby and Shavitz to tour the Triangle area and available manufacturing facilities. A representative "took us around the whole area for 3 days,"

---

[2]The "Triangle" area in North Carolina includes Chapel Hill, Raleigh, and Durham and is the home of Research Triangle Park, a large high-tech business park similar to Silicon Valley in California or Route 128 in Massachusetts.

Quimby said. "He showed us tons of plants and real estate. He made us a great offer and we were impressed."

When they got back to Maine, Quimby called the Maine Department of Commerce to give it a chance to keep Burt's Bees in the state. "If they had offered us half the deal North Carolina did," Quimby said, "I would have taken it." The Maine Department of Commerce asked her to call back in a couple of months because the person in charge of business recruiting was out on maternity leave. Quimby marveled, "We were the second largest employer in the town and they didn't respond to us at all. We finally heard from the governor of Maine when he read an article about us in *Forbes*[3] that mentioned we were leaving the state. By then it was too late."

Trimming the Azalea Bush: The Economics of the Move

Roxanne Quimby likened Burt's Bees' move to transplanting an azalea bush in full bloom. She said, "I realized I had to trim and prune radically to allow it to survive."

In Maine, Burt's Bees biggest resource was cheap labor—production line workers earned $5 an hour. Therefore, most of its products were very labor-intensive and all were handmade.

In North Carolina, the company's biggest resource was skilled labor. But skilled labor is expensive, so Burt's Bees wouldn't be able to keep making labor-intensive items. It would have to automate everything and change its product line to skin care products (see Exhibit B for industry employment statistics).

EXHIBIT B

Occupations Employed by Standard Industrial Classification (SIC) 284: Soap, Cleaners, and Toilet Goods

Occupation	% of Industry Total, 1994	% Change to 2005 (Projected)
Packaging and filling machine operators	8.5	−30.1
Hand packers and packagers	6.3	−20.1
Assemblers, fabricators, and hand workers	5.7	16.5
Sales and related workers	4.9	16.5
Freight, stock and material movers, hand	3.6	−6.8
Secretaries, executive, legal and medical	3.5	6.0
Chemical equipment controllers, operators	3.0	4.8
Industrial machinery mechanics	2.7	28.1
Machine operators	2.6	2.6
Industrial truck and tractor operators	2.6	16.5
Chemists	2.5	28.1
Crushing and mixing machine operators	2.5	16.4
General managers and top executives	2.5	10.5
Traffic, shipping, and receiving clerks	2.2	12.1
Marketing, advertising, and PR managers	2.0	16.5
Science and mathematics technicians	1.8	16.5
Bookkeeping, accounting, and auditing clerks	1.8	16.5
Maintenance repairers, general utility	1.7	4.8
Inspectors, testers and graders, precision	1.6	16.5
General office clerks	1.6	−.7
Order clerks, materials, merchandise and service	1.5	13.9
Machine feeders and offbearers	1.5	4.8
Clerical supervisors and managers	1.5	19.1
Professional workers	1.4	39.7
Industrial production managers	1.4	16.4
Stock clerks	1.4	−5.3
Managers and administrators	1.3	16.4
Adjustment clerks	1.2	39.8
Accountants and auditors	1.2	16.5
Management support workers	1.1	16.4
Engineering, mathematical, and science managers	1.1	32.2
Truck drivers, light and heavy	1.0	20.1

Source: *Manufacturing USA: Industry Analyses, Statistics, and Leading Companies,* 5th ed., vol. I, ed. A. J. Darnay, Gale Research Inc. (1996), p. 837.

[3]D.W. Linder, "Dear Dad," *Forbes,* December 6, 1993, pp. 98–99.

Skin care products (for general industry statistics, see Exhibits C and D) require only blending and filling, almost all of which can be done by machinery. "To justify the move to North Carolina from a cost and manufacturing perspective, we would have to make more 'goop,'" Quimby stated. "I looked at my list of prospective new products, and there wasn't anything on the list that we made in 1988."

EXHIBIT C

General Industry Statistics for SIC 2844: Toilet Preparations[a]

	Establishments		Employment			Compensation		Production ($million)			
Year	Total	With ≤ 20 Employees	Total (00s)	Production Workers (00s)	Production Hours (mil)	Payroll ($mil)	Wages ($/hour)	Cost of Materials	Value Added by Manufacture	Value of Shipments	Capital Investment
1988	687	277	64.9	40.5	78.1	1,551.3	9.08	4,445.1	12,053.2	16,293.6	292.6
1989	676	282	63.6	39.4	75.4	1,615.5	9.69	4,758.2	11,979.2	16,641.9	313.7
1990	682	284	63.6	38.1	74.3	1,620.6	10.14	4,904.6	12,104.2	17,048.4	280.4
1991	674	271	57.4	35.6	69.8	1,616.3	10.81	5,046.3	12,047.4	18,753.5	299.5
1992	756	305	60.1	37.2	75.6	1,783.3	10.82	5,611.3	13,167.2	19,706.4	507.3
1993	778	299	61.7	38.6	79.7	1,857.8	10.59	6,152.6	13,588.8	19,736.0	472.6

[a]*Manufacturing USA: Industry Analyses, Statistics, and Leading Companies,* 5th ed., vol. I, ed. A. J. Darnay, Gale Research Inc. (1996), p. 833.

Sources: 1982, 1987, 1992 *Economic Census; Annual Survey of Manufactures,* pp. 83–86, 88–91, 93–94. Establishment counts for noncensus years are from *County Business Patterns.*

EXHIBIT D

Comparison of Toilet Preparations Industry (SIC 2844) to the Average of All U.S. Manufacturing Sectors, 1994[a]

Selected Measurement	All Manufacturing Sectors Average	SIC 2844 Average	Index
Employees per establishment	49	77	157
Payroll per establishment	$ 1,500,273	$2,397,065	160
Payroll per employee	$ 30,620	$ 31,191	102
Production workers per establishment	34	47	137
Wages per establishment	$ 853,319	$ 1,061,646	124
Wages per production worker	$ 24,861	$ 22,541	91
Hours per production worker	2,056	2,062	100
Wages per hour	$ 12.09	$ 10.93	90
Value added per establishment	$4,602,255	$17,781,454	386
Value added per employee	$ 93,930	$ 231,375	246
Value added per production worker	$ 134,084	$ 377,541	282
Cost per establishment	$ 5,045,178	$8,648,566	171
Cost per employee	$ 102,970	$ 112,536	109
Cost per production worker	$ 146,988	$ 183,629	125
Shipments per establishment	9,576,895	26,332,221	275
Shipments per employee	195,460	342,639	175
Shipments per production worker	279,017	559,093	200
Investment per establishment	$ 321,011	$ 654,570	204
Investment per employee	$ 6,552	$ 8,517	130
Investment per production worker	$ 9,352	$ 13,898	149

[a]*Manufacturing USA: Industry Analyses, Statistics, and Leading Companies,* 5th ed., vol. I, ed. A. J. Darnay, Gale Research Inc. (1996), p. 833.

Quimby planned on retaining Burt's Bees environmental ethic by using primarily natural ingredients—and no chemical preservatives—in its skin care products. Still, though, Burt's Bees would have to become an entirely new company and abandon the product line responsible for its success.

Quimby also realized she and Shavitz couldn't remain the sole owners of the company if she wanted it to grow. Since the inception of Burt's Bees, Roxanne and Burt had held 70 percent and 30 percent of its stock, respectively. Quimby knew the employees she hoped to attract would be highly motivated by stock grants. She also knew sharing ownership would mean feeling accountable to others and having to justify her sometimes unorthodox decisions. Quimby had fought her whole life to avoid accountability and her autonomy was a reason for Burt's Bees' success.

Conclusion

Quimby walked around the empty North Carolina factory. She tried to imagine the empty space filled with machinery and workers, but her mind kept going back to the old schoolhouse in Maine. As she saw it, Quimby had three choices:

1. *Stay in North Carolina:* Quimby could commit to North Carolina and try to get over her doubts. Burt's Bees had promising leads on a plant manager from Revlon and a sales and marketing manager with experience at Lancome, Vogue, and Victoria's Secret. The two would largely fill Quimby's expertise deficit.

2. *Move back to Maine:* Quimby could halt all purchasing and hiring and move back to Maine. She could minimize the sunk costs by acting quickly. Additionally, Burt's Bees could keep its original product line. Maine's governor had told her to call if she changed her mind. She could pursue a deal Maine to mitigate the company's tax, transport, and employment costs.

3. *Sell the company:* Although having only $3 million in sales might be an obstacle, Burt's Bees had received a lot of attention and would be enticing to many prospective buyers. Quimby knew she didn't want to be at Burt's Bees forever and said, "I feel like at some point, this business isn't going to need me anymore. My child will grow up and want to move away from its mother. There are other things I want to do."

Chapter Four

Clean Commerce and Sustainable Enterprise Movements Are an Opportunity Sea Change[1]

LEARNING OUTCOMES: After reading this chapter you will be able to understand:

4-1 Acting on new opportunities and strategies

4-2 How to look through a sustainability lens

4-3 Illustrations of clean and sustainable approaches

4-4 Entrepreneurial views and opportunities within these new approaches

As noted by one of the most famous venture capitalists, John Doerr, the clean commerce and sustainable enterprise movements could be the most promising opportunities of this century. What new opportunities are being spawned by this seismic shift? How can entrepreneurs create and seize the opportunities? It is hard to find an industry or manufacturer that is not affected by these trends. Businesses now experience increased global regulatory pressure, demands for heightened transparency, and growing public concern about the environment and health.

Clean Commerce and the Sustainability Lens: Seeing and Acting on New Opportunities and Strategies

As indicated in the Timmons Model of Entrepreneurial Process in Chapter 3, sustainability is becoming a key strategy for new ventures. Entrepreneurs now need to look at their industries

through a *sustainability lens* to identify new opportunities and devise means of acting on them.

Sustainability Defined

Sustainability means that resource utilization should not deplete existing (natural) capital. . . that is, resources should not be used at a rate faster than the rate of replenishment, and waste generation should not exceed the carrying capacity of the surrounding ecosystem. . .

Dr. Karl-Henrik Robèrt, 1997
Oncologist and founder, The Natural Step
www.naturalstep.org

Sustainability includes the concept of economic viability. Revenues and earnings must sustain ongoing business success, and like any business profits must be reinvested into product and service improvements to drive future growth. But sustainability also refers to the role new ventures play in supporting communities, improving human health, and protecting ecological systems.

Defining the Concept: How to Look through a Sustainability Lens

Consistent with the Timmons Model, emphasis on opportunity, and the resources an entrepreneurial

---

[1]We are extremely appreciative of Associate Professor Andrea Larson of the Darden Graduate School of Business Administration, University of Virginia, and Dr. Karen O'Brien of Advancing Green Chemistry for the contribution of their pioneering work in this chapter. Leaders in this emerging field, the authors have shared a very insightful look at what the clean commerce and sustainability movement means and how that translates into enormous opportunities for the next generation of global entrepreneurs.

team brings to bear means today entrepreneurial leaders are successfully mobilizing resources and offering new products and alternative business models. There are three strategic facets of looking through a sustainability lens:

- Weak ties.
- Systems thinking.
- Thinking like a molecule.

Reviewing each of these facets of the sustainability lens will illuminate new tactics.

Weak Ties

You will need new partners to help you see and analyze issues and opportunities. This requires that you establish *weak ties* to individuals and organizations previously off your radar screen.[2] They are called *weak* not because they lack substance or will let you down, but because they lie outside your traditional network of relationships. Through these ties you can gain access to fresh ideas, emergent perspectives, and new scientific data that are now salient to new venture opportunities and success.

Systems Thinking

A sustainability lens requires systems thinking. Companies generally design their strategy while implicitly assuming narrowly defined system boundaries: the firm, the market, or the industry. The reality is we all work in a complex and interconnected world and those who grasp this and seek to leverage this understanding can discover new and previously unappreciated and lucrative areas in which to act.

The 12 Principles of Green Chemistry

1. *Prevent waste:* Design chemical syntheses to prevent waste, leaving no waste to treat or clean up.
2. *Design safer chemicals and products:* Design chemical products to be fully effective yet have little or no toxicity.
3. *Design less hazardous chemical syntheses:* Design syntheses to use and generate substances with little or no toxicity to humans and the environment.
4. *Use renewable feedstocks:* Use raw materials and feedstocks that are renewable rather than depleting. Renewable feedstocks are often made from agricultural products or are the wastes of other processes; depleting feedstocks are made from fossil fuels (petroleum, natural gas, or coal) or are mined.
5. *Use catalysts, not stoichiometric reagents:* Minimize waste by using catalytic reactions. Catalysts are used in small amounts and can carry out a single reaction many times. They are preferable to stoichiometric reagents, which are used in excess and work only once.
6. *Avoid chemical derivatives:* Avoid using blocking or protecting groups or any temporary modifications if possible. Derivatives use additional reagents and generate waste.
7. *Maximize atom economy:* Design syntheses so that the final product contains the maximum proportion of the starting materials. There should be few, if any, wasted atoms.
8. *Use safer solvents and reaction conditions:* Avoid using solvents, separation agents, or other auxiliary chemicals. If these chemicals are necessary, use innocuous chemicals. If a solvent is necessary, water is a good medium, as well as certain ecofriendly solvents that do not contribute to smog formation or destroy the ozone.
9. *Increase energy efficiency:* Run chemical reactions at ambient temperature and pressure whenever possible.
10. *Design chemicals and products to degrade after use:* Design chemical products to break down to innocuous substances after use so that they do not accumulate in the environment.
11. *Analyze in real time to prevent pollution:* Include in-process, real-time monitoring and control during syntheses to minimize or eliminate the formation of by-products.
12. *Minimize the potential for accidents:* Design chemicals and their forms (solid, liquid, or gas) to minimize the potential for chemical accidents, including explosions, fires, and releases to the environment.

Source: P. T. Anastas and J. C. Warner, *Green Chemistry: Theory and Practice* (New York: Oxford University Press, 1998).

---

[2]M. Granovetter, "The Strength of Weak Ties," *American Journal of Sociology* 6 (1973), pp. 1360–1380.

Thinking Like a Molecule

In systems thinking we ask you to take the large perspective and look at an entire eco-system. Here we are asking you to look at your immediate environment, or to think small, while not losing the perspective of the larger environment you are operating in.

Green chemistry is the utilization of principles that embrace the reduction and elimination of hazardous substances in the design, manufacture, and application of chemical products. These principles can be applied to organic chemistry, inorganic chemistry, biochemistry, analytical chemistry with the focus being on minimizing the risks and maximizing the efficiency of any chemical reaction. Thinking like a molecule is a mind-set that can be used to reengineer entire systems to discover ways of meeting market needs without being limited by traditional chemical choices or processes.

Illustrating the Concept: Method

The entrepreneurial firm NextWorth (NextWorth. com) was founded in 2004 to act as a used iPod trade-in company. Entrepreneur David Chen soon discovered that proper disposal of electronic waste was a key component of the business model. "We took responsible environmental stewardship as a given. Once we started marketing our methods, sales grew dramatically," says David, where annual revenue has more than doubled in 2011, which David attributes to driving sustainability principles. NextWorth has taken green into mainstream retail with goods available at major retailers, like Target, where consumers are using NextWorth because they are reasonably priced, nontoxic, and work.

Consider cleaning wipes, a product traditionally made from petroleum-derived plastics. Eighty-three tons of cleaning wipes are thrown away every year in the United States, and U.S. plastics manufacturers told Method, an environmentally sensitive cleaning products company, that single-use, non-woven cleaning cloths could not be made from PLA (polylactic acid), a plant-based biomaterial recently commercialized by Cargill's NatureWorks subsidiary. Entrepreneur Adam Lowry was undeterred. Lowry found innovative Chinese subcontractors to formulate biomass-based, microfiber plastic wipes that are both compostable and biodegradable. It was not long before those U.S. subcontractors were calling Adam back to say they had figured out how to do it. Working with domestic manufacturers is a sourcing strategy more consistent with the sustainability concept of reducing transportation fuel use and facilitating supplier management.

At every turn, method seeks to be a catalyst for broader systemic change. The company uses biodiesel-fueled trucks, has developed solar-powered forklifts for its main Chicago warehouse, and is already carbon-neutral through offsets. In the laundry detergent category, the company has led the industry move to 2X and 3X ultra-condensed laundry detergent, which reduces packaging materials, shipping cost, and water use.

Co-development of innovations with suppliers drives Method's ability to remain on the competitive edge. Most early suppliers were small firms that wanted to be innovative and to learn new processes and designs. Many of these have scaled up successfully with Method's tremendous growth, continuing to provide creative input. In 2009 Method became one of the first cradle-to-cradle–endorsed companies, with 37 cradle-to-cradle–certified products at launch, among the most of any company in the world, now up to 60 certified products and counting. The competitive picture emerges of a David-esque network of suppliers taking on the Goliaths of P&G, Johnson & Johnson, and Unilever.

"Find it, don't build it," guides the company's strategy. Method keeps R&D inside, holding onto a talented internal team. Manufacturing is outsourced. To stay innovative, Method will partner with anyone who can help it deliver "healthy, happy home revolution"–a phrase that places interestingly wide boundaries around the brand. Lowry also comments that rigid environmental rhetoric always frustrated him; he advises, "Don't let perfection be the enemy of progress" in the environmental and sustainability markets. He also recommends that entrepreneurs get people involved who have nothing to do with the business. "Get people involved who design other cool stuff" was his comment to a classroom of Stanford MBA students in 2007.

The sustainability lens is sharpened by using weak ties, systems thinking, and thinking like a molecule will clearly guide this venture. As ecological, health, and community concerns grow more important in society, Method represents a business model that fully integrates ecological and sustainability principles into product and strategy design. This is what entrepreneurs do: they create a better future.

Illustrating the Concept: NatureWorks

How would it feel to show up Monday morning, check your e-mail, and learn that Walmart—the

Greentech Alliance

Scientific breakthroughs in biology and materials technology mean that there has never been a better time to start and grow a great green venture. The legendary Silicon Valley-based venture capital firm Kleiner, Perkins, Caufield & Byers (KPCB) is actively investing in Greentech innovation and entrepreneurs.

To further these aims, in November 2007 KPCB announced a global collaboration with Generation Investment Management (Generation), a firm cofounded by Al Gore, former vice president of the United States, Nobel Prize winner, and a leading advocate for climate change initiatives. The collaboration works to find, fund, and accelerate green business, technology, and policy solutions with the greatest potential to help the current climate crisis. The partnership provides funding and global business-building expertise to a range of businesses, both public and private, and to entrepreneurs.

This alliance represents a landmark alignment of resources to effect global change to protect the environment. It combines the research expertise of both organizations with a track record of successful investments in public and private companies, from early-stage to large-capitalization business. It aligns the convening power of Gore, the KPCB Greentech Innovation Network, and the Generation Advisory Board toward a common goal. In addition, KPCB's presence in Asia and the United States, combined with Generation's presence in the United States, Europe, and Australia, will support global-scale solutions.

Source: www.kpcb.com.

ultimate supply chain captain–was going to begin sourcing your product? Not a bad start to the week. All the more so if you are CEO of a relatively small subsidiary struggling to make a profit by producing a relatively unknown commodity: corn-based plastic.

This Monday morning scenario actually happened at NatureWorks, an entrepreneurial venture under the technical and managerial direction of Patrick Gruber. Born of a joint venture between agricultural processing giant Cargill and Dow Chemical, NatureWorks had been struggling to realize the vision of its original founders for 10 years: replacing oil-based plastics (for packaging, films, and fabrics) with plant-based (biomass) plastics. Employing 230 people and carrying some $750 million of capital investment by Cargill, in 2005 the company was operating at a lower capacity than expected. NatureWorks was not yet profitable, and the refrain "make the bleeding stop" was beginning to sound like a broken record. And then Walmart called. As part of the mega-retailer's new strategy to source environmentally sustainable products, Walmart would begin purchasing deli containers made from NatureWorks' corn-based plastic.

NatureWorks' new plastic is the result of an entrepreneurial process where materials engineers and industrial chemists designed a product that has a health focus, environmental attributes, and functional performance built in. Consequently the company has assumed leadership in the emerging market for greener plastics. NatureWorks' product is another excellent example of what happens when you think like a molecule and employ green chemistry techniques. This strategic approach has you question the nature and value of material inputs to your products, the efficiency of your manufacturing and formulation processes, and the ultimate fate of your outputs and products. "Cradle to cradle" is a sustainability concept: At the end of a product's useful life, its constituent materials (understood as assets, not waste) become inputs for new products or return safely into the earth. Thinking like a molecule allows you to understand the complete cradle-to-cradle life cycle of your products and manufacturing processes–not just the visible outcomes, but the microscopic ones as well.

In 2009 NatureWorks teamed with Ashland Distribution, a leading distributor in thermoplastics in North America, Europe, and China to expand products and sales.

The E-Factor

Included in green chemistry tools is the idea of the "atom economy," where manufacturers make as full use as possible of every input molecule in the final output product. If you consider that on average 94 percent of the resources that go into making a product are discarded as waste, this principle has profound system-wide ramifications.[3]

[3]The definition of E-factor is evolving at this writing. Pharmaceutical companies engaged in green chemistry are still debating whether to include input factors such as energy, water, and other nontraditional inputs.

The pharmaceutical industry, an early adopter of green chemistry principles in industrial processing, uses a metric called *E-factor* to measure the ratio of inputs to outputs in any given product. In essence, an E-factor measures how many weight units of output one gets per weight unit of input. This figure gives companies a sense of process efficiency and inherent costs associated with waste, energy, and other resources' rates of use. Applying green chemistry principles to pharmaceutical production processes has enabled pharmaceutical companies to dramatically lower their E-factors–and significantly raise profits.

Merck and Co., for example, "discovered a highly innovative and efficient catalytic synthesis for sitagliptin, the active ingredient in Januvia, their new treatment for type 2 diabetes. This revolutionary synthesis creates 220 pounds less waste for each pound of sitagliptin manufactured, and increases the overall yield by nearly 50 percent. Over the lifetime of Januvia, Merck decreased waste generated by 23 percent (from 2005 to 2008). Twenty-nine percent of generated waste is reused in industry and 26 percent burned as energy source to power machinery and industrial furnaces. Only 3 percent of waste goes into landfills."[4]

This is a great example of how green chemistry places human and ecological health at the heart of profitable product design and manufacturing. Moreover, because it calls for increased reliance on renewable inputs, at a macro level, green chemistry provides the means of shifting away from a petrochemical-based economy to a biobased economy. This has profound consequences for a wide range of issues, from environmental health, to worker safety, to national security and the farm economy. While no single science supplies all the answers, green chemistry plays a foundational role in enabling companies to see concrete benefits from greener design.

Drivers of New Entrepreneurial Opportunities

As we pointed out earlier, the Timmons Model of Entrepreneurial Process represents sustainability as the bedrock of new ventures. Granted, not all ventures currently include explicit environmental and sustainable considerations, but this reflects a past in which these issues did not have to be part of the business model. We now live in a world constrained by the capacities of natural systems to adapt to our activity.

The major challenge of this century is how to create prosperity for more people worldwide given climate change, water shortages, urban air pollution, energy supply challenges, and the necessity of feeding and providing decent lifestyles for a world population that is expected to double by 2050. Economic models that served as the foundation of the Industrial Revolution assumed limitless natural resources and infinite capacity for nature to absorb waste streams from commercial and industrial activity. Feedback from natural systems, communicated by the scientific communities that monitor pollution and ecological health, tells us that this growth model can no longer guide us.

We are inundated by media reports on the mounting challenges from environmental constraints. In fact, the revolution in communications is a major contributor to the opening of new opportunities for entrepreneurs in this field. Because information is now widely distributed and universally accessible, consumers can access new scientific findings and perspectives well in advance of government action and regulations. With climate change, for example, U.S. companies began to take action to protect their shareholders well in advance of governmental acceptance that climate change was even happening. Similarly, caution is beginning to prevail in the arena of consumer goods and environmental health. When a material in a common product comes under increasing scrutiny as a hazard, such as a material in imported children's toys, the consumer is increasingly disinclined to wait for the U.S. Environmental Protection Agency (EPA) to test, assess, and ban the substance. Instead, end users now have the means and motivation to search out alternative products. Thus the entrepreneur who reads these trends and gets ahead of them can be ready when the market begins to shift–and indeed can help shift the market just by offering safe alternatives.

As with the REACH regulations in the European Union (regulatory requirements for chemicals enacted in 2006),[5] changing global standards and international regulations are shifting the playing field as well. "Why is this substance banned in Europe and Japan but sold in the United States?" an American consumer may wonder. It is becoming increasingly difficult to manufacture different qualities of goods for diverse regulatory regimes, so it is best to meet the highest global standard. This not only simplifies supply chains but allows companies

---

[4]http://www.epa.gov/greenchemistry/pubs/pgcc/winners/gspa06.html.
[5]http://ec.europa.eu/enterprise/reach/index_en.htm.

to avoid being caught selling "substandard" or even contaminated products in one country and "clean" products in another.

Europe and Japan are setting a high bar for international manufacturing standards. The Directive on the Restriction of the Use of Certain Hazardous Substances in Electrical and Electronic Equipment (commonly referred to as the Restriction of Hazardous Substances Directive [RoHS]) was adopted in February 2003 by the European Union. RoHS took effect in July 2006 and is mandated to become law in each member state. This directive restricts the use of six hazardous (and commonly used) materials in the manufacture of various types of electronic and electrical equipment. RoHS is closely linked with the EU's Waste Electrical and Electronic Equipment Directive (WEEE), which sets collection, recycling, and recovery targets for electronics. Under WEEE, responsibility for the disposal of waste electrical and electronic equipment is placed on manufacturers. Both of these directives are part of an EU legislative initiative to solve the problem of increasing amounts of toxic electronic waste.

There are other powerful drivers behind entrepreneurs using a sustainability lens. For example, green building design and construction are now mainstream markets and will continue to grow as the need for energy efficient housing increases. The Leadership in Energy and Environmental Design (LEED) standards provide sustainable building rating systems under the U.S. Green Building Council. Each LEED certified building has the potential to be awarded silver, gold, or platinum levels of design and material use, a way companies now differentiate themselves and recoup costs through greater efficiency over time. Buildings with LEED certification realize benefits such as operating cost reductions due to energy and water savings, employee productivity gains, better recruitment and retention, and higher resale value.

Another area of rapid market growth is clean energy technology including wind, solar photovoltaics, fuel cells, and biofuels. Debate over climate change has shifted from whether it is happening to what to do about it. Venture investments in energy technologies were estimated to have tripled in 2006 to $2.4 billion.[6] Clean Technology venture investment increased 65 percent from 2009 to first half of 2010. North American companies raised 1.46 billion to support solar, biofuels, and Smart Grid systems investments in North America, Europe, China, and India. Close to 40 percent growth across the wind, solar, fuel cell, and biofuel markets indicates that opportunity abounds.

As ecological and economic pressures grow worldwide, the true entrepreneurial leader will be viewed as someone with a vision from which he or she creates new ventures that protect the integrity of natural systems, whether we are referring to atmospheric systems, watersheds and streams, urban housing/job/health systems, or human immune systems. Entrepreneurial visions that allow successful co-evolution of business with natural systems will have more durability and be better grounded in the new realities.

Consistent with the Timmons Model, today a growing number of entrepreneurs are creating this new competitive market space by effectively mobilizing resources, offering successful products, and devising alternative business models. These leaders are integrating sustainable principles into their operations and strategies and offer a distinct entrepreneurial and innovative business model for the future. It is an evolving model for positive and creative business adaptation to the increasingly problematic impact humans have on the natural environment.

Implications for 21st Century Entrepreneurs

The implications of these trends for 21st century entrepreneurs are profound. The opportunities exist today and are growing worldwide as people adapt and evolve in response to more complex social, economic, and environmental pressures. Resource constraints and the limits of ecological systems to absorb our waste are not transitory challenges. Sustainability is not a fad. Clean commerce is a necessity given global population growth, rising economic aspirations in emerging economies, and a growing appreciation of our role in affecting the intricate balance of the earth's natural systems. A wave of entrepreneurial creativity and innovation is already under way, inspired by the sustainability lens. As Jeff Timmons has stated, "The force of one generation's entrepreneurs becomes the next generation's business paradigm." This is happening as new businesses and technologies emerge to address environmental and human health concerns. As the entrepreneurs behind NextWorth, Method, and NatureWorks illustrate, by driving change in consumer product design and materials innovation, entrepreneurship trends in environmental sustainability are the leading indicators of business and social change.

---

[6]J. Makower; R. Pernick; and C. Wilder, "Clean Energy Trends," March 2007, www.cleanedge.com.

Entrepreneurs have important opportunities to supply mid-sized and larger firms with newly designed products that meet environmental and sustainability criteria. Larger firms can move the market, but often they must buy innovations from smaller, more nimble entrepreneurial firms. Given the creative skill set required in this transition, newer entrepreneurial leaders will be the ones to offer new solutions to large firms and consumers. The transition to sustainable and clean commerce requires fresh perspective on new technology, products, and markets. Providing these has historically been, and remains today, the role of the entrepreneur.

Chapter Summary

- Some of the most fertile opportunities lie in the areas of greatest tension. If you can see them and act on them, you will differentiate your company and set the industry standard to best suit your venture's capabilities.

- The three strategic facets of looking through a sustainability lens are weak ties, systems thinking, and thinking like a molecule.

- Employing green chemistry techniques can not only reduce process costs and the risk of production and product liability, but can generate new products and open new markets.

- Green chemistry places human and ecological health at the heart of profitable product design and manufacturing. It uses the creativity of nature's biological processes to create molecules, materials, and processes that are safe and high performing.

- Consistent with the Timmons Model, emphasis on opportunity, and the resources a visionary entrepreneurial team brings to bear, today many entrepreneurial leaders are looking through a sustainability lens and creating new competitive market spaces.

- The entrepreneur who reads these trends and gets ahead of them can be ready when the market begins to shift–and indeed can help shift the market just by offering safe alternatives.

- Because it is becoming increasingly difficult to manufacture different qualities of goods for diverse regulatory regimes, it is best to meet the highest global standard–not only to simplify supply chains but to avoid being caught selling "substandard" or even contaminated products in one country and "clean" products in another.

- Although old-school business leaders may be inclined to fight against sustainability measures, entrepreneurs will instead spend their time coming up with new processes and products ahead of such regulations–and by doing so will ultimately lead the market.

- Entrepreneurial opportunities exist today and are growing worldwide as creative business leaders adapt and evolve in response to more complex social, economic, and environmental pressures.

Study Questions

1. In what ways does looking through a sustainability lens change how an entrepreneur approaches a new venture opportunity?

2. Explain how thinking like a molecule is related to the entrepreneurial process.

3. Why has the clean commerce domain become one of the hottest for venture capital investors?

4. How has the communications revolution become a major driver of entrepreneurial thinking and opportunities in sustainable, green business models?

5. How can entrepreneurs use the increasingly stringent product, raw material, and manufacturing process laws (particularly in Japan and in Europe) to their advantage?

Internet Resources

www.sustainablebusiness.com *SustainableBusiness.com provides global news and networking services to help green business grow, covering all sectors: renewable energy, green building, sustainable investing, and organics.*

www.greenbiz.com *GreenBiz is a free information resource on how to align environmental responsibility with business success. It includes news and resources for large and small businesses through a combination of websites, workshops, daily news feeds, electronic newsletters, and briefing papers.*

www.cleanedge.com *Clean Edge is a leading research and publishing firm helping companies, investors, and governments understand and profit from clean technologies.*

www.cleantech.com *The Cleantech Network founded Cleantech as a viable investment category in 2002 and has played an influential role in the development of this*

fast-growth investment category. The network brings capital and innovation together through Cleantech Forums and membership services.

www.environmentalhealthnews.org *Environmental Health Sciences is a not-for-profit organization founded in 2002 to help increase public understanding of emerging scientific links between environmental exposures and human health.*

Case

Jim Poss

Preparation Questions

1. Analyze this case using the Timmons entrepreneurship framework (entrepreneur–opportunity–resources). Particularly note the entrepreneur's traits and how he gathered resources for his venture.

2. Discuss Jim's fund-raising strategies. What other options might SPC consider for raising money? Is SPC a good investment?

3. Discuss SPC's growth strategy. What additional market(s) would you recommend it pursue?

Jim Poss stopped at a Logan Airport newsstand to flip through the June 2004 *National Geographic* cover story that declared, "The End of Cheap Oil."

Jim's enterprise, Seahorse Power Company (SPC), was an engineering startup that encouraged the adoption of environmentally friendly power generation methods. Jim was sure its first product, a patent-pending solar-powered trash compactor, could make a real difference.

In the United States, 180 million garbage trucks consume over 1 billion gallons of diesel fuel a year. By compacting trash on-site and off-grid, the mailbox-sized "BigBelly" could cut pickups by 400 percent. The prototype—designed on the fly at a cost of $10,000—had been sold to Vail Ski Resorts in Colorado for $5,500. It had been working as promised since February, saving the resort time and money on round trips to a lodge accessible only by snow machine.

Jim viewed the $4,500 loss on the sale as a marketing and proof-of-concept expense. But with a 20-machine production run under way, SPC had to reduce component costs and increase production efficiencies.

Jim put the magazine back and walked to the New York Shuttle gate. An investor group in the city had called another meeting, and Jim planned to ask some hard questions about their proposed deal. He thought they should write him the check they had been promising—and let him run SPC the way he saw fit—or decline to invest so he could locate other sources for the company's $250,000 seed round.

Green Roots

As a kid, Jim enjoyed fashioning gadgets from components he had amassed by dismantling appliances and electronic devices. He also spent a lot of time cross-country skiing with his father. Jim said that by 12th grade, he knew where he was headed:

> I had read *Silent Spring*[1] and that got me thinking about the damage we are doing to the earth. And once I started learning about the severity of our problems—that was it. By the end of my first semester at Duke University, I had taken enough environmental science to see that helping businesses to go green was going to be a huge growth industry.

Jim thought the way to get businesses to invest in superior energy systems was to make doing so profitable for them. He had a double major in environmental science and policy, and geology—with a minor in engineering. He graduated in 1996 and found work analyzing soil and rock samples, but did not stay long:

> Within 6 months I found a fun job redesigning the production capabilities at a small electronics firm. Soon after that, I started working for this company called Solectria; that was right up my alley.

As a sales engineer at the Massachusetts designer and manufacturer of sustainable transportation and energy solutions, Jim helped clients configure electric drive systems for vehicles. He developed an expertise in using spreadsheets to calculate the most efficient layout of motors, controllers, power converters, and other hardware. By 1999, he had decided to move on:

> I found an interesting job in San Francisco as a production manager for a boat manufacturing company—coordinating the flow of parts from seven or eight subcontractors. When the [Internet] bubble burst, the boat company wasn't able to raise capital to expand. My work soon became relatively mundane, so I left.

This time, Jim headed back to school:
I knew that I could run a good company—something in renewable energy, and maybe something with

This case was prepared by Carl Hedberg under the direction of Professor William Bygrave. © Copyright Babson College, 2004. Funding provided by the Franklin W. Olin Graduate School and a gift from the class of 2003.

[1]*Silent Spring*, written in 1962 by Rachel Carson, exposed the hazards of the pesticide DDT, eloquently questioned humanity's faith in technological progress, and helped set the stage for the environmental movement. Appearing on a CBS documentary shortly before her death from breast cancer in 1964, the author remarked, "Man's attitude toward nature is today critically important simply because we have now acquired a fateful power to alter and destroy nature. But man is a part of nature, and his war against nature is inevitably a war against himself. . . . [We are] challenged as mankind has never been challenged before to prove our maturity and our mastery, not of nature, but of ourselves."

gadgets. I still had a lot to learn, so I applied to the MBA program at Babson College. I figured that I could use the second-year EIT[2] module to incubate something.

Opportunity Exploration

Between his first and second years at Babson, Jim applied for a summer internship. He sent a proposal to the Spire Corporation, which made highly engineered solar electric equipment, about investigating the feasibility of solar-powered trash compactors. Jim discussed his idea with a Spire director and got a call from Spire's president:

> Roger Little had talked with the board member I knew and said that while they weren't interested in having me write a case study on some solar whatever-it-was, . . . they'd like me to write some business plans for Spire—based on their existing opportunities and existing operations. I said, "Sure, I'll take it."

That summer, Jim worked with Spire's executive team to complete three business plans. When they asked him to stay on, he agreed to work 15 hours per week—on top of his full-time MBA classes. He kept bringing up his idea for a solar-powered trash compactor with the Spire executives, who kept dismissing it. "Finally," he recalled, "they just said that they don't get into end-user applications."

Early in his second year, Jim attended a product design fair featuring young engineers from Babson's sister school, the Franklin W. Olin School of Engineering. There, he met Jeff Satwicz. When Jim got involved with a project that required engineering capabilities, he sought out Jeff:

> I went up the hill to Olin to ask Jeff if he'd like to help design a folding grill for tailgating—he said, "Sure."

Although Jim did not stay with the grill team, he had forged a link with an entrepreneurial engineer. Certain of his trajectory, Jim incorporated the Seahorse Power Company (SPC)—a nod to his aspiration of developing power systems that could harness the energy of ocean waves and currents.

Understanding that sea-powered generators were a long way off, Jim investigated ways to serve well-capitalized ventures that were developing alternative-energy solutions.

Everybody kept telling me that wind was where it's at—and they were right; it's the fastest-growing energy source in the world. All the venture capitalists are looking at wind power. I realized, though, that if I was going to make wind plants, I'd have to raise $200 million to $500 million—with no industry experience. Impossible. So instead, I started looking at what these [wind-plant ventures] needed.

The DAQ Buoy

Jim discovered that The Cape Wind Project, a company working to build a wind farm on Nantucket Sound, had erected a $2.5 million, 200-foot tower to collect wind and weather data. Jim felt there was a better way:

> My idea was to deploy data buoys that could be moved around a site to capture a full range of data points. I spent about 6 months writing a business plan on my data acquisition buoy—the DAQ. I figured that to get to the prototype stage I'd need between $5 million and $10 million. This would be a pretty sophisticated piece of equipment, and a lot of people worried that if a storm came up and did what storms typically do to buoys, we'd be all done. I was having a hard time getting much traction with investors.

Finding the Waste

Even while he searched for a big-concept opportunity, Jim remembered his solar compactor idea. In the spring semester, he decided to try it as an EIT endeavor. Although he knew producing such a device was feasible, he did not get excited about the project until he examined the trash industry:

> I looked at the market size and realized that I had been messing around with expensive, sophisticated business models that didn't offer close to the payback this compactor would.

U.S. companies spent $12 billion on trash receptacles in 2000, and $1.2 billion on compaction equipment in 2001. The average trash truck gets less than 3 miles to the gallon and costs over $100 an hour to operate. There are lots of off-grid sites[3] with high trash volumes—resorts, amusement parks, and beaches—requiring multiple pickups a day. That is a tremendous waste of labor and energy.

Joining Jim in the EIT module was first-year MBA candidate Alexander Perera. Alex had an undergraduate degree in environmental science from Boston

[2]The Entrepreneurship Intensity Track (EIT) was a compressed and highly focused entrepreneurial curriculum for graduate students at Babson College. The program provided a select group of MBAs with the necessary skills to take a business idea through the critical stages of exploration, investigation, and refinement. The program tailored students' education to best fit their perceived market opportunity, enabling them to launch their business during the spring of their second year.

[3]Sites without electrical power.

University, plus industry experience in renewable energy and energy efficiency. The pair reasoned that if a solar compactor could offer significant savings as a trash collection device, its market could include retail and food establishments, cities, and hotels (Exhibit A).

Gearing Up

By the end of spring semester, they had a clear sense of the market and the nature of the opportunity—plus seed funding of $22,500: $10,000 from Jim's savings, and $12,500 through Babson's hatchery program. Competitors—dumpster and compaction equipment manufacturers—did not have a system like the one they were designing. Nevertheless, Jim and Alex knew that if their solar-powered compactor proved reliable and saved money, established companies would seek to replicate or acquire the technology behind it.

Jim sought out the best patent attorneys, but most were outside his budget. In May 2003, he got a break when he presented his idea at an investor forum:

> I won $1,500 in patent services from Brown and Rudnick.[4] That might not have taken me too far, but they have a very entrepreneurial mindset. They gave me a flat rate for the patent—which is not something many firms will do. I paid the $7,800 up front, we filed a provisional patent in June, and they agreed to work with me as I continued to develop and modify the machine.

Jim's efforts had again attracted the interest of Jeff Satwicz, who brought in Bret Richmond, a fellow Olin student with experience in product design, welding, and fabrication. When the team conducted some reverse engineering to see if their idea was feasible, Jim said they were pleasantly surprised:

> I found a couple of kitchen trash compactors . . . for about 125 bucks. We took them apart, and that's when I realized how easy this was going to be. . . . Of course, nothing is ever as easy as you think it's going to be.

Pitching without Product

To conduct some field research, they called on businesses that would be the most likely early adopters of their product. Alex described an unexpected turn of events:

> Literally the first place I called was the ski resort in Vail, Colorado. Some eco-terrorists had recently burned down one of their lodges to protest their expansion on the mountain, and they were also dealing with four environmental lawsuits related to some kind of noncompliance.
> This guy Luke Cartin at the resort just jumped at the solar compactor concept. He said, "Oh, this is cool. We have a lodge at Blue Sky Basin that is an hour and a half round trip on a snow cat. We pick up the trash out there three or four times a week, sometimes every day. We could really use a product like that. . ."

Jim added that after a couple of calls, they were in business without a product:

I explained that we were students and that we had not actually built one of these things yet (sort of). Luke asked me to work up a quote for three machines. They had been very open about their costs for trash pickup, and I figured that they'd be willing to pay six grand apiece. I also had a rough idea that our cost of materials would fall somewhat less than that.

> Luke called back and said that they didn't have the budget for three, but they'd take one. I was actually really happy about that, because I knew by then that making just one of these was going to be a real challenge.

In September, SPC received a purchase order from Vail Resorts. When Jim called the company to work out a payment plan, Luke surprised them again:

> He said, "We'll just send you a check for the full amount, minus shipping, and you get the machine here by Christmas." That was great, but now we were in real trouble because we had to figure out how to build this thing quickly, from scratch—and on a tight budget.

EXHIBIT A

Target Customers

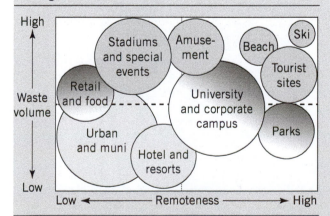

[4]Brown Rudnick Berlack Israels, LLP, Boston, Massachusetts.

Learning by Doing

The team set out to design and develop the machine that SPC had now trademarked as the "BigBelly Solar-Powered Trash Compactor." Although his team was unfamiliar with computer-aided design (CAD) software, Jim saw that as an opportunity:

> These guys were doing engineering diagrams on paper with pens and pencils—but now we were going to need professional stuff. I said that we could all learn CAD together, and if they made mistakes, great, that's fine; we'd work through it.

They also had to crunch the numbers to design a machine that would work as promised. They began sourcing the internal components and looking for a design, fabrication, and manufacturing subcontractor that could produce the steel cabinet quickly. Although SPC would oversee the entire process from design to assembly, quotes ranged from $80,000 to $400,000. Jim noted that SPC had an even bigger problem:

> On top of the price, the lead times that they were giving me were not going to cut it; I had to get this thing to Colorado for the ski season!
>
> So we decided to build it ourselves. I went to a local fabricator trade show and discovered that although they all have internal engineering groups, some were willing to take a loss on the research and development side in order to get the manufacturing contract.
>
> We chose Boston Engineering since they are very interested in developing a relationship with Olin engineers. They gave me a hard quote of $2,400 for the engineering assistance, and $2,400 for the cabinet. By this time we had sourced all the components we needed, and we began working with their

engineer to size everything up. Bob Treiber, the president, was great. He made us do the work ourselves out at his facility in Hudson (Massachusetts), but he also mentored us, and his firm did a ton of work pro bono.

Fulfillment and Feedback

The Christmas deadline came and went. By late January 2004, Jim was working from four in the morning to nearly 11 at night. In February, they fired up the device, tested it, and shipped it (Exhibit B). Jim met it in Colorado, helped unwrap it, and put a few finishing touches on it. Although it worked, even at zero degrees, it had never been tested in the field. Jim left after a few days, and for 2 weeks, heard nothing.

Jim wrestled with how he could check in with SPC's first customer without betraying his angst. He finally called under the guise of soliciting feedback:

> They said that they had dropped the machine off a forklift and it fell on its face. "Oh man," I thought; "if it had fallen on its back, that would have been okay, but this was bad—real bad." And then Luke tells me that it was a bit scratched—but it worked fine. He told me how happy they were that we had made it so robust. When I asked how heavy the bags were that they were pulling out of the thing, he said, "I don't know; we haven't emptied it yet. . ." I was astounded.

The Vail crew did discover that the single collection bag was too heavy—a two-bin system would work better. The resort also suggested that the inside cart

EXHIBIT B

The BigBelly Arrives in Vail

be on wheels, that the access door be in the back, and that the compactor give a wireless notification when it was full.

As the SPC team incorporated these ideas into their next generation of "SunPack" compactors, they also engineered a second product that they hoped would expand their market to include manufacturers of standard compaction dumpsters. The "SunPack Hippo" would be a solar generator designed to replace the 220-V AC-power units that ran industrial compactors. The waste hauling industry had estimated that among commercial customers that would benefit from compaction, between 5 and 20 percent did not adopt it because of the cost of electrical wiring. SPC planned to market the system through manufacturing and/or distribution partnerships.

Protecting the Property

Although the interstate shipment of the BigBelly had given SPC a legal claim to the name and the technology, Jim kept his patent attorneys apprised of developments and modifications. SPC had applied for a provisional patent in June 2003, and had 1 year to broaden and strengthen it prior to the formal filing. As that date approached, the attorneys worked to craft a document that protected the inventors without being so broad that it could be successfully challenged in court.

SPC's patents covered as many aspects of SunPack products as possible, including energy storage, battery charging, energy draw cycle time, sensor controls, and wireless communication. The filing also specified other off-grid power sources besides solar, such as foot pedals, windmills, and water wheels.

Jim felt they had a good head start in an industry segment they had created. Now they had to prove their business model.

The Next Generation

While the first machine had cost more to build than it sold for, the unit had proven the concept and enabled useful feedback. SPC's production run of 20 machines, however, would have to show that the machines could be made profitably. That would mean cutting the cost of materials by more than 75 percent to around $2,500 per unit. SPC estimated that although a $5,000 price made the system far more expensive than a traditional trash receptacle, it could pay for itself by trimming the ongoing cost of collection (Exhibit C).

The team had determined that leasing the Big-Belly would alleviate new-buyer jitters by having

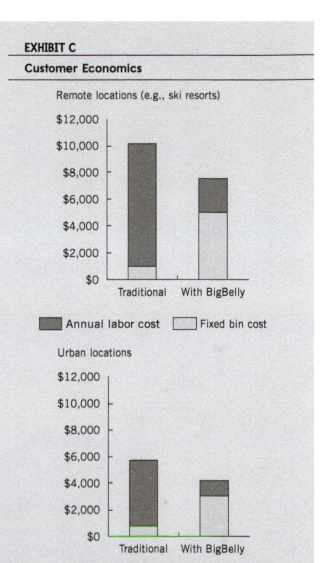

EXHIBIT C

Customer Economics

Remote locations (e.g., ski resorts)

Urban locations

Legend: Annual labor cost ∎   Fixed bin cost ▢

SPC retain the risk of machine ownership—which could increase margins by 10 percent. Over the next 5 years, SPC expected to expand its potential customer pool by reducing the selling price to around $3,000—along with a corresponding drop in material costs (Exhibit D).

To save money, the SPC team designed their new machines with 30 percent fewer steel parts. They also halved the solar panel's size and the 2-week battery storage capacity, and replaced the screw compaction system with a simpler, cheaper, and more efficient sprocket and chain mechanism (Exhibit E).

To offer an effective service capability, the team mostly sold to New England customers. One concern was vandalism. Team members explained that the solar panel was protected by a replaceable sheet of Lexan,[5] that the mechanical parts were out of

[5] A clear, high-impact-strength plastic used in many security applications.

EXHIBIT D

BigBelly Economics

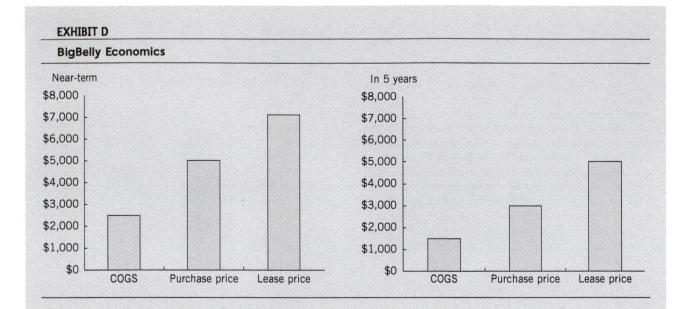

Near-term

In 5 years

EXHIBIT E

BigBelly CAD Schematic

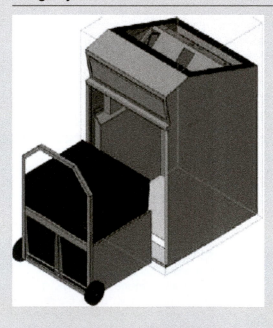

reach, and that the unit was quite solid. Jim said that didn't alleviate fears:

> One state park ranger was worried that it would get tossed into the lake, so I assured him that the units would be very heavy. He said, "So they'll sink really fast . . ."

Still, Jim said, the overall response was very favorable:

> We have pre-sold nearly half of our next run to places like Acadia National Park in Maine, Six Flags Amusement Park in Massachusetts, Harbor Lights in Boston, beaches on Nantucket, and Harvard University. Fifty percent down payment deposits should be

coming in soon, but that won't cover what we'll need to get this done.

Projections and Funding

During this "early commercialization period," Jim was committed to controlling expenses by using on-campus and contractor facilities as much as possible. The company hoped to close on an A-round of $250,000[6] by early summer to pay for cost reduction engineering, sales and marketing, and working capital. The following year, the company expected to raise a B-round of between $700,000 and $1 million.

SPC projected a positive cash flow in 2006 on total revenues of just over $4.7 million (Exhibit F). The team felt that if their products continued to perform well, their market penetration estimates would be highly achievable (Exhibit G). Jim estimated that by 2008, SPC would become an attractive merger or acquisition candidate.

In January 2004, as Jim began work on drafting an SBIR[7] grant proposal, his parents invested $12,500. That same month, while attending a wind

[6]Based on a pre-money valuation of $2.5 million. The principal and interest on this seed-round note would convert into equity at the A-round with an additional 30 percent discount to A-round investors. Seed-round investors would have the right to reinvest in the A-round to offset dilution.

[7]The Small Business Innovation Research (SBIR) Program was a source of government grant funding driven by 10 federal departments and agencies that allocated a portion of their research and development capital for awards to innovative small businesses in the United States.

EXHIBIT F

SPC Financial Projections

	2004	2005	2006	2007	2008
BigBelly unit sales	50	300	1,200	3,600	9,000
BigBelly revenues	$225,000	$1,200,000	$4,200,000	$10,800,000	$22,500,000
Hippo royalty revenues	0	120,000	525,000	1,620,000	3,937,500
Total income	225,000	1,320,000	4,725,000	12,420,000	26,437,500
COGS	146,250	660,000	2,100,000	4,860,000	9,000,000
Gross income	78,750	660,000	2,625,000	7,560,000	17,437,500
SG&A	400,000	1,600,000	2,600,000	5,000,000	11,000,000
EBIT	($321,250)	($940,000)	$25,000	$2,560,000	$6,437,500

EXHIBIT G

Market Size and Penetration

	2004	2005	2006	2007	2008
Top-Down					
SunPack market[a] ($ billions)	$1.0	$1.0	$1.0	$1.0	$1.0
SunPack % penetration	0.0%	0.1%	0.5%	1.2%	2.6%
Bottom-Up					
Total potential customers[b]	30,000	30,000	30,000	30,000	30,000
Potential units/customer	20	20	20	20	20
Total potential units	600,000	600,000	600,000	600,000	600,000
Cumulative units sold	50	350	1,550	5,150	14,150
Cumulative % penetration	0.0%	0.1%	0.3%	0.9%	2.4%

[a]Assume $600,000 BigBelly market (5 percent of $12 billion waste receptacles sold to target segments) plus a $400,000 power unit market ($1.2 billion compacting dumpsters sold/$12,000 average price X $4,000 per power unit).

[b]Assume 400 resorts, 600 amusement parks, 2,000 university campuses, 5,000 commercial campuses, 2,200 hotels, 4,000 municipalities, 57 national parks, 2,500 state parks and forests, 3,700 RV parks and campgrounds, and 17,000 fast-food and retail outlets.

energy conference, Jim overheard someone saying he wanted to invest his recent entrepreneurial windfall in socially responsible ventures:

> I gave him my 3-minute spiel on the compactor. He said that it sounded interesting, but that he was into wind power—after all, this *was* a wind power conference. "Well then," I said, "have I got a business plan for you!"

Jim sent the investor the most recent version of the data acquisition buoy business plan. That led to a meeting where the investor ended up explaining to Jim why the DAQ was such a good idea. Jim said that the investor also understood the difficulty of funding the venture:

> [The investor] said, "Well, I sure wish you were doing the data acquisition buoy, but I can also see why you're not." I assured him that my passion was, of course, offshore wind, and that it was something I was planning to do in the future. So he agreed to invest $12,500 in the compactor—but only because he wanted to keep his foot in the door for what SPC was going to do later on.

In February, after the favorable review from Vail, Jim called on his former boss at Spire. Roger Little was impressed, and Spire invested $25,000. In April, the team earned top honors in the 2004 Douglas Foundation Graduate Business Plan Competition at Babson College. The prize—$20,000 cash plus $40,000 worth of services—came with a good deal of favorable press, too.

Although SPC could now begin to move ahead on the construction of the next 20 cabinets, Jim was still looking for an unusual investor:

> This is not a venture capital deal, and selling this idea to angels can be a challenge because many are not sophisticated enough to understand what we are doing. I had one group, for example, saying that this wouldn't work because most trash receptacles are located in alleys—out of the sun.
>
> Here we have a practical, commonsense business, but since it is a new technology, many investors are unsure of how to value it. How scalable is it? Will our patent filings hold up? Who will fix them when they break?

Earlier that spring, Jim had presented to a gathering of angels interested in socially responsible enterprises. Jim said one group seemed eager to move ahead:

> They liked that Spire had invested, and they seemed satisfied with our projections. When I told them that we had a $25,000 minimum, they said not to worry—they were interested in putting in $50,000 now and $200,000 later. In fact, they started talking about setting up funding milestones so that they could be our primary backers as we grew. They wanted me to stop fund-raising, focus on the business, and depend on them for all my near-term financing needs.
>
> At this point I felt like I needed to play hardball with these guys, show them where the line was. My answer was that I wasn't at all comfortable with that, and that I would be comfortable when I had $200,000 in the bank—my bank. They backed off that idea, and by the end of the meeting, they agreed to put in the $50,000; but first they said they had to perform some more due diligence.

Momentum

By May 2004, the Seahorse Power Company had six team members,[8] all of whom had been given equity in the company in exchange for their services. The investor group expressed concern with this arrangement, saying the team could walk away when the going got tough. Jim said he would not change it:

> They wanted my people to have "skin in the game" because they might get cold feet and choose to get regular jobs. I told them that SPC workers are putting in 20 hours a week for free when they could be out charging consulting rates of $200 an hour. They have plenty of skin in this game, and I'm not going to ask them for cash. Besides, if we could put up the cash, we wouldn't need investors, right?

As Jim settled into his seat for the flight to New York, he thought about the investors' other primary contention: His pre-money valuation was high by a million:

> These investors—who still haven't given us a dime—are saying they can give me as much early-stage capital as SPC would need, but at a pre-money of $1.5 million and dependent on us hitting our milestones. With an immediate funding gap of about $50,000, it's tempting to move forward with these guys so we can fill current orders on time and maintain our momentum. On the other hand, I've already raised some money on the higher valuation, and maybe we can find the rest before the need becomes really critical.

[8]Three of the most recent equity partners were Richard Kennelly, a former director at Conservation Law Foundation where he concentrated on electric utility deregulation, renewable energy, energy efficiency, air quality, and global warming; Kevin Dutt, an MBA in operations management and quantitative methods from Boston University with extensive work experience in improving manufacturing and operational practices in a range of companies; and Steve Delaney, an MBA from Tuck School of Business at Dartmouth College with a successful track record in fund-raising, business development, market strategy, finance, and operations.

Chapter Five

Opportunity Recognition

LEARNING OUTCOMES: After reading this chapter you will be able to understand:

5-1 Scalability and how it applies in building a business

5-2 How investors fund early stage companies

5-3 Typical financing cycles for early stage companies

5-4 How opportunities are defined

5-5 The role of ideas, experience, creativity, and timing

5-6 The difference between an idea and an opportunity

5-7 How venture opportunities are evaluated

5-8 How to screen industries and markets for new opportunities

5-9 Harvest issues

5-10 Competitive advantage, strategic differentiation, and how they apply

5-11 The role of management teams

5-12 How and where to gather information

Think Scalability

New Venture Creation means thinking about scale—the ability to build a business beyond a sole proprietorship and to build one that can grow with the right resources and people while building equity for you and your investors.

This chapter focuses on the process of moving from opportunity to scalable company by covering the approaches and benchmarks successful entrepreneurs, venture capitalists, angel investors, and others use to develop successful companies.

Only about 5 percent of ventures emerge from the pack to grow into big companies. Pattern recognition of these attributes is what best identifies their attributes versus a formula or execution checklist.

The Patterns to Recognize

1. Most new ventures are works in process and are messy and chaotic; what you begin with has little correlation of what you end with.

2. Business plans are required but obsolete the minute they are finished.

3. The key to succeeding is failing quickly.

4. Successful entrepreneurs know luck is a key part of success.

5. The best entrepreneurs specialize in making only new mistakes.

6. Knowing what not to do is as important as knowing what to do.

How Investors Fund Early Stage Companies

Exhibit 5.1 shows an example life cycle a company funded through venture capital, with the funding amounts and valuation ultimately differing significantly based on industry norms and current valuations. As an entrepreneur you need to understand this cycle, who the capital suppliers are for you industry across the financing rounds, and how the investors will be evaluating your company. We will cover this in greater detail in Chapter 13, and for now the key takeaway is different players in different funding stages will have different capacities and preferences for the kind of venture they will back.

When Is an Idea an Opportunity?

The Essence: Five Attributes It is important to know the difference between features, products, and companies. Real business opportunities have the following attributes:

1. They create or add significant value to a customer or end user.

2. They address a true market problem with some form of competitive advantage.

EXHIBIT 5.1

The Capital Markets Food Chain for Entrepreneurial Ventures

Stage of Venture	R&D	Seed	Launch	High Growth
Company enterprise value at stage	Less than $1 million	$1 million–$5 million	> $1–$50 +million	More than $100 million
Sources	Founders High net worth individuals FFF[a] SBIR[c]	FFF[a] Angel funds Seed funds SBIR	Venture capital series A, B, C . . .[b] Strategic partners Very high net worth individuals	IPOs Strategic acquirers Private equity Private equity
Amount of capital invested	Up to $200,000	$10,000–$500,000	$500,000–$20 million	$10–$50 +million
% company owned at IPO	10%–25%	5%–15%	40%–60% by prior investors	15%–25% by public
Share price and number[d]	$.01–$.50 1–5 million	$.50–$1.00 1–3 million	$1.00–$8.00+/− 5–10 million	$12–$18+ 3–5 million

[a]Friends, families, and fools.

[b]Venture capital series A, B, C . . . (average size of round)

		A	@ $5.1 million—startup
Round		B	@ $8.1 million—product development
(Q4 2004)		C+	@ $11.3 million—shipping product

Valuations vary markedly by industry (e.g., 2x[s]).

Valuations vary by region and VC cycle.

[c]Small Business Innovation Research, a N&F Program. The SBA provides a number of financial assistance programs for small businesses, including 7(a) loan guarantees, 504 long-term finance loans, and disaster assistance loans.

[d]At post–IPO.

3. The need for the product or service is pervasive, the customer has a high sense of urgency, and is willing to pay for a solution.

4. They have robust market, growth, margin, and profitability characteristics that can be proven.

5. The founders and management team have collective domain experience that matches the opportunity.

A strong management team recognizes these opportunities and takes advantage of them when the "window of opportunity"[1] is available. A strong team recognizes these fleeting moments and develops competitive advantage to give the business additional leverage to exploit the market opportunity.[2]

Spawners and Drivers of Opportunities

Many of today'xs most exciting opportunities have grown from technological innovation. The performance of smaller firms in technological innovation is remarkable–95 percent of the radical innovations since World War II have come from new and small firms. A National Science Foundation study found that smaller firms generated 24 times as many innovations per research and development dollar as did firms with 10,000 or more employees.[3]

Technology and regulatory changes have profoundly altered the way we conceive of opportunities. Cable television with its hundreds of channels came of age in the 1990s and brought with it new opportunities for small companies to achieve cost-effective and substantial reach in the sale and distribution of goods through infomercials and pay-per-view. New opportunities in sales have recently arisen: For example, Red Box movies and Netflix allow people affordable and convenient ways to get the entertainment they want and have put movie rental stores out of business. The Internet has created even more diverse and cost-effective methods of customer reach as demonstrated by Amazon, Priceline, eBay, YouTube, and social networks led by Facebook and Twitter.

[1]The window of opportunity is defined as the period of revenue growth in the life cycle of the target industry when the slope of the revenue curve is increasing. The window of opportunity begins to close as that revenue curve levels off.

[2]J.A. Timmons, *New Business Opportunities* (Acton, MA: Brick House, 1989).

[3]R. Leifer, C. McDermott, G.C. O'Connor, L. Peters, M. Rice, and R.W. Veryzer, *Radical Innovation: How Mature Companies Can Outsmart Upstarts* (Boston, MA: Harvard Business School Press, 2000).

EXHIBIT 5.2

Summary of Opportunity Spawners and Drivers

Root of Change/Chaos/Discontinuity	Opportunity Creation
Regulatory changes	Cellular, airlines, insurance, telecommunications, medical, pension fund management, financial services, banking, tax and SEC laws, new societal and/or environmental standards and expectations
10-fold change in 10 years or less	Moore's law—computer chips double productivity every 18 months: financial services, private equity, consulting, Internet, biotech, information age, publishing
Reconstruction of value chain and channels of distribution	Superstores—Staples, Home Depot; all publishing; autos; Internet sales and distribution of all services
Proprietary or contractual advantage	Technological innovation: patent, license, contract, franchise, copyrights, distributorship
Existing management/investors burned out/undermanaged	Turnaround, new capital structure, new breakeven, new free cash flow, new team, new strategy; owners' desires for liquidity, exit; telecom, waste management service, retail businesses
Entrepreneurial leadership	New vision and strategy, new team equals secret weapon; organization thinks, acts like owners
Market leaders are customer obsessed or customer blind	New, small customers are low priority or ignored: hard disk drives, paper, chemicals, mainframe computers, centralized data processing, desktop computers, corporate venturing, office superstores, automobiles, software, most services

In our service-dominated economy (70 percent of businesses are service businesses, vs. 30 percent 40 years ago), customer service, rather than the product itself, can be the critical success factor. One study by the Forum Corporation in Boston showed that 70 percent of customers leave because of poor service and only 15 percent because of price or product quality. The tremendous shift to offshore manufacturing in India, China, and Mexico of labor- and transportation-intensive products has dramatically altered the nature of selling manufactured goods in the United States.

Exhibit 5.2 summarizes the major types of discontinuities, asymmetries, and changes that can result in high-potential opportunities. Creating such changes through technical innovation (PCs, wireless telecommunications, Internet servers, software), influencing and creating the new rules of the game (airlines, telecommunications, financial services and banking, medical products, music and video), and anticipating how the associated industries respond are central to recognizing opportunities.

Search for Sea Changes

Exhibit 5.3 summarizes some categories for thinking about such changes. Moore's law (the computing power of a chip doubles every 18 months)

has been a gigantic driver of computing power. Breakthroughs in gene mapping and cloning, biotechnology, nanotechnology, and changes brought about by the Internet will continue to create huge opportunities for decades. Beyond the macro view of sea changes, how can one think about opportunities in a more practical, less abstract sense? What are some parameters of business and revenue models that increase the odds of scaling a business?

The Role of Ideas

Ideas as Tools

A good idea is nothing more than a tool in the hands of an entrepreneur. Finding a good idea is the *first* of many steps in the process of converting an entrepreneur's creativity into an opportunity. The importance of the idea is often overrated at the expense of underemphasizing the need for products or services that can be sold in enough quantity to real customers.

Further, the new business that simply bursts from a flash of brilliance is rare. Usually a series of trial-and-error iterations are necessary before a crude and promising product or service fits with what the customer is willing to pay for. Howard

EXHIBIT 5.3

Ideas versus Opportunities: Search for Sea Changes

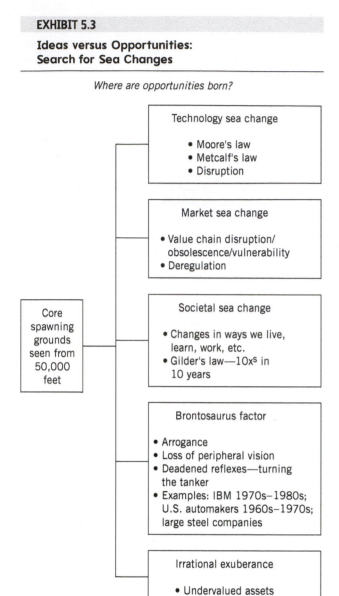

Where are opportunities born?

Core spawning grounds seen from 50,000 feet

Technology sea change
- Moore's law
- Metcalf's law
- Disruption

Market sea change
- Value chain disruption/obsolescence/vulnerability
- Deregulation

Societal sea change
- Changes in ways we live, learn, work, etc.
- Gilder's law—$10x^s$ in 10 years

Brontosaurus factor
- Arrogance
- Loss of peripheral vision
- Deadened reflexes—turning the tanker
- Examples: IBM 1970s–1980s; U.S. automakers 1960s–1970s; large steel companies

Irrational exuberance
- Undervalued assets

Head made 40 different metal skis before he finally made the model that worked consistently. With surprising frequency, major businesses are built around totally different products than those originally envisioned. Consider these examples:

- When 3-M chemist Spence Silver invented a new adhesive that would not dry or permanently bond to things, he had no idea what to do with it. It was not until another 3-M chemist, Arthur Fry, needed a bookmark for his choir book that the idea for applying the glue to small pieces of paper was found, and Post-it Notes were born.[4]

- Polaroid Corporation was founded with a product based on the principle of polarized light. It was thought that polarized lamps would prevent head-on collisions between cars by preventing the "blinding" glare of oncoming headlights. But the company grew to its present size based on another application of the same technology: instant photography.

- William Steere, CEO of Pfizer, described the discovery of Viagra, the fastest-selling drug in history, as having "a certain serendipity" behind it. The drug was originally developed by Pfizer to treat angina; its real potency was discovered as a side effect.[5]

As one entrepreneur expressed it,

Perhaps the existence of business plans and the language of business give a misleading impression of business building as a rational process. But as any entrepreneur can confirm, starting a business is very much a series of fits and starts, brainstorms and barriers. Creating a business is a round of chance encounters that leads to new opportunities and ideas, mistakes that turn into miracles.[6]

Pattern Recognition

The Experience Factor

Time after time, experienced entrepreneurs exhibit an ability to recognize patterns quickly—and opportunities—while the idea is still taking shape. The late Herbert Simon, Nobel laureate, and Richard King, Mellon University Professor of Computer Science and Psychology at Carnegie-Mellon University, wrote extensively about pattern recognition. Simon described the recognition of patterns as a creative process that is not simply logical but intuitive and inductive as well. It involves, he said, the creative linking, or cross-association, of two or more in-depth "chunks" of experience, know-how, and contacts.[7] He contended that it takes 10 years or more for people to accumulate what he called the "50,000 chunks" of experience that enable them to be highly creative and recognize patterns—familiar circumstances that can be translated from one place to another.

[4]P.R. Nayak and J.M. Ketterman, *Breakthroughs: How the Vision and Drive of Innovators in Sixteen Companies Created Commercial Breakthroughs That Swept the World* (New York, NY: Rawson Associates, 1986), chapter 3.

[5]T. Corrigan, "Far More than the Viagra Company: Essential Guide to William Steere," *Financial Times* (London), August 31, 1998, p. 7.

[6]J. Godfrey, *Our Wildest Dreams: Women Entrepreneurs, Making Money, Having Fun, Doing Good* (New York, NY: Harper Business, 1992), p. 27.

[7]H.A. Simon, "What We Know about the Creative Process" in *Frontiers in Creative and Innovative Management*, ed. R.L. Kuhn (Cambridge, MA: Ballinger, 1985), pp. 3–20.

Thus the process of sorting through ideas and recognizing a pattern can also be compared to the process of fitting pieces into a three-dimensional jigsaw puzzle. It is impossible to assemble such a puzzle by looking at it as a whole unit. Rather, one needs to see the relationships between the pieces and be able to fit together some that are seemingly unrelated before the whole is visible.

Recognizing ideas that can become entrepreneurial opportunities stems from a capacity to see what others do not. Consider the following examples of the common thread of pattern recognition and new business creation by linking knowledge in one field or marketplace with different technical, business, or market know-how:

- In 1973 Thomas Stemberg worked for Star Market in Boston, where he became known for launching the first line of low-priced generic foods. Twelve years later, he applied the same low-cost, large-volume supermarket business model to office supplies. The result was Staples, the first office superstore and today a multibillion-dollar company.[8]
- During travel throughout Europe, the eventual founders of Crate & Barrel frequently saw stylish and innovative products for the kitchen and home that were not yet available in the United States. When they returned home, the founders created Crate & Barrel to offer these products for which market research had, in a sense, already been done. In Crate & Barrel, the knowledge of consumer buying habits in one geographical region, Europe, was transferred successfully to another, the United States.

Enhancing Creative Thinking

Creative thinking is of great value in recognizing opportunities, as well as other aspects of entrepreneurship. The notion that creativity can be learned or enhanced holds important implications for entrepreneurs. Most people can certainly spot creative flair. Children seem to have it, and several studies suggest that creativity actually peaks around the first grade because a person's life tends to become increasingly structured, defined by others and by institutions. Further, the development of intellectual discipline and rigor in thinking takes on greater importance in school than during the formative years, and most of our education beyond grade school stresses a logical, rational mode of orderly reasoning and thinking.

Approaches to Unleashing Creativity

Since the 1950s, much has been learned about the working of the human brain. Today there is general agreement that the two sides of the brain process information in different ways. The left side performs rational, logical functions, while the right side operates the intuitive and nonrational modes of thought. A person uses both sides, actually shifting from one mode to the other. Approaching ideas creatively and maximizing the control of these modes of thought can be of value to the entrepreneur.

More recently, professors have focused on the creativity process. For instance, Michael Gordon stressed the importance of creativity and the need for brainstorming in a presentation on the elements of personal power. He suggested that using the following 10 brainstorming rules could enhance creative visualization:

1. Define your purpose.
2. Choose participants.
3. Choose a facilitator.
4. Brainstorm spontaneously, copiously.
5. No criticisms, no negatives.
6. Record ideas in full view.
7. Invent to the "void."
8. Resist becoming committed to one idea.
9. Identify the most promising ideas.
10. Refine and prioritize.

Team Creativity

Teams of people can generate creativity that may not exist in a single individual. The creativity of a team of people is impressive, and comparable or better creative solutions to problems evolving from the collective interaction of a small group of people have been observed.

Students interested in exploring this further may want to do the creative squares exercise at the end of the chapter.

Big Opportunities with Little Capital

Within the dynamic free enterprise system, opportunities are apparent to a limited number of individuals—and not just to the individuals with financial resources. Ironically, successful entrepreneurs such as Howard Head attribute their success to the discipline of limited capital resources. Thus, in the 1990s, many entrepreneurs learned

---

[8]J. Pereira, "Focus, Drive and an Eye for Discounts: Staples of Stemberg's Business Success," *The Wall Street Journal*, September 6, 1996, p. A9B. Used by permission of Dow Jones & Co. Inc. via The Copyright Clearance Center.

the key to success is in the art of bootstrapping, which "in a startup is like zero inventory in a just-in-time system: it reveals hidden problems and forces the company to solve them."[9] Consider the following:

- A 1991 study revealed that of the 110 start-ups researched, 77 had been launched with $50,000 or less; 46 percent were started with $10,000 or less as seed capital. Further, the primary source of capital was overwhelmingly personal savings (74 percent) rather than outside investors with deep pockets.[10] This pattern of frugality in startups is as true today as it was then.

- In the 1930 s Josephine Esther Mentzer assisted her uncle by selling skin care balm and quickly created her own products with $100 initial investment. After convincing the department stores rather than the drugstores to carry her products, Estee Lauder was on its way to becoming a $4 billion corporation.[11]

- Putting their talents (cartooning and finance) together, Roy and Walt Disney moved to California and started their own film studio—with $290 in 1923. In 2009, the Walt Disney Co. had a market capitalization exceeding $60 billion.[12]

- While working for a Chicago insurance company, a 24-year-old sent out 20,000 inquiries for a black newsletter. With 3,000 positive responses and $500, John Harold Johnson published *Jet* for the first time in 1942. By the 1990s, Johnson Publishing published various magazines, including *Ebony*.[13]

- With $100, Nicholas Graham, age 24, went to a local fabric store, picked out some fabrics, and made $100 worth of ties. Having sold the ties to specialty shops, Graham was approached by Macy's to place his patterns on men's underwear. So Joe Boxer Corporation was born, and "6 months into Joe Boxer's second year, sales had already topped $1 million."[14]

- Cabletron founders Craig Benson and Bob Levine literally started their company in a garage and grew it to over $1.4 billion in revenue in under 10 years.

- Vineyard Vines is a creative necktie company that was started on Martha's Vineyard with $40,000 of credit card debt.

Real Time

Opportunities exist or are created in real time and have what we call a window of opportunity. For an entrepreneur to seize an opportunity, the window must be open and remain open long enough to achieve market-required returns.

Exhibit 5.4 illustrates a window of opportunity for a generalized market. Markets grow at different rates over time, and as a market quickly becomes larger, more opportunities are possible. The curve shown describes the rapid growth pattern typical of such new industries as microcomputers and software, cellular phones, quick oil changes, and biotechnology. For example, in the cellular phone industry, most major cities began service between 1983 and 1984. By 1989, there were more than 2 million subscribers in the United States, and the industry continued to experience significant growth.

In considering the window of opportunity, the length of time the window will be open is important. It takes a considerable length of time to determine whether a new venture is a success or a failure. And if it is to be a success, the benefits of that success need to be harvested.

Exhibit 5.5 shows that for venture-capital-backed firms, the lemons (i.e., the losers) ripen in about 2.5 years, while the pearls (i.e., the winners) take 8 years. An extreme example of the length of time it can take for a pearl to be harvested is the experience of a Silicon Valley venture capital firm that invested in a new firm in 1966 and was finally able to realize a capital gain in early 1984.

Relation to the Framework of Analysis

Successful opportunities, once recognized, fit with the other forces of new venture creation. This iterative process of assessing and reassessing the fit among the central driving forces in the creation of a new venture was shown in Chapter 3. Of utmost importance is the fit of the lead entrepreneur and the management team with an opportunity. It is easy to see why there are thousands of exceptional opportunities that will fit with a wide variety of entrepreneurs but that might not fit neatly into the frameworks in Exhibit 5.6.

[9]A. Bhide, "Bootstrap Finance," *Harvard Business Review*, November–December 1992, p. 112.
[10]E. B. Roberts, *Entrepreneurs in High Technology: Lessons from MIT and Beyond* (New York, NY: Oxford University Press, 1991), p. 144, table 5-2.
[11]T. Lammers and A. Longsworth, "Guess Who? Ten Big-Timers Launched from Scratch," *INC.*, September 1991, p. 69.
[12]Financial data from Dow Jones Interactive, http://www.djnr.com.
[13]Ibid.
[14]R.A. Mamis, "The Secrets of Bootstrapping," *INC.*, September 1991, p. 54.

EXHIBIT 5.4

Changes in the Placement of the Window of Opportunity

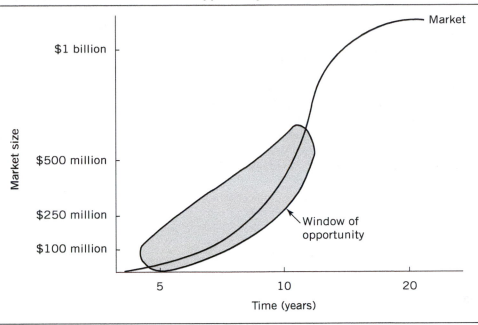

EXHIBIT 5.5

Lemons and Pearls

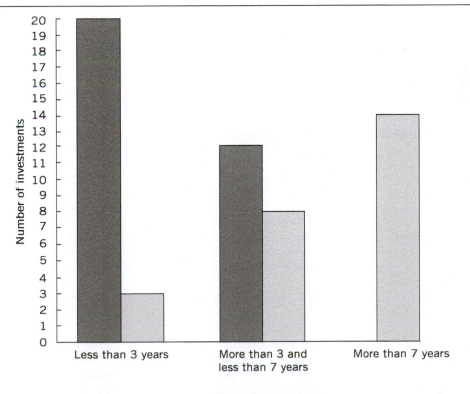

EXHIBIT 5.6

Criteria for Evaluating Venture Opportunities

	Attractiveness	
Criteria	**Highest Potential**	**Lowest Potential**
Industry and Market	Changes way people live, work, learn, etc.	Incremental improvement only
Market:	Market driven; identified; recurring revenue niche	Unfocused; onetime revenue
Customers	Reachable; purchase orders Remove serious pain point	Loyal to others or unreachable
User benefits	Less than one-year payback Solves a very important problem/need	Three years plus payback
Value added	High; advance payments	Low; minimal impact on market
Product life	Durable	Perishable
Market structure	Imperfect, fragmented competition or emerging industry	Highly concentrated or mature or declining industry
Market size	$100+ million to $1+ billion sales potential	Unknown, less than $20 million or multibillion-dollar sales
Growth rate	Growth at 30%–50% or more	Contracting or less than 10%
Market capacity	At or near full capacity	Undercapacity
Market share attainable (Year 5)	20% or more; leader	Less than 5%
Cost structure	Low-cost provider; cost advantages	Declining cost
Economics		
Time to breakeven/positive cash flow	Under 1½–2 years	More than 4 years
ROI potential	25% or more; high value	Less than 15%–20%; low value
Capital requirements	Low to moderate; fundable/bankable	Very high; unfundable or unbankable
Internal rate of return potential	25% or more per year	Less than 15% per year
Free cash flow characteristics:	Favorable; sustainable; 20%–30% or more of sales	Less than 10% of sales
Sales growth	Moderate to high (+15% to +20%)	Less than 10%
Asset intensity	Low/sales $	High
Spontaneous working capital	Low, incremental requirements	High requirements
R&D/capital expenditures	Low requirements	High requirements
Gross margins	Exceeding 40% and durable	Under 20%
After-tax profits	High; greater than 10%; durable	Low
Time to break-even profit and loss	Less than two years; breakeven not creeping or leaping	Greater than four years; breakeven creeping or leaping up
Harvest Issues		
Value-added potential	High strategic value	Low strategic value
Valuation multiples and comparables	Price/earnings = +20x; +8 −10x EBIT; +1.5−2x revenue: Free cash flow +8−10x	Price/earnings ≤ 5x, EBIT ≤ 3−4x; revenue ≤ .4
Exit mechanism and strategy	Present or envisioned options	Undefined; illiquid investment
Capital market context	Favorable valuations, timing, capital available; realizable liquidity	Unfavorable; credit crunch
Competitive Advantage Issues		
Fixed and variable costs	Lowest; high operating leverage	Highest
Control over costs, prices, and distribution	Moderate to strong	Weak
Barriers to entry:	Knowledge to overcome	
Proprietary protection	Have or can gain	None
Response/lead time	Competition slow; napping	Unable to gain edge
Legal, contractual advantage	Proprietary or exclusivity	None
Contracts and networks	Well-developed; accessible	Crude; limited
Key people	Top talent; an A team	B or C team
Sustainability	Low social and environmental impact	High social and/or environmental costs and consequences

(continued)

EXHIBIT 5.6 (concluded)

Criteria for Evaluating Venture Opportunities

Criteria	Attractiveness	
	Highest Potential	**Lowest Potential**
Management Team		
Entrepreneurial team	All-star combination; free agents	Weak or solo entrepreneur; not free agents
Industry and technical experience	Top of the field; super track record	Underdeveloped
Integrity	Highest standards	Questionable
Intellectual honesty	Know what they do not know	Do not want to know what they do not know
Fatal Flaw Issue	Nonexistent	One or more
Personal Criteria		
Goals and fit	Getting what you want; but wanting what you get	Surprises; only making money
Upside/downside issues	Attainable success/limited risks	Linear; on same continuum
Opportunity costs	Acceptable cuts in salary, etc.	Comfortable with status quo
Desirability	Fits with lifestyle	Simply pursuing big money
Risk/reward tolerance	Calculated risk; low risk/reward ratio	Risk averse or gambler
Stress tolerance	Thrives under pressure	Cracks under pressure
Strategic Differentiation		
Degree of fit	High	Low
Team	Best in class; excellent free agents	B team; no free agents
Service management	Superior service concept	Perceived as unimportant
Timing	Rowing with the tide	Rowing against the tide
Technology	Groundbreaking; one of a kind	Many substitutes or competitors
Flexibility	Able to adapt; commit and decommit quickly	Slow; stubborn
Opportunity orientation	Always searching for opportunities	Operating in a vacuum; napping
Pricing	At or near leader	Undercut competitor; low prices
Distribution channels	Accessible; networks in place	Unknown; inaccessible
Room for error	Forgiving and resilient strategy	Unforgiving, rigid strategy

Screening Opportunities

Opportunity Focus

To effectively screen an opportunity there must be a focus on possible positive and negative outcomes if pursued. The screening process should not begin with strategy (which derives from the nature of the opportunity), financial and spreadsheet analysis (which flow from the former), or estimations of how much the company is worth and who will own what shares.[15]

These starting points, and others, usually place the cart before the horse. Also, many entrepreneurs who start businesses–particularly those for whom the ventures are their first–run out of cash faster than they bring in customers and profitable sales. There are lots of reasons why this happens, but one thing is certain: These entrepreneurs have not focused on the right opportunity.

Over the years, those with experience in business and in specific market areas have developed rules to guide them in screening opportunities. For example, during the initial stages of the irrational exuberance about the dot-com phenomenon, number of "clicks" changed to attracting "eyeballs," which changed to page view. Many investors got caught up in false metrics. Those who survived the NASDAQ crash of 2000-2001 understood that dot-com survivors would be the ones who executed

[15]J.A. Timmons, D.F. Muzyka, H.H. Stevenson, and W.D. Bygrave, "Opportunity Recognition: The Core of Entrepreneurship" in *Frontiers of Entrepreneurship Research: 1987*, ed. N. Churchill et al. (Babson Park, MA: Babson College, 1987), p. 409.

transactions. Number of customers, amounts of the transactions, and repeat transactions became the recognized standards.[16]

Screening Criteria: The Characteristics of High-Potential Ventures

Venture capitalists, savvy entrepreneurs, and investors also use this concept of boundaries in screening ventures. Exhibit 5.6 summarizes criteria used by venture capitalists to evaluate opportunities, many of which tend to have a high-technology bias. As will be seen later, venture capital investors reject 60 to 70 percent of the new ventures presented early in the review process, based on how the entrepreneurs satisfy these criteria.

However, these criteria are not the exclusive domain of venture capitalists. The criteria are based on good business sense that is used by successful entrepreneurs, angels, private investors, and venture capitalists. Consider the following examples of great small companies built without a dime of professional venture capital:

- Paul Tobin, who built Cellular One in eastern Massachusetts from the ground up to $100 million in revenue in 5 years, started Roamer Plus with less than $300,000 of internally generated funds from other ventures. Within 2 years, it grew to a $15 million profitable annual sales rate.

- Entrepreneur and educator Ed Marram founded Geo-Systems without any money but with one paying customer. He sold the company in 2005 after 29 years of double-digit revenue growth.

- In 1986 Pleasant Rowland founded the Pleasant Company as a mail-order catalog company selling the American Girls Collection of historical dolls. She had begun the company with the modest royalties she received from writing children's books, and did not have enough capital to compete in stores with the likes of Mattel's Barbie.[17] By 1992 she had grown the company to $65 million in sales. Mattel acquired it in 1998 for $700 million, and under Rowland's continued management, the company had sales of $300 million in 1999 and 2000.[18]

- At age 66, Charlie Butcher had to decide whether to buy out an equal partner in his 100-year-old industrial polish and wax business (Butcher Polish) with less than $10 million in sales. This niche business had high gross margins, very low working capital (WC) and fixed-asset requirements for increased sales, substantial steady growth of more than 18 percent per year, and excellent products. He acquired the company with a bank loan and seller financing, and increased sales to over $50 million by 1993. The company continues to be highly profitable. Butcher vows never to utilize venture capital money or to take the company public.

The point here is focus on the opportunity and, implicitly, the customer, the marketplace, and the industry. Exhibit 5.6 shows how higher- and lower-potential opportunities can be placed based on their potential outcomes. The criteria provide some quantitative ways in which an entrepreneur can make judgments about the industry and market, competitive advantage, economic status and harvest potential, management team, and whether these issues add up to a compelling opportunity. For example, dominant strength in any one of these criteria can readily translate into a winning entry, whereas a single flaw can be fatal.

Market Issues

Higher-potential businesses can identify a market niche for a product or service that meets an important customer need and provides high value-added benefits to customers. This invariably means the product or service eliminates or drastically reduces a major pain point for a customer or end user; customers are often willing to pay a premium for convenience and efficiency. Customers are reachable and receptive to the product or service, with no brand or other loyalties. The life of the product or service exists beyond the time needed to recover the investment and earn a profit.

Lower-potential opportunities are represented by a poor understanding of customer requirements and market demands. They also frequently target expensive-to-reach customers that are loyal to existing brands in slow growth markets.

Market Structures Market structure is significant and is indicated by the number of sellers, distribution channels, market size and growth rate,

---

[16]E. Parizeau, partner, Norwest Venture Partners, in a speech to Babson College MBAs, December 2000.
[17]M. Neal, "Cataloger Gets Pleasant Results," *Direct Marketing*, May 1992, p. 33.
[18]B. Dumaine, "How to Compete with a Champ," *Fortune*, January 10, 1994, p. 106.

level of differentiation, number of buyers, sensitivity of demand, and other forces around competitive advantage.

A fragmented or emerging industry often contains vacuums and asymmetries that create unfilled market niches and markets where resource ownership and cost advantages can be achieved. In addition, those where information or knowledge gaps exist and where competition is profitable, but not so strong as to be overwhelming, are promising. An example of a market with an information gap is that experienced by an entrepreneur who encountered a large New York company that wanted to sell a small, old office building in downtown Boston. This office building, with a book value of about $200,000, was viewed by the financially oriented firm as a low-value asset, and the company wanted to dispose it off so that the resulting cash could be put to work for a higher return. The buyer, who had done more homework than the out-of-town sellers, bought the building for $200,000 and resold it in less than 6 months for more than $8 million.

Industries that are highly concentrated, perfectly competitive, or declining, are typically more likely to fail. The capital requirements and costs to achieve distribution and marketing presence can be prohibitive, while price cutting and other competitive strategies in highly concentrated markets can be a significant barrier to entry. Response by established competitors can come through product strategy, legal tactics, and distribution control can cause significant response.

Market Size   A minimum market size of $100 million in sales is attractive. In the medical and life sciences today, this target boundary is $500 million. Such a market size means it is possible to achieve significant sales by capturing roughly 5 percent or less and thus not threatening competitors. For example, to achieve a sales level of $1 million in a $100 million market requires only 1 percent of the market.

However, such a market can also be too large. A multibillion-dollar market in maturity with long established players can translate into competition from existing players resulting in lower margins and profitability. Further, an unknown market, or one that is less than $10 million in sales is also unattractive.

Growth Rate   A successful market is always growing. An annual growth rate of 30 to 50 percent creates niches for new entrants as companies will focus on growth through new customers versus

taking share from competitors. A $100 million market growing at 50 percent per year has the potential to become a $1 billion industry in only a few years, and if a new venture can capture just 2 percent of sales in that first year, it can attain sales of $1 million. If it just maintains its market share over the next few years, sales will grow significantly.

Market Capacity   Another signal of desirable market opportunity is full capacity in a growth situation; that is, fulfilling demand the existing suppliers cannot meet. Timing is vital, which means the entrepreneur should be asking, can a new entrant fill that demand before the other players decide to?

Market Share Attainable   The potential to be a leader in the market and capture at least a 20 percent share can create a high value for a company. For example, a firm with less than $15 million in sales became dominant in its small market niche with a 70 percent market share. The company was acquired for $23 million in cash.

Cost Structure   The goal for a firm is to become the low-cost provider and avoid declining revenue conditions. Attractive opportunities exist in industries where economies of scale work to the advantage of the new venture. Firms with lower cost customer acquisition costs also allow room for increased profitability.

Economics

Profits after Tax   High and durable gross margins usually translate into strong and durable after-tax profits. Attractive opportunities have potential for durable profits of 10 to 20 percent, and those with after-tax profits of less than 5 percent are quite fragile.

Time to Breakeven and Positive Cash Flow   As mentioned previously, breakeven and positive cash flow for attractive companies take place within 2 years. After 3 years, the positive attributes of the opportunity diminish accordingly.

ROI Potential   An important corollary to forgiving economics is reward. Attractive opportunities have the potential to yield a return on investment of 25 percent or more per year. High and durable gross margins and after-tax profits usually yield larger earnings per share and high return on stockholders' equity, thus generating a satisfactory harvest price for a company.

Capital Requirements   Ventures that can be funded and have capital requirements that are low to moderate are attractive. High growth businesses that can be started with little or no capital are rare, but they do exist. In today's venture capital market, the first round of financing is typically $1 million to $2 million for a startup.[19] Some higher-potential ventures, such as those in the service sector or "cash sales" businesses, have lower capital requirements than do high-technology firms with large research and development expenditures.

Avoid ventures that require unrealistic amounts of startup funding. An extreme example is a venture that a team of students recently proposed to repair satellites. The students believed that the required startup capital was in the $50 million to $200 million range. Projects of this magnitude are in the domain of the government and large corporations, rather than that of the entrepreneur and the venture capitalist.

Internal Rate of Return (IRR) Potential   Is the risk-reward relationship attractive enough? The response to this question can be quite personal, but the most attractive opportunities often have the promise of–and deliver on–a very substantial upside of 5 to 10 times the original investment in 5 to 10 years. Of course, the extraordinary successes can yield 50 to 100 times or more, but these are exceptions. A minimum 25 percent annual compound rate of return is considered healthy.

Free Cash Flow (FCF) Characteristics   Free cash flow (FCF) is a way of understanding a number of crucial financial dimensions of any business: the robustness of its economics; its capital requirements, both working and fixed assets; its capacity to service external debt and equity claims; and its capacity to sustain growth.[20] We define unleveraged FCF as earnings before interest but after taxes (EBIAT) *plus* amortization (A) and depreciation (D) *less* spontaneous WC requirements *less* capital expenditures (CAPex), or FCF = EBIAT + [A + D] – [+ or − WC] – CAPex. EBIAT is driven by sales, profitability, and asset intensity. Low-asset-intensive, high-margin businesses generate the highest profits and sustainable growth.[21] We will explore this in detail in Chapter 12, Entrepreneurial Finance.

Gross Margins   The potential for high and durable gross margins (i.e., the unit selling price less all direct and variable product costs) is important. Gross margins exceeding 40 to 50 percent provide a tremendous built-in cushion and are more forgiving of mistakes. High and durable gross margins, in turn, mean that a venture can reach breakeven earlier, preferably within the first 2 years. For example, if gross margins are just 20 percent, for every $1 increase in fixed costs (e.g., insurance, salaries, rent, and utilities), sales need to increase $5 just to stay even. If gross margins are 75 percent, however, a $1 increase in fixed costs requires a sales increase of just $1.33.

Time to Breakeven—Cash Flow and Profit and Loss (P&L)   New businesses that can quickly achieve a positive cash flow and become self-sustaining are highly desirable. It is often the second year before this is possible, but the sooner the better. Obviously, simply having a longer window does not mean the business will be lousy. Federal Express is an example of a higher-potential business that made good use of a longer window of opportunity. In fact, they went through an early period of enormous negative cash flows of around $1 million a month.

Harvest Issues

Value-Added Potential   New ventures that are based on strategic value in an industry, such as valuable technology, are preferable. Thus one characteristic of businesses that command a premium price is that they have high value-added strategic importance to their acquirer, such as distribution, customer base, geographic coverage, proprietary technology, contractual rights, and the like. Such companies might be valued at 4, 5, or even 6 times (or more) last year's *sales*, whereas perhaps 60 percent to 80 percent of companies might be purchased at 0.75 to 1.25 times sales.

Valuation Multiples and Comparables   Consistent with the previous point, there is a large spread in the value the capital markets place on private and public companies. Part of your analysis is to identify some historical boundaries for valuations placed on companies in the market/industry/technology area you intend to

---

[19]J.A. Timmons, W. Bygrave, and N. Fast, "The Flow of Venture Capital to Highly Innovative Technology Ventures," *Study for the National Science Foundation, reported in Frontiers of Entrepreneurship Research: 1984* (Babson Park, MA: Babson College, 1984).

[20]For a more detailed description of free cash flow, see W. Sahlman, "Note on Free Cash Flow Valuation Models," HBS 9-288-023, Harvard Business School, 1987.

[21]W.A. Sahlman, "Sustainable Growth Analysis," HBS 9-284-059, Harvard Business School, 1984.

pursue. The rules outlined in Exhibit 5.6 are variable and should be thought of as a boundary and a point of departure.

Exit Mechanism and Strategy   Businesses that are eventually sold–privately or to the public–or acquired, usually are started and grown with a harvest objective in mind. Attractive companies that realize capital gains from the sale of their businesses have or envision a harvest or exit mechanism. Planning is critical because, as is often said, it is much harder to get out of a business than to get into it. Giving some serious thought to the options and likelihood that the company can eventually be harvested is an important aspect of the entrepreneurial process.

Capital Market Context   The context in which the sale or acquisition of the company occurs is largely driven by the capital markets at that particular time. Timing can be a critical component of the exit mechanism because, as one study indicated, since World War II, the average bull market on Wall Street has lasted just 6 months. For a keener appreciation of the critical difference the capital markets can make, one only has to recall the stock market crash of October 19, 1987, the bank credit crunches of 1990-1992 and 2007, or the bear market of 2001-2003. By the end of 1987, the valuation of the Venture Capital 100 index had dropped 43 percent, and private company valuations followed. Initial public offerings are especially vulnerable to the vicissitudes of the capital markets; here the timing is vital. Some of the most successful companies seem to have been launched when debt and equity capital were most available and relatively cheap.

Competitive Advantages Issues

Variable and Fixed Costs   An attractive opportunity usually requires the lowest marketing and distribution costs and can be the lowest-cost producer. Being unable to achieve and sustain a position as a low-cost producer shortens the life expectancy of a new venture.

Degree of Control   Attractive opportunities have potential for moderate to strong control over prices, costs, and channels of distribution. Fragmented markets where there is no dominant competitor have this potential. These markets usually have a market leader with a 20 percent market share *or less*.

Lack of control over such factors as product development and component prices can make an opportunity unattractive.

Anywhere a competitor has share of 40 percent or more usually implies a market where power and influence over suppliers, customers, and pricing create a serious barrier and risk for a new firm. However, if a dominant competitor is at full capacity, is slow to innovate or to add capacity in a large and growing market, or routinely ignores the customer, there may be an entry opportunity.

Entry Barriers   If an industry has low entry barriers it is unattractive, so a firm needs to be diligent in examining these. Things like a favorable window of opportunity, proprietary protection, regulatory advantage, or other legal or contractual advantage is attractive. Other advantages are response or lead times and knowledge of industries and contacts that only come with experience.

Management Team Issues

Entrepreneurial Team   Attractive opportunities have existing teams that are strong and contain industry superstars. The team has proven profit and loss experience in the same technology, market, and service area, and members have complementary and compatible skills.

Industry and Technical Experience   A management track record of accomplishment in the industry, with the technology, or in the market area, with successful business outcomes is highly desirable.

Integrity   Trust and integrity are the oil and glue that make economic interdependence possible. Having an unquestioned reputation in this regard is a major long-term advantage for entrepreneurs and should be sought in all personnel and backers.

Intellectual Honesty   There is a fundamental issue of whether the founders know what they do and do not know, as well as whether they know what to do about shortcomings or gaps in the team and the enterprise.

Personal Criteria

Goals and Fit   Is there a good match between the requirements of business and what the founders want out of it?

Upside/Downside Issues An attractive opportunity has significant upside and limited downside risk. An entrepreneur needs to be able to absorb the financial downside in such a way that he or she can rebound without becoming indentured to debt obligations. If an entrepreneur's financial exposure in launching the venture is greater than his or her net worth–the resources he or she can reasonably draw upon, and his or her alternative disposable earnings stream if it does not work out–the deal may be too big. An existing business needs to consider if a failure will be too demeaning to the firm's reputation and future credibility, aside from the obvious financial consequences.[22]

Opportunity Cost In pursuing any venture opportunity costs need to be evaluated as a potentially successful entrepreneur's talents are highly valued by established firms as well. Any new pursuit's outcome needs to be weighed against forgone economic opportunities to truly understand the costs.

Risk/Reward Tolerance Successful entrepreneurs take only calculated risks and avoid risks they do not need to take. The real issue is fit, recognizing that risk is part of a startup and the right balance needs to be struck.

Strategic Differentiation

Degree of Fit To what extent is there a good fit among the driving forces (founders and team, opportunity, and resource requirements) and the timing given the external environment?

Team There is no substitute for an absolutely top-quality team. The execution of and the ability to adapt and to devise constantly new strategies are vital to survival and success.

Timing From business to historic military battles to political campaigns, timing is often the one element that can make a significant difference. Time can be an enemy or a friend; being too early or too late can be fatal. The key is to row with the tide, not against it.

Technology A breakthrough, proprietary product is no guarantee of business success, but it can create a competitive advantage.

Flexibility Maintaining the capacity to commit and un-commit quickly, to adapt, and to abandon if

necessary is a major strategic weapon, particularly when competing with larger organizations.

Pricing One common mistake of new companies with high value-added products or services in a growing market is to underprice. In a 30 percent gross margin business, a 10 percent price increase results in a 20 percent to 36 percent increase in gross margin and will lower the breakeven sales level for a company with $900,000 in fixed costs to $2.5 million from $3 million. At the $3 million sales level, the company would realize an extra $180,000 in pretax profits.

Distribution Channels Access to distribution channels is sometimes overlooked or taken for granted. New channels of distribution can leapfrog traditional channels, but at the same time take long periods of time to set up and develop.

Room for Error How forgiving is the business and the financial strategy? How wrong can the team be in estimates of revenue costs, cash flow, timing, and capital requirements? How bad can things get with the firm still able to survive?

Gathering Information

Finding Ideas

Factors suggest that finding a potential opportunity is most often a matter of being the right person, in the right place, at the right time. How can you increase your chances of being the next Anita Roddick of The Body Shop? Numerous sources of information can help generate ideas.

Existing Businesses Purchasing an ongoing business is an excellent route to a new venture can save time and money and risk as well. Investment bankers, trust officers and business brokers are knowledgeable about businesses for sale. However, brokers do not advertise the very best private businesses for sale, and the real gems are usually bought by the individuals or firms closest to them, such as management, directors, customers, suppliers, or financial backers. Bankruptcy judges have a continual flow of ventures in serious trouble. Excellent opportunities may be buried beneath all the financial debris of a bankrupt firm.

Franchises Franchising is another way to enter an industry, by either starting a franchise operation or

---

[22]This point was made by J. Willard Marriott, Jr., at Founder's Day at Babson College, 1988.

becoming a franchisee. This is a fertile area, in the United States 10.5 percent of all businesses are franchised operations and franchising represents a $1.3 trillion business model.[23] See Chapter 10 for a fuller discussion of franchises, including resource information.

Patents   Patent brokers specialize in marketing patents that are owned by individual inventors, corporations, universities, or other research organizations to those seeking new commercially viable products. Some brokers specialize in international product licensing, and occasionally a patent broker will purchase an invention and then resell it.

Product Licensing   A good way to obtain exposure to many product ideas available from universities, corporations, and independent investors is to subscribe to information services such as the *American Bulletin of International Technology, Selected Business Ventures* (published by General Electric), *Technology Mart, Patent Licensing Gazette*, and the National Technical Information Service. In addition, corporations, not-for-profit research institutions, and universities are sources of licenses.

Corporations.   Corporations engaged in research and development often have inventions or services that they do not exploit commercially. These inventions either do not fit existing product lines or marketing programs or do not represent sufficiently large markets to be interesting to large corporations. A good number of corporations license these kinds of inventions, either through patent brokers, product-licensing information services, or their own patent marketing efforts.

Not-for-Profit Research Institutes.   Many nonprofit organizations do research and development under contract to government and private industry that can be licensed for further development, manufacturing, and marketing.

Universities.   A number of universities are active in research in the physical sciences and seek to license inventions that result from this research either directly or through an associated research foundation that administers a patent program.

Industry and Trade Contacts

Trade Shows and Association Meetings   Trade shows and association meetings in a number of industries can be an excellent way to examine the products of many potential competitors, meet distributors and sales representatives, learn about product and market trends, and identify potential products.

Customers   Potential customers of a certain type of product can identify a need and suggest where existing products might be deficient or inadequate.

Distributors and Wholesalers   Similar to customers, contacting people who distribute a certain type of product can yield extensive information about the strengths and weaknesses of existing products and the kinds of product improvements and new products.

Competitors   Examining competitive products can show whether an existing design is protected by patent and whether it can be improved or imitated.

Former Employers   A number of businesses are started with products or services, or both, based on technology and ideas developed by entrepreneurs while others employed them. In some cases, research laboratories were not interested in commercial exploitation of technology, or the previous employer was not interested in the ideas for new products, and the rights were given up or sold.

Professional Contacts   Ideas can also be found by contacting such professionals as patent attorneys, accountants, commercial bankers, and venture capitalists who come into contact with those seeking to license patents.

Consulting   A method for obtaining ideas that has been successful for technically trained entrepreneurs is to provide consulting and one-of-a-kind engineering designs for people in fields of interest. For example, an entrepreneur wanting to establish a medical equipment company can do consulting or can design experimental equipment for medical researchers. These kinds of activities often lead to prototypes that can be turned into products needed by a number of researchers.

Networking   Networks can be a stimulant and source of new ideas, as well as a source of valuable contacts with people. Much of this requires personal initiative on an informal basis; but around the country, organized networks can facilitate and accelerate the process of making contacts and finding new business ideas.

---

[23]Economic Census, 2007; Franchise Statistics, U.S. Census Bureau, 2007.

Shaping Your Opportunity

You will need to invest in thorough research to shape your idea into an opportunity. Data available about market characteristics, competitors, and so on are frequently inversely related to the real potential of an opportunity; that is, if market data are readily available and if the data clearly show significant potential, then a large number of competitors will enter the market and the opportunity will diminish.

Published Sources

The first step is a complete search of materials in libraries and on the Internet. You can find a huge amount of published information, databases, and other sources about industries, markets, competitors, and personnel. Some of this information will have been uncovered when you search for ideas, and here are sources that should help get you started.

Guides and Company Information

Valuable information is available in special issues and on the websites of *Bloomberg Businessweek, Forbes, INC., The Economist, Fast Company*, and *Fortune;* and online at the following:

- Hoovers.com.
- ProQuest.com.
- Bloomberg.com.
- Harrisinfo.com.

Additional Internet Sites

- *Fast Company* (http://www.fastcompany.com).
- Ernst & Young (http://www.ey.com).
- Entrepreneur.com & magazine (http://www.entrepreneur.com).
- EDGAR database (http://www.sec.gov). Note that subscription sources, such as Thomson-Research (http://www.thomsonfinancial.com), provide images of other filings as well.
- Venture Economics (http://www.ventureeconomics.com).

Journal Articles via Computerized Indexes

- Factiva with Dow Jones, *Reuters, The Wall Street Journal.*
- EBSCOhost.
- FirstSearch.
- Ethnic News Watch.
- LEXIS/NEXIS.

- *New York Times.*
- InfoTrac from Gale Group.
- ABI/Inform and other ProQuest databases.
- RDS Business Reference Suite.
- *The Wall Street Journal.*

Statistics

- Stat-USA (http://www.stat-usa.gov)–U.S. government subscription site for economic, trade and business data, and market research.
- U.S. Census Bureau (http://www.census.gov)– the source of many statistical data including:
- Statistical Abstract of the United States.
- American FactFinder–population data.
- Economic Programs (http://www.census.gov/econ/www/index.html)–data by sector.
- County business patterns.
- Zip code business patterns.
- CRB Commodity Year Book.
- Manufacturing USA, Service Industries USA, and other sector compilations from Gale Group.
- Economic Statistics Briefing Room (http://www.whitehouse.gov/fsbr/esbr.html).
- Federal Reserve Bulletin.
- Survey of Current Business.
- FedStats (http://www.fedstats.gov/).
- Global Insight (http://www.globalinsight.com).
- International Financial Statistics–International Monetary Fund.
- World Development Indicators–World Bank.
- Bloomberg Database.

Consumer Expenditures

- New Strategist Publications.
- Consumer Expenditure Survey.
- Euromonitor.

Projections and Forecasts

- ProQuest.
- InfoTech Trends.
- Guide to Special Issues and Indexes to Periodicals (*Grey House Directory of Special Issues*).
- RDS Business Reference Suite.
- Value Line Investment Survey.

Market Studies

- LifeStyle Market Analyst.
- MarketResearch.com.

- Scarborough Research.
- Simmons Market Research Bureau.

Other Sources

- Wall Street Transcript.
- Brokerage house reports from Investext, Multex, and so forth.
- Company annual reports and websites.

Other Intelligence

Everything entrepreneurs need to know will not be found in libraries because this information needs to be highly specific and current. This information is most likely available from people–industry experts, suppliers, and the like (see the nearby box). Summarized next are some useful sources of intelligence.

Trade Associations   Trade associations, especially the editors of their publications and information officers, are good sources of information.[24] Trade shows and conferences are prime places to discover the latest activities of competitors.

Employees   Employees who have left a competitor's company often can provide information about the competitor and be hired by competing firms. Consideration of ethics in this situation is important, the number of experienced people in any industry is limited, and competitors must prove that a company hired a person intentionally to get specific trade secrets in order to challenge any hiring legally.

Consulting Firms   Consulting firms frequently conduct industry studies and then make this information available. Frequently, in such fields as computers or software, competitors use the same design consultants, and these consultants can be sources of information.

Market Research Firms   Firms doing market studies, such as those listed under published sources above, can be sources of intelligence.

Key Customers, Manufacturers, Suppliers, Distributors, and Buyers   These groups are often a prime source of information.

Public Filings   Federal, state, and local filings, such as filings with the Securities and Exchange Commission (SEC), Patent and Trademark Office, or Freedom of Information Act filings, can reveal a surprising amount of information. There are companies that process inquiries of this type.

Reverse Engineering   Reverse engineering can be used to determine costs of production and sometimes even manufacturing methods. An example of this practice is the experience of Advanced Energy Technology of Boulder, Colorado, which learned firsthand about such tactics. No sooner had it announced a new product, which was patented, when it received 50 orders, half of which were from competitors asking for only one or two of the items.

Networks   The networks mentioned in Chapter 3 as sources of new venture ideas also can be sources of competitor intelligence.

Other   Classified ads, buyers guides, labor unions, real estate agents, courts, local reporters, and so on can all provide clues.[25]

Internet Impact: Research

The Internet has become *the* resource for entrepreneurial research and opportunity exploration. The rapid growth of data sources, websites, sophisticated search engines, and consumer response forums allows for up-to-date investigations of business ideas, competitive environments, and value chain resources.

Google is currently the top search engine in the world. One of the reasons for Google's success is its increasingly deep and wide platform of tools. Keep in mind Google not only enables search of the Web, but the means to view the text of U.S. patents, scholarly papers, archives of news stories, and blogs on hundreds of subjects.

As virtual communities of people who share a common interest or passion, blogs can be a tremendously valuable resource of insights and perspectives on potential opportunities. Proactive, low- or no-cost research can also be conducted with e-mailed questionnaires or by directing potential subjects to a basic website set up to collect responses. In addition, the Internet provides entrepreneurs and other proactive searchers with the extraordinary capability to tap wisdom and advice from experts on virtually anything–anywhere in the world.

---

[24]Ibid., pp. 46, 48.
[25]Ibid., pp. 369–418.

Chapter Summary

- Ideas are a dime a dozen. Perhaps one out of a hundred becomes a truly great business, and one in 10 to 15 becomes a higher-potential business. The complex transformation of an idea into a true opportunity is akin to a caterpillar becoming a butterfly.
- High-potential opportunities invariably solve an important problem, want, or need that someone is willing to pay for now. In renowned venture capitalist Arthur Rock's words, "I look for ideas that will change the way people live and work."
- There are decided patterns in superior opportunities, and recognizing these patterns is an entrepreneurial skill aspiring entrepreneurs need to develop.
- Rapid changes and disruptions in technology, regulation, information flows, and the like cause opportunity creation. The journey from idea to high-potential opportunity requires navigating an undulating, constantly changing, three-dimensional relief map while inventing the vehicle and road map along the way.

- Some of the best opportunities actually require some of the least amounts of capital, especially via the Internet.
- The best opportunities often don't start out that way. They are crafted, shaped, molded, and reinvented in real time and market space. Fit with the entrepreneur and resources, the timing, and the balance of risk and reward govern the ultimate potential.
- The highest-potential ventures are found in high-growth markets, with high gross margins, and robust FCF characteristics, because their underlying products or services add significantly greater value to the customer, compared with the next best alternatives.
- Trial and error, or learning by doing alone, is not enough for developing breakthrough ventures, which require experience, creativity, and conceptualizing.

Study Questions

1. How does an idea differ from a good opportunity?
2. Why do people say, "Ideas are a dime a dozen?"
3. How does experience help people create opportunities, and where do most good opportunities come from? Why is learning by trial and error not good enough?
4. List the idea sources most relevant to your personal interests, and search for them online.
5. What conditions and possible societal and economic changes could and drive future opportunities? List as many as you can think of that could occur in the next 10 years.
6. Evaluate your best idea against the summary criteria in Exhibit 5.6. What is its potential? What has to happen for it to be made into a high-potential business?
7. Draw a value chain and FCF chain for an industry dominated by a few large players. How can you use technology to capture (save) a significant portion of the margins and FCFs?

Internet Resources

www.emc.score.org *The Service Corps of Retired Executives is a nonprofit whose more than 11,000 volunteers work with the U.S. Small Business Administration to help small businesses across the country.*

www.mitef.org *Through its worldwide network of chapters, this affiliate of the Massachusetts Institute of*

Technology annually produces more than 400 events, activities, and workshops to connect, inspire and inform technology entrepreneurs, business leaders, and enthusiasts.

www.inc.com *The website of the magazine Inc. contains many useful stories and resources for small businesses and entrepreneurs.*

The Next Sea Changes

Sea changes such as electricity, the airplane, the integrated circuit, and wireless communications have been the wellheads of major industries. What technological and societal sea changes over the next 20 to 30 years will spawn the next generation of new industries?

Purpose

This exercise is meant to help you answer that question by broadening your horizon of technological literacy and enriching your vision of the next quarter century—the time in which you have the best chance to seize the mega-opportunities that lie ahead.

We ask you to research and think about the future directions of technology and how scientific inquiries under way today can produce innovations that get commercialized and create entirely new industries.

The following steps will help you, but do not rely solely on them. Use Google and other resources to find as many other information sources as possible. Follow both the data you find and your instincts. If you find an area of science and technology that excites you—or that you think can change the way people will live, work, learn, and/or relax—pursue it.

STEP 1

Go to the www.kickstarter.com. Are any of the "Recently Funded" or Most Popular" deals sea change ideas. Why? Why not?

STEP 2

Select one or two of the Kickstarter deals that interest you the most and one or two you know the least about but find the most interesting. Using Google and other tools, identify products, companies, or market segments that are driven by the entrepreneurs behind these innovations.

STEP 3

Meet with two to five of your classmates and share what you have learned, your observations and insights about how industries are born, and new fields you think might arise.

- What patterns and common characteristics did you find? What are the lead times and early indicators?

- What technologies could have the greatest impacts on how people live, work, and learn?

- What entrepreneurs created the firms that utilize these discoveries? What are their backgrounds, skills, and experience? Are there any common denominators?

- Have you changed your views about where and when the next biggest opportunities will emerge?

STEP 4

- What existing technologies, products, and services are they most likely to disrupt and replace?

- What societal trends can be combined with them to create entirely new industries?

STEP 5

In class, or in informal groups, discuss and explore the implications of your findings from the exercise.

- What two or three future sea changes do you anticipate?

- What other exploration do you need to do?

- How can you better prepare yourself to be able to recognize and seize these future opportunities now, in 10 years, and in 15 years?

- What implications do you see for the personal entrepreneurial strategy you began to develop in Chapter 2—especially with regard to projects to work on, next education and work experience, and brain trust and mentor additions?

Opportunity-Creating Concepts and the Quest for Breakthrough Ideas

After fully digesting the discussions in this chapter, prepare an industry analysis utilizing the criteria listed in Exhibit 5.6. Just do a first cut analysis. Map out your value chain on one to two pages at most and address the other questions/issues in bullet points on no more than two pages. This is designed to get you to a specific way of thinking.

Your task is to complete a *simple, clear, and articulate value chain analysis* of an industry you find interesting. Analyze the value chain as it *currently exists*. Next complete an *information flow analysis* of that value chain through its various stages. Then *create a value cluster* of the industry. Think multidimensionally, not just linearly, and describe or visually depict the impact of the multiple dimensions on the flow of both goods/services *and* information. Explain how this value cluster adds or intensifies value for that industry, as compared to the linear chain. Finally, provide a *succinct analysis of the margins in this value cluster*, with particular emphasis on the extremes (highs/lows).

Also consider the following:

- What deconstructors and reconstructors drive the value chain and opportunity in this industry?

- What is your best estimate of the composition of the FCF, profit, and value chains in a business in the industry?

- Which prevailing industry practices, conventions, wisdom in marketing, distribution, outsourcing customer services, IT, and capital investment are significant in the business?

- What new practices, conventions, and so forth are now in place, and what are their half-lives?

- What are the growth segments?

- Where do the pundits (Forrester, IDG, and other Wall Street analysts) think the next growth market will be?

- What are the parameters and characteristics of that market?

If you plan to bring a high-tech product to market, you might consider the framework discussed in *Crossing the Chasm: Marketing and Selling High-Tech Products to Mainstream Customers* by Geoffrey Moore and Regis McKenna and look at the value chain and the specific industry segment(s) you plan to focus on. Also consider reviewing Clayton M. Christensen's writings on disruptive innovation, including *The Innovator's Dilemma* and Steve Blank and Bob Dorf, *The Startup Owner's Manual*.

Idea Generation Guide

Before you start the process of generating ideas for new ventures, reflect on the old German proverb: "Every beginning is hard." If you allow yourself to think creatively, you will be surprised at how many interesting ideas you can generate.

The aim of this exercise is to generate as many interesting ideas as possible. *Do not evaluate them or worry about their implementation.* The rest of the book will allow you to evaluate your ideas to see if they are opportunities and to consider your own personal entrepreneurial strategy.

And remember—in any creative endeavor there are no right answers.

Name:

Date:

STEP 1

Generate a List of as Many New Venture Ideas as Possible. Think of the biggest, most frustrating, and painful task or situation you continually face as a consumer or user, especially ones you think people would pay to eliminate or minimize. These are often the seeds of real opportunities. Thinking about any unmet or poorly filled customer needs that have resulted from regulatory changes, technological changes, knowledge and information gaps, lags, asymmetries, inconsistencies, and so forth will help you compile your list. Also think about various products and services (and their substitutes) and the providers of these products or services. Identifying weaknesses or vulnerabilities with the products/services and/or their producers may give you ideas for new ventures.

STEP 2

Expand Your List if Possible. Think about your personal interests, your desired lifestyle, your values, what you feel you are likely to do very well, and contributions to society you would like to make.

STEP 3

Ask at Least Three People Who Know You Well to Look at Your List, and Revise It Based on Their Remarks.
See the discussion about getting feedback in Chapter 2.

STEP 4

Jot Down Insights, Observations, and Conclusions That Have Emerged about Your Business Ideas or Your Personal Preferences. Which ones address the greatest pain point/aggravation/frustration that you and others you have spoken with would gladly pay to eliminate?

Exercise 4

Quick Screen

This is an opportunity screening tool that weighs the components of opportunities and is useful in assessing an idea and comparing a number of opportunities.

The criteria, as listed in the guide, were created from many years of analyzing venture-backed companies. The potential of any opportunity is weighed on a spectrum that encourages the entrepreneur to focus on the high potential venture. Remember, there is no perfect deal so you should not expect to score all criteria in the high potential category. We have found that when seeking advice from trusted adviser the Quick Screen provides a map for probing the expert's perspectives. However, the most important source of information comes from potential customers. While the Quick Screen quantifies comparisons among opportunities it is intended to be directional, not absolute. There is no score that will assure success. Rather, the Quick Screen will focus your attention on the strengths and weaknesses of your idea and encourage you to

proceed with the deal, fixing the weaknesses, emphasizing strengths, or abandoning the idea.

Begin by having each member of the new venture team independently fill out the Quick Screen and then compare scores. This will lead to a great deal of discussion. Debate should conclude with a team Quick Screen.

We recommend you then interview 20 or more potential customers, describing your offering and asking the customer to compare your description to the solution they are currently using.

Compare customer interview data with your team Quick Screen. List the gaps between your assessment and that of the customer. If there is a gap you need to do further interviewing, either shape your opportunity or improve the manner in which you describe the offering.

Note: The authors have weighed criteria based on our experience. Some entrepreneurs have decided to adjust the weights.

Criteria	Highest Potential	Lowest Potential	Quick Screen Score Weight 1, less important; 2, average importance; 3, high importance
Industry and Market	Changes way people live and work	Incremental improvement	3
Market need	Market driven	Unfocused	2
	Market identified	One time revenue	2
	Recurring revenue	—	2
Customers	Reachable; purchase orders	Loyal to others, unreachable	3
User benefits	Less than 1-year payback	3 years plus payback	3
Value added	High; advance payments	Low; minimal impact on market	2
Product life	Durable	Perishable	2
Market Structure	Imperfect, fragmented competition or emerging in industry	Highly concentrated or mature or declining industry	2
Market size	$100 million to $1 billion sales	Unknown, less than $20 million or multibillion sales	2
Growth Rate	Growth at 30%–50% or more	Contracting or less than 10%	2
Market capacity	At or near full capacity	Undercapacity	2
Market share attainable (Year 5)	20% or more; leader	Less than 5%	2
Cost structure	Low-cost provider; cost advantages	Declining cost	2
Economics			
Time to breakeven—CF	Under 2 years; breakeven point not creeping	More than 4 years, breakeven creeping	3
Time to breakeven—P&L	Under 2 years; break-even point not creeping	More than 4 years, break-even creeping	2
ROI potential	High; 25% or more	Low; less than 15%–20%	2
Capital requirements	Low to moderate; fundable	Very high; unfundable	2
Internal rate of return potential	25%	Less than 15%	2
Free cash flow characteristics	Favorable; sustainable; 20%–30% or more of sales	Less than 10%	2
Sales growth	Moderate to high (15%–20%)	Less than 10% of sales	2
Asset intensity	Low/sales $	High	3
Spontaneous working capital	Low, incremental requirements	High requirements	2
R&D/capital expenditures	Low	High	2
Gross margins	Exceeding 40% and durable	Under 20%	3
After-tax profits	High; greater than 10%; durable	Low	2
Harvest Issues			
Value-added potential	High strategic value	Low strategic value	2
Valuation multiples and comparables	20 × P/E	< = 5 × P/E	2
	8–10 × EBIT	3–4 × EBIT	2
	1.5–2 × revenue	< = 0.4 × revenue	2
	8–10 × free cash flow	—	2
Exit mechanism and strategy	Present or envisioned options	Undefined; illiquid investment	2

(continued)

Criteria	Highest Potential	Lowest Potential	Quick Screen Score Weight I, less important; 2, average importance; 3, high importance
Capital market context	Favorable valuations, timing, capital available; realizable liquidity	Unfavorable; credit crunch	2
Competitive Advantage issues			2
Fixed and variable costs	Lowest; high operating leverage	Highest	2
Control over costs, prices, and distribution	Moderate to strong	Weak	2
Barriers to entry:			2
Proprietary protections	Have or can gain	None	2
Response/lead time	Competition slow, napping	Unable to gain edge	2
Legal, contractual advantage	Proprietary or exclusivity	None	2
Contracts and networks	Well-developed; accessible	Crude; limited	2
Key people	Top talent, A team	B or C team	2
Management team			
Entrepreneurial team	All-star combination, free agents	Weak or solo entrepreneur	2
Industry and technical experience	Top of the field, super track record	Underdeveloped	2
Integrity	Highest standards	Questionable	2
Intellectual honesty	Know what they do not know	Do not want to know what they do not know	2
Fatal-flaw issue	Nonexistent	One or more	3
Personal criteria			
Goals and fit	Getting what you want but wanting what you get	Surprises	2
Upside/downside issues	Attainable success/limited risks	Linear	2
Opportunity costs	Acceptable cuts in salary, etc.	Comfortable with status quo	I
Desirability	Fits with lifestyle	Simply pursuing big money	3
Risk/reward tolerance	Calculated risk; low risk/reward ratio	Risk adverse or gamble	2
Stress tolerance	Thrives under pressure	Cracks under pressure	2
Strategic differentiation			2
Technology	Groundbreaking, one-of-a-kind	Many substitutes or competition	2
Degree of fit	High	Low	2
Team	Best in class, excellent free agents	B team; no free agents	2
Service management	Superior service concept	Perceived as unimportant	I
Timing	Rowing with the tide	Rowing against the tide	2
Flexibility	Able to adapt, commit and decommit quickly	Slow, stubborn	2
Opportunity orientation	Always searching for opportunities	Operating in a vacuum, napping	3
Pricing	At or near leader	Undercut competitor; low prices	2
Distribution channels	Accessible, networks in place	Unknown, inaccessible	2
Room for error	Forgiving strategy	Unforgiving, rigid structure	2

Case

Burt's Bees

The biggest businesses have revolutionized civilization, changed the way we live. That's my aspiration: to change the world for the better through my company.

Roxanne Quimby

Introduction

By April 1997 Burt's Bees employed 20 and was on track to post-sales of $6 million to $8 million for the year. Its average margin was 35 percent. The company distributed to every state, had products in more than 3,000 stores nationwide, and had just entered Europe and Japan. It had also gotten its products into such conventional retailers as Eckerds, the Drug Emporium, and Fred Meyer. Roxanne Quimby, the president and founder of Burt's Bees, explained:

> We're starting to get a lot of inquiries from mainstream stores. They don't have an artistic inclination for merchandising, though, so we give them premade floor stands and displays to help with the backdrop and give meaning to the products for the consumer.

Shifting the Product Line

Burt's Bees' success was due to the changes it made in its product line in the two years following its 1994 move from Maine to North Carolina. Since the company had invested heavily in cosmetics manufacturing equipment, and the manufacturing processes for skin care products were fairly simple, it replaced many of its traditional products with skin care products. Quimby stated:

> We kept the lip balm, moisturizer, and baby powder, but that's it. There's not a single thing we made in 1987 that we still make today. We had to make more "goop" once we bought the blending and filling equipment. By the time we opened as a fully operational facility in North Carolina in 1994, we were still at $3 million but had totally different products. In terms of the marketing spin, that was predetermined by our environmental ethic (Exhibit A for the company's mission statement). We draw the line

at chemical preservatives. Our products had to be all-natural. If we ever step over that line, we have a whole lot of competition.

By January 1997, Burt's Bees had over 70 "Earth Friendly, Natural Personal Care Products" (Exhibit B).

Despite Burt's Bees' success making personal care products, the company faced a dilemma: Should it open its own stores? And, if it did, could it continue the success it had enjoyed as just a manufacturer?

A Retail Experiment

In late 1996, Quimby began what she called a "retail experiment" by opening a Burt's Bees retail store in Carrboro, North Carolina, so she could develop a large-scale retail concept for the company. Quimby laughed:

> I worked at the Carrboro store for 10 hours the other day and sold only $400 worth of products while our vice president of marketing and sales sold something like $30,000 worth of products in 15 minutes on QVC. But I'm testing a very valuable concept. I'm interested in controlling the whole chain from manufacturing to retail. I don't like being separated from the end user. . . . I like to just be in the store so I can observe customers and how they evaluate and respond to the products. I don't know whether we would open lots of company stores or start franchising or what, but that's what I'm trying to figure out.

The Market and Competition

Sales of skin care and bath products were growing rapidly. For example, sales of bath gels, washes, and scrubs grew 114 percent from 1994 to 1995, making it the fastest growing in the entire health and beauty industry,[1] which only grew 64 percent over the same time.[2] Skin care and bath products accounted for $1.8 billion of the health and beauty market's $14.2 billion in sales for 1995.[3]

---

[1]Bath Gels, Washes, and Scrubs is a subset of the Bath Sundries product category, which is a subset of the overall Health & Beauty market. The Bath Sundries product category grew 32 percent in dollar volume between 1994 and 1995. The Health & Beauty category includes products such as meal supplements, tooth whiteners, thermometers, antacids, mouthwashes, razors, feminine hygiene, deodorant, acne preparations, and analgesics.

[2]"A Sofi Year for HBC," *Progressive Grocer*, May 1996, pp. 263–64.

[3]"Skincare: New Body Washes Make a Splash," *Progressive Grocer*, May 1996, pp. 263–264.

© Copyright Jeffry A. Timmons, 1997. Rebecca Voomes wrote this case under the direction of Jeffry A. Timmons, Franklin W. Olin Distinguished Professor of Entrepreneurship, Babson College. Funding provided by the Ewing Marien Kauffman Foundation. All rights reserved.

EXHIBIT A

Burt's Bees' Mission Statement

Who We Are	What We Believe	What's In It?	What's It In?
We are Burt's Bees, a manufacturer of all-natural, Earth-friendly personal care products including:	We believe that work is a creative, sustaining and fulfilling expression of the Inner Being.	Our ingredients are the best that Mother Nature has to offer: herbs, flowers, botanical oils, beeswax, essential oils and clay. Safe effective ingredients that have withstood the test of time.	Bottles, jars, tubes, caps, closures, bags, dispensers, containers, "convenient" throwaway plastic. Our planet is awash in trash!

We are Burt's Bees, a manufacturer of all-natural, Earth-friendly personal care products including:

herbal soaps

aromatherapy bath oils

powders

bath salts

salves

balms

We make these products in our facility in North Carolina, and sell them through more than 3,000 stores across the country, including three company-owned stores in Burlington, VT; Carrboro, NC; and Ithaca, NY.

What We Believe

We believe that work is a creative, sustaining and fulfilling expression of the Inner Being.

We believe that what is right is not always popular and what is popular is not always right.

We believe that no one can do everything but everyone can do something.

We believe that the most complicated and difficult problems we face as a civilization have the simplest solutions.

We believe that Mother Nature has the answers and She teaches by example.

We believe that by imitating Her economy, emulating Her generosity and appreciating Her graciousness, we will realize our rightful legacy on the magnificent Planet Earth.

What's In It?

Our ingredients are the best that Mother Nature has to offer: herbs, flowers, botanical oils, beeswax, essential oils and clay. Safe effective ingredients that have withstood the test of time.

What's Not In It?

We leave out the petroleum-synthesized fillers like mineral oil and propylene glycol. We don't use artificial preservatives such a methyl paraben or diazolidinyl urea. Take a closer look and read the label.

We Deliver What Others Only Promise!

What's It In?

Bottles, jars, tubes, caps, closures, bags, dispensers, containers, "convenient" throwaway plastic. Our planet is awash in trash!

How does Burt's Bees Reduce, Reuse, and Recycle?

We Reduce. You'll find very little plastic here. We're exploring the use of simple, safe, effective and time-tested materials made of cotton, paper, metal and glass.

We Reuse. Many of our containers can be used again and again. Use our cotton bags to hold jewelry or other small items. Try our tins for pins, pills, tacks, clips, nails, screws, and nuts and bolts. Our canisters make attractive pencil holders and our glass jars will safely store your herbs and spices.

We Recycle. Bring back your empties. What we can't reuse we will recycle at our engineering recycling system at our plant in Raleigh, North Carolina.

WE LOOK DIFFERENT & WE ARE DIFFERENT

Companies were quick to try to capitalize on this growth, with such firms as The Body Shop, Bath & Body Works, Garden Botanika, and Origins battling for market dominance. Most new skin care and bath products claimed to be "all natural" and appealed primarily to young women who did not purchase traditional personal care products found in mainstream department stores. Donald A. David, the editor of *Drug and Cosmetic Industry* journal, wrote in late 1996,

There is a "market glut" in the soaps and scents business stimulated by the competition between The Body Shop and Bath & Body Works. Indeed, the retail outlets out there under the banners of these two companies (and their hard-charging competitors Garden Botanika, Crabtree & Evelyn, Aveda, Nature's Elements, and H2O Plus) now number over 1,400 in the U.S. alone, a staggering number even if it isn't added to the ranks of scent-purveying store chains such as Victoria's Secret, Frederick's of Hollywood, The Gap, Banana Republic, and dozens more.... A shakeout seems inevitable. For example, when last heard from, Nature's Element was in Chapter II, Garden Botanika's stock price plunged two-thirds in value three months after an initial public offering, and The Body Shop and H2O Plus have been plagued by lagging profits.... Without having to deal with everyday product sales figures, this market watcher believes that the glut does not augur well for soaps and bath lines, wherever they are sold.[4] [Exhibit C]

[4] D.A. David, "Glut Indeed," *Drug and Cosmetic Industry,* November 1996, p. 22.

EXHIBIT B

Burt's Bees 1997 Product List

Product Collection	Product Name	Suggested Retail Price
Burt's Beeswax Collection	Beeswax Lip Balm (tin or tube)	$2.25–2.50
	Beeswax Face Soap 1.9 oz	$5.00
	Beeswax Moisturizing Creme 1 oz	$6.00
	Beeswax Moisturizing Creme 2 oz	$10.00
	Beeswax Pollen Night Creme 0.5 oz	$8.00
	Beeswax Royal Jelly Eye Creme 0.25 oz	$8.00
Wise Woman Collection	Comfrey Comfort Salve 1 oz	$4.00
	Calendula Massage Oil 4 fl oz	$8.00
	Mugwort & Yarrow Massage Oil 4 fl oz	$8.00
	Bladderwrack Massage Oil 4 fl oz	$8.00
	Comfrey Massage Oil 4 fl oz	$8.00
	Comfrey or Calendula Massage Oil 8 fl oz	$11.00
Ocean Potion Collection	Dusting Powder 5 oz	$14.00
	Dusting Powder Canister 3.5 oz	$6.00
	Emollient Bath & Body Oil 4 fl oz	$8.00
	Seaweed Soap 3.5 oz	$5.00
	Detox Dulse Bath 2 oz	$2.00
	Dead Sea Salts 25 oz	$12.00
	Sea Clay Mud Pack 6 oz	$10.00
Green Goddess Collection	Bath Salts 25 oz	$10.00
	Clay Mask 3 oz	$6.00
	Cleansing Gelee 4 oz	$8.00
	Beauty Bar 3.5 oz	$5.00
	Moisturizing Creme 2 oz	$10.00
	Dusting Powder 5 oz	$12.00
	Emollient Milk Bath 1 oz	$2.50
	Circulation Bath 1 oz	$2.50
	Foot Freshening Powder 3 oz	$8.00
	Flaxseed Eye Rest	$9.00
Farmer's Market Collection	Orange Essence Cleansing Creme 4 oz	$8.00
	Coconut Foot Creme 4 oz	$8.00
	Carrot Nutritive Creme 4 oz	$14.00
	Lemon Butter Cuticle Crème 1 oz	$5.00
	Citrus Facial Scrub 2 oz	$6.00
	Apple Cider Vinegar Toner 4 fl oz	$5.00
	Sunflower-Oatmeal Body Soak 1 oz	$2.50
	Avocado Hair Treatment 4 oz	$8.00
	Wheat Germ Bath & Body Oil 4 fl oz	$6.00
	Fruit Flavored Lip Gloss .25 oz	$3.50
Baby Dee Collection	Dusting Powder 5 oz	$12.00
	Dusting Powder Canister 2.5 oz	$8.00
	Skin Creme 2 oz	$10.00
	Buttermilk Soap 3.5 oz	$5.00
	Buttermilk Bath 1 oz	$3.00
	Apricot Baby Oil 4 fl oz	$6.00
	Apricot Baby Oil 8 fl oz	$10.00
Farmer's Friend Collection	Garden Soap 6 oz	$5.00
	Hand Salve 3 oz	$6.50

(continued)

EXHIBIT B   (concluded)

Product Collection	Product Name	Suggested Retail Price
	Hand Salve .30 oz	$2.00
	Lemon Grass Insect Lotion 2 fl oz	$5.00
Furry Friends Collection	Oat Straw Pet Soap 3.5 oz	$6.00
	Rosemary & Nettles Coat Conditioner 4 oz	$8.00
	Lemon Oil Dry Shampoo 1.5 oz	$4.00
	Tea Tree Pest Powder 3 oz	$6.50
	Calendula Hot Spot Ointment 1.5 oz	$6.00
	Burt's Bones 5.5 oz	$5.00
	Wheat Grass Seeds 1 oz	$3.00
	Cat Nip Toy	TBD
Kitchen Cupboard Collection	Kitchen Soap 6 oz	$6.00
	Kitchen Crème 2 oz	$6.50
	Lemon Oil Cuticle & Nail Soak 1 oz	$3.00
Bay Rum Collection	Exfoliating Soap 3.5 oz	$5.00
	Shaving Soap 3 oz	$5.00
	Cologne 3.25 fl oz	$16.00
	Shave Brush	$6.50
	Razor	$5.00
Sugar Body Scrubs Collection	Lavender Sugar Body Scrub 1 oz	$3.00
	Rose Sugar Body Scrub 1 oz	$3.00
	Vanilla Sugar Body Scrub 1 oz	$3.00
Rebound Collection	Deodorizing Body Powder 3 oz	$6.00
	Invigorating Foot Bath 1 oz	$2.50
	Stimulating Massage Oil 4 fl oz	$8.00
	Therapeutic Bath Crystals 1 lb	$8.00

EXHIBIT C

Retail Statistics for Cosmetic and Toiletry Sales (% of Total Sales by Retail Outlet)

Retail Outlet	1990	1994
Food stores	27%	25%
Drugstores	26%	23%
Mass merchandisers	16%	20%
Department stores	16%	17%
Direct sales	7%	8%
All other	8%	8%

Source: "Retail Statistics," Stores, October 1996, pp. 108–10. Courtesy of Stores Magazine/Deloitte.

Even if Burt's Bees stayed out of the retail market, competition was also fierce in manufacturing. The largest health and beauty products manufacturers (Exhibits D and E), including Gillette, Lever Brothers, Chesebrough-Pond's, Jergens, Freeman, and St. Ives, had been introducing their own "natural" skin care and bath products to ensure their continued market dominance.

EXHIBIT D

25 Largest Manufacturers in the Toilet Preparations Industry (SIC 2844), 1996

Rank	Company Name	Sales ($ million)	Employees (000)
1	Johnson & Johnson	15,734	81.5
2	Colgate-Palmolive	7,588	28.0
3	Amway	4,500	10.0
4	Helene Curtis Industries Inc.	1,266	3.4
5	Alberto-Culver Co.	1,216	8.5
6	Cosmair Inc.	1,000	0.4
7	Forever Living Products International	939	0.9
8	Perrigo Co.	669	3.9
9	Clairol Inc.	350	2.0
10	Freedom Chemical Co.	300	1.0
11	Neutrogena Corp.	282	0.8
12	Benckiser Consumer Products	230	1.5
13	John Paul Mitchell Systems	190	< 0.1
14	Del Laboratories Inc.	167	1.1
15	Johnson Co.	140	0.9
16	Dep Corp.	138	0.4
17	Kolmar Laboratories	130	0.8
18	Guest Supply Inc.	116	0.7
19	Redmond Products Inc.	115	0.2
20	Cosmolab Inc.	110	0.7
21	Accra Pac Group Inc.	100	0.8
22	Sebastian International Inc.	100	0.4
23	Andrew Jergens Co.	97	0.6
24	Houbigant Inc.	97	0.6
25	Cumberland-Swan Inc.	80	0.8

Source: A.J. Damay, ed., *Manufacturing USA: Industry Analyses, Statistics, and Leading Companies,* 5th ed (Farmington, MI: Gale Research, 1996), p.834.

EXHIBIT E

1995 Top 9 Hand and Body Lotions

Rank	Brand	1995 Sales ($ million)	1995 Market Share (%)	Manufacturer
1	Intensive Care	149.9	18.6	Chesebrough-Pond's
2	Jergens	89.9	11.2	Andrew Jergens
3	Lubriderm	77.9	9.7	Warner-Wellcome
4	Nivea	44.1	5.5	Beiersdorf
5	Suave	43.0	5.3	Helene Curits
6	Eucerin	41.1	5.1	Beiersdorf
7	Curel	36.8	4.6	Bausch & Lomb
8	Neutrogena	34.5	4.3	Neutrogena
9	St. Ives	34.4	4.3	St. Ives

Conclusion

Quimby had always planned on selling Burt's Bees, but she did not think anyone would consider buying the company until it reached at least $25 million in sales. Unfortunately, she could not decide how it should get to $25 million in sales. Should it become a retailer? If so, how could it establish a presence in such a crowded market? If not, where did its future lie? If Burt's Bees remained a manufacturer and direct seller, how could it grow its annual revenue from $6 to $8 million and $25 million?

Chapter Six

Opportunities for Social Entrepreneurship

LEARNING OUTCOMES: After reading this chapter you will be able to understand:

6-1 Definitions of Social Entrepreneurship

6-2 Types of Social Entrepreneurship

6-3 The Timmons model applied to Social Entrepreneurship

6-4 Wicked problems

6-5 Resources

What Is Social Entrepreneurship?

Social entrepreneurship does not have a single definition; Exhibit 6.1 covers the most commonly accepted definitions. Perhaps the best summarization comes from Jeff Stamp, an assistant professor at the University of North Dakota: "All ventures require investment; all ventures require return. The social question is who pays and what is the return horizon."

The *entrepreneurial process* (Chapter 3) is all about entrepreneurship resulting in the "creation, enhancement, realization, and renewal of value." The result of social entrepreneurship is no different, but it helps clarify the definition of value. Specifically, social value is derived from entrepreneurial activities that seek to address problems related to people and the planet—regardless of profit orientation. In other words, social entrepreneurship seeks creative and valuable solutions to such issues as education, poverty, health care, global warming, water shortages, and energy.

Types of Social Entrepreneurship

The shaded area of Exhibit 6.2 depicts the territory of social entrepreneurship, where entrepreneurs develop ventures to solve a pressing social problem. This first section helps create an understanding of the language, territory, and definitions of social entrepreneurship relative to the traditional view of entrepreneurship.

Social Purpose Ventures

Social purpose ventures (Exhibit 6.2, quadrant 1) are founded to solve a social problem through an economically viable entity. A great example is the Jim Poss case of Chapter 4. Poss founded Seahorse Power Company to help the environment through his BigBelly solar trash compactor. According to Poss,

> The problem at large is that there are 180,000 garbage trucks in the United States that burn over a billion gallons of diesel fuel every year. These are heavy particulates—cancer-causing, asthma-causing pollutants. Obviously greenhouse gases are being emitted. Those 180,000 garbage trucks also cost about $50 billion a year. So (waste companies) are pouring a lot of money into a system that is incredibly inefficient. The (trash) pickup frequency is driven by the container—the receptacle. So when it's full you have to make a garbage truck trip. We use technology (in the receptacle) to reduce the pickup frequency by about a factor of 5.[1]

Poss considers himself a social entrepreneur. He started studying the environment in 1992, and he

We are extremely grateful to Professor Heidi Neck of Babson College for this pioneering contribution to the edition, as well as David Boss, Heidi's able MBA research assistant, for his data collection efforts. Heidi's research and curriculum development in this area have advanced much of our thinking at Babson and for the book.

[1]Interview with Jim Poss at Babson College on November 28, 2007.

EXHIBIT 6.1

Popular Definitions of Social Entrepreneurship (or Social Entrepreneur)

Definition	Author
Social entrepreneurs play the role of change agents in the social sector by (1) adopting a mission to create and sustain social value (not just private value); (2) recognizing and relentlessly pursuing new opportunities to serve that mission; (3) engaging in a process of continuous innovation, adaptation, and learning; (4) acting boldly without being limited by resources currently in hand; and (5) exhibiting heightened accountability to the constituencies served and for the outcomes created.	Greg Dees, 1998[a]
Social entrepreneurship is a process involving the innovative use and combination of resources to pursue opportunities to catalyze social change and/or address social needs.	Johanna Mair and Ignasi Marti, 2006[b]
Innovative, social value–creating activity that can occur within or across the nonprofit, business, or government sectors.	James Austin, Howard Stevenson, and Jane Wei-Skillern, 2006[c]
A process that includes the identification of a specific social problem and a specific solution (or set of solutions) to address it; the evaluation of the social impact, the business model, and the sustainability of the venture; and the creation of a social mission–oriented for-profit or a business-oriented nonprofit entity that pursues the double (or triple) bottom line.	Jeffrey Robinson, 2006[d]
Social entrepreneurship is (1) about applying practical, innovative, and sustainable approaches to benefit society in general, with an emphasis on those who are marginalized and poor; (2) a term that captures a unique approach to economic and social problems—an approach that cuts across sectors and disciplines; (3) grounded in certain values and processes that are common to each social entrepreneur.	The Schwab Foundation for Social Entrepreneurship[e]

[a]"The Meaning of Social Entrepreneurship," p. 4; http://www.caseatduke.org/documents/dees_SE.pdf.

[b]"Social Entrepreneurship Research. A Source of Explanation, Prediction, and Delight," *Journal of World Business,* 41, p. 37.

[c]"Social and Commercial Entrepreneurship. Same, Different, Both?" *Entrepreneurship Theory & Practice,* January 2006, p. 2.

[d]"Navigating Social and Institutional Barriers to Market: How Social Entrepreneurs Identify and Evaluate Opportunities," in J. Mair, J. Robinson, and K. Hockerts (eds.), *Social Entrepreneurship,* p. 95.

[e]http://www.schwabfound.org/whatis.htm.

EXHIBIT 6.2

Typology of Ventures

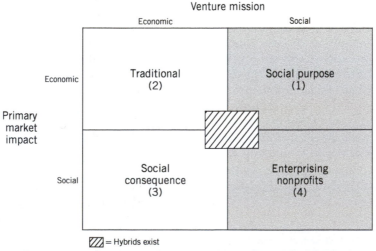

Venture mission

	Economic	Social
Economic	Traditional (2)	Social purpose (1)
Social	Social consequence (3)	Enterprising nonprofits (4)

Primary market impact

 = Hybrids exist

Source: H. Neck, C. Brush, and E. Allen, "Exploring Social Entrepreneurship Activity in the United States: For-Profit Ventures Generating Social and Economic Value," Working Paper, Babson College.

felt starting a business was the best way to tackle some of the world's environmental problems. In 2009, Philadelphia replaced 700 trashcans with 500 BigBelly compactors and recycling units and reduced the number of weekly trash collection trips from an average of 17 to 5. This alone reduces the operating costs by almost 70 percent, around $13 million (http://earth911.com/news/2010/05/25/solar-powered-trash-cans-save-cities-millions/).

Poss's mission is social, to help the environment, but recognizes the importance of sustainable business economics: "If you have a business that can sustain itself economically and do something environmentally beneficial, then it can be on its own growth path without the need for fund-raising every year to sustain."[2]

Enterprising Nonprofits

Confusion abounds regarding the notion that social entrepreneurship is reserved for nonprofit organizations. For examples such as Jim Poss, the term "enterprising nonprofits" is used in quadrant 4 in Exhibit 6.2.

We might argue that any nonprofit startup is entrepreneurial. However, consistent with the focus of this book and research in entrepreneurship, the scaling and sustainability of new ventures are important to the economy (as with for-profit ventures) and to systemic change (as with nonprofit organizations). It is not enough, from both an economic and social perspective, to simply start a venture; it must be scalable and sustainable. With longevity, innovation, and an eye toward growth, significant impact can be made.

There are two types of enterprising nonprofits. The first type utilizes earned-income activities, a form of venturing, to generate all or a portion of total revenue. In many ways enterprising nonprofits apply the principles of entrepreneurship to generate revenue and sustain their mission-driven organizations. The second type has a focus on growth and economic sustainability. Such an enterprising nonprofit may incorporate outside investment, in the form of philanthropy, to scale the organization for increased social impact.

KickStart International is an example of an enterprising nonprofit using earned-income activities and venture philanthropy. Martin Fisher and Nick Moon founded KickStart in 1991 with a mission to end poverty in sub-Saharan Africa. They started in Kenya and today have offices in Tanzania and Mali. Though Fisher and Moon have introduced many technologies related to irrigation, oil processing, and building, their greatest success to date is with their micro-irrigation pump known as the MoneyMaker. This low-cost irrigation system has helped rural farmers in Kenya increase their crop production by a factor of 10, allowing the farmers to produce crops not only for family survival but for profitable return. Their metrics supporting success are inspiring. By early 2010 KickStart featured the following statistics on its website:[3]

- 162,700 pumps are in use by poor farmers.
- 90,400 new jobs have been created.
- The pumps generate $105 million per year in new profits and wages.
- 523,200 people out of poverty.
- Over 104,600 enterprises have been created throughout Kenya, Tanzania, and Mali.

Winner of the *Fast Company* social capitalist awards for 2007 and 2008, KickStart and its enterprising ways are making great strides in their mission of fighting poverty.

A study was conducted by the Yale School of Management and the Goldman Sachs Foundation Partnership on Nonprofit Ventures to better understand how and why enterprising nonprofits pursue earned-income activities.[4] Of the 519 nonprofit organizations participating in the study, 42 percent were operating earned-income ventures; 5 percent had tried but with little success; and 53 percent had never tried to pursue any type of revenue-generating activity beyond fund-raising, grant writing, and other activities. Some of the study's key findings were interesting. Nonprofits pursuing earned-income activities:[5]

- Have more employees. Fifty-five percent of the enterprising nonprofits had 1,001 employees compared to 36 percent that had never participated in any type of venturing activity.
- Believe they are more entrepreneurial. Seventy-seven percent of the enterprising nonprofits characterized themselves as entrepreneurs compared to 46 percent that had never participated in any type of venturing activity.
- Typically do not wait for complete financing before starting a business.

[2] Ibid.
[3] http://www.kickstart.org/tech/technologies/micro-irrigation.html.
[4] C. W. Massarsky and S. L. Beinhecker, "Enterprising Nonprofits: Revenue Generation in the Nonprofit Sector," 2002.
[5] Ibid., pp. 5–12.

- Have budgets of $5 million to $25 million. This is an important figure because the majority of nonprofits in the United States never exceed a budget of $1 million.
- Do so to fund other programs (66 percent), become self-sustaining (52 percent), or diversify revenue streams (51 percent). Other reasons include job creation and building community.
- Have a strong desire to see their ventures grow and replicate–but only 55 percent had actually written a business plan. However, 56 percent said they would find help writing a business plan valuable.

Hybrid Models of Social Entrepreneurship

Many types of ventures within the domain of social entrepreneurship do not fit nicely into quadrants 1 or 4 in Exhibit 6.2. In fact there are probably more hybrid arrangements than social ventures and enterprising nonprofits combined. In a recent survey, 2,000 entrepreneurs were asked about the primary goals of their business.[6] Entrepreneurs chose one from the following four options:

- For profit–primarily achieving economic goals.
- For profit–primarily achieving social goals.
- For profit–equally emphasizing social and economic goals.
- Not for profit, serving a social mission.

How do you think 2,000 random entrepreneurs in the United States, not necessarily classified as social entrepreneurs, responded to this question?

As you might expect, the majority of the entrepreneurs (49 percent) were traditional enterprisers (quadrant 2). They identified themselves as having a for-profit venture with purely economic goals. Another 9 percent classified their ventures as for profit with a pure social purpose–similar to Jim Poss and his BigBelly solar trash compactor. Only 8 percent of the surveyed entrepreneurs identified themselves as not for profit. Most interesting were the 31 percent of entrepreneurs that claimed to be for profit with social and economic goals. These findings show that new ways of organizing are emerging: dual-purpose organizations with missions that equally emphasize economic and social goals.

Scojo Vision, an eyewear company, is an example of a hybrid model. Founded in New York by two entrepreneurs, Scott Berrie and Jordon Kassalow, the company mission addresses economic and social needs. In addition to stylish lines of eyewear, they have created a program that brings eye care and affordable reading glasses to rural areas of Latin America and India. The program, run by the Scojo Foundation, trains women entrepreneurs to build businesses by selling inexpensive reading glasses to workers that depend on their vision for their livelihood, such as tailors, textile workers, and weavers.[7]

Recently a new classification of organization has emerged called "for benefit." A growing army of volunteers and interested social entrepreneurs are participating in a community called the Fourth Sector Project.[8] The fourth sector emerges from a rather unchanged historical classification of businesses that have served either the private or public sector. There are for-profit entities, nonprofit (nongovernmental) social organizations, and governmental organizations. The Fourth Sector Project seeks to recognize a new model, the for-benefit model, as sectors begin to blur.

Hybrid models are *not* examples of corporate social responsibility (CSR), which is a term that is growing in popularity in theory and in practice. CSR emphasizes helping and serving communities while still making a profit. Corporations with CSR practices impact the communities in which they operate, but it is not the core component of their business models. For example, Dow Chemical donates Styrofoam to Habitat for Humanity for new home insulation. Starbucks builds relationships with local farmers, pays fair market prices, and extends credit so local farmers can grow their coffee bean businesses. Anheuser-Busch commercials encourage consumers to drink responsibly to prevent alcohol abuse and drunk driving. In 2005 Walmart announced long-term goals to be supplied by 100 percent renewable energy, create zero waste, and sell environmentally friendly products.

The Timmons Model Interpreted for Social Entrepreneurship

Chapter 3 introduced the Timmons Model of the entrepreneurial process. The three major components of the Timmons Model–opportunity, resources, and teamwork–certainly apply to social entrepreneurship; but the model requires a few contextual

---

[6]Questions related to social entrepreneurship were included in the Global Entrepreneurship Monitor survey for the United States sponsored by Babson College. Social entrepreneurship results are included in H. Neck, C. Brush, and E. Allen, "Exploring Social Entrepreneurship Activity in the United States: For-Profit Ventures Generating Social and Economic Value," Working Paper, Babson College.
[7]http://www.scojo.com/eyewear.aspx.
[8]See http://www.fourthsector.net/ for more information.

changes. Social opportunities are driven not only by markets but also by mission and social need. The brain trust aspect of the team–the external stakeholders–is especially important because collaboration across boundaries is paramount in social entrepreneurship. Similar to traditional startups, the art of bootstrapping is a necessary method of resource acquisition. Yet capital markets exist for social entrepreneurs, and available funds are increasing in both the for-profit and not-for-profit sectors. The concepts of fit and balance remain because sustainability and growth are the essence of *any* entrepreneurial endeavor.

Wicked Problems and Opportunity Spaces

Opportunities in social sectors, including environmental issues, are driven by large, complex problems that we are going to call "wicked problems." In the early 1970s the notion of wicked problems emerged out of the complexity of resolving issues related to urban and governmental planning.[9] An examination of the characteristics of a wicked problem (as opposed to a "tame" problem;[10] see Exhibit 6.3) reveals the considerable challenges facing social entrepreneurs.

The recent and rapid increase in the U.S. elderly population is an excellent example of a wicked problem; due to advancements in health care, especially in disease control, humans are living longer. Between 2010 and 2020 we will see, for the first time in history, people over the age of 65 outnumbering children under age 5.[11] In 1903, 15 percent of white females lived to the age of approximately 80; but today close to 70 percent of white females live to be 80 years old.[12]

This aging population creates significant challenges for society. Pensions and retirement incomes will need to last longer. Health care costs are likely to increase. The service economy will capture an increasing percentage of GDP as the elderly require more help from services as opposed to products. Also consider that the workforce pays for many social benefits of the elderly. In a wider scope, the aging population decreases the percentage of taxpayers supporting the growing number of non-working retirees.

As with many such issues, this massive societal challenge represents a growing opportunity space for alert social entrepreneurs. Let us consider one aspect of this issue using the characteristics of wicked problems as the backdrop. Most elderly people want to maintain their independence as long as possible, so for many moving to an assisted living facility or nursing home is the last and least desired option. Furthermore, as the population ages and baby boomers enter their declining years, the availability of such assisted living facilities will decrease. A solution may be to create the next generation of smart homes that allow the elderly to stay in their own homes yet reap the benefits and security of assisted living. Let us assume the technology is in place and retrofitting existing homes is possible. Is this a good solution? On the surface yes, but consider other challenges:

- The elderly are not universally comfortable with technology.
- Older people may not have money to pay for the smart features.

EXHIBIT 6.3

Wicked versus Tame Problems

Characteristics of Wicked Problems	Characteristics of Tame Problems
I. You do not understand the problem until you have developed a solution.	Have well-defined and stable problem statements.
2. Wicked problems have no stopping rule.	Have definite stopping points—when a solution is reached.
3. Solutions to wicked problems are not right or wrong.	Have solutions that can be objectively evaluated as right or wrong.
4. Every wicked problem is unique and novel.	Belong to a class of similar problems that are all solved in a similar way.
5. Every solution to a wicked problem is a "one-shot operation."	Have solutions that can be easily tried and abandoned.
6. Wicked problems have no given alternative solutions—infinite set.	Come with a limited set of alternative solutions.

Source: J. Conklin, *Dialogue Mapping: Building Shared Understanding of Wicked Problems*, chapter I.

---

[9]H. Rittel and M. Webber, "Dilemmas in a General Theory of Planning," *Policy Sciences* 4 (1973), pp. 155-169.
[10]Ibid., p. 160.
[11]www.state.gov/g/oes/rls/or/81537.htm.
[12]Ibid.

- Elderly people staying in their own homes may require assistance to reach hospitals in cases of emergency; so more elderly at home may stretch the 911 emergency response system.
- Cities and towns may be expected to create services for a larger elderly population, and these services may be funded by additional property taxes.

The list could go on, but the point is that sometimes we do not understand a whole problem until a solution is developed (Exhibit 6.3, #1). But let us continue with the idea of smart homes for the elderly. How much independence should be built into the homes? What is the trade-off of using both floors in a two-story home versus just one? Does the entire home need to be smart? Wicked problems do not have a predetermined stopping rule (Exhibit 6.3, #2), so the social entrepreneur is forced to make rational choices based on a rigorous evaluation of trade-offs. The social entrepreneur must accept that a wicked problem is never fully solved and the solution is not likely to meet all expectations; this is also known as *satisficing* behavior. As characteristic #3 states, there are no right or wrong solutions.

Independent living for the elderly is a unique social problem (#4), and interpretation of the dilemma is in the eye of the beholder. The problem in this example affects not only older people but also other stakeholders. Potential solutions to wicked problems are known to have consequences over an extended period. A smart home may be a good idea for an elderly person wanting to maintain her independence, but consider the amount of work involved in retrofitting a home. What systems need to be installed? What changes to the home structure are anticipated? Finally how difficult will it be to sell an "elder smart" home on the market, and would it be easy or desirable to take the "smartness" out of the home after the death of the independent elder? Perhaps there are many other consequences of making a home smart in this context, but for a wicked problem only time will tell. Elderly independence is just one aspect of the social problem we will encounter as the population ages. There are innumerable possibilities, and wicked problem theory tells us that there is no finite solution (#6). Perhaps some see this as a limitation; but social entrepreneurs see an ocean of possibilities and opportunities.

To get a better understanding of the social challenges facing the planet, the United Nations' Millennium Development Goals are a good starting point. The goals were developed in 2000 in a historically significant event when world leaders came together to address universally pressing social

---

EXHIBIT 6.4

United Nations Millennium Development Goals

1. Eradicate extreme poverty and hunger.
2. Achieve universal primary education.
3. Promote gender equality and empower women.
4. Reduce child mortality.
5. Improve maternal health.
6. Combat HIV/AIDS, malaria, and other diseases.
7. Ensure environmental sustainability.
8. Develop a global partnership for development.

Source: The Millennium Development Goals Report 2005 (http://www.un.org/millenniumgoals/background.html).

issues. The collaboration resulted in the inspiring United Nations Millennium Declaration. According to then Secretary-General Kofi Annan, the eight goals (Exhibit 6.4) with a target achievement date of 2015 form a blueprint agreed to by all the world's countries and all the world's leading development institutions–a set of simple but powerful objectives that every man and woman in the street, from New York to Nairobi to New Delhi, can easily support and understand.[13]

Though these goals represent the UN's view of our most pressing social problems, the available opportunities for social entrepreneurs (in for-profit and nonprofit areas) are vast and promising. An opportunity is merely the positive view of a problem or challenge. We know from previous chapters that entrepreneurs think differently and identify opportunities that others cannot see. What opportunities can you identify?

Resources

Not unlike the traditional entrepreneurial ventures discussed throughout this text, resource acquisition is critical to the success of social ventures, enterprising nonprofits, and even hybrid forms. Most social entrepreneurs will admit that access to capital is a burgeoning challenge as more social ventures emerge, especially with high growth aspirations and visions of international scalability. Bootstrapping is prevalent among passionate social entrepreneurs, who are often quiet in their approach as they struggle to build sustainable business models.

Social venture capital (SVC) is a subset of the traditional venture capital market. SVCs seek to invest in for-profit ventures not only for financial return but also for social and environmental return also known as the *double bottom line* or *triple bottom line*.[14] Within

---

[13]*The Millennium Development Goals Report 2005*, p. 3, http://www.un.org/millenniumgoals/background.html.

the social venture capital territory are three types of funds. First there is the "focused" fund. For example, Expansion Capital Partners with offices in San Francisco and New York invests solely in expansion-stage clean technology businesses related to energy, water, transportation, and manufacturing. Similarly, Commons Capital, operating outside Boston, invests in early-stage companies operating in one of four areas of social concern: education, health care, energy, and the environment. Both companies explicitly promote the environmental and social focus of their funds. The second type of fund is the "community" fund; its purpose is typically economic development and job creation in impoverished areas. CEI Ventures, headquartered in Portland, Maine, invests in businesses operating in underserved markets. Each company in the CEI portfolio is required to hire employees with low-income backgrounds from the community in which the business is operating. The case at the end of the chapter is an example of this type of SVC. The third type of fund is what has been referred to as "VC with a conscience."[15] These funds stipulate that a certain percentage will be invested in socially responsible businesses related to their target investment areas. For example, Solstice Capital operates offices in Boston, Massachusetts, and Tucson, Arizona. It invests 50 percent of its fund in information technology and the remaining 50 percent in socially responsible companies. According to its website, "Socially responsive investments can generate superior venture capital returns and make a positive contribution to the natural and social environments."[16]

Venture philanthropy provides value-added funding for nonprofit organizations to increase their potential for social impact. Though the origin of venture philanthropy has been attributed to John D. Rockefeller III in 1969 when he spoke before Congress in support of tax reform, the modern version looks more like venture capital but with a social return on investment.[17] There are various definitions of venture philanthropy, and the European Venture Philanthropy Association (EVPA) has adopted several tenets of venture philanthropy that are similar across all definitions—in both Europe and the United States, where the venture philanthropy concept is gaining unprecedented popularity (Exhibit 6.5).

EXHIBIT 6.5

Accepted Principles of Venture Philanthropy from the European Venture Philanthropy Association

Characteristic	Description
High engagement	Venture philanthropists have a close, hands-on relationship with the social entrepreneurs and ventures they support, driving innovative and scalable models of social change. Some may take board places in these organizations, and all are far more intimately involved at strategic and operational levels than are traditional nonprofit funders.
Multiyear support	Venture philanthropists provide substantial and sustained financial support to a limited number of organizations. Support typically lasts for 3 to 5 years, with an objective of helping the organization to become financially self-sustaining by the end of the funding period.
Tailored financing	As in venture capital, venture philanthropists take an investment approach to determine the most appropriate financing for each organization. Depending on their own missions and the ventures they choose to support, venture philanthropists can operate across the spectrum of investment returns.
Organizational capacity building	Venture philanthropists focus on building the operational capacity and long-term viability of the organizations in their portfolios, rather than funding individual projects or programs. They recognize the importance of funding core operating costs to help these organizations achieve greater social impact and operational efficiency.
Nonfinancial support	In addition to financial support, venture philanthropists provide value-added services such as strategic planning, marketing and communications, executive coaching, human resource advice, and access to other networks and potential funders.
Performance measurement	Venture philanthropy investment is performance-based, placing emphasis on good business planning, measurable outcomes, achievement of milestones, and high levels of financial accountability and management competence.

Source: R. John, "Venture Philanthropy: The Evolution of High-Engagement Philanthropy in Europe," Working Paper. Oxford Said Business School, Skoll Center for Entrepreneurship, 2006.

[14]C. Clark, "RISE Capital Market Report: The Double Bottom Line Private Equity Landscape in° 2002–2003," Columbia Business School, 2003.
[15]Ibid.
[16]http://www.solcap.com/objective.html.
[17]R. John, "Venture Philanthropy: The Evolution of High-Engagement Philanthropy in Europe," Working Paper, Oxford Said Business School, Skoll Center for Entrepreneurship, 2006.

Social Entrepreneur Wins Nobel Peace Prize in 2006

This is not charity. This is business: business with a social objective, which is to help people get out of poverty.

Muhammad Yunus

Muhammad Yunus is the banker to the poor. He revolutionized the banking industry in the late 1970s when he started offering microloans with no collateral to the poorest of the poor in Bangladesh. Over 25 years later he and his Grameen Bank were introduced to the mainstream as recipients of the Nobel Peace Prize for their contributions to social and economic development by breaking the cycle of poverty through microcredit.

The idea is simple yet powerful. Borrowers are organized into groups of five, but not all members can borrow at once. Two borrowers may receive a microloan at one time; but not until these two borrowers begin to pay back the principal plus interest can the other members become eligible for their own loans. The average interest rate is 16 percent, and the repayment rate is an unprecedented 98 percent, which is attributed to group pressure, empowerment, and motivation. The loans are tiny–typically enough to buy a goat, tools, or a small piece of machinery that can be used to produce new sources of income.

The Grameen Bank was founded by Yunus with the following objectives:

- Extend banking facilities to poor men and women.

- Eliminate the exploitation of the poor by money lenders.

- Create opportunities for self-employment for the vast multitude of unemployed people in rural Bangladesh.

- Bring the disadvantaged, mostly women from the poorest households, within the fold of an organizational format they can understand and manage by themselves.

- Change the age-old vicious circle of low income, low savings, and low investment into the virtuous circle of low income, injection of credit, investment, more income, more savings, more investment, and more income.

As of October 2007 the Grameen Bank had served 7.34 million borrowers, of whom 97 percent were women. The bank operates 2,468 branches and employs 24,703 people. Since 1983 the Grameen Bank has disbursed $6.55 billion to the poor and has been profitable every year except 1983, 1991, and 1992.

New Profit Inc., based in Cambridge, Massachusetts, exemplifies venture philanthropy using venture capital methodology. With 38 employees, New Profit has a venture fund that has, as of 2010, invested in 27 nonprofit organizations, and reached out to over 1.4 million people (http://www. newprofit.com/cgi-bin/iowa/about/3.html). The average investment in each organization has been $1 million over a 4-year period. However, New Profit tends to stay with organizations longer than 4 years to achieve sustainability and desired scale. In addition to providing growth capital financing, portfolio organizations receive strategic support from a New Profit portfolio manager and New Profit's signature partner, Monitor Group, a global advisory and financial services firm. Monitor Group, through a collaborative and unprecedented partnership, provides New Profit portfolio organizations with pro bono consulting as well as giving New Profit additional operating resources. It is estimated that since 1999 Monitor Group has provided New Profit and its portfolio organizations more than $50 million in pro bono services (http://newprofit. com/cgi-bin/iowa/about/org/29.html?org=1).

Given the value-added investment capability of New Profit, this venture philanthropy organization is able to double the impact of each investment dollar from donors. Thus donors (or investors) of New Profit know that for every $1 they invest, the nonprofit portfolio organization actually receives $1.98 due to services, support, and intellectual capital delivered by the New Profit team in conjunction with Monitor Group (see Exhibit 6.6).

EXHIBIT 6.6

New Profit Doubles a $1 Investment

$1.00	Financial capital donated to New Profit portfolio organization
−0.00	New Profit expense or management fee (overhead and operating costs are covered by New Profit's board of directors)
+0.48	Value of New Profit portfolio manager
+0.50	Value of Monitor Group services donated
$1.98	Total investment to New Profit portfolio organization

Source: New Profit collateral materials, 2008.

New Profit has significantly increased the social impact of many nonprofit organizations across various sectors, including education, workforce development, and health care. The innovative approach of venture philanthropists such as New Profit illustrates the power of entrepreneurial principles to scale nonprofit organizations to achieve unparalleled social reach.

The Importance of the Brain Trust in Social Entrepreneurship

The third component of the Timmons Model of the Entrepreneurial Process is the team. As we have discussed, social entrepreneurship seeks to solve wicked problems, and such problems cannot be solved alone or even with a small startup team. The environment to solve social problems requires a spirit of collaboration; and therefore in the social entrepreneurship context the brain trust is particularly important.

The brain trust in social entrepreneurship can include the community, investors, the government, customers, suppliers, and manufacturers. The list is endless in many respects and depends on the venture. Social ventures, while working toward a positive mission, must still deliver value for key stakeholders. What the value is and to whom will vary, but it is important that the social entrepreneur understand the interactions among brain trust stakeholders as well as the potential value derived from being associated with the venture.

Think back to the Jim Poss example at the beginning of the chapter. Poss must understand the value proposition for each stakeholder. In a municipality, for example, the company responsible for waste management needs to see money saved by reducing the frequency of trash pickups. Poss must show the mayor of the city that the BigBelly supports green initiatives. For city planners, Poss can address space-saving and aesthetic features. But what about labor unions? What if reducing the number of trash pickups cuts the number of trucks and drivers needed? Every social innovation likely has a downside; the social entrepreneur needs to consider not only the value added but also the value loss to various stakeholder groups and assess consequences.

Concluding Thoughts: Change Agent Now or Later?

Bank of America recently commissioned a report on philanthropy that found that entrepreneurs, on average, give 25 percent more to charitable causes than other types of wealthy donors.[18] Of course this spirit of giving among entrepreneurs should be recognized and applauded; but is such giving sufficient? The story of a successful entrepreneur building a company, creating personal wealth, and *then* making significant charitable contributions is common. Social entrepreneurs, however, do not wait to give, but build businesses where economic value and societal contribution are two sides of the same coin. Social entrepreneurs use fundamental principles of entrepreneurship to promote positive change and permanent impact to help create and sustain our future.

---

[18]C. Preston, "Entrepreneurs Are among Most Generous Wealthy, Report Finds," *Chronicle of Philanthropy* 20, no. 5 (December 13, 2007).

Chapter Summary

- The primary difference between traditional entrepreneurship and social entrepreneurship is the intended mission.
- There are two types of enterprising nonprofits. The first type utilizes earned-income activities, while the second has a focus on growth and economic sustainability.
- The primary mission of both social ventures and enterprising nonprofits is social regardless of market impact. The hybrid model equally emphasizes social and economic goals.

- Social opportunities are driven not only by markets but also by mission and social need.
- With social entrepreneurship, the team in the Timmons Model is expanded to include stakeholders external to the venture.
- As more social ventures emerge, access to capital becomes a greater challenge.
- Social venture capitalists seek to invest in for-profit ventures for financial return as well as for social and environmental return.

Study Questions

1. What are the differences among socially responsible ventures, social ventures, and enterprising nonprofits?

2. Why are corporate social responsibility (CSR) activities not considered to be part of the domain of social entrepreneurship?

3. What are three characteristics of wicked problems?

4. What is meant by the concept of double bottom line with regard to socially focused investing?

5. What is an example of a wicked problem facing humanity, and what types of opportunities might arise for social entrepreneurs in that space?

Internet Resources

http://www.netimpact.org *Net Impact is a global network of leaders who are changing the world through business.*

http://www.echoinggreen.org *Since 1987, Echoing Green has provided seed funding and support to nearly 450 social entrepreneurs with bold ideas for social change in order to launch groundbreaking organizations around the world.*

http://www.se-alliance.org *An increasing number of organizations are working toward sustainable social innovation by applying the power of market-based strategies to advance social change. The Social Enterprise Alliance serves as a single point of reference and support and a source of education and networking lenders, investors,* *grant makers, consultants, researchers, and educators who recognize the increasing impact of social enterprise.*

http://www.svn.org *Founded in 1987 by Josh Mailman and Wayne Silby, Social Venture Network (SVN) is a nonprofit network committed to building a just and sustainable world through business.*

www.skollfoundation.org *The Skoll Foundation's mission is to advance systemic change to benefit communities around the world by investing in, connecting, and celebrating social entrepreneurs. Social entrepreneurs are proven leaders whose approaches and solutions to social problems are helping to better the lives and circumstances of countless underserved or disadvantaged individuals.*

Northwest Community Ventures Fund

Preparation Questions

1. Does the for-profit avenue chosen by Eileen O'Brien make sense for Grassroots Business Initiatives, Inc.?

2. When is it OK to forgo economic profit in order to increase social returns? How can social returns be measured? Can social and environmental benefits be given a monetary value?

3. What is the upside for Michelle Foster if NCV succeeds? What are the professional risks she faces?

4. How should Foster position herself and her team prior to raising a follow-on fund?

Michelle Foster glanced at the unclaimed nametags. Stormy weather had hurt attendance at the conference on funding alternatives for growing businesses, which was sponsored in part by Foster's equity fund, Northwest Community Ventures (NCV). To follow its mandate to invest in rural Oregon and Washington, the fund depended on such outreach venues as the conference to attract and build trust with rural entrepreneurs unfamiliar with traditional venture capital.

In early 2005 NCV had just over 8 years remaining on its 10-year charter. Nevertheless, Foster was already thinking about raising a follow-on fund. Like most venture-fund managers, she planned to start seeking investors for her next fund long before her current fund's performance could be gauged.

Foster was concerned whether she could attract institutional investors to NCV's brand of socially responsible venture capital—especially if they could get better returns elsewhere at lower risk. Her primary challenge, however, was her deteriorating relationship with Eileen O'Brien, the founder of NCV's high-profile, nonprofit parent organization.

Grassroots Business Initiatives, Inc.

The civil rights rallies and marches O'Brien attended while growing up in the late 1960s steeled her resolve to make a real difference. When she came

to coastal Oregon 10 years later, she knew she had found a place to begin a new sort of journey.

The rural coastal community was in dire straits. The farming, fishing, and forestry industries were vibrant, but most of the hardworking business owners—and almost all their workers—were living at or below the poverty line. The tall, self-assured redhead soon became a force in the state as she searched for ways to improve lives while maintaining the waters, farms, and forests that supported the rural communities. In 1979 she founded Grassroots Business Initiatives (GBI), a community development corporation (CDC) set up to invest in small businesses, foster employment opportunities, and develop the Oregon's natural resource industries.

Although O'Brien had no formal business training, she was a quick study and adept at finance. For nearly 25 years, she and her team[1] had done well by being creative:

> As part of our effort to strengthen GBI financially, we began to develop innovative programs around economic development that could supplement and diversify our income stream. These programs were subsidized by federal and state agencies, as well as foundations. We made our loans conditional on things like improved wage rates, benefits, and working conditions. We generated income from the "spread" between our cost of capital—1 percent was typical for 10-year foundation money—and the rate at which we could lend it out.

Lending money to business organizations not only helped foster economic development initiatives, but also gave GBI a powerful voice to effect change within the business community. By 2000, the organization had assets under management of nearly $75 million. But O'Brien sensed a big change coming:

> The Bush administration was making it clear that in addition to tax cuts for the wealthy, they were going

---

This case was prepared by Carl Hedberg under the direction of Professor Natalie Taylor. Copyright Babson College, 2005. Funding provided by the F.W. Olin Graduate School and a gift from the class of 2003. All rights reserved.

[1]By 2005 GBI employed 75 individuals dedicated to O'Brien and her mission. Ironically, because GBI generally attracted liberal-minded social progressives, the organization had become a highly effective community development corporation whose workers collectively exhibited strong antibusiness sentiments. This culture was reinforced during the late 1990s as scandals on Wall Street and corporate America became headline news. GBI's board of directors had been chosen by O'Brien for their commitment to the values she embraced. Though some of the banks who supported her organization sat on her board, conservative business individuals were the exception.

to cut back or dismantle government programs that we have always relied on. Also, Congress was saying that it might support changes in the Community Reinvestment Act.[2]

O'Brien knew many nonprofits were pursuing social entrepreneurship[3] to fund their efforts:

If we lose government funding, there is no way that private sector donations, along with our lending practices, could come close to covering our expenses. And if we were forced to become aggressive fund-raisers, those efforts would severely distract us from our community development objectives. For us, it made total sense to close that gap with a for-profit investment fund.

Community Development Venture Capital

In the early 1990s, O'Brien and a few of her community development peers realized that although they could use conditional loans to advance modest social initiatives, their roles as lenders did not afford them greater influence. They also noted an absence of equity capital to support growth in rural markets. Using grant money from foundations, this loose coalition of creative lenders developed a structure for a socially progressive equity fund. Their concept, community development venture capital (CDVC), was one of several types of community development financial institutions (CDFIs) that CDCs were using to advance rural reinvestment objectives (Exhibit A).

Like traditional venture capital funds (Appendix A), CDVCs aimed to invest in companies that had

[2]The Community Reinvestment Act (CRA), enacted by Congress in 1977, was intended to encourage depository institutions to help meet the credit needs of the communities in which they operated—including channeling some of their investment funds into CDCs and similar entities. Banks with less than $250 million in assets could qualify for certain CRA exemptions. In 2005 a controversial FDIC proposal was advanced to exempt many more banks by raising that minimum threshold to $1 billion in assets.

[3]Social entrepreneurship—nonprofits raising money through businesslike arrangements to support a social mission—was a growing trend, but not entirely new. Goodwill Industries had long raised money through businesses to support its core mission, sometimes using its clients to help operate those businesses. At the heart of social entrepreneurship was the notion that many nonprofits had marketable assets that could be tapped to generate revenue to support and promote their missions. These assets included expertise, services, products, logos, volunteer networks, and even their reputation or standing in the community. Children's Television Workshop, for example, licensed *Sesame Street* characters for books, toys, and other products. By the early 2000s Girl Scouts of America was selling more than $200 million in cookies each year to support the organization. (Source: *Developments* newsletter, University of Pittsburgh, 2002.)

EXHIBIT A

Community Development Financial Institutions (CDFI)

In 2005 community development corporations in the United States were operating 800–1,000 CDFIs, including

- 500 community development loan funds.
- 80 venture capital funds.
- 275 community development credit unions.
- 50 community development banks.

There were five generally recognized types of CDFIs:

- *Community development banks* provide capital to rebuild economically distressed communities through targeted lending and investment.

- *Community development credit unions* promote ownership of assets and savings and provide affordable credit and retail financial services to low-income people with special outreach to minority communities.

- *Community development loan funds* aggregate capital from individual and institutional social investors at below-market rates and lend it primarily to nonprofit housing and business developers in economically distressed communities.

- *Community development venture capital funds* provide equity and debt with equity features for community real estate and medium-sized business projects. Their typical target internal rate of return (IRR) is 10 to 12 percent, as opposed to 25 to 35 percent for mainstream VC funds.

- *Microenterprise development loan funds* foster social and business development through loans and technical assistance to low-income people who run very small businesses or are self-employed and unable to access conventional credit.

solid business models, outstanding managers, and excellent growth potential. However, CDVCs differed from mainstream venture capital in multiple ways (Exhibit B), with the most striking being that they sought a double bottom line. Their goal was to realize not only financial returns on their investments, but also returns to their communities in the form of such things as job creation for low-income workers, inner-city property revitalization, and opportunities for women and minorities.[4] In addition, their lower investment threshold—as little as $100,000 per investment—meant they could be a resource for talented entrepreneurs working in rural America.

[4]CDVC funds also tended to invest in more diverse industry sectors than traditional venture funds, which often focused their investments in technology or biotechnology—two sectors that did not provide many jobs for entry-level workers. By 2000 manufacturing had made up 49 percent of all CDVC investments, with services, retail trade, and software development following at 17, 7, and 6 percent, respectively.

EXHIBIT B

Community Development Venture Capital versus Traditional Venture Capital

Aspect	CDVC Funds[a]	VC Funds
Total capital under management	About $300 million	About $134 billion
Average investment size per round	$186,000	$13.2 million
Typical time frame before exit	5–8 years	3–5 years
Typical IRR goal range	10%–12%	25%–35%
Funding sources	Government foundations, banks, endowments, wealthy individuals	Pension funds, trusts and foundations, university endowments

[a]Further distinctions:

Socially responsible venture capital (SRVC) firms look for the following criteria in potential investments:

- *Diversity:* Women/minority owners/founders, businesses, diverse suppliers, employees, partners, etc.
- *Workforce:* Benefits, profit sharing, employee ownership, healthy work environment.
- *Environmental:* Beneficial products/services, pollution prevention, recycling, alternative energy, building design.
- *Products:* Socially beneficial, quality, innovative, safe.

Socially responsible investing also avoided such industries as tobacco, adult entertainment, gambling, and firearms.

A New Model for Economic Development

In 2001, O'Brien persuaded her board of directors to support the creation of a $10 million socially responsible venture capital fund. NCV criteria were designed to make equity investments in areas that could have the most positive impact (Exhibit C). O'Brien felt sure this fund would be a good fit:

> GBI has been built on the strength of our talent to guide and nurture rural businesses, and this is an opportunity to give us a voice in the boardrooms of high-potential ventures that can have a real impact in these communities. As a limited partner in the fund, we'd participate in long-term capital gains that would likely be far above what our lending programs can provide.

When a banker on her board emphasized the importance of bringing in an experienced individual to manage the fund, O'Brien agreed and set out to recruit a top venture capital professional willing to make some trade-offs.

Michelle Foster

Michelle Foster was born in southern California to liberal parents who grew up in the 60s. Although she embraced their values, Foster chose a different career track. After earning her MBA at Babson

EXHIBIT C

NCV Investment Criteria

In traditional VC markets, criteria used to evaluate companies include the following:

- *Management:* Experienced within domain, able to understand demands of growth, receptive to working with VC investor as partner, realistic about own skills/experience and willing to change roles if needed; management team should be complete.
- *Market:* Large, fast-growing; identified pain point of customers.
- *Barrier to entry:* Typically intellectual property protection to defend product/service against competitors.
- *Financial:* Capital requirements appropriate to venture finance (e.g., not too capital intensive); high gross margins.
- *Business model:* Scalable, consistent with current market conditions.

In more rural markets, most of these criteria still apply but with the following differences:

- *Management:* Management possesses strong domain experience but may not have worked with VCs before and may need education; management teams often are incomplete.
- *Market:* Unlike technology markets (denominated in $billions), markets served by more rural companies tend to be smaller (denominated in $hundred millions) with less dramatic growth (low–mid double-digit rather than triple-digit for technology markets).
- *Barriers to entry:* For mid- and later-stage companies not operating in technology markets, barriers tend to be existing brands and current scale of business.

College in Wellesley, Massachusetts, she landed a position at a prestigious venture capital fund in Boston and worked her way up to partner.

Although Foster loved the job, she wanted more than the exclusive financial orientation of the deal maker's life and began looking for opportunities closer to her native California. In the fall of 2001 she spotted an unusual offering in Portland, Oregon. Foster recalled that she and the founder hit it off immediately:

> EILEEN'S background and sensibilities were very similar to what my parents were all about. She joked that in person I was not nearly as scary as my résumé made me out to be. So she was getting a VC with a soul, and I saw this as a fabulous opportunity to bring my deep experience to a position that involved a lot more than just meeting financial objectives. This seemed like a match made in heaven.

> O'Brien agreed:

> I could see that Michelle was a seasoned business-person, but she was also a good listener. Not only that, she totally got what we were trying to accomplish with this innovative fund.

Foster accepted the position in November 2001—at less than half her salary in Boston. She commented on the risks and trade-offs:

> The Portland area is so beautiful, and the pace of life is a pleasant change from what I had been doing on the East Coast. But this was also a serious career decision. While I knew that NCV had a very challenging rural investment mission, I also saw it as an enormous opportunity to do something interesting and innovative—beyond what the CDVC industry had done to date. This looked like an excellent opportunity to prove that venture capital investments could realize a return and make a real difference in underserved markets.

> At the same time, I was aware that since no one at GBI had venture investment experience, I would have to set the tone and would probably spend a good deal of time explaining my decisions. But that was what I was being hired for—to be the expert. I was also a bit uncertain about what it would mean to be part of the unique nonprofit culture that existed at GBI.

The recession that followed the 9/11 terrorist attacks made it very hard for mainstream venture capitalists to raise new funds from traditional sources such as pension funds.[5] Although NCV got funding primarily from foundations and banks with socially progressive mandates that were less sensitive to market conditions, it took Foster 18 months to raise a $10 million fund.

The economic slowdown was also hurting the parent company—especially its cash flow. GBI clients and portfolio companies were struggling, deal flow had dried up, and recession-fighting interest rate cuts had dramatically reduced CDC's income from lending.

The Investing Staff

Since joining NCV, Foster had been looking for an associate with venture experience and a willingness to put lifestyle ahead of money. In February 2004 she found such a person. John Coolidge had an MBA from Stanford and some early nonprofit experience, and had spent the last 3 years working for an international consulting firm. He explained that although he had loved that job, he knew he needed to make a change:

> I was always working with two clients simultaneously over a broad range of functional areas like growth strategy, marketing effectiveness, organizational strategy, and lean manufacturing. Within a short time I had gained a large breadth of experience across several sectors.

> It was a fantastic experience, but on the negative side, there were many weeks where I worked 70–80 hours while traveling two or three days. My wife and I had had our son while I was in business school, and it became a struggle to balance home life and my career. When our daughter was born in November 2003, I knew I had to make a change. After taking 4 weeks off for paternity leave, I went back and gave notice. I felt it was time to find a way to merge the social purpose and business sides of my career track.

Still, when a financial services firm in San Francisco made a lucrative job offer, Coolidge considered it. Then a wee-hours heart-to-heart talk turned the tide:

> I was really close to accepting that Citibank job. The kids had finally nodded off at around 1 in the morning, so for the first time my wife and I had a chance to really talk. When she asked me if I was going to be excited to go to work on my first day, I just sort of froze. When I said no, she said, "Well, that settles it; you're not going to take that job." . . . Soon after, I was on the Internet and found the listing for what sounded like the perfect job up north in Oregon.

Coolidge was even more intrigued after his interview with Foster. Although working for NCV would mean a big pay cut, he found the firm's social mission and business model very attractive. Coolidge and his wife also loved the area:

---

[5]For groups seeking to raise private equity, there were two adverse consequences of the precipitous fall in the equity markets in 2001. The first was that because the IPO market had dried up virtually overnight, the harvest horizon had become highly uncertain. The second consequence of falling share prices was that as the aggregate portfolios of pension fund managers shrank, the denominator (which defined the percentage of total investments allocated to venture capital and private equity) also shrank. This resulted in a considerable overallocation for that asset class. Consequently pension fund managers had simply stopped investing their money in venture capital until the allocation percentage was back within a range set by their investing policies. (Source: Jeffry Timmons, Forte Ventures case, 2004.)

The quality of life is fantastic here. We were able to get a house that would have been way out of our price range in San Francisco. I can ride my bike to work, and we live in a great town with good schools. I look out the window at the fishing boats and the harbor seals, and realize how much the consulting business had conditioned me to believe that there wasn't any other way to live besides working long hours and making lots of money.

For her part, Foster thought Coolidge's enthusiasm and background trumped his lack of venture capital experience:

What's great about John's background is he made certain decisions that were based on quality of family life and a desire to integrate his values into his work. So there were enough linkages with where I was coming from, and John was obviously motivated and smart. I needed someone whose motivations were not purely financial—someone willing to adapt. I felt that John's nonprofit policy background would keep him from running shrieking from the boardroom when those for-profit versus nonprofit cultural issues flared up.

Developing Deal Flow

Together Foster and Coolidge handled the responsibilities of the fund's investing team (Exhibit D). Although most mainstream venture capital firms could generate deal flow without much marketing,[6] NCV actively promoted its fund to a variety of groups across the region, generating leads through economic development organizations, other VC firms, and banks.

NCV also utilized business directories, chamber-of-commerce listings, and local and regional newspapers to identify and attract a range of prospects—from companies actively seeking expansion capital to promising rural enterprises that had never considered venture capital as a funding option. From these sources, the team could identify the rough universe of companies that fit their investment criteria.[7]

---

[6]Venture capitalists attended industry networking forums such as The Venture Forum, purchased listings in publications such as *Galante's Guide to Venture Capital*, and participated in panel sessions and in business plan competitions.

[7]The databases and publication on hand listed approximately 20,000 companies in the rural markets in Washington State and in Oregon. Assuming that the list spanned 80 percent of the potential companies, NCV estimated the total size of the business market to be 25,000. If 20 percent of this market (5,000) represented companies with VC characteristics and an estimated 20 percent of this subset (1,000) could fulfill progressive investment goals, then NCV had to find and invest in 152 companies out of an eligible market of 1,000—that is, NCV had to find and invest in approximately 1 in 66 companies (1,000 companies divided by 15 investments).

EXHIBIT D

Investing Staff (President, Associate) Responsibilities

Deal sourcing: Identify, qualify, and secure interest from companies seeking capital.

Due diligence: Research a company's market, management, product/service, and financial forecasts to understand the potential risk of and return from investing in it.

Negotiation (pricing, terms): Negotiate investment terms (price, security, and key legal/financial terms) with company owners and managers.

Decision making:

- Management decision—weigh risks and opportunities, chemistry with management, and other factors to decide whether to invest in a company.
- Board review—present investment recommendation to board of directors for vote.

Corporate governance and stakeholder management: Through seat on board of directors, help govern the company, balancing interests of various stakeholders—investors/shareholders, management/staff, and community/environmental.

Operational assistance: Help company reach targets in its business plan.

Return management: Help management achieve financial and social returns within the agreed-upon timeframes; facilitate exit opportunities that maximize those returns.

Reporting: Prepare periodic fund and management reports:

- Every 6 to 8 weeks, report to board on fund operations and fund/portfolio performance.
- Make filings with and report to Small Business Administration as required.
- Report quarterly and annually to investors (limited partners or LPs) on performance (financial, social) of fund's portfolio.

Fund-raising: Prepare fund-raising documents for successor fund (typically 3 to 5 years after start of existing fund); identify and present to prospective investors to secure capital commitments.

Among NCV's important outreach efforts were their educational seminars. Cosponsored by banks and service providers, and hosted and marketed by local economic development groups, these conferences presented a broad view of the growth and funding strategies available to promising businesses. Foster felt these forums—which targeted rural entrepreneurs—were unusual in the VC industry:

Our programs provide content that generally doesn't get covered in other forums; we are very transparent in everything we do. People will ask, "What is your valuation expectation?" or "What return do you expect?" Or sometimes they do not quite understand how venture capital works. We explain how we do not lend money like a bank, but that we price deals to target a high IRR because of the typical loss rates in venture capital. By *assuming* the risk—whereas banks mitigate risk—we share in the upside because we're sharing in the downside. Once they see the challenges of our work, they begin to understand why we usually require a substantial equity piece.

Cool Winds

Foster and her team worked on the second floor of a red brick, harbor-side shipping warehouse that O'Brien had made into GBI's headquarters. Even during a coastal storm, the view was beautiful—and often more tranquil than the team's experience inside the building. Foster offered her take on the chilly reception that was now in its third year:

> Even though I had agreed to a huge cut in salary to do this, I am still making $5,000 more than Eileen. She's always been fine with that, but there is definitely resentment from some of her senior staff since they have been with her for many years, and their salaries are maybe only 65 percent of my base, and none of them have the potential upside that I do with carried interest.[8] But hey—we're talking two completely different models here: nonprofit versus a venture capital operation.

Foster and Coolidge were not bothered by their colleagues' resentment. But they were concerned that O'Brien had begun pushing for significant input on funding decisions. They soon realized she expected NCV to accept her suggestions without resistance. Foster, who was sensitive to the top-down culture that O'Brien had established, had found tactful ways of deflecting her attempts at direct oversight and was moderately successful until O'Brien decided to take a firm stand.

Turbulence

By the end of 2003 NCV had investigated 187 potential deals. Seven were under active consideration, 163 had been turned down, and 15 were considered dormant (neither under active consideration nor turned down). Two firms had received equity investments.

One was the Portland Baking Company (PBC), a women-owned and -managed manufacturer of all-natural cakes and confections. The business had been operating for 5 years when founder Mary Bishop decided to set up an online store to sell high-margin gift packages. When sales doubled to $600,000 in 8 months, the company sought funding to exploit its most lucrative online channel: corporations. PBC received $400,000 from NCV, as well as a $200,000 economic-development loan set up through GBI. The company planned to use the money to hire additional employees and to install an automated packaging system.

The other was Sostenga, Inc., a catalog/e-commerce business that marketed sustainable energy systems to farms and off-the-grid residences. The company, founded by Manuel Gracioso and his brother Ricardo in 1996, had been growing quickly due to a resurgence of interest in alternative energy. Sostenga had received $350,000 from NCV for inventory purchases and marketing expenditures.

When Foster and Coolidge began due diligence on Sostenga, O'Brien told Foster she had reservations about the investment. While she favored the deal's minority and environmental aspects, she was concerned that Sostenga could grow without adding people. As an alternative, O'Brien suggested that Foster revisit a call center (offering lower-income jobs) that had been rejected weeks before. Foster felt it was time to push back:

> Ever since we started, Eileen has been floating in and out of my office to "check up" on progress with deals she has become fond of, or to promote opportunities that fit her progressive social agenda. I finally told her, "Look, you hired me because of my experience. The quid pro quo for me agreeing to work for a lower salary is that GBI needs to give me the benefit of the doubt on deal-related decision making."
>
> After all, GBI has no experience in this business, either directly or on their board. How can I be expected to take direction from a group that doesn't know what financial success looks like?

O'Brien was looking for cash flow to mitigate her first loss in 20 years[9] and noted that management fees at the venture fund more than covered expenses.[10] Foster said she remained committed to running the fund in a manner commensurate with industry standards:

> How we spend our management fees is discretionary. As fund managers we decide what equipment we need, what conferences we want to attend, and what newsletters and news services we buy. Sure, in theory, we could operate very leanly and have

---

[8]Carried interest is the share of residual capital gains from a venture capital fund, minus expenses and allocations to limited partners. Carried interest payments were designed to create a significant economic incentive for venture capital fund managers to achieve capital gains. The term originated in the early days of VC, when general partners put up nothing in return for 20 percent of the profits; thus the limited partners "carried the interest" of the general partners.

[9]Although deficits were not uncommon for nonprofits in general and CDCs in particular, GBI was one of the few in the country that had consistently covered its expenses.

[10]Annual management fees of 2 percent of the capital under management covered salaries, office expenses and other overhead, and all costs associated with locating, reviewing, and consummating investment opportunities. Money left over at the end of the year in traditional venture funds was typically disbursed as bonuses to the fund managers. Foster was anticipating little or no remaining capital at the end of the year.

excess cash that could flow upward to the parent, but our job is to use those fees to find and close good deals. . . not to subsidize the parent.

WHEN I said to Eileen that our investors didn't invest so that she could fund a loss with our fees, she brought up the whole moral issue of supporting her nonprofit side of this business. But what about the ethical issue with regard to our fiduciary responsibility to other NCV limited partners?

Another difficult situation arose when Foster and Coolidge considered investing in an organic products manufacturer contingent on replacing the founder with a more experienced CEO. O'Brien had known the man for years, and GBI planned to participate in the loan portion of the investment package. Foster explained that despite pressure from her board of directors—which O'Brien chaired—she refused to back down:

> We've got such challenging mandates already; we can't shy away from the best course of action just because it makes people uncomfortable. Sure, I liked the guy too; he just wasn't the one to take that business to the next level.
>
> As tension creating as this all became, this would have been a fairly clear issue for traditional VCs. That happens a lot around here: A solution that to me seems basically straightforward can become a big crisis for the parent and this board.
>
> As it turned out, that particular investment wasn't going to happen. But practically speaking, if we could have structured the deal, then I probably would have suffered whatever wrath there would have been and gone ahead and replaced the guy.

Getting to Scale

As with any type of investment, the long-term success of socially responsible VC firms such as NCV would depend on how they met their investors' needs and expectations. In the early 2000s, CDVCs still largely depended on public-sector funds and socially progressive foundations (Exhibit E). Referring to NCV's 10-year financial expectations (Exhibit F), Foster said the success of such CDVCs could open the door to a whole new class of rural investment vehicles targeting communities in underserved regions—but only if they could attract a more traditional base of limited partners:

> Should we expect mainstream institutional investors to subsidize socially responsible ventures in perpetuity? A 10 to 12 percent return might be reasonable from the point of view of GBI and mission-driven foundations, but if you can't get a pension fund or a bank to make a significant contribution, the market is telling you it's not the appropriate risk-reward.

EXHIBIT E

Funding Sources for CDVCs

Banks and financial institutions	31%
Federal government	25%
Foundations and family trusts	17%
State and local government	11%
Individuals	6%
Corporations and partnerships	6%
Parent entities	3%
Other	1%
	100%

Source: J. B. Rubin, "CDVC; Double Bottom-Line Approach to Poverty Alleviation," Harvard Business School, 2001.

> I tend to think that an IRR in that range is not sustainable long-term for the risk level that an early-stage fund like this takes on. Our theory is that if we target a materially higher IRR in the range of 15 to 22 percent, we'd be able attract the sort of limited partners that could fund a $50 million to $100 million CDVC effort.

Sustaining Momentum

Foster felt spinning her follow-on fund off from GBI would offer her more flexibility to craft and replicate the CDVC model—especially if this economic development vision of addressing underserved regions and sectors caught on. The question was how she could present the idea to O'Brien as a win for GBI. And if O'Brien refused to have GBI step back into the role of a passive limited partner, how could she improve the current working structure?

At a CDVC peer group meeting in San Diego, Foster found that her colleagues—many of whom had no previous venture capital experience—were struggling as well:

> The overall perception of CDVCs right now seems to be that we are minor-league players who value our social agenda over market-rate returns. That will change only if we can demonstrate that our focus on underserved communities and underserved sectors can be a market advantage—and even a lucrative source of proprietary deal flow.

By the time Foster started back from the NCV seminar in Eugene, the storm had given way to clear skies. The conference had not been fully attended, but had yielded a couple of interesting leads. While she was confident that NCV could source the deals it needed from its challenging geographic base, Foster needed to determine how to best position herself and her team for the future.

EXHIBIT F

NCV 10-Year Projections

	Year 1	Year 2	Year 3	Year 4	Year 5	Year 6	Year 7	Year 8	Year 9	Year 10
Capital Calls	$1,000,000	$3,000,000	$4,000,000	$2,000,000	—	—	—	—	—	—
Management Fees[a]	300,000	300,000	300,000	300,000	$ 300,000	$ 300,000	$ 300,000	$ 300,000	$ 300,000	$ 300,000
Investments	—	600,000	2,800,000	4,000,000	1,900,000	700,000	—	—	—	—
Divestments	—	—	—	575,000	1,800,000	5,500,000	6,400,000	8,500,000	7,200,000	5,500,000
Distributions to Investors	—	—	—	275,000	1,500,000	5,200,000	5,460,000	7,350,000	6,180,000	4,650,000
Carried Interest	—	—	—				940,000	1,150,000	1,020,000	850,000

[a]Annual management fees include president, $90,000; associate, $70,000; administrative assistant, $40,000.

Appendix A
Note on the Venture Capital Investing Process

Venture-capital advocates say VC fosters innovation by enabling investors and entrepreneurs to share the risks and rewards of starting, funding, and running potentially high-growth companies.

The process begins when a group of people identifies a good opportunity for venture-capital investment and decides to raise a fund to pursue it. Next, the group writes a prospectus articulating its strategy, qualifications, and track record, which it uses to raise money for its fund. Raising money is a networking and sales undertaking that typically gains momentum only after an institutional investment advisor—known as a gatekeeper—commits capital to the fund.[II]

DIAGRAM 6–A

Classic Venture Capital Investing Process

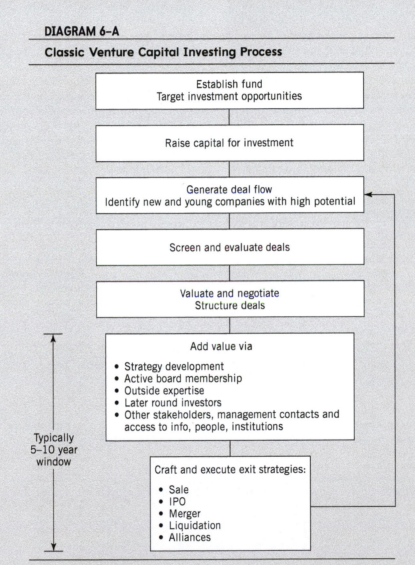

Establish fund
Target investment opportunities

Raise capital for investment

Generate deal flow
Identify new and young companies with high potential

Screen and evaluate deals

Valuate and negotiate
Structure deals

Add value via
- Strategy development
- Active board membership
- Outside expertise
- Later round investors
- Other stakeholders, management contacts and access to info, people, institutions

Craft and execute exit strategies:
- Sale
- IPO
- Merger
- Liquidation
- Alliances

Typically 5–10 year window

Note: This diagram and additional discussion of venture funding may be found in Chapter 13 of this text.

[II]Institutional investors such as corporations, foundations, and pension funds invest as limited partners in hundreds of venture capital and buyout funds. Many of these investors, having neither the resources nor the expertise to evaluate and manage fund investments, delegate these duties to investment advisors with expertise in the venture capital industry. These advisors pool the assets of their various clients and invest those proceeds on behalf of their limited partners into a venture or buyout fund currently raising capital. For this service, the advisors collect a fee of 1 percent of committed capital per annum. Because these investment experts exert a tremendous amount of influence over the allocation of capital to new and existing venture teams and funds, they are referred to as "gatekeepers."

Once the money is raised, the VC firm sets about identifying and evaluating business opportunities; negotiating and closing investments; providing its portfolio companies with technical and management assistance; and helping them attract resources, including additional capital, directors, managers, and suppliers (Diagram 6-A).

Given the numerous factors (e.g., management talent, market timing, strategic vision) required for a startup to reach a profitable exit event such as an acquisition or an initial public offering (IPO), home runs are rare. Only about 1 out of every 15 VC investments realize a return of 10 times or more on invested capital.

Venture capital funds typically are structured as limited partnerships set up for specific terms of years. The venture capitalists are the general partners and the investors are the limited partners (Diagram B). The general partners organize the fund and manage its investments, while the limited partners are passive investors and have limited liability for actions the fund takes. As compensation for their direct participation and risk exposure, general partners can reap substantial capital gains—known as carried interest—as the fund exits its investments.

Between 1980 and the early 2000s, there were two recessions (in 1981-1982 and in 1990-1992) and a stock market panic in late 1987 that sent share prices plummeting 22 percent in a single day. Nevertheless, according to Venture Economics—a private equity database compiler—venture investments during that time yielded a 19.3 percent average annual return after fees and expenses. Over the same period, the S&P 500 and the Russell 2000 index of small companies generated average annual returns, respectively, of 15.7 percent and 13.3 percent.

Equity funds are typically conceived, invested, and exited in 8- to 12-year cycles, with preparation for follow-on funds beginning in years 3 and 4. That time frame is largely driven by the reality that, on average, it takes 5 to 7 years to build and harvest a successful portfolio investment.

Successful funds yield a significant financial upside. In the early 2000s, the average total pay packages (salary plus bonus) for managing general partners and senior partners were $1.24 million and $1.04 million, respectively. Carried interest distributions to a general partner of a top firm averaged $2.5 million over a fund's life.

DIAGRAM 6-B

Flows of Venture Capital

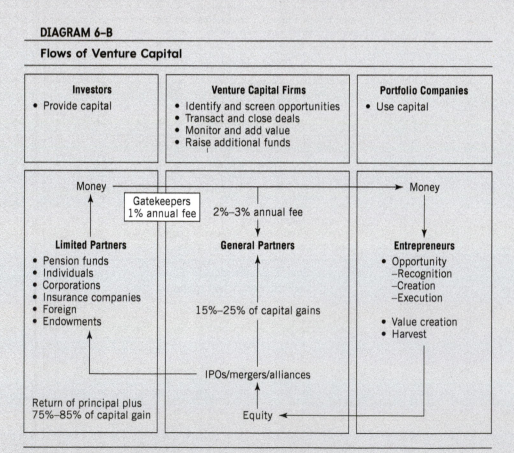

Note: This diagram and additional discussion of venture funding may be found in Chapter 13 of this text.

Chapter Seven

The Business Plan

LEARNING OUTCOMES: After reading this chapter you will be able to understand:

7-1 Why write a business plan?

7-2 Developing the business plan

7-3 Working with investors to add value to the plan

7-4 How to do the plan

7-5 Resources and exercises

Why Do a Business Plan?

Let us put one urban legend to rest–to raise money from a real investor you need a business plan; to embark on a perilous startup journey without serious planning is antithetical to how investors operate. Creating a business plan is a great way for you and your current team to analyze the opportunity while gaining experience working together.

Developing the Business Plan

The business plan itself is the culmination of a usually lengthy, arduous, creative, and iterative process covered in Chapters 5 and 6. The plan will carefully articulate the market, business model, investment requirements, risks, and returns of the opportunity.

The plan is the start of your relationship with investors as they work with the management team to understand the opportunity. Even without outside capital this process and experience is vital. The collisions between founders and investors that occur during meetings, discussions, and investigations reveal a great deal to all parties and begin to set the mood for their relationship and negotiations. Getting to know each other

much more closely is a crucial part of the evaluation process.

The Plan Is Obsolete at the Printer

The authors have argued for three decades that the plan is obsolete the instant it emerges from the printer. The business plan should be thought of as a work in progress which must be completed if you are trying to raise outside capital, attract key advisors, directors, team members, or the like.

Some Tips from the Trenches

The most valuable lessons in preparing a business plan and raising venture capital come from entrepreneurs who have already succeeded in their own endeavors. Tom Huseby is the founder of SeaPoint Ventures outside Seattle and an entrepreneur who raised venture capital as CEO of two telecommunications companies, Innova and Metawave, that exited through public offerings. Tom has some great insight from his own experiences sitting on both sides of the venture capital table–as an entrepreneur and as a VC:

RE: Venture Capitalists

- There are a lot of venture capitalists. Once you meet one you could end up meeting all 700-plus of them.
- Getting a no from venture capitalists is as hard as getting a yes; qualify your targets and force others to say no.
- Be vague when describing other potential venture capitalists.
- Do not ever meet with an associate or junior member twice without also meeting with a partner in that venture capital firm.

RE: The Plan

- Stress your business concept in the executive summary.
- The numbers do not matter; but the economics of the business do.
- Prepare several copies of published articles, contracts, market studies, purchase orders, and the like.
- Prepare very detailed résumés and reference lists of key players in the venture.
- If you cannot do the details, make sure you hire someone who can.

RE: The Deal

- Make sure your current investors are as desperate as you are.
- Create a market for your venture.
- Never say no to an offer price.
- Use a lawyer who is experienced at closing venture deals.
- Do not stop selling until the money is in the bank.
- Make it a challenge.
- Be honest.

RE: The Fund-Raising Process

- It is more difficult than you expect.
- Anticipate the worst and be persistent through the process despite setbacks.

This is a particularly valuable advice for any entrepreneur seeking outside capital and planning to deal with investors.[1]

How to Determine If Investors Can Add Value

The right investors add a great deal of value to the venture through experience, wisdom, and networks, and entrepreneurs can use the fund-raising process to both learn about the kind of value each investor can add and to make their plan more attractive.

Two powerful forces are unleashed in this process. First, as a founder, you will begin to discern just how smart, knowledgeable, and creative the investors are about the proposed business. The second force implicit message to investors when you

ask good questions and listen, rather than become argumentative and defensive.

Who Develops the Business Plan?

Do not hire outsiders to do your plan. Writing the business plan allows the founders to develop their venture at a detailed level. No quality investor will spend time with a team that outsourced this critical exercise.

Segmenting and Integrating Information

All businesses are unique, and there is no fixed outline that will work across all industries. An effective way to organize information is to segment key components into sections, such as the target market, the industry, the competition, the financial plan, and so on, and then integrate the information into a plan.

Establishing Action Steps

The following steps outline how to write a business plan. These action steps are presented in the Business Plan Guide exercise at the end of this chapter.

- *Segmenting information.* An overall plan for the project needs to be devised to include who is responsible for each section as well as important draft deadlines.
- *Creating an overall schedule.* Create a more specific list of tasks; identify priorities and who is responsible for them. Determine when they will be started and completed.
- *Creating an action calendar.* Tasks on the *do* list then need to be placed on a calendar and re-evaluated to be sure the overall schedule works, and everyone understands due dates.
- *Doing the work and writing the plan.* The necessary work needs to be done and the plan written. If the work is done well the plan will be straightforward to put together.

Preparing a Business Plan

A Complete Business Plan

It may seem to an entrepreneur who has completed the exercises in Chapter 6 and spent hours

---

[1]See also W.A. Sahlman, "How to Write a Great Business Plan," *Harvard Business Review*, July–August 1997, pp. 98–108, for an excellent article about business plans.

informally thinking and planning, that jotting down a few things is all that needs to be done. *However, there is a great difference between screening an opportunity and developing a business plan.*

There are two important differences in the way these issues need to be addressed. First, a business plan can have two uses: (1) inducing someone to part with $500,000 to $10 million or more, and (2) guiding the policies and actions of the firm over a number of years. Therefore, strategies and statements need to be well thought out, unambiguous, and capable of being supported.

Exhibit 7.1 is a sample table of contents for a business plan. The information shown is included in most effective business plans and is a good framework to follow. Organizing the material into sections makes dealing with the information more manageable. Also, while the amount of detail and the order of presentation may vary for a particular venture according to its circumstances, most effective business plans contain this information in some form.

EXHIBIT 7.1

Business Plan Table of Contents

I. **EXECUTIVE SUMMARY**
   Description of the Business Concept and the Business Opportunity and Strategy.
   Target Market and Projections.
   Competitive Advantages.
   The Team.
   The Offering.

II. **THE INDUSTRY AND THE COMPANY AND ITS PRODUCT(S) OR SERVICE(S)**
   The Industry.
   The Company and the Concept.
   The Product(s) or Service(s).
   Entry and Growth Strategy.

III. **MARKET RESEARCH AND ANALYSIS**
   Customers.
   Market Size and Trends.
   Competition and Competitive Edges.
   Estimated Market Share and Sales.
   Ongoing Market Evaluation.

IV. **THE ECONOMICS OF THE BUSINESS**
   Gross and Operating Margins.
   Profit Potential and Durability.
   Fixed, Variable, and Semivariable Costs.
   Months to Breakeven.
   Months to Reach Positive Cash Flow.

V. **MARKETING PLAN**
   Overall Marketing Strategy.
   Pricing.
   Sales Tactics.
   Service and Warranty Policies.
   Advertising and Promotion.
   Distribution.

VI. **DESIGN AND DEVELOPMENT PLANS**
   Development Status and Tasks.
   Difficulties and Risks.
   Product Improvement and New Products.
   Costs.
   Proprietary Issues.

VII. **MANUFACTURING AND OPERATIONS PLAN**
   Operating Cycle.
   Geographical Location.
   Facilities and Improvements.
   Strategy and Plans.
   Regulatory and Legal Issues.

VIII. **MANAGEMENT TEAM**
   Organization.
   Key Management Personnel.
   Management Compensation and Ownership.
   Other Investors.
   Employment, Other Agreements, Stock Options, and Bonus Plans.
   Board of Directors.
   Other Shareholders, Rights, and Restrictions.
   Supporting Professional Advisors and Services.

IX. **SUSTAINABILITY AND IMPACT**
   Issues of Sustainability of the Venture.
   Impact on the Environment.
   Impact on the Community and Nation.

X. **OVERALL SCHEDULE**

XI. **CRITICAL RISKS, PROBLEMS, AND ASSUMPTIONS**

XII. **THE FINANCIAL PLAN**
   Actual Income Statements and Balance Sheets.
   Pro Forma Income Statements.
   Pro Forma Balance Sheets.
   Pro Forma Cash Flow Analysis.
   Break-Even Chart and Calculation.
   Cost Control.
   Highlights.

XIII. **PROPOSED COMPANY OFFERING**
   Desired Financing.
   Offering.
   Capitalization.
   Use of Funds.
   Investor's Return.

XIV. **APPENDIXES**

Chapter Summary

- The business plan is more of a process and work in progress than an end in itself.
- Given today's change of pace in all areas affecting an enterprise, the plan is obsolete the moment it emerges from the printer.
- The business plan is a blueprint that helps those involved convert ideas into opportunities, articulate and manage risks and rewards, and set a realistic time schedule.

- The numbers in a business plan do not matter, but the economics of the business model matter enormously.
- The plan is not the business.
- Preparing and presenting the plan to prospective investors is one of the best ways for the team to have a trial marriage, to learn about the venture strategy, and to determine which investors can add the greatest value.

Study Questions

1. What is a business plan, for whom is it prepared, and why?
2. What should a complete business plan include?
3. Who should prepare the business plan?
4. How is the plan used by potential investors, and what are the four anchors they are attempting to validate?
5. What is a dehydrated business plan, and when and why can it be an effective tool?

6. Explain the expression, "The numbers in the plan do not matter."
7. How can entrepreneurs use the business plan process to identify the best team members, directors, and value-added investors?
8. Prepare an outline of a business plan tailored to the specific venture you have in mind.

Internet Resources

http://www.sba.gov/starting_business *Features a "Business Plan Road Map of Success" tutorial.*

http://www.businessplans.org *Helpful resources c/o Business Resource Software.*

Exercise 1
The Business Plan Guide

An Exercise and Framework

This Business Plan Guide follows the order of presentation outlined in Exhibit 7.1. Based on a guide originally developed at Venture Founders Corporation by Leonard E. Smollen and the late Brian Haslett, and on more than 30 years of observing and working with entrepreneurs and actually preparing and evaluating hundreds of plans, it is intended to make this challenging task easier.

There is no single best way to write a business plan; the task will evolve in a way that suits you and your situation. While there are many ways to approach the preparation for and writing of a business plan, it is recommended that you begin with the market research and analysis sections. In writing your plan, you should remember that although one of the important functions of a business plan is to influence investors, rather than

preparing a fancy presentation, you and your team need to prove to yourselves and others that your opportunity is worth pursuing and to construct the means by which you will do it. Gathering information, making hard decisions, and developing plans come first.

The Business Plan Guide shows how to present information succinctly and in a format acceptable to investors. Although it is useful to keep in mind who your audience is and that information not clearly presented will most likely not be used, it also is important not to be concerned just with format. The Business Plan Guide indicates specific issues and shows you what needs to be included in a business plan and why.

You may feel as though you have seen much of this before. You should. The guide is based on the analytical framework described in the book and builds upon the Venture Opportunity Screening Exercises in Chapter 6. If you have not completed the Opportunity Screening Exercises, it is helpful to do so before proceeding.

The Business Plan Guide will allow you to draw on data and analysis developed in the Venture Opportunity Screening Exercises as you prepare your business plan.

As you proceed through the Business Plan Guide, remember that statements need to be supported with data whenever possible. Note also that it is sometimes easier to present data in graphic, visual form. Include the source of all data, the methods and/or assumptions used, and the credentials of people doing research. If data on which a statement is based are available elsewhere in the plan, be sure to reference where.

Remember that the Business Plan Guide is just that—a guide. It is intended to be applicable to a wide range of product and service businesses. Certain critical issues are unique to any industry or market. In the chemical industry, for example, some special issues of significance currently exist, such as increasingly strict regulations at all levels of government concerning the use of chemical products and the operation of processes, diminishing viability of the high capital cost, special-purpose chemical processing plants serving a narrow market, and long delivery times of processing equipment. In the electronics industry, the special issues may be the future availability and price of new kinds of large-scale integrated circuits. Common sense should rule in applying the guide to your specific venture.

The Guide

Name:

Venture:

Date:

STEP I

Segment Information into Key Sections.

Establish priorities for each section, including individual responsibilities and due dates for drafts and the final version. When you segment your information, it is vital to keep in mind that the plan needs to be logically integrated and that information should be consistent. Because the market opportunity section is the heart and soul of the plan, it may be the most difficult section to write; but it is best to assign it a high priority and to begin working there first. Remember to include such tasks as printing in the list.

Section or Task	Priority	Person(s) Responsible	Date to Begin	First Draft Due Date	Date Completed or Final Version Due Date

STEP 2

List Tasks That Need to Be Completed.

Devise an overall schedule for preparing the plan by assigning priorities, persons responsible, and due dates to each task necessary to complete the plan. It is helpful to break larger items (fieldwork to gather customer and competitor intelligence, trade show visits, etc.) into small, more manageable components (such as phone calls required before a trip can be taken), and to include the components as a task. *Be as specific as possible.*

Task	Priority	Person Responsible	Date to Begin	Date of Completion

STEP 3

Combine the List of Segments and the List of Tasks to Create a Calendar.

In combining your lists, consider if anything has been omitted and whether you have been realistic in what people can do, when they can do it, what needs to be done, and so forth. To create your calendar, place an X in the week when the task is to be started and an X in the week it is to be completed and then connect the Xs. When you have placed all tasks on the calendar, look carefully again for conflicts or lack of realism. In particular, evaluate whether team members are overscheduled.

Task	Week														
	1	2	3	4	5	6	7	8	9	10	11	12	13	14	15

STEP 4

A Framework to Develop and Write a Business Plan.
As has been discussed, the framework here follows
the order of presentation of the table of contents
shown in Exhibit 7.1. While preparing your own plan,
you will most likely want to consider sections in a different order from the one presented in this exhibit.
(Also, when you integrate your sections into your final
plan, you may choose to present material somewhat
differently.)

Cover

The cover page includes the name of the company, its
address, its telephone number, the date, and the securities offered. Usually the name, address, telephone
number, and the date are centered at the top of the
page and the securities offered are listed at the bottom. Also suggested on the cover page at the bottom is
the following text:

> This business plan has been submitted on a confidential
> basis solely for the benefit of selected, highly qualified in-
> vestors in connection with the private placement of the
> above securities and is not for use by any other persons.
> Neither may it be reproduced, stored, or copied in any
> form. By accepting delivery of this plan, the recipient
> agrees to return this copy to the corporation at the ad-
> dress listed above if the recipient does not undertake to
> subscribe to the offering. Do not copy, fax, reproduce, or
> distribute without permission.

Table of Contents

Included in the table of contents is a list of the sections, subsections, and any appendixes, and the pages
on which they can be found (Exhibit 7.1).

I. Executive Summary   The first section in the
body of the business plan is usually an executive summary. The summary is usually short and concise (1 or 2
pages). The summary articulates what the opportunity conditions are and why they exist, who will execute the opportunity and why they are capable of
doing so, and how the firm will gain entry and market
penetration—it answers the questions we asked in
Chapter 5: "For *what* reason does this venture exist
and for *whom?*"

Essentially the summary for your venture needs to
mirror the criteria shown in Exhibit 5.6 and the Venture
Opportunity Screening Exercises in Chapter 6. This is
your chance to clearly articulate how your business is
durable and timely, and how it will create or add value
to the buyer or end user.

The summary is usually prepared after the other sections of the business plan are completed. As the other
sections are drafted, it is helpful to note one or two key
sentences and some key facts and numbers from each.

The summary is important for those ventures trying
to raise or borrow money. Many investors, bankers,
managers, and other readers use the summary to
determine quickly whether they find the venture of
interest. Therefore, unless the summary is appealing
and compelling, it may be the only section read, and
you may never get the chance to make a presentation
or discuss your business in person.

Leave plenty of time to prepare the summary.
(Successful public speakers have been known to spend
an hour of preparation for each minute of their speech.)

The executive summary usually contains a paragraph or two covering each of the following:

A. ***Description of the business concept and the business***. Describe the business concept for the business
you are or will be in. Be sure the description of your
concept explains how your product or service will
fundamentally change the way customers currently
do certain things. For example, Arthur Rock, the
lead investor in Apple Computer and Intel, has
stated that he focuses on concepts that will change
the way people live and/or work. You need to identify when the company was formed, what it will do,
what is special or proprietary about its product,
service, or technology, and so forth. Include summary information about any proprietary technology, trade secrets, or unique capabilities that give
you an edge in the marketplace. If the company
has existed for a few years, a brief summary of its
size and progress is in order. Try to make your
description using 25 or fewer words, and briefly
describe the specific product or service.

B. ***The opportunity and strategy***. Summarize what the
opportunity is, why it is compelling, and the entry
strategy planned to exploit it. Clearly state the main
point or benefit you are addressing. This information
may be presented as an outline of the key facts,
conditions, competitors' vulnerabilities ("sleepiness,"
sluggishness, poor service, etc.), industry trends (is it
fragmented or emerging?), and other evidence and
logic that define the opportunity. Note plans for
growth and expansion beyond the entry products or
services and into other market segments (such as
international markets) as appropriate.

C. ***The target market and projections***. Identify and
briefly explain the industry and market, who the
primary customer groups are, how the product(s)
or service(s) will be positioned, and how you plan
to reach and service these groups. Include information about the structure of the market, the size and
growth rate for the market segments or niches you
are seeking, your unit and dollar sales estimates,
your anticipated market share, the payback period
for your customers, and your pricing strategy
(including price vs. performance/value/benefits
considerations).

D. ***The competitive advantages***. Indicate the significant competitive edges you enjoy or can create as
a result of your innovative product, service, and
strategy; advantages in lead time or barriers to
entry; competitors' weaknesses and vulnerabilities;
and other industry conditions.

E. ***The team***. Summarize the relevant knowledge, experience, know-how, and skills of the lead entrepreneur and any team members, noting previous accomplishments, especially those involving profit and loss responsibility and general management and people management experience. Include significant information, such as the size of a division, project, or prior business with which the lead entrepreneur or a team member was the driving force.

F. ***The offering***. Briefly indicate the dollar amount of equity and/or debt financing needed, how much of the company you are prepared to offer for that financing, what principal use will be made of the capital, and how the investor, lender, or strategic partner will achieve its desired rate of return. Remember, your targeted resource provider has a well-defined appetite, and you must understand the "Circle of Venture Capital Ecstasy" (Exhibit 5.1).

II. The Industry and the Company and Its Product(s) or Service(s)

A major area of consideration is the company, its concept for its product(s) and service(s), and its interface with the industry in which it will be competing. This is the context into which the marketing information, for example, fits. Information needs to include a description of the industry, a description of the concept, a description of your company, and a description of the product(s) or service(s) you will offer, the proprietary position of these product(s) or service(s), their potential advantages, and entry and growth strategy for the product(s) or service(s).

A. ***The industry***.

- Present the current status and prospects for the industry in which the proposed business will operate. Be sure to consider industry structure.

- Discuss briefly market size, growth trends, and competitors.

- Discuss any new products or developments, new markets and customers, new requirements, new entrants and exits, and any other national or economic trends and factors that could affect the venture's business positively or negatively.

- Discuss the environmental profile of the industry. Consider energy requirements, supply chain factors, waste generation, and recycling capabilities. Outline any new green technologies or trends that may have an impact on this opportunity.

B. ***The company and the concept***.

- Describe generally the concept of the business, what business your company is in or intends to enter, what product(s) or service(s) it will offer, and who are or will be its principal customers.

- By way of background, give the date your venture was incorporated and describe the identification and development of its products and the involvement of the company's principals in that development.

- If your company has been in business for several years and is seeking expansion financing, review its history and cite its prior sales and profit performance. If your company has had setbacks or losses in prior years, discuss these and emphasize current and future efforts to prevent a recurrence of these difficulties and to improve your company's performance.

C. ***The product(s) or service(s)***.

- Describe in some detail each product or service to be sold.

- Discuss the application of the product or service and describe the primary end use as well as any significant secondary applications. Articulate how you will solve a problem, relieve pain, or provide a benefit or needed service.

- Describe the service or product delivery system.

- Emphasize any unique features of the product or service and how these will create or add significant value; also, highlight any differences between what is currently on the market and what you will offer that will account for your market penetration. Be sure to describe how value will be added and the payback period to the customer—that is, discuss how many months it will take for the customer to cover the initial purchase price of the product or service as a result of its time, cost, or productivity improvements.

- Include a description of any possible drawbacks (including problems with obsolescence) of the product or service.

- Define the present state of development of the product or service and how much time and money will be required to fully develop, test, and introduce the product or service. Provide a summary of the functional specifications and photographs, if available, of the product.

- Discuss any head start you might have that would enable you to achieve a favored or entrenched position in the industry.

- Describe any features of the product or service that give it an "unfair" advantage over the competition. Describe any patents, trade secrets, or other proprietary features of the product or service.

- Discuss any opportunities for the expansion of the product line or the development of related products or services. (Emphasize opportunities and explain how you will take advantage of them.)

D. *Entry and growth strategy.*

- Indicate key success variables in your market-ing plan (e.g., an innovative product, timing advantage, or marketing approach) and your pricing, channel(s) of distribution, advertising, and promotion plans.

- Summarize how fast you intend to grow and to what size during the first 5 years and your plans for growth beyond your initial product or service.

- Show how the entry and growth strategy is derived from the opportunity and value-added or other competitive advantages, such as the weakness of competitors.

- Discuss the overall environmental and social sustainability of your growth plan. Consider the effect on the community if the growth strategy involves offshore manufacturing or outsourced labor.

III. Market Research and Analysis

Information in this section needs to support the assertion that the venture can capture a substantial market in a growing industry and stand up to competition. Because of the importance of market analysis and the critical dependence of other parts of the plan on this information, you are advised to prepare this section of the business plan before any other. Take enough time to do this section very well and to check alternative sources of market data.

This section of the business plan is one of the most difficult to prepare, yet it is one of the most important. Other sections of the business plan depend on the market research and analysis presented here. For example, the predicted sales levels directly influence such factors as the size of the manufacturing operation, the marketing plan, and the amount of debt and equity capital you will require. Most entrepreneurs seem to have great difficulty preparing and presenting market research and analyses that show that their ventures' sales estimates are sound and attainable.

A. *Customers.*

- Discuss who the customers for the product(s) or service(s) are or will be. Note that potential customers need to be classified by relatively homo-geneous groups having common, identifiable characteristics (e.g., by major market segment). For example, an automotive part might be sold to manufacturers and to parts distributors sup-plying the replacement market, so the discus-sion needs to reflect two market segments.

- Show who and where the major purchasers for the product(s) or service(s) are in each market segment. Include national regions and foreign countries, as appropriate.

- Indicate whether customers are easily reached and receptive, how customers buy (wholesale, through manufacturers' representatives, etc.), where in their organizations buying decisions are made, and how long decisions take. Describe customers' purchasing processes, including the bases on which they make pur-chase decisions (e.g., price, quality, timing, delivery, training, service, personal contacts, or political pressures) and why they might change current purchasing decisions.

- List any orders, contracts, or letters of com-mitment that you have in hand. These are the most powerful data you can provide. List also any potential customers who have expressed an interest in the product(s) or service(s) and indicate why. Also list any potential customers who have shown no interest in the proposed product or service, and explain why they are not interested and explain what you will do to overcome nega-tive customer reaction. Indicate how fast you believe your product or service will be accepted in the market.

- If you have an existing business, list your princi-pal current customers and discuss the trends in your sales to them.

B. *Market size and trends.*

- Show for 5 years the size of the current total market and the share you will have, by market segment, and/or region, and/or country, for the product or service you will offer, in units, dollars, and potential profitability.

- Describe also the potential annual growth for at least 3 years of the total market for your product(s) or service(s) for each major cus-tomer group, region, or country, as appropriate.

- Discuss the major factors affecting market growth (e.g., industry trends, socioeconomic trends, government policy, environmental impacts, and population shifts) and review pre-vious trends in the market. Any differences between past and projected annual growth rates need to be explained.

C. *Competition and competitive edges.*

- Make a realistic assessment of the strengths and weaknesses of competitors. Assess the sub-stitute and/or alternative products and services and list the companies that supply them, both domestic and foreign, as appropriate.

- Compare competing and substitute products or services on the basis of market share, quality, price, performance, delivery, timing, service, warranties, and other pertinent features.

- Compare the fundamental value that is added or created by your product or service, in terms of economic benefits to the customer and to your competitors.

- Discuss the current advantages and disadvantages of these products and services and say why they are not meeting customer needs.

- Indicate any knowledge of competitors' actions that could lead you to new or improved products and an advantageous position. For example, discuss whether competitors are simply sluggish or nonresponsive or are asleep at the switch.

- Identify the strengths and weaknesses of the competing companies and determine and discuss each competitor's market share, sales, distribution methods, and production capabilities.

- Review the financial position, resources, costs, and profitability of the competition and their profit trends. Note that you can utilize Robert Morris Associates data for comparison.

- Indicate who are the service, pricing, performance, cost, and quality leaders. Discuss why any companies have entered or dropped out of the market in recent years.

- Discuss the three or four key competitors and why customers buy from them, and determine and discuss why customers leave them. Relate this to the basis for the purchase decision examined in IIIA.

- From what you know about the competitors' operations, explain why you think they are vulnerable and you can capture a share of their business. Discuss what makes you think it will be easy or difficult to compete with them. Discuss, in particular, your competitive advantages gained through such "unfair" advantage as patents.

D. *Estimated market share and sales.*

- Summarize what it is about your product(s) or service(s) that will make it salable in the face of current and potential competition. Mention, especially, the fundamental value added or created by the product(s) or service(s).

- Identify any major customers (including international customers) who are willing to make, or who have already made, purchase commitments. Indicate the extent of those commitments, and why they were made. Discuss which customers could be major purchasers in future years and why.

- Based on your assessment of the advantages of your product or service, the market size and

trends, customers, competition and their products, and the trends of sales in prior years, estimate the share of the market and the sales in units and dollars that you will acquire in each of the next 3 years. Remember to show assumptions used.

- Show how the growth of the company sales in units and its estimated market share are related to the growth of the industry, the customers, and the strengths and weaknesses of competitors. Remember, the assumptions used to estimate market share and sales need to be clearly stated.

- If yours is an existing business, also indicate the total market, your market share, and sales for 2 prior years.

E. *Ongoing market evaluation.*

- Explain how you will continue to evaluate your target markets; assess customer needs and service; guide product improvement, pricing, and new product programs; plan for expansions of your production facility; and guide product/service pricing.

IV. The Economics of the Business   The economic and financial characteristics, including the apparent magnitude and durability of margins and profits generated, need to support the fundamental attractiveness of the opportunity. The underlying operating and cash conversion cycle of the business, the value chain, and so forth need to make sense in terms of the opportunity and strategies planned.

A. *Gross and operating margins.*

- Describe the magnitude of the gross margins (i.e., selling price less variable costs) and the operating margins for each of the product(s) and/or service(s) you are selling in the market niche(s) you plan to attack. Include results of your contribution analysis.

B. *Profit potential and durability.*

- Describe the magnitude and expected durability of the profit stream the business will generate—before and after taxes—and reference appropriate industry benchmarks, other competitive intelligence, or your own relevant experience.

- Address the issue of how perishable or durable the profit stream appears to be. Provide reasons why your profit stream is perishable or durable, such as barriers to entry you can create, your technological and market lead time, and environmental sustainability, which in some cases can be a driver for cost reduction.

C. *Fixed, variable, and semivariable costs.*

- Provide a detailed summary of fixed, variable, and semivariable costs, in dollars and as percentages of total cost as appropriate, for the product or service you offer and the volume of purchases and sales upon which these are based.

- Show relevant industry benchmarks.

D. *Months to breakeven.*

- Given your entry strategy, marketing plan, and proposed financing, show how long it will take to reach a unit breakeven sales level.

- Note any significant stepwise changes in your breakeven that will occur as you grow and add substantial capacity.

E. *Months to reach positive cash flow.**

- Given the above strategy and assumptions, show when the venture will attain a positive cash flow.

- Show if and when you will run out of cash. Note where the detailed assumptions can be found.

- Note any significant stepwise changes in cash flow that will occur as you grow and add capacity.

V. Marketing Plan   The marketing plan describes how the sales projections will be attained. The marketing plan needs to detail the overall marketing strategy that will exploit the opportunity and your competitive advantages. Include a discussion of sales and service policies; pricing, distribution, promotion, and advertising strategies; and sales projections. The marketing plan needs to describe *what is* to be done, *how* it will be done, *when* it will be done, and *who* will do it.

A.   *Overall marketing strategy.*

- Describe the specific marketing philosophy and strategy of the company, given the value chain and channels of distribution in the market niche(s) you are pursuing. Include, for example, a discussion of the kinds of customer groups that you already have orders from or that will be targeted for initial intensive selling effort and those targeted for later selling efforts; how specific potential customers in these groups will be identified and how they will be contacted; what features of the product or service, such as service, quality, price, delivery, warranty, or training, will be emphasized to generate sales; if any innovative or unusual marketing concepts will enhance customer acceptance, such as leasing where only sales were previously attempted; and so forth.

- Indicate whether the product(s) or service(s) will initially be introduced internationally, nationally, or regionally; explain why; and if appropriate, indicate any plans for extending sales later.

- Discuss any seasonal trends that underlie the cash conversion cycle in the industry and what can be done to promote sales out of season.

- Describe any plans to obtain government contracts as a means of supporting product development costs and overhead.

B.   *Pricing.*

- Discuss pricing strategy, including the prices to be charged for your product and service, and compare your pricing policy with those of your major competitors, including a brief discussion of payback (in months) to the customer.

- Discuss the gross profit margin between manufacturing and ultimate sales costs, and indicate whether this margin is large enough to allow for distribution and sales, warranty, training, service, amortization of development and equipment costs, price competition, and so forth, and still allow a profit.

- Explain how the price you set will enable you to (1) get the product or service accepted, (2) maintain and increase your market share in the face of competition, and (3) produce profits.

- Justify your pricing strategy and differences between your prices and those for competitive or substitute products or services in terms of economic payback to the customer and value added through newness, quality, warranty, timing, performance, service, cost savings, efficiency, and the like.

- If your product is to be priced lower than those of the competition, explain how you will do this and maintain profitability (e.g., through greater value added via effectiveness in manufacturing and distribution, lower labor costs, lower material costs, lower overhead, or other cost component).

- Discuss your pricing policy, including a discussion of the relationship of price, market share, and profits.

C.   *Sales tactics.*

- Describe the methods (e.g., own sales force, sales representatives, ready-made manufacturers' sales organizations, direct mail, or distributors) that will be used to make sales and distribute the product or service and both the initial plans and longer-range plans for a sales force. Include a discussion of any special requirements (e.g., refrigeration).

- Discuss the value chain and the resulting margins to be given to retailers, distributors, wholesalers, and salespeople and any special policies regarding discounts, exclusive distribution rights, and so on given to distributors or sales representatives, and compare these to those given by your competition. (See the Venture Opportunity Screening Guide Exercises.)

- Describe how distributors or sales representatives, if they are used, will be selected, when they will start to represent you, the areas they will cover and the head count of dealers and representatives by month, and the expected sales to be made by each.

- If a direct sales force is to be used, indicate how it will be structured and at what rate (a head count) it will be built up; indicate if it is to replace a dealer or representative organization and, if so, when and how.

- If direct mail, magazine, newspaper, or other media, telemarketing, or catalog sales are to be used, indicate the specific channels or vehicles, costs (per 1,000), expected response rates, and so on. Discuss how these will be built up.

- Show the sales expected per salesperson per year and what commission, incentive, and/or salary they are slated to receive, and compare these figures to the average for your industry.

- Present a selling schedule and a sales budget that includes all marketing promotion and service costs.

D. *Service and warranty policies.*

- If your company will offer a product that will require service, warranties, or training, indicate the importance of these to the customers' purchasing decisions and discuss your method of handling service problems.

- Describe the kind and term of any warranties to be offered; whether service will be handled by company service people, agencies, dealers and distributors; or returns to the factory.

- Indicate the proposed charge for service calls and whether service will be a profitable or breakeven operation.

- Compare your service, warranty, and customer training policies and practices to those of your principal competitors.

E. *Advertising and promotion.*

- Describe the approaches the company will use to bring its product or service to the attention of prospective purchasers.

- For original equipment manufacturers and for manufacturers of industrial products, indicate the plans for trade show participation, trade magazine advertisements, direct mailings, the preparation of product sheets and promotional literature, and use of advertising agencies.

- For consumer products, indicate what kind of advertising and promotional campaign will introduce the product, including sales aids to dealers, trade shows, and so forth.

- Present a schedule and approximate costs of promotion and advertising (direct mail, telemarketing, catalogs, etc.), and discuss how these costs will be incurred.

F. *Distribution.*

- Describe the methods and channels of distribution you will employ. Discuss the availability and capacity of these channels.

- Indicate the sensitivity of shipping cost as a percentage of the selling price.

- Note any special issues or problems that need to be resolved or present potential vulnerabilities.

- If international sales are involved, note how these sales will be handled, including distribution, shipping, insurance, credit, and collections.

VI. Design and Development Plans   The nature and extent of any design and development work and the time and money required before a product or service is marketable need to be considered in detail. (Note that design and development costs are often underestimated.) Design and development might be the engineering work necessary to convert a laboratory prototype to a finished product; the design of special tooling; the work of an industrial designer to make a product more attractive and salable; or the identification and organization of employees, equipment, and special techniques, such as equipment, new computer software, and skills required for computerized credit checking, to implement a service business.

A. *Development status and tasks.*

- Describe the current status of each product or service and explain what remains to be done to make it marketable.

- Describe briefly the competence or expertise that your company has or will require to complete this development.

- List any customers or end users who are participating in the development, design, and/or testing of the product or service. Indicate results to date or when results are expected.

B. *Difficulties and risks.*

- Identify any major anticipated design and development problems and define approaches to their solution.

- Discuss the possible effect on the cost of design and development, on the time to market introduction, and so forth, of such problems.

C. *Product improvement and new products.*

- In addition to describing the development of the initial products, discuss any ongoing design and development work that is planned to keep the product(s) or service(s) that can be sold to the same group of customers. Discuss customers who have participated in these efforts and their reactions, and include any evidence that you may have.

- With regard to ongoing product development, outline any compliance issues relating to new, pending, or potential environmental legislation.

D. *Costs.*

- Present and discuss the design and development budget, including costs of labor, materials, consulting fees, and so on.

- Discuss the impact on cash flow projections of underestimating this budget, including the impact of a 15 percent to 30 percent contingency.

E. *Proprietary issues.*

- Describe any patent, trademark, copyright, or intellectual property rights you own or are seeking.

- Describe any contractual rights or agreements that give you exclusivity or proprietary rights.

- Discuss the impact of any unresolved issues or existing or possible actions pending, such as disputed rights of ownership, relating to proprietary rights on timing and on any competitive edge you have assumed.

VII. Manufacturing and Operations Plan

The manufacturing and operations plan needs to include such factors as plant location, the type of facilities needed, space requirements, capital equipment requirements, and labor force (both full- and part-time) requirements. For a manufacturing business, the manufacturing and operations plan needs to include policies on inventory control, purchasing, production control, and which parts of the product will be purchased and which operations will be performed by your workforce (called make-or-buy decisions). A service business may require particular attention to location (proximity to customers is generally a must), minimizing overhead, and obtaining competitive productivity from a labor force.

A. *Operating cycle.*

- Describe the lead/lag times that characterize the fundamental operating cycle in your business.

(Include a graph similar to the one found in the Venture Opportunity Screening Exercises.)

- Explain how any seasonal production loads will be handled without severe dislocation (e.g., by building to inventory or using part-time help in peak periods).

B. *Geographical location.*

- Describe the planned geographical location of the business. Include any location analysis, and so on, that you have done.

- Discuss any advantages or disadvantages of the site location in terms of labor (including labor availability, whether workers are unionized, wage rates, and outsourcing), closeness to customers and/or suppliers, access to transportation, state and local taxes and laws (including zoning and environmental impact regulations), access to utilities (energy use and sustainability), and so forth.

C. *Facilities and improvements.*

- For an existing business, describe the facilities, including plant and office space, storage and land areas, special tooling, machinery, and other capital equipment currently used to conduct the company's business, and discuss whether these facilities are adequate and in compliance with health, safety, and environmental regulations. Discuss any economies of scale.

- For a startup, describe how and when the necessary facilities to start production will be acquired.

- Discuss whether equipment and space will be leased or acquired (new or used) and indicate the costs and timing of such actions and how much of the proposed financing will be devoted to plant and equipment.

- Explain future equipment needs in the next 3 years.

- For startups expecting to outsource manufacturing, indicate the location and size of the firm, and discuss the advantages, risks, and monitoring regime.

- Discuss how and when, in the next 3 years, plant space and equipment will be expanded and capacities required by future sales projections and any plans to improve or add existing plant space. Discuss any environmental impacts related to those expansion requirements. If there are any plans to move the facility, outsource labor, or move production overseas, discuss the impact on the local community. Indicate the timing and cost of such acquisitions.

D. *Strategy and plans.*

- Describe the manufacturing processes involved in production of your product(s) and any decisions with respect to subcontracting of component parts, rather than complete in-house manufacture.

- Justify your proposed make-or-buy policy in terms of inventory financing, available labor skills, and other nontechnical questions, as well as production, cost, and capability issues.

- Discuss which potential subcontractors and/or suppliers are likely to be and any information about, or any surveys that have been made of, these subcontractors and suppliers.

- Present a production plan that shows cost/volume/inventory level information at various sales levels of operation with breakdowns of applicable material, labor, purchased components, and factory overhead.

- Describe your approach to quality control, production control, and inventory control; explain what quality control and inspection procedures the company will use to minimize service problems and associated customer dissatisfaction.

E. *Regulatory and legal issues.*

- Discuss any relevant state, federal, or foreign regulatory requirements unique to your product, process, or service such as licenses, zoning permits, health permits, and environmental approvals necessary to begin operation.

- Note any pending regulatory changes that can affect the nature of your opportunity and its timing.

- Discuss any legal or contractual obligations that are pertinent as well.

VIII. Management Team This section of the business plan includes a description of the functions that will need to be filled, a description of the key management personnel and their primary duties, an outline of the organizational structure for the venture, a description of the board of directors, a description of the ownership position of any other investors, and so forth. You need to present indications of commitment, such as the willingness of team members to initially accept modest salaries, and of the existence of the proper balance of technical, managerial, and business skills and experience in doing what is proposed.

A. *Organization.*

- Present the key management roles in the company and the individuals who will fill each position. (If the company is established and of sufficient size, an organization chart needs to be appended.)

- If it is not possible to fill each executive role with a full-time person without adding excessive overhead, indicate how these functions will be performed (e.g., using part-time specialists or consultants to perform some functions), who will perform them, and when they will be replaced by a full-time staff member.

- If any key individuals will not be on board at the start of the venture, indicate when they will join the company.

- Discuss any current or past situations where key management people have worked together that could indicate how their skills complement each other and result in an effective management team.

B. *Key management personnel.*

- For each key person, describe in detail career highlights, particularly relevant know-how, skills, and track record of accomplishments, that demonstrate his or her ability to perform the assigned role. Include in your description sales and profitability achievements (budget size, number of subordinates, new product introductions, etc.) and other prior entrepreneurial or general management results.

- Describe the exact duties and responsibilities of each of the key members of the management team.

- Complete résumés for each key management member need to be included here or as an exhibit and need to stress relevant training, experience, and concrete accomplishments, such as profit and sales improvement, labor management success, manufacturing or technical achievements, and meeting budgets and schedules.

C. *Management compensation and ownership.*

- State the salary to be paid, the stock ownership planned, and the amount of equity investment (if any) of each key member of the management team.

- Compare the compensation of each key member to the salary he or she received at his or her last independent job.

D. *Other investors.*

- Describe here any other investors in your venture, the number and percentage of outstanding shares they own, when they were acquired, and at what price.

E. *Employment and other agreements and stock option and bonus plans.*

- Describe any existing or contemplated employment or other agreements with key members.

- Indicate any restrictions on stock and investing that affect ownership and disposition of stock.

- Describe any performance-dependent stock option or bonus plans.

- Summarize any incentive stock option or other stock ownership plans anticipated or in effect for key people and employees.

F. *Board of directors.*

- Discuss the company's philosophy about the size and composition of the board.

- Identify any proposed board members and include a one- or two-sentence statement of each member's background that shows what he or she can bring to the company.

G. *Other shareholders, rights, and restrictions.*

- Indicate any other shareholders in your company and any rights, restrictions, or obligations, such as notes or guarantees, associated with these. (If they have all been accounted for previously, simply note that there are no others.)

H. *Supporting professional advisors and services.*

- Indicate the supporting services that will be required.

- Indicate the names and affiliations of the legal, accounting, advertising, consulting, and banking advisors selected for your venture and the services each will provide.

IX. Sustainability and Impact
This section should address the social, economic, and environmental sustainability of your business model. Because customers (and investors) are increasingly interested in supporting companies that are proactive with regard to these issues, building a sustainable, socially responsible venture from the start can have competitive as well as economic advantages.

- Outline any environmental issues related to your business with regard to resources, waste generation, and legislative compliance.

- Discuss the nature of any opportunities for green impact, such as carbon reduction, recycling, and any green technologies or production capabilities that could enhance sustainability.

- Describe the nature of subcontractors and suppliers you plan to do business with.

- Describe any sustainability advantages you have or can develop, and how these might relate to building customer loyalty and community support for your product(s) or service(s).

- Summarize the employment opportunities that your business is likely to create, and describe any plans for outsourcing or using offshore labor and how that might impact the community and your labor pool.

- Examine the potential environmental impact of your business as it grows.

X. Overall Schedule
A schedule that shows the timing and inter-relationship of the major events necessary to launch the venture and realize its objectives is an essential part of a business plan. The underlying cash conversion and operating cycle of the business will provide key inputs for the schedule. In addition to being a planning aid, by showing deadlines critical to a venture's success, a well-presented schedule can be extremely valuable in convincing potential investors that the management team is able to plan for venture growth in a way that recognizes obstacles and minimizes investor risk. Because the time to do things tends to be underestimated in most business plans, it is important to demonstrate that you have correctly estimated these amounts in determining the schedule. Create your schedule as follows:

1. Lay out (use a bar chart) the cash conversion cycle of the business for each product or service expected, the lead and elapsed times from an order to the purchase of raw materials, or inventory to shipping and collection.

2. Prepare a month-by-month schedule that shows the timing of product development, market planning, sales programs, production, and operations, and that includes sufficient detail to show the timing of the primary tasks required to accomplish an activity.

3. Show on the schedule the deadlines or milestones critical to the venture's success, such as these:

   - Incorporation of the venture.
   - Completion of design and development.
   - Completion of prototypes.
   - Obtaining sales representatives.
   - Obtaining product display at trade shows.
   - Signing distributors and dealers.
   - Ordering materials in production quantities.
   - Starting production or operation.
   - Receipt of first orders.
   - Delivery on first sale.
   - Receiving the first payment on accounts receivable.

4. Show on the schedule the "ramp-up" of the number of management personnel, the number of production and operations personnel, and plant or equipment and their relation to the development of the business.

5. Discuss in a general way the activities most likely to cause a schedule slippage, what steps will be

taken to correct such slippages, and the impact of schedule slippages on the venture's operation, especially its potential viability and capital needs.

XI. Critical Risks, Problems, and Assumptions

The development of a business has risks and problems, and the business plan invariably contains some implicit assumptions about them. You need to include a description of the risks and the consequences of adverse outcomes relating to your industry, your company and its personnel, your product's market appeal, and the timing and financing of your startup. Be sure to discuss assumptions concerning sales projections, customer orders, and so forth. If the venture has anything that could be considered a fatal flaw, discuss why it is not. The discovery of any unstated negative factors by potential investors can undermine the credibility of the venture and endanger its financing. Be aware that most investors will read the section describing the management team first and then this section.

Do not omit this section. If you do, the reader will most likely come to one or more of the following conclusions:

1. You think he or she is incredibly naive or stupid, or both.

2. You hope to pull the wool over his or her eyes.

3. You do not have enough objectivity to recognize and deal with assumptions and problems.

Identifying and discussing the risks in your venture demonstrate your skills as a manager and increase the credibility of you and your venture with a venture capital investor or a private investor. Taking the initiative on the identification and discussion of risks helps you to demonstrate to the investor that you have thought about them and can handle them. Risks then tend not to loom as large black clouds in the investor's thinking about your venture.

1. Discuss the assumptions and risks implicit in your plan.

2. Identify and discuss any major problems and other risks, such as these:

    ▪ Running out of cash *before* orders are secured.

    ▪ Potential price cutting by competitors.

    ▪ Any potentially unfavorable industry trends.

    ▪ Design or manufacturing costs in excess of estimates.

    ▪ Sales projections not achieved.

    ▪ An unmet product development schedule.

    ▪ Difficulties or long lead times encountered in the procurement of parts or raw materials.

    ▪ Difficulties encountered in obtaining needed bank credit.

    ▪ Larger-than-expected innovation and development costs.

    ▪ Running out of cash *after* orders pour in.

3. Indicate what assumptions or potential problems and risks are most critical to the success of the venture, and describe your plans for minimizing the impact of unfavorable developments in each case.

XII. The Financial Plan

The financial plan is basic to the evaluation of an investment opportunity and needs to represent your best estimates of financial requirements. The purpose of the financial plan is to indicate the venture's potential and to present a timetable for financial viability. It also can serve as an operating plan for financial management using financial benchmarks. In preparing the financial plan, you need to look creatively at your venture and consider alternative ways of launching or financing it.

As part of the financial plan, financial exhibits need to be prepared. To estimate cash flow needs, use cash-based, rather than accrual-based, accounting (i.e., use a real-time cash flow analysis of expected receipts and disbursements). This analysis needs to cover 3 years, including current- and prior-year income statements and balance sheets, if applicable; profit and loss forecasts for 3 years; pro forma income statements and balance sheets; and a breakeven chart. On the appropriate exhibits, or in an attachment, specify assumptions behind such items as sales levels and growth, collections and payables periods, inventory requirements, cash balances, and cost of goods. Your analysis of the operating and cash conversion cycle in the business will enable you to identify these critical assumptions.

Pro forma income statements are the plan-for-profit part of financial management and can indicate the potential financial feasibility of a new venture. Because usually the level of profits, particularly during the startup years of a venture, will not be sufficient to finance operating asset needs, and because actual cash inflows do not always match the actual cash outflows on a short-term basis, a cash flow forecast indicating these conditions and enabling management to plan cash needs is recommended. Further, pro forma balance sheets are used to detail the assets required to support the projected level of operations and, through liabilities, to show how these assets are to be financed. The projected balance sheets can indicate if debt-to-equity ratios, working capital, current ratios, inventory turnover, and the like are within the acceptable limits required to justify future financings that are projected for the venture. Finally, a breakeven chart showing the level of sales and production that will cover all costs, including those costs that vary with production level and those that do not, is very useful.

A. ***Actual income statements and balance sheets.*** For an existing business, prepare income statements and balance sheets for the current year and for the prior 2 years.

B. *Pro forma income statements.*

- Using sales forecasts and the accompanying production or operations costs, prepare pro forma income statements for at least the first 3 years.

- Fully discuss assumptions (e.g., the amount allowed for bad debts and discounts, or any assumptions made with respect to sales expenses or general and administrative costs being a fixed percentage of costs or sales) made in preparing the pro forma income statement and document them.

- Draw on Section XI of the business plan and highlight any major risks, such as the effect of a 20 percent reduction in sales from those projected or the adverse impact of having to climb a learning curve on the level of productivity over time, that could prevent the venture's sales and profit goals from being attained, plus the sensitivity of profits to these risks.

C. *Pro forma balance sheets.* Prepare pro forma balance sheets semiannually in the first year and at the end of each of the first 3 years of operation.

D. *Pro forma cash flow analysis.*

- Project cash flows monthly for the first year of operation and quarterly for at least the next 2 years. Detail the amount and timing of expected cash inflows and outflows. Determine the need for and timing of additional financing and indicate peak requirements for working capital. Indicate how necessary additional financing is to be obtained, such as through equity financing, bank loans, or short-term lines of credit from banks, on what terms, and how it is to be repaid. Remember that these numbers are based on cash, not accrual, accounting.

- Discuss assumptions, such as those made on the timing of collection of receivables, trade discounts given, terms of payments to vendors, planned salary and wage increases, anticipated increases in any operating expenses, seasonality characteristics of the business as they affect inventory requirements, inventory turnovers per year, capital equipment purchases, and so forth. Again, these are real time (i.e., cash), not accruals.

- Discuss cash flow sensitivity to a variety of assumptions about business factors (e.g., possible changes in such crucial assumptions as an increase in the receivable collection period or a sales level lower than that forecast).

E. *Breakeven chartx*

- Calculate breakeven and prepare a chart that shows when breakeven will be reached and any stepwise changes in breakeven that may occur.

- Discuss the breakeven shown for your venture and whether it will be easy or difficult to attain, including a discussion of the size of breakeven sales volume relative to projected total sales, the size of gross margins and price sensitivity, and how the breakeven point might be lowered in case the venture falls short of sales projections.

F. *Cost control.* Describe how you will obtain information about report costs and how often, who will be responsible for the control of various cost elements, and how you will take action on budget overruns.

G. *Highlights.* Highlight the important conclusions, including the maximum amount and timing of cash required, the amount of debt and equity needed, how fast any debts can be repaid, and so forth.

XIII. Proposed Company Offering

The purpose of this section of the plan is to indicate the amount of money that is being sought, the nature and amount of the securities offered to investors, a brief description of the uses that will be made of the capital raised, and a summary of how the investor is expected to achieve its targeted rate of return. It is recommended that you read the discussion about financing in Part IV.

The terms for financing your company that you propose here are the first steps in the negotiation process with those interested in investing, and it is very possible that your financing will involve different kinds of securities than originally proposed.

A. *Desired financing.* Based on your real-time cash flow projections and your estimate of how much money is required over the next 3 years to carry out the development and/or expansion of your business as described, indicate how much of this capital requirement will be obtained by this offering and how much will be obtained via term loans and lines of credit.

B. *Offering.*

- Describe the type (e.g., common stock, convertible debentures, debt with warrants, debt plus stock), unit price, and total amount of securities to be sold in this offering. If securities are not just common stock, indicate by type, interest, maturity, and conversion conditions.

- Show the percentage of the company that the investors of this offering will hold after it is completed or after exercise of any stock conversion or purchase rights in the case of convertible debentures or warrants.

- Securities sold through a private placement and that therefore are exempt from SEC registration should include the following statement in this part of the plan:

The shares being sold pursuant to this offering are restricted securities and may not be resold readily. The prospective investor should recognize that such securities might be restricted as to resale for an indefinite period of time. Each purchaser will be required to execute a Nondistribution Agreement satisfactory in form to corporate counsel.

C.   *Capitalization.*

- Present in tabular form the current and proposed (postoffering) number of outstanding shares of common stock. Indicate any shares offered by key management people and show the number of shares that they will hold after completion of the proposed financing.

- Indicate how many shares of your company's common stock will remain authorized but unissued after the offering and how many of these will be reserved for stock options for future key employees.

D.   *Use of funds.* Investors like to know how their money is going to be spent. Provide a brief description of how the capital raised will be used. Summarize as specifically as possible what amount will be used for such things as product design and development, capital equipment, marketing, and general working capital needs.

E.   *Investors' return.* Indicate how your valuation and proposed ownership shares will result in the desired rate of return for the investors you have targeted and what the likely harvest or exit mechanism (IPO, outright sale, merger, MBO, etc.) will be.

XIV. Appendixes   Include pertinent information here that is too extensive for the body of the business plan but that is necessary (product specs or photos; lists of references, suppliers of critical components; special location factors, facilities, or technical analyses; reports from consultants or technical experts; and copies of any critical regulatory approval, licenses, etc.).

STEP 5

Integrate Sections.
Integrate the discrete sections you have created into a coherent business plan that can be used for the purpose for which it was created.

STEP 6

Get Feedback.
Once written, it is recommended that you get the plan reviewed. No matter how good you and your team are, you will most likely overlook issues and treat aspects of your venture in a manner that is less than clear. A good reviewer can give you the benefit of an outside objective evaluation. Your attorney can make sure that there are no misleading statements in your plan and that it contains all the caveats and the like.

The Virtual Brain Trust

Finding the right date or partner for life is a daunting challenge. Everyone agrees that certain chemistry can make or break a relationship. This is certainly true in new ventures. Today all the various social networking Web sites and the worldwide connectivity of the Internet have opened up vast new opportunities to identify and build the most important part of the external team—the venture's brain trust. As you have seen (and will continue to see) in the text, cases, and discussions, ventures rarely succeed in isolation. Invariably there are one or a few external mentors, advisors (who are often also investors), coaches, and sources of great knowledge, insights, and contacts the venture desperately needs but does not have. Members of your brain trust must be direct and honest and have your best interests at heart. These can be very valuable individuals.

Consider the following example. In 1994 Gary Mueller and his brother George, both still in graduate school and in their 20s, were developing a business plan to launch a company they would call Internet Securities, Inc. (www.internetsecurities.com). Begun as a course project, their venture sought to develop a subscription service to provide financial, stock and bond market, economic, and related information—first from Poland and Russia and later from other emerging markets—all delivered over the Internet. The talented, motivated, and very entrepreneurial brothers had some good contacts, but this was their first serious venture, and there were many things they knew they did not know. One basic issue was how to package, price, and sell this new service to clients such as investment banks, commercial banks, financial service firms, large accounting firms, and the like. The core question they asked was this: Who knows more about this than anyone in the world?

That is the key question to ask as you begin your search for potential members of your own brain trust. In the case of the Muellers, Professor Timmons knew the founder of what became First Call: Jeff Parker, who had created a new venture in the early 1980s that put the first desktop computer (an Apple II) on the desks of bond traders on Wall Street. This highly successful company led to other new ventures and a wealth of knowledge, networks, and experience in this market. Connecting the Muellers with Parker made a number of key results occur. For one thing, Parker agreed to invest $1 million and become chairman of the board. This was a great asset for the company because of the know-how and credibility he brought to the venture. It also meant that the Muellers were able to conserve equity by not having to raise venture capital. A venture capitalist wanted to invest more money, but for a controlling interest of the venture; Parker asked for 25 percent. This seasoned entrepreneur also knew the best people in the business from a sales perspective and was able to recruit his former national sales manager to ISI. This made a huge difference—early on with pricing and selling strategies, and later in achieving early revenue targets.

You can see here the potential and importance of the external brain trust. This exercise will help you to begin to identify and connect with potential brain trust advisors who can become invaluable to your venture's success.

STEP 1

Identify and List the Gaps at This Stage of the Venture.

Applying the Timmons Model to your opportunity and potential venture has put a zoom lens on each critical aspect of your venture—the opportunity, the resources, and the team (internal and external)—and has revealed important gaps and the extent of the fit in the venture. Remember, many gaps are uncovered by an honest assessment of the confidence you have in the critical assumptions you have made in your plan; the weaker your confidence, the greater the need for brain trust support. These missing pieces in the puzzle will point to the facts, people, information, access, insights, and the like that your venture needs and that no team members currently possess; without these pieces, the venture will likely fail; with them, the odds for success rise. Make a list of these critical gaps and needs.

STEP 2

Think: Who Knows What We Do not?

This step will draw on your personal networks. With the Internet you can articulate carefully what expertise/knowledge/experience you are looking for, and then start asking the people you know, who can eventually lead you to a source. Networking sites such as Facebook, MySpace, and LinkedIn can be especially fruitful search platforms. Match this list of potential brain trust members to the list of critical gaps and needs.

STEP 3

Revisit Step 1 as the Venture Develops.

During the course, as you work on your business plan, you can apply this method to various aspects of your zoom lens. Dive into the nuances of the opportunity, the team, and the minimal required resources you need to improve the fit by filling the gaps and managing risk and reward. Much will change as your idea evolves into a bona fide opportunity and then into a live venture: attracting key team members, valuing the business, raising capital, structuring and negotiating the deal, and other key negotiations with key hires and suppliers. Trying to learn all the things necessary to succeed the first time by doing it all yourself is a high-risk, high-tuition path that will delight your competitors! Reaching out to connect with people who can help you the most makes a huge difference—and is clearly one of the most vital entrepreneurial competencies.

A Cautionary Word: Scammers and Predators

Unfortunately the Internet has its share of scammers and predators. Be vigilant and thorough in checking out potential contacts! Ewing M. Kauffman always advised that "you should trust people" rather than assume they are all out to cheat you, lie to you, scam you, or steal from you. It is certainly true that at least 95 percent of the people you will encounter in your journey can be trusted. Just keep in mind the old adage: Trust everyone, but always cut the deck!

Newland Medical Technologies

Preparation Questions

1. Discuss the process used by Sarah Foster and her partners to bring their medical device to market. How might they have avoided some of the pitfalls they encountered?

2. Examine Newland's strategy in light of the special circumstances in its industry. How do you recommend the company proceed?

3. In light of your plan for Newland Medical, how can Foster balance her personal and professional goals?

It seemed the perfect plan. With two angel investors steering her medical device company toward an acquisition, Foster and her husband decided to start a family. However, by fall 2005 (the middle of her first trimester), everything had changed. The co-founder and president of Newland Medical Technologies had to seriously reconsider the course she had set for her company and make some tough choices to balance motherhood with her professional passions.

Opportunity Recognition

Sarah Foster had been working with hip implant designs for Johnson & Johnson in Massachusetts for 2 years when her division was moved to Iowa. Foster and her husband, a professor at a local college, loved Boston, so she used her engineering degrees from MIT and Stanford (Exhibit A) to get another job. Still, she never lost sight of her primary career objective:

> I had been looking for a medical device opportunity ever since I left Johnson & Johnson. Then a friend of mine—a urologist at the Brigham and Women's Hospital in Boston—told me how there was a need for better stents[1] in urology, since most of the

industry focus has been in cardiac work. He pointed out that even though it was commonly known that the ureter naturally dilates in the presence of a foreign body, no stent products had taken full advantage of this fact. We felt that gently stimulating a wider dilation would improve urine flow and might even help pass kidney stones.

Kidney stones, or ureteral stones, affected nearly 10 percent of the U.S. population, causing severe pain when they lodged in the ureter and obstructed urine flow.

A patient arriving at a hospital with kidney stones was usually considered an emergency. The emergency-room physician would administer pain medication and consult a urologist. The immediate and near-term treatment had to be safe and effective but keep options open for later procedures.

By the late 1990s, most urologists were meeting these needs with the "Double-J"—a standard polyurethane stent inserted into the ureter to relieve pain by allowing urine to flow around the stone. With the Double-J, stones often remained in the ureter; the choice of procedure to remove them was related to their size and location, as well as access to sophisticated equipment.

Patients with stones smaller than 5 mm typically waited in pain for up to several weeks for them to pass. Larger stones were broken up using ultrasound and laser technologies—leaving fragments too small to retrieve but big enough to ensure a painful passing. Basketing was a secondary procedure that was very effective in removing individual stone fragments, but it required a skilled surgeon and an extended operating time (Exhibit B).

In the winter of 1999, Foster and Dr. Grainer began brainstorming a sheath-covered stent that could be deployed in the same manner and with the same materials as the Double-J. Once inside the ureter, the sheath would be removed, and their stent would enlarge the passageway with a series of expansion bulbs along its length (Exhibit C). While their aim was to relieve urine flow to a greater degree than competitive products, during their initial trials on pigs they noticed that as the device was slowly withdrawn from the ureter, stones became trapped in the basket-like bulbs. Direct and nontraumatic removal of stones from the ureter had never been done before; now they had their product.

This case was prepared by Carl Hedberg under the direction of Professor Stephen Spinelli. © Copyright Babson College, 2005.

[1]A medical stent was an expandable wire mesh or polyurethane tube that was inserted into a hollow structure of the body to keep it open or to provide strength. Stents were used on diverse structures such as coronary arteries, other blood vessels, the common bile duct, the esophagus, the trachea, and the ureter—the tract that conducts urine flow from the kidney to the bladder.

EXHIBIT A

Résumé: Sarah Choi Foster

Education

2002–2004	**F.W. OLIN BUSINESS SCHOOL AT BABSON COLLEGE**	**Wellesley, MA**

M.B.A., May 2003, cum laude, Babson Fellow.
- Consulted with Boston Scientific, Inc.; competitive analysis and e-commerce initiatives.
- Entrepreneurship Intensity Track program, Hatchery company.

1996–1997	**STANFORD UNIVERSITY**	**Stanford, CA**

M.S. degree in Mechanical Engineering, Design, June 1997.
Concentration: Mechatronics (Mechanical Electronics) &
Design for Manufacturability.
- Design projects: 3M-sponsored portable overhead projector, smart tag–playing robot, automated 3D foam facsimile machine, automated paper palm-tree maker.

1992–1996	**MASSACHUSETTS INSTITUTE OF TECHNOLOGY**	**Cambridge, MA**

B.S. degree in Mechanical Engineering, May 1996. Minor in Music.

Experience

2003–present	**NEWLAND MEDICAL TECHNOLOGIES, INC.**	**Boston, MA**

President and Founder
- Raised $600 K to bring an FDA-approved patented product to market.
- Built team; currently running the business.

2002	**PERCEPTION ROBOTICS, INC.**	**Waltham, MA**

Kauffman Intern, Product Manager Intern
- Analyzed potential e-commerce partners for an interactive retail software system.
- Helped develop new product value proposition for Web cameras.

1999–2002	**THE GILLETTE COMPANY**	**Boston, MA**

Design Engineer, Shaving and Technology Lab
- Managed design process and testing of high-volume plastic packaging for various toiletries.
- Designed Economy Gel antiperspirant container from market requirement to mold production.

1998–1999	**JOHNSON & JOHNSON PROFESSIONAL, INC.**	**Raynham, MA**

Project Engineer, Hip R&D
- Served as lead engineer to design hip implant products; two patents granted, three pending.
- Launched the Bipolar and Calcar Hip instrumentation systems, developed with customers.

1997–1998	**DEFENSE INTELLIGENCE AGENCY/PENTAGON**	**Washington, DC**

Analyst, Strategic Industries Branch.

1995	**MISSILE & SPACE INTELLIGENCE CENTER**	**Huntsville, AL**

Intern, Surface to Air Missile Division

Other:

Unigraphics, ProENGINEER, SolidWorks ANSYS, C, working knowledge of Korean and German. Interests include symphony playing, triathlons, downhill skiing, cycling, and woodworking.

EXHIBIT B

Anatomy and Stone Removal Procedures

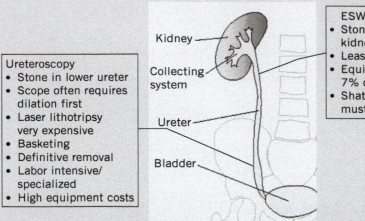

Kidney

Collecting
system

Ureter

Bladder

Ureteroscopy
• Stone in lower ureter
• Scope often requires
  dilation first
• Laser lithotripsy
  very expensive
• Basketing
• Definitive removal
• Labor intensive/
  specialized
• High equipment costs

ESWL (Shockwave)
• Stone in upper ureter or
  kidney
• Least invasive
• Equipment expensive (only
  7% of hospitals have them)
• Shattered fragments created
  must be passed

EXHIBIT C

The SRS: Insertion and Expanded Forms

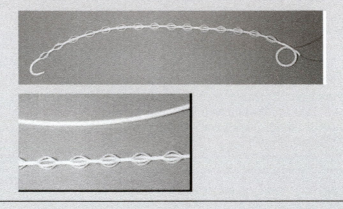

The SRS

To emphasize what they now saw as its *primary* attribute, Foster and Grainer named their device the Stone Removal Stent (SRS). A new series of animal trials led to the following procedure outline:

1. A guide wire was inserted up the ureter.
2. The SRS was slipped over the guide wire and pushed into place.
3. The sheath around the SRS was removed to open the baskets.
4. In 1 to 2 days, the SRS caused the ureter to passively dilate and enlarge the passageway.
5. The SRS was slowly withdrawn, whereby stones were either trapped in the baskets, fell into the baskets upon removal, or were swept out alongside the SRS.

Throughout 2000 and into 2001, Foster took charge as Grainer returned to his full-time practice. She raised money from friends and family to secure a patent, while examining various aspects of the opportunity in order to assemble a business plan for professional investors.

Target Market

Foster found the target market included kidney-stone patients who received primary ureteroscopy and extracorporeal shock-wave lithotripsy (ESWL) therapy (the two most common procedures), as well as stenting to relieve urine flow. ESWL machines cost from $500,000 to $1.5 million, which only the largest medical centers could afford. As a result, only 7 percent of U.S. hospitals had one and only 400

EXHIBIT D

Procedure Market Tree

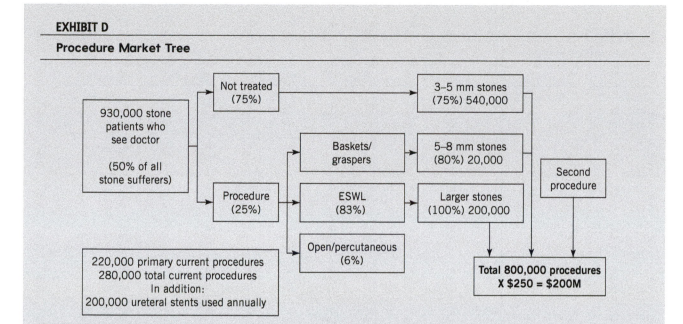

were in the field. Over $2 billion was spent every year on treating kidney stones. The average per patient annual expenditure was around $7,000, excluding pharmaceuticals.

Foster found that in the early 2000s there were approximately 260,000 primary and secondary procedures each year in the United States. Because the SRS had proven effective in capturing smaller stones that were currently left painfully untreated, she added in 75 percent of those for a total U.S. market of 800,000 target procedures (Exhibit D). At a price of $250 each, the SRS represented a $200 million opportunity.

Customers

The SRS' two main customers would be urologists and medical centers. The urologist determined the procedure and chose the device. The actual buyer was the hospital, where purchasing administrators closely watched costs. One way hospitals cut costs was to order packages of devices and services from diversified suppliers such as Johnson & Johnson.

Urologists generally were not keen on new devices and procedures. Their concerns included patient comfort and safety, risk, and reimbursement. Urologists would be most influenced by endorsements from respected colleagues and data from clinical studies. In 2001 there were just over 7,100 licensed urologists in the United States, each averaging 140 stone patients per year.

Attracting the Competition

The main competitors were market leaders in basket retrieval and ureteral stent devices (Exhibit E). Stents like the Double-J were simple devices, produced by many manufacturers.

Revenue leader Boston Scientific had made many acquisitions, suggesting to Foster that its internal R&D structure was not producing enough innovations. Unit leader ACMI was undergoing a restructuring and leadership change that indicated a lull in innovations. Neither company had a presence in the ESWL market.

Makers of ESWL machines and laser lithotripters also supplied ESWL accessories such as water bags and fluids. Foster reasoned that large sellers like Dornier MedTech and Siemens Medical Systems might be interested in a product like the SRS, which worked in conjunction with ESWL. In a sense, though, every stent competitor was a potential distributor, research and development partner, or parent. Major industry players could significantly affect the speed of adoption of new devices.

Unlike most ventures, Foster's would not go up against top competitors, so investors would not look at such typical metrics as revenues, gross margins, and projected net income. Foster wanted to establish a following among top medical practitioners—even if she had to give the stents away. Foster felt that once the SRS had proven market demand, her company would have an excellent chance of being acquired.

EXHIBIT E

Competitor Profiles

	Location	Employees	Revenues	Products	Price Points	Perception
Cook Urological (private)	Spencer, IN	300, incl mnf (4,000 all Cook)	$25.lM	Stents, baskets, wires, and other lithotripsers	Medium	Good products and innovative—strong company (#1 in biliary market)
BARD (urological)	Covington, GA	8,100 (all BARD)	$95M w/out Foleys ($360M total) 1999	Stents, baskets, laser, and other lithotripsers	Low-end	Slow, no innovation
Microvasive (Boston Scientific)	Natick, MA	14,400 (all BSC)	$143M $133M (stones) 1999	Stents, baskets, laser, and other lithotripsers	High-end	Innovative (with acquisitions), good sales force, good products
Surgitek (ACMI) (private)	Southboro, MA (HQ); Racine, WI (Urology)		$17M stents	Stents, baskets, scopes, lasers	Low-end	Based on quantity, but no innovation, hungry for new products
Applied Medical	Rancho Santa Margarita, CA	375, incl mnf	$31M (all three divisions) 2001	Various dilators and specialty items	High-end	Interesting, good, clever products, not full product line

Startup

Working part-time, Foster completed the business plan in late summer 2001. Because she could not predict the timing or price of an acquisition, her financial projections for the company she had named Newland Medical Technologies followed a standard scenario of steady growth (Exhibit F). By spring 2002, she had raised just over $600,000 in seed capital from friends, family, Grainer, and her own savings. When she began to discuss assembling a management team, Foster was surprised to learn that Grainer thought she would serve as president and CEO.

To do it the right way, I was going to need some practical business education. In the fall of 2002, I was accepted into the MBA program at the F.W. Olin Graduate School of Business (at Babson College in Wellesley, Massachusetts). I then switched jobs, to a position with a well-defined, short-range end point.

Patent work took nearly a year and drained a third of the capital Foster had raised. After some additional R&D work on the stent, Foster applied for Food and Drug Administration (FDA) approval. Given her past experience with Johnson & Johnson, and some good advice from an expert at Babson College, the SRS was approved in just under 3 months. Foster recalled the strategy:

Professor Boulnois[2] had come up with the idea of taking a two-tiered approach. First we got the SRS approved as a basic drainage stent—no problem there. When we filed our follow-on application with a different indication—stone removal—we got lucky because we had the same reviewer for both applications. She saw that it was the identical device that she had just approved, with a new indication, and because of that, we received that next approval in less than 30 days.[3]

[2] Dr. Jean-Luc Boulnois, an adjunct professor at Babson College, was founder and president of Interactive Consulting, Inc., a management consulting firm specializing in business development for European early-stage medical technology companies entering the U.S. market.

[3] By the early 2000s, the Centers for Medicare & Medicaid Services (CMS) had become a bottleneck challenge for many ventures seeking to commercialize a medical device product. The CMS was charged with the subjective task of evaluating the costs and benefits of particular technologies—an evolving field with plenty of room for debate. Reimbursement issues could be so complex and complicated that receiving payment for new products had become the greatest stumbling block for early entrants—and CMS was only one piece of the coverage approval puzzle. To achieve reimbursement coverage and payment throughout the country for a new technology, medical device ventures were required to weave their way through a maze of several hundred payers. Moreover, new products had to struggle to get assigned a unique code that would distinguish them from existing technologies. Even after that code was assigned, it might take several years for Medicare to recognize that device as a new cost. Since health care facilities would not use products that had not received proper payment approvals, it was not unusual for reimbursement gaps to derail the implementation of viable, FDA approved medical device innovations.

EXHIBIT F

Newland Pro Forma Income Statement

	2004	2005	2006	2007	2008
Net Revenues	0	721,000	8,380,000	22,327,000	34,811,625
Total Cost of Goods Sold (see below)	0	335,160	2,692,135	6,620,487	9,434,219
Percentage of Revenues	—	46.5%	32.1%	29.7%	27.1%
Gross Profit	0	385,840	5,687,865	15,706,513	25,377,406
Percentage of Revenues	—	53.5%	67.9%	70.3%	72.9%
Operating Expenses	—	—	—	—	—
Sales & Marketing	166,200	939,900	1,573,016	2,379,059	2,858,596
Research & Development	225,240	448,795	600,140	947,216	1,105,338
General & Administrative	153,800	315,700	680,055	1,057,531	1,398,100
Total Operating Expenses	545,240	1,704,395	2,853,211	4,383,806	5,362,034
Net Earnings before Taxes	(545,240)	(1,318,555)	2,834,654	11,322,707	20,015,372
Taxes	0	0	498,899	4,529,083	8,006,149
Net Earnings	(545,240)	(1,318,555)	2,335,755	6,793,624	12,009,223

Cost of Goods Sold Breakdown (e.g., 2005)

Direct Costs

Average Material Cost per Unit	8
Average Labor Cost per Unit	14
Sterilizing and Packaging per Unit	8
Manufacturer per Unit Markup (20%)	6
Total per Unit Direct Costs	36
Direct Costs: 6,200 Units (2005)	223,200

Indirect Costs

Salaries and Benefits	84,750
Facility; Shipping	7,210
Depreciation	20,000
Total Indirect Costs	111,960
Cost of Goods & Services	335,160

While attending the Olin School, Foster looked for the $1.7 million she estimated Newland would need to commercialize the SRS device. A business development foundation in Rhode Island agreed to put up $65,000—as long as 20 percent was spent directly in Rhode Island. As a result, Foster began working with a Rhode Island company to produce prototypes in a manner that would satisfy FDA production and quality requirements. The company handled all aspects of the manufacturing from extrusion to packaging.

By the time Foster graduated in January 2004, she had two additional team members—an engineer she knew from a previous job and a business-development person she met at a business-plan forum. Since she had no money to pay them, she offered to "back pay" their earned salaries from the next round of funding she expected to raise.

At a business plan competition in spring 2004, a fellow Babson graduate recommended that Foster speak with his uncle, a local philanthropist and retired venture investor.

Peter Cunningham is in his seventies, and he had told his nephew Bill that he wasn't doing any more investments. But Bill said, "You've got to meet this woman and see what she is doing."

Cunningham invested $250,000 and attracted two other local angels, who each invested $75,000. The capital was a long way from full funding, but it provided sustaining salaries for the team and a one-room incubator space in Boston's south end—halfway between two major medical research centers. The company's proximity to those research labs would prove immediately critical.

Setbacks

Foster got to know the researchers at the animal testing facilities at New England Medical and they advanced Newland's research at almost no cost:

The labs were doing their cardio work on pigs in the morning and working with the urinary tract system most every afternoon. They were curious about the SRS capabilities and were willing to add our stent to their work with the ureters.

While pre-FDA approval trials had confirmed that the SRS would perform as expected in the ureter, the latest tests revealed some serious design flaws. Foster explained:

The first five stents we designed wouldn't fit in the ureter. So our focus became making the baskets small enough to fit inside a sheath. We made a bunch, and when 15 in a row deployed successfully and worked as expected, I immediately began to move forward on developing the business plan. Then when we got FDA approval and the reimbursement codes, I figured we were ready to go out into the market.

The problem was Dr. Grainer and I hadn't talked to enough doctors early on when we were still in that design stage. For example, we chose an insertion guide wire that was larger than the standard—but one that an advisor said ought to be fine. We had created a device that worked—it could stay in the body, it dilated the ureter, patients didn't feel any pain, and it caught stones—but because our design was far more difficult to place than a standard stent, we had failed to create a salable product.

On top of that, the manufacturer was incapable of being a one-stop shop. As a result, Newland had to assemble a supply chain of specialists. This gave Newland more control over quality at each level of production, but Foster knew that passing off work-in-process between several companies would extend lead times and increase the possibility of communication challenges.

Rebirth and Conception

In late 2004 the team—bolstered by 60 successful patient trials and very positive feedback from physicians—began their full-scale effort to build a critical mass of advocates and attract at least one major distributor. They got a significant boost in March 2005, when Boston-based Taylor Medical Supply (TMS) agreed to test Newland's stent in a few major U.S. markets.

Meanwhile, Foster focused on raising funds to help get Newland back to where she thought it had been months earlier. At an angel investor breakfast in late May, she met two potential investors. Chris Fallon had made his money when his banking software company was acquired by a major financial corporation. Claudia Grimes was the cofounder of an adventure sports vacation portal that had been snapped up by a multinational travel agency.

Both investors felt Newland was at an excellent point for a lucrative early-stage acquisition. Foster explained,

There are a few times when you can sell a medical device company like ours: after a product development milestone like proof of concept on animals, after FDA approval, after a series of successful clinical trials, and after your first million or so in sales.

Chris and Claudia were certain that since we had a patented product that had FDA approval and payment codes, it was an excellent time for us to sell. They could see we were ready for market, and they were talking about putting up at least $200,000 apiece—as long as we pursued an acquisition strategy. Although an early-stage acquisition (pre-sales) was never in our plan, the more we thought about it, the more it sounded like an attractive option.

Taylor Medical Supply was not pleased with what it saw as an abrupt strategy shift. Foster thought it was angry because of how it learned about the change:

Things had started to move very fast. We chose an investment banker whose initial task was to act as an intermediary between Newland and potential buyers. He called TMS to let them know we were pursing an acquisition, and to ask if they wanted in on it. They were definitely taken aback. They told the investment banker that from their perspective we'd been moving toward a distribution deal. That was news to me; they had never seemed more than lukewarm about taking on our device. Not only did they decline to put in an offer, but they suspended their test marketing of the SRS. Still, they did indicate that initial feedback from their clients had been very positive.

With endorsements from two prominent medical centers, and a few promising acquisition prospects, momentum seemed to be building for a speedy harvest. Encouraged by Newland's progress, that summer, Foster and her husband ran the numbers—with an allowance for misconceptions—and concluded it was an excellent time to start a family. On paper, their planned parenthood coincided well with the harvest schedule that Newland's newest investors were espousing. The couple was a bit shocked, but thoroughly delighted, when Foster became pregnant that very month. Well, she mused, maybe the acquisition strategy would proceed as rapidly. It did not.

A Fork in the Road with a Baby on Board

By the fall Foster was having a hard time dealing with Fallon and Grimes. They had a good deal of latitude in setting the acquisition strategy that Foster and her original investors had signed off on, and they began demanding changes in the deal structure that would provide them with better returns.

In mid-October 2005, their investment banker got an offer from a middle-tier medical supply distributor. The $9.5 million term sheet provided a generous 5-year earn-out for Foster and her team—provided they stayed on to develop a line of innovative stents. It also required Foster to serve as president and was contingent upon FDA approval of Newland's latest innovation—now in early trials[4]—although it provided no funds to make that happen. When Fallon and Grimes said that more capital would require additional equity, Foster finally confided in her original investors:

> I had kept Chris Cunningham and his group apprised of our decision to seek an acquisition, and they had agreed with that. But these two entrepreneur angels were so difficult to work with, and neither of them had any experience in the medical industry. Maybe that's not a crucial requirement, but overall, they just didn't seem to get what we were about. Mr. Cunningham looked at me and said, "Well, if what has been stopping you from tossing these two aside was the money, you should have come to me earlier."

But for Foster this was not just about the money: it was about developing new medical products that could make a difference. Nevertheless, she felt that if Newland could strike a deal with a large company that would give its current investors a decent return and provide it with resources to develop new products, that was what it should do. On the other hand, staying the course and building a line of innovative products would significantly increase Newland's acquisition value.

If not for her pregnancy, Foster would have returned to Newland's original strategy—and to her passion for building an innovative medical device enterprise. To pursue that course now, however, she would be facing the prospect of being a new mother *and* running a growing business. With an offer on the table and funds running short, she knew she had to make some tough decisions.

---

[4]Newland Medical was working on a line of stents designed to hold the ureter open against, for example, external compression from a tumor. Newland's ureteral structural stents would be significantly more resistant to compression than any product that was currently on the market. These devices would allow patients with locally and regionally invasive tumors (typically end-stage and terminal) to survive longer with healthy kidney function. Taking into account national occurrence rates for diseases that tended to exert pressure on urinary passageways, the team estimated that this represented a $25 million market opportunity.

PART THREE

The Founder and Team

Entrepreneurial founders must take a personal role in attracting, motivating, inspiring, and retaining an effective team of both specialists and generalists. The quality of that team has never been more fundamental and important than it is now. Some have characterized this time as the communication era, characterized by galloping innovation—fueled by the ability of inventive engineers and creative entrepreneurs to instantly access and share information worldwide. Within this ever-growing globalized world, private and venture capital investors have a renewed appreciation for new ventures. In this section we will look at the leadership issues inherent in building a company from scratch and the significant recruiting, sales, and management skills the founders must bring to bear as the enterprise grows through various stages.

One of the most critical aspects of entrepreneurship is being able to attract the right people: team players whose skills and know-how are critical to the success of the enterprise. Ambiguity, risk, and the ability to shift with competitive landscapes require that entrepreneurial teams be greater than the sum of their parts. The solo entrepreneur may make a living, but generally the team builder develops an organization and a company with sustainable value and attractive harvest options. The vision these founders are trying to accomplish provides the unwritten ground rules that become the fabric, character, and purpose behind the venture. Effective lead entrepreneurs are able to build a culture around the business mission and the brand by rewarding success, supporting honest failure, sharing the wealth with those who helped to create it, and setting high ethical standards of conduct. Chapter 9, "Ethical Decision Making and the Entrepreneur," addresses the complex and thorny issues of ethics and integrity for the entrepreneur, and how those decisions and choices can have a significant impact on future success.

Chapter Eight

The Entrepreneurial Leader and the Team

LEARNING OUTCOMES: After reading this chapter you will be able to understand:

8-1 The entrepreneurial leader

8-2 Stages of growth

8-3 Managing for rapid growth

8-4 Entrepreneurial culture

8-5 What entrepreneurial leaders need to know

8-6 Leadership competencies

8-7 Forming and building teams

8-8 Slicing the equity pie

The Entrepreneurial Leader

People want to be led–not managed; this is why the battle for mind share and talent, time and again, is being won by entrepreneurial leaders. Do you love where you work and whom you work for? Would you recommend it to your best friends and family? Why? There is a familiar ring to the answers; they boil down to the leadership and culture of the company. Entrepreneurs focus on this need, creating energy and excitement inside the companies they start.

Successful entrepreneurial leaders display the high work ethic, integrity, honesty, and fairness that attract and keep the best talent. Their creativity and innovativeness, especially in recognizing opportunities and producing new product or service ideas, invariably wins the confidence and enthusiasm of followers. They are quick to give credit and recognize good performance, and they always accept more than their share of the blame when things do not work out.

This is vital in new ventures because the key to their success is the talent and quality of the lead entrepreneur and founding team. There is little time or priority in a startup for coaching, training, mentoring, and development of new hires.

People Know Leaders When They Experience Them

For years, research has shown that peers are more accurate in identifying and ranking leaders than outside observers, researchers, and experts. They know when someone is truly committed, they can distinguish the exceptionally creative and inventive entrepreneur with an eye for opportunity, and it is obvious when they care and show respect for others.

Stages of Growth

A Theoretical View

Clearly entrepreneurship is not static. Exhibit 8.1 represents a *theoretical* view of the process of gestation and growth of new ventures and the transitions that occur at different boundaries in this process. This smooth, S-shape curve in the exhibit is rarely replicated in the real world. If we actually tracked the progress of most emerging companies, the curve would be a ragged and jagged line with many ups and downs; these companies would experience some periods of rapid progress followed by setbacks and accompanying crises.

In this illustration, venture stages are shown in terms of time, sales, and number of employees. It is at the boundaries between stages that new ventures

EXHIBIT 8.1

Stages of Venture Growth, Crucial Transitions, and Core Management Mode

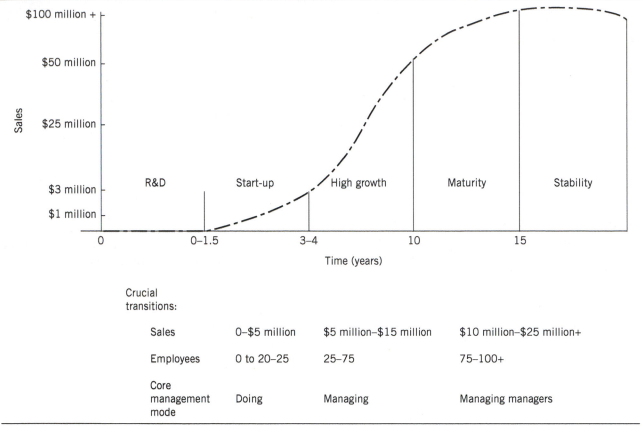

Crucial transitions:			
Sales	0–$5 million	$5 million–$15 million	$10 million–$25 million+
Employees	0 to 20–25	25–75	75–100+
Core management mode	Doing	Managing	Managing managers

seem to experience transitions. Thus the exhibit shows the crucial transitions during growth and the key management tasks of the chief executive officer or founders. Most important and most challenging for the founding entrepreneur or a chief executive officer is coping with crucial transitions and the change in leadership focus–going from leading to leading managers–as a firm grows to roughly 30 employees, then 50, and then 75 plus.

The *research and development stage,* sometimes referred to as the nascent stage, is characterized by a single aspiring entrepreneur, or small team, doing the investigation and due diligence for their business idea. The nascent stage can be as short as a few months or can last years. Research indicates that if an idea is not turned into a going concern within 18 months, the chances of a startup fall dramatically. Nascent entrepreneurs have many fits and starts, and the business model can change often in the process.

The *startup stage* usually covers the first 2 or 3 years and is by far the most perilous stage requiring the drive and talent of a lead entrepreneur. The

level of sales reached varies widely but typically ranges between $2 and $20 million.

A new company then begins its *high-growth stage*–characterized by a continually increasing rate of growth or the slope of the revenue curve. It is in this stage that new ventures tend to exhibit a failure rate exceeding 60 percent.

As with the other stages, the length of time it takes to go through the high-growth stage, as well as the magnitude of change occurring during the period, varies greatly. The high-growth stage offers one of the most difficult challenges though the entire process as new layers of management are created to enable scale. For example, sales of Litton's microwave oven division had reached $13 million, and it had 275 employees. The long-range plan called for building sales volume to $100 million in 5 to 7 years. The head of the division said, "Having studied the market for the previous 2 years, I was convinced that the only limit on our growth was our organization's inability to grow as rapidly as the market opportunities."[1]

[1]W.W. George, "Task Teams for Rapid Growth," *Harvard Business Review,* March–April 1977.

From the high-growth stage, a company then moves to what is called the *maturity stage* where the company is no longer fighting for survival, but rather remains at a steady level of profitable growth. The *stability stage* usually follows.

Managing for Rapid Growth

The transition from rapid growth to maturity and stability is even less recognizable and assured within today's inconsistent markets. Increased rates of new technology adoption and the reduced importance of asset density to gain business model scale make the maturity and stability stages less enduring. This means entrepreneurship has become a core competency of the modern firm.

Managing for rapid growth involves a leadership orientation not found in mature and stable environments. (This topic will be addressed again in Chapter 16.) For one thing, the tenet that one's responsibility must equal one's authority is often counterproductive in a rapid-growth venture. Results usually require close collaboration of a manager with people other than his or her subordinates, and managers invariably have responsibilities far exceeding their authority. In rapid-growth firms, power and control are delegated and leadership is shared. Everyone is committed to making the pie larger, and power and influence are derived not only from achieving one's own goals but also from contributing to the achievements of others.

Successful entrepreneurial leaders understand their interdependencies and have learned to incorporate mutual respect, openness, trust, and benefit into their leadership style. Fundamental to this progressive style is the awareness and practice of reciprocity for mutual gain.[2] Exhibit 8.2 characterizes probable crises that growing ventures will face.

Entrepreneurial Culture   There exists in growing new ventures a common value system, which is difficult to articulate, is even more elusive to measure, and is evident in behavior and attitudes. There is a belief in and commitment to growth, achievement, improvement, and success, as well as the sense among members of a joint effort. Team goals, along with market trends, determine group priorities rather than individual pettiness. Managers appear unconcerned about status, power, and personal control. They are more concerned with overseeing tasks, goals, and roles rather than the current status of the organizational chart or interior design of the office. Likewise, they are more concerned about the evidence, competence, and logic of arguments affecting important decisions than the status or formal position of the argumentative individuals.

What Entrepreneurial Leaders Need to Know

Much of business education traditionally has emphasized and prepared students for life in administration. Entrepreneurial programs need to emphasize skills necessary for life in entrepreneurship:

EXHIBIT 8.2

Entrepreneurial Transitions

Modes/Stages	Planning	Doing	Leading	Leading Managers
Sales	$0	0–$5 million	$5 million–$15 million	$10 million or more
Employees	0–5	0–30	30–75	75 and up
Transitions	Characteristics:	Characteristics:	Probable crises:	Probable crises:
	Founder-driven	Founder-driven	Erosion of creativity	Failure to clone
	Wrenching changes	creativity	of founders	founders
	Highly influential	Constant change,	Confusion over	Specialization/eroding
	informal advisor	ambiguity, and	ambiguous roles,	of collaboration vs.
	Resource desperation	uncertainty	responsibilities,	practice of power,
	Very quick or very	Time compression	and goals	information, and
	slow decision making	Informal	Desire for delegation	influence
		communications	vs. autonomy	Need for operating
		Counterintuitive	and control	controls and
		decision making	Need for	mechanisms
		and structure	organization and	Conflict among
		Relative inexperience	operating policies	founders

---

[2]D.L. Bradford and A.R. Cohen, *Influence without Authority* (New York, NY: John Wiley & Sons, 1990).

managing conflict, resolving differences, balancing multiple viewpoints and demands, and building teamwork and consensus.

In talking about larger firms, Kanter identifies necessary power and persuasion skills, skill in managing problems accompanying team and employee participation, and skill in understanding how change is designed and constructed in an organization. Kanter notes:

> [I]ndividuals do not have to be doing "big things" in order to have their cumulative accomplishments eventually result in big performance for the company. . . . They are only rarely the inventors of the "breakthrough" system. They are only rarely doing something that is totally unique or that no one, in any organization, ever thought of before. Instead, they are often applying ideas that have proved themselves elsewhere, or they are rearranging parts to create a better result, or they are noting a potential problem before it turns into a catastrophe and mobilizing the actions to anticipate and solve it.[3]

A study of midsized growth companies having sales between $25 million and $1 billion and sales or profit growth of more than 15 percent annually over 5 years, confirms the importance of many of these same fundamentals of entrepreneurial management.[4] For one thing, these companies practiced opportunity-driven management. According to the study, they achieved their first success with a unique product or distinctive way of doing business and often became leaders in market niches by delivering superior value to customers rather than through low prices. These firms not only offer great customer service, but emphasize financial control by managing every element of their business.

In a book that follows up on the implementation issues of how one gets middle managers to pursue and practice entrepreneurial excellence (first made famous in *In Search of Excellence* by Tom Peters and Bob Waterman), two authors note that some of the important fundamentals practiced by team-builder entrepreneurs—who are more intent on getting results than just getting their own way—also are emulated by effective middle managers.[5] Or as John Sculley of Apple Computer explained,

> The heroic style—the lone cowboy on horseback—is not the figure we worship anymore at Apple. In the new corporation, heroes won't personify any single set of achievements. Instead, they personify the process. They might be thought of as gatekeepers, information carriers, and teams. Originally heroes at Apple were the hackers and engineers who created the products. Now, more teams are heroes.[6]

The ability to shape and guide a cohesive team is particularly critical in high-tech firms. In his book *The Innovator's Dilemma*, Clayton Christensen finds that even aggressive, innovative, and customer-driven organizations can been rendered nearly obsolete if they fail to take decisive, and at times radical, actions to stay competitive.[7] The point of greatest peril in the development of a high-tech market, writes Geoffrey Moore in his book *Crossing the Chasm*, lies in making the transition from an early market, dominated by a few visionary customers, to a mainstream market that is dominated by a large block of customers who are predominantly pragmatists in orientation.[8] In Exhibit 8.3, Ed Marram, Entrepreneur-in-Residence at Babson College, depicts the aspects of leadership as a company grows to maturity.

Lead entrepreneurs whose companies successfully break into the mass market must then find a way to manage the hyper and revenues that result from demand.[9] Several entrepreneurial managers who have skillfully negotiated these high-tech waters are as well-known as the companies they founded: think Dell, Gates, Jobs, and Ellison. What sort of skills and personality are required to achieve such high levels of performance in a dynamic and uncertain marketplace? As portrayed in Stephen Covey's classic work, *The 7 Habits of Highly Effective People*, these individuals are curious, proactive team builders who have a passion for continuous improvement and renewal in their lives and in their ventures. Maybe most important in this context: These leaders have "the ability to envision, to see the potential, to create with their minds what they cannot at present see with their eyes. . . . "[10]

Other Leadership Competencies

Entrepreneurial leaders need a sound foundation in what are considered traditional management skills. Interestingly, in the study of practicing entrepreneurs mentioned earlier, no one assigned much importance to capital asset pricing models, beta coefficients,

---

[3]R.M. Kanter, *The Change Masters* (New York: Simon & Schuster, 1983), pp. 354–355.
[4]The study was done by McKinsey & Company. See "How Growth Companies Succeed," reported in *Small Business Report*, July 1984, p. 9.
[5]D.L. Bradford and A.R. Cohen, *Managing for Excellence* (New York: John Wiley & Sons, 1984), pp. 3–4.
[6]J. Sculley and J. Byrne, *Odyssey: Pepsi to Apple . . . A Journey of Adventures, Ideas, and the Future* (New York: HarperCollins, 1987), p. 321.
[7]C.M. Christensen, *The Innovator's Dilemma* (Harvard Business Review Press, 1997).
[8]G. Moore, *Crossing the Chasm* (New York: HarperCollins, 2002).
[9]G. Moore, *Inside the Tornado: Marketing Strategies from Silicon Valley's Cutting Edge* (New York: HarperCollins, 1999).
[10]S.R. Covey, *The 7 Habits of Highly Effective People* (New York: Simon & Schuster, 1989).

EXHIBIT 8.3

Management Factors and Stages

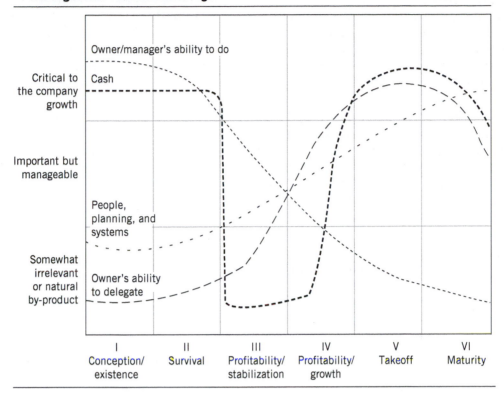

	I	II	III	IV	V	VI
	Conception/ existence	Survival	Profitability/ stabilization	Profitability/ growth	Takeoff	Maturity

linear programming, and so forth–the prevailing and highly touted "new management techniques."[11]

The following list is divided into two cross-functional areas (administration and law and taxation) and four key functional areas (marketing, operations/production, finance, entrepreneurial leadership, law and taxes, and information technology).

Marketing

- *Market research and evaluation.* Ability to analyze and interpret existing and competitive market research results, and to design and conduct studies within your own market, especially through questionnaire design and sampling techniques. One successful entrepreneur stated that what is vital "is knowing where the competitive threats are and where the opportunities are and an ability to see the customers' needs."

- *Customer relations.* A drive to build a relationship with customers and react to changing demand.

- *Marketing planning.* Skill in planning overall sales, advertising, and promotion programs, and in setting into action effective distributor or sales representative systems.

- *Product pricing.* Ability to determine competitive pricing and margin structures and to position products and pricing policies to maximize profits.

- *Sales management.* Ability to organize, supervise, and motivate a direct sales force, analyze market trends, and account for sales potential to obtain maximum market share.

- *Direct selling.* Skills in identifying, meeting, and closing sales with new customers.

- *Service management.* Ability to understand potential service requirements, handle customer complaints, and create and lead an effective service organization.

- *Distribution management.* Ability to use an understanding of shipping costs and scheduling techniques to organize and manage the flow of product from manufacturing to distribution channels to customers.

- *Profit management.* Ability to recognize the flow of margin that follows the flow of goods.

- *Product management.* Ability to integrate market information, perceived needs, research

---

[11]J.A. Timmons, and H.H. Stevenson, "Entrepreneurship Education in the 80s: What Entrepreneurs Say," In *Entrepreneurship: What It Is and How to Teach It*, ed. J. Kao and H.H. Stevenson. Boston, MA: Harvard Business School Press, 1985, pp. 115–134.

and development, and advertising into a rational product plan through an understanding of market penetration and breakeven.

- *New product planning.* Skills in introducing new products, including market testing, prototype testing, and development of price/sales/merchandising and distribution plans for new products.

Operations/Production

- *Manufacturing management.* Knowledge of the production process, machines, personnel, and space required to produce products within time, cost, and quality constraints.
- *Inventory control.* Familiarity with techniques of controlling in-process and finished goods inventories of materials.
- *Cost analysis and control.* Ability to calculate labor and materials costs, develop and manage standard cost systems, conduct variance analyses, and calculate overtime labor needs.
- *Quality control.* Ability to set up inspection systems and standards for effective control of quality of incoming, in-process, and finished materials; ability to benchmark continuous improvement.
- *Production scheduling and flow.* Ability to analyze work flow and to plan and manage production processes, and to calculate schedules for rising sale levels.
- *Purchasing.* Ability to identify appropriate sources of supply, to negotiate supplier contracts, and to manage the incoming flow of material into inventory; should be familiar with order quantities and discount advantages.
- *Job evaluation.* Ability to analyze worker productivity and needs for additional help, and the ability to calculate cost-saving aspects of temporary versus permanent help.

Finance

- *Raising capital.* Ability to decide how best to acquire funds for startup and growth; ability to forecast fund's needs and to prepare budgets; should be familiar with formal and informal sources and vehicles of short- and long-term financing.
- *Managing cash flow.* Ability to project cash requirements, set up cash controls, and manage the firm's cash position, and the ability to identify how much capital is needed, when and where cash will run out, and when breakeven will occur.

- *Credit and collection management.* Ability to develop credit policies and screening criteria and to age receivables and payables; should have an understanding of the use of collection agencies and when to start legal action.
- *Short-term financing alternatives.* Understanding of payables management and the use of interim financing, such as bank loans, factoring of receivables, pledging and selling notes and contracts, bills of lading, and bank acceptance; should be familiar with financial statements and budgeting/profit planning.
- *Public and private offerings.* Ability to develop a business plan and an offering memo that can be used to raise capital; should be familiar with the legal requirements of public and private stock offerings, management of shareholder relations, and how to negotiate with financial sources.
- *Bookkeeping, accounting, and control.* Ability to determine appropriate bookkeeping and accounting systems as the company starts and grows, including various ledgers and accounts and possible insurance needs.
- *Other specific skills.* Ability to read and prepare an income statement and balance sheet, as well as cash flow analysis and planning, including breakeven analysis, contribution analysis, profit and loss analysis, and balance sheet management.

Entrepreneurial Leadership

- *Stakeholder management.* Ability to accurately define the value of varying stakeholder groups and manage the company to deliver value.
- *Problem solving.* Ability to anticipate and research potential problems, analyze them for real causes, and plan effective action to solve them; should be familiar with how to thoroughly deal with details of particular problems and follow through.
- *Communications.* Ability to communicate effectively and clearly—orally and in writing—to media, public, customers, peers, and subordinates.
- *Planning.* Ability to set realistic and attainable goals, identify obstacles and develop detailed action plans to achieve those goals, and schedule personal time systematically.
- *Decision making.* Ability to make decisions on the best analysis of incomplete data effectively and appropriately.

- *Project management.* Skills in organizing project teams, setting project goals, defining project tasks, and monitoring task completion in the face of problems and cost/quality constraints.
- *Negotiating.* Ability to balance value given with value received, while recognizing existing and potential working relationships.
- *Managing outside professionals.* Ability to identify, manage, and guide appropriate legal, financial, banking, accounting, consulting, and other necessary outside advisors.
- *Personnel administration.* Ability to set up payroll, hiring, compensation, and training.

Law and Taxes

- *Corporate and securities law.* Familiarity with the Uniform Commercial Code, including forms of organization and the rights and obligations of officers, shareholders, and directors; and familiarity with Security and Exchange Commission, state, and other regulations concerning the securities of the firm, both registered and unregistered, and the advantages and disadvantages of different instruments.
- *Contract law.* Familiarity with procedures and requirements of government and commercial contracts, licenses, leases, and other agreements, particularly employment agreements and agreements governing the vesting rights of shareholders and founders.
- *Law relating to patent and proprietary rights.* Skills in preparation and revision of patent applications, and the ability to recognize strong patent, trademark, copyright, and privileged information claims such as intellectual property.
- *Tax law.* Familiarity with state and federal reporting requirements, including specific requirements of a particular form of organization, of profit and other pension plans, and the like.
- *Real estate law.* Familiarity with leases, purchase offers, purchase and sale agreements, and so on, necessary for the rental or purchase and sale of property.
- *Bankruptcy law.* Knowledge of bankruptcy law, options, and the forgivable and nonforgivable liabilities of founders, officers, and directors.

Information Technology

- Information and management systems tools from laptop to Internet: sales, supply chain, inventory, payroll, and so on.

Internet Impact: Virtual Teams and Collaboration

The ever-expanding number of devices designed to exploit Internet accessibility is having a profound impact on team building and collaboration. As a pervasive global network, the Internet provides a means for geographically dispersed parties to work from the same system, using the same information, in a real-time environment.

Using Web-based communications, organizations can now quickly and effectively keep value chain participants in the loop–from concept through design and delivery–without ever meeting in the same physical space.

The Internet also has become an effective tool for collaborative design, development, and data maintenance. Internet-based collaboration not only can nullify a development team's physical separation, enhance productivity, and shorten design cycles, but also opens up the talent base to include special application freelancers, as well as engineers under the employ of consultants, vendors, clients, and business partners.

- Business to business, business to consumer, and business to government via the Internet.
- Sales, marketing, manufacturing, and merchandising tools.
- Financial, accounting, and risk analysis and management tools (e.g., Microsoft's Office platform).
- Telecommunications and wireless solutions for corporate information, data, and process management.

As has been said before, not all entrepreneurs will find they are greatly skilled in all of these areas; and if they are not, they will most likely need to acquire these skills through apprenticeship, partners, or advisors. However, while many outstanding advisors, such as lawyers and accountants, are of enormous benefit to entrepreneurs, they are not always businesspeople, and often cannot make the best business judgments for those they represent.

Forming and Building Teams

Rewards and Incentives: Slicing the Founder's Pie

One of the most frequently asked questions from startup entrepreneurs is, How much stock ownership should go to whom? (Chapter 12 examines the various methodologies used by venture capitalists and investors to determine what share of the company is required by the investor at different rounds of investment.)

First, start with a philosophy and set of values that boil down to Ewing Marion Kauffman's great principle: The key is making the pie as large as possible. Second, the ultimate goal of any venture capital–backed company is to realize a harvest at a price 5 to 10 times the original investment. Thus the company will be sold either via an initial public offering (IPO) or to a larger company. It is useful to work backward from the capital structure at the time of the IPO to envision and define what will happen and who will get what. Finally, especially for young entrepreneurs in their 20s or 30s, this will not be their last venture. The single most important thing is that it succeeds. Make this happen, and the future opportunities will be boundless. All this can be ruined if the founder/CEO simply gets greedy and over-controlling, keeping most of the company to himself or herself, rather than creating a larger shared pie.

An Approach to Rewards and Equity

There are five fundamental realities with nearly any new venture:

1. Cash is king, and there is never enough.
2. You will be out of cash much sooner than you think.
3. Sales are what count most.
4. Talent is the key to success.
5. Equity creation and realization determine the payoff.

Therefore, thinking through how the founders will compensate themselves and the team, new talent, and the brain trust is an essential early task of the founders. Keeping in mind some worthwhile principles can guide this effort and create a blueprint and expectations for the future.

Principle 1: Share the wealth with the high performers who contribute to its creation. This implies wider than normal stock ownership and a healthy stock option or comparable performance unit pool. Investors typically like to see a future pool of 10 to 20 percent of the fully diluted company set aside for attracting future talent and creating incentives and rewards for high performance. At the end of this chapter is an exercise, "Slicing the Equity Pie," in which we provide some guidelines and suggest you work through the likely capital structure and ownership of the venture,

recognizing that this will take time, and that a 5- to 7-year vesting schedule will help remediate any hiring mistakes.

Principle 2: The fairness concept, treat other people as you would want to be treated. Is this equity and compensation a deal you would consider fair and reasonable if you were in the other person's situation? This does not imply that everyone should have equal ownership. This is where the brain trust can be valuable in helping to guide the numbers that represent the marketplace for talent in your area, whether it is marketing, financial, or technical. Imagine what these numbers would be like in Silicon Valley for a highly talented technical person versus a rural, small city in the upper Midwest or northern New England. If you can't get a good view of the range in the marketplace, you don't have the right brain trust yet for advice and have not done enough homework.

Principle 3: Reward results, and especially those who create revenue, and attract and grow key talent. This may seem obvious; but it is amazing to us how other criteria can creep in the way. For example, a smart, articulate, and strong-minded technical genius who is the first-time founder of a company can suffer the delusion that his or her technical contribution alone will drive the success of the company and thus should command 15 to 25 percent or more of the company's equity. An ownership structure like that will make it virtually impossible to raise venture capital and attract key talent to the company. This principle also implies a vesting schedule, usually of at least 5 and sometimes 7 years or more, whereby the stock is restricted and earned by one's performance. Key people who do not work out earn only the stock they are entitled to, and the rest is still available to the company to reward and motivate others.

Principle 4: Sweat equity matters—a lot! The early stages of a company require very hard work and many sacrifices. Thus a good test for founders is the will of prospective team members to sacrifice, tempered by the realities of the competition you face to attract talent.

Principle #5: Chemistry–chemistry–chemistry. The most brilliant talent, the most creative product or service, and the most well-developed and financed business plan on the planet will not succeed unless there is strong chemistry among the founding team that is then embedded into the company's culture. The abilities to respect one another and to work well together, especially when the road is the bumpiest, steepest, and darkest, are crucial.

As you and prospective team members begin to talk seriously about doing a venture together, it can be useful to agree on some governing principles. You may have others to add, but these will serve the process well. Without these underlying principles the process often bogs down into endless negotiations and a stillborn venture. These will not guarantee you will agree on an ownership structure, but they can certainly help.

Considerations of Value

The contributions of team members will vary in nature, extent, and timing. In developing the reward system, particularly the distribution of stock, contributions in certain areas are of particular value to a venture. Consider:

- *Idea.* In this area, the originator of the idea, particularly if trade secrets or special technology for a prototype was developed or if product or market research was done.
- *Business plan preparation.* One preparing an acceptable business plan, in terms of dollars and hours expended.
- *Commitment and risk.* A team member may invest a large percentage of his or her net worth in the company, be at risk if the company fails, have to make personal sacrifices, put in long hours and major effort, risk his or her reputation, accept reduced salary, or already have spent a large amount of time on behalf of the venture.
- *Skills, experience, track record, or contacts.* A team member may bring to the venture skills, experience, track record, or contacts in such areas as marketing, finance, and technology. These are of critical importance and may not be readily available.
- *Responsibility.* The importance of a team member's role to the success of the venture.

Being the originator of the idea or expending a great amount of time or money in preparing the business plan is frequently overvalued. If these factors are evaluated in terms of the real success of the venture down the road, it is difficult to justify much more than 15 to 20 percent of equity for them. Commitment and risk, skills, experience, and responsibility contribute much more to successful ventures.

The previous list is valuable in attempting to weigh fairly the relative contributions of each team member. Contributions in each of these areas have some value; it is up to a team to agree on how to assign value to contributions and, further, to leave enough flexibility to allow for changes.

Chapter Summary

- The growing enterprise requires that the founder and team develop competencies as entrepreneurial leaders.
- Founders who succeed in growing their firms beyond $10 million in sales learn to adapt and grow quickly themselves as leaders, or they do not survive.
- Founders of rapidly growing firms defy the conventional wisdom that entrepreneurs cannot manage growing beyond the startup.
- A strong team is usually the difference between a great success and a marginal or failed company.
- Ventures go through stages of growth from startup, through rapid growth, to maturity, to decline and renewal.
- Core philosophies, values, and attitudes—particularly sharing the wealth and ownership with those who create it—are key to team building.
- The fit concept is central to anticipating management gaps and building the team.
- The faster the rate of growth, the more difficult and challenging are the issues, and the more flexible, adaptive, and quick-learning the organization must be.
- Numerous pitfalls await the entrepreneur in team building and need to be avoided.
- Entrepreneurs create and invent new and unique approaches to organizing and leading teams.
- As ventures grow, the core competencies need to be covered by the team.
- Compensating and rewarding team members requires both a philosophy and technical know-how and can have enormous impact on the odds of success.

Study Questions

1. What are the differences between an entrepreneurial leader and an administrator or manager?

2. How do founders grow their ventures beyond $10 million in sales, and why is the team so important?

3. Define the stages that most companies experience as they grow, and explain the leadership issues and requirements anticipated at each stage.

4. Describe what is meant by team philosophy and attitudes. Why are these important?

5. What are the most critical questions a lead entrepreneur needs to consider in thinking through the team issue? Why? What are some common pitfalls in team building?

6. What are the critical rewards, compensation, and incentive issues in putting a team together? Why are these so crucial and difficult to manage?

7. How does the lead entrepreneur allocate stock ownership and options in the new venture? Who should get what ownership, and why?

8. Can you compare and describe the principal differences in leadership, management, and organization between the best growing companies of which you are aware and large, established companies? Why are there differences?

9. What drives the extent of complexity and difficulty of issues in a growing company?

10. What would be your strategy for changing and creating an entrepreneurial culture in a large, nonentrepreneurial firm? Is it possible? Why or why not?

Internet Resources

http://entrepreneurialleadership.org *This study, sponsored by the Society of Industrial and Organizational Psychologists (siop.org) and* Fast Company *magazine, examines the different styles of leadership exhibited by entrepreneurs and how those styles affect organizational culture.*

http://www.managementhelp.org *The Free Management Library offers comprehensive resources regarding the leadership and management of yourself, other individuals, groups, and organizations. Its content is relevant to the vast* majority of people, whether they are in large or small for-profit or nonprofit organizations.

http://fed.org *As a private foundation, the Foundation for Enterprise Development seeks to foster the advancement of entrepreneurial scientific and technology enterprises.*

http://www.eonetwork.org/ *The Entrepreneurs' Organization (EO) is a membership organization designed to engage leading entrepreneurs to learn and grow. We are a global community of business owners, all of whom run companies that exceed $1M (U.S.) in revenue.*

Leadership Skills and Know-How Assessment

Name:

Venture:

Date:

Part I—Management Competency Inventory

Part I of the exercise involves filling out the Management Competency Inventory and evaluating how critical certain management competencies are either (1) for the venture or (2) personally over the next 1 to 3 years. *How you rank the importance of management competencies, therefore, will depend on the purpose of your managerial assessment.*

STEP I

Complete the Management Competency Inventory on the following pages. For each management competency, place a check in the column that best describes your knowledge and experience. Note that a section is at the end of the inventory for *unique skills* required by your venture; for example, if it is a service or franchise business, there will be some skills and know-how that are unique. Then rank from I to 3 particular management competencies as follows:

I = Critical

2 = Very desirable

3 = Not necessary

	Competency Inventory				
Marketing	**Rank**	**Thorough Knowledge and Experience (Done Well)**	**Some Knowledge and Experience (So-So)**	**No Knowledge or Experience (New Ground)**	**Importance (I–3 Years)**
Market Research and Evaluation *Finding and interpreting industry and competitor information; designing, and conducting market research studies; analyzing and interpreting market research data; etc.*					
Market Planning *Planning overall sales, advertising, and promotion programs; planning and setting up effective distributor or sales representative systems; etc.*					

		Competency Inventory			
	Rank	Thorough Knowledge and Experience (Done Well)	Some Knowledge and Experience (So–So)	No Knowledge or Experience (New Ground)	Importance (1–3 Years)
Product Pricing *Determining competitive pricing and margin structures and breakeven analysis; positioning products in terms of price; etc.*					

Customer Relations Management (CRM)

Customer Service *Determining customer service needs and spare-part requirements; managing a service organization and warranties; training; technical backup, telecom and Internet systems and tools; etc.*					
Sales Management *Organizing, recruiting, supervising, compensating, and motivating a direct sales force; analyzing territory and account sales—potential; managing sales force; etc.*					
Direct Selling *Identifying, meeting, and developing new customers, suppliers, investors, brain trust and team; closing sales; etc.*					
Direct Mail/Catalog Selling *Identifying and developing appropriate direct mail and catalog sales and related distribution; etc.*					

	Competency Inventory				
	Rank	Thorough Knowledge and Experience (Done Well)	Some Knowledge and Experience (So–So)	No Knowledge or Experience (New Ground)	Importance (1–3 Years)
Electronic and Telemarketing *Identifying, planning, and implementing appropriate telemarketing programs; Internet-based programs; etc.*					

Supply Chain Management

Distribution Management *Organizing and managing the flow of product from manufacturing through distribution, channels to customers; knowing the margins throughout the value chain; etc.*					
Product Management *Integrating market information, perceived needs, research and development, and advertising into a rational product plan; etc.*					
New Product Planning *Planning the introduction of new products, including market testing, prototype testing, and development of price, sales, merchandising, and distribution plans; etc.*					

Operations/ Production

	Competency Inventory			
Rank	Thorough Knowledge and Experience (Done Well)	Some Knowledge and Experience (So–So)	No Knowledge or Experience (New Ground)	Importance (1–3 Years)
Manufacturing Management *Managing production to produce products within time, cost, and quality constraints; knowledge of manufacturing resource planning; etc.*				
Inventory Control *Using techniques of controlling in-process and finished goods inventories; etc.*				
Cost Analysis and Control *Calculating labor and materials costs; developing standard cost systems; conducting variance analyses; calculating overtime labor needs; managing and controlling costs; etc.*				
Quality Control *Setting up inspection systems and standards for effective control of quality in incoming, in-process, and finished goods; etc.*				
Production Scheduling and Flow *Analyzing work flow; planning and managing production processes; managing work flow; calculating schedules and flows for rising sales levels; etc.*				
Purchasing *Identifying appropriate sources of supply; negotiating supplier contracts; managing the incoming flow of material into inventory; etc.*				

	Rank	Thorough Knowledge and Experience (Done Well)	Some Knowledge and Experience (So–So)	No Knowledge or Experience (New Ground)	Importance (1–3 Years)
Job Evaluation					
Analyzing worker productivity and needs for additional help; calculating cost-saving aspects of temporary vs. permanent help; etc.					

Finance

	Rank	Thorough Knowledge and Experience (Done Well)	Some Knowledge and Experience (So–So)	No Knowledge or Experience (New Ground)	Importance (1–3 Years)
Accounting					
Determining appropriate bookkeeping and accounting systems; preparing and using income statements and balance sheets; analyzing cash flow, breakeven, contribution, and profit and loss; etc.					
Capital Budgeting					
Preparing budgets; deciding how best to acquire funds for startup and growth; forecasting funds needs; etc.					
Cash Flow Management					
Managing cash position, including projecting cash requirements; etc.					
Credit and Collection Management					
Developing credit policies and screening criteria; etc.					
Short-Term Financing					
Managing payables and receivables; using interim financing alternatives; managing bank and creditor relations; etc.					

Competency Inventory

	Rank	Competency Inventory			
		Thorough Knowledge and Experience (Done Well)	Some Knowledge and Experience (So–So)	No Knowledge or Experience (New Ground)	Importance (I–3 Years)
Public and Private Offering Skills *Developing a business plan and offering memo; managing shareholder relations; negotiating with financial sources; deal structuring and valuation; etc.*					

Entrepreneurial Leadership

	Rank	Thorough Knowledge and Experience (Done Well)	Some Knowledge and Experience (So–So)	No Knowledge or Experience (New Ground)	Importance (I–3 Years)
Problem Solving *Anticipating problems and planning to avoid them; analyzing and solving problems; etc.*					
Culture and Communications *Communicating effectively and clearly, both orally and in writing, to customers, peers, subordinates, and outsiders; treating others as you would be treated, sharing the wealth, giving back; etc.*					
Planning *Ability to set realistic and attainable goals, identify obstacles to achieving the goals, and develop detailed action plans to achieve those goals.*					
Decision Making *Making decisions based on the analysis of incomplete data; etc.*					

| | Competency Inventory | | | |
	Rank	Thorough Knowledge and Experience (Done Well)	Some Knowledge and Experience (So–So)	No Knowledge or Experience (New Ground)	Importance (1–3 Years)
Ethical Competency Ability to define and give life to an organization's guiding values; to create an environment that supports ethically sound behavior; and to instill a sense of shared accountability among employees.					
Project Management *Organizing project teams; setting project goals; defining project tasks; monitoring task completion in the face of problems and cost/quality constraints; etc.*					
Negotiating *Working effectively in negotiations; etc.*					
Personnel Administration *Setting up payroll, hiring, compensation, and training functions; identifying, managing, and guiding appropriate outside advisors; etc.*					
Management Information Systems *Knowledge of relevant management information systems available and appropriate for growth plans; etc.*					

	Competency Inventory				
	Rank	Thorough Knowledge and Experience (Done Well)	Some Knowledge and Experience (So–So)	No Knowledge or Experience (New Ground)	Importance (I–3 Years)
Information Technology and the Internet *Using spreadsheet, word processing, and other relevant software; using e-mail, management tools, and other appropriate systems.*					

Interpersonal Team

Entrepreneurial Leadership/ Vision/Influence *Actively leading, instilling vision and passion in others, and managing activities of others; creating a climate and spirit conducive to high performance; etc.*					
Helping *Determining when assistance is warranted and asking for or providing such assistance.*					
Feedback *Providing effective feedback or receiving it; etc.*					
Conflict Management *Confronting differences openly and obtaining resolution; using evidence and logic; etc.*					
Teamwork and Influence *Working with others to achieve common goals; delegating responsibility and coaching subordinates; etc.*					

		Competency Inventory		
Rank	**Thorough Knowledge and Experience (Done Well)**	**Some Knowledge and Experience (So–So)**	**No Knowledge or Experience (New Ground)**	**Importance (1–3 Years)**
Building a Brain Trust *Connecting with experts and seeking advice and value.*				
Law				
Corporations *Understanding the Uniform Commercial Code, including forms of organization and the rights and obligations of officers, shareholders, and directors; etc.*				
Contracts *Understanding the requirements of government and commercial contracts, licenses, leases, and other agreements; etc.*				
Taxes *Understanding state and federal reporting requirements; understanding tax shelters, estate planning, fringe benefits, and so forth; etc.*				
Securities *Understanding regulations of the Security and Exchange Commission and state agencies concerning the securities, both registered and unregistered; etc.*				
Patents and Proprietary Rights *Understanding the preparation and revision of patent applications; recognizing strong patent, trademark, copyright, and privileged information claims; etc.*				

		Competency Inventory			
	Rank	Thorough Knowledge and Experience (Done Well)	Some Knowledge and Experience (So–So)	No Knowledge or Experience (New Ground)	Importance (1–3 Years)
Real Estate *Understanding agreements necessary for the rental or purchase and sale of property; etc.*					
Bankruptcy *Understanding options and the forgivable and non-forgivable liabilities of founders, officers, directors, and so forth; etc.*					
Unique Skills List unique competencies required: *1.* *2.* *3.*					

Part II—Competency Assessment

Part II involves assessing management strengths and weaknesses, deciding which areas of competence are most critical, and developing a plan to overcome or compensate for any weaknesses and to capitalize on management strengths.

STEP 1

Assess competency strengths and weaknesses:

- Which skills are particularly strong?

- Which skills are particularly weak?

- What gaps are evident? When?

STEP 2

Circle the areas of competence most critical to the success of the venture, and cross out those that are irrelevant.

STEP 3

Consider the implications for you and for developing the venture management team:

- What are the implications of this particular constellation of strengths and weaknesses?

- Who in your team can overcome or compensate for each critical weakness?

- How can you leverage your critical strengths?

- What are the time implications of these actions? For you? For the team?

- How will you attract people to fill the critical gaps in your weaknesses?

STEP 4

Obtain feedback. If you are evaluating your management competencies as part of the development of a personal entrepreneurial strategy and planning your apprenticeship, refer back to the Crafting a Personal Entrepreneurial Strategy Exercise in Chapter 2. Complete this exercise if you have not done so already.

Slicing the Equity Pie

After considering the issues and criteria discussed in this chapter, in this exercise the lead entrepreneur will begin to think through the tricky and delicate compensation and equity allocations. Once the company or limited liability corporation (LLC) is ready to be legally formed, these decisions need to be made.

First, we urge you to anchor these deliberations in several principles and realities:

- The best companies share their wealth with the high performers that create and build it via creative incentives and rewards.

- Fairness is a prime consideration.

- When it comes to founders' salaries, less is more.

- The value-added contributions of the key players will drive ownership.

Second, it is useful to think about the capital structure and ownership of the company at an eventual IPO—even if you never go this route. As we saw in the capital markets food chain in Chapter 5, post-IPO the ownership will be roughly 50 percent in the hands of outside investors (angels, family, venture capitalists, etc.) and 20 to 25 percent in the hands of the public; the rest (25–30 percent) will be owned by the founders, management, and directors/advisors, including the option pool. It would also be common for a company to have 15 to 20 million shares of stock outstanding, post-IPO on a fully diluted basis. Thus the ownership in shares might approximate the following:

Public investors	=	4–5 million shares
Private investors	=	7.5–10 million shares
Founders:		
CEO	=	1–2 million shares
Marketing VP	=	500 K–1 million shares
CFO	=	200–400 K shares
Rest	=	1.5–2 million shares

Advisors and directors may have 0.25–1 percent, or roughly 10 K to 200 K shares, depending on their perceived value and the negotiation.

The Founder's Assignment

STEP 1

Draft a one-page summary of what you believe at this initial point the salaries and stock ownership (members' ownership in an LLC) will look like at the launch of your venture. Be specific about dollars, number of shares, and percentages for each.

STEP 2

Discuss your draft with at least three members of your brain trust who have been founders/principals in, or legal advisors to, a company that has gone public. This is to test your thinking, assumptions, and assessment of the potential contributions of the team.

STEP 3

After digesting their reactions and suggestions, make appropriate revisions.

STEP 4

Ask each founding team member (if you have any at this point) to do the same. Then share each draft and attempt to reach a consensus.

Be sure to avoid the temptation, as pointed out in this chapter, to simply make everyone equal. Although this can and does work, it often does not, and it is a way of avoiding the reality that not everyone will have equal responsibility, risk, and contributions.

Case

Maclean Palmer

Preparation Questions

1. Evaluate Maclean Palmer's decision to create a new venture capital fund and his progress to date.
2. What do you think of his team?
3. Outline the major risks you see, the due diligence questions you would focus on, and whom you would contact as a pension fund analyst or prospective limited in the fund.
4. Outline in detail what you would include in a private placement memorandum to market the fund to potential investors.
5. Who should invest in a venture capital fund?

Maclean Palmer

Maclean Palmer strode out onto a Martha's Vineyard beach to enjoy the warm sun. That August afternoon in 2000, Palmer and the four partners he had chosen in his quest to start up a $200 million private equity fund had made a collective decision that would change their lives forever.

In less than 2 months, the partners would quit their jobs, sell their homes, and move their families to Boston to begin crafting an offering memorandum for the fund. With 2000 shaping up to be the largest venture fund-raising year in history, they felt they could not have picked a better time to strike out on their own.

The Venture Capital Investing Process

Venture capital advocates say VC fosters innovation by enabling investors and entrepreneurs to share the risks and rewards of starting, funding, and running potentially high-growth companies.

The process begins when a group of people identifies a good opportunity for venture capital investment and decides to raise a fund to pursue it. Next, the group writes a prospectus articulating its strategy, qualifications, and track record, which it uses to raise money for its fund. Raising money is a networking and sales undertaking that typically gains momentum only after an institutional investment advisor—known as a gatekeeper—commits capital to the fund.

Once a venture capital firm has raised money, it starts identifying and evaluating promising companies, negotiating and making investments in them,

The Gatekeepers

Institutional investors such as corporations, foundations, and pension funds invest as limited partners in hundreds of venture capital and buyout funds. Many delegate the duty of evaluating and managing fund investments to advisors with expertise in the venture capital industry. These advisors pool their clients' assets and invest the proceeds into venture or buyout funds. For this, the advisors collect a fee of 1 percent of committed capital per annum. Because these investment experts have a large influence over the allocation of capital to venture funds, they are called gatekeepers.

tracking and coaching them, providing them with technical and management assistance, and helping them attain additional capital, directors, management, suppliers, and other resources (Exhibit A). Given the numerous factors (e.g., management talent, market timing, strategic vision) required for a startup to reach a profitable exit event such as an acquisition or an initial public offering (IPO), home runs are rare. Only about one out of every 15 VC investments realize a return of 10 times or more on invested capital.

Venture capital is part of the mostly private, imperfect capital markets for new, emerging, and middle-market companies (i.e., those with $20 million to $150 million in sales).[1]

Private venture capital funds typically are structured as limited partnerships. The venture capitalists are the general partners and the investors are the limited partners (Exhibit B). The general partners organize the fund and manage its investments, while the limited partners are passive investors and have limited liability for actions the fund takes. As compensation for their direct participation and risk exposure, general partners can reap substantial capital gains—known as carried

This case was prepared by Carl Hedberg under the direction of Professor Jeffry Timmons, the Franklin W. Olin Distinguished Professor of Entrepreneurship at the Arthur M. Blank Center for Entrepreneurship, Babson College. © Copyright Babson College, 2004. Funding provided by the Franklin W. Olin Foundation. All rights reserved.

[1] W.D. Bygrave and J.A. Timmons, *Venture Capital at the Crossroads* (Boston, MA: Harvard School Press, 1992). Note: middle-market company figures reflect the range in the early 2000s.

EXHIBIT A

Classic VC Investing Process

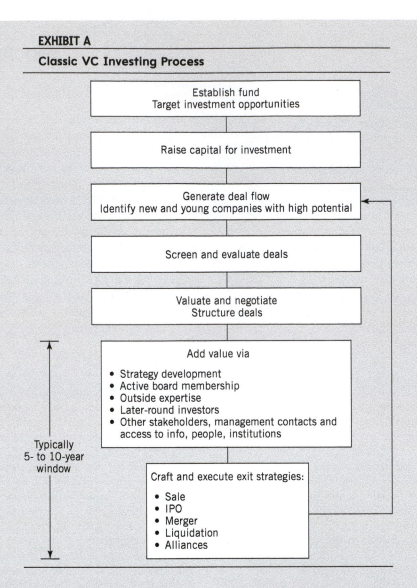

interest—when the fund's portfolio companies get bought or go public.

The partnership structure stipulates a specific term of years for a fund. Extending that requires the consent of the general partners and two-thirds of the limited partners. The fee structure between the general and limited partners varies considerably and, as a result, affects funds' attractiveness.[2]

Between 1980 and mid-2000, there were two recessions (in 1981–1982 and in 1990–1992) and a stock market panic in October 1987 that sent share prices plummeting 22 percent in a day. Nevertheless, according to Venture Economics, which compiles private equity data, venture investments during that time yielded a 19.3 percent average annual return after fees and expenses. Over the same period, the S&P 500 and the Russell 2000 index of small companies generated average annual returns, respectively, of 15.7 percent and

13.3 percent. The latest 5-year trends showed venture returns far ahead of the returns on buyout funds and blue chip stocks. Fueled by these figures and the Internet boom, 2000 was shaping up to be a record breaker for venture fund-raising (Exhibit C).

Equity funds had been conceived, invested, and exited in 8- to 12-year cycles, with preparation for follow-on funds beginning in years 3 and 4. That was because it took 5 to 7 years to build and harvest a successful portfolio investment.

By the late 1990s, however, some companies were skipping from a first round of venture financing to a successful IPO in 2 years or less. This radically altered the frequency and capitalization of follow-on venture funds. For example, between 1994 and 2000, Spectrum Equity Investors (Boston/Menlo Park) raised four funds totaling just over $3 billion. Between 1998 and 2001, venture firms raised over $200 billion—more than they had raised in the previous 40 years.

[2]Ibid.

EXHIBIT B

Flows of VC

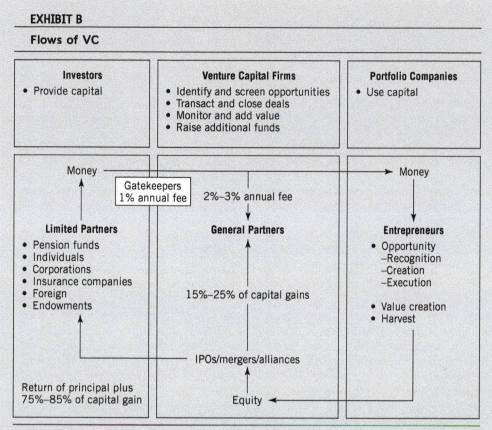

Note: These exhibits are discussed further in Chapter 13, Obtaining Venture and Growth Capital.

EXHIBIT C

Funds, Fund Commitments, and Average Fund Size

	Venture Capital				Buyout and Mezzanine			
Year/Qtr	First-Time Funds	Total Funds	Average Fund Size ($mil)	Total Raised ($billions)	First-Time Funds	Total Funds	Average Fund Size ($mil)	Total Raised ($billions)
1994	25	138	56.5	7.8	31	103	202.9	20.9
1995	36	155	63.9	9.9	32	105	253.3	26.6
1996	54	163	74.2	12.1	38	112	300.9	33.7
1997	79	232	76.3	17.7	39	140	355.7	49.8
1998	82	277	109.7	30.4	42	166	386.1	64.1
1999	146	424	139.5	59.2	44	157	410.8	64.5
Q1 2000	45	165	132.1	21.8	9	42	300	12.6
Q2 2000	51	183	168.3	30.8	10	50	212	10.6

Source: National Venture Capital Association (http://www.nvca.org/nvca2_II_02.html).

Concepting

With 5 years of investing experience as a principal at Point West Partners in San Francisco—along with 17 years of operating experience—Maclean Palmer, 40, decided in 1999 to develop his own fund:

As an ethnic minority, I had always been committed to minority business development, and I knew that there was a large pool of talented minority executives out there that traditional VCs weren't calling on to run portfolio companies. These executives have a tremendous amount of operating experience, and

I figured there should be a way to build significant postinvestment value by bridging that operating experience with a solid investing strategy. I began to ask, "What should be the profile and experience of the team that could exploit that opportunity?"

For advice, Palmer called Wanda Felton, a director of private equity investments at Credit Suisse First Boston. During the early 1990s, Felton had performed due diligence for Hamilton Lane, a Philadelphia-based gatekeeper with an interest in first-time funds in the minority space. She and Palmer met while judging a business plan competition, and later worked together when she helped the Point West group raise its fourth fund.

Outlining what she felt were important criteria for assessing first-time private equity offerings (Exhibit D), Felton sensed Palmer had a salable concept:

> For a limited partner, putting money into a first-time fund has all the risks associated with a typical startup investment. On top of that, this type of deal is a 10-year-plus commitment with no ability to get out. LPs, therefore, look for groups that can demonstrate that they have worked successfully together in the past, will stay together, and have a common view of how they'll run their portfolio businesses. Since Maclean was talking about developing a new team, this collective experience was of course something his fund would not have.
>
> Still, Maclean was describing a focused, "management-centric" concept—meaning that his core strategy would be to identify and recruit top-level ethnic minority managers from Fortune 1,000 companies to run—and add value to—his fund's investments. . . . This was intriguing, and it certainly differentiated him from the majority of private equity firms.

Next, Palmer contacted Grove Street Advisors (GSA) partner David Mazza, an expert in the venture executive search field and a champion of first-time funds.

The Advocates

In 1997, Mazza had introduced Babson MBA Palmer—then a Kauffman Fellow (see box) at Advent International in Boston—to the venture group at Point West Partners. When Palmer (Appendix A: Team Profiles) contacted Mazza in 1999 with an idea for a fund that would back talented minority executives in mainstream ventures, Mazza immediately sensed the possibilities:

> I'm being told by the chairman of General Motors that if we could start three or four well-run ethnic-minority-owned supplier businesses, we could build

---

EXHIBIT D

Due Diligence on New Funds

The Business

What is the overall strategy?

Is there a market opportunity, and can it be executed in the current environment and during the expected commitment period?

Has the team articulated a strategic and operating business strategy for portfolio companies?

Do they have a viable exit plan?

Probably most crucial: How has the general partner group demonstrated that they can add investment value to their portfolio companies?

The Team

Do the general partner and the team have enough private equity investing experience and resources to execute the strategy?

Will the team have access to deal flow within the stated strategy?

Is the team stable?

Has the team worked together before?

Do they have a common view as to how they will run the businesses?

Do they have a meaningful track record in the stated strategy?

---

them to $300 million to $400 million companies over the next 4 to 5 years—easily and profitably. That's an opportunity you don't always hear—and it's because of the minority aspect. In the automotive industry, 10 percent of all supplier contracts have to be set aside for minority businesses—that's life, and traditional venture capital firms like Kleiner, Bessemer and Sequoia can't effectively go after that market; but someone like Palmer could.

The Kauffman Fellowship

In 1993, the Ewing Marion Kauffman Foundation (www.kauffman.org) established the Kauffman Fellows Program (www.kauffmanfellows.org) to educate and train emerging leaders in the venture capital industry. Like a medical residency, the fellowship was an apprenticeship program that featured a structured educational curriculum, an individual learning plan, facilitated mentoring, peer learning and networking, and leadership development in specific areas of interest.

Kauffman Fellows were students of the Center for Venture Education and could serve as either temporary or permanent full-time associates of a venture firm during their fellowship.

Mazza added that the capabilities of nontraditional funds were something that gatekeepers like Hamilton Lane and GSA had been advocating for years:

> Traditional institutional investors always look for the same things. They think that the guys who made money before are going to make it again; that's wrong—it's a different world now. The reality is that white boys aren't the only people who know how to make money. Sure, there are still going to be the guys making money in biotech and in semiconductors, but more and more we are seeing women entrepreneurs, African American entrepreneurs, Hispanic entrepreneurs. The trouble is, there has been no money going in that direction except for government funding programs—and those are not set up to provide critical post-money support.

GSA cofounder Clint Harris referred to his firm's detailed evaluation model (Exhibit E) as he explained that identifying and supporting emerging talent was similar to the work of assessing new venture opportunities:

> As with startups and entrepreneurs, the difference between the average investment manager and the top performers is huge. And just like with successful venture investing, we look at a lot of offerings and

meet with a lot of teams. We tend to say no quickly; when we do spot talent, we start small, help them along. As they gain experience and credibility as successful investors, we write bigger and bigger checks.

Although GSA felt Palmer had the background, drive, and personality to lead the charge, the influential player was adamant about the need to bring in known, experienced players. Mazza elaborated:

> I told Maclean that what he really needed to do was create an effort that became so prominent that if you were a top entrepreneur, a CEO, an Oprah, or a Steadman Graham—and you weren't part of it—you'd feel like you were out of it. That's the deal.
>
> This would have to be a very high-profile group with private equity expertise and some buyout experience. I wanted to see some names that people could immediately identify with—either on the advisory board or in the partnership ranks.

Palmer, however, felt way too much emphasis was being placed on the minority aspect of what he was trying to develop. He also had his own vision about the sort of partners he needed to attract:

> GSA made it clear that if they were going to make any kind of substantial investment in my concept, then they would prefer that I focused on finding partners

EXHIBIT E

GSA Evaluation Process

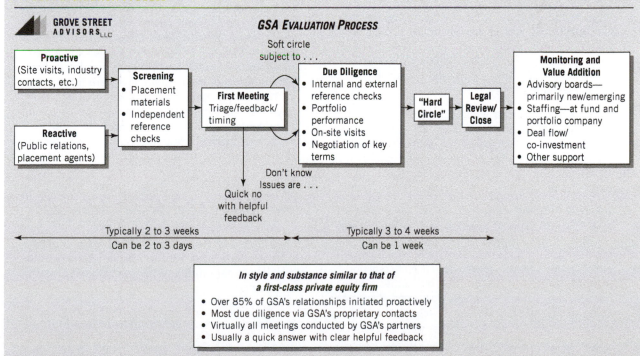

Source: Used by permission of Grove Street Advisors, LLC.

with lots of deal experience. That was, of course, one thing I had to look at, but I don't think that prior experience working together is necessarily the most important consideration in building a team of people who I expect to be partners with for 20 or 30 years. Although experience and track record are key, who my partners are as people is much more important to me than what they have accomplished up until now.

Recruiting an "American" Lineup

Palmer thoroughly investigated dozens of potential minority candidates. When asked about his first two choices, Wharton MBA Clark Pierce,[3] 38, and Harvard MBA Andrew Simon, 30, Palmer referred to their respective résumés (Appendix A: Team Profiles), adding,

Clark was a principal with Ninos Capital with 7 years of mezzanine experience. What attracted me most about him was that we knew each other well and had complementary skill sets.... Andrew had excellent fundamentals and I liked the way he thought.

In the spring of 1999, Wanda Felton introduced Palmer to 61-year-old Ray Turner, who had just retired from a senior executive position at a Fortune 50 heavy industry corporation and already had turned down 7 CEO jobs and 38 offers to serve on boards of directors. Turner recalled his first meeting with the nascent group:

The four of us met on a Saturday morning at Logan Airport, and we spent a lot of time talking beyond just intellect. It was about character. I told them that if this was all about excellence, then I would consider playing—but if not, I didn't want to touch it. These were young, bright guys, and I was energized by how committed they were.

Felton explained that while Turner's sterling credentials (Appendix A: Team Profiles) would help raise the profile of the group, his understanding of operations and his ability to connect with and evaluate senior-level managers would add the most value to the team:

The pool of ethnic minority business talent—people with 20 or 30 years of experience—is something we haven't had in this country until very recently. Although there is now a huge cadre of senior managers—minority men and women who have risen to real positions of authority—they are not altogether visible because they have their heads down and they are doing their jobs. As a member of organizations like

the Executive[4] Leadership Council, Ray has the ability to tap into that group.

For the position of vice president, Palmer recruited Harvard MBA Dario Cardenas, 31, a young man whose name had come up on everyone's short list of the most talented Hispanic candidates in the country. Cardenas had earned that reputation in part because of his service—at just 23 years old—as the youngest elected mayor of a major U.S. city (Appendix A: Team Profiles). Palmer explained that there was an advantage to bringing together people who were previously unknown to each other:

One way to think about a private equity firm is that it is only as good as the combined talents and networks of its team members. For this reason, I wanted to set up a group that could bring to the table a diverse set of skills, contacts, and perspectives. What we wound up with was 57 years of operating and 25 years of private equity experience, leading deals of over $200 million, with $100 million returned on just four of 16 investments.

Clint Harris was impressed with the team Palmer had recruited, but remained concerned about their ability to evaluate and add significant value to companies:

These guys had a good track record—which we verified with calls to their former colleagues, people at companies that they had invested in, and members of boards that they had served on. We could see that these were very bright and talented junior partner guys—as talented as any general partners that we had worked with—and Ray Turner was a real plus. In fact, a single half-hour call to my former suite mate at HBS—now CEO of General Motors—was all the due diligence I needed to learn that Ray would be a tremendous asset to the team, that he was totally committed, and that these young guys were top notch.

That said, it takes time and investing results for anyone to learn the equity investment business, and to calibrate on their judgment and skills. These guys didn't have much of a track record, and in that respect they were on the thin edge of what we like to see.

Grove Street Advisors—Gatekeeper

Back in 1997 Clint Harris and Catherine Crocket parlayed their extensive venture capital relationships into an investment management practice for institutional clients.

---

[3]Palmer and Pierce had first met in 1995. Seeing that they shared many of the same values and aspirations, they had kept in touch professionally and socially.

[4]The Executive Leadership Council was an independent, nonpartisan, nonprofit corporation founded in 1986 to provide African-American executives with a network and leadership forum designed to add perspective and direction to the achievement of excellence in business, economic, and public policies for the African-American community, corporate America, and the public.

EXHIBIT F

Life Cycle of Private Equity Managers

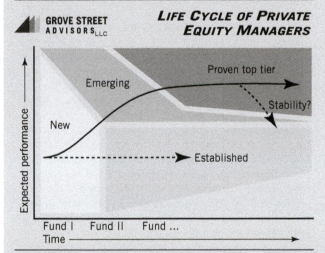

Source: Used by permission of Grove Street Advisors, LLC.

EXHIBIT G

Gatekeeper Dilemma

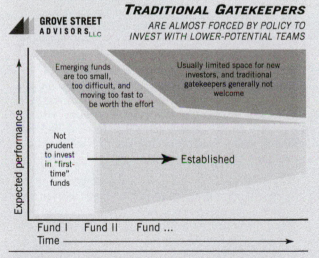

Source: Used by permission of Grove Street Advisors, LLC.

Harris explained that the risk-averse approach of traditional fee-for-service investment advisors had shut their clients out of top-tier funds (Exhibits F–H):

Gatekeepers generally view first-time funds as too risky and therefore imprudent investments. With teams now raising new funds before they have proven track records, it becomes very difficult to evaluate a team based on their investments. By the time these teams do emerge as top-tier players, their funds are often closed to all but the people who have been supporting them all along. As an advisor and a fund of funds, the only way that we

EXHIBIT H

Critical Issues and Development Stage

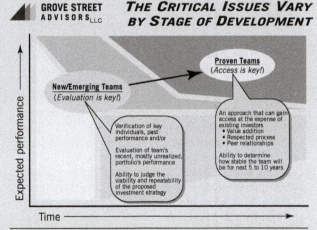

Source: Used by permission of Grove Street Advisors, LLC.

can hope to be on top 10 years from now is to identify and nurture the best new and emerging investment managers out there.

Our idea was to offer these institutional investors a vehicle that could effectively identify, evaluate, and invest in a portfolio of very high-quality new and emerging fund managers.

With no track record, Harris and Crocket had assumed they would start with a small client before going after a big state pension fund. Then, in the spring of 1998, the Grove Street pair met with Barry Gonder, senior investment officer for the California Public Employees Retirement System (CalPERS). After filling out their team with the addition of Dave Mazza—founder of the largest and best-known executive search practice serving the venture capital industry—and proposing the creation of a dedicated fund of funds they would call California Emerging Ventures I (CEV I), GSA succeeded in beating out several other firms for the $350 million account.

Almost immediately, GSA began opening venture capital doors for its sole client. By early 2001, CalPERS had increased its GSA capital stake to $750 million, and the advisor group had placed CEV I money with nearly 45 top venture capital firms. Harris explained that with a third of the total investment pool earmarked for new and emerging teams, his group was naturally drawn to nontraditional niche opportunities:

The paradox with demanding that mainstream investment standards are met is that those standards severely limit deal flow. We had our antennae up for minority and women investment opportunities, not for social reasons, but because we had the conviction that if we were able to find a strong enough team, they would attract a proprietary deal flow by way of their demographic network. We also knew that there were a lot of pension fund managers out there that were very interested in minority funding opportunities—opportunities that were being ignored by the mainstream.

At the heart of GSA's effectiveness was a broad base of business and venture capital industry contacts that enabled them to consistently conduct a level of due diligence on private equity managers that had not been seen before.

GSA interviewed, reviewed, and assessed hundreds of potential new fund managers and concepts—and passed on all but a few.

Although Palmer had not recruited a senior partner with a proven return performance of "50 IRR over 20 years," the GSA group remained solidly behind his efforts. Now that Palmer had assembled a team that was demographically similar to the entrepreneurial slice of America he aimed to target, he knew his next step was to foster a cohesive group dynamic.

Bonding the Team

Over the next few months, Palmer organized a number of in-depth strategy and bonding sessions (Exhibit I). Although these gatherings addressed issues related to the team's investment business, their main focus was on building rapport and understanding:

At our first get-together each of us told our whole personal and professional story. Once we had a collective sense of who we were, we began to talk in general terms about what we wanted to build. It had to be something we all believed in—something that would last over the long term—and be able to survive economic down cycles. Then we asked, "Does the market want what we envision, and do we have the collective talent to succeed?"

In the summer of 2000, Palmer took his wife and two young children to Martha's Vineyard for his first 2-week vacation in 15 years. He used part of that time to further bond the team:

I invited everyone—partners and their families—to visit with us on the island for 3 days. I explained to their wives why I was asking their spouses to do this. I felt that I needed to look them in the eye and tell them that there were no guarantees, that there would be hard, lean times, and that we'd be working harder than we ever had before.

The team was experienced enough to understand that success with this venture would yield a financial upside that was commensurate with the risks and challenges they would be taking on. At that time, the average total pay package—salary plus bonus—for managing general partners and senior-level partners was $1.24 million and $1.04 million, respectively. In addition, effective equity investors stood to reap even greater rewards in the form of carried interest distributions as their investments matured; managing general partners were bringing home an average of $2.5 million in carry, compared with $1.0 million by senior-level partners.[5]

The team estimated that their startup expenses for 1 year of fund-raising would be just under $400,000 (Exhibit J)—funded out of pocket or through personal loans. They felt that if they could articulate an opportunity that leveraged their collective skill set (and resonated with potential investors), they could cut their fund-raising time and be in business by late fall of 2001.

The Opportunity

The fund that Palmer and his team were setting up would execute buyout investments in a broad range of profitable, small- to middle-market private companies that served or operated in the minority marketplace. When these companies needed managers, Palmer and his team would tap into the "hidden" pool of experienced minority executives.

The team understood that many prospective LPs would align them with previous minority-focused investment efforts that were run by groups with little private equity experience. Clint Harris noted that many of those funds had lost sight of what should have been their main objective:

Minority funds in the past were often driven by political and social agendas; money got wasted and didn't do any good—and burned investors have very long memories. When this happens, it's not just the failure of the team and the fund; it's the failure of the good intentions to do social investing for the wrong reasons.

The team frequently encountered a tendency by some limited partner prospects to pigeonhole the fund as one that would invest exclusively in existing minority enterprises. For instance, Judith Elsea, then the Ewing Marion Kauffman Foundation's chief investment officer, noted that some prospective

---

[5] *Venture Capital Journal*, November 1, 2000; *The Compensation Game: While Opportunities Abound, Firms Entice Partner-Level VCs to Stick Around.* Data was according to a compensation survey of over 100 private equity firms, conducted by William M. Mercer Inc. Performance & Rewards Consulting.

EXHIBIT I

Meeting Notes

Agenda—Introduction and Strategy Session

All connected to the same Rope.

Date: **July 21, 2000**

Vilma Martinez — Roy's Contact

9:00 a.m.	**Introduction**
	• Progress to date – *Team / Research / LPs /*
	• Team introductions – *Detailed / Worst trouble...*
10:30 a.m.	**Discussion of fund strategy** – *Broaden MKT ⟶ Serve, Employ, Located / Basket for General Mkt Deals*
	• Fund size – $150M (⟶ $200M 9/16/00)
	• Deal stages – *Growth Equity ⟶ Buyouts*
	• Industries – *Focus on Ind w/ strong # prospects*
	• Geography – *Midwest presence - access to deal flow*
MKT •	• Deal flow – *Growth equity ⟶ Buyouts*
	• Portfolio company management - *style / 2 per BOD*
	• Side fund - *Charles Tribbett / Exc. of executives / Operating Affiliates ⟶ Second side fund*
11:30 a.m.	**Firm operating philosophy** - *End product ⟹ View of the firm and internal culture*
	• Management philosophy - *Open / all-hands, all-eyes / veto / No mng partner*
	• Roles - *1-2 Admin / 4N-IB, GMs, banks, etc / Att. PR resp.*
	• Decision making - *consensus*
	• Due diligence - *set parameters / evolve over time*
	• Partner meetings - *format*
	• Portfolio management - */ lead, / backup*
12:30 p.m.	**Review draft budget** - *Startup* Timing
12:45 p.m.	**Discussion of fund-raising strategy**
	• First close goals –
	• LP targets and amount for first close – *who / # amounts*
	• Placement agent? - *see notes from Wanda*
1:30 p.m.	**Open issues for the team** - *How do we get to a decision on whether to do this = timing / concerns / additional info needed*
2:00 p.m.	**Next steps**
Strategic Partner —	• Decision on doing it with or without Wind Point = *Financial + Startup capital / Continuity and timing of close / Don't pay for what you don't use*
	• Timing for other decisions
	• PPM draft—need team resumes and track record info
	• Side fund—executive recruitment
	• Pick counsel—for mgmt company, GP&LP documents
	• Negotiate economics - *f/u w/ each individual and come back w/ proposal to*
	• Start-up logistics - *who / when / groups location / steps*
	• Firm name? - *Input ...*

limited partners would be challenged to conduct due diligence:

This team is proposing something different by addressing markets that are not as heavily trafficked by private equity groups. But while those markets are arguably underserved, they are also in areas where a lot of institutional investors don't

have a lot of experience—or big networks where people would be easy to check out.

Palmer felt that the entire discussion was missing the point:

I'm not worrying about what other minority firms are doing or have done, but I know that as soon as we sit down with potential investors, they are going

EXHIBIT J

Startup Estimates

October 2000 to October 2001

Variable Expenses

Salaries	90,000[a]
Legal	44,000
Travel	20,000
Rent	62,500[b]
Phone	10,000
Postage and printing	14,000
Meals	10,000
Entertainment	20,000
	$270,500

Fixed Expenses

Computers/networking/printers	40,000
Phone system	20,000
Office supplies	5,000
Office furniture	50,000
	$ 115,000
Total startup expenses	$385,500

[a]Salaries: Three partners @ $40,000 each. Half salary for 6 months.

[b]Rent: 2,500 square feet @ $25/sf.

to think we are investing exclusively in minority ventures. We are going to have to craft our presentation in a way that gets people to stop thinking about that and instead see what we are doing as a generic way to go make money, a solid private equity strategy—no mirrors or hidden agendas.

Since much of their deal flow would involve established and later-stage opportunities, David Mazza cautioned against being too quick to initiate operations:

I told them that a $50 million buyout fund was only going to get them into trouble. We like to see a bare minimum of $100 million, and prefer $200 to $250 million.

The Beginning

Now that the team had committed to move to Boston, Palmer decided that when they and their families arrived in September, he would welcome them with a van tour of the city. Then they would start crafting the offering prospectus and raising the fund.

Appendix A
TEAM PROFILES

Maclean Palmer, Jr.

Maclean Palmer, Jr. (41) has over 5 years of *direct* private equity experience and over 17 years of operating experience. He was a managing director in the San Francisco office of Point West Partners from 1997 to 2000. There, Palmer originated deals, executed transactions, and managed portfolio companies. He focused on growth equity and buyout investments in the telecommunications, business-to-business services, industrial manufacturing, and auto sectors. Palmer led Point West investments in three competitive local exchange carriers (CLECs): Cobalt Telecommunications, MBCS Telecommunications, and Concept Telephone. He continues to represent Point West on the board of directors of both MBCS and Concept Telephone.

From 1995 to 1997, Palmer was a vice president in the Boston office of Advent International. There, he focused on industrial and technology investments and led Advent's investment in ISI, a financial and business information services provider. From 1986 to 1995, Palmer held various management and engineering positions for three startup companies financed by private equity investors. Palmer also held engineering positions with Borg Warner Corporation from 1984 to 1986 and with the diesel division of a major automotive firm from 1983 to 1984.

Palmer sits on the board of JT Technologies, a minority-owned firm that develops battery and ultra-capacitor technology, and the board of the Cooper Enterprise Fund, a minority-focused fund based in New York.

Palmer holds a BSME from the Automotive Institute, an MBA cum laude from Babson College, and was awarded a Kauffman Fellowship in the program's inaugural class.

Ray S. Turner

Ray S. Turner (61) worked for a multinational heavy-industry manufacturer in the Fortune 50 from 1977 to March 2000. He was group vice president, North America Sales, Service, and Marketing from October 1998 to March 2000, and vice president and general manager for North America Sales and Manufacturing from 1990 to 1998.

Prior to his career at that corporation, Turner spent several years in a variety of positions in engineering, materials management, manufacturing, sales, personnel, and labor relations. He serves on the board of directors of two Fortune 100 corporations.

Turner received a bachelor's degree in business administration from Western Michigan University. He also completed the Executive Development Program at Harvard Business School and an Advanced International General Management Program in Switzerland.

Clark T. Pierce

Clark T. Pierce (38) has over 7 years of mezzanine and private equity experience and over 4 years of corporate finance experience. As a principal with Ninos Capital, a publicly traded mezzanine investment fund, he was responsible for leading all aspects of the investment process, including deal origination and evaluation, due diligence, deal, execution, and portfolio company management.

From 1993 to 1995, Pierce managed Ninos Capital's Specialized Small Business Investment Company ("SSBIC"). This SSBIC was a $45 million investment vehicle directed toward minority-owned and -controlled companies. Prior to Ninos Capital, Pierce spent 1 year with Freeman Securities as a vice president in the Corporate Finance Group. From 1989 to 1991, Pierce was an associate with Chase Manhattan Bank, N.A.

Pierce received a BA from Morehouse College, a JD from George Washington University, and an MBA from the Wharton Business School at the University of Pennsylvania.

Andrew L. Simon

Andrew L. Simon (30) has 4 years of direct private equity experience and 3 years of strategy consulting experience. During his career, Simon has worked on private equity investments in numerous industries, including contract manufacturing, industrial products, health care, financial services, and direct marketing. Most recently he was a senior associate in the New York office at McCown De Leeuw & Co., Inc. ("MDC"), where he focused on growth and leveraged equity investments, including recapitalization and buy-and-build acquisitions.

From 1995 to 1997, Simon was an associate in the Boston office of Trident Partners and from 1992 to 1995, he was a senior analyst at Marakon Associates. In addition, Simon has worked for Littlejohn & Co., an LBO firm focused on restructuring, Physicians Quality Care, a venture-backed health care services company, and Lotus Development.

Simon earned an AB degree from Princeton University's Woodrow Wilson School and earned his MBA, with honors, from Harvard Business School, where he was a Toigo Fellow.

Dario A. Cardenas

From 1999 to 2000, Fidel A. Cardenas (31) was a managing director with MTG Ventures, a private equity firm focused on acquiring and operating manufacturing and service companies. There, he was responsible for deal origination, transaction execution, and portfolio company management. From 1992 to 1997, Cardenas was a principal with MTG Advisors, where he focused on strategy consulting and executive coaching. During that time, Cardenas was elected to two terms as mayor of Sunny Park, California, the first at 23. He has also served as assistant deputy mayor for public safety for the City of Los Angeles and as an analyst for McKinsey and Company.

Cardenas received a BA in Political Science from Harvard, cum laude, and his MBA from Harvard Business School.

Chapter Nine

Ethical Decision Making and the Entrepreneur

LEARNING OUTCOMES: After reading this chapter, you will be able to understand:

9-1 An overview of ethics

9-2 Ethical stereotypes

9-3 Can ethics be taught?

9-4 The usefulness of academic ethics

9-5 Foundations for ethical decision making

9-6 Advice and tips from the trenches

9-7 Thorny issues for entrepreneurs

9-8 The ecological shareholder

Overview of Ethics

The vast majority of successful entrepreneurs believe that high ethical standards and integrity are exceptionally important to long-term success. For example, Jeffry Timmons and his colleague Howard H. Stevenson conducted a study among 128 presidents and founders attending the Harvard Business School's Owner-President Management (OPM) program in 1983.[1] Their firms typically had sales of $40 million, and sales ranged from $5 to $200 million. These entrepreneurs were also very experienced, with an average age in the mid-40s, and about half had founded their companies. They were asked to name the most critical concepts, skills, and know-how for success for their companies at the time and what they would be in 5 years. The answer to this question was startling enough that the Sunday *New York Times* reported the findings: 72 percent of the presidents responding stated that high ethical standards were the single most important factor in long-term success.[2]

A May 2003 study by the Aspen Institute found that MBA students are concerned their schools are not doing enough to prepare them for the ethical dilemmas of the business world. Seventeen hundred MBA students from the United States, Canada, and Britain were surveyed and the results were addressed in the May 21, 2003 issue of *Chronicle of Higher Education*. Ethical lapses like those of Enron executives erode the confidence in business activity at all levels.

A provocative article published in the *Harvard Business Review* asserted that the ethics of business were not those of society but rather those of the poker game.[3] The author of the article argued, "Most businessmen are not indifferent to ethics in their private lives, everyone will agree. My point is that in their office lives they cease to be private citizens; they become game players who must be guided by a somewhat different set of ethical standards."

Laws have not only authority but also limitations. While laws are made with forethought and with the deliberate purpose of ensuring justice, it can be difficult to anticipate new conditions. Statutes do not always have the effect they were intended to have; they sometimes conflict with one another and they are incapable of making judgments where multiple, sometimes contradictory ethical considerations hang in the balance.

The authors are most grateful to Professors James Klingler and William Bregman, Center for Entrepreneurship at Villanova University, Villanova, PA, for their contributions to our thinking on this challenging and important subject. We have included their insightful and practical work throughout this revised chapter. Their work has influenced how we now think about and present this material.

[1] J.A. Timmons and H.H. Stevenson, "Entrepreneurship Education in the 1980s," presented at the 75th Anniversary Entrepreneurship Symposium, Harvard Business School, Boston, 1983. *Proceedings*, pp. 115–34.

[2] For an overview of the philosophical underpinnings of ethics and a decision-making framework, see "A Framework for Ethical Decision Making," J. L. Livingstone et al., Babson College Case Development Center, 2003.

[3] Reprinted by permission of *Harvard Business Review*. An excerpt from "Is Business Bluffing Ethical?" by A. Z. Carr, January–February 1968, pp. 145–152. Copyright © 1967 by the President and Fellows of Harvard College.

Ethical Stereotypes

The United States provides an inviting climate for those starting their own enterprises with a regulatory environment encourages an atmosphere that allows free market forces, private initiative, individual responsibility, and freedom to flourish.

These laws have had the equally desirable effect of encouraging those in many industries to develop codes of ethics, in large part because they wished to have the freedom to set their own rules rather than to have rules imposed on them by legislatures.

Many entrepreneurs were regarded as ruthless in the unfettered economic climate of the 19th century, when industrial sabotage, child workers, and the exploitation of black labor were common. Yet institutions such as the Morgan Library and the Rockefeller Foundation show that even American entrepreneurs of that era wanted to give back to society through education, culture, and art. The extraordinary legacy of Andrew Carnegie is another example.

Carnegie's case is interesting based on his total change of attitude that came after he amassed his fortune. Carnegie, the son of a Scottish weaver, created a personal fortune of $300 million in the production of crude steel between 1873 and 1901, the equivalent of $130 billion in today's dollars. Carnegie believed that competition "insures the survival of the fittest in every department." Carnegie also felt that "the fact that this talent for organization and management is rare among men is proved by the fact that it invariably secures enormous rewards for its possessor."[4] After 1901, when he sold Carnegie Steel to United States Steel, Carnegie personally supervised donations in the United States and Great Britain of more than $300 million. Among these gifts were over 2,800 libraries, an Endowment for International Peace, and the Carnegie Institute of Pittsburgh.

Can Ethics Be Taught?

Just as the 1990s ushered in a new era of worldwide entrepreneurship, Andrew Stark asserts that the world of business ethics has redefined itself:

> Advocates of the new business ethics can be identified by their acceptance of two fundamental principles. While they agree with their colleagues that ethics and interest can conflict, they take that observation as the starting point, not the ending point,

of an ethicist's analytical task.... Second, the new perspective reflects an awareness and acceptance of the messy work of mixed motives.[5]

The challenge facing this new group of business ethicists is to bridge the gap between the moral philosophers and the managers. The business ethicists talk of "moderation, pragmatism, minimalism"[6] in their attempt to "converse with real managers in a language relevant to the world they inhabit and the problems they face."[7] With this focus on the practical side of decision making, courses on ethics can be useful to entrepreneurs and all managers.

Ethics Can and Should Be Taught

In an article that examines the ancient tradition of moral education, the decline of moral instruction beginning in the 19th century, and the renaissance of interest in ethics in the 1960s, Derek Bok, former president of Harvard University, argues that ethics can and should be taught by educational institutions and that this teaching is both necessary and of value. Dr. Bok's comments may be summarized as follows:

> Universities by nature encourage diverse communities, often divided and confused over their own values, as well as the values of others. A learning environment that pays little attention to moral development may find that many of its students fall under the incorrect impression that ethical dilemmas are simply matters of personal opinion beyond external judgment or careful analysis. Universities should be the last institutions to discourage a thorough study in ethical behaviors and philosophies.[8]

Some of America's top business schools seem to agree. Harvard and Wharton both include business ethics as a substantial part of their MBA curricula, and Georgetown, Virginia, and Minnesota all have endowed chairs in the field. Fully 90 percent of the nation's business schools now offer some training in the area, demonstrating widespread recognition of the need to provide future leaders with a strong ethical foundation.

The Entrepreneur's Competitive Edge: The Art of Self-assessment

As discussed in Chapters 2 and 8, one of the core principles of this book is the importance of self-assessment and self-awareness. Entrepreneurs who truly know themselves and understand not only their own morals and values, but also those of the

---

[4]"Introduction to Contemporary Civilization in the West," *The Gospel of Wealth* (New York: Century, 1900), p. 620.
[5]A. Stark, "What's the Matter with Business Ethics?" *Harvard Business Review*, May–June 1993, p. 46.
[6]Ibid., p. 48.
[7]Ibid.
[8]D. Bok, "Is Dishonesty Good for Business?" *Business & Society Review*, Summer 1979, p. 50.

people they surround themselves with, make the best decisions. This manifests itself in a number of ways. First, they can invite people of similar philosophies into their team and brain trust. Second, this produces teams that are honest about their own capabilities and shortcomings, which instills trust and confidence. This is critical because of the environment in which their decisions will be made. Often in entrepreneurship, particularly in the launch and growth stages of a new venture, the environment is chaotic, unpredictable, and frequently unforgiving.

Take Time to Reflect   To make good decisions you must identify and understand yourself and the scope and the effects of your own self-interest. Knowing your biases and weaknesses offers an opportunity for personal development and to clearly define your personal and business goals and objectives.

Take the time now, while life is relatively calm, to determine what is important to you and why. During these times you can consider your stakeholders, your personal motivations, and the impact those can have on your decision making. Because your judgment will be less clouded prior to launch, the planning process for your new venture should include a good bit of introspection.

Recognize Self-interest   Our perceptions are filtered by who we are: our experiences, beliefs, and preferences–all the things that make us unique and shape what is important to us.

Henry Brooks Adams, a historian and author as well as the great-grandson of John Adams and the grandson of John Quincy Adams, summed up the peril faced by a person who overwhelmingly pursues his or her own self-interest when he wrote, "Never esteem anything as of advantage to you that will make you break your word or lose your self-respect." The pursuit of self-interest without realizing the pitfalls it presents can be costly and even dangerous. Here are some major influences to consider:

Emotion: What you love, hate, or fear will influence your perception and therefore your decisions. The people whom you feel most strongly about can have a tremendous influence on your decisions. Like divorces, partnership breakups can become so emotionally charged with self-interest that decisions made ignore the best outcome for anyone involved.

Motivation: Entrepreneur and investor Khalil Tuzman, in his "Entrepreneur's Survival Kit," lists five individual motivators: to attain wealth, to achieve recognition or fame, to feel courageous, to be healthy, and to find contentment. If the motivation is to win at any cost, for example, fair play and ethics will have far less influence over your decisions than they should.

Stakeholders: Who will be affected by your decisions and how? Recognize that the closer they are to you, the more effect they will have on your decision making.

The Usefulness of Academic Ethics

The study of ethics does seem to make students more aware of the pervasiveness of ethical situations in business settings, and helps to bring perspective to ethical situations. Further, the study of ethics has been shown to affect, to some degree, both beliefs and behavior.

One study used the Kohlberg construct, a sequence of stages devised to break down moral instincts and behaviors.[9] These stages are presented in Exhibit 9.1. Being moral in Stage 1 is synonymous with being obedient, and the motivation is to avoid condemnation. In Stage 2, the individual seeks advantage. Gain is the primary purpose, and interaction does not result in binding personal relationships. The orientation of Stage 3 is toward pleasing others and winning approval. Proper roles are defined by stereotyped images of majority behavior. Such reciprocity is confined to primary group relations. In Stage 4, cooperation is viewed in the context of society as a whole. External laws coordinate moral schemes, and the individual feels committed to the social order. We thus subscribe to formal punishment by police or the courts. In Stage 5, there is acknowledgment that reciprocity can be inequitable. New laws and social arrangements now may be invoked as corrective mechanisms. All citizens are assured of fundamental safety and equality. Cognitive structures at the Stage 6 level automatically reject credos and actions that the individual considers morally reprehensible, and the referent is a person's own moral framework, rather than stereotyped group behavior. Because most people endorse a law does not guarantee its moral validity; when confronting social dilemmas, the individual is guided by internal principles that

---

[9]Lawrence Kohlberg was a professor at Harvard University. He became famous for his work there as a developmental psychologist and then moved to the field of moral education. His work was based on theories that human beings develop philosophically and psychologically in a progressive fashion. Kohlberg believed and demonstrated in several published studies that people progressed in their moral reasoning (i.e., in their bases for ethical behavior) through a series of six identifiable stages.

EXHIBIT 9.1

Classification of Moral Judgment into Stages of Development

Stage	Orientation	Theme
1	Punishment and obedience	Morality of obedience
2	Instrumental relativism	Simple exchange
3	Interpersonal concordance	Reciprocal role taking
4	Law and order	Formal justice
5	Legitimate social contract	Procedural justice
6	Universal ethical principle	Individual conscience

Source: Adapted from Kohlberg (1967).

may transcend the legal system. Although these convictions are personal, they are also universal because they have worth and utility apart from the individual espousing them. Kohlberg's final stage thus represents more than mere conformity with state, teacher, or institutional criteria. Rather, it indicates one's capacity for decision making and problem solving in the context of personal ethical standards. In the study, those who took a course in business ethics showed a progression up the ethical scale, while those who had not taken a course did not progress.

Foundations for Ethical Decision Making

Some may find it surprising to learn that there is no perfect approach to dealing with ethically charged situations. In fact, people who subscribe to a "one best" approach can find themselves making decisions that, after the fact, others view as unethical. Similarly, lacking an understanding of the different approaches may lead to missteps because the decision maker fails to recognize the ethical implications of a particular situation.

When considering what to do in a situation with ethical overtones, it is useful to be familiar with different approaches to ethics. These varied approaches become ethical screens—similar to the opportunity screens presented in Chapter 6. Taking a multifaceted approach can prevent someone from unknowingly making an ethical mistake. We will briefly consider three widely used approaches.

Aristotle, the Greek philosopher, provided one of the oldest approaches to ethics. To him it seemed that the aim of each person should be to perfect his or her inherent human nature, and if successful, become a person of virtue. By striving to be virtuous, and by emulating what people who are widely considered to be virtuous do in similar situations, we can, over time, develop habits of virtue. In modern terms, this is akin to choosing to observe and emulate exemplary role models.

Two issues arising from this approach can lead an entrepreneur to make poor decisions. The first is choosing the wrong person to emulate, such as former Enron CEO Jeff Skilling. The second is that neither the actions actually taken nor the consequences of the actions are directly addressed—only that the "court of opinion" holds the actions to have been virtuous.

A second approach to ethics focuses on the consequences or outcomes of actions. This approach is called utilitarianism, and its most often cited proponent is John Stewart Mill, a 19th-century English philosopher. It holds that the ethical person will always choose actions that will provide for the greatest good (or least bad) for the greatest number of people. When considering what action to take, an ethical entrepreneur acting from a utilitarian perspective would mentally calculate the impact of the action on each stakeholder. Therefore, it is not the action that is being judged as ethical or unethical, but rather the collective impact of that action. A familiar way of expressing this is the saying that "the ends (consequences) justify the means (actions taken)."

A number of issues can make the utilitarian approach difficult to adhere to or can to actions that may be considered unethical. First, it permits decisions that may hurt some stakeholders, as long as the majority benefits from the action. Second, a narrow view of who the stakeholders are may lead to unethical decisions because we may fail to consider a stakeholder such as the environment. Third, the proximity of stakeholders, or the degree to which they demand attention, may cause the decision maker to ignore (or forget) them. Fourth, there is a thin line between seeking the greatest good for the greatest number and seeking the greatest good for you. Self-interest can justify many deplorable actions because they maximize personal outcomes to the exclusion of all else. The last important issue stems from the fact that people are judged as ethical or unethical based on the actions they take, not by how they calculate the utility of the outcomes. We must have a means of considering the action apart from the outcomes. That leads into our third approach, deontology.

Deontology means duty—one's duty to act. According to Immanuel Kant, the 18th-century German philosopher, deontology focuses on the precepts that should determine action. This approach is pursued without concern for the outcomes of actions, but according to whether the action is something that an ethical person would do. Actions, then, are undertaken because they are right in themselves, whether or not the outcomes benefit or harm the person taking the actions. People therefore should act in ways that one would hope become the universal laws of society. In situations where one's duty to society conflicts with one's self-interest, one must act in accordance with the duty to society regardless of the consequences. For example, if lying is not what you would want to have as a universal law in society, then you should never lie, even if lying would benefit you personally or benefit your stakeholders.

Applying the Foundations

So how can we use these approaches? We suggest that you use them as decision-making screens to view the outcome and impact of any action you might take. A good place to start would be the most widely used approach, utilitarianism. Carefully enumerate the stakeholders, being sure to include everyone, not just the convenient ones or the ones making the most noise. When you have decided on an action, apply the Aristotelian approach by asking, "What would a really ethical entrepreneur in this situation do?" You might ask people in your network and brain trust to tell you what they have done in similar situations. Finally, look at the action you are taking alone–separate from the consequences. Is this action pure? That is, is it something that you would be proud to have as the headline your mother reads when she Googles you?

Using these screens will not guarantee an ethical decision. Considering different approaches to the same issue will help prevent ethical myopia–a narrowly defined ethical perspective that can lead to trouble.

The Fog of War and Entrepreneurship: A Unique Context

The environment around a new venture is often chaotic. Lessons can be learned from an even more chaotic environment: combat. There is a concept called "the fog of war" that goes back to the 19th century, when Prussian general Carl von Clausewitz wrote,

> War is the realm of uncertainty; three-quarters of the factors on which action is based are wrapped in a fog of greater or lesser uncertainty.

When bullets are flying and lives are at stake, critical decisions must be made without the benefit of a perfect understanding of the whole picture. In the same way, the fog of the startup battle that a typical entrepreneur faces could include intense pressures from outside influences like the following:

- Your spouse says you are not home enough.
- Your Aunt Tillie, your father, and your mother-in-law have each put in $50,000 . . . which is gone.
- Everything takes too long and costs too much.
- Your business is not working as it was supposed to.
- You are doing nothing but damage control.
- You have slowed down payments to creditors, who are now screaming and making threats.
- You have maxed out your refinanced line of credit and your credit cards, and you have discounted receivables and inventories to get the cash in sooner. Still, you figure you have just 18 business days of cash left.
- Investors will put in money, but they want two more seats on the board and a much larger percentage of ownership.
- The bank reminds you that you and your spouse have signed personal guarantees.
- The 80-ton dinosaur in your industry just moved into your market.
- The malcontent troublemaker you fired is suing you.

Now, in the midst of these sorts of pressures, make a decision that might have serious financial and ethical consequences that could follow you the rest of your life.

Action under Pressure

An entrepreneur will have to act on issues while under serious time constraints and when struggling for survival. In addition, the entrepreneur will most likely decide ethical questions that involve obligations on many fronts–to customers, employees, stockholders, family, partners, self, or a combination of these. As you will see in the ethically charged situations presented at the end of the chapter, walking the tightrope and balancing common sense with an ethical framework can be precarious.

To cope with the inevitable conflicts, an entrepreneur should develop an awareness of his or her own explicit and implicit ethical beliefs, those of his or her team and investors, and those of the milieu within which the company competes for survival. As the successful entrepreneurs quoted earlier believe, in the long run, succumbing to the temptations of situational ethics will, in all likelihood, result in a tumble into the quicksand, not a safety net—just ask Steve Madden or the executives at Enron, Tyco, and Arthur Andersen.

Advice and Tips from the Trenches

Many of the lessons learned in the military and on the battlefield can be instructive to entrepreneurs struggling with the chaos and uncertainties that go with the territory. Consider the following.

Experience Is Critical   Military troops are not sent into combat on the day they enlist. They receive relevant training and engage in stressful and chaotic simulations that are as close as possible to the real thing. In a new venture, an entrepreneur who has done it before has experience to help with chaos. In areas where they lack direct experience, entrepreneurs can compensate with a key hire, team member, mentor, consultant, board member, or professional.

Have a Plan B   Although designing "what if" scenarios is most often associated with the quantitative side of running a proactive business (costs, pricing, margins, and the like), thinking through contingency plans, particularly during the launch and growth stages, is an excellent way to avoid rash or ethically questionable decisions in the heat of a challenge. One technique to facilitate scenario dialog and planning is to have a brown-bag lunch with your partners and pose some tough ethical dilemmas you may face. Ask, "what would each of you do?"

Develop and Use Objective Standards   When faced with decisions on the fly—especially ones involving ethical issues—it can be helpful to have a clear and objective means to assess the situation. For example, at Everon IT, a remote IT services venture based in Boston, critical metrics for incoming, outgoing, and ongoing calls are projected large on the facing wall of the service area. Other walls feature motivational posters, challenge goals, employee accolades, and descriptions of goal-related rewards ranging from dinners for all to lavish vacation retreats. With everyone pulling together to meet and beat well-defined milestones, the office is charged with a sense of mission and purpose.

Find a Pessimist You Can Trust   Every lead entrepreneur should have a trusted, no-nonsense advisor in the brain trust who can provide brutally honest assessments when things seem to be off base. When these cautious, somewhat pessimistic advisors express their approval of a given decision or strategy, that validation can be a real confidence booster.

Do not Forget the Mirror and Those Internet Headlines   Looking in the mirror can be a powerful, challenging exercise. You have just read the morning headlines all over the Internet that describe in intimate detail all of your actions and behaviors concerning a recent decision that—most unexpectedly—became highly visible and public. Is this the person you want to be known as? Is this a person the people you love and respect the most would admire and support? Is this a person you want your best friends and your family to know about? If you are not fully comfortable with your answers to these questions and what you see in the mirror as a result of an ethical decision you have to make, then you do not have an acceptable answer yet. Do not give up—but clean it up!

Thorny Issues for Entrepreneurs

Although the majority of entrepreneurs take ethics seriously, researchers in this area are still responding to David McClelland's call for inquiry: "We do not know at the present time what makes an entrepreneur more or less ethical in his dealings, but obviously there are few problems of greater importance for future research."[10] One article outlined the topics for research (Exhibit 9.2). Clearly an opportunity for further research still exists.

Different Views

Different reactions to what is ethical may explain why some aspects of venture creation go wrong, both during startup and in the heat of the battle, for no apparent reason. Innumerable examples can be cited to illustrate that broken partnerships often can be traced to apparent differences in the personal ethics among the members of a management team. So too with investors. While the experienced venture capital investor seeks entrepreneurs with a reputation for integrity, honesty, and ethical behavior, the definition is necessarily subjective and depends in part on the beliefs of the investor and in part on the prevailing ethical climate in the industry sector in which the venture is involved.

---

[10]D. McClelland, Achieving Society (New York: Van Nostrand, 1961), p. 331.

EXHIBIT 9.2

Selected Ethical Dilemmas of Entrepreneurial Management

Dilemma: Elements	Issues That May Arise
Promoter: Entrepreneurial euphoria Impression management Pragmatic vs. moral considerations	What does honesty mean when promoting an innovation? Does it require complete disclosure of the risks and uncertainties? Does it require a dispassionate analysis of the situation, with equal time given to the downside as well as the upside? What sorts of influence tactics cross the line from encouragement and inducement to manipulation and coercion?
Relationship: Conflicts of interest and roles Transactional ethics Guerrilla tactics	Tension between perceived obligations and moral expectations. Changes in roles and relationships: pre- vs. postventure status. Decisions based on affiliative concerns rather than on task-based concerns. Transition from a trust-based work environment to one that is more controlled.
Innovator: "Frankenstein's problem" New types of ethical problems Ethic of change	Side effects and negative externalities force a social reconsideration of norms and values. Heightened concern about the future impact of unknown harms. Who is responsible for the assessment of risk? Inventor? Government? Market? Breaking down traditions and creating new models.
Other dilemmas: Finders–keepers ethic Conflict between personal values and business goals Unsavory business practices	Is there a fair way to divide profits when they are the result of cooperative efforts? Should the entrepreneur take all the gains that are not explicitly contracted away? Managing an intimate connection between personal choices and professional decisions. Coping with ethical pressures with creative solutions and integrity. Seeking industry recognition while not giving in to peer pressure to conform.

Source: Adapted from J.G. Dees and J.A. Starr, "Entrepreneurship through an Ethical Lens," in *The State of the Art of Entrepreneurship,* ed. D.L. Sexton and J.D. Kasarda (Boston: PWS-Kent, 1992), p. 96.

Problems of Law

For entrepreneurs, situations where one law directly conflicts with another are increasingly frequent. For example, a small-business investment company in New York City got in serious financial trouble. The Small Business Administration stated the company should begin to liquidate its investments because it would otherwise be in defiance of its agreement with the SBA. However, the Securities and Exchange Commission stated that this liquidation would constitute unfair treatment of stockholders, due to resulting imbalance in their portfolios. After a year and a half of agonizing negotiation, the company was able to satisfy all the parties, but compromises had to be made on both sides.

Another example of conflicting legal demands involves conflicts between procedures of the civil service commission code and the Fair Employment Practice Acts. The code states that hiring will include adherence to certain standards, a principle that was introduced in the 20th century to curb the patronage abuses in public service. Recently the problem of encouraging and aiding minorities has led to the Civil Service Commission Fair Employment Practice Acts, which require the same public agencies that are guided by CSC standards to hire without prejudice, and without the requirement that a given test shall serve as the criterion of selection. Both these laws are based on valid ethical intent, but the resolution of such conflicts is no simple matter.

Further, unlike the international laws governing commercial airline transportation, there is no international code of business ethics. When doing business abroad, entrepreneurs may find that those with whom they do business have little in common with them—no common language, no common historical context for conducting business, and no common set of ethical beliefs about right and wrong and everything in between. For example, in the United States, bribing a high official to obtain a favor is considered both ethically and legally unacceptable; in parts of the Middle East, it is the only way to get things done.

Examples of the Ends-and-Means Issue

A central question in any ethical discussion concerns the extent to which a noble end may justify ignoble means-or whether using unethical means for assumed ethical ends may subvert the aim in some way. As an example of a noble end, consider the case of a university agricultural extension service whose goal was to help small farmers increase their crop productivity. The end was economically constructive and profit oriented only in the sense that the farmers might prosper from better crop yields. However, to continue being funded, the extension service was required to predict the annual increases in crop yield it could achieve at a level of detail it could not do. Unless it could show detailed increases in crop yields its funding was at risk. In this case the extension service decided to provide the detailed figures because they felt that even though the presentation of overly optimistic predictions was unethical, the objectives of those running the organization were highly ethical. The funding source finally backed down in its demand, ameliorating the immediate problem. But if it had not, the danger existed that the individuals in this organization, altruistic though their intentions were, would begin to think that falsification was the norm and forget that actions that run contrary to ethical feelings gradually build a debilitating cynicism.

Another example is the merger of a small rental service business with a midsize conglomerate. In this case, a partner in the rental firm became involved in a severe automobile accident and suffered multiple injuries shortly before the merger and was unable to return to work. The partner also knew that the outlook for his health in the immediate future was unpredictable. For the sake of his family, he was eager to seek some of the stock acquired in the merger and liquidate a large portion of his assets. However, federal law does not allow quick profit taking from mergers and therefore did not allow such a sale. The partner consulted the president and officers of the larger company, and they acquiesced to his plans to sell portions of his stock and stated their conviction that no adverse effect on the stock would result. Still unsure, the partner then checked with his lawyer and found that the federal law in question had almost never been prosecuted. Having ascertained the risk and having probed the rationale of the law as it applied to his case, the partner sold some of the stock acquired in the merger to provide security for his family. Although he subsequently recovered completely, this could not have been foreseen.

In this instance, the partner decided that a consideration of the intrinsic purpose of the law allowed him to act as he did. In addition, he made as thorough a check as possible of the risks involved in his action. He was not satisfied with the decision he made, but he believed it was the best he could do at the time.

An Example of Integrity

The complicated nature of entrepreneurial decisions is also illustrated in the following example. At age 27, an entrepreneur joined a new computer software firm with sales of $1.5 million as vice president of international marketing of a new division. His principal goal was to establish profitable distribution for the company's products in the major industrialized nations. Stock incentives and a highly leveraged bonus plan placed clear emphasis on profitability rather than on volume. In one European country, the choice of distributors was narrowed to 1 from a field of more than 20. The potential distributor was a top firm, with an excellent track record and management, and the chemistry was right. In fact, the distributor was so eager to do business with the entrepreneur's company that it was willing to accept a 10 percent commission rather than the normal 15 percent royalty. The other terms of the deal were acceptable to both parties. In this actual case, the young vice president decided to give the distributor the full 15 percent commission, even though it would have settled for less. This approach was apparently quite successful because, in 5 years, this international division grew from zero to $18 million in very profitable sales, and a large firm acquired the venture for $80 million. In describing his reasoning, the entrepreneur said his main goal was to create a sense of long-term integrity. He said further,

I knew what it would take for them to succeed in gaining the kind of market penetration we were after. I also knew that the economics of their business definitely needed the larger margins from the 15 percent, rather than the smaller royalty. So I figured that if I offered them the full royalty, they would realize I was on their side, and that would create such goodwill that when we did have some serious problems down the road—and you always have them—then we would be able to work together to solve them. And that is exactly what happened. If I had exploited their eagerness to be our distributor, then it only would have come back to haunt me later on.

The Ecological Stakeholder

While working through the chaos and constantly considering how to get the most out of each dollar spent, it is important to remember the effects of your decisions, not only on team members, investors, and other stakeholders, but also on the environment. Environmental ethics can play a tricky role in entrepreneurship–there are so many challenges which already drain time, money, and patience that business owners sometimes struggle to consider the short- and long-term effects of their decisions on the natural world.

Code of Ethical Responsibility

Ethical Performance: Everyone's Responsibility

As an employee or independent contractor of The MENTOR Network, you have an obligation to be honest in all of your dealings with the individuals we serve, their families, fellow employees, independent contractors, vendors, and third parties. You must know and comply with applicable laws, regulations, licensing requirements, contractual obligations, and all company policies and procedures. Maintaining ethical standards is everyone's responsibility. If you know of a problem, you cannot remain silent. Step forward and be part of the solution.

For those employees and independent contractors involved in the coordination of services for individuals in care, the company expects you to

■ Conduct yourself according to professional and ethical standards.
■ Take responsibility for identifying, developing, and fully utilizing knowledge and abilities for professional practice.
■ Obtain training/education and supervision to assure competent services.
■ Not misrepresent professional qualifications, education, experience, or affiliations, and maintain the credentials required in order to deliver the type and intensity of services provided.
■ Be aware of your own values and their implications for practice.
■ Solicit collaborative participation by professionals, the individuals served, and family and community members to share responsibility for consumer outcomes.
■ Work to increase public awareness and education of the human service industry.
■ Advocate for adequate resources.
■ Work to ensure the efficiency and effectiveness of services provided.
■ Maintain boundaries between professional and personal relationships with individuals served.
■ Report ethical violations to appropriate parties.

Ethical Performance: Leadership/Supervisory Responsibility

Leadership requires setting a personal example of high ethical standards in the performance of your job. Managers set the tone for the company. Managers are responsible for making sure that all employees, independent contractors, and vendors receive a copy of the code and assisting them in applying the code's ethical standards.

Conclusion

The company depends on everyone we work with to safeguard our standards and ethics. Although ethical requirements are sometimes unclear, the following questions will provide a good guideline for those in doubt about their conduct.

■ Will my actions be ethical in every respect?
■ Will my actions fully comply with the law and company standards?
■ Will my actions be questioned by supervisors, associates, family, or the general public?
■ How would I feel if my actions were reported in the newspaper?
■ How would I feel if another employee, contractor, customer, or vendor acted in the same way?
■ Will my actions have the appearance of impropriety?

Source: The MENTOR Network (www.thementornetwork.com). Founded in 1980, The MENTOR Network is a national network of local human service providers offering an array of quality, community-based services to adults and children with developmental disabilities or acquired brain injury; to children and adolescents with emotional, behavioral, and medically complex challenges; and to elders in need of home care.

Because there are no immediate or tangible returns, it is easy to overlook these concerns. The reality is that environmental regulations and public perceptions are becoming increasingly important, and will most likely have an effect on your venture at some point. It is best to assess possible issues from the very beginning. Ask yourself: What kinds of facilities will I need? How can I run those facilities to reduce or prevent harmful emissions? If building new facilities, how can I implement newer, cleaner technologies to help create more efficient and safer working environments? What materials will I need to create my product? Will they be safe for the environment, and will they be recyclable, biodegradable, or destined for the landfill?

Chapter Summary

- The vast majority of CEOs, investors, and entrepreneurs believe that a high ethical standard is the single most important factor in long-term success.
- Historically, ethical stereotypes of businesspeople ranged widely, and today the old perceptions have given way to a more aware and accepting notion of the messy work of ethical decisions.
- Ethical issues and discussion are now a part of curricula at many of the top business school programs in the United States and abroad.

- Entrepreneurs can rarely, if ever, finish a day without facing at least one or two ethical issues.
- To make effective and ethical decisions you must understand yourself and be able to identify the scope and effects of your self-interest.
- Numerous ethical dilemmas challenge entrepreneurs at the most crucial moments of survival, like a precarious walk on a tightrope.

Study Questions

1. What conclusions and insights emerged from the ethics exercise?
2. Why have ethical stereotypes emerged, and how have they changed?
3. Why is ethics so important to entrepreneurial and other success?
4. Why do many entrepreneurs and CEOs believe ethics can and should be taught?
5. What are the most thorny ethical dilemmas that entrepreneurs face, and why?
6. Describe an actual example of how and why taking a high ethical ground results in a good decision for business.

Internet Resources

http://www.managementhelp.org/ethics/ethics.htm *A range of papers and articles on ethics from the Free Management Library.*

http://www.pdcnet.org/beq.html *Business Ethics Quarterly publishes scholarly articles from a variety of disciplinary orientations that focus on the general subject of the application of ethics to the international business community.*

http://www.business-ethics.org *An international institute fostering global business practices to promote equitable economic development, resource sustainability, and just forms of government.*

http://www.business-ethics.com/ *Business Ethics is an online publication that offers information, opinion, and analysis of critical issues in the field of corporate responsibility.*

Ethics

In this exercise, decisions will be made in ethically ambiguous situations and then analyzed. As in the real world, all the background information on each situation will not be available, and assumptions will need to be made.

It is recommended that the exercise be completed before reading the following material, and then revisited after you have completed the chapter.

Name:

Date:

Part I

STEP 1

Make decisions in the following situations.

You will not have all the background information about each situation; instead you should make whatever assumptions you feel you would make if you were actually confronted with the decision choices described. Select the decision choice that most closely represents the decision you feel you would make personally. You should choose decision choices even though you can envision other creative solutions that were not included in the exercise.

Situation 1. You are taking a very difficult chemistry course, which you must pass to maintain your scholarship and to avoid damaging your application for graduate school. Chemistry is not your strong suit, and because of a just-below-failing average in the course, you must receive a grade of 90 or better in the final examination, which is 2 days away. A janitor who is aware of your plight informs you that he found the master copy of the chemistry final in a trash barrel and saved it. He will make it available to you for a price, which is high, but which you could afford. What would you do?

_____ *(a)* I would tell the janitor thanks, but no thanks.

_____ *(b)* I would report the janitor to the proper officials.

_____ *(c)* I would buy the examination and keep it to myself.

_____ *(d)* I would not buy the examination myself, but I would let some of my friends, who are also flunking the course, know that it is available.

Situation 2. You have been working on some complex analytical data for 2 days now. It seems that each

time you think you have them completed, your boss shows up with a new assumption or another "what if" question. If you only had a copy of a new software program for your personal computer, you could plug in the new assumptions and revise the estimates with ease. Then a colleague offers to let you make a copy of some software that is copyrighted. What would you do?

_____ *(a)* I would readily accept my friend's generous offer and make a copy of the software.

_____ *(b)* I would decline to copy it and plug away manually on the numbers.

_____ *(c)* I would decide to go buy a copy of the software myself for $300 and hope I would be reimbursed by the company in a month or two.

_____ *(d)* I would request another extension on an already overdue project date.

Situation 3. Your small manufacturing company is in serious financial difficulty. A large order of your products is ready to be delivered to a key customer, when you discover that the product is simply not right. It will not meet all performance specifications, will cause problems for your customer, and will require rework in the field; but this, you know, will not become evident until after the customer has received and paid for the order. If you do not ship the order and receive the payment as expected, your business may be forced into bankruptcy. And if you delay the shipment or inform the customer of these problems, you may lose the order and also go bankrupt. What would you do?

_____ *(a)* I would not ship the order and place my firm in voluntary bankruptcy.

_____ *(b)* I would inform the customer and declare voluntary bankruptcy.

_____ *(c)* I would ship the order and inform the customer after I received payment.

_____ *(d)* I would ship the order and not inform the customer.

Situation 4. You are the cofounder and president of a new venture, manufacturing products for the recreational market. Five months after launching the business, one of your suppliers informs you it can no longer supply you with a critical raw material because you are not a large-quantity user. Without the raw material your business cannot continue. What would you do?

_____ *(a)* I would grossly overstate my requirements to another supplier to make the supplier think I am a much larger potential customer in order to secure the raw material from that supplier, even though this would mean the supplier will no longer be able to supply another, noncompeting small manufacturer who may thus be forced out of business.

_____ *(b)* I would steal raw material from another firm (noncompeting) where I am aware of a sizable stockpile.

_____ *(c)* I would pay off the supplier because I have reason to believe that the supplier could be persuaded to meet my needs with a sizable under-the-table payoff that my company could afford.

_____ *(d)* I would declare voluntary bankruptcy.

Situation 5. You are on a marketing trip for your new venture, calling on the purchasing agent of a major prospective client. Your company is manufacturing an electronic system that you hope the purchasing agent will buy. During your conversation, you notice on the cluttered desk of the purchasing agent several copies of a cost proposal for a system from one of your direct competitors. This purchasing agent has previously reported mislaying several of your own company's proposals and has asked for additional copies. The purchasing agent leaves the room momentarily to get you a cup of coffee, leaving you alone with your competitor's proposals less than an arm's length away. What would you do?

_____ *(a)* I would do nothing but await the man's return.

_____ *(b)* I would sneak a quick peek at the proposal, looking for bottom-line numbers.

_____ *(c)* I would put the copy of the proposal in my briefcase.

_____ *(d)* I would wait until the man returns and ask his permission to see the copy.

Part II

STEP I

Based on the criteria you used, place your answers to each of the situations just described along the continuum of behavior shown here:

	Duty	Contractual	Utilitarian	Situational
Situation 1				
Situation 2				
Situation 3				
Situation 4				
Situation 5				

STEP 2

After separating into teams of 5 to 6 people, record the answers made by each individual member of your team on the form here. Record the answers of each team member in each box and the team's solution in the column on the far right:

Member Name:						Team Answer
Situation 1						
Situation 2						
Situation 3						
Situation 4						
Situation 5						

STEP 3

Reach a consensus decision in each situation (if possible) and record the consensus that your team has reached in the previous chart. Allow 20 to 30 minutes.

STEP 4

Report to the entire group your team's conclusions and discuss with them how the consensus, if any, was reached. The discussion should focus on the following questions.

- Was a consensus reached by the group?

- Was this consensus difficult or easy to achieve? Why?

- What kinds of ethical issues emerged?

- How were conflicts, if any, resolved? Or were they left unresolved?

- What creative solutions did you find to solve the difficult problems without compromising your integrity?

STEP 5

Discuss with the group the following issues.

- What role do ethical issues play? How important are they in the formation of a new venture management team?

- What role do ethical issues play and how important are they in obtaining venture capital? That is, how do investors feel about ethics and how important are they to them?

- What feelings bother participants most about the discussion and consensus reached? For example, if a participant believes that his or her own conduct was considered ethically less than perfect, does he or she feel a loss of self-respect or a sense of inferiority? Does he or she fear others' judgment, and so on?

- What does it mean to do the right thing?

STEP 6

Define each group member's general ethical position and note whether his or her ethical position is similar to or different from yours:

Member	Position	Different/ Similar

STEP 7

Decide whom you would and would not want as business partners based on their ethical positions:

Would Want	Would Not Want

Ethical Decisions—What Would You Do?

The following statements are often made even by practicing, experienced entrepreneurs: "How can we think about ethics when we haven't enough time even to think about running our venture?" "Entrepreneurs are doers, not thinkers—and ethics is too abstract a concept to have any bearing on business realities." "When you're struggling to survive, you're not worried about the means you use—you're fighting for one thing: survival." But when you do not have enough time, ethics is the one thing you need to make time for.

By considering some likely ethical scenarios, an individual can become more aware of his or her own value system and how making ethical decisions can be affected by the climate in which these decisions are made. We urge you to fully engage in the Ethical Decisions exercise that follows. These three vignettes pose practical and not infrequently encountered sorts of ethical dilemmas based on actual occurrences. One excellent way to complete this exercise is to take two or three friends to lunch—particularly those you imagine might make excellent venture partners. Over lunch, discuss in detail each of the vignettes—what you would and should do. Try to apply the ideas from the chapter. At the end, see if you can reach conclusions about what you have learned and what you plan to do differently.

Here are three interesting real-life ethical decision situations for your consideration.

Rim Job

Jeremy, a successful entrepreneur in the automotive industry, is a certified car fanatic who is passionate about having the latest, hottest look for his street rod. A line of new wheel rims is all the rage, and after checking the prices ($1,500 each), he decides to contact the manufacturer directly and see if he can make a better deal. He is told that they are sold only through speed shops and custom shops, and that his area does not have a sales representative. If he would agree to become a representative and get $10,000 worth of wholesale orders, the manufacturer would sell him a set of the rims at cost, in addition to paying him his commission. Jeremy agrees. Now he knows how he will get his new rims.

First Jeremy goes to the biggest and best speed shop nearby and asks for the rims by name. The owner says he has never heard of them. Jeremy, after telling the owner that they are really a popular product and that he is the sales rep, leaves some literature and says he will call again. Meanwhile he hires four male students from a local college to each go into the shop once in the next 2 weeks and to ask for the rims by

name. They are to indicate that they would buy them if they were available. For this he pays each student $100. He then returns after 3 weeks, and the owner reports that the rims must be as hot as Jeremy says—kids have been asking for them. He orders $15,000 worth of rims to be delivered over 6 months. Jeremy is able to buy a set of rims from the manufacturer for $335 each and receives a $380 sales commission on the total sale. The speed shop owner sells $30,000 worth of the rims and reorders after 4 months. Jeremy remains the sales representative collecting commissions, but he does not actively promote the rims.

Were Jeremy's actions ethical? Why or why not? What should he have done?

Empty Suits

Fred was excited to make his pitch to some angel investors; but he felt a bit uneasy because although he had used the terms *team* and *we* throughout his business plan, he was the only one involved in his venture. He had not yet been able to attract any members to his team, but he had had several conversations with prospects. His personal contact in the angel group told him that his venture was likely to be funded, but there would be considerable focus on his team; a lot was riding on the meeting. For the presentation to the group he had four of his best friends, not at all connected to the business, dress in their best business suits, accompany him to the presentation, take seats in the back of the room, and say nothing. He hoped to make the impression that he had a team. He did a great job in the meeting, and his "team" filed out after him.

Was Fred being ethical? Why or why not? How should he have handled the situation?

A Moving Disclosure

Susan has been wrestling with moving her patio furniture manufacturing plant to Georgia from upstate Michigan, where her mother and father founded the company 58 years ago. Everything about her business will be easier there: closer to her markets, lower labor costs, lower raw materials costs, lower shipping costs, no problems with weather, and access to a labor pool that better fits her business. She finally makes the decision to move, but the site she has chosen will not be available for 6 months. Even though her company is a public company (she owns 35 percent) and her board is pushing her to maintain high production levels in Michigan as long as possible, she decides that in deference to her parents and their legacy in the community, she must tell her employees. Four days after signing the lease for the new site in Georgia, she holds a meeting on the shop floor and tells her employees. That afternoon she holds a press conference.

Was Susan ethical? Why or why not?

What are the implications and lessons from your discussion of the three cases? What role do ethical issues play in forming a team, selecting advisors and investors, and other entrepreneurial activities?

PART FOUR

Financing Entrepreneurial Ventures

A financing strategy should be driven by corporate and personal goals, financial requirements, and ultimately by the available alternatives. In the final analysis, these alternatives are governed by the viability of the business and the entrepreneur's skill in managing and orchestrating the fund-raising process. This process, in turn, is constrained by when the company will run out of funds given its current cash burn rate.

More alternatives for financing a company exist now than ever before. Many contend that money remains plentiful for well-managed emerging firms with the promise of profitable growth. Savvy entrepreneurs should remain vigilant for the myopic temptation to "take the money and run."

Although some of these alternatives look distinct and separate, a financing strategy probably will encompass a combination of both debt and equity capital. In considering which financial alternatives are best for a venture at any particular stage of growth, it is important to draw on the experience of other entrepreneurs, professional investors, lenders, accountants, and other professionals.

Chapter Ten

Resource Requirements

The Entrepreneurial Approach to Resources

Entrepreneurial resources include (1) people, such as the management team, the board of directors, lawyers, accountants, and consultants; (2) financial resources; (3) assets, such as plant and equipment; and (4) the business plan. Successful entrepreneurs view these resources differently than large organizations.

Howard H. Stevenson has contributed to understanding the unique approach to resources of successful entrepreneurs. The decisions on what resources are needed, when they are needed, and how to acquire them are strategic decisions that fit with the other driving forces of entrepreneurship. Furthermore, Stevenson has pointed out that entrepreneurs seek to use the minimum possible amount of all types of resources at each stage in their ventures' growth. Rather than own the resources they need, entrepreneurs seek to control resources.

Entrepreneurs with this approach reduce some of the risk in pursuing opportunities:

- *Less capital.* The amount of capital required is smaller due to the quest for parsimony. The financial exposure is therefore reduced, as is the dilution of the founder's equity.

- *Staged capital commitments.* Capital infusions are staged to match critical milestones and value inflection points that will signal whether it is prudent to keep going, raise additional capital, or abort the venture.

- *More flexibility.* Entrepreneurs who take control of their resources without owning them are in a better position to commit and de-commit quickly,[1] as one significant price of resource ownership is an inherent inflexibility. It is extremely difficult to accurately predict the resources needed to exploit the opportunity. For example, consider the future challenges of a company that permanently commits to a certain technology, software, or management system.

- *Low sunk cost.* In addition, sunk costs are lower if the firm exercises its option to abort the venture at any point. Consider, in contrast, the enormous upfront capital commitment of a nuclear power plant and the cost of abandoning such a project.

- *Lower costs.* Lower fixed costs positively impact breakeven; however, be aware of the risk that variable costs may rise.

- *Reduced risk.* In addition to reducing total exposure, other risks, such as the risk of resource obsolescence, are also lower. For example, venture leasing has been used by biotechnology companies to supplement sources of equity financing and to maintain greater flexibility.

---

[1]H.H. Stevenson, M.J. Roberts, and H.I. Grousbeck, *New Business Ventures and the Entrepreneur* (Homewood, IL: Richard D. Irwin, 1985).

Bootstrapping Strategies: Marshaling and Minimizing Resources

Minimal financing is colloquially referred to as boot-strapping or a lack of resource intensity. *Bootstrapping* is defined as a multistage commitment of resources with a minimum commitment at each stage or decision point.[2] When discussing his philosophy on bootstrapping, Greg Gianforte (who retired at the age of 33 after he and his partners sold their software business, Brightwork Development Inc., to McAfee Associates for more than $10 million) stated, "A lot of entrepreneurs think they need money. . . . when actually they haven't figured out the business equation."[3] According to Gianforte, lack of money, employees, and equipment—even lack of product—is actually a huge advantage because it forces the bootstrapper to concentrate on selling to bring cash into the business. Thus, to persevere, entrepreneurs ask at every step how they can accomplish a little more with a little less in order to pursue the opportunity.

Using Other People's Resources

Use of other people's resources (OPR), particularly in the startup and early growth stages of a venture, is an important approach for entrepreneurs. While ownership of these resources is not important, having the use of a resource and being able to control or influence the deployment of a resource are critical.

OPR include, for example, money invested or lent by friends, relatives, business associates, or other investors. Resources such as people, space, equipment, or other material lent, provided inexpensively or free by customers or suppliers, or secured by bartering future services, opportunities, and the like can also be included. In fact, using OPR can be as simple as reading free booklets and pamphlets, such as those published by accounting firms, or using low-cost educational programs or government-funded management assistance programs. Extending accounts payable is a common example of leveraging resources to increase cash flow for startups and growing firms.

How can you as an entrepreneur begin to tap into these resources? Howard H. Stevenson and

William H. Sahlman suggest that you have to do "two seemingly contradictory things: seek out the best advisors–specialists if you have to–and involve them more thoroughly, and at an earlier stage, than you have in the past. At the same time, be more skeptical of their credentials and their advice."[4] A recent study found that social capital, including having an established business network and encouragement from friends and family, is strongly associated with entrepreneurial activity.[5] In addition to networking with family, friends, classmates, and advisors, Stevenson and Sahlman suggest that the human touch enhances the relationship between the entrepreneur and the venture's advisors.[6] Accuracy in social perception, skill at impression management, persuasion and influence, and a high level of social adaptability may be relevant to the activities necessary for successful new ventures.[7] Paola Dubini and Howard Aldrich have contributed to the growing body of knowledge about how these "social assets" may benefit the bottom line of a new venture; see Exhibit 10.1 for the strategic principles they have identified.

Outside People Resources

Board of Directors

Initial work in evaluating the need for people resources is done when forming a new venture team (see Chapter 8). Once you have selected your team and determined your needs, you will most likely want to bring in additional outside resources.

The decision of whether to have a board of directors–and if so, defining the process of choosing and finding the right people–are often troublesome for new ventures.[8]

The Decision Corporate structures require a board of directors elected by shareholders, and investors will occupy some of these positions. Noncorporate structures do not require formal boards.

Beyond that, deciding whether to involve outsiders merits careful thought. They can provide missing experience, know-how, and networks; but

---

[2]Ibid.

[3]E. Barker, "Start with Nothing," *INC.*, February 2002.

[4]H.H. Stevenson and W.H. Sahlman, "How Small Companies Should Handle Advisors." In *The Entrepreneurial Venture* (Boston, MA: Harvard Business School Press, 1992), p. 296. See also a *Harvard Business Review* reprint series called "Boards of Directors: Part I" and "Board of Directors: Part II" (Boston: *Harvard Business Review*, 1976).

[5]B. Honig and P. Davidsson, "The Role of Social and Human Capital among Nascent Entrepreneurs," *Academy of Management Proceedings*, 2001, pp. 1–7.

[6]Ibid., p. 301.

[7]R.A. Baron and G.D. Markman, "Beyond Social Capital: How Social Skills Can Enhance Entrepreneurs' Success," *Academy of Management Executive* 14, no. 1 (2000), pp. 106–17.

[8]The authors are indebted to Howard H. Stevenson of the Harvard Business School, and to Leslie Charm and Carl Youngman, formerly of Doktor Pet Centers and Command Performance hair salons, respectively, for insights into and knowledge of boards of directors.

EXHIBIT 10.1

Hypotheses Concerning Networks and Entrepreneurial Effectiveness

Effective entrepreneurs are more likely than others to systematically plan and monitor network activities.

- Effective entrepreneurs are able to *chart their present network* and to discriminate between production and symbolic ties.
- Effective entrepreneurs are able to *view effective networks as a crucial aspect for ensuring the success of their company.*
- Effective entrepreneurs are able to *stabilize and maintain networks* to increase their effectiveness and their efficiency.

Effective entrepreneurs are more likely than others to undertake actions toward increasing their network density and diversity.

- Effective entrepreneurs set aside time for purely random activities—things done with no specific problem in mind.
- Effective entrepreneurs are able to *check network density,* so as to avoid too many overlaps (because they affect network efficiency) while still attaining solidarity and cohesiveness.
- Effective entrepreneurs multiply, through extending the reachability of their networks, the stimuli for better and faster adaptation to change.

Source: Adapted from P. Dubini and H. Aldrich, "Executive Forum: Personal and Extended Networks Are Central to the Entrepreneurial Process," *Journal of Business Venturing* 6, no. 5 (September 1991), pp. 310–12. Copyright 1991, with permission from Elsevier.

---

having a board will require greater external disclosure of operating and financial plans, and can complicate some financing and ownership decisions.

When Art Spinner of Hambro International was interviewed by *INC.*, he explained,

> Entrepreneurs worry about the wrong thing. . . . that the boards are going to steal their companies or take them over. Though entrepreneurs have many reasons to worry, that's not one of them. It almost never happens. In truth, boards don't even have much power. They are less well equipped to police entrepreneurs than to advise them.[9]

As Spinner suggests, the expertise that board members bring to a venture can be invaluable. David Gumpert cites the crucial roles of the advisory board recruited by his partner and he for what was originally NetMarquee, an online direct marketing agency. He describes the importance of intentionally choosing a board by focusing on "holes" that need to be filled, while also being mindful of financial constraints. According to Gumpert, "The board continually challenged us—in terms of tactics, strategy, and overall business philosophy." These challenges benefited their company by (1) preventing dumb mistakes, (2) keeping management focused on what really mattered, and (3) stopping management from getting gloomy.[10]

Selection Criteria: Add Value with Know-How and Contacts

Filling in the gaps relates to one criterion of a successful management team: intellectual honesty—that is, knowing what you know and what you need to know. In a study of boards, and specifically venture capitalists' contribution to them, entrepreneurs seemed to value operating experience over financial expertise.[11] In addition, the study reported, "Those CEOs with a top-20 venture capital firm as the lead investor, on average, did rate the value of the advice from their venture capital board members significantly higher—but not outstandingly higher than the advice from other outside board members."[12]

As a director of 11 companies and an advisor to two other companies, Art Spinner suggests the following as a simple set of rules to guide you toward a productive relationship with your board.

- Treat your directors as individual resources.
- Always be honest with your directors.
- Set up a compensation committee.
- Set up an audit committee.
- Never set up an executive committee.[13]

New ventures are finding that, for a variety of reasons, people who could be potential board members are increasingly cautious about getting involved.

Liability   Motivated by a wave of corporate scandals in the United States, Congress passed the Sarbanes-Oxley Act (SOX) in 2002. SOX requires companies to file paperwork with the Securities

---

[9]"Confessions of a Director: Hambro International's Art Spinner Says Most CEOs Don't Know How to Make Good Use of Boards; Here He Tells You How," *INC.*, April 1991, p. 119.

[10]D.E. Gumpert, "Tough Love: What You Really Want from Your Advisory Board," http://www.entreworld.org/content/entrebyline, 2001.

[11]J. Rosenstein, A.V. Bruno, W.D. Bygrave, and N.T. Taylor, "The CEO, Venture Capitalist, and the Board," *Journal of Business Venturing*, 1988, pp. 99–113.

[12]Ibid., pp. 99–100.

[13]"Confessions of a Director," *INC.*, April 1991, p. 119. Reprinted with permission. © 1991 by Goldbirsh Group, Inc., 38 Commercial Wharf, Boston, MA 02110.

and Exchange Commission faster, to create a more transparent means of collecting and posting financial data, and to test their procedures for posting accurate, timely information. The potential consequences of running afoul of this law are ominous: They include prison time and huge fines for the company's top officers.

Although startups are usually not subject to the technical requirements of the act, the spirit of the law creates higher disclosure standards for small and growing firms. For instance, many startups who pursue Initial Public Offerings will adhere to public company reporting and SOX reporting standards in advance of going public.

Directors of a company can also be held personally liable for its actions and those of its officers. While courts have held that if a director acts in good faith, he or she can be excused from liability, it can be difficult for a director to *prove* that he or she has acted in good faith, especially in a startup situation. One solution to limit board and officer liability is through directors and officers indemnity insurance.

Paying the Board   The Mellon Financial Corporation's annual Board of Directors Compensation and Governance Practices Survey[14] found that new governance practices are reshaping the boardroom of corporate America, with significant increases in director pay, responsibility, and accountability. The survey results reflect the compensation practices of 150 of the largest U.S-based companies (many of which are publicly traded). Analysis provides information on both cash and equity-based compensation, retainers, meeting fees, and board- or committee-based leadership differentials. Key findings include:

- The median board retainer was $35,000, a slight increase from the previous year.
- The median total cash compensation including the retainer was $40,000, up 17 percent from the previous year.
- The median annual equity award value was $68,200, down from $81,400 in 2008.
- Approximately 80 percent of these companies had either an outside Chairman of the Board or Lead Director, 63 percent of which provided additional compensation.[15]

Alternatives to a Formal Board

Advisors and other nonboard equivalents can be a useful alternative to having a formal board of directors. Since a board of advisors is designed to dispense advice rather than make decisions it limits liability and a firm can solicit objective observations and feedback from these advisors.

Attorneys

The Decision   Nearly all companies need and use the services of attorneys–entrepreneurial ventures perhaps more than most.[16] Because it is critical that entrepreneurs fully understand the legal aspects of any decisions and agreements they make, they should never outsource that knowledge to their attorney. Babson College Adjunct Professor Leslie Charm put it this way: "You must understand the meaning of any document you're considering, as well as your attorneys, because at the end of the day, when you close that deal, you are the one who has to live with it, not your lawyers." In addition, Charm noted that attorneys should be viewed as teachers and advisors; use them to explain legalese and articulate risk and ramifications; and in negotiations, use them to help to close the deal.

Various authors describe the importance of choosing and managing legal counsel. By following some legal basics and acquiring appropriate legal services, companies can achieve better legal health, including fewer problems and lower costs over the long term.[17] According to FindLaw, Inc., some of the legal work can be done by entrepreneurs who do not have law degrees by using self-help legal guides and preprinted forms. According to this organization, the factors to consider in choosing an attorney include availability, comfort level with the attorney, experience level and appropriateness to work, cost, and whether the lawyer knows the industry and has connections to investors and venture capital.[18]

Entrepreneurs will most likely need to get assistance with the following legal areas.

- *Incorporation.* Issues such as liabilities of founders, officers, and directors and the form of organization chosen for a new venture are important. Corporate tax laws are another constantly changing field that require specialized legal skill.

[14]The Mellon Financial Corporation, *Board of Directors Compensation and Governance Practices Survey*, February 16, 2005.

[15]"Bay Area 150: Board of Directors Compensation Practices 2009 Survey," http://www.compensia.com/surveys/BayArea150_Directors_1009.pdf.

[16]The author wishes to acknowledge the input provided by Gerald Feigen of the Center for Entrepreneurial Studies, University of Maryland, from a course on entrepreneurship and the law he has developed and teaches at George Washington University Law School, and John Van Slyke of Alta Research.

[17]J. Adamec, "A Business Owner's Guide to Preventive Law," http://www.inc.com, 1997.

[18]FindLaw, Inc., "Selecting an Attorney," http://www.findlaw.com, 2000.

- *Franchising and licensing.* Innumerable issues concerning future rights, obligations, and ramifications in the event of nonperformance by a franchisee, lessee, or a franchisor or lessor require specialized legal advice.
- *Contracts and agreements.* Firms need assistance with contracts, licenses, leases, and other agreements such as the vesting of shareholders.
- *Formal litigation, liability protection, and so on.* In today's climate most entrepreneurs will find themselves as defendants in lawsuits and require counsel.
- *Real estate, insurance, and other matters.* As an entrepreneur you will be involved in various kinds of real estate transactions that require the services of an attorney.
- *Copyrights, trademarks, and patents.* Intellectual property is a specialized field requiring specific expertise.
- *Employee plans.* Benefit and stock ownership plans have become complicated to administer and use effectively and require legal advisors with expertise in these areas.
- *Tax planning and review.* Entrepreneurs who can worry more about finding good opportunities, as opposed to tax shelters, are infinitely better off.
- *Federal, state, and other regulations and reports.* Understanding the impact of and complying with regulations requires specialized resources and legal advice.
- *Mergers and acquisitions.* Specialized legal knowledge is required when buying or selling a company.
- *Bankruptcy.* Not all business ventures succeed. Legal advice is crucial for any company navigating the bankruptcy course, since the owners, officers, and often the directors can be held personally liable for those obligations.
- *Other matters.* These matters can range from assistance with collecting delinquent accounts to labor relations.
- *Personal needs.* As entrepreneurs accumulate net worth legal advice in estate, tax, and financial planning is important.

Selection Criteria: Add Value with Know-How and Contacts   In a survey of the factors that enter into the selection of a law firm or an attorney, 54 percent of respondents said personal contact with a member of the firm was the main factor.[19]

Reputation was a factor for 40 percent, a prior relationship with the firm was important for 26 percent of the respondents, and fees were mentioned by only 3 percent of respondents.

Many areas of the country have attorneys who specialize in new ventures and in firms with high growth potential. The best place to start in selecting an attorney is with acquaintances of the lead entrepreneur, of members of the management team, or of directors. Recommendations from accountants, bankers, and associates are also useful. Other sources are partners in venture capital firms, partners of a leading accounting firm, a bar association, or the *Martindale-Hubbell Law Directory*, a listing of lawyers. To be effective, an attorney needs to have the experience and expertise to deal with specific issues facing a venture. Stevenson and Sahlman state that the vast resources of a large law firm or national accounting firm may be the best course of action.

Bankers and Other Lenders

The Decision   Specific financial needs may help you decide if a banker or another lender is needed. Not all institutions work well with entrepreneurial companies and at the end of the day, having an excellent banker will be more important than having the very best bank. The entrepreneur should know what he or she needs from a lender, be it needs that are asset-based, such as money for equipment, facilities, inventory, or working capital to fund short-term operations.

Selection Criteria   Starting with the recommendations of lawyers, venture capitalists, accountants and other entrepreneurs is ideal. We suggest exploring multiple possibilities to improve your chance of finding the right lender and the right institution.

Accountants

The Decision   Today, virtually all the larger accounting firms have discovered the enormous client potential of new and entrepreneurial ventures. A significant part of their business strategy is to cater specifically to these firms. Accountants often are unfairly maligned, especially after the fallout of the Enron/Arthur Andersen case. The activities that accountants engage in have grown and no longer consist of solely adding numbers.[20] Accountants who are experienced as advisors to emerging companies can provide valuable services in addition to audits and taxation advice.

---

[19]B.W. Ketchum, Jr., "You and Your Attorney," *INC.*, June 1982, p. 52.
[20]J. Andresky Fraser, "How Many Accountants Does It Take to Change an Industry?" http://www.inc.com, April 1, 1997.

Selection Criteria: Add Value with Know-How and Contacts   In selecting accountants, the first step is for the venture to decide whether to go with a smaller local firm, a regional firm, or one of the major accounting firms. Although each company should make its own decision, in general, CEOs prefer working with smaller regional accounting firms because of lower costs and better personal attention.[21] In making this decision, you will need to address several factors:[22]

- *Service.* Levels of service offered and the attention likely to be provided need to be evaluated. Chances are, for most startups, both will be higher in a small firm than a large one. But if an entrepreneur of a higher-potential firm seeking venture capital or a strategic partner has aspirations to go public, a national firm is a good place to start.

- *Needs.* Needs, both current and future, have to be weighed against the capabilities of the firm. Larger firms are more equipped to handle highly complex or technical problems, while smaller firms may be preferable for general management advice and assistance because the principals are more likely to be involved in handling the account. In most instances, companies in the early stages of planning or that do not plan to go public do not require a top-tier accounting firm. However, one exception to this might be startups that are able to attract formal venture capital funds from day 1.[23]

- *Cost.* Most major firms will offer very cost-competitive services to startups with significant growth and profit potential. That does not mean you will be talking to a partner. If a venture needs the attention of a partner in a larger firm, services of the larger firm are more expensive. However, if the firm requires extensive technical knowledge, a larger firm may have more experience and be more efficient. Many early-growth phase companies are not able to afford to hire a leading national accounting firm, and therefore a small local firm is best. According to Tim McCorry of McCorry Group Inc., these firms should tell you when you are ready to move on to a larger firm that provides more extensive services.[24]

The Decision   The recent trend in the accounting market has led to increased competition, spiraling capital costs, declining profit margins, and an increase in lawsuits.[25] Entrepreneurs should shop around in such a buyer's market for competent accountants who provide the most suitable and appropriate services. Sources of reference for good attorneys are also sources of reference for accountants. Trade groups are also valuable sources.

Consultants

Selection Criteria[26]   Consultants are hired to solve particular problems and to fill gaps not filled by the management team. There are many skilled consultants who can give valuable assistance and the advice needed by the entrepreneur can be quite technical and specific or general and far-ranging.

Startups usually require help with critical one-time tasks and decisions that will have lasting impact on the business. In a study of how consultants are used and their impact on venture formation, Karl Bayer, of Germany's Institute for Systems and Innovation Research of the Fraunhofer-Society, interviewed 315 firms. He found that 96 used consultants and they are employed by startups for the following reasons:

1. To compensate for a lower level of professional experience.
2. To target a wide market segment.
3. To undertake projects that require a large startup investment in equipment.[27]

Existing businesses face ongoing issues resulting from growth. Many of these issues are so specialized that this expertise is rarely available on the management team. Obtaining market research, evaluating when and how to go about computerizing business tasks, deciding whether to lease or buy major pieces of equipment, and determining whether to change inventory valuation methods can be involved.

A fresh, outside view can help pinpoint issues and provide necessary expertise, but not everyone can use consultants effectively. Bayer reported that the use of consultants had a negative effect on sales 3 to 5 years later. In addition, his surveys overwhelmingly

[21]S. Greco and C. Caggiano, "Advisors: How Do You Use Your CPA?" *INC.*, September 1991.

[22]N.C. Churchill and L.A. Werbaneth, Jr., "Choosing and Evaluating Your Accountant." In *Growing Concerns*, ed. D.E. Gumpert (New York: John Wiley & Sons and *Harvard Business Review*, 1984), p. 265.

[23]J.A. Fraser, "Do I Need a Top-Tier Accounting Firm?" http://www.inc.com/incmagazine, June 1, 1998.

[24]Ibid., p. 2.

[25]Fraser, "How Many Accountants Does It Take To Change an Industry?"

[26]The following is excerpted in part from D.E. Gumpert and J.A. Timmons, *The Encyclopedia of Small Business Resources* (New York: Harper & Row, 1984), pp. 48–51.

[27]K. Bayer, "The Impact of Using Consultants during Venture Formation on Venture Performance." In *Frontiers of Entrepreneurship Research: 1991*, ed. N.H. Churchill et al. (Babson Park, MA: Babson College, 1991), pp. 298–299.

reported (two-thirds of the 96) that "the work delivered by the consultants . . . [was] inadequate for the task."[28] Bayer suggests that the entrepreneur can adequately prepare a consultant so that gaps are filled and the firm benefits in the long run, but it takes diligence.

Mie-Yun Lee of BuyerZone.com offers useful hints for establishing an effective consultation relationship: (1) Define, define, define–invest whatever time is necessary to define and communicate the expected outcome of the project; (2) when choosing a consultant, expect a long-term relationship because it takes time to get the consultant up to speed on your business; and (3) outsourcing is not a magic bullet that relieves you of work; communication is critical to success.[29]

The Decision   Nowhere are the options as numerous, the quality as variable, and the costs as unpredictable as in the area of consulting. The number of people calling themselves management consultants is large and growing steadily. Various private and nonprofit organizations provide management assistance to help entrepreneurs; and others, such as professors, engineers, and so forth, provide consulting services part-time. Such assistance also may be provided by other professionals, such as accountants and bankers.

Again, the right chemistry is critical in selecting consultants. One company president who was asked what he had learned from talking to clients of the consultant he finally hired said, "They couldn't really pinpoint one thing, but they all said they would not consider starting and growing a company without him!"

As unwieldy and risky as the consulting situation might appear, there are ways to limit the choices. Consultants tend to have specialties. While some consultants claim wide expertise, most will indicate the types of situations with which they feel most comfortable and skillful. In seeking a consultant, consider the following:[30]

- Good consultants are not geographically bound; they will travel and can work via electronic sources.
- The best referral system is word of mouth and always check references carefully.
- People skills are essential and therefore should be assessed early.

A written agreement, specifying the consultant's responsibilities, the assignment's objectives, the length of time the project will take, and the type and amount of compensation, is highly recommended. Some consultants work on an hourly basis, some on a fixed-fee basis, and some on a retainer-fee basis. While the quality of many products roughly correlates with their price, this is not so with consulting services. It is difficult to judge consultants solely on the basis of their fees.

Financial Resources

Analyzing Financial Requirements

Once the opportunity has been assessed, a new venture team has been formed, and all resource needs have been identified, it is time for an entrepreneur to evaluate the type, quantity, and timing of financial resources.

As has been noted previously, there is a temptation to place the cart before the horse. Entrepreneurs are tempted to begin their evaluation of business opportunities–particularly their thinking about formal business plans–by analyzing spreadsheets, rather than first focusing on defining the opportunity, deciding how to seize it, and preparing financial requirement estimates.

However, when the time comes to analyze financial requirements, it is important to realize that cash is the lifeblood of a venture. As James Stancill, Professor of Finance at the University of Southern California's Marshall School of Business, has said, "Any company, no matter how big or small, moves on cash, not profits. You can't pay bills and employees with profits, only cash."[31] Financial resources are almost always limited, and important and significant trade-offs need to be made in evaluating a company's needs and the timing of those needs.

Stancill points out:

> Usual measures of cash flow–net income plus depreciation (NIPD) or earnings before interest and taxes (EBIT)–give a realistic indication of a company's cash position only during a period of steady sales.[32]

Take cash flow projections. An entrepreneur could answer a question such as, what if sales grow at just 5 percent, instead of 15 percent, and what if

---

[28]Ibid., p. 301.

[29]M. Lee, "Finding the Right Consultant," http://www.inc.buyerzone.com, February 2, 2000.

[30]J. Finnegan, "The Fine Art of Finding a Consultant," http://www.inc.com.incmagazine, July 1, 1997.

[31]Reprinted by permission of *Harvard Business Review*. An excerpt from "When Is There Cash in Cash Flow?" by J.M. Stancill, March–April 1987, p. 38. Copyright © 1987 by the President and Fellows *of* Harvard College.

[32]Stancill, "When Is There Cash in Cash Flow?" p. 38.

only 50 percent, instead of 65 percent, of amounts billed are paid every 30 days? The impact on cash flow of changes in these projections can be seen.

Taking the time to thoroughly assess the cash requirements of a venture under several different what-if scenarios is enormously valuable. Assumptions about fixed and variable costs, market estimates, and probable startup resource requirements can be combined to create detailed monthly cash flows in order to precisely determine the economic character of a business. These assumptions can then be manipulated to simulate financial success under different operating conditions, and establish realistic projections of the money required and likely rewards of a new venture.

Internet Impact: Resources

Fund-Raising for Nonprofits

A dynamic online service model has emerged that is changing the way nonprofits conduct their fund-raising auctions. Historically, coordinating and staffing those venues has always been a challenge, particularly because volunteer turnover requires the retraining of a majority of the workforce each time an auction is held. In addition, physical auctions are typically catered affairs that are attended by only a small percentage of an organization's support base.

cMarket, Inc., a venture-funded startup based in Cambridge, Massachusetts, has developed an online service model that allows nonprofits to promote their causes, build their donor base, provide value to corporate sponsors, and improve the results of their fund-raising programs. In 2008, they hosted 2,259 online charity auctions, accounting for $20 million in charitable giving in the U.S.[33] Jon Carson, president of cMarket, Inc., noted, "Now any non-profit—without training or in-house technical people—can hold a fund-raising event that reaches the inbox of its entire constituency."

In 2004, the company's first full year of operations, cMarket signed over 400 clients. Then in May 2005 the company announced a partnership with Network for Good. Founded in 2001 by the Time Warner Foundation and AOL, the Cisco Foundation and Cisco Systems, and Yahoo!, Network for Good is an independent, nonprofit organization that works to advance nonprofit adoption of the Internet as a tool for fund-raising, volunteer recruitment, and community engagement.

Chapter Summary

- Successful entrepreneurs use ingenious bootstrapping approaches to marshal and minimize resources.
- Control of resources rather than ownership of resources is the key to a "less is more" resource strategy.
- Entrepreneurs are also creative in identifying other people's money and resources, thereby spreading and sharing the risks.

- Selecting outside advisors, directors, and other professionals boils down to one key criterion: Do they add value through their know-how and networks?
- Today, access to financial and nonfinancial resources is greater than ever before and is increasing because of the Internet.
- Building a brain trust of the right mentors, advisors, and coaches is one of the entrepreneur's most valuable "secret weapons."

Study Questions

1. Entrepreneurs think and act ingeniously when it comes to resources. What does this mean, and why is it so important?
2. Describe at least two creative bootstrapping resources.
3. Why will the Internet become an increasingly important gateway to controlling resources?
4. In selecting outside advisors, a board, consultants, and the like, what are the most important criteria, and why?

[33]http://stepbystepfundraising.com/online-charity-auctions-upward-trend/.

Internet Resources

http://www.gmarketing.com/ *Guerilla Marketing offers creative marketing tips to help you outsmart the competition.*

http://online.wsj.com/small-business *Small business resources from* The Wall Street Journal.

http://www.score.org *SCORE, "Counselors to America's Small Business," is a popular source of free and confidential small business advice for entrepreneurs.*

http://smallbusiness.findlaw.com *This site provides comprehensive access to small-business lawyers and legal information.*

Exercise I
Build Your Brain Trust

Building a cadre of mentors, advisors, coaches, and directors can be the difference between success and failure of a venture. Building this brain trust will require professionalism, thoroughness, salesmanship, and tenacity. You gain the trust and confidence of these mentors through your performance and integrity.

This exercise is intended to provide a framework for, and key steps in thinking through, your requirements and developing a brain trust for your ventures.

Part I: Gap and Fit Analysis vis-à-vis the Timmons Model

1. At each phase of development of a venture, different know-how and access to experience, expertise, and judgment external to the founding team are often required. A key risk–reward management tool is the gap and fit analysis using the model.

   ✓ Who has access to key know-how and resources that we do not?

   ✓ What is missing that we need in order to obtain a very good chance?

   ✓ Who can add the most value/insights/solid experience to the venture now and in the next 2 years, and how?

   ✓ Who are the smartest, most insightful people given what we are trying to do?

   ✓ Who has the most valuable perspective and networks that could help the venture in an area that you know least about?

2. Break down the Timmons Model to focus on each dimension:

   ▪ *Core opportunity.* If they are not on your team now, who are the people who know more than anyone else on the planet about the revenue and cost model and underlying drivers and assumptions? How to price, get sales, marketing, customer service, and distribution? IT and e-business? The competition? The free cash flow characteristics and economics of the business?

   ▪ *Resources.* Who can help you get the necessary knowledge of and access to people, networks, money, and key talent?

   ▪ *Team.* Who has 10 to 20 years more experience than you do in building a venture from ground zero?

   ▪ *Context.* Who understands the context, changes, and timing of the venture in terms of the capital markets, any key regulatory requirements, and the internal drivers of the industry/technology/market?

3. Conclusions: What and who can make the biggest difference in the venture? Usually just one to three key people or resources can make a huge difference.

Part II: Identify and Build the Brain Trust

1. Once you have figured out what and who can make the greatest difference, you need to arrange for introductions. Faculty, family friends, roommates, and the like are good places to start.

2. If you cannot get the introductions, then you have to go with your wits and creativity to get a personal meeting.

   ✓ Be highly prepared and articulate.

   ✓ Send an executive summary and advance agenda.

✓ Know the reasons and benefits that will be most appealing to this person.

✓ Follow up and follow through—send a hand-written note, not just another e-mail message.

3. Ask for blunt and direct feedback to such questions as these:

✓ What have we missed here? What flaws do you see in our team, our marketing plan, our financial requirements, our strategy, and so forth?

✓ Are there competitors we do not know about?

✓ How would you compete with me?

✓ Who would reject and accept us for an investment? Why?

✓ Who have we missed?

✓ Whom else should we talk with?

You will gain significant insight into yourself and your venture, as well as how knowledgeable and insightful the potential brain trust member is about your business, from the questions he or she asks, and from your own. You will soon know whether the person is interested and can add value.

4. Grow the brain trust to grow the venture. Think 2 years ahead and add to the brain trust people who have already navigated the difficult waters you expect to travel.

Exercise 2

How Entrepreneurs Turn Less into More

Entrepreneurs are often creative and ingenious in boot-strapping their ventures and in getting a great deal out of limited resources. This assignment can be done alone, in pairs, or in trios. Identify at least two or three entrepreneurs whose companies exceed $3 million in sales and are less than 10 years old and who have started their companies with less than $25,000 to $50,000 of initial seed capital. Interview them with a focus on their strategies and tactics that minimize and control (not necessarily own) the necessary resources:

1. What methods, sources, and techniques did they devise to acquire resources?

2. Why were they able to do so much with so little?

3. What assumptions, attitudes, and mind-sets seemed to enable them to think and function in this manner?

4. What patterns, similarities, and differences exist among the entrepreneurs you interviewed?

5. What impact did these minimizing bootstrapping approaches have on their abilities to conserve cash and equity and to create future options or choices to pursue other opportunities?

6. How did they devise unique incentive structures in the deals and arrangements with their people, suppliers, and other resource providers (their first office space or facility, brochures, etc.)?

7. In lieu of money, what other forms of currency did they use, such as bartering for space, equipment, or people or giving an extra day off or an extra week's vacation?

8. Can they think of examples of how they acquired (gained control of) a resource they could afford to pay for with real money and did not?

9. Many experienced entrepreneurs say that for first-time entrepreneurs it can be worse to start with too much money rather than too little. How do you see this, and why?

10. Some of the strongest new companies are started during an economic recession, among tight credit and capital markets. It is valuable to develop a lean-and-mean, make-do, less-is-more philosophy and sense of frugality and budgetary discipline. Can you think of any examples of this? Do you agree or disagree? Can you think of opposite examples, such as companies started at or near the peak of the 1990s economic boom with more capital and credit than they needed?

You will find as background reading the feature articles on bootstrapping in *INC* magazine, *Success* magazine, *Fast Company*, and others to be very useful.

Chapter Eleven

Franchising

LEARNING OUTCOMES: After reading this chapter, you will be able to understand:

11-1   Job creation versus wealth creation

11-2   Franchising history

11-3   The franchising process

11-4   Evaluating a franchise

11-5   Components of a franchise offering

Introduction

In this chapter we will explore franchising and how it fits within the Timmons Model. We will consider the scope of franchising and examine the criteria for determining whether an offering makes sense to use a franchise model. We will cover approaches and models that will be helpful in considering franchise opportunities.

Franchising fits our definition of entrepreneurship from Chapters 2 and 3, which is, entrepreneurship is opportunity recognition for the purpose of wealth creation. Just as opportunity, thought, and action are essential elements of an entrepreneurial venture, so too are they important components of a franchise opportunity.

At its most fundamental level, franchising is a large-scale growth opportunity based on a partnership rather than on individual effort. Once a business is operating successfully, according to the Timmons Model, it is appropriate to think about franchising as a growth and financing tool.

Job Creation versus Wealth Creation

As a franchise entrepreneur, we control the growth of our franchise opportunity. This means the ability to own one to dozens of pizza restaurants using the same systematic process, depending on the goals and resources of the franchisee.

The ability to create wealth in any venture starts with the initial opportunity assessment. For example, a franchise company may decide to limit its number of stores per geographic territory. Therefore, the expansion market is limited from the start for potential franchisees. Some companies are designed to reward successful franchisees with the opportunity to buy more stores in a particular market or region. Franchisees who achieve prosperity with single units are rewarded with additional stores. The entrepreneurial process is encouraged, and wealth is created.

Franchising: A History of Entrepreneurship

The franchise entrepreneurial spirit in the United States has never been more alive than today. More than 4,500 franchise businesses with 600,000 outlets populate the marketplace and these businesses make up 36 percent of all retail sales nationwide. Internationally, franchising represents as much as 10 percent of retailing in the United Kingdom, France, and Australia. The belief that franchising can be an exciting entrepreneurial venture is supported by the continued success of established franchise systems, the proliferation of new franchises, and the profitability reported by franchisees and franchisors.[1] The process of wealth creation through franchising continues to evolve as we witness an increase in not only the number of multiple-outlet franchisors,[2] but also in the number of franchisees that operate multiple outlets in different franchise systems.

---

[1]S. Spinelli, Jr., B. Leleux, and S. Birley, "An Analysis of Shareholder Return in Public Franchisors," Society of Franchising presentation, 2001.

[2]S. Shane, "Hybrid Organizational Arrangements and Their Implications for Firm Growth and Survival: A Study of New Franchisors," *Academy of Management Journal* 39 (1996), pp. 216-234.

Evidence of the success of franchising as an entrepreneurial opportunity-exploiting and wealth-creating vehicle comes from one of the largest franchisors in the world–the UK conglomerate Allied Domecq, which owns Dunkin' Donuts, Baskin-Robbins, and Togo's restaurants. Bob Rosenberg,[3] son of Dunkin' Donuts founder Bill Rosenberg, grew the Dunkin' system from a few hundred to more than 3,000 outlets before selling to Allied Domecq. Bob continued to operate Allied Domecq's North American retail operation for 10 years, doubling its size, until he retired in 1998. Bob believes, "Allied Domecq's franchise operation can double again in the United States, and the potential in Europe and Asia is exponential." Clearly franchising can be a global business model that is adaptable to most locales.

Another company that signaled the prevalence of franchising in contemporary business is Jiffy Lube International. Although most franchisors tend to think in terms of national scale, the team that grew Jiffy Lube purchased the then-small mom-and-pop company based in Ogden, Utah, and immediately added *International* to the company's name, sensing that globalization of the business model and service offering could be successful outside the United States.

When people hear the names Ray Kroc and Anita Roddick, most people certainly identify the founders of McDonald's and The Body Shop as entrepreneurs and their trademarks and brands as some of the most successful in the world. Exhibit 11.1 reveals several aspects of contemporary franchises.

Anyone exploring entrepreneurial opportunities should give serious consideration to the franchising option. As franchisor or franchisee, this option can be a viable way to share risk and reward, create and grow an opportunity, and raise human and financial capital.

Franchising: Assembling the Opportunity

As we saw in earlier chapters, the Timmons Model identifies the three components of opportunity as market demand, market size and structure, and margin analysis (the 3Ms). The franchise organization must understand the nature of demand as it resides both in the individual consumer and in the society. At the most fundamental level, the primary target audience (PTA) is the defining quality of the opportunity recognition process. Without a customer, there is no opportunity; without an opportunity, there is no venture; without a sustainable opportunity, there can be no franchise.

As we discussed earlier in this chapter, our goal is to look at franchising because it presents opportunities for both franchisees and franchisors. We will now investigate several aspects of franchise opportunity recognition: PTA identification; service concept; service delivery system (SDS) design; training and operational support; field support, marketing, advertising, and promotion; and product purchase provision. Prospective franchisees should understand the nature and quality of each of these franchise components. Existing franchisors might study their offerings in light of this information. Those considering growth through franchising must pay attention to the details of their systems' offerings.

Primary Target Audience

Defining the target customer is essential because it dictates many diverse functions of the business. Most importantly, it measures primary demand. Once the PTA is defined, secondary targets may be identified. The degree of market penetration in the secondary target is less than that of the primary target. Although measuring market demand is not an exact science, a franchisor must continually collect data about its customers. Even after buying a franchise, the franchisee compares local market demographics with national profiles to estimate the potential of the

EXHIBIT 11.1

Franchise Facts about Some of the Largest U.S. Franchisors[a]

Franchise system age	21 years
Number of outlets per franchisor	2,652
Annual revenue	$871 million
Franchise fee	$28,559
Royalty rate	5.58%
Advertising rate	2.89%
License agreement term	14 years

[a]The average for 91 firms is used for all categories.

---

[3]Bob Rosenberg is now an adjunct professor at Babson College and teaches in the entrepreneurship division. The authors have consulted with Professor Rosenberg on a number of issues in entrepreneurship, including franchising.

local market in terms of the number of outlets that can be developed. Revenue projections are made from the identification of the target audiences and the degree of market penetration that can be expected based on historical information. Three major areas of data collection can be integral to refining the PTA.

Demographic Profiles   A demographic profile is a compilation of personal characteristics that enables the company to define the "average" customer. Most franchisors perform market research as a central function, developing customer profiles and disseminating this information to franchisees. Such research may include current user and non-user profiles. Typically a demographic analysis includes age, gender, income, home address (driving or walking distance from the store), working address (driving or walking distance from the store), marital status, family status (number and ages of children), occupation, race and ethnicity, religion, and nationality. Demographics must be put into context by looking at concept-specific data such as

average number of automobiles for a Midas franchise or percentage of disposable income spent on clothes for a Gap franchise.

Psychographic Profiles   Psychographic profiles segment potential customers based on social class, lifestyle, and personality traits. Economic classes in the United States are generally divided into seven categories:

1. Upper uppers	1 percent
2. Lower uppers	2 percent
3. Upper middles	12 percent
4. Middle class	32 percent
5. Working class	38 percent
6. Upper lowers	9 percent
7. Lower lowers	7 percent

Lifestyle addresses such issues as health consciousness, fashion orientation, or being a "car freak." Personality variables such as confidence, conservation, and independence are used to segment markets.

Behavioral variables segment potential customers by their knowledge, attitude, and use of products in order to project usage of the product or service. By articulating detailed understanding of the target market, specifically why these consumers will buy the product or service, you gain great insight into the competitive landscape. Why will a consumer spend money with us rather than with a competitor?

Geographic Profiles   The scope of a franchise concept can be local, regional, national, or international. The U.S. national market is typically divided into nine regions: Pacific, Mountain, West North Central, West South Central, East North Central, East South Central, South Atlantic, Middle Atlantic, and New England. Regions are further divided by population density and described as urban, suburban, or rural.

The smart franchise uses the ever-growing system of franchisees and company outlets to continuously gather data about customers. This helps dynamically shape the vision and therefore the strategic exploitation of the opportunity. The analysis of system data must include a link to the vision of the concept and to the vision's possibilities. For example, if we launched an earring company 10 years ago, we could have defined the target market as women of ages 21 to 40, and the size of the market as the number of women within this age group in the United States. But perhaps looking beyond the existing data and anticipating the larger market that now exists can shape our vision. The target market for earrings could be defined as women and men of ages 12 to 32, with an average

---

Theory into Practice: Market Demand—Radio Shack's Moving Target Market

Target markets are dynamic, often metamorphosing very quickly. Radio Shack had to change its business to reflect the shift in its target market. In the 1970s and 1980s Radio Shack grew by addressing the needs of technophiles–young men with penchants for shortwave radios, stereo systems, walkie-talkies, and the like. The national retail chain supplied this audience with the latest gadgets and did very well.

Then, starting in the early 1990s, technology became more sophisticated. Personal electronic equipment began to include cell phones, hand-held computers, and electronic organizers. The market for these products was expanding from a smaller group of technophiles to a larger group of middle-aged males who loved gadgets and who had more disposable income. Yet Radio Shack remained Radio Shack. Its audience dwindled while the personal electronics market boomed.

In the early 1990s Radio Shack refocused its business to target this new demographic. Its advertising addressed the needs of the 44-year-old upper-middle-class male versus the 29-year-old technophile because that 29-year-old who formerly shopped at Radio Shack was now 44. He was not going to make a radio, but he would buy a cell phone. Radio Shack made dramatic changes in its marketing and inventory.

of three pairs of earrings per individual, not two. The identification of the target market requires that we combine demographic data with our own unique vision for the venture.

The focus on PTA development as the core to franchise opportunity recognition is essential to estimating the consumer appeal of a franchise and to establish validity of the opportunity. We will consider a set of criteria that will help define the due diligence process in assessing how a franchise has exploited the opportunity. This discussion holds value for an overall understanding of franchising for existing franchisors and potential franchisors and franchisees alike.

Evaluating a Franchise: Initial Due Diligence

Before looking at the details of a franchise offering, the prospective franchisee must sift through the offerings of the 4,500 franchises in the United States. Exhibit 11.2 provides a franchise screening template designed to make a preliminary assessment of the key variables that constitute a franchise offering. The exercise is crafted to help map the risk profile of the franchise and highlight areas that will most likely need further investigation.

This exercise is not designed to yield a "go or no go" decision. Rather, prospective franchisees should use it to help evaluate if a franchise meets their personal risk/return profile. Franchisors should also review the exercise to examine the risk signals they may be sending to prospective franchisees.

Franchisor as the High-Potential Venture

In this section we focus principally on franchisors and their rewards. In a study of publicly traded franchisors, the size and scope of the firms that achieved public capital are impressive. The capital marketplace has rewarded many franchisors that have met the criteria for a high-potential franchise and they, in turn, have performed well in return to shareholders. Exhibit 11.3 illustrates the performance of public franchisors compared with the Standard and Poor's 500. This analysis of total return to shareholders (dividends and stock price appreciation) demonstrates that while the S&P index was hit hard by the economic downturn after 2001, the public franchisor index was not. Although the stock market slide following the

period of irrational exuberance in the late 1990s was precipitated by excessively high dot-com valuations, the correction tended to depress share prices across the board. The relative buoyancy of the franchisor index can be attributed to the index being heavily weighted in the food category. During a recession, when household budgets are tight, consumers seek out dining establishments that offer the best value, which is the primary driver of many food-based franchise organizations.

Even more interesting are those exceptional performers among high-achieving franchisors. Take, for example, the quintessential franchise, McDonald's Corporation. McDonald's is the world's largest food service organization with more than 30,000 restaurants in 122 countries as of May 2007. Its global infrastructure includes a network of suppliers and resources that allows it to achieve economies of scale and great value to customers. In 2006 system-wide sales reached $21.6 billion, operating income was $4.6 billion, and earnings per share increased 3.3 percent. A local management team runs each market.

Allied Domecq's unique strategy combines two or three brand concepts in a single operation, attempting to optimize return on investment through more efficient use of resources. Launched in 1950, Dunkin' Donuts, now the world's largest chain of coffee and donut shops, has grown to more than 7,000 locations throughout the United States and 70 countries. Founded in 1971, Togo's is California's fastest-growing chain of sandwich eateries and is now spreading across the country. Baskin-Robbins' 31 flavors are offered in more than 5,500 locations from California to Moscow.

Key Components of a Franchise Offering

In this section we describe the major aspects of delivering a franchise system, where both concept and delivery has created wealth for the franchisors, and this is where prospective franchisees need to focus much of their time. If you are looking to be a franchisor to expand your offering, review the following in terms of how you might construct the offering, knowing that prospective franchisees will go deep on these franchise components.

Service Delivery System

The road map for marshaling resources for the franchise comes from establishing the SDS. The

EXHIBIT II.2

Franchise Risk Profile Template

Criteria	Low Risk/Average Market Return 15–20%	Acceptable Risk/ Incremental 30% Return	High Risk/Marginal 40–50% Return	Extreme Risk/Large Return 60–100%
Multiple Market Presence	National	Regional	State	Local
Outlet Pro Forma Disclosed or Discerned	Yes, 90% apparently profitable	Yes, 80% apparently profitable	Yes, 70% apparently profitable	No, less than 70% profitable
Market Share	No. I and dominant	No. I or 2 with a strong competitor	Lower than No. 2	Lower than No. 3 with a dominant player
National Marketing Program	Historically successful creative process, national media buys in place	Creative plus regional media buys	Creative plus local media buys	Local media buys only
National Purchasing Program	More than 3% gross margin advantage in national purchasing contract	I–3% gross margin advantage vs. independent operators	Regional gross margin advantages only	No discernible gross margin advantages
Margin Characteristics	50%+ gross margin; 18%+ net outlet margin	40–50% gross margin; 12–17% net outlet margin	30–40% gross margin; less than 12% net outlet margin	Declining gross margin detected; erratic net outlet margin
Business Format	Sophisticated training, documented operations manual, identifiable feedback mechanism with franchisees	Initial training and dynamically documented operations manual, some field support	Training and operations but weak field support	Questionable training and field support and static operations
Term of the License Agreement	20 years with automatic renewal	15 years with renewal	Less than I5 years or no renewal	Less than I0 years
Site Development	Quantifiable criteria clearly documented and tied to market specifics	Markets prioritized with general site development criteria	General market development criteria outlined	Business format not tied to identifiable market segment(s)
Capital Required per Unit	$15,000–$25,000 working capital	Working capital plus $50,000–$100,000 machinery and equipment	Working capital plus machinery and equipment plus $500,000–$1,000,000 real estate	Erratic, highly variable, or ill-defined
Franchise Fee and Royalties	PDV[a] of the fees is less than the demonstrated economic advantages (reduced costs or increased revenue) of the franchise vs. stand-alone		PDV of the fees is projected to be less than the expected economic advantages (reduced costs or increased revenue) of the franchise vs. stand-alone	PDV of the fees is not discernibly less than the expected value of the franchise

[a]PDV is an abbreviation for present discounted value. If franchising is a risk reduction strategy, then the discount of future revenue should be less. Concurrently, the economies of scale in marketing should increase the amount of revenue a franchise can generate versus a stand-alone, operation.

opportunity dictates that we perform certain tasks to meet consumer demand, and the assets put into place to meet these demands are the resources needed to launch the franchisee. In the franchise entrepreneurial alliance, the franchisor develops a method for delivering the product or service that fills customer demand and this SDS is well defined, documented, and proven. The ability of the organization to develop and transfer the SDS is the creation of the firm's competitive advantage.

The Timmons Model first looks at opportunity assessment, which demands clear understanding of

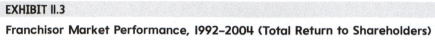

EXHIBIT II.3

Franchisor Market Performance, 1992–2004 (Total Return to Shareholders)

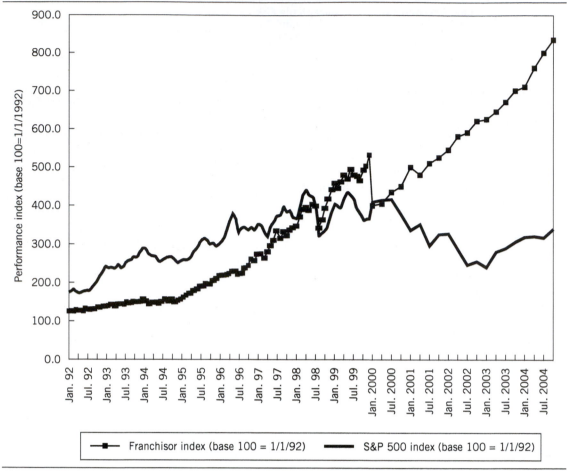

the target market and customer. Next it looks at resource marshaling or, in franchising, the establishment of the SDS. The SDS is the fundamental means by which customers will be served, and the fashion, often proprietary in design, in which the service delivery resources are arrayed to create competitive advantage in the marketplace. Highly successful and visible examples of business format innovations are the drive-through in fast-food restaurants and the bi-level facilities in quick oil change facilities.

Because the SDS is truly the essence of the successful franchise, the detailed attention given to it should not be underestimated. For the concept innovator, the common phrase, "the devil is in the details," never takes on more meaning than when designing the SDS for the franchise. Steve Spinelli can corroborate this fact from experiences while expanding the Jiffy Lube franchise. One particular component of Jiffy Lube's expansion plans paints a vivid picture of the intricacy of the development of the SDS and reveals what a great benefit this design paid over time.

Jiffy Lube franchises must meet specific location criteria: high-volume car traffic, side of the street located for inbound or outbound traffic, high-profile retail area, and the far corner of any given street or block, among other requirements. Through trial and error, Jiffy Lube has determined the optimal location of the structure on any given property. Once these aspects are met, the building specifications follow. Structural specifications regarding the angle of the building and the width, depth, and angle of the entrance allow the optimal number of cars to stack in line waiting for the car in front to complete the service. On several occasions, facilities that met location criteria were failing to perform as expected. Analysis of the situation determined that the bend in the driveway was too sharp, preventing customers from driving their cars completely into the line and giving the inaccurate impression that the lot was full. Driveways were adjusted to accommodate an increased number of cars waiting for service.

Another part of the complete Jiffy Lube SDS was the design of the maintenance bay. Considering the limitations inherent in the use of hydraulic lifts, Jiffy Lube faced the dilemma of providing 30 minutes of labor in only 10 minutes. To deliver this 10-minute service, three technicians would need to work on a car at once without the use of a lift. This quandary led to the design of having cars drive into the bay and stop above an opening in the floor. This allowed one technician to service the car from below, another to service the car underneath the hood, and a third to service the car's interior. Without developing such a disruptive system,[4] Jiffy Lube would not have been able to succeed as it did.

The soundness of the decision to use the drive-through and bi-level system was confirmed when competitors, gas stations and car dealers, failed to deliver a "quick lube" using hydraulic lifts and traditional bays. The sum of Jiffy Lube's intricately designed parts created the value of the SDS. The accompanying box highlights the specific design around Wendy's SDS that creates value.

Training and Operational Support

Formal franchisor training programs transfer knowledge of the SDS to the franchisee's managers and line workers. Continuous knowledge gathering and transfer are important both before launch and on an ongoing basis. The license agreement defines the specific manner in which this franchisor responsibility will be performed. Training will vary with the specifics of the franchise, but should include organized and monitored on-the-job experience in the existing system for the new franchisee and as many of the new staff members as the franchisor will allow. Established and stable franchise systems such as Jiffy Lube and Dunkin' Donuts require such operational experience in the existing system for as long as a year before the purchase of the franchise. Once the franchise is operational, the franchisee may be expected to do the on-site training of new hires. Field support from the franchisor is often a signal of franchise stability and a reflection of the strength of the franchise partnership.

As discussed previously, the trade name and trademark are valuable assets in a franchise system as a franchisee's success relies on the sales of products that are based on the brand equity and strength of the franchisor. As important as a sound SDS design is to the concept's foundation for success, the prospective training regimen is equally important. Without appropriately instructed individuals, an exceptional product will never reach the consumer's hands.

Theory into Practice: The SDS—How Wendy's Used Its Business Format to Enter a "Saturated" Market

In 1972 Dave Thomas entered what many experts called a crowded hamburger fast-food market. His concept was to offer a "Cadillac hamburger" that was hot, fresh, and delivered more quickly than the competitors'. To execute Thomas's mission, Wendy's introduced the first drive-through in a national fast-food chain. Because Wendy's menu offered double and triple patties in addition to the traditional single-patty hamburger, its kitchens were designed to mass-produce hamburgers and deliver them to the front counter or drive-through window with minimal effort. To ensure a cooked just-in-time hamburger, each Wendy's restaurant included a large front window that enabled grill cooks, were placed in clear view of the customer, to observe the flow of customers onto the premises.

Notwithstanding the huge market share owned by McDonald's and Burger King, Wendy's was able to successfully enter the fray because of the manner in which it arranged its resources to create competitive advantage. In Wendy's, the sum of the intricacies—the drive-through window, the position of the cooks and kitchen, and the double and triple patties, has allowed the chain to compete and prosper in the fast-food hamburger market.

Dave Thomas's vision and personal impact on the fast-food industry were significant. When he passed away in January 2002, Wendy's received thousands of e-mail messages from customers expressing condolences.

Field Support

Akin to the training program mentioned above is ongoing field support. This will take at least two forms: A franchisor's representative will visit the franchisee's location in person, and the franchisor will retain resident experts at corporate headquarters in each of the essential managerial disciplines that are available for consultation. Ideally the license agreement will provide for scheduled visits by the franchisor's agents to the franchisee's outlet with prescribed objectives, such as performance review, field training, facilities inspection, local

---

[4]A disruptive business system is one that fundamentally changes the value proposition. McDonald's and Dairy Queen created the fast-food concept. Midas, Aamco, and Jiffy Lube pioneered targeted specialization in automotive service.

marketing review, and operational audits. Unfortunately some franchisors use their field role as a diplomatic or pejorative exercise rather than for training and support. The greater the substance of the field functions, the easier it is for the franchisee to justify the royalty cost.

One means of understanding the franchisor's field support motivation is to investigate the manner in which the field support personnel are compensated. If field staff members are paid commensurately with franchisee performance and ultimate profitability, then politics will play a diminished role. Key warning signs in this regard come when bonuses are paid for growth in the number of stores versus individual store growth, or for franchisor supplied product use by franchisee.

Marketing, Advertising, and Promotion

Marketing activities are certainly some of the most sensitive areas in the ongoing franchise relationship because they imprint the trade name and trademark in the mind of the consumer to gain awareness–the most important commodity of the franchise. If the delivery of the product validates the marketing message, then the value of the franchise is enhanced; but if it is not congruent, there can be a detrimental effect at both the local and national levels. As the number of outlets grows, marketing budgets increase and spread across the growing organization.

Generally marketing programs are funded and implemented at three different levels: national, regional, and local. A national advertising budget is typically controlled by the franchisor, and each franchisee contributes a percentage of top-line sales to the advertising fund. The franchisor then produces for use by the franchisees and, depending on the size of the fund, also buys media time or space on behalf of the franchisees. Because it is impossible to allocate these services equally between franchisees of different sizes across different markets, the license agreement will specify the use of "best efforts" to approximate equal treatment between franchisees. Although "best efforts" will invariably leave some franchisees with more advertising exposure and some with less, over time this situation should balance itself. This is one area of marketing that requires careful monitoring by both parties.

Regional marketing, advertising, and promotion are structured on the basis of an area of dominant influence (ADI). All the stores in a given ADI

(e.g., Greater Hartford, Connecticut) should contribute a percentage of their top-line sales to the ADI advertising cooperative.[5] The cooperative's primary function is usually to buy media using franchisor-supplied or franchisor-approved advertising and to coordinate regional site promotions. If the franchise has a regional advertising cooperative requirement in the license agreement, it should also have standardized ADI cooperative bylaws, which will outline things like voting rights and expenditure parameters.

The third and final scenario for marketing is typically dubbed local advertising or local store marketing. At this level, the franchisee is contractually obligated to make direct advertising expenditures. There is often a wide spectrum of permissible advertising expenditures, depending on the franchisor guidelines in the license agreement.

The franchisor should monitor and enforce marketing expenditures. For example, the customer of a franchisee leaving one ADI and entering another will have been affected by the advertising of adjacent regions. In addition, advertising expenditures not made are lost marketing impressions, reducing the marketing leverage inherent in franchising.

Supply

In most franchise systems, major benefits include bulk purchasing and inventory control. In the license agreement, there are several ways to account for this economy of scale advantage. Because of changing markets, competitors and U.S. antitrust law make it impossible for the franchisor to be bound to best-price requirements. The franchise should employ a standard of best efforts and good faith to acquire both national and regional supply contracts.

Depending on the nature of the product or service, regional deals might make more sense than national deals. Regional content may provide greater advantages to the franchisee because of shipping weight and cost or service requirements. The savvy franchisor will recognize this and implement a flexible purchase plan. When local advantages exist and the franchisor does not act appropriately, the franchisees will fill the void. The monthly ADI meeting then becomes an expanded forum for franchisees to voice their appreciations and concerns. The results of such ad hoc organizations can be reduced control of quality and expansion of franchisee association outside the confines of the license agreement. Advanced activity of this nature can often

---

[5]Advertising cooperatives in franchising are common. A cooperative is a contractual agreement whereby franchisees in a geographic area are bound to contribute a percentage of their revenue to a fund that executes a marketing plan, usually including media purchases. The cooperative is typically governed by the participating franchisees and sometimes includes representation from the franchisor and advertising agency.

fractionalize a franchise system and even render the franchisor obsolete. In some cases, the franchisor and franchisee-operated buying cooperatives peaceably coexist, acting as competitors and lowering the costs to the operator. However, the dual buying co-ops usually reduce economies of scale and dilute system resources. They also provide fertile ground for conflict within the franchise alliance.

For quality control purposes, the franchisor will reserve the right to publish a product specifications list. The list will clearly establish the quality standards of raw materials or goods used in the operation. From those specifications, a subsequent list of approved suppliers is generated. This list can evolve into a franchise "tying agreement," which occurs when the business format franchise license agreement binds the franchisee to the purchase of a specifically branded product. This varies from the product specification list because brand, not product content, is the qualifying specification. The important question here is: Does the tying arrangement of franchise and product create an enhancement for the franchisee in the marketplace? If so, then are arm's-length controls in place to ensure that pricing, netted from the enhanced value, will yield positive results? Unfortunately this is impossible to precisely quantify. However, if the tying agreement

is specified in the license agreement, then the prospective franchise owner is advised to make a judgment before purchasing the franchise. With this sort of decision at hand, the franchisor should prove the value of the tying agreement or abandon it.

Another subtle form of tying agreements occurs when the license agreement specifies an approved suppliers list that ultimately includes only one supplier. If adding suppliers to the list is impossible, there is a de-facto tying arrangement. In addition, another tying arrangement can occur when the product specification is written so that only one brand can qualify. A franchisor should disclose any remuneration gained by the franchisor or its officers, directly or indirectly, from product purchase in the franchise system. In this case, the franchisor's market value enhancement test is again proof of a credible arrangement.

Franchise Relationship Model

Now that we have established the nature and components of the franchise relationship, we can connect these principles to the franchise relationship model (FRM), which we have developed over the past 8 years (Exhibit 11.4). The FRM connects the

EXHIBIT 11.4

Franchise Relationship Model

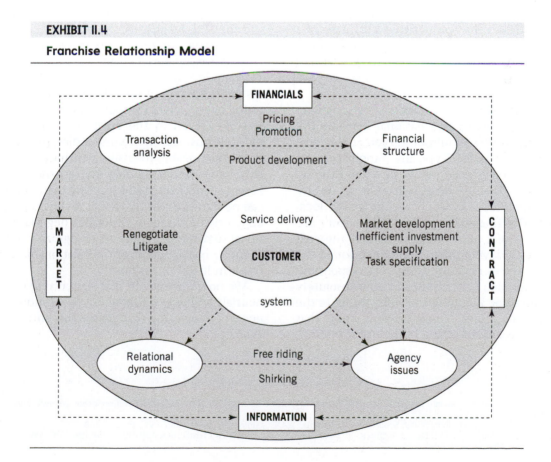

entrepreneurial framework provided by the Timmons Model to the specific processes that are unique to franchising. We have argued that franchising is a powerful entrepreneurial method because it fits the Timmons Model and because it creates wealth. The FRM illustrates both how a concept innovator (i.e., potential franchisor) can most efficiently construct a franchising company and how a concept implementer (i.e., potential franchisee) can determine which company to join. The FRM further helps to distinguish between those tasks best executed under a corporate umbrella and those best done by the individual franchisee. Just as franchising is a risk-reduction tool for the entrepreneur, the FRM is also a tool that both franchisors and franchisees can use to judge the efficiency or success potential of a franchise opportunity. By overlaying the FRM template onto any given franchise, we can forecast where bottlenecks will impede success or where improvements can be made that will offer competitive advantage.

The FRM is a puzzle, a series of franchise principles, each of which fits into the others to form a powerful interlocking business concept that solidifies itself as the linkages are implemented more efficiently. Although the process starts in the center with the customer, moves to the SDS, and follows from there, the outer perimeter of means and mechanisms drives the competitive advantage of a franchise system. The major areas of concern other than the customer and the SDS are transaction analysis, financial structure, agency issues, and relational dynamics.

Transaction analysis considers which transactions are better served at a national level by the franchisor and which should be served at the local level by the franchisee.[6] Typically franchisor functions are centered on economies of scale. Franchisee functions include those that require on-site entrepreneurial capacity such as hiring and local promotion. The financial structure flows from pro forma analysis of customer demand and the cost associated with development and execution of the SDS. Agency issues concern delegating responsibility to a partner.[7] No franchisor can know absolutely that the franchisee is "doing the right thing" at the store level. Franchisees cannot possibly know that the franchisor is always acting in their best interest.

Relational dynamics is the area that allows the partnership between franchisor and franchisee to continuously change and develop as the business continues to expand.[8] Any partnership that strictly adheres to a contract will end in litigation.

The FRM (Exhibit 11.4) is dynamic: As events affect one aspect of the model, all other aspects must be reviewed in an iterative process. For example, if renegotiation of the license agreement were to result in a reduced royalty, the financial model would be altered. A change in royalty could dictate a change in the services that the franchisor provides. Any change creates a cascading effect throughout the system–a reconstruction of the puzzle.

The FRM begins with opportunity recognition and shaping (customer) and then articulates the competitive advantages and costs of the SDS that will extract the demand and create a return on investment. The competitive sustainability of the franchise is embedded in the delineation of responsibilities between franchisor and franchisee and in the conscious design of the SDS. The franchisor's tasks are centrally executed and focus on economies of scale; the franchisee concentrates on those responsibilities that require local on-site entrepreneurial intensity (transaction analysis). The emergent financial structure is the manifestation of the interaction between the primary target customer and the SDS. By sharing the burden of the SDS and the potential for return on investment, the franchise entrepreneurial alliance is formed.

Central to the long-term stability of the franchise system is the proper selection of partners and monitoring of key partner responsibilities (agency issues). However, even in the most stable relationship, a dynamic business environment dictates adjustments in the relationship to ensure continued competitive advantage. Understanding the partner's tolerance zone in performance and reacting to market changes can be standardized by formal review programs and kept unstructured by informal negotiations (relational dynamics). Failure to recognize the need for dynamic management of the relationship can often result in litigation, as noted.

We now understand that franchising is entrepreneurial, and we understand the unique components of franchising that enable this entrepreneurial alliance.

---

[6]O.E. Williamson, "Comparative Economic Organizations: The Analysis of Discrete Structural Alternatives," *Administrative Science Quarterly* (June 1991), pp. 269-288.

[7]F. Lafontaine, "Agency Theory and Franchising: Some Empirical Results," *RAND Journal of Economics* 23 (1992), pp. 263-268.

[8]I.R. Macneil, "Economic Analysis of Contractual Relations: Its Shortfalls and Need for a 'Rich Classification Apparatus,'" *Northwestern University Law Review*, February 1980, pp. 1018-1063.

Internet Impact: Resources

The Network Enhanced

The essence of franchising is the creation of value in a trademark. Efficiently sharing information is a key to leveraging the experiences of each franchisee for the betterment of all franchisees. Because franchising is governed (primarily) by a long-term contract, the players in the system are motivated to share knowledge because enhanced performance builds the commonly held trademark.

Franchises have been pioneers in monitoring systems and feedback loops. Most franchising organizations have invested significantly in Internet and extranet systems. Originally (well before the Internet), these systems were primarily "policing" devices established to make sure franchisees followed the prescribed business format and then paid their royalties. Today these systems go far beyond the original control function.

McDonald's recently began testing an outsourcing of its restaurant drive-through ordering systems. A McDonald's franchisee created this system and now shares it with 300 other franchisees in a beta test. Early results show a significant increase in both speed of delivery and order accuracy.

Chapter Summary

Franchising is an inherently entrepreneurial endeavor. In this chapter we argue that opportunity, scale, and growth are at the heart of the franchise experience. The success of franchising is demonstrated by the fact that it accounts for more than one-third of all U.S. retailing. Equally important is the demonstrated performance of the top franchise companies, which consistently outperform the Standard & Poor's 500. Franchising shares profits, risk, and strategic implementation between the franchisor and the franchisee. Unique aspects of franchising as entrepreneurship are the wide spectrum of opportunity that exists and the matching of scale to appetite for a broad spectrum of entrepreneurs. For those interested in creating a franchise, the FRM articulates the dynamic construction of the franchisor–franchisee alliance. For the prospective franchisee, the franchise risk profile helps the budding entrepreneur assess the risk–return scenario for any given franchise opportunity.

Study Questions

1. Can you describe the difference between the franchisor and the franchisee? How are these differences strategically aligned to create competitive advantage?

2. We describe franchising as a "pathway to entrepreneurship" that provides a spectrum of entrepreneurial opportunities. What does this mean to you?

3. What are the most important factors in determining whether franchising is an appropriate method of rapidly growing a concept?

4. What are the five components of the FRM? Can you describe the interactive nature of these components?

5. Why do you think the public franchisors consistently outperform the S&P 500?

6. What would be the most attractive aspects of franchising to you? What is the least attractive part of franchising?

Internet Resources

http://bison1.com/ *Our favorite site for franchising information.*

http://www.businessfranchisedirectory.com/ *A searchable database of franchise information and opportunities.*

http://www.franchisehelp.com/ *Help for those looking into a franchise: how it works and when to invest.*

http://www.aafd.org/ *The AAFD is a national nonprofit trade association focused on market-driven solutions to improve the franchising community.*

http://www.franchise.org/ *The International Franchise Association (IFA).*

Mike Bellobuono had a lot to consider. Bagel industry sales had exploded, and Connecticut-based Bagelz, had established seven retail locations in three years. Bellobuono knew the company needed to grow quickly or risk an inability to compete against larger players.

There was a lot at stake for President Joe Amodio, Vice President Wes Becher, Territory Development Manager Jamie Whalen, and Director of Operations Mike Bellobuono. Bagelz's four-member management team had planned on keeping stores company-owned until they met Fred DeLuca, who suggested franchising and offered financing. DeLuca, who founded Subway, could be a tremendous asset for Bagelz. But the four were used to operating as a small, closely knit team and were afraid partnering with DeLuca would result in their losing control of Bagelz.

If they decided to franchise, Bellobuono wondered if they would be able to find franchisees that had the finances, motivation, and ability to successfully run Bagelz stores. He knew disgruntled franchisees would poorly represent the company, and he wasn't sure if accelerated growth was worth the headaches and the possibility that unhappy franchisees would damage the company's reputation. He was also worried that franchisees wouldn't maintain the high standard of Bagelz's seven company-owned stores. He thought about what happened to Jack-in-the-Box, another large fast-food franchise company. In January 1993, a customer had gotten sick and died from bacteria in an undercooked hamburger. The company hired independent inspectors to review every franchise and ensure that all complied with the Board of Health's regulated cooking process. No additional violations were found, but franchisees experienced declines in revenues of up to 35 percent.[1]

On the other hand, if they decided not to franchise, they risked being locked out of certain geographical areas. Bruegger's Bagels was opening units all over New England (Exhibit A), and Manhattan Bagel had gone public, giving it access to large amounts of capital for expansion. If the company decided against franchising, the team wondered if Bagelz would be able to withstand the onslaught of competition that was sure to occur. They wanted to make the right decision, but there was much to consider, and the offer to partner with DeLuca would not stay on the table for long. The bagel wars were heating up, and Bellobuono knew they had to develop a superior growth strategy.

Mike Bellobuono's Background

Bellobuono graduated from Babson College with a BS in May of 1991. He was working for a lawn service, but he and his college friend Jamie Whalen were looking at bagel and chicken franchises. As part of a class project during Bellobuono's senior year, they had done an in-depth study of the food service industry (Exhibit B). It led them to believe that the industry would experience continued growth, and that bagels and chicken would be the next high-growth segments.

Then, Bellobuono met Wes Becher and Joe Amodio. The two had opened a bagel store called Bagelz that had done so well they opened a second store and planned to develop additional locations. (See Exhibit C for Bagelz's income statement.) After considering alternatives, Bellobuono decided he liked both the company and the taste of Bagelz bagels best.

Whalen's father, who had originally approached Bellobuono about the possibility of Bellobuono becoming a partner with Whalen, was extremely supportive of the decision. Bellobuono and Whalen had been friends all their lives. The elder Whalen and Bellobuono had become so close that Bellobuono thought of him as his second father, and Mr. Whalen looked at Bellobuono as the perfect business partner for his son. He eagerly endorsed Bellobuono's idea and even thought Whalen should leave school one year early to do this. Bellobuono's father, however, was somewhat less than enthused at first:

> My father wanted me to go to law school or work for Aetna, where I had a job offer, but to me, working for someone else was never an option. When I told him about Bagelz he said, "Bagels? You went to business school and now you're going to sell bagels?" He wasn't exactly convinced that I was making the right decision, but he supported my decision anyway.

Due Diligence

Bellobuono approached Bruegger's about opening bagel stores in Connecticut, but the company thought it had no market potential. He then considered Manhattan Bagel, which thought Connecticut was a viable market, before deciding to invest in

This case was prepared by Andrea Alyse with assistance from Dan D'Heilly under the direction of Professor Stephen Spinelli. © Copyright Babson College, 1996. Funding provided by the Ewing Marion Kauffman Foundation. All rights reserved.
[1]"E-Coli Scare Deals Blow to Seattle Burger Sales," *Restaurant Business*, March 20, 1993; and "Fallout of E-Coli Episode Still Troubles Foodmarket," *Nation's Restaurant News*, March 20, 1995.

EXHIBIT A

Bruegger's Bagels Growth Statistics

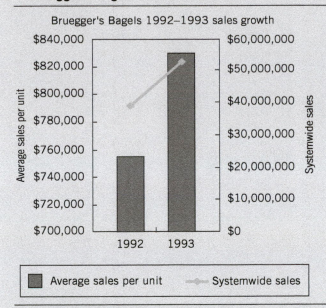

Bruegger's Bagels 1992–1993 sales growth

Average sales per unit · Systemwide sales

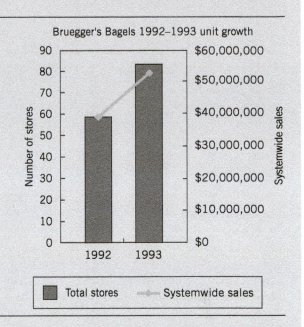

Bruegger's Bagels 1992–1993 unit growth

Total stores · Systemwide sales

EXHIBIT B

Food Service Industry Growth

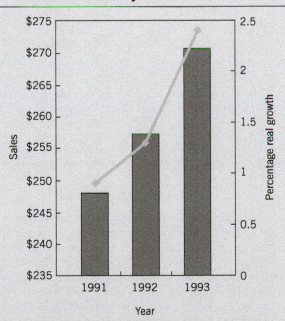

Bagelz because of its competitive advantages. Irving Stearns, Bagelz's chief bagel maker, had been in the business for more than 20 years and knew everything there was to know about bagels. Bellobuono also liked the flexibility of Bagelz's management, which was quick to spot and react to market trends. For example, Bagelz offered customers five different

kinds of flavored coffees at a time when all their competitors offered only regular and decaffeinated. Finally, with Bagelz, he was on the ground floor.

Bagelz

Bellobuono and Whalen contacted Amodio and Becher about buying a franchise. They soon learned that franchisers had to adhere to the U.S. Federal Trade Commission (FTC) Disclosure Rule, which requires them to disclose certain specified information to all prospective franchisees (Exhibit D). Most franchisers used a Uniform Franchise Offering Circular (UFOC), which contains a description of the business, estimated development costs, fee schedules, franchisee and franchiser obligations, other businesses affiliated with the franchise, and pending lawsuits. Producing this document was expensive and time consuming, but without it, Amodio and Becher couldn't sell franchises. However, Bellobuono and Whalen persisted until Amodio and Becher agreed to sell them a store as a limited partnership.

Bellobuono and Whalen opened the Manchester store in December 1991. Then Becher, impressed by Bellobuono and Whalen's dedication, approached the two about becoming full partners in the company. Becher said that although he had several prospective investors, he wanted to offer the two a partnership because he and Amodio were looking for investors who would work for Bagelz, not simply finance it. Whalen and Bellobuono arranged financing through their fathers, and the two became full partners the

EXHIBIT C

Bagelz Per Store Earning Claims 1993[a]

	Weekly	Annually	Percentage of Total Revenue per Store (%)
Total revenue per store	$8,000.00	$ 416,000.00	100
Cost of goods sold			
Salaries and wages	2,000.00	104,000.00	25
Food	1,680.00	87,360.00	21
Beverages	800.00	41,600.00	10
Paper supplies	320.00	16,640.00	4
Total COGS	$4,800.00	$249,600.00	60
Gross profit on sales	$3,200.00	$ 166,400.00	40
Operating expenses			
Payroll tax	136.00	7,072.00	1.70
Payroll service	20.00	1,040.00	0.25
Rent	480.00	24,960.00	6.00
Connecticut Light and Power	200.00	10,400.00	2.50
Connecticut Natural Gas	120.00	6,240.00	1.50
Telephone	24.00	1,248.00	0.30
Advertising	200.00	10,400.00	2.50
Local advertising	80.00	4,160.00	1.00
Insurance	80.00	4,160.00	1.00
Linen and laundry	16.00	832.00	0.20
Repairs and maintenance	80.00	4,160.00	1.00
Rubbish removal	40.00	2,080.00	0.50
Office supplies	40.00	2,080.00	0.50
Uniforms	16.00	832.00	0.20
Professional fees	40.00	2,080.00	0.50
Miscellaneous	20.00	1,040.00	0.25
Total operating expenses	$ 1,592.00	$ 82,784.00	19.90
Total income from operations	$ 1,608.00	$ 83,616.00	20.10

[a]All figures have been estimated based on industry data and do not necessarily represent the actual financial performance of a Bagelz store operation.

next year. Bellobuono, Becher, Whalen, and Amodio handled all aspects of the partnership. Each store was visited by one of the four members of the team daily to ensure that operations were running smoothly and to solve any difficulties that arose. Becher, Whalen, and Bellobuono focused on the day-to-day operations, and Amodio on growing the company:

Joe was the leader and a fly-by-the-seat-of-the-pants type of guy. Joe would point in a direction, and we three would make it happen. Joe had an incredible talent for salesmanship, a kind of way about him that enabled him to achieve the seemingly impossible. One Christmas we were in New York City, and we were in this restaurant. The owner was depressed because the restaurant was empty. Joe said he could fill the restaurant if the owner sat

him by the window. He proceeded to put on quite a show, performing in the window, carrying on, gesturing, and waving, which drove people in who wanted to see what all the excitement was about. And you know what? He filled the restaurant in under an hour. But Joe wasn't finished yet. He then got the entire place to sing "The Twelve Days of Christmas," and when people forgot the words of a section of the song, he had them running out into the street asking people if they knew the words and could help out—I mean strangers, in the middle of New York City. It was unbelievable! Even the ending was like a fairy tale: As the crowd got to the twelfth day of Christmas, Joe was tipping his hat at the door and making his exit. To this day whenever he goes into that restaurant his dinner is free; the owner never forgot what Joe did for him.

EXHIBIT D

U.S. Federal Trade Commission Disclosure Rule

I. Rule Overview

A. **Basic Requirement:** Franchisors must furnish potential franchisees with written disclosures providing important information about the franchisor, the franchised business and the franchise relationship, and give them at least 10 business days to review it before investing.

B. **Disclosure Option:** Franchisors may make the required disclosures by following either the Rule's disclosure format or the UFOC Guidelines prepared by state franchise law officials.

C. **Coverage:** The Rule primarily covers business-format franchises, product franchises, and vending machine or display rack business opportunity ventures.

D. **No Filing:** The Rule requires disclosure only. Unlike state disclosure laws, no registration, filing, review or approval of any disclosures, advertising or agreements by the FTC is required.

E. **Remedies:** The Rule is a trade regulation rule with the full force and effect of federal law. The courts have held it may only be enforced by the FTC, not private parties. The FTC may seek injunctions, civil penalties and consumer redress for violations.

F. **Purpose:** The Rule is designed to enable potential franchisees to protect themselves before investing by providing them with information essential to an assessment of the potential risks and benefits, to meaningful comparisons with other investments, and to further investigation of the franchise opportunity.

G. **Effective Date:** The Rule, formally titled "Disclosure Requirements and Prohibitions Concerning Franchising and Business Opportunity Ventures," took effect on October 21, 1979, and appears at 16 C.F.R. Part 436.

II. Rule Requirements

A. **General:** The Rule imposes six different requirements in connection with the "advertising, offering, licensing, contracting, sale or other promotion" of a franchise in or affecting commerce:

1. **Basic Disclosures:** The Rule requires franchisors to give potential investors a basic disclosure document at the earlier of the first face-to-face meeting or 10 business days before any money is paid or an agreement is signed in connection with the investment (Part 436.1(a)).

2. **Earnings Claims:** If a franchisor makes earnings claims, whether historical or forecast, they must have a reasonable basis, and prescribed substantiating disclosures must be given to a potential investor in writing at the same time as the basic disclosures (Parts 436.1(b)–(d)).

3. **Advertised Claims:** The Rule affects only ads that include an earnings claim. Such ads must disclose the number and percentage of existing franchisees who have achieved the claimed results, along with cautionary language. Their use triggers required compliance with the Rule's earnings claim disclosure requirements (Part 436.1(e)).

4. **Franchise Agreements:** The franchisor must give investors a copy of its standard-form franchise and related agreements at the same time as the basic disclosures, and final copies intended to be executed at least 5 business days before signing (Part 436.1(g)).

5. **Refunds:** The Rule requires franchisors to make refunds of deposits and initial payments to potential investors, subject to any conditions on refundability stated in the disclosure document (Part 436.1(h)).

6. **Contradictory Claims:** While franchisors are free to provide investors with any promotional or other materials they wish, no written or oral claims may contradict information provided in the required disclosure document (Part 436.1(f)).

B. **Liability:** Failure to comply with any of the six requirements is a violation of the Franchise Rule. "Franchisors" and "franchise brokers" are jointly and severally liable for Rule violations.

1. A "franchisor" is defined as any person who sells a "franchise" covered by the Rule (Part 436.2(c)).

2. A "franchise broker" is defined as any person who "sells, offers for sale, or arranges for the sale" of a covered franchise (Part 436.2(j)), and includes not only independent sales agents, but also subfranchisors that grant subfranchises (44 FR 49963).

III. Business Relationships Covered

A. **Alternate Definitions:** The Rule employs parallel coverage definitions of the term "franchise" to reach two types of continuing commercial relationships: traditional franchises and business opportunities.

B. **"Traditional Franchises":** There are three definitional prerequisites to coverage of a business-format or product franchise (Parts 436.2(a)(1)(i) and (2)):

1. **Trademark:** The franchisor offers the right to distribute goods or services that bear the franchisor's trademark, service mark, trade name, advertising or other commercial symbol.

2. **Significant Control or Assistance:** The franchisor exercises significant control over, or offers significant assistance in, the franchisee's method of operation.

(continued)

EXHIBIT D   (continued)

3. Required Payment: The franchisee is required to make any payment to the franchisor or an affiliate, or a commitment to make a payment, as a condition of obtaining the franchise or commencing operations. (NOTE: There is an exemption from coverage for required payments of less than $500 within 6 months of the commencement of the franchise (Part 436.2(a)(3)(iii))).

C. Business Opportunities: There are also three basic prerequisites to the Rule's coverage of a business opportunity venture (Parts 436.2(a)(1)(ii) and (2)):

1. No Trademark: The seller simply offers the right to sell goods or services supplied by the seller, its affiliate, or a supplier with which the seller requires the franchisee to do business.

2. Location Assistance: The seller offers to secure retail outlets or accounts for the goods or services to be sold, to secure locations or sites for vending machines or rack displays, or to provide the services of someone who can do so.

3. Required Payment: The same as for franchises.

D. Coverage Exemptions/Exclusions: The Rule also exempts or excludes some relationships that would otherwise meet the coverage prerequisites (Parts 436.2(a)(3) and (4)):

1. Minimum Investment: This exemption applies if all payments to the franchisor or an affiliate until 6 months after the franchise commences operation are $500 or less (Part 436.2(a)(iii)).

2. Fractional Franchises: Relationships adding a new product or service to an established distributor's existing products or services, are exempt if (i) the franchisee or any of its current directors or executive officers has been in the same type of business for at least 2 years, and (ii) both parties anticipated, or should have, that sales from the franchise would represent no more than 20 percent of the franchisees sales in dollar volume (Parts 436.2(a)(3)(i) and 436.2(h)).

3. Single Trademark Licenses: The Rule language excludes a "single license to license a [mark]" where it "is the only one of its general nature and type to be granted by the licenser with respect to that [mark]" (Part 436.2(a)(4)(iv)). The Rule's Statement of Basis and Purpose indicates it also applies to "collateral" licenses [e.g., logo on sweatshirt, mug] and licenses granted to settle trademark infringement litigation (43 FR 59707-08).

4. Employment and Partnership Relationships: The Rule excludes pure employer—employee and general partnership arrangements. Limited partnerships do not qualify for the exemption (Part 436.2(a)(4)(i)).

5. Oral Agreements: This exemption, which is narrowly construed, applies only if no material term of the relationship is in writing (Part 436.2(a)(3)(iv)).

6. Cooperative Associations: Only agricultural co-ops and retailer-owned cooperatives "operated 'by and for' retailers on a cooperative basis," and in which control and ownership is substantially equal are excluded from coverage (Part 436.2(a)(4)(ii)).

7. Certification/Testing Services: Organizations that authorize use of a certification mark to any business selling products or services meeting their standards are excluded from coverage (e.g., Underwriters Laboratories) (Part 436.2(a)(4)(iii)).

8. Leased Departments: Relationships in which the franchisee simply leases space in the premises of another retailer and is not required or advised to buy the goods or services it sells from the retailer or an affiliate of the retailer are exempt (Part 436.2(a)(3)(ii)).

E. Statutory Exemptions: Section 18(g) of the FTC Act authorizes "any person" to petition the Commission for an exemption from a rule where coverage is "not necessary to prevent the acts or practices" that the rule prohibits (15 U.S.C. § 57a(g)). Franchise Rule exemptions have been granted for service station franchises (45 FR 51765), many automobile dealership franchises (45 FR 51763; 49 FR 13677; 52 FR 6612; 54 FR 1446), and wholesaler-sponsored voluntary chains in the grocery industry (48 FR 10040).

IV. Disclosure Options

A. Alternatives: Franchisors have a choice of formats for making the disclosures required by the Rule. They may use either the format provided by the Rule or the UFOC format prescribed by the North American Securities Administrators' Association ("NASAA").

B. FTC Format: Franchisors may comply by following the Rule's requirements for preparing a basic disclosure document (Parts 436.1(a)(1)–(24)), and if they make earnings claims, for a separate earnings claim disclosure document (Parts 436.1(b)(3), (c)(3), and (d)). The Rule's Final Interpretive Guides provide detailed instructions and sample disclosures (44 FR 49966).

C. UFOC Format: The UFOC format may also be used for compliance in any state.

1. Guidelines: Effective January 1, 1996, franchisors using the UFOC disclosure format must comply with the UFOC Guidelines, as amended by NASAA on April 25, 1993. (44 FR 49970; 60 FR 51895).

2. Cover Page: The FTC cover page must be furnished to each potential franchisee, either in lieu of the UFOC cover page in nonregistration states or along with the UFOC (Part 436.1(a)(21); 44 FR 49970-71).

(continued)

EXHIBIT D   (continued)

3. Adaptation: If the UFOC is registered or used in one state, but will be used in another without a franchise registration law, answers to state-specific questions must be changed to refer to the law of the state in which the UFOC is used.

4. Updating: If the UFOC is registered in a state, it must be updated as required by the state's franchise law. If the same UFOC is also adapted for use in a nonregistration state, updating must occur as required by the law of the state where the UFOC is registered. If the UFOC is not registered in a state with a franchise registration law, it must be revised annually and updated quarterly as required by the Rule.

5. Presumption: The Commission will presume the sufficiency, adequacy and accuracy of a UFOC that is registered by a state, when it is used in that state.

D. UFOC versus Rule: Many franchisors have adopted the UFOC disclosure format because roughly half of the 13 states with franchise registration requirements will not accept the Rule document for filing. When a format is chosen, all disclosure must conform to its requirements. Franchisors may not pick and choose provisions from each format when making disclosures (44 FR 49970).

E. Rule Primacy: If the UFOC is used, several key Rule provisions will still apply:

1. Scope: Disclosure will be required in all cases required by the Rule, regardless of whether it would be required by state law.

2. Coverage: The Rule will determine who is obligated to comply, regardless of whether they would be required to make disclosures under state law.

3. Disclosure Timing: When disclosures must be made will be governed by the Rule, unless state law requires even earlier disclosure.

4. Other Material: No information may appear in a disclosure document not required by the Rule or by nonpreempted state law, regardless of the format used, and no representations may be made that contradict a disclosure.

5. Contracts: Failure to provide potential franchisees with final agreements at least 5 days before signing will be a Rule violation regardless of the disclosure format used.

6. Refunds: Failure to make promised refunds also will be a Rule violation regardless of which document is used.

V. Potential Liability for Violations

A. FTC Action: Rule violations may subject franchisors, franchise brokers, their officers, and agents to significant liabilities in FTC enforcement actions.

1. Remedies: The FTC Act provides the Commission with a broad range of remedies for Rule violations:

a. Injunctions: Section 13(b) of the Act authorizes preliminary and permanent injunctions against Rule violations (15 U.S.C. § 53(b)). Rule cases routinely have sought and obtained injunctions against Rule violations and misrepresentations in the offer or sale of any business venture, whether or not covered by the Rule.

b. Asset Freezes: Acting under their inherent equity powers, the courts have routinely granted preliminary asset freezes in appropriate Rule cases. The assets frozen have included both corporate assets and the personal assets, including real and personal property, of key officers and directors.

c. Civil Penalties: Section 5(m)(1)(A) of the Act authorizes civil penalties of up to $10,000 for each violation of the Rule (15 U.S.C. § 45(m)(1)(A)). The courts have granted civil penalties of as much as $870,000 in a Rule case to date.

d. Monetary Redress: Section 19(b) of the Act authorizes the Commission to seek monetary redress on behalf of investors injured economically by a Rule violation (15 U.S.C. § 57b). The courts have granted consumer redress of as much as $4.9 million in a Rule case to date.

e. Other Redress: Section 19(b) of the Act also authorizes such other forms of redress as the court finds necessary to redress injury to consumers from a Rule violation, including rescission or reformation of contracts, the return of property and public notice of the Rule violation. Courts may also grant similar relief under their inherent equity powers.

2. Personal Liability: Individuals who formulate, direct and control the franchisor's activities can expect to be named individually for violations committed in the franchisor's name, together with the franchisor entity, and held personally liable for civil penalties and consumer redress.

3. Liability for Others: Franchisors and their key officers and executives are responsible for violations by persons acting in their behalf, including independent franchise brokers, subfranchisors, and the franchisor's own sales personnel.

B. Private Actions: The courts have held that the FTC Act generally may not be enforced by private lawsuits.

1. Rule Claims: The Commission expressed its view when the Rule was issued that private actions should be permitted by the courts for Rule violations (43 FR 59723; 44 FR 49971). To date, no federal court has permitted a private action for Rule violations.

(continued)

EXHIBIT D   (concluded)

2. State Disclosure Law Claims: Each of the franchise laws in the 15 states with franchise registration and/or disclosure requirements authorizes private actions for state franchise law violations.

3. State FTC Act Claims: The courts in some states have interpreted state deceptive practices laws ("little FTC Acts") as permitting private actions for Rule violations.

VI. Legal Resources

A. Text of Rule: 16 C.F.R. Part 436.

B. Statement of Basis and Purpose: 43 FR 59614–59733 (Dec. 21, 1978) (discusses the evidentiary basis for promulgation of the Rule, and shows Commission intent and interpretation of its provisions—particularly helpful in resolving coverage questions).

C. Final Interpretive Guides: 44 FR 49966–49992 (Aug. 24, 1979) (final statement of policy and interpretation of each of the Rule's requirements—important discussions of coverage issues, use of the UFOC and requirements for basic and earnings claims disclosures in the Rule's disclosure format).

D. Staff Advisory Opinions: Business Franchise Guide (CCH) 6380 et seq. (interpretive opinions issued in response to requests for interpretation of coverage questions and disclosure requirements pursuant to 16 C.F.R. §§ 1.2–1.4).

By 1993, Bagelz had seven stores with the goal of saturating Connecticut by the year 2000. Bruegger's wasn't there yet, and Manhattan had only a few locations, but Bellobuono knew it was coming:

> We were Bagelz, and we wanted to make Connecticut our turf, so that you knew that if you were going to go into Connecticut, you would have to fight us.

The Bagel Industry

Legend maintains that the first bagel was created for the king of Poland as celebration bread, when the king's army repelled a 1683 Turkish invasion. Jewish immigrants introduced the bagel in the United States, and for decades bagels were perceived as a strictly ethnic food with limited appeal.

Traditionally bagels were made from water, flour, yeast, and salt, combined and formed into rings. The rings were boiled in water to create the crust and shiny appearance, then baked in brick ovens to produce a crispy outside and a soft, chewy inside, considerably denser than most breads. As bagels gained acceptance, the industry grew at an accelerating rate. Modern bakers often use machine-formed bagels and large stainless-steel ovens, complete with rotating racks for faster, more uniform baking. As competition between bagel shops has increased in the United States, the traditional bagel recipe has been adapted to increase a variety of flavors.

Lender's, now a division of Pinnacle Foods Inc., first marketed a mass-produced, frozen, supermarket bagel in 1962. Before this time, bagels had been sold only as fresh. By 1991, Lender's had sales of $203 million, and Sara Lee, Lender's closest competitor, which had entered the frozen bagel market in 1985, had sales of $22.4 million.

In the 1980s, Lender's and Bagel Nosh opened bagel shops nationally, but they did not succeed. By the early 1990, bagels were gaining acceptance across the country, most notably on the East Coast. As of mid-1992, 51 percent of all bagel sales in the United States came from 15 cities. Frozen supermarket bagels achieved sales of $211.9 million in 1992, up 4 percent from 1991, but sales of fresh bagels, the most rapidly growing segment, increased 28 percent to $95 million. For 1993, sales of frozen bagels were projected to increase 6 percent to $224.4 million, and sales of fresh bagels were projected to increase 17 percent to $111 million. Consumer awareness and consumption of bagels had increased steadily, but most dramatically throughout the past six years (Exhibit E illustrates the increase in per capita bagel

EXHIBIT E

Bagel Consumption

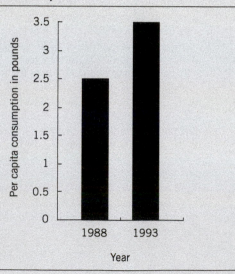

consumption for 1988 to 1993). Breakfast accounted for 65 percent of all bagel sales, and with increased consumer health awareness, bagels had become a natural, low-fat, high-carbohydrate alternative to other menu items such as doughnuts and muffins.

Fred DeLuca

In the spring of 1993, Fred DeLuca contacted the Bagelz team. DeLuca was well known in the franchise industry. While still in college, he had opened his first Subway location in 1965. Nine years later he began franchising, and by 1995 Subway had grown to more than 10,000 locations. In addition, *Entrepreneur Magazine* rated Subway the No. 1 franchise in its annual franchising 500 six times between 1988 and 1994:

> WE never thought that he wanted to do business with us. We were just excited to meet him. When we realized he was interested in making a deal, we were astonished.

It was then that the team first seriously considered franchising.

To Franchise or Not to Franchise?

DeLuca had offered to buy into Bagelz and turn it into a world-class franchise, but first he wanted to be sure that the bagel team was fully aware of, and ready to meet, all potential difficulties involved with franchising:

> Fred wanted to know why we wanted to franchise. He said, "Do you know what you are getting yourself into? Are you sure you really want to deal with all the problems that arise from franchising?"

The team weighed both the pros and cons of becoming a franchiser. They evaluated two basic strategies: either to grow rapidly throughout Connecticut as a chain, or to franchise and grow nationally.

They were afraid of losing control if they franchised, but knew it would be difficult to grow quickly otherwise. They were also afraid they wouldn't be able to lock out the competition: Manhattan Bagel planned to expand into Connecticut, and Bruegger's had been named one of the 50 fastest-growing U.S. restaurants (Exhibit F). Last, Bellobuono and the team feared that DeLuca would lose interest. Then Subway began receiving increasing amounts of negative publicity regarding the company's support of its franchisees. One particularly disturbing article appeared in *The Wall Street Journal,*[2] and Bellobuono and the team began to wonder if aligning with DeLuca could hurt Bagelz. They knew, however, that time was running out and they needed to decide the best future direction for their company.

[2] B. Welch, "Franchise Realities: Sandwich-Shop Chain Surges, But to Run One Can Take Heroic Effort," *The Wall Street Journal,* September 16, 1992, p. A1.

50 Fastest-Growing Restaurants, 1992–1993

Name of Restaurant	City and State	Type of Restaurant	Does the Company Franchise?	Projected 1992–1993 % Change in Systemwide Sales	Projected 1992–1993 % Change in Units	Projected 1992–1993 % Change in Average Unit Sales
1 Boston Chicken	Naperville, IL	Fast food	Y	261.0%	161.4%	9.2%
2 Lone Star Steakhouse & Saloon	Wichita, KS	Casual steakhouse	Y	136.3	95.7	3.6
3 Italian Oven	Latrobe, PA	Casual Italian dinnerhouse	Y	126.2	60.0	11.7
4 Romano's Macaroni Grill	Dallas	Casual Italian dinnerhouse	N	107.7	86.7	0.2
5 Hooters	Atlanta	Casual dinnerhouse	Y	87.2	16.0	25.0
6 Papa John's	Louisville	Delivery/take-out pizza	Y	80.4	81.8	8.7
7 Outback Steakhouse	Tampa	Casual steakhouse	Y	77.9	71.8	6.7
8 Checkers Drive-In	Clearwater, FL	Drive-through hamburgers	Y	68.1	81.2	5.2
9 Taco Cabana	San Antonio, TX	Patio-style Mexican	Y	65.1	87.7	−4.2
10 Hot 'n Now	Irvine, CA	Drive-through hamburgers	N	64.0	80.9	3.6
11 Wall Street Deli	Memphis	Self-serve deli and buffet	N	56.2	26.4	5.0
12 Mick's	Atlanta	Casual dinnerhouse	N	53.8	50.0	1.5
13 Applebee's	Kansas City, MO	Casual dinnerhouse	Y	50.5	44.4	5.3
14 Starbucks	Seattle	Coffee specialist	N	50.0	63.7	6.7
15 Grady's American Grill	Dallas	Casual dinnerhouse	N	45.1	52.6	1.2
16 Bertucci's Brick Oven Pizza	Woburn, MA	Casual Italian dinnerhouse	N	45.0	42.9	5.9
17 Fresh Choice	Santa Clara, CA	Self-serve buffet	N	44.4	63.6	4.9
18 Miami Subs Grill	Fort Lauderdale, FL	Fast food	Y	42.9	23.2	3.5
19 Stacey's Buffet	Largo, FL	Self-serve buffet	Y	39.0	50.0	−5.3
20 Longhorn Steaks	Atlanta	Casual steakhouse	Y	37.4	32.5	−2.8
21 Panda Express	South Pasadena, CA	Fast-food Oriental	N	36.8	40.0	2.9
22 Bruegger's Bagel Bakery	Burlington, VT	Fast food	Y	36.5	44.8	9.5
23 California Pizza Kitchen	Los Angeles	Casual dinnerhouse	N	26.4	51.7	5.6
24 Old Country Buffet	Eden Prairie, MN	Self-serve buffet	N	33.7	28.6	4.3
25 Sfuzzi	Dallas	Casual Italian dinnerhouse	N	33.3	25.0	3.0
26 Claim Jumper	Irvine, CA	Dinnerhouse	N	33.3	30.0	4.3
27 Nathan's Famous	Westbury, NY	Fast food	Y	31.4	20.3	−4.0
28 Morton's of Chicago	Chicago	Upscale steakhouse	N	31.1	20.0	9.2
29 The Cheesecake Factory	Redondo Beach, CA	Casual dinnerhouse	N	29.9	60.0	1.2

(continued)

EXHIBIT F (concluded)

50 Fastest-Growing Restaurants, 1992–1993

Name of Restaurant	City and State	Type of Restaurant	Does the Company Franchise?	Projected 1992–1993 % Change in Systemwide Sales	Projected 1992–1993 % Change in Units	Projected 1992–1993 % Change in Average Unit Sales
30 Au Bon Pain	Boston	Bakery café	Y	28.8	11.0	5.5
31 Ruby Tuesday	Mobile, AL	Casual dinnerhouse	N	28.2	25.6	6.2
32 Schlotzsky's Deli	Austin, TX	Fast food	Y	27.0	17.7	2.9
33 Blimpie	New York	Fast food	Y	26.6	27.9	0.0
34 Cracker Barrel	Lebanon, TN	Family restaurant	N	25.1	20.7	3.7
35 The Cooker Bar & Grille	Columbus, OH	Casual dinnerhouse	N	24.5	45.0	0.0
36 Subway	Milford, CT	Fast food	Y	22.7	13.9	6.0
37 The Spaghetti Warehouse	Garland, TX	Casual Italian dinnerhouse	N	21.7	37.0	11.5
38 Dunkin' Donuts	Randolph, MA	Fast food	Y	21.3	16.6	4.5
39 Sirloin Stockade	Hutchinson, KS	Budget steakhouse	Y	21.3	7.6	15.0
40 Cinnabon	Seattle	Fast food	Y	21.2	8.6	5.2
41 T.G.I. Friday's	Dallas	Casual dinnerhouse	Y	20.2	18.3	0.0
42 Don Pablo's	Bedford, TX	Casual Mexican dinnerhouse	N	19.8	47.4	2.7
43 Rally's	Louisville	Drive-through hamburgers	Y	19.6	20.0	−4.5
44 Chili's	Dallas	Casual dinnerhouse	Y	19.0	15.5	3.2
45 Damon's—The Place for Ribs	Columbus, OH	Casual dinnerhouse	Y	18.3	4.0	2.9
46 Red Robin	Irvine, CA	Casual dinnerhouse	Y	18.1	19.0	−3.5
47 Bain's Deli	King of Prussia, PA	Fast food	Y	17.9	8.0	10.3
48 On the Border Cafe	Dallas	Casual Mexican dinnerhouse	Y	17.9	46.7	0.0
49 Bojangles	Charlotte, NC	Fast food	Y	17.2	20.3	5.7
50 Ruth's Chris Steak House	New Orleans	Upscale steakhouse	Y	17.1	8.8	4.8

Source: *Restaurant Business,* July 20, 1994.

Chapter Twelve

Entrepreneurial Finance

LEARNING OUTCOMES: After reading this chapter, you will be able to understand:

12-1 Venture financing

12-2 Financial management myopia

12-3 Entrepreneurial finance versus corporate finance

12-4 Determining capital requirements

12-5 Financial and fund-raising strategies

Venture Financing: The Entrepreneur's Achilles' Heel[1]

There are three core principles of entrepreneurial finance: (1) More cash is preferred to less cash, (2) cash sooner is preferred to cash later, and (3) less risky cash is preferred to more risky cash. Although these principles are simple, everyone from entrepreneurs to chief executive officers seems to forget them. Take, for example, the following predicaments:

- Reviewing the year-end results just handed to you by your chief financial officer you see that the company loss is even larger than you had projected 3 months earlier. For the fourth year in a row, you will have to walk into the boardroom and deliver bad news. A family-owned business since 1945, the company has survived and prospered with average annual sales growth of 17 percent, and the company's market share has actually increased during recent years despite the losses. With the annual growth rate in the industry averaging less than 5 percent, your

mature markets offer few opportunities for sustaining higher growth. How can this be happening? Where do you and your company go from here? How do you explain to the board that for 4 years you have increased sales and market share but produced losses? How will you propose to turn the situation around?

- During the past 20 years, your cable television company has experienced rapid growth through the expansion of the business and acquisitions. The next decade of expansion was fueled by the high leverage common in the cable industry, and valuations soared. Ten years later your company had a market value in the $500 million range. You had a mere $300 million in debt, and you owned 100 percent of the company. Just 2 years later, your $200 million net worth has dropped to zero. In addition, you now face the personally exhausting and financially punishing restructuring battle to survive; personal bankruptcy is a very real possibility. How could this happen? Can the company be salvaged?[2]

- At mid-decade your company was the industry leader, exceeding your business plan targets for annual sales, profitability, and new stores. This and doubling sales and profitability each year has propelled your stock price from $15 at the initial public offering to the mid $30s. Meanwhile you still own a large chunk of the company. Then the shocker—at decade's end your company loses $78 million on just over $90 million in sales. The value of

---

[1]This section was drawn from J.A. Timmons, "Financial Management Breakthrough for Entrepreneurs."
[2]For more detail, see B.C. Hurlock and W.A. Sahlman, "Star Cablevision Group: Harvesting in a Bull Market," HBS Case 293-036, Harvard Business School Publishing.

your stock plummets. A brutal restructuring follows in which the stock is stripped from the original management team, including you, and you are ousted from the company you founded and loved. Why did the company spin out of control?

- As the chair of a rapidly growing telecommunications firm, you are convening your first board meeting after a successful public stock offering. As you think about the agenda, your plans are to grow the company to $25 million in sales in the next 3 years, which is comfortable given the $18 million in sales last year, the $4 million of cash in the bank, and no debt on the balance sheet. Early in the meeting, one of the two outside directors asks the controller and the chief financial officer his favorite question: "When will you run out of cash?" The chief financial officer is puzzled at first; then he is indignant, if not outraged, by what he considers an irrelevant question. After all, he reasons, our company has plenty of cash and we do not need a bank line. However, 16 months later, without warning from the chief financial officer, the company is out of cash and has overdrawn its $1 million credit line by $700,000. The board fires the president, the chief financial officer, and the senior audit partner from a major accounting firm. The chairman has to take over the helm and must personally invest half a million dollars in the collapsing company to keep it afloat. At this point it is the bank that is indignant and outraged. You have to devise an emergency battle plan to get on top of the financial crisis. How can this be done?

Financial Management Myopia: It Cannot Happen to Me

All of these situations have three things in common. First, they are real companies and these are actual events.[3] Second, each of these companies was led by successful entrepreneurs who knew enough to prepare audited financial statements. Third, in each example, the problems stemmed from financial mismanagement, a case of just plain not understanding the complex dynamics and interplay between financial management and business strategy. Why is this so?

Getting Beyond "Collect Early, Pay Late"

During our nearly 40 years as educators, authors, directors, founders, and investors in entrepreneurial

companies, we have met a few thousand entrepreneurs and managers. By their own admission, they felt uncomfortable, and in some cases intimidated, by their lack of expertise in financial analysis and its relationship to management and strategy. This is why entrepreneurs and nonfinancial managers are sometimes at a disadvantage when it comes to these complex and dynamic financial interrelationships. Even seasoned managers fail to grasp the concept that increasing sales and healthy profitability frequently lead to negative cash flow. If this happens, how do you finance it?

Critical Financing Issues

Exhibit 12.1 illustrates the central issues in entrepreneurial finance. These include the creation of value, the slicing and dividing of the value pie

EXHIBIT 12.1

Central Issues in Entrepreneurial Finance

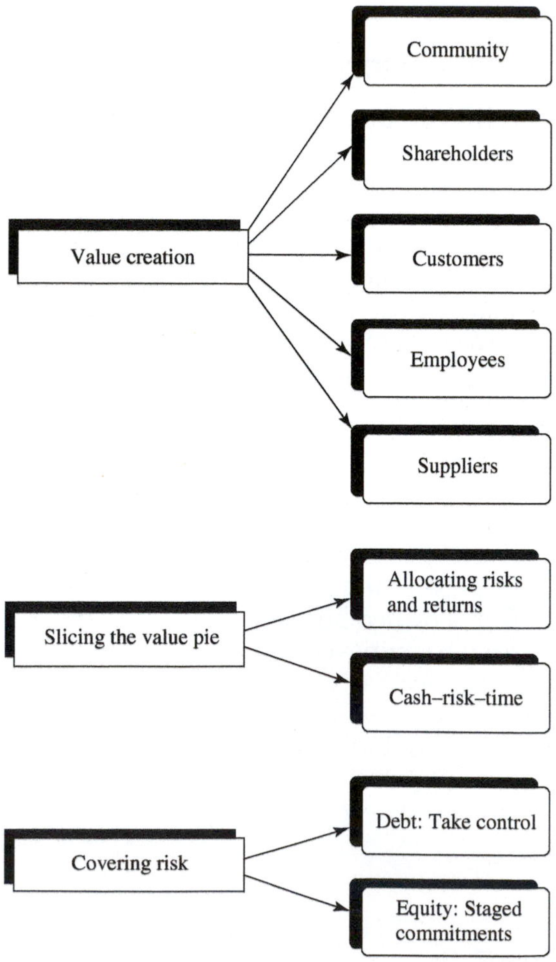

[3]Their outcomes have ranged from demise to moderate success to radical downsizing followed by dramatic recovery.

EXHIBIT 12.2

Initial Losses by Small New Ventures

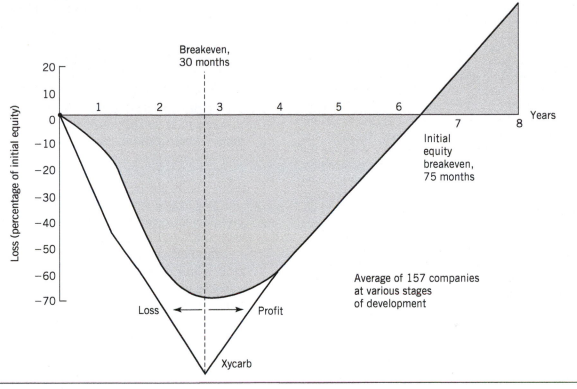

Source: Indivers.

among those who have a stake or have participated in the venture, and the handling of the risks inherent in the venture. Developing financing and fundraising strategies are important for the survival of high potential ventures.

As a result, entrepreneurs face certain critical issues and problems that bear on the financing of entrepreneurial ventures, such as these:

- *Creating value.* Who are the constituencies for whom value must be created or added to achieve a positive cash flow?

- *Slicing the value pie.* How are deals, both for startups and for the purchases of existing ventures, structured and valued?

- *Covering risk.* How much money is needed to start, acquire, or expand the business, and can it be obtained on acceptable terms? What sources of financing are available, and how will appropriate financing be negotiated and obtained?

A clear understanding of the financing requirements of a new venture is especially vital for the

entrepreneur. New and emerging companies are gluttons for capital, yet are usually not very debt worthy. To make matters worse, fast growth only leads to an even greater appetite for cash.

This phenomenon is best illustrated in Exhibit 12.2 where loss as a percentage of initial equity is plotted against time.[4] The shaded area represents the cumulative cash flow of 157 companies from their inception. For these firms, it took 30 months to achieve operating breakeven and 75 months, or going into the *seventh* year, to recover the initial equity. As can be seen from the illustration, *cash goes out for a long time before it starts to come in.* This phenomenon is at the heart of the financing challenges facing new and high revenue growth companies.

Entrepreneurial Finance versus Corporate Finance

While there is some common ground between these two disciplines, there are important limits to some financial theories as applied to new ventures. Entrepreneurial finance has always been skeptical

---

[4]Special appreciation is due to Bert Twaalfhoven, founder and chairman of Indivers, the Dutch firm that compiled this summary and that owns the firm on which the chart is based. Mr. Twaalfhoven is also a key figure in the promotion of entrepreneurship in Europe.

about the reliability and relevance of modern finance theory, including the capital asset pricing model (CAPM) and beta.[5] New research by corporate finance theorists is supporting that position. As reported in a *Harvard Business Review* article,

> One of the strongest attacks is coming from a man who helped launch modern finance, University of Chicago Professor Eugene Fama. His research has cast doubt on the validity of a widely used measure of stock volatility: beta. A second group of critics is looking for a new financial paradigm; they believe it will emerge from the study of nonlinear dynamics and chaos theory. A third group, however, eschews the scientific approach altogether, arguing that investors aren't always rational and that managers' constant focus on the markets is ruining corporate America. In their view, the highly fragmented U.S. financial markets do a poor job of allocating capital and keeping tabs on management.[6]

Challenging further the basic assumptions of corporate finance, the author continued, "These three concepts, the efficient market hypothesis, portfolio theory, and CAPM, have had a profound impact on how the financial markets relate to the companies they seek to value...They have derailed and blessed countless investment projects."[7] Nancy Nichols concluded that "despite tidy theories, there may be no single answer in a global economy."[8]

It is noteworthy that even one of the most prestigious modern finance theorists, Nobel laureate Robert Merton of Harvard University, lends credibility to this position. His works and theories of finance were the basis for Long Term Capital Management, Inc., which collapsed in the late 1990s and threatened to topple the entire financial system.

Acquiring knowledge of the limits of financial theories and of differences between the domains of entrepreneurial and corporate finance is a core task for entrepreneurs. Consider the following:

Cash Flow and Cash: Cash flow and cash are the king and queen of entrepreneurial finance. Accrual-based accounting, earnings per share, depreciation, use of the tax codes and rules of the Securities and Exchange Commission are not. Enron is an example of how these can be manipulated.

Time and Timing: Financing alternatives for an enterprise are often sensitive to timing. In entrepreneurial finance, the timeframe for financing moves is shorter and more compressed, and these moves are subject to wider, more volatile swings in pricing.

Capital Markets: Capital markets for private entrepreneurial ventures are less efficient and more opaque based on their private nature. All the underlying characteristics and assumptions used by popular financial theories and models, such as the CAPM, do not hold up for startups, even up to an IPO.

Strategies for Raising Capital: Strategies that optimize or maximize the amount of money raised can be counter-productive for new and emerging companies. Thus the concept of "staged capital commitments," where money is staged into the company based on reaching "value inflection points." Smart entrepreneurs raise capital when the valuation is in their favor and the capital can be used to reduce their company's risk.

Downside Consequences: The consequences of financial decisions are eminently more personal for the owners of new and emerging ventures than for the managers of large companies. The downside for entrepreneurs running out of cash is monumental and relatively catastrophic because personal guarantees of bank or other loans are common.

Determining Capital Requirements

How much money does my venture need? When is it needed? How long will it last? Where and from whom can it be raised? How should this process be orchestrated and managed? These are vital questions to any entrepreneur at any stage in the development of a company. These questions are answered in the next two sections.

Financial Strategy Framework

The financial strategy framework shown in Exhibit 12.3 is a way to begin crafting financial and fund-raising strategies.[9] The exhibit provides a flow and logic with which an otherwise confusing task can be attacked. The opportunity leads and drives the business strategy, which in turn drives the financial requirements, the sources and deal structures, and the financial strategy. Once an entrepreneur has

---

[5]See P.A. Gompers and W.A. Sahlman, *Entrepreneurial Finance* (New York: John Wiley & Sons, 2002).
[6]N.A. Nichols, "In Question: Efficient? Chaotic? What's the New Finance?" *Harvard Business Review*, March–April 1993, p. 50.
[7]Ibid., p. 52.
[8]Ibid., p. 60.
[9]This framework was developed for the Financing Entrepreneurial Ventures course at Babson College and has been used in the Entrepreneurial Finance course at the Harvard Business School.

EXHIBIT 12.3

Financial Strategy Framework

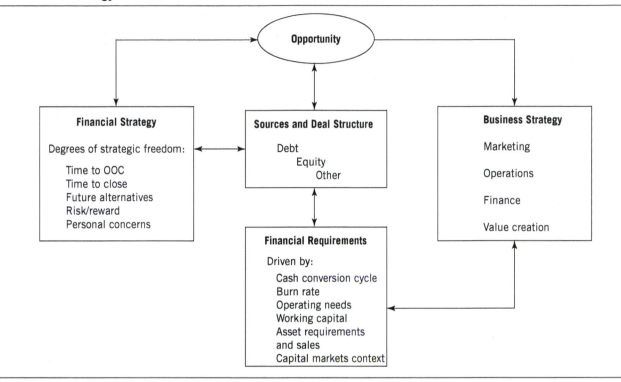

defined the core of the market opportunity and the strategy for seizing it, he or she can begin to examine the financial requirements in terms of assets and operating capital.

Each fund-raising strategy, along with its accompanying deal structure, commits the company to actions that incur actual and real-time costs and may enhance or inhibit future financing options. Similarly, each source has particular requirements and costs–both apparent and hidden–that carry implications for both financial strategy and financial requirements. The premise is that successful entrepreneurs are aware of potentially punishing situations, and that they are careful to "sweat the details" and proceed with a certain degree of wariness as they evaluate, select, negotiate, and craft business relationships with potential funding sources. In doing so, they are more likely to find the right sources, at the right time, and on the right terms and conditions. They are also more likely to avoid potential mismatches, costly sidetracking for the wrong sources, and the disastrous marriage to these sources that might follow.

Certain changes in the financial climate, such as the aftershocks of October 1987, March 2000, and the Great Recession, can cause repercussions across financial markets and institutions serving smaller companies. These take the form of greater caution by both lenders and investors as they seek to increase their protection against risk. When the financial climate becomes harsher, an entrepreneur's capacity to devise financing strategies and effectively deal with financing sources can be stretched to the limit. For example, the subprime credit crisis in the summer of 2007 caused mayhem across the capital markets. For instance, a 400-unit residential complex in the Southeast was built between 2003 and 2004 with a purchase and sale agreement executed in June 2007 with a price of over $40 million, generating a superb return to the founders and investors. The deal was expected to close by mid-September, but unfortunately the buyer's financing fell through, a victim of much tighter and less liquid credit markets.

Free Cash Flow: Burn Rate, Fume Date, and Time to Clear

The core concept in determining the external financing requirements of the venture is free cash flow. Three vital corollaries are the burn rate, fume date that the company runs out of money, and time to clear, or how long it takes to close financing and have the check clear. These have a major impact on the entrepreneur's choices and relative bargaining power with various sources of equity and debt capital, which is represented in Exhibit 12.4.

EXHIBIT 12.4

Entrepreneur's Bargaining Power Based on Time to OOC

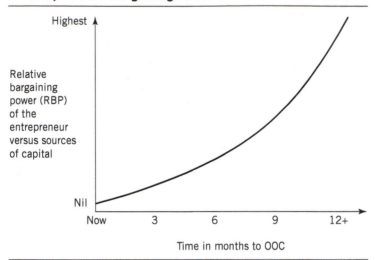

The cash flow generated by a company or project is defined as follows:

	Earnings before interest and taxes (EBIT)
Less	Tax exposure (tax rate times EBIT)
Plus	Depreciation, amortization, and other noncash charges
Less	Increase in operating working capital
Less	Capital expenditures

Economists call this result free cash flow. The definition takes into account the benefits of investing, the income generated, the cost of investing, the amount of investment in working capital, plant and equipment required to generate a given level of sales, and net income. This definition can fruitfully be refined further. Operating working capital is defined as follows:

	Transactions cash balances
Plus	Accounts receivable
Plus	Inventory
Plus	Other operating current assets (e.g., prepaid expenses)
Less	Accounts payable
Less	Taxes payable
Less	Other operating current liabilities (e.g., accrued expenses)

Finally, this expanded definition can be collapsed into a simpler one:[10]

	Earnings before interest but after taxes (EBIAT)
Less	Increase in net total operating capital (FA + WC)

where the increase in net total operating capital is defined as follows:

	Increase in operating working capital
Plus	Increase in net fixed assets

Crafting Financial and Fund-Raising Strategies

Critical Variables

When financing is needed, a number of factors affect the availability of the various types of financing and their suitability and cost:

- Accomplishments and performance to date.
- Investor's perceived risk.
- Industry and technology.
- Venture upside potential and anticipated exit timing.
- Venture anticipated growth rate.
- Venture age and stage of development.
- Investor's required rate of return or internal rate of return.
- Amount of capital required and prior valuations of the venture.
- Founders' goals regarding growth, control, liquidity, and harvesting.
- Relative bargaining positions.
- Investor's required terms and covenants.

---

[10]This section is drawn directly from "Note on Free Cash Flow Valuation Models," HBS 288-023, pp. 2–3.

Numerous other factors, especially an investor's or lender's view of the quality of a business opportunity and the management team, will also play a part in a decision to invest in or lend to a firm.

Generally a company's operations can be financed through debt and some form of equity financing.[11] Moreover, it is generally believed that a new or existing business needs to obtain both equity and debt financing if it is to have a sound financial foundation for growth without excessive dilution of the entrepreneur's equity.

Short-term debt of 1 year or less is used by a business for working capital and is repaid out of the proceeds of its sales. Longer-term borrowings of 1 to 5 years are used for working capital or to finance the purchase of property or equipment that serves as collateral for a loan. Equity financing is used to fill the nonbankable cash gaps where money cannot be borrowed, preserve ownership, and lower the risk of loan defaults.

A new venture will have difficulty obtaining bank debt without a substantial cushion of equity financing.[12] As far as a lender is concerned, a startup has little proven capability to generate sales, profits, and cash to pay off short-term debt and even less ability to sustain profitable operations over a number of years to retire long-term debt. In addition, asset values can erode with time; in the absence of adequate equity capital and good management, they may provide little real loan security to a bank.[13]

An existing business seeking expansion capital or funds for a temporary use has a much easier job obtaining both debt and equity. Sources such as banks, professional investors, and leasing and finance companies often seek out such companies as good investment prospects. Furthermore, an existing and expanding business will find it easier to raise equity capital from private or institutional sources.

Financial Life Cycles

One useful way to begin identifying equity financing alternatives, and when and if certain alternatives are available, is to consider the financial life cycle of firms. Exhibit 12.5 shows the types of capital available over time for different types of firms at different stages of development.[14] It also summarizes, at different stages of development, the principal sources and costs of risk capital.

As can be seen in the exhibit, sources have different preferences and practices, including how much money they will provide, when in a company's life cycle they will invest, and the cost of the capital or expected annual rate of return they are seeking. The available sources of capital change for companies at different stages and rates of growth, and there will be variations in different parts of the country.

Another key factor affecting the availability of financing is the upside potential of a company. For example, of the 3 million new businesses of all kinds launched in the United States in 2008, 5 percent or fewer achieved the growth and sales levels of high-potential firms. Foundation firms will total about 8 percent to 12 percent of all new firms, which will grow more slowly but exceed $1 million in sales and may grow to $20 million with 50 to 500 employees. Remaining are the traditional, stable, lifestyle firms. High-potential firms (those that grow rapidly and are likely to exceed $25 million or more in sales) are strong prospects for a public offering and have the widest array of financing alternatives, including combinations of debt and equity, while foundation firms have fewer, and lifestyle firms are limited to the personal resources of their founders and whatever net worth or collateral they can accumulate.

In general, investors believe the younger the company, the more risky the investment. This is a variation of the old saying in the venture capital business: The lemons ripen in two-and-a-half years, but the plums take 7 or 8.

International Finance and Trade

Like the global supply chains it has already fostered, the Internet has dramatically improved the facilitation and movement of financial instruments and trade documents. The result has been an acceleration of transactions and cash collections that has strengthened cash flow, boosted investment income, and bolstered balance sheets.

---

[11]In addition to the purchase of common stock, equity financing is meant to include the purchase of both stock and subordinated debt, or subordinated debt with stock conversion features or warrants to purchase stock.

[12]For lending purposes, commercial banks regard such subordinated debt as equity. Venture capital investors normally subordinate their business loans to the loans provided by the bank or other financial institutions.

[13]The bank loan defaults by the real estate investment trusts (REITs) in 1975 and 1989–1991 are examples of the failure of assets to provide protection in the absence of sound management and adequate equity capital.

[14]W. H. Wetzel, Jr., of the University of New Hampshire, originally showed the different types of equity capital that are available to three types of companies. The exhibit is based on a chart by Wetzel, which the authors have updated and modified. See W. H. Wetzel, Jr., "The Cost of Availability of Credit and Risk Capital in New England." In *A Region's Struggling Savior: Small Business in New England*, ed. J.A. Timmons and D.E. Gumpert (Waltham, MA: Small Business Foundation of America, 1979).

EXHIBIT 12.5

Financing Life Cycles

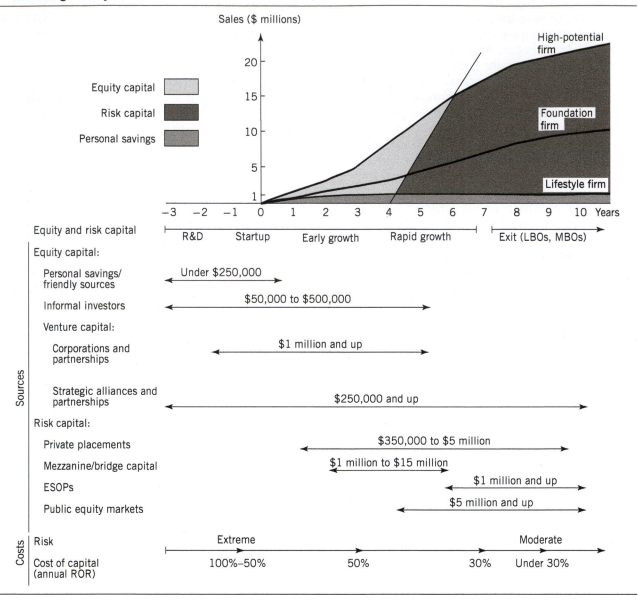

Source: Adapted and updated for 2008 from W.H. Wetzel, Jr., "The Cost of Availability of Credit and Risk Capital in New England," in *A Region's Struggling Savior: Small Business in New England*, ed. J.A. Timmons and D.E. Gumpert (Waltham, MA: Small Business Foundation of America, 1979), p. 175.

Major financial institutions now offer sophisticated trade portals that support document creation and transmission, making it possible for all parties to a transaction (exporter, importer, bank, freight forwarder, ocean carrier, and cargo insurer) to exchange information through the same secure site. Letters of credit, for example, frequently carry discrepancies such as misspelled names, inaccurate descriptions of products, and faulty dates. Amending those errors has typically meant additional bank fees and higher port charges, slower movement through overseas customs, and the possibility of failing to perform within the legal timetable of the letter of credit. Electronic trade documentation helps avoid discrepancies in the first place and supports quick and easy corrections when needed.

In a similar way, the U.S. Export–Import Bank has leveraged the speed and ease of the Internet to structure stand-alone deals between its approved exporters and large finance companies that in the past worked only with regular clients. This is giving first-time and early-stage trade ventures that meet Ex–Im Bank's credit standards access to major suppliers of trade credit and insurance.

Chapter Summary

- Cash is king and queen. Happiness is a positive cash flow. More cash is preferred to less cash. Cash sooner is preferred to cash later. Less risky cash is preferred to more risky cash.

- Lack of financial know-how and unanticipated issues are often the entrepreneurs' Achilles' heels.

- Entrepreneurial finance is the art and science of quantifying value creation, slicing the value pie, and managing and covering financial risk.

- Determining capital requirements, crafting financial and fund-raising strategies, and managing and orchestrating the financial process are critical to new venture success.

- Harvest strategies are as important to the entrepreneurial process as value creation itself. Value that is unrealized may have no value.

Study Questions

1. Define the following and explain why they are important: burn rate, free cash flow, fume something, time to clear, financial management myopia.

2. Why is entrepreneurial finance simultaneously both the least and most important part of the entrepreneurial process? Explain this paradox.

3. What factors affect the availability, suitability, and cost of various types of financing? Why are these factors critical?

4. What is meant by *free cash flow*, and why do entrepreneurs need to understand this?

Internet Resources

http://www.businessfinance.com/*Funding sources for small businesses.*

http://www.exim.gov/*The Export–Import Bank supports the financing of U.S. goods and services.*

Midwest Lighting, Inc.

Preparation Questions

1. Evaluate the company. How much do you believe it is worth? Bring to class a written bid showing how much you would pay for it if you were Scott and Peterson.

2. What should they do to resolve the ownership situation?

3. How would you finance the purchase of the company?

4. Assume you do purchase the company: What specific actions would you plan to take on the first day? By the end of the first week? By the end of six months? Explain how and why.

As early as 1996, Jack Peterson had become discouraged by conflicts with his partner, David Scott, and had sought advice on how to remedy the situation. By 2005, Peterson thought he and Scott had just grown too far apart to continue together and had to find a mutually agreeable way to separate. One alternative was for one partner to buy the other out, but Scott seemed to have no interest in such an arrangement.

Peterson recalled the executive committee's annual planning meeting in January 2005:

It was a total disaster. There were loud arguments and violent disagreements. It was so bad that no one wanted to ever participate in another meeting. We were all miserable.

What was so difficult was that each of us truly thought he was right. On various occasions other people in the company would support each of our positions. These were normally honest differences of opinion, but politics also started to enter in.

Company Description

Midwest Lighting, Inc. (MLI) manufactured custom-engineered fluorescent lighting fixtures for commercial and institutional applications. Sales in 2005 were approximately $5.5 million, with profits of just over $144,000.

Most sales were standard items, but 10 percent were custom-designed or custom-built fixtures, and 15 percent were slightly modified versions of standard products. In 2005, MLI shipped 82,500 fixtures. Although individual orders ranged from one unit to over 2,000 units, the average order size was approximately 15 to 20 fixtures. Modified and custom-designed fixtures averaged about 25 per order. Jack Peterson, MLI's president, described the company's market position:

Our product-marketing strategy is to try to solve lighting problems for architects and engineers. We design products which are architecturally styled for specific types of building constructions. If an architect has an unusual lighting problem, we design a special fixture to fit his needs. Or if he designs a lighting fixture, we build it to his specifications. We try to find products that satisfy particular lighting needs that are not filled by the giant fixture manufacturers. We look for niches in the marketplace.

Most of our bids for orders are probably compared with bids from half a dozen other firms across the country. Since a higher percentage of our orders are for premium-priced products, we are not as price sensitive as producers of more commonplace lighting fixtures. It is difficult for a small firm to compete in that market. As many as 30 companies might bid on one standard fixture job.

MLI owned a modern manufacturing facility outside Pontiac, Michigan. Production consisted of stamping, cutting, and forming sheet metal; painting; and assembling the fixture with the electrical components from outside suppliers. The company employed 130, with 42 in sales, engineering, and administration, and 88 in production and assembly.

Since 2003, the company had sold nationwide through regional distributors. Going national was the primary reason sales had increased over the last few years despite a weak construction market. (See Exhibit A for historical sales, earnings, unit sales, and employment.)

Background

Midwest Lighting, Inc., was formed in Flint, Michigan, in 1956 by Daniel Peterson and Julian Walters. Each owned half the company. Peterson was responsible for finance and engineering and Walters for sales and design. They subcontracted all manufacturing.

After several years, differences in personal work habits led Daniel Peterson to buy out Walters's interest and bring in Richard Scott, who had been one of his sheet metal subcontractors, as his new partner. Scott became president and Peterson became treasurer. Peterson retained a little more than half the company's shares and all voting control because of his prior experience with the company.

In 1960, MLI began manufacturing and moved to a multi-floor 50,000-square-foot plant in Flint. Over the next decade, Peterson and Scott were content to let the company remain at a steady level of about $1.2 million in sales and about $18,000 in profit after taxes.

EXHIBIT A

Historical Performance

Year	Net Sales	Profit after Tax	No. of Fixtures Shipped	Total Employees	Hourly Employees
2005	$5,515,239	$144,011	82,500	130	88
2004	4,466,974	126,266	72,500	118	73
2003	3,717,225	133,160	65,000	103	65
2002	3,669,651	79,270	67,500	103	63

Daniel Peterson's son, Jack, joined MLI as a salesman in 1983 after graduating from MIT and Colorado Business School. Richard Scott's son, David, who graduated from Trinity College, became an MLI salesman in 1984 when he was discharged from the service. The two sons were acquaintances but not close friends.

In 1986, Daniel Peterson had a heart attack and withdrew from management of the business, leaving Richard Scott to run the company.

Jack Peterson moved inside to learn about other parts of the company in 1987. His first work assignments were in manufacturing and sales service. David Scott joined his father in the manufacturing area a year later. Jack Peterson became sales manager, David Scott became manufacturing manager, and, at Richard Scott's suggestion, another person was added as financial manager. These three shared responsibility for running the company and worked well together, but major decisions were still reserved for Richard Scott, who spent less and less time in the office.

As the new group began revitalizing the company, a number of employees who had not been productive and were not responding to change were given early retirement or asked to leave. When the man who had been Richard Scott's chief aide could not work with the three younger managers, they ultimately decided he had to be discharged. Richard Scott became so angry that he rarely entered the plant again.

For several years, the three managers guided the company as a team. However, there were some spirited discussions over the basic strategic view of the company. As sales manager, Jack Peterson pressed for responding to special customer needs. This, he felt, would be their strongest market niche. David Scott argued for smooth production flows and less disruption. He felt they could compete well in the "semistandard" market.

In 1988, Jack Peterson co-founded a company in the computer field. The company rented extra space from MLI, and MLI provided management and administrative support, helping it with bidding and keeping track of contracts. Although David Scott was not active in this company, Peterson split his partial ownership in this new company with Scott because they were partners and because Peterson was spending time away from MLI with the company.

In 1989 the fathers restructured the company's ownership to reflect the management changes. The fathers converted their ownership to nonvoting class A stock, and then each transferred 44 percent of his nonvoting stock to his son. Daniel Peterson relinquished his voting control and Jack Peterson and David Scott were each issued 50 percent of the class B voting shares.

The computer company began to weaken the relationship between Peterson and Scott. At the same time Scott and the financial manager began to have strong disagreements, arising primarily from errors in cost analysis that led the financial manager to question some of Scott's decisions. There were also differences of opinion over relations with the workforce and consistency of policy. Scott preferred to control the manufacturing operation. Peterson felt Scott could be more consistent, less arbitrary, and more supportive of the workforce. When the computer company was sold in 1995, the financial manager joined it as treasurer and resigned from MLI.

Growing Conflict

The departure of the financial manager led to a worsening of the relationship between Peterson and Scott. With Scott's acquiescence, Peterson had been made company president in 1990, but the three managers had really operated as a team. Now Peterson was upset that they had lost an excellent financial manager, partially due, in his opinion, to the disagreements with Scott. Also, there was no longer a third opinion to help resolve conflicts.

The pressure of growth created more strains between Peterson and Scott. Sales had reached $2.3 million and had begun to tax MLI's manufacturing capacity. Peterson felt changing production methods would alleviate some of the problems, but Scott disagreed. Both, however, agreed to look for additional space.

The transition to a new factory outside Pontiac, Michigan, in 1997 eased the stresses between the partners. A major corporation had purchased an indirect competitor to obtain its product lines and sold MLI the 135,000-square-foot plant. MLI also agreed to manufacture some of the other company's light fixtures as a subcontractor. The plant was in poor condition, and David Scott took over the project of renovating it and continuing production of the other company's lines. That was also the year that Richard Scott died. Daniel and Jack Peterson and David Scott were now the only directors.

Jack Peterson remained in Flint running the MLI operation alone until the company could consolidate the entire operation in Pontiac. Peterson described this interlude:

> The next year was a sort of cooling-off period. David was immersed in the project with the new factory and I was busy with the continuing operation. David had always enjoyed projects of this sort and was quite satisfied with this arrangement.
>
> Then, in 1998, we hired a plant manager to run the Pontiac plant and David came back to work in Flint. By that time, of course, a lot of things had changed. All of Flint had been reporting to me. I had somewhat reshaped the operation and the people had gotten used to my management style, which was different from David's.
>
> David's reaction was to work primarily with the design and engineering people, but he really wasn't involved very much with the daily manufacturing anymore. He developed a lot of outside interests, business and recreation, that took up much of his time.
>
> I was very happy with the arrangement because it lessened the number of conflicts. But when he did come back, the disagreements that did rise would be worse. I guess I resented his attempts to change things when he only spent a small amount of his time in the company.
>
> Then, in 2000, we made the decision to sell the Flint plant and put the whole company in Pontiac. We were both involved in that. Most of the key people went with us. David and I were very active in pulling together the two groups and in integrating the operations.
>
> That began a fairly good time. I was spending my time with the sales manager trying to change the company from a regional company to a national one and was helping to find new representatives all over the country. David Scott spent his time in the engineering, design, and manufacturing areas. There was plenty of extra capacity in the new plant, so things went quite smoothly. In particular, David did an excellent job in upgrading the quality standards of the production force we had acquired with the plant. This was critical for our line of products and our quality reputation.
>
> This move really absorbed us for almost two years. It just took us a long time to get people working together and to produce at the quality level and rate we wanted. We had purchased the plant for an excellent price with a lot of new equipment and had started deleting marginal product lines as we expanded nationally. The company became much more profitable.

During the company's expansion, a group of six people formed the operating team. Scott concentrated on applications engineering for custom fixtures and new product design. In addition, there were a sales manager, financial manager, engineering manager, the plant manufacturing manager, and Peterson. Disagreements began again. Peterson recounted the problems:

> Our operating group would meet on a weekly or biweekly basis, whatever was necessary. Then we would have monthly executive committee meetings for broader planning issues. These became a disaster. Scott had reached the point where he didn't like much of anything that was going on in the company and was becoming very critical. . .
>
> He and I also began to disagree over which topics we should discuss with the group. I felt that some areas were best discussed between the two of us, particularly matters concerning personnel, and that other matters should be left for stockholders meetings.

Search for a Solution

When Peterson returned from a summer vacation in August 2005, he was greeted by a string of complaints from sales agents and managers. He decided the problem had to be resolved and sought an intermediary:

> I knew that Scott and I weren't communicating and that I had to find a mediator Scott trusted. I had discussed this before with Allen Burke, our accountant. He was actually far more than our accountant. Allen is a partner with a Big Six accounting firm and is active in working with smaller companies. Allen was a boyhood friend who had grown up with Scott. I felt he had very high integrity and was very smart. Scott trusted him totally and Allen was probably one of Scott's major advisors about things.
>
> When I first talked to Burke in March, he basically said, "Well, you have problems in a marriage and you make it work. Go make it work, Peterson." He wasn't going to listen much.
>
> Then in early September, I went back to say that it wasn't going to work anymore. I asked him for his help. Allen said that Scott had also seen him to complain about the problems, so Allen knew that the situation had become intolerable.

Both directly and through Burke, Peterson pressured Scott to agree to a meeting to resolve the situation. Although Scott was also unhappy about their conflicts, he was hesitant to meet until he had thought through his options.

Peterson felt there were several principal reasons for Scott's reluctance. One of them leaving the company was becoming a possibility and Peterson knew Scott's only work experience was with MLI managing manufacturing operations he had known for years. Second, Peterson thought Scott was very uncertain about financial analysis, which made evaluating alternative courses of action difficult. Last was Scott's emotional tie to the company.

As the possibility of selling the company grew, Scott's reluctance waxed and waned. Just before Thanksgiving, Scott told Peterson he wanted to fire the financial manager and become the treasurer so he could look at the figures for a year or so and be able to make a better decision. Peterson felt the financial manager was essential and Scott was trying to buy time. He convinced Scott to retain the financial manager.

After another month, Peterson and Scott realized they had no estimate of the company's value. Both felt getting one might alter the attractiveness of potential alternatives.

Valuing the Company

Before making his decision, Peterson reviewed his thoughts. He began with the company's current position. The financial statements for 2005 were already completed. (These are shown, together with the results of 2004 and 2003, as Exhibits 2 and 3.)

Peterson had also begun developing the bank support to fund a buyout. The company's banker said he would lend Peterson funds secured by his other personal assets, but that since he had not worked with Scott, the bank would not finance a buyout led by Scott. In addition, the bank would continue the company's existing line of credit, which was secured by MLI's cash and accounts receivable. Under it, MLI could borrow 100 percent of cash plus 75 percent of receivables. Both types of borrowing would be at 1 percent over the prime rate (then about 6 percent).

Peterson worked with the financial manager to develop financial projections and valuation assessments. To be conservative, Peterson had made each year's sales projections about 10 percent lower than his actual sales forecasts. Because fixed costs would not rise appreciably with modest sales increases, improvements in sales volume would boost profits. He felt he should consider how these various changes would impact his financing requirements and his assessment.

Peterson sought out common valuation techniques, but found they weren't precise. Private manufacturing companies were typically valued at five to ten times after-tax earnings. Book net asset value also helped establish worth, but it was often adjusted to reflect differences between assets' market and balance-sheet values. For MLI, this was significant because it had obtained the new plant at an excellent price. Peterson felt it was probably worth $250,000 more than book value.

To Peterson, the variations in worth suggested by these different methods not only reflected the uncertainty of financial valuation techniques but also showed that a business had different values to different people. His estimate would have to incorporate more personal and subjective elements.

Personal Financial Considerations

One important consideration was what amount of personal resources each could and should put at risk. Both Peterson and Scott were financially very conservative. Neither had ever had any personal long-term debt–even for a house. Peterson could pledge a maximum of $815,000 of assets outside of MLI to secure borrowing, but for him to risk his entire worth to purchase Scott's share of the company, he needed to be very comfortable that the price was reasonable. Peterson described his feelings: "You get very protective about what you have outside the company. The problem you always have with a small company is that most of your worth is tied up in it and you may have very little to fall back on if something goes sour. We both have never been big leverage buyers or anything like that."

Several other considerations tempered Peterson's willingness to pay a very high price. He disliked the one-hour commute to the plant in Pontiac. He also thought his management experience and engineering undergraduate degree and MBA gave him flexibility in the job market. This was important because he felt he would still have to work if he left MLI.

On the other hand, some factors encouraged Peterson to be aggressive. Peterson knew his father would be very disappointed if he lost the company, and Peterson himself had strong emotional ties to MLI. Peterson also developed a point of view that in some ways he was buying the entire company, rather than just half: "I'm sitting here with a company that I have no control over because of our disagreements. If I buy the other half share, I'm buying the whole company—I'm buying peace of mind, I could do what I want, I wouldn't have to argue. So I'd buy a 'whole peace of mind' if I bought the other half of the company."

Finally, Peterson considered his competitive position versus Scott. Although Scott had not accumulated

EXHIBIT B

Statement of Earnings

	Year Ended December 31		
	2005	**2004**	**2003**
Net sales	$5,515,239	$4,466,974	$3,717,225
Cost of goods sold:			
Inventories at beginning of year	928,634	741,481	520,640
Purchases	1,999,283	1,594,581	1,387,226
Freight in	24,400	33,244	26,208
Direct labor	537,693	450,710	410,609
Manufacturing expenses	1,221,536	1,002,715	842,054
	4,711,545	3,822,731	3,186,736
Inventories at end of year	1,032,785	928,634	741,481
	3,678,760	2,894,098	2,445,255
Gross profit	1,836,479	1,572,876	1,271,970
Product development expenses	164,683	161,011	127,874
Selling and administrative expenses	1,390,678	1,143,925	926,001
	1,555,360	1,304,936	1,053,875
Operating income	281,119	267,940	218,095
Other expense (income):			
Interest expense	70,324	47,238	40,520
Payments to retired employee	12,500	12,500	25,000
Miscellaneous	(1,154)	(1,939)	(7,741)
	81,670	57,799	57,779
Earnings before income taxes	199,449	210,141	160,316
Provision for income taxes	55,438	83,875	61,250
Earnings before extraordinary income	144,011	126,266	99,066
Extraordinary income—life insurance proceeds in excess of cash surrender value			34,094
Net earnings	$ 144,011	$ 126,266	$ 133,160
Earnings per share of common stock	$ 23.94	$ 20.99	$ 16.46

292

EXHIBIT B (continued)

Statement of Earnings

	Year Ended December 31		
	2005	**2004**	**2003**
Assets			
Current assets:			
Cash	$ 64,060	$ 4,723	$ 88,150
Accounts receivable:			
Customers	750,451	538,438	397,945
Refundable income taxes	28,751	2,845	6,611
Other			404,556
	779,203	541,283	
Less allowance for doubtful receivables	4,375	4,375	4,375
	774,828	536,908	400,181
Inventories			
Raw materials	364,738	324,438	346,340
Work in progress	668,048	604,196	395,141
	1,032,785	928,634	741,481
Prepaid insurance and other	17,760	25,168	32,588
Total current assets	1,889,433	1,495,431	1,262,400
Property, plant, and equipment:			
Buildings and improvements	426,783	407,108	368,913
Machinery and equipment	263,116	216,341	169,274
Motor vehicles	40,723	40,723	36,776
Office equipment	53,583	54,881	46,186
	784,204	719,053	621,149
Less accumulated depreciation	341,605	291,805	231,519
	442,599	427,248	389,630
Land	13,876	13,876	13,876
	456,475	441,124	403,506
Other assets:			
Cash surrender value of life insurance policies (less loans of $24,348 in 2004, $24,488 in 2003, and $24,290 in 2002)	102,473	96,519	90,711
Total assets	$ 2,448,380	$ 2,033,074	$ 1,756,618

(continued)

293

EXHIBIT B (continued)

Statement of Earnings

	Year Ended December 31		
	2005	2004	2003
Liabilities and Stockholders' Equity			
Current liabilities			
Current maturities of long-term debt	15,230	13,198	11,250
Note payable: bank	406,250	250,000	
Note payable: officer		37,500	48,750
Accounts payable	486,978	369,010	391,504
Amount due for purchase of treasury stock			93,750
Accrued liabilities	193,238	145,168	111,196
Total current liabilities	1,101,695	814,875	656,450
Long-term debt	220,653	236,403	244,638
Stockholders' Equity			
Contributed capital:			
6% cumulative preferred stock; authorized 10,000 shares of $12.50 par value: issued 2,000 shares	13		
	25,000	25,000	25,000
Common stock:			
Class A (nonvoting)			
Authorized 15,000 shares of $12.50 par value: issued 8,305 shares	103,813	103,813	103,813
Class B (voting)			
Authorized 5,000 shares of $12.50 par value: issued and outstanding 20 shares	250	250	250
	129,063	129,063	129,063
Retained earnings	1,115,495	971,484	845,218
	1,244,558	1,100,546	974,280
Less shares reacquired and held in treasury, at cost: 2,000 shares 6% cumulative preferred stock	25,000	25,000	25,000
2,308 shares Class A common stock	93,750	93,750	93,750
	118,750	118,750	118,750
	1,125,808	981,796	855,530
Total liabilities and stockholders' equity	$2,448,155	$2,033,074	$1,756,618

294

EXHIBIT B (continued)

Statement of Earnings

	Year Ended December 31		
	2005	**2004**	**2003**
Statement of Changes in Financial Position			
Working capital provided:			
From operations:			
Earnings before extraordinary income	144,011	126,266	99,066
Add depreciation not requiring outlay of working capital	69,973	63,323	55,334
Working capital provided from operation	213,984	189,589	154,400
Extraordinary income from life insurance proceeds		6,619	34,094
Capitalized equipment lease obligation			64,846
Proceeds from cash surrender value of life insurance policies			
Total working capital provided	213,984	196,208	253,340
Working capital applied:			
Additions to property, plant, and equipment	85,324	100,940	58,884
Increase in cash surrender value of life insurance policies; net of loans	5,954	5,808	7,443
Reduction of long-term debt	15,750	14,854	11,244
Purchase of 2,308 shares of nonvoting Class A stock			93,750
Total working capital applied	107,028	121,601	171,320
	106,956	74,606	82,020
Increase in working capital			
Net change in working capital consists of:			
Increase (decrease) in current assets:			
Cash	59,338	(83,428)	81,068
Accounts receivable: net	237,920	136,726	(4,435)
Inventories	104,151	187,153	220,841
Prepaid expenses	(7,633)	(7,420)	(6,225)
	393,776	233,031	291,249

(continued)

295

EXHIBIT B (concluded)

Statement of Earnings

	Year Ended December 31		
	2005	2004	2003
Increase (decrease) in current liabilities:			
Current portion of long-term debt	2,033	1,948	625
Note payable to bank	156,250	250,000	
Note payable to officer	(37,500)	(11,250)	
Accounts payable	117,968	(22,494)	130,104
Amount due for purchase of treasury stock		(93,750)	93,750
Contribution to profit-sharing trust			(25,000)
Accrued liabilities	48,070	33,971	9,751
Total	286,820	158,425	209,230
Increase in working capital	106,956	74,606	82,019
Working capital at beginning of year	680,556	605,950	523,931
Working capital at end of year	787,513	680,556	605,950

EXHIBIT C

Pro Forma Financial Statements

	Historical Percentages			Projected Percentages			Thousands of Dollars		
	2003	2004	2005	2006	2007	2008	2006	2007	2008
Net sales	100.00	100.00	100.00	100.0	100.0	100.0	$6,000	$6,375	$6,750
Cost of goods sold	65.80	64.79	66.70	67.0	67.0	67.0	4,020	4,271	4,523
Gross income	34.22	35.21	33.30	33.0	33.0	33.0	1,980	2,104	2,228
Operating, general, and admin.	28.61	29.28	28.25	28*	28.0	28.0	1,680	1,785	1,890
Profit before taxes	5.61	5.93	5.05	5.0	5.0	5.0	300	319	338
Taxes†	38.20	39.90	27.80	39†	39.0	39.0	121	124	131
Net earnings							$ 179	$ 195	$ 206

*Projected percentages reflect an assumption that one partner will leave the company, and include a $30,000 cost reduction for the reduced salary requirements of a replacement.
†Effective tax rate.

Source: income statement projections (prepared by Jack Peterson).

the personal resources that Peterson had, he had a brother-in-law with a private company that Peterson knew had the ability to match Peterson's resources and might be willing to back Scott financially. The brother-in-law would also be giving Scott financial advice in evaluating his alternatives and setting a value for the company. Scott also probably had fewer job prospects if he sold out. His undergraduate study was in liberal arts, and his entire experience was with MLI. Peterson also thought Scott might have some doubts about his ability to manage the company on his own.

The Meeting

After another conversation with Allen Burke, Scott called Peterson at home one evening: "Peterson, I realize that you are right—I can't live in this tense environment any longer. I've spoken with Allen, and he has agreed to meet with both of us to discuss our situation, and to attempt to identify some possible solutions. Would Friday at 9:00 be convenient for you?"

Chapter Thirteen

Obtaining Venture and Growth Capital

LEARNING OUTCOMES: After reading this chapter, you will be able to understand:

13-1 The capital markets food chain

13-2 Preserve your equity

13-3 Timing

13-4 Angels and Informal Investors

13-5 Venture capital: Gold mines and tar pits

13-6 What is venture capital?

13-7 The venture capital industry

13-8 Other equity sources

13-9 Keeping current about capital markets

The Capital Markets Food Chain

Consider the capital markets for equity a "food chain," whose participants have differing appetites in terms of risk and deal size they invest in (Exhibit 13.1). This topology will help entrepreneurs identify the myriad sources of capital based on the venture's development, the amount of the raise, and the level of risk.

The bottom row in Exhibit 13.1 shows this ultimate progression from R&D stage to Initial Public Offering (IPO), where the capital markets are typically willing to pay $12 to $18 per share for new issues of small companies. Obviously these prices are lower when the so-called IPO window is tight or closed, as in 2001. Prices for the few offerings that do exist (1 to 3 per week vs. more than 50 per week in June 1996) are $5 to $9 per share. In hot IPO periods, 1999 for instance, offering prices reached as high as $20 per share. While these numbers provide a relative metric for comparison, keep in mind the price per share can fluctuate dramatically based on the number of outstanding shares and valuation at IPO.

The private equity capital markets for mergers and acquisitions, as one would expect, suffered severely from the July–August credit meltdown in 2007. In 2006, for example, worldwide deals matched the 1999 and 2000 peaks of $4 trillion worldwide, and April 2007 saw $695 billion in deals closed, again according to *The Wall Street Journal* and Dealogic. In August this amount plummeted to $222 billion–a direct casualty of the credit and capital markets meltdown that began in mid-July.

One of the toughest decisions for founders is whether to sell equity to catalyze the value creation process. The row "% Company Owned at IPO" shows that by the time a company goes public, the founders may have sold 70 to 80 percent of their equity. As long as the market capitalization of the company is at least $100 million, the founders have created significant value for investors and themselves. During the peak of the dot-com mania in the late 1990s, companies went public with market capitalizations of $1 billion regularly. Founders' shares were frequently worth $200 million, which were staggering, unprecedented valuations and not sustainable. Take Sycamore Networks for example. From startup to IPO in less than 24 months, founders Desh Deshpanda and Don Smith achieved paper value in the billions each.[1] By late 2004 the founders had lost more than 90 percent of the value of their stock based on market corrections.

In the remainder of the chapter, we will discuss these various equity sources and how to identify and deal with them. Exhibit 13.2 summarizes the typical venture capital food chain, where in the first

---

[1]A. Pham, "MassFirm Takes $14B Rocket Ride," *The Boston Globe*, October 23, 1999.

EXHIBIT 13.1

The Capital Markets Food Chain for Entrepreneurial Ventures

Stage of Venture	R&D	Seed	Launch	High Growth
Company Enterprise Value at Stage	Less than $1 million	$1 million–$5 million	More than $1 million–$50 million-plus	More than $100 million
Sources	Founders	FFF[a]	Venture capital series A, B, C . . .	IPOs
	High net worth individuals	Angel funds	Strategic partners	Strategic acquires
	FFF	Seed funds	Very high net worth individuals	Private equity
	SBIR	SBIR	Private equity	
Amount of Capital Invested	Less than $50,000–$200,000	$10,000–$500,000	$500,000–$20 million	$10 million–$50 million-plus
% Company Owned at IPO	10–25%	5–15%	40–60% by prior investors	15–25% by public
Share Price and Number[b]	$.01–$.50	$.50–$1.00	$1.00–$8.00	$12–$18 +
	1–5 million	1–3 million	+/−5–10 million	3–5 million

[a]Friends, families, and fools.

[b]At post-IPO.

EXHIBIT 13.2

The Venture Capital Food Chain for Entrepreneurial Ventures

Venture capital series A, B, C, . . . (Average size of round):
Example of three staged rounds

Round*
"A" @ $1–$4 million: start-up
"B" @ $6–$10 million: product development
"C"[1] @ $10–$15 million: shipping product

*Valuations vary markedly by industry.

[1]Valuations vary by region and venture capital cycle.

three rounds, referred to as series A, B, and C, we see the amount of capital invested increasing as the company risk is mitigated and valuation increases.

Preserve Your Equity

One of the toughest trade-offs for any young company is to balance the need for startup and growth capital with preservation of equity. Holding on to as much as you can for as long as you can is generally good advice for entrepreneurs. As was evident in Exhibit 12.5, the earlier the capital enters, regardless of the source, the more expensive it is.

Creative bootstrapping strategies can preserve equity as long as it is done in an optimal way so the opportunity does not get away from the company.

Three central issues should be considered when obtaining investment capital: (1) Does the venture need outside equity capital? (2) Do the founders want outside equity capital? and finally, (3) Who should invest?

After reviewing the Venture Opportunity Screening Exercises in Chapter 5, the business plan you prepared in Chapter 7, and free cash flow from Chapter 12, you will be in a position to assess the need for additional capital. Deciding whether the capital infusion will be debt or equity is situation specific and we will cover debt as an alternative to equity in Chapter 15.

Once the amount of additional capital has been quantified, the management needs to consider the desirability of an equity investment. As covered in Chapter 10, bootstrapping continues to be an attractive source of financing. For instance, *INC* magazine suggested that entrepreneurs in certain industries tap vendors and suppliers by getting them to extend credit as[2] the equivalent of cash in the bank.

Other entrepreneurs interviewed by *INC.* suggested getting customers to pay quickly.[3] Rebecca McKenna, an entrepreneur, built a software firm that reached $8 million in sales in 2001 in the

[2]R.A. Mamis, "The Secrets of Bootstrapping," *INC.*, September 1992, p. 72.
[3]Ibid., p. 76.

health care industry. The robustness of economic benefits to her customers justified a 25 percent advance payment with each signed contract, and this upfront cash was a major source of her bootstrap financing. An equity investment requires that the management team firmly believes investors can add value to the venture.

The single most important criterion for selecting investors is what they can contribute to the value of the venture beyond just financing. Angels or wealthy individuals are often sought because the amount needed may be less than the minimum investment required by institutional sources. Entrepreneurs should note that "only 30 percent to 40 percent of the companies seeking private equity actually wind up getting it at the end of the process."[4]

Timing

A venture should not wait to look for capital until it has a serious cash shortage. For a startup, especially one with no experience raising money, it is likely to take 6 months or more to raise money. In addition to the problems with cash flow, the lack of planning implicit in waiting until there is a cash shortage can undermine the credibility of the management team. When raising money you need either a credibly audacious plan or significant results while if a venture tries to obtain equity capital too early, the equity position of the founders may be unnecessarily diluted and the discipline instilled by financial leanness goes away.

Angels and Informal Investors

Who They Are

The greatest source of seed and startup capital comes from successful entrepreneurs and executives who have achieved wealth from their gains on stock in midsize and large companies. In 2006, according to the Center for Angel Investing at the University of New Hampshire, there were 234,000 active angels in the United States. In terms of the number of deals they finance angels dwarf the venture capital industry; in 2006, angels funded 51,000 companies compared to just 3,522 for the entire U.S. venture capital industry. The total amount of capital they invested was $26.1 billion, about the same as the venture capital investments that year.

By 2007 there were an estimated 207 angel groups around the country.

New Hampshire's Bill Wetzel has found that these angels are mainly American self-made millionaires, have made it on their own, have substantial business and financial experience, and are likely to be in their 40s or 50s. They are also well educated: 95 percent hold college degrees from 4-year colleges, and 51 percent have graduate degrees. Of the graduate degrees, 44 percent are in a technical field and 35 percent are in business or economics. According to Scott Peters, cofounder and co-CEO of Angel Society, 96 percent of angels are men. One growing effort to involve female entrepreneurs is Chicago-based Springboard Enterprises; by 2007 Springboard had become a leading forum for women entrepreneurs seeking startup and growth capital.

The typical informal investor will invest from $10,000 to $250,000 in any one deal and are particularly appropriate for the following:[5]

- Ventures with capital requirements of between $50,000 and $500,000.
- Ventures with sales potential of between $2 million and $20 million within 5 to 10 years.
- Small, established, privately held ventures with sales and profit growth of 10 to 20 percent per year.
- Special situations, such as very early financing of high-technology inventors that have not developed a prototype.
- Companies that project high levels of free cash flow within 3 to 5 years.

Usually these informal investors will be knowledgeable and experienced in the market and technology areas where they invest. If the right angel is found they will add a lot more to a business than just money. Generally the evaluations of potential investments by such wealthy investors tend to be less thorough than those undertaken by organized venture capital groups, and such noneconomic factors as the desire to be involved with entrepreneurship may be important to their investment decisions and there is a clear geographic bias of working within a 1-hour driving radius of the investors' base.

Finding Informal Investors

Finding these backers is not easy. One expert noted, "Informal investors, essentially individuals of means and successful entrepreneurs, are a diverse and

---

[4]Ibid.

[5]R. Harrison and C. Mason, *Informal Venture Capital: Evaluating the Impact of Business Introduction Service* (Hemel Hempstead, Woodhead Faulkner, 1996).

dispersed group with a preference for anonymity. Creative techniques are required to identify and reach them."[6] In most larger cities, there are law firms and private placement firms that syndicate investment packages as Regulation D offerings to networks of private investors or through crowd-funding resources.

Contacting Investors

The best way to meet an investor is through a personal introduction, followed by a meeting where the entrepreneur needs to make a concise presentation of the key features of the proposed venture by answering the following questions:

- What is the market opportunity?
- Why is it compelling?
- How will/does the business make money?
- How soon can the business reach positive cash flow?
- Why is this the right team at the right time?
- How does an investor exit the investment?

Evaluation Process

An informal investor will want to review a business plan, meet the full management team, see any product prototype or design that may exist, and so forth. The investor will conduct background checks on the venture team and its product potential and the process is similar to the due diligence of professional investors but may be less formal and structured.

The Decision

If the investor decides to invest, he or she will have an investment agreement drafted by an attorney. This agreement may be somewhat simpler than those used by venture capital firms. All the cautions and advice about investors and investment agreements that are discussed later in the chapter apply here as well.

Most likely, the investment agreement with an informal investor will include some form of a "put," whereby the investor has the right to require the venture to repurchase his or her stock after a specified number of years at a specified price. If the venture is not harvested, this put will provide an investor with a cash return.

For access to important documents for venture agreements, please see the website for this textbook for downloadable sample term sheets.[7]

Venture Capital: Gold Mines and Tar Pits

There are only two classes of investors in new and young private companies: value-added investors and all the rest. One of the keys to raising risk capital is to seek investors who will truly add value to the venture beyond the money. Carefully screening potential investors to determine how they might fill some gaps in the founders' know-how and networks can yield significant results.

A young founder of an international telecommunications venture landed a private investor who also served as an advisor. The following are examples of how this private investor provided critical assistance: Introduced the founder to other private investors, to foreign executives (who became investors and helped in a strategic alliance), and to the appropriate legal and accounting firms; served as a sounding board in crafting and negotiating early rounds of investments; and identified potential directors and other advisors familiar with the technology and relationships with foreign investors and cross-cultural strategic alliances.

Numerous other examples exist of venture capitalists being instrumental in opening doors to key accounts and vendors that otherwise might not take a new company seriously. Venture capitalists may also provide valuable help in such tasks as negotiating contracts, licensing or royalty agreements, making key contacts with banks and leasing companies, finding key people to build the team and helping to craft a strategy. Norwest Venture Partners brought in Ashley Stephenson to run a portfolio company and then backed him in a second venture. "Most venture capitalists have a short list of first-class players. Those are the horses you back," says Norwest partner Ernie Parizeau.

What Is Venture Capital?[8]

The word *venture* suggests that this type of capital involves a degree of risk and even something of a gamble. Specifically, "The venture capital industry

---

[6]W.H. Wetzel, Jr., "Informal Investors–When and Where to Look." In *Pratt's Guide to Venture Capital Sources*, 6th ed., ed. S.E. Pratt (Wellesley Hills, MA: Capital Publishing, 1982), p. 22.

[7]To access *New Venture Creation* online, go to http://highered.mcgraw-hill.com/sites/0072498404/information_center_view0/.

[8]Unless otherwise noted, this section is drawn from W.D. Bygrave and J.A. Timmons, *Venture Capital at the Crossroads* (Boston, MA: Harvard Business School Press, 1992), pp. 13-14. Copyright 1992 by William D. Bygrave and Jeffry A. Timmons.

EXHIBIT 13.3

Classic Venture Capital Investing Process

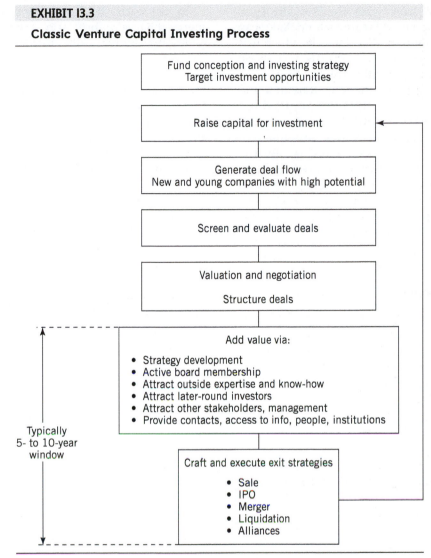

Source: Reprinted by permission of Harvard Business School Press. From *Venture Capital at the Crossroads* by W.D. Bygrave and J.A. Timmons. Boston, MA, 1992. Copyright © 1992 by the Harvard Business School Publishing Corporation; all rights reserved.

supplies capital and other resources to entrepreneurs in business with high growth potential in hopes of achieving a high rate of return on invested funds."[9] The whole investing process involves many stages, which are represented in Exhibit 13.3. Throughout the investing process, venture capital firms seek to add value in several ways: identifying and evaluating business opportunities, including management, entry, or growth strategies; negotiating and closing the investment; tracking and coaching the company; providing technical and management assistance; and attracting additional capital, directors, management, suppliers, and other key stakeholders and resources. The process begins with the conception of a target investment opportunity or class of opportunities, which leads to a written proposal or prospectus to raise a venture capital fund. Once the money is raised, the value creation process moves from generating deals to crafting and executing harvest strategies and back to raising another fund. The process usually takes up to 10 years to unfold, but exceptions in both directions often occur.

The Venture Capital Industry

Although the roots of venture capital can be traced from investments made by wealthy families in the 1920s and 1930s, most industry observers credit Ralph E. Flanders, then president of the Federal

---

[9]"Note on the Venture Capital Industry (1981)," HBS Case 285-096, Harvard Business School, 1982, p. 1.

Reserve Bank of Boston, with the idea. In 1946 Flanders joined a top-ranked team to fund American Research and Development Corporation which was the first firm, as opposed to individuals, to provide risk capital for new and rapidly growing firms.

Despite the success of American Research and Development, the venture capital industry did not experience a growth spurt until the 1980s. In 1979, venture capital investing activities amounted to $460 million invested in 375 companies. By the late 1980s, the industry had ballooned to more than 700 venture capital firms, which invested $3.94 billion in 1,729 portfolio companies. The sleepy cottage industry of the 1970s was transformed into a vibrant and dynamic market for private risk and equity capital.

The Booming 1990s

As we can see in Exhibits 13.4 and 13.5, the industry experienced an eightfold increase in the 1990s. While the absolute dollars committed and invested by 2000 were huge, the rate of increase in the 1980s was much greater, from $1 billion in 1979 to $31 billion in 1989.

By the early 2000s, not only had the commitments changed, but also a new structure was emerging, increasingly specialized and focused. Exhibit 13.6 summarizes some of the important changes in the industry, which have implications for entrepreneurs seeking money and for those investing it. The major structural trends that emerged at the end of the 1980s continued through the 1990s:

1. The average fund size grew larger and larger, and funds of more than $500 million accounted for nearly 80 percent of all capital under management.

2. The average size of investments correspondingly grew much larger as well. Unheard of previously, startup and early rounds of $20 million, $40 million, even $80 million were common in the dot-com and telecom feeding frenzy of the late 1990s.

3. The specialization pattern, which began in the 1980s, expanded to mainstream as funds like Oak Venture Partners abandoned its long-time health care investing for information technology.

EXHIBIT 13.4

Venture Capital Fund Commitments (1980–2006)

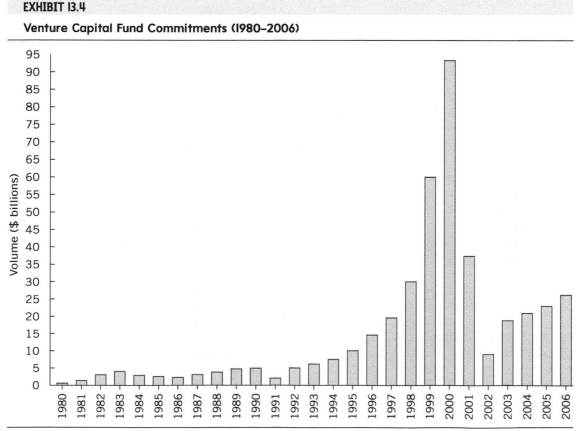

Source: 2006 *National Venture Capital Association Yearbook.*

EXHIBIT 13.5

Total Venture Capital under Management (1979–2006)

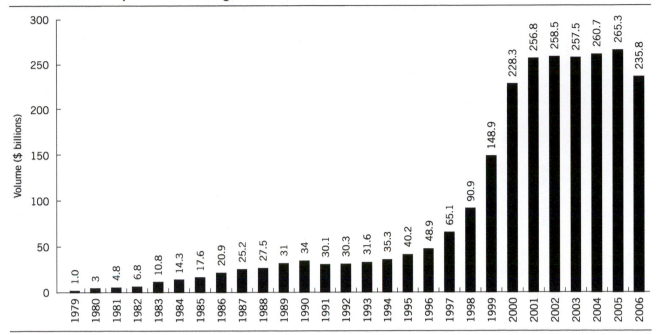

Source: 2006 *National Venture Capital Association Yearbook.*

Beyond the Crash of 2000: The Venture Capital Cycle Repeats Itself

The crash of the NASDAQ began in March 2000, resulting in more than a 60 percent drop in value by late summer 2001. This major decline in equity values began a shakeout in the private equity and public stock markets. The repercussions and consequences are still being felt in 2014. Many high-flying companies went public in 1998 and 1999 at high prices, saw their values soar beyond $150 to $200 per share, then came plummeting down to low single-digit prices. For example, Sycamore Networks went public in October 1999 at $38 per share, soared to nearly $200 per share in the first week, and was trading around $3.50 per share by the summer of 2005.

Similarly, beginning in the late summer of 2000, many young telecommunication companies saw their stocks begin to decline rapidly, losing 90 percent or more of their value in less than a year. These downdrafts swept across the entire venture capital and private equity markets. By mid-2001 the amount of money being invested had dropped by half from the record highs of 2000, and valuations plummeted. Not since the periods 1969–1974 and 1989–1993 had entrepreneurs experienced such a downturn.

The reality is that venture capital, like any asset class, is cyclical and tends to repeat itself. Scarcity of capital leads to high returns, which attract an over-abundance of new capital, which drives returns down.

The Sine Curve Lives Circa 2005

Historically the venture capital cycle of ups and downs has had the shape of a sine curve; an "S" on its side. Fortunately, after a period of painful adjustments, too much time spent working on troubled portfolio companies, and too few exits in 2002 to 2003, the industry began to rebound in 2004, when, for instance, the total number of companies invested in rose for the first time since the 2000 bubble: from 2,825 to 2,873. Referring back to Exhibits 13.4 and 13.5, we see that the industry has been making steady gains. Fund commitments in 2006 were up to $26.3 billion and total venture capital under management, while down slightly, exceeded $235 billion. Exhibit 13.7, which captures a bit more granularity on the nature of venture investments since 1990, shows that total investments increased from $18.95 billion in 2003 to $26.3 billion in 2006. The average deal size likewise increased from $6.65 million to $7.4 million.[10]

As we discussed earlier in this chapter, anytime there is a robust IPO market such as in 2007, the returns on venture capital invariably get much better, and home runs like Google and YouTube

[10]*Venture Capital Journal,* February 2005, pp. 29-30.

EXHIBIT 13.6

New Heterogeneous Structure of the Venture Capital Industry

	Megafunds	Mainstream	Second Tier	Specialists and Niche Funds	Corporate Financial and Corporate Industrial
Estimated Number and Type (2005)	106 Predominantly private, independent funds	76 Predominantly private and independent; some large institutional SBICs and corporate funds	455 Mostly SBICs; some private independent funds	87 Private, independent	114
Size of Funds under Management	More than $500 million	$250–$499 million	Less than $250 million	$50–$100 million	$50–$100 million plus
Typical Investment	Series B, C . . . $5–$25 million plus	Series A, B, C . . . $1–$10 million	Series A, B $500,000–$5 million	Series A, B $500,000–$2 million	Series A, B, C . . . $1–$25 million
Stage of Investment	Later expansion, LBOs, start-ups	- Later expansion, LBOs, some start-ups; mezzanine	Later stages; few start-ups; specialized areas	Seed and start-up; technology or market focus	Later
Strategic Focus	Technology: national and international markets; capital gains; broad focus	Technology and manufacturing; national and regional markets; capital gains; more specialized focus	Eclectic—more regional than national; capital gains, current income; service business	High-technology national and international links; "feeder funds," capital gains	Windows on technology; direct investment in new markets and suppliers; diversification; strategic partners; capital gains
Balance of Equity and Debt	Predominantly equity	Predominantly equity; convertible preferred	Predominantly debt; about 91 SBICs do equity principally	Predominantly equity	Mixed
Principal Sources of Capital	Mature national and international institutions; own funds; insurance company and pension funds; institutions and wealthy individuals; foreign corporation and person funds; universities	Mature national and international institutions; own funds; insurance company and pension funds; institutions and wealthy individuals; foreign corporation and pension funds; universities	Wealthy individuals; some smaller institutions	Institutions and foreign companies; wealthy individuals	Internal funds
Main Investing Role	Active lead or colead; frequent syndications; board seat	Less investing with some solo investing	Initial or lead investor; outreach; shirtsleeves involvement	Later stages, rarely start-ups; direct investor in funds and portfolio companies	

Note: Target rates of return vary considerably, depending on stage and market conditions. Seed and start-up investors may seek compounded after-tax rates of return in excess of 50 to 100 percent; in mature, later-stage investments they may seek returns in the 30–40 percent range. The rule of thumb of realizing gains of 5 to 10 times the original investment in 5 to 10 years is a common investor expectation.

Source: 2001 *National Venture Capital Association Yearbook.* Revised and updated for 2008.

EXHIBIT 13.7

U.S. Venture Capital Investment by Year (1990–2006)

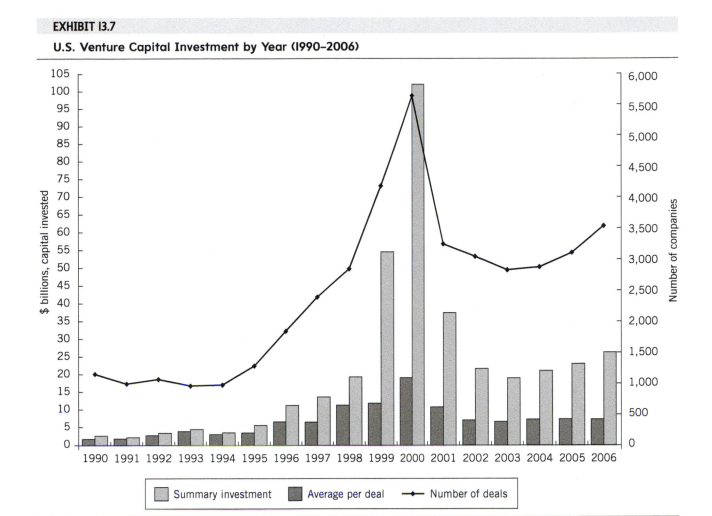

Source: PricewaterhouseCoopers/Venture Economics/National Venture Capital Association/Money Tree™ Report. Updated August 2007. Used by permission of PricewaterhouseCoopers.

start a new cycle of investing activity. Institutional investors, such as pension funds, foundations, and others, are anxious to get in on the party, so more money pours into the industry. This occurred in the extreme in 2000, as shown in Exhibit 13.7. With annual investing of $25–$30 billion, the industry appears to have reached somewhat of an equilibrium–an oxymoron in this tumultuous world of entrepreneurship. The net impact for high-potential entrepreneurs is positive as the availability of capital remains robust.

Venture Capital Investing Is Global

Venture capital has existed in Europe since the late 1970s and began to take root in other parts of the world in the 1980s and 1990s. In many countries, such as Germany and France, banks would often be the first to create funds. In England

private firms, often with U.S. associations, were launched. By the early 1980s even Sweden had begun a private venture industry. In the old Soviet Union, venture capital firms were usually formed by Americans working with local business and financial connections.

In the new century explosive growth of emerging economies has led to similar venture fund creation in Latin America, China, India, and even Vietnam. Leading U.S. venture capital firms such as Kleiner Perkins, Caufield & Byers, IDG Venture Capital, and Venrock have launched country-dedicated funds. IDG, for instance, has been active in China since 1992. Several new funds are being formed in India and China, and some spectacular returns have been achieved from investments such as Baidu, China's equivalent of Google. This is all very good news for American entrepreneurs because investors will now welcome business plans for enterprises that pursue these global markets.

EXHIBIT 13.8

Flows of Venture Capital

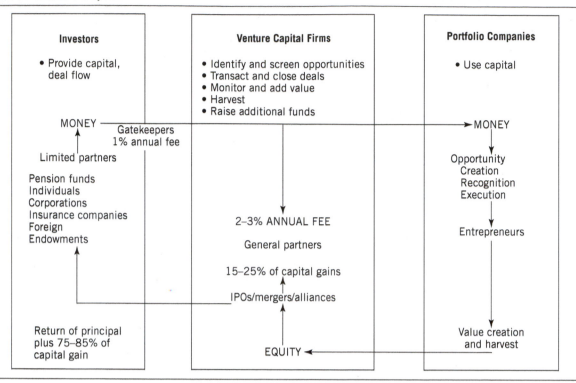

Exhibit 13.8 represents the core activities of the venture capital process. At the heart of this dynamic flow is the collision of entrepreneurs, opportunities, investors, and capital.[11] Because the venture capitalist brings, in addition to money, experience, networks, and industry contacts, a professional venture capitalist can be very attractive to a new venture. Moreover, a venture capital firm has deep pockets and contacts with other groups that can facilitate the raising of money as the venture develops.

The venture capital process occurs in the context of mostly private, quite imperfect capital markets for new, emerging, and middle-market. The availability and cost of this capital depend on a number of factors:

- Perceived risk, in view of the quality of the management team and the opportunity.
- Industry, market, attractiveness of the technology, and fit.
- Upside potential and downside exposure.
- Anticipated growth rate.
- Age and stage of development.

- Amount of capital required.
- Founders' goals for growth, control, liquidity, and harvest.
- Fit with investors' goals and strategy.
- Relative bargaining positions of investors and founders given the capital markets at the time.

However, less than 4 percent of those contacting venture capital firms receive financing from them. Despite the increase in funds in the recent boom years, observers comment that the repeat fund-raisers "stay away from seed and early-stage investments largely because those deals tend to require relatively small amounts of capital, and the megafunds, with $500 million-plus to invest, like to make larger commitments."[12] Further, an entrepreneur may give up 15 percent to 75 percent of his or her equity for seed/startup financing. Thus after several rounds of venture financing have been completed, an entrepreneur may own no more than 10 percent to 20 percent of the venture.

The venture capitalists' stringent criteria for their investments limit the number of companies

[11]Bygrave and Timmons, *Venture Capital at the Crossroads*, p. 11.
[12]Vachon, "Venture Capital Reborn," p. 35.

receiving venture funds. Venture capital investors look for opportunities with very high growth potential where they can quintuple their investment in five years; they place a premium on the quality of management in a venture; and they like to see a management team with complementary business skills headed by someone who has previous entrepreneurial or profit-and-loss (P&L) management experience. In fact, these investors are searching for the "superdeal." Superdeals meet the investment criteria outlined in Exhibit 13.9.

Identifying Venture Capital Investors

Venture capital funds have an established capital base and professional management. Their investment policies cover a range of preferences in investment size and the maturity, location, and industry of a venture. Capital for these investments can be provided by wealthy families, financial institutions and endowments. Most are organized as partnerships, where the fund managers are general partners and the investors are limited partners. Most investments are in the range of $500,000 to $1.5 million, with funds with more than $500 million investing $5 to $10 million.

Sources and Guides   If an entrepreneur is searching for a venture capital investor, a good place to start is with *Pratt's Guide to Venture Capital Sources,* published by Venture Economics, as well as Ventureone.com, which are two of several directories of venture capital firms. Entrepreneurs also can seek referrals from accountants, lawyers, investment and commercial bankers, and businesspeople knowledgeable about professional investors. Especially good sources of information are other entrepreneurs who have recently raised money.

EXHIBIT 13.9

Characteristics of the Classic Superdeal from the Investor's Perspective

Mission
- Build a highly profitable and industry-dominant market leading company.
- Go public or merge within four to seven years at a high price–earnings (P/E) multiple.

Complete Management Team
- Led by industry "superstar."
- Possess proven entrepreneurial, general management, and P&L experience in the business.
- Have leading innovator or technologies/marketing head.
- Possess complementary and compatible skills.
- Have unusual tenacity, imagination, and commitment.
- Possess reputation for high integrity.

Proprietary Product or Service
- Has significant competitive lead and "unfair" and sustainable or defensible advantages.
- Has product or service with high value-added properties resulting in early payback to user.
- Has or can gain exclusive contractual or legal rights.

Large, Robust, and Sustainable Market
- Will accommodate a $100 million entrant in 5 years.
- Has sales of $200 million or more, is growing at 25% per year, and has a billion-dollar potential.
- Has no dominant competitor now.
- Has clearly identified customers and distribution channels.
- Possesses forgiving and rewarding economics, such as
  - Gross margins of 40% to 50% or more.
  - 10% or more profit after tax.
  - Early positive cash flow and break-even sales.

Deal Valuation and ROR
- Has "digestible" first-round capital requirements (i.e., greater than $1 million and less than $10 million).
- Able to return 10 times original investment in 5 years at P/E of 15 times or more and a market cap of $200–$300 million.
- Has possibility of additional rounds of financing at substantial markup.
- Has antidilution and IPO subscription rights and other identifiable harvest/liquidity options.

Source: Reprinted by permission of Harvard Business School Press. From *Venture Capital at the Crossroads* by W.D. Bygrave and J.A. Timmons. Boston, MA, 1992. Copyright © 1992 by the Harvard Business School Publishing Corporation; all rights reserved. Revised and updated for 2008.

Sometimes professional investors find entrepreneurs. Rather than wait for a deal to come to them, a venture capital investor may decide on a product or technology it wishes to commercialize and then put its own deal together. Kleiner Perkins used this approach to launch Genentech and Tandem Computer Corporation, as did Greylock and J. H. Whitney in starting MassComp.

What to Look For   Entrepreneurs are well advised to screen prospective investors to determine their activity around stage, industry, technology, and capital requirements. It is also useful to determine which investors have money to invest, which are actively seeking deals, and which have the time and people to investigate new deals. Depending on its size and investment strategy, a fund that is a year or two old will generally be in an active investing mode.

Early-stage entrepreneurs need to seek investors who (1) are considering new financing proposals and can provide the required level of capital; (2) are interested in companies at the particular stage of growth; (3) understand the industry; (4) can provide good business advice, moral support, and contacts in the business and financial community; (5) are reputable, fair, and ethical people with whom the entrepreneur gets along; and (6) have successful track records advising and building smaller companies.[13]

What to Look Out For   There are also some things to be wary of in finding investors. These warning signs are worth avoiding unless an entrepreneur is so desperate that he or she has no real alternatives:

- *Attitude.* Entrepreneurs need to be wary if they cannot get through to a general partner in an investment firm and keep getting handed off to a junior associate, or if the investor thinks he or she can run the business better than the lead entrepreneur or the management team.

- *Overcommitment.* Entrepreneurs need to be wary of lead investors who indicate they will be active directors but who also sit on the boards of a dozen other startups and early-stage companies or are money for a new fund.

- *Inexperience.* Entrepreneurs need to be wary of dealing with venture capitalists who have an MBA; are under 30 years of age; have worked only on Wall Street or as a

consultant; have no operating, hands-on experience in new and growing companies; and have a predominantly financial focus.

- *Unfavorable reputation.* Entrepreneurs need to be wary of funds that have a reputation for early and frequent replacement of the founders or those where more than one-fourth of the portfolio companies are in trouble or failing to meet projections in their business plans.

- *Predatory pricing.* During adverse capital markets (e.g., 1969-1974, 1988-1992, 2000-2003), investors who unduly exploited these conditions by forcing large share price decreases in the new firms and punishing terms on prior investors do not make the best long-term financial partners.

How to Find Out   How does the entrepreneur learn about the reputation of the venture capital firm? The best source is the CEO or founder of prior investments. Besides the successful deals, ask for the names and phone numbers of CEOs the firm invested in whose results were only moderate to poor, and where the portfolio company had to cope with significant adversity. Talking with these CEOs will reveal the underlying fairness, character, values, ethics, and potential of the venture capital firm as a financial partner, as well as how it practices its investing philosophies.

Dealing with Venture Capitalists[14]

Do not forget that venture capitalists see lots of business plans and proposals, frequently more than a 100 a month, typically investing in less than 1% of these. The following suggestions may be helpful in working with them.

If possible, obtain a personal introduction from someone that is well-known to the investors, such as a director or founder of one of their portfolio companies, a limited partner in their fund, or a lawyer who has worked with them and who knows you well. After identifying the best targets, you should create demand for your company by marketing it. Have several prospects and be vague about whom else you are talking with. Remember it is also much harder to get a "no" than to get a "yes", so be aware you can spend an enormous amount of time getting to an answer.

One of the best pieces of advice is to get to a "no" quickly. That is, eliminate the fund as a source

[13]For more specifics, see H. A. Sapienza and J. A. Timmons, "Launching and Building Entrepreneurial Companies: Do the Venture Capitalists Build Value?" in *Proceedings of the Babson Entrepreneurship Research Conference,* May 1989, Babson Park, MA. See also J. A. Timmons, "Venture Capital: More Than Money," in *Pratt's Guide to Venture Capital Sources.* 13th ed., ed. J. Morris (Needham, MA: Venture Economics, 1989), p. 71.
[14]The authors express appreciation to Thomas Huseby of SeaPoint Ventures in Washington for his valuable insights in the following two sections.

of investment. This may sound counter-intuitive, but frequently firms are reluctant to give you a firm "no" and will simply string you along. They do this so the door is not permanently shut on them should the deal heat up.

When pushed by the investors to indicate what other investors you are talking to, simply put it this way: "All our advisors believe that information is highly confidential to the company, and our team agrees. We are talking to other high-quality investors like yourselves. The ones with the right chemistry who can make the biggest difference in our company and are prepared to invest first will be our partner. Once we have a term sheet and deal on the table, if you also want co-investors we are more than happy to share these other investors' names." Failing to take such a tack usually puts you in an adverse negotiating position.

Most investors who have serious interest will have some clear ideas about how to improve your strategy, product line, positioning, and a variety of other areas. Consequently, you need to be prepared for them to take apart your business plan and to put it back together. They are likely to have their own format and their own financial models. Working with them on this is a good way to get to know them.

Never lie. As one entrepreneur put it, "You have to market the truth, but do not lie." Other good pieces of advice include: Do not stop selling until the money is in the bank. Let the facts speak for themselves. Be able to deliver on the claims, statements, and promises you make or imply in your business plan and presentations. Tom Huseby adds some final wisdom: "It's much harder than you ever thought it could be. You can last much longer than you ever thought you could. They have to do this for the rest of their lives!" Finally, never say no to an offer price. There is an old saying that your first offer may be your best offer.

Questions the Entrepreneur Can Ask

The presentation to investors when seeking venture capital is appropriately demanding. Venture capitalists have an enormous legal and fiduciary responsibility to their limited partners as well as their self-interests. Expect them to be thorough in their due diligence and questioning to assess the intelligence, integrity, nimbleness, and creativity of the entrepreneurial mind in action as covered in Chapter 2.

Once the presentation and questioning is complete, the founders can learn a great deal about the

investors and enhance their own credibility by asking a few simple questions:

- Tell us what you think of our strategy, how we size up the competition, and our game plan. What have we missed? Whom have we missed?
- Are there competitors we have overlooked? How are we vulnerable and how do we compete?
- How would you change the way we are thinking about the business and planning to seize the opportunity?
- Is our team as strong as you would like? How would you improve this and when?
- Give us a sense of what you feel would be a fair range of value for our company if you invested $___?

Their answers will reveal how much they have done and how knowledgeable they are about your industry, technology, competitors, and the like. This will provide robust insight as to whether and how they can truly add value to the venture. At the same time, you will get a better sense of their forthrightness and integrity: Are they direct, straightforward, but not oblivious to the impact of their answers?

Due Diligence: A Two-Way Street

It can take several weeks or even months to complete the due diligence on a startup. The verification of facts, backgrounds, and reputations of key people, market estimates, technical capabilities of the product, proprietary rights, and the like is a painstaking investigation for investors. They will want to talk with your directors, advisors, former bosses, and previous partners. Prepare extra copies of published articles, reports, studies, market research, contracts or purchase orders, technical specifications, and the like that can support your claims.

One recent research project examined how 86 venture capital firms nationwide conducted their intensive due diligence. To evaluate the opportunity, the management, the risks, and the competition, and to weigh the upside against the downside, firms spent from 40 to 400 hours, with the typical firm spending 120 hours. That is nearly 3 weeks of full-time effort. At the extreme, some firms engaged in twice as much due diligence.[15] Central to this investigation were careful checks of the management's references and verification of track record and capabilities.

---

[15]G.H. Smart, "Management Assessment Methods in Venture Capital," unpublished doctoral dissertation, 1998 (Claremont, CA: Claremont Graduate University), p. 109.

Do your own due diligence on the venture fund. Ask for the names and phone numbers of their successful deals and some that did not work, as well as the names of founders they ended up replacing. Who are their legal and accounting advisors? Examine the chemistry between the management team and the general partner that will have responsibility for the investment. If you do not have a financial partner you respect and can work closely with, then you are likely to regret ever having agreed to the investment.

Other Equity Sources

Small Business Administration's 7(a) Guaranteed Business Loan Program

The Small Business Administration has a wide variety of programs and assistance for aspiring entrepreneurs, including the 7(a) loan program. For ventures that are not candidates for venture capital, such as all lifestyle and foundation firms, it would be useful to explore their website. Descriptions and links to training, resources, and other assistance programs for women, minorities, Native Americans, and most aspiring small businesses are available here.

Promoting small businesses by guaranteeing long-term loans, the Small Business Administration's 7(a) Guaranteed Business Loan Program has been supporting startup and high-potential ventures since 1953[16] and provides 40,000 loans annually. The 7(a) program is almost exclusively a guarantee program, but under it the Small Business Administration also makes direct loans to women, veterans of the armed forces, and minorities, as well as other small businesses. The program entails banks and certain nonbank lenders making loans that are then guaranteed by SBA for between 50 percent and 90 percent of each loan, with a maximum of $1 million. Eligible activities under 7(a) include acquisition of borrower-occupied real estate, fixed assets such as machinery and equipment, and working capital for items such as inventory or cash flow needs.[17]

SBA programs have a noteworthy effect on the economy and entrepreneurship. The $1 million guarantees, the largest of all the SBA programs, have helped many entrepreneurs start, stay in, expand, or purchase businesses.

Small Business Investment Companies

SBICs, or small business investment companies, a specialized type of debt financing, are licensed by the SBA and can invest capital of $4 in loans for each $1 of private equity.[18] The impact of SBICs is evidenced by many major U.S. companies that received early financing from SBICs, including Intel, Apple Computer, Staples, Federal Express, Sun Microsystems, Sybase, Inc., Callaway Golf, and Outback Steakhouse.[19] The SBIC program was established in 1958 to address the need for venture capital by small emerging enterprises and to improve opportunities for growth.[20] An SBIC's equity capital is generally supplied by one or more commercial banks, wealthy individuals, and the investing public. The benefit of the SBIC program is twofold: (1) Small businesses that qualify for assistance from the SBIC program may receive equity capital, long-term loans, and expert management assistance, and (2) venture capitalists participating in the SBIC program can supplement their own private investment capital with funds borrowed at favorable rates through the federal government. According to the National Association of Small Business Investment Companies through December 2000 there were 404 operating SBICs with more than $16 billion under management. Since 1958 the SBIC program has provided approximately $27 billion of long-term debt and equity capital to nearly 90,000 small U.S. companies.

SBICs are limited by law to taking minority shareholder positions and can invest no more than 20 percent of their equity capital in any one situation. Because SBICs borrow much of their capital from the SBA and must service this debt, they prefer to make some form of interest-bearing investment. Four common forms of financing are long-term loans with options to buy stock, convertible debentures, straight loans, and, in some cases, preferred stock. In 2000 the average financing by bank SBICs was $4 million. The median for all SBICs was $250,000.[21] Due to their SBA debt, SBICs tend not to finance startups and early-stage companies but invest in more established companies.

Small Business Innovation Research

The risk and expense of conducting serious research and development are often beyond the

[16]Data were compiled from the Small Business Administration, http://www.sba.gov.
[17]D.R. Garner, R.R. Owen, and R.P. Conway, *The Ernst & Young Guide to Raising Capital* (New York: John Wiley & Sons, 1991), pp. 165–166.
[18]This section was drawn from J.A. Timmons, *Planning and Financing the New Venture* (Acton, MA: Brick House Publishing, 1990), pp. 49–50.
[19]The National Association of Small Business Investment Companies (NASBIC), http://www.nasbic.org.
[20]Small Business Administration, http://www.sba.gov.
[21]The National Association of Small Business Investment Companies (NASBIC), http://www.nasbic.org.

means of startups and small businesses. The Small Business Innovation Research (SBIR) is a federal government program designed to strengthen the role of small businesses in federally funded R&D and to help develop a stronger national base for technical innovation.

The SBIR program provides R&D capital for innovative projects that meet specific needs of any one of 11 federal government agencies, including the Departments of Agriculture, Commerce, Education, Energy, and Homeland Security; the Environmental Protection Agency; and the National Science Foundation. SBIR is a competitive, three-phase process. Phase I provides funds to determine the feasibility of the technology. During Phase II, the necessary R&D is undertaken to produce a well-defined product or process. Phase III involves the commercialization of the technology using non-SBIR funds.

An SBIR small business is defined as an independently owned and operated, for-profit organization with no more than 500 employees. In addition, the small business must be at least 51 percent owned by U.S. citizens or lawfully admitted resident aliens, not be dominant in the field of operation in which it is proposing, and have its principal place of business in the United States.

Corporate Venture Capital

During the Internet boom in the late 1990s, corporate investors were very active. In 2000 alone, large corporations invested $17 billion in small and mid-size opportunities. When the bubble burst, many of these funds scaled back or shut down entirely. But as we have seen, business investing is highly cyclical, and in 2006 corporate-based venture capitalists were back, investing $1.9 billion in 671 deals.

While corporate venture capitalists are similar to traditional VCs in that they look for promising young companies on the verge of a spike in sales, corporations tend to be more risk-averse and specialized. Because investing in a relevant technology is a way of outsourcing research and development, fit is usually an important aspect of the funding decision. When working with corporate investors make sure you consider the corporations' philosophy and culture, as well as their investment track record with small businesses, before agreeing to any deal.

Mezzanine Capital

At the point where the company has overcome many of the early-stage risks, it may be ready for mezzanine capital.[22] The term *mezzanine financing* refers to capital that is between senior debt financing and common stock. In some cases it takes the form of redeemable preferred stock, but in most cases it is subordinated debt that carries an equity "kicker" consisting of warrants or a conversion feature into common stock. This subordinated-debt capital has many characteristics of debt but also can serve as equity to underpin senior debt. It is generally unsecured, with a fixed coupon and maturity of 5 to 10 years. A number of variables are involved in structuring such a loan: the interest rate, the amount and form of the equity, exercise and conversion price, maturity, call features, covenants, and options. These variables provide a wide range of possible structures to suit the needs of both the issuer and the investor.

Offsetting these advantages are a few disadvantages around mezzanine capital compared to equity capital. As debt, the interest is payable on a regular basis, and the principal must be repaid if not converted into equity. This is a large claim against cash and can be burdensome if the expected growth or profitability does not materialize and cash becomes tight. In addition, the subordinated debt often contains covenants relating to net worth, debt, and dividends that must be adhered to.

Mezzanine investors generally look for companies that have a demonstrated performance record, with revenues exceeding $10 million. Because the financing will involve paying interest, the investor will carefully examine existing and future cash flow and projections.

Mezzanine financing is utilized in a wide variety of industries, ranging from basic manufacturing to high technology. As the name implies, however, it focuses more on the broad middle spectrum of business rather than on high-tech, high-growth companies. Companies preparing for IPO's, along with specialty retailing, broadcasting, communications, environmental services, distributors, and consumer or business service industries are attractive to mezzanine investors.

Private Placements

Private placements are an attractive source of equity capital for a private company that has ruled out the possibility of going public. If the goal of the company is to raise a specific amount of capital in a short time, this equity source may be the answer. In this transaction, the company offers stock to a few private investors rather than to the general

---

[22]This section was drawn from D.P. Remey, "Mezzanine Financing: A Flexible Source of Growth Capital." In *Pratt's Guide to Venture Capital Sources,* ed. D. Schutt (New York: Venture Economics Publishing, 1993), pp. 84–86.

public. A private placement has a limited audience, hence requires less regulatory paperwork compared to a public offering.

If the management team knows enough investors, then the private placement could be distributed among a small group of insiders, or the company may decide to have a broker circulate the proposal among a few investors who have expressed interest in small companies. The following four groups of investors might be interested in a private placement:[23]

1. Let us say you manufacture a product and sell to dealers, franchisors, or wholesalers. These are the people who know and respect your company and depend on you to supply the product they sell. They might consider it to be in their interest to buy your stock if they believe it will help assure continuation of product supply, and perhaps give them favored treatment if you bring out a new product or product improvement.

2. A second group of prospective buyers for your stock are professional investors who are always on the lookout to buy a good, small company in its formative years and ride it to success. Very often these sophisticated investors choose an industry and a particular product or service in that industry they believe will blossom. If your management, or one key individual, has earned a high

reputation as a star in management, technology, or marketing, these risk-minded investors will be interested.

3. Other investors are searching for opportunities to buy shares of smaller growth companies in the expectation that the company will go public.

4. Private placements also often attract venture capitalists who hope to benefit when the company goes public or is sold.

Initial Public Stock Offerings

Commonly referred to as an IPO, an initial public offering raises capital through federally registered and underwritten sales of the company's shares. Numerous federal and state securities laws and regulations govern these offerings; thus it is important that management consult with lawyers and accountants who are familiar with the current regulations.

In the past, such as during the strong bull market for new issues that occurred in 1983, 1986, 1992, 1996, 1999, and 2006, it was possible to raise money for an early-growth venture or even for a startup. These boom markets are easy to identify because the number of new issues jumped from 78 in 1980 to an astounding 523 in 1983, representing a sharp increase from about $1 billion in 1980 to about 12 times that figure in 1983 (Exhibit 13.10).

EXHIBIT 13.10

Initial Public Offerings (1980–2003)

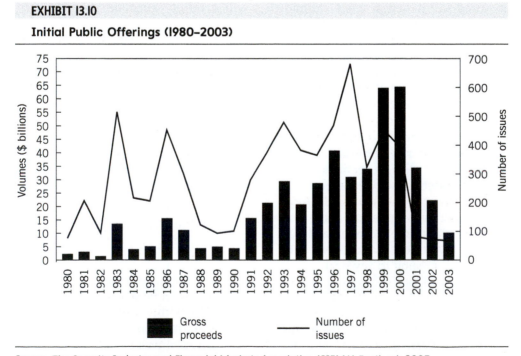

Source: The Security Industry and Financial Markets Association (SIFMA) Factbook 2007.

---

[23]The following examples are drawn directly from Garner, Owen, and Conway, *The Ernst & Young Guide to Raising Capital*, pp. 51–52.

EXHIBIT 13.11

Analysis of Recent IPO History

Year	Number of U.S. IPOs	Number of U.S. Venture-Backed IPOs	Total Venture-Backed Offer Size ($million)	Average Venture-Backed Offer Size ($million)	Total Venture-Backed Post-Offer Value ($million)	Average Venture-Backed Post-Offer Value ($million)
1996	771	268	11,605.6	43.1	56,123.0	208.6
1997	529	131	4,501.4	35.9	20,838.8	159.1
1998	301	75	3,515.4	48.3	16,837.4	224.5
1999	461	223	18,355.5	76.4	114,864.6	493.0
2000	340	226	19,343.0	93.3	106,324.3	470.5
2001	81	37	3,088.2	87.3	15,078.5	407.5
2002	71	22	1,908.5	86.8	8,219.6	373.6
2003	82	29	2,022.7	75.6	8,257.5	273.0
2004	246	93	11,014.9	131.5	61,087.6	699.6
2005	168	56	3,366.5	60.1	13,260.3	236.8
2006	168	57	4,284.1	75.2	17,724.9	311.0

Source: Thomson Venture Economics and National Venture Capital Association, June 12, 2007.

Another boom came 3 years later in 1986, when the number of new issues reached 464. Although in 1992 the number of new issues (396) did not exceed the 1986 amount, a record $22.2 billion was raised in IPOs. Accounting for this reduction in the number of new issues and the increase in the amounts raised, one observer commented, "The average size of each 1983 deal was a quarter of the $70 million average for the deals done in 1992."[24] In other, more difficult financial environments, such as following the 2001 recession, the new-issues market became very quiet for entrepreneurial companies, especially compared to the hot market of 1999. As a result, exit opportunities for venture capital were limited.

In 1991, as the IPO market began to heat up, but as the United Nations deadline for Saddam Hussein ensued, the new issues market turned downward. Simply stated, the market for IPOs is highly influenced by macro-economics and turns hot or cold quickly.

A classic recent example occurred in 2000 as the NASDAQ collapsed and the IPO market shut down. A company we will call NetComm had raised more than $200 million in private equity and debt, was on track to exceed $50 million in revenue, and was 18 months away from positive cash flow. It would require another $125 million in capital to reach this point. The company had completed registration and was ready for an IPO in May 2000, but it was too late. Not only was the IPO canceled, but also subsequent efforts to merge the company failed and the company was liquidated for 20 cents on the dollar in the fall of 2000. Dozens of companies experienced a similar fate during this period and in 2004 activity rebounded significantly. The number of issues nearly tripled from the previous year, from 85 to 247. In 2006, 207 IPOs generated gross proceeds of $45.9 billion. As shown in Exhibit 13.11, 2002 ended with just 22 venture-backed IPOs from U.S. companies for a total offer size of $1.9 billion, down significantly from the 2000 record of $19.3 billion. A recovery was evident in 2004, although there has been less activity in 2005 and 2006.

The more mature a company is when it makes a public offering, the better the terms of the offering. A higher valuation can be placed on the company, and less equity will be given up by the founders for the required capital. There are a number of reasons an entrepreneurial company would want to go public. The following are some of the advantages:

- To raise more capital with less dilution than occurs with private placements or venture capital through a higher valuation.
- To improve the balance sheet or to reduce or to eliminate debt, thereby enhancing the company's net worth.
- To obtain cash to pursue opportunities for growth.
- To access other suppliers of capital with increased bargaining power.
- To improve credibility with customers, vendors, key people, and prospects.

---

[24]T.N. Cochran, "IPOs Everywhere: New Issues Hit a Record in the First Quarter," *Barron's*, April 19, 1993, p. 14. Though softened in 1997, the IPO market by any prior standard remains robust.

- To achieve liquidity for owners and investors.
- To create options to acquire other companies with stock rather than cash.
- To create equity incentives for new and existing employees.

However, IPOs can be disadvantageous for a number of reasons:

- The legal, accounting, and administrative costs of raising money via a public offering are more disadvantageous than other ways of raising money.
- A large amount of management effort, time, and expense are required to comply with SEC regulations and reporting requirements and to maintain the status of a public company. This diversion of management's time and energy from the tasks of running the company can hurt its performance and growth.
- Management can become more interested in maintaining the price of the company's stock and computing capital gains than in running the company. Short-term activities to maintain or increase a current year's earnings can take precedence over longer-term programs to build the company and increase its earnings.
- The liquidity of a company's stock achieved through a public offering may be more apparent than real. Without a sufficient number of shares outstanding and a strong "market maker" there may be limited liquidity for the shares.
- The investment banking firms willing to take a new or unseasoned company public may not be the ones with whom the company would like to do business and establish a long-term relationship.

Private Placement after Going Public[25]

Sometimes a company goes public and then, for any number of reasons, the high expectations that attracted lots of investors turn sour. Your financial picture worsens, there is a cash crisis and the price of your stock in the public marketplace sinks. You find that you need new funds to work your way out of difficulties, but public investors are disillusioned and not likely to cooperate if you bring out a new issue.

Still, other investors are sophisticated enough to see beyond today's problems; they know the company's fundamentals are sound. Although the public has turned its back on you, these investors may

be receptive if you offer a private placement to tide you over. In such circumstances you may use a wide variety of securities, common stock, convertible preferred stock, or convertible debentures.

Regulation D is the result of the first cooperative effort by the SEC and the state securities associations to develop a uniform exemption from securities registration for small issuers. Many states allow for qualification under state law in coordination with the qualification under Regulation D.

Although Regulation D outlines procedures for exempt offerings, there is a requirement to file certain information (Form D) with the SEC. Form D is a relatively short form that asks for certain general information about the issuer and the securities being issued, as well as some specific data about the expenses of the offering and the intended use of the proceeds. Regulation D also provides exemptions from registration when securities are being sold in certain circumstances. The various circumstances are commonly referred to by the applicable Regulation D rule number and their application are as follows:

> *Rule 504.* Issuers that are not subject to the reporting obligations of the Securities Exchange Act of 1934 (nonpublic companies) and that are not investment companies may sell up to $1 million worth of securities over a 12-month period to an unlimited number of investors.
>
> *Rule 505.* Issuers that are not investment companies may sell up to $5 million worth of securities over a 12-month period to no more than 35 nonaccredited purchasers and to an unlimited number of accredited investors. Such issuers may be eligible for this exemption even though they are public companies (subject to the reporting requirements of the 1934 Act).
>
> *Rule 506.* Issuers may sell an unlimited number of securities to no more than 35 nonaccredited but sophisticated purchasers and to an unlimited number of accredited purchasers. Public companies may be eligible for this exemption.

Employee Stock Ownership Plans (ESOPs)

ESOPs are another potential source of funding used by existing companies that have high confidence in the stability of their future earnings and cash flow. An ESOP is a program in which the employees become investors in the company, thereby creating an internal source of funding. An ESOP is a

---

[25]Garner, Owen, and Conway, *The Ernst & Young Guide to Raising Capital*, pp. 52–54.

tax-qualified retirement benefit plan and in essence borrows money, usually from a bank or insurance company, and uses the cash proceeds to buy the company's stock. The stock becomes collateral for the bank note while the owners or treasury have cash that can be used for a variety of purposes. For the lender 50 percent of the interest earned on the loan to the ESOP is tax exempt. The company makes annual tax-deductible contributions to the ESOP in an amount needed to service the bank loan. "The combination of being able to invest in employer stock and to benefit from its many tax advantages makes the ESOP an attractive tool."[26]

Keeping Current about Capital Markets

One picture is vivid from all this: Capital markets, especially for closely held, private companies right through the IPO, are very dynamic, volatile,

asymmetrical, and imperfect. Keeping abreast of what is happening in the capital markets in the 6 to 12 months before a major capital infusion can save valuable time and money; here are some of the best sources currently available to keep you informed:

The European Private Equity and Venture Capital Association (www.evca.com).

The Angel Capital Association (www.angelcapitalassociation.org).

Bloomberg Businessweek magazine (www.businessweek.com).

INC. magazine (www.inc.com).

Red Herring magazine (www.redherring.com).

Business 2.0 magazine (www.money.cnn.com).

Private Equity Analyst (www.privateequity.dowjones.com).

[26]Ibid., p. 281.

Chapter Summary

- Appreciating the capital markets as a food chain looking for companies to invest in is key to understanding motivations and requirements.
- Entrepreneurs have to determine the need for outside investors, whether they want outside investors, and if so whom.
- America's unique capital markets include a wide array of private investors, from "angels" to venture capitalists.
- The search for capital can be very time-consuming, and whom you obtain money from is more important than how much.

- It is said that the only thing that is harder to get from a venture capitalist than a "yes" is a "no."
- Fortunately for entrepreneurs, the modest revival of the venture capital industry has raised the valuations and the sources available. Entrepreneurs who know what and whom to look for—and look out for—increase their odds of success.

Study Questions

1. What is meant by the following, and why are these important: cover your equity; angels; venture capital; valuation; due diligence; IPO; mezzanine; SBIC; private placement; Regulation D; Rules 504, 505, and 506; and ESOP?
2. What does one look for in an investor, and why?
3. How can founders prepare for the due diligence and evaluation process?
4. Describe the venture capital investing process and its implications for fund-raising.

5. Most venture capitalists say there is too much money chasing too few deals. Why is this so? When does this happen? Why and when will it reoccur?
6. What other sources of capital are available, and how are these accessed?
7. Explain the capital markets food chain and its implications for entrepreneurs and investors.

Internet Resources

http://www.businesspartners.com *Business Partners is a global Internet-based service that connects entrepreneurs, early-stage companies, and established corporations with angel investors, venture capital, corporate investors, potential partners, and target data on mergers and acquisitions.*

http://www.nvca.org *The National Venture Capital Association.*

http://www.vcjnews.com/ *The online version of* Venture Capital Journal.

http://www.ventureone.com/ *One of the world's leading venture capital research firms.*

http://www.sba.gov/index.html *Small business resources and funding information from the Small Business Administration (SBA).*

http://initial-public-offerings.com/ *Compilation of IPO-related websites. Find information relating to IPOs, SEC filings, and upcoming IPOs.*

Wiki–Google Search

Try these keywords and phrases:
venture capital
private equity

growth capital
angel capital
risk capital

Case

Forte Ventures

Preparation Questions

1. Evaluate the situation facing the Forte founders in April 2001 and the Private Placement Memorandum (PPM) (Appendix A).

2. What should Maclean Palmer and his partners do, and why?

3. What are the economics of the venture capital business? Assume Forte is a "top quartile" fund in terms of performance. What will the cumulative paychecks and distributions to the limited partners and the general partners be over 10 years?

Forte Ventures

> Bite off more than you can chew, then chew it.
>
> Roger Babson, Speech to the
> Empire Club of Canada, 1922

Maclean Palmer hung up the phone and took another quick glance at the article:

> **April 6, 2001: Bear Market Drives IPOs into Hibernation**
> Further deterioration in the capital markets amidst growing concern about the health of the U.S. and global economy resulted in a dismal start to the 2001 IPO market . . .

Palmer wondered whether he had bitten off more than he could chew in seeking to raise a first-time $200 million venture fund. Were the venture capital and private equity markets collapsing? Should Forte shut down, minimize losses, and revisit the fund-raising when the markets revived? Or should it press on? As he tapped in the number for the next prospect, Palmer smiled ruefully.

What a difference a year makes . . .

Last winter, venture investments in new funds were at an all-time high, and the capital markets were riding the Internet wave. His partners had quit their jobs, sold their homes, and moved to Boston to start Forte with him.

Convincing institutional investors to commit money to a long-term, illiquid, nonrecourse investment run by an unproven team was the challenge all new venture groups faced in raising money. By spring 2001, however, a weakening economy had made that challenge tougher.

With IPOs declining, and venture firms using money to support their portfolio companies rather than make new investments, institutional investors had severely tightened their criteria for evaluating new funds. In addition, Forte was encountering objections to the strategy it felt gave it an edge. Dave Mazza, a partner at Grove Street Advisors (GSA), explained:

> The backdrop to all of this is that there have been a lot of African American–led funds; they've been predominantly SBICs, and few of them have come close to the top quartile performance that we have come to expect from private equity investors. We didn't have any question about what this team's motives were, but in the minds of some limited partners, they are always going to equate the two.

Still, the news was not all bad for Forte. The GSA group—which had been early supporters of Palmer's concept—had recently committed $10 million and pledged $15 million more once Forte had commitments of $50 million.

The support from the influential gatekeeper had boosted state pension funds' interest in Forte. Still, Palmer and his partners, who were bootstrapping this effort from their savings, knew their targeted first closing of $100 million was probably a long way off.

The Offering

The team had spent the last quarter of 2000 developing their offering memorandum for a $200 million venture fund (Appendix A). As private equity fund managers, they would receive both management fees and performance-based incentives. The typical management fee was in the range of 1.5 to 2.5 percent of the total assets under management. The incentive was generally 20 percent of the investment returns over a predetermined baseline—known as the preferred, or hurdle, rate.

While the plan said Forte preferred to back ethnic minority managers and opportunities, it emphasized that Forte's core mission was wealth creation. Palmer summarized the concept:

> We have put a new spin on a very successful private equity strategy that we believe has been proven successful in good and bad markets—a fundamental long-term investing approach using a management-centric strategy. And since virtually no one is out there recruiting these seasoned ethnic minority managers, that gives us a unique advantage.

We will then partner with these managers and go out to buy a small middle-market company—but not necessarily an existing ethnic minority-owned business or even an ethnic minority marketplace. At the end of the day, we're going to do exactly what a firm like Point West does; it's just that we'll be tapping a different network.

Unfortunately, Forte was trying to raise capital in an increasingly tenuous environment.

The Venture Capital Climate in 2001

By April 2001 the Internet bubble had clearly burst. Three federal funds rate cuts had failed to stimulate the economy. Many companies had pre-announced revenue and/or earnings shortfalls and issued cautious outlooks for the coming months. The year looked to be dismal for venture fund-raising and 5-year private equity fund performance (Exhibits A and B).

EXHIBIT A

Funds, Fund Commitments, and Average Fund Size

	Venture Capital				Buyout and Mezzanine			
Year/Quarter	First-Time Funds	Total Funds	Commitments ($billions)	Average Fund Size ($mil)	First-Time Funds	Total Funds	Commitments ($billions)	Average Fund Size ($mil)
QI 1999	32	86	9.1	106	16	48	10	208
Q2 1999	27	92	9.5	103	10	40	12.9	323
Q3 1999	38	103	11.4	111	10	41	13.9	339
Q4 1999	59	194	29.6	153	12	62	25.5	411
QI 2000	33	150	21.7	145	6	35	14.3	409
Q2 2000	56	167	29.2	175	13	42	22.8	543
Q3 2000	37	113	26.6	235	7	32	12.8	400
Q4 2000	51	147	23.8	162	8	34	20.6	606
QI 2001	29	95	16.1	169	7	33	8.9	270

EXHIBIT B

Five-Year Performance Trends

THOMSON
VENTURE ECONOMICS ™

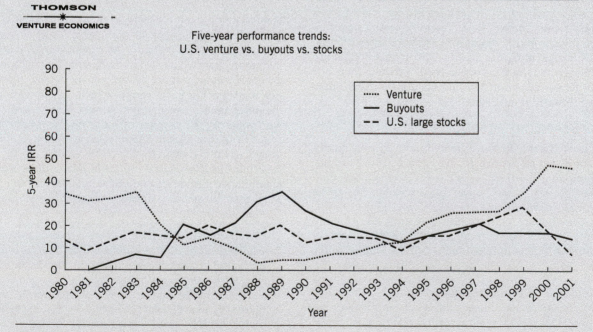

Five-year performance trends:
U.S. venture vs. buyouts vs. stocks

Source: Thomson Venture Economics/NVCA. Used by permission.

The negative news and outlook caused the NASDAQ, S&P 500, and S&P Technology Sector to fall 12.1 percent, 25.5 percent, and 24.8 percent, respectively, in the first quarter. One result was that the IPO market dried up. The first quarter of 2000 produced 142 IPOs with gross proceeds of $32.15 billion. In contrast, the first 3 months of 2001 generated just 20 IPOs with gross proceeds of $8.21 billion—85 percent of which came from three offerings.

Falling share prices also shrank the values of pension fund managers' portfolios, making their investments in private equity, including venture capital, too large a share of their overall investments. As a result, they had to stop investing in venture funds until the amount they had allocated to them was back within the range set by their investing policies.

Palmer and his partners also faced another negative dynamic.

Fund-Raising: Perceptions and Realities

Because Forte had begun courting investors just as the capital markets started weakening, it was not surprising that the prospective limited partners it encountered were unwilling to bet on an untested team. Palmer and his partners could appreciate their position: Profitable allocations were part of their job, and backing what could appear to be a long shot could get a pension fund manager fired. Palmer said Forte's fund-raising pitch emphasized the team and their commitment to success:

We were selling on the fact that we had put a lot of thought into deciding whom we wanted to be partners with. If we were willing to do it—literally burn all the boats and move to Boston before we ever raised a dime—we figured that ought to say something about our level of confidence and dedication.

Judith Elsea, at the time the chief investment officer with the Ewing Marion Kauffman Foundation, discussed her response to their prospectus:

What made Forte different from many minority-centric funds of the past was that they had a good deal of operating experience, so once they got the deals, they'd know what to do with them. The challenge was that many limiteds saw the team as a group whose investment activities would be outside of their sphere of contacts.

Even with GSA's support, advice and referrals, by spring 2001, Forte was making little headway. Mazza commented on the deteriorating fund-raising environment:

The limited partner excuses are coming in a few flavors: The market is terrible, Forte doesn't have a senior star equity player, and we are tapped out. They are all in real bad moods because they're losing a lot of money, and even though this fund is a good bet—and certainly doesn't have anything to do with their market losses—it is just about the worst time in the world to be raising a fund.

GSA founder Clint Harris reiterated that the ability of new funds to attract investors was unfortunately closely related to market conditions:

The bar has gone way up. If a new group like Forte had come to us a year earlier, we probably could have gotten them a check for half of the $200 million they're looking for.

The Worsening Storm

As Palmer hung up from yet another prospect that was planning to hold off on new investments, he had a hard time looking away from a tally of first-quarter market indices:

Index	1Q 2001%
PVCI[a]	−31.4
Dow Jones	−8.02
S&P 400	−12.42
S&P 500	−11.85
S&P 600	−6.57
NASDAQ	−25.51
Russell 1000	−12.56
Russell 2000	−6.51
Russell 3000	−12.5

[a]The Warburg Pincus/Venture Economics Post-Venture Capital Index (PVCI) is a market cap weighted index of the stock performance of all venture-backed companies taken public over the previous 10-year period.

Appendix A

FORTE VENTURES, L.P.: PRIVATE PLACEMENT MEMORANDUM (PPM)

I. Executive Summary

Introduction

Forte Ventures, L.P. (the "Fund" or the "Partnership"), is being formed principally to make equity investments in a broad range of profitable, small to middle-market private companies that are owned or managed by ethnic minorities. The Fund will also invest in businesses that serve or operate in the minority marketplace. Forte's core investment principles are to support or recruit high-quality management teams who are focused on wealth creation and to invest in businesses that, because of their strategic position, have attractive growth prospects. Forte's overriding investment thesis is to leverage its investment and operating expertise, as well as its extensive contacts and knowledge of the minority marketplace, in order to allocate capital to fundamentally sound businesses in an underserved market. Forte believes that it is uniquely positioned to execute this investment thesis and provide attractive returns to the Fund's Limited Partners.

Forte is currently offering limited partnership interests in Forte Ventures, L.P., to institutional investors and a limited number of qualified individuals with the objective of raising $200 million. The Fund will be managed by Maclean E. Palmer, Jr., Ray S. Turner, Clark T. Pierce, and Andrew L. Simon (the "Principals").

Forte's private equity transactions will take several forms, including recapitalizations, leveraged buyouts, industry consolidations/buildups, and growth equity investments. Forte will seek investments opportunistically with particular focus on industry sectors in which the Firm's Principals have substantial prior experience. These sectors currently include auto, auto aftermarket, business-to-business services, growth manufacturing, branded consumer products, OEM industrial products, health care, information technology services, and telecommunications.

Forte's Success Factors

Forte believes the Partnership represents an attractive investment opportunity for the following reasons:

- *Experienced team of investment professionals.* Messrs. Palmer, Pierce, and Simon have over 17 years of *direct* private equity experience. At their previous firms—Advent International, Point West Partners, Ninos Capital, Trident Partners, and McCown De Leeuw—Palmer, Pierce, and Simon

executed all aspects of private equity transactions. They have led investments in a variety of industries and have considerable experience in manufacturing, business services and outsourcing, health care, consumer products, financial services, and telecommunications. In addition, Palmer and Pierce led 13 transactions for their prior firms and were co-lead on three others, investing over $169 million.

- *Operating experience of principals.* Forte's team brings a combined 57 years of operating experience to the firm in addition to their investing expertise. The Principals have found that this experience and insight are invaluable in assessing investment opportunities, recruiting management teams, and adding value to portfolio companies post investment. The Principals will continue to leverage their operating experience through active involvement with portfolio management teams to develop and implement value creation strategies that will drive growth and deliver superior returns.

- *Proven investment track record.* As highlighted in the following table, Palmer has fully exited three of six equity transactions returning $75.2 million on $16.4 million invested, yielding a cash on cash return of 4.73 and an internal rate of return (IRR) of 113 percent. Pierce has fully exited one of ten mezzanine transactions returning $10.6 million on $5.3 million invested, yielding a cash on cash return of 2.03 and an IRR of 23 percent. For another three transactions where values have been established but are as yet unrealized, Palmer and Pierce have collectively generated $46.1 million on investments of $24 million for an imputed cash on cash return of 1.93. The Principals believe there is substantial remaining value to be realized from these three unrealized investments, as well as the remaining nine unrealized investments.

- *Implementation of a proven and successful strategy.* Forte will implement a proven and effective two-part strategy that has been utilized by the Principals to generate excellent investment returns:

  - Support or recruit high-quality management teams with demonstrated records of success who are focused on creating shareholder value.

  - Invest in fundamentally sound businesses that, because of their strategic position, have sustainable margins and attractive growth prospects.

Summary Investment Track Record

	Number of Deals	Invested Capital ($million)	Value Realized ($million)	Value Unrealized ($million)	IRR (%)	Cash on Cash
Equity Investments						
Valuation Status						
Realized[a]	3	$ 16.4	$75.2		113%	4.7×
Established but unrealized	1	$ 8.0		$ 19.1	109%	2.4×
Unrealized[a]	2	$50.0		$50.0		1.0×
Total	6	$74.4	$75.2	$69.1	112%	1.9×
Mezzanine Investments						
Valuation Status						
Realized	1	$ 5.3	$ 10.6		23%	2.0×
Established but unrealized	2	$ 16.0	$ 10.5	$ 16.5	29%	1.7×
Unrealized[a]	7	$73.5		$68.4		0.9×
Total	10	$94.8	$ 21.1	$84.9	26%	1.1×

[a]Includes one investment each for which Palmer or Pierce had significant, but not full, responsibility.

The Principals believe that the ongoing refinement of this strategy in the target marketplace will contribute to the success of the Fund's investments. In addition, Forte's strategy will utilize, where appropriate, the minority status of the firms it invests in as a means to accelerate growth. However, it should be noted that because Forte intends to invest in fundamentally sound businesses, the minority status of its portfolio companies will not influence or be a substitute for the goal of building world-class operational capabilities in each portfolio company.

- *Attractiveness of minority companies and the minority marketplace.* Minority-managed or -controlled companies and the minority marketplace represent attractive investment opportunities for the following reasons:

  - The number of seasoned minority managers with significant P&L experience has grown appreciably over the past 15 years and provides a sizable pool from which Forte can recruit.[1,2]

  - The number of minority-controlled companies with revenues in excess of $10 million has increased dramatically over the past 15 years, and these companies need equity capital to continue their impressive growth rates.[3,4]

  - Rapid growth in the purchasing power of minority consumers, currently estimated at over $1.1 trillion of retail purchasing power and growing at seven times the rate of the overall U.S. population, presents an attractive investment opportunity for companies serving the minority marketplace.[5]

- Numerous corporations have initiatives in place to increase their purchasing from minority suppliers; however, these corporations are being forced to reduce their supplier bases to remain competitive. Minority-controlled companies that serve these corporations need significant equity capital to support the growth rates demanded by their customers. Without this capital infusion, minority suppliers will be unable to remain competitive in an environment of supplier rationalization, and corporations will be unable to reach the targets they have set for their minority purchasing.[6]

- The minority marketplace is overlooked and underserved by private equity investors. Despite the numerous investment opportunities, Forte estimates that less than 1 percent of the $250 billion in private equity capital is targeted at the minority marketplace.

- *Access to multiple sources of proprietary deal flow.* Over their years in private equity and operating positions, the Principals have developed an extensive network for sourcing and developing potential transactions and identifying and recruiting management teams. Forte expects the majority of its opportunities will be negotiated or initiated transactions developed from the following sources:

  - Proprietary investment ideas generated by the Principals involving world-class minority management talent.

  - Growth-stage opportunities led by minority management teams or companies serving the minority marketplace.

[1]July 2000 interview with senior Russell Reynolds & Associates executives.
[2]"What Minorities Really Want," *Fortune* magazine, vol. 142, no. 2 (July 10, 2000).
[3]U.S. Census Bureau, the Survey of Minority Owned Businesses, 1997.
[4]National Minority Supplier Development Council Survey, 1999.
[5]SBA Office of Advocacy, 1997 Economic Census.
[6]National Minority Supplier Development Council Survey, 1999.

- Traditional buyouts and corporate divestitures to minority-led management teams or companies serving the minority marketplace.

- The existing pool of minority-controlled enterprises.

- Corporations seeking to increase their minority purchasing.

- Proactive calling efforts to generate proprietary deal flow that leverages the relationships of the Principals.

- Investment banks and other financial intermediaries.

- *Principals' extensive knowledge of the minority marketplace.* The Principals have direct experience sourcing and executing deals in the target marketplace through their involvement in two minority-focused funds. In addition, the Principals believe that the combination of their in-depth knowledge of the target marketplace, their operating experience, and their ability to identify and recruit exceptional management teams affords Forte a distinct competitive advantage.

II. Investment Strategy

Overview

The combined experience of Forte's Principals has helped them evolve a twofold investment strategy:

- To support or recruit high-quality management teams with demonstrated records of success and provide them the opportunity for significant equity ownership in order to align their interests with the Fund.

- To acquire or invest in fundamentally sound companies in the minority marketplace that, because of their strategic positions, have sustainable margins and attractive growth prospects.

In executing this strategy during both the pre- and postinvestment stages of a transaction, Forte's Principals will consistently take the following steps:

- Maintain a disciplined approach to valuation and structuring.

- Conduct a thorough due diligence examination to identify the stress points in the business model.

- Obtain controlling equity positions, possibly with co-investors, or significant equity positions with certain supermajority rights.

- Implement focused value creation plans and performance monitoring metrics.

- Align companies with strategic and corporate partners to control costs and accelerate growth and thus value creation.

- Exercise value-added operating leadership by supporting management in the development and achievement of business goals.

- Create liquidity through carefully timed and executed transactions.

Forte has developed an investment strategy that builds on the strengths of the Principals' prior experiences. It is also a strategy that has produced excellent results. The Principals expect the Fund's capital to be invested in approximately 3 to 4 years from the date of the first close. Forte will primarily seek to invest in established companies generally ranging in value from $25 million to $75 million and will typically invest $10 million to $35 million in any given investment.

Investment Focus

Forte will seek investments opportunistically with particular focus on industry sectors in which the Firm's Principals have substantial prior experience. These sectors currently include auto, auto aftermarket, business-to-business services, growth manufacturing, branded consumer products, OEM industrial products, health care, information technology services, and telecommunications. The Principals' depth of industry knowledge has led to a substantial flow of potential investments and an ability to rapidly and thoroughly evaluate proposed opportunities. It has also provided numerous industry contacts to call upon for assistance in due diligence and has been helpful in supporting management plans for growth and development. Furthermore, the Principals' industry expertise will enable Forte to be an attractive participant in corporate partnerships.

Forte's specific industry knowledge has evolved over time, and new industries will be added as the firm opportunistically explores new areas for potential investment. It is expected that Forte will leverage its analytical skills and network of contacts to continue developing logical extensions of its current preferences as well as new areas of focus in which high rates of growth and outstanding management are present. The following charts are representative of the Principals' prior allocation of investment dollars by stage and industry sector as well as Forte's expected allocations for the Fund.

Types of Investment Opportunities

Forte believes that the most attractive investments generally share several important characteristics:

- A proven and highly motivated management team that owns or wishes to acquire a significant equity interest in the company.

- A strong competitive market position or the ability to build one.

- Presence in an industry with attractive dynamics and an investment structure that supports sustainable earnings growth.

Prior Allocations by Forte Principals ($ weighted)

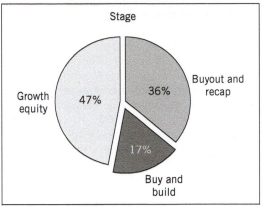
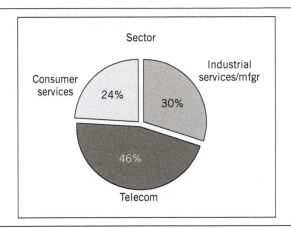

Projected Allocations in Forte Ventures ($ weighted)

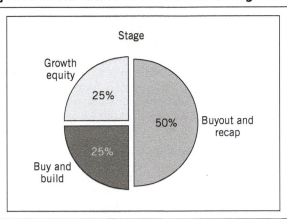
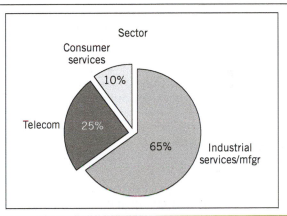

- An established track record of solid financial performance and resistance to earnings downturns during economic or industry cycles.

- The potential to increase operating earnings through focused value creation efforts.

Because Forte's priorities start with the capability of the management team and a company's growth prospects, the actual form of a transaction is often secondary. Forte will seek to participate in the following types of transactions:

- *Leveraged buyouts:* Forte will initiate LBOs and participate in buyouts organized by management and other investment partners.

- *Recapitalizations:* Forte will assist in organizing recapitalizations of businesses in which management retains significant ownership. Forte will participate as either a majority or minority partner.

- *Growth capital investments:* Forte will provide capital to companies in need of equity to support attractive growth opportunities.

- *Industry consolidations/buildups:* Forte will support management teams that seek to build significant companies through acquisition within fragmented industries.

The Principals' prior transactions are indicative of the mix of transactions that will be pursued. Five of these prior transactions were LBOs, two were recapitalizations, three were consolidations/buildups, and five were growth capital investments.

III. Selected Investment Summaries

Cobalt Telecommunications

The Company   Cobalt Telecommunications (Cobalt or the "Company") provides small to medium-sized businesses a resold package of local, long-distance, Internet, paging, and cellular telecommunications services from a variety of providers. The Company added value by aggregating the charges onto one customized bill, as well as providing one source for all customer support.

The Investment   While at Point West Partners, Palmer became the lead investor in Cobalt in December 1997 with an investment of $2 million. In October 1998 he led another $2 million investment in the Company.

The Situation Cobalt was formed to capitalize on the deregulation of the local telecom marketplace. The Company's vision was to provide a higher level of customer service and a full suite of voice and data products to a neglected, but very profitable, customer segment. The Company needed financing to build its customer support and service-provisioning infrastructure, as well as recruit and support an agent-based sales channel.

Role of Forte Principal Mr. Palmer worked with Cobalt management to develop the Company's strategy of concentrating its sales activity within a focused geography in the western Boston suburbs. Palmer also identified a low-cost, yet robust, billing and customer support platform that proved to be the key component of the Company's low-cost and efficient back office. Palmer recruited the Company's CFO prior to the investment, and he played a key role in the Company's acquisition efforts. He also worked with the Company to initiate price increases and cost reductions to improve gross margins. After recognizing weaknesses in the existing Sales VP, Palmer also identified and recruited a new VP of Sales and Marketing and worked with him to accelerate the performance of the Company's sales channels, as well as introduce a new telemarketing channel. The new sales focus enabled Cobalt to increase its sales by over 600 percent in 1 year.

Liquidity Event In the summer of 1999 Palmer led the effort to identify potential strategic acquirers for the Company after it was determined that an attractive purchase price could be achieved. After an intense 3-month process, the Company received and accepted an offer to be acquired by Macklin USA (NASDAQ: MLD). Palmer led the negotiations with Macklin and achieved, to Forte's knowledge, the highest multiple that has been paid to date for a pure reseller of telecom services. The transaction closed in December 1999 with a return to Point West Partners valued at 4.2× cash on cash and an 83 percent IRR.

MBCS Telecommunications

The Company MBCS Telecommunications (MBCS or the "Company") is a switch-based provider of local, long-distance, Internet, data, and high-speed access services to small to medium-sized businesses. The Company has offices in five markets in the Ameritech region and is expanding its switch network in each of these markets.

The Investment Palmer led Point West Partners' initial $3 million investment in MBCS in July 1998, and made a follow-on investment of $5 million in March 2000.

The Situation MBCS had received a first-round investment in July 1997, which was used to finance the Company's growth in long-distance services and to recruit additional management. In 1998 the Company was seeking investors with telecom expertise to aid in the transition into local voice and data services.

Role of Forte Principal Palmer worked with the Company to identify and select a low-cost, yet robust, billing and customer support platform that saved over $1 million in potential capital expenditures. This system has proven to be a key component in supporting MBCS's growth from 20,000 to over 70,000 customers. Palmer also played a key role in recruiting senior management team members, and advised and assisted management in two of the Company's three acquisitions. Most recently, Palmer has been a leader in the Company's fund-raising efforts, introducing the Company to senior lenders and investment bankers and guiding the management team through the selection and approval process.

Valuation Events In March 2000 MBCS received a third round of financing that was led by a new investor at a valuation that represented a 2.63 step up over the previous round (on a fully diluted basis). In September 2000 MBCS acquired a data services and high-speed access provider in a stock-for-stock transaction that valued LDM at a 1.63 step up over the third round.

X-Spanish Radio

The Company X-Spanish Radio Networks, Inc. (X-Spanish or the "Company"), was built by acquiring radio stations in California, Arizona, Texas, and Illinois. These stations form a Spanish language radio network. The programming is satellite delivered from the Company's main studio located in Sacramento, California.

The Investment Mr. Pierce led Ninos Capital's $5.25 million initial investment in X-Spanish in November 1994.

The Situation X-Spanish's overall strategy was to acquire radio stations at attractive prices in desirable markets and keep operating costs low by delivering the programming via satellite to the entire network. To execute the strategy the Company needed capital to purchase additional stations. Over a 4-year period X-Spanish was able to acquire 15 radio stations and build a loyal audience, which led to increasing advertising revenues.

Role of Forte Principal Pierce sourced, structured, priced, and underwrote Ninos's investment in X-Spanish. He also performed a complete due diligence review of the Company, the management team, and the Company's competitive position in each of its target markets. Pierce's due diligence review included the technical performance of the stations, the demand for advertising in the target markets, and the "stick" value of the radio stations. In his board observer role, he monitored the Company's strategic plan, operating performance, and acquisition opportunities and was involved in the strategic decisions of the Company, including potential acquisitions and capital raising.

Liquidity Event   X-Spanish was sold to a financial buyer in November 1998, and this investment resulted in a 23 percent IRR to Ninos Capital.

Krieder Enterprises

The Company   Krieder Enterprises, Inc. (Krieder or the "Company"), is the largest manufacturer of nail enamel in bulk in the United States. Krieder is a leading supplier of enamel to the world's leading cosmetics companies.

The Investment   Pierce led Ninos Capital's $4 million initial investment in Krieder in April 1995 to finance a buyout.

The Situation   To gain market share and improve its competitive position, the Company needed to build infrastructure, upgrade and improve its manufacturing facilities, strengthen its laboratory and technical capabilities, increase the level of customer service, and build an organization that could support the planned growth. The buyout allowed the Company to evolve from an entrepreneurial managed company to a professionally managed one.

Role of Forte Principal   Mr. Pierce sourced, structured, priced, and underwrote Ninos's investment in Krieder. He also performed a complete due diligence review of the equity sponsor, the Company, the management team, and the Company's competitive position within its industry. In his board observer role, he evaluated and analyzed the Company's growth plans, acquisition candidates and deal structures, expansion of the manufacturing facilities, and the implementation of an MIS system.

Liquidity Event   For the 3-year period 1997 to 1999, the Company's revenues and EBITDA grew at CAGRs of 20 percent and 33 percent, respectively. In January 1999 Ninos's investment was repaid along with an additional $1 million distribution. Ninos's warrant position is currently valued in excess of $3.5 million. The combination of the repayment and the warrant value yield a 29 percent IRR on this investment.

Cidran Food Service

The Company   Cidran Food Services II, L.P. (Cidran or the "Company"), owned and operated 130 Burger King restaurants in Louisiana, Arkansas, and Mississippi. Cidran owned and operated over 80 percent of the Burger King restaurants in Louisiana.

The Investment   Pierce led Ninos Capital's $12 million investment in Cidran in December 1998 to complete a recapitalization of the company and provide growth capital.

The Situation   The Company was recapitalized to repurchase the equity interests of several minority shareholders and to allow the Company to continue execution of its strategic plan. This plan required continuously upgrading and improving restaurants, aggressively opening new restaurants, and selectively pursuing acquisitions.

Role of Forte Principal   Pierce sourced, structured, priced, and underwrote Ninos's investment in Cidran. He performed a complete due diligence review of the Company, the management team, and the Company's competitive position in its markets. Through active participation in investor meetings, he evaluated and reviewed the Company's strategic planning and budgeting process, the operating performance at the store-level, various advertising and marketing initiatives, new store-level development, and acquisition opportunities.

Liquidity Event   In June 2000 Pierce led Ninos's voluntary reinvestment in a combination of all the Cidran sister companies. The new company is called Cidran Services LLC ("Cidran Services"). As part of the reinvestment, Ninos sold its 5 percent warrant position back to Cidran in June 2000, which resulted in an IRR of 28 percent.

IV. Investment Process

Sourcing Investment Opportunities

The majority of the Principals' prior investments were originated by the Principals themselves. The Principals have developed sources and techniques for accessing quality investment opportunities, and the Principals' deal flow ability represents an important asset. Investment opportunities for the Fund are expected to emerge from a broad range of categories:

- Operating executives, entrepreneurs, board members, and other investment professionals with whom the Principals have forged relationships. The Principals have developed relationships with hundreds of potential partners and referral sources that understand the Principals' investment approach.

- Original concepts developed and implemented by the Principals.

- Service professionals (e.g., attorneys, accountants, and consultants).

- Professional financial community contacts and relationships (major investment banks, small and regional investment banks, and business brokers).

This network is maintained and developed by a combination of personal visits and telephone calls, as well as frequent mailings.

Evaluation of Investment Opportunities

The Principals possess strong analytical skills and seasoned judgment, reflecting over 17 years of collective investing experience and over 57 years of operating experience. The Principals will leverage this experience in selecting attractive investment opportunities. When considering investment opportunities, a team of Forte professionals will be assembled to conduct a thorough due diligence investigation of the target company, including its history, management, operations, markets, competition, and prospects. The deal team works closely with the target company's management to develop a thorough understanding of their individual goals and objectives as well as their capabilities. Each Forte managing director will also spend considerable time interacting with the CEO. The deal team will also spend considerable time conducting extensive reference checks on the senior team, especially the CEO. If the Principals determine that the management team requires strengthening, professional searches will be initiated during due diligence.

The deal team will independently assess the market by studying available research reports, attending industry trade conferences, conducting competitive interviews, and performing original market and industry research. The deal team will also conduct customer interviews and, in most cases, participate in sales calls, both with and without company personnel. Forte will augment the efforts of the deal team with outside resources such as attorneys, accountants, and function-specific consultants as appropriate. Market research consultants may also be engaged to validate management's market forecasts.

The Principals, because of their operating experience, work with all levels of an organization to understand the capabilities of each manager as well as the internal dynamics of the organization. In the considerable amount of time devoted to the management team, the deal team develops knowledge of each manager's objectives to ensure that they can be aligned in a common strategy to maximize growth and shareholder value.

Transaction Structuring

While engaged in due diligence, the deal team simultaneously structures the transaction, which includes valuing the company, negotiating with the seller, securing the financing, and arranging management's equity participation. As in the past, the Principals will price transactions based on conservative operating assumptions and capital structures. Forte will risk-adjust target rates of return for various investments based on general industry and financial risk, as well as specific operating characteristics of individual investments. Using these risk adjustment factors, the deal team will model a variety of possible operating results and exit outcomes.

Forte considers only investments where multiple exit alternatives are clearly identified at the time of the transaction. The Principals' years of transaction experience enhance their ability to successfully negotiate outcomes that satisfy Forte's investment goals. Generally the management team will invest its own funds on the same terms as Forte and participate in a performance-based option plan to augment their ownership interests. The management team's ownership will be carefully structured to ensure that the objectives of all the participants are aligned to the ultimate goal of maximizing the return on the investment.

Development and Implementation of a Focused Value Creation Plan

Prior to closing a transaction, Forte's Principals will work in partnership with the management team to develop a 3- to 4-year value creation plan. These plans will usually be anchored by systemic growth, which is most often achieved through management team development and operating and systems improvements that enhance the company's ability to serve its customers, as well as sales force development, new customer recruitment, and new product development.

Developing and Monitoring Investments

The Principals' post-transaction activities will involve extensive interaction with each portfolio company and its management, with the value creation plan serving as the blueprint for increasing shareholder value. Forte believes that its strategy of investing in small to middle-market companies with growth potential necessitates the dedication of Forte management resources to a significantly greater extent than might be required if Forte were investing in larger or slower-growing enterprises. The Principals' involvement will include regular communications with management, typically in the form of weekly flash reports, informal meetings and conversations, monthly or quarterly board meetings, and annual budgeting review sessions. The Principals also actively participate in strategic planning sessions and industry trade conferences. In addition, the Firm will assist each portfolio company on a project or functional basis as required. Forte will hold weekly staff meetings where each portfolio company is reviewed at least monthly to ensure full communication and input from all Forte professionals. Objectives for developing each company will be developed by Forte, and management will be encouraged to pursue activities to enhance investment value. Semiannual comprehensive reviews of the entire portfolio will also be conducted to ensure that prior objectives have been met and adequate progress has been targeted for the upcoming period. The Principals will also assist portfolio companies in addressing strategic issues through the creation and effective use of a strong board of directors. Two Forte Principals will generally sit on each portfolio company board, and the Principals will augment these boards through the recruitment of outside industry-specific directors, often from the group of successful executives with whom the Principals have previously worked.

Achieving Investment Liquidity

Forte's investment strategy focuses heavily on the ultimate exit strategy at the time each investment is made. Forte will regularly consider opportunities for investor liquidity as part of its formal semiannual portfolio company planning process or as specific circumstances arise.

The Principals have successfully led the exit of four investments and achieved significant realizations from two others. The four exited investments were strategic sales, and the Principals also have direct involvement in companies that have gone public or been acquired by other equity sponsors.

Internal Planning

At the end of each year, Forte will undertake an annual planning process during which it will evaluate its investment strategy and the financial and human resources needed to execute that strategy. Several days will be set aside by the Principals to set priorities and the targets for the coming year, as well as to give consideration to longer-term trends affecting Forte's business. The output of this planning process will provide a formal agenda for a second meeting of all Forte professionals. Forte believes that an emphasis on internal planning and evaluation will result in continued refinement of its investment strategy and identification and development of new partners to provide for the firm's long-term continuity.

V. Investment Team

Forte Ventures, L.P., will be managed by the General Partner. The Principals of the General Partner are Maclean E. Palmer, Jr., Ray S. Turner, Clark T. Pierce, and Andrew L. Simon. Two of the Principals have known each other for over 5 years and developed a working relationship through their prior firms' co-investment in two deals. These two Principals have demonstrated the ability to generate superior returns for investors and have experience initiating investment opportunities, structuring and negotiating investments, and actively working with portfolio company management teams to maximize returns. Two members of Forte's team also bring over 57 years of operating experience covering a broad range of industry sectors including auto and other heavy industries, high-tech electronics, and health care. The team's operating experience was garnered from Fortune 100 companies as well as startup and fast-growth companies financed by private equity investors.

Managing Directors

Maclean E. Palmer, Jr.
Maclean Palmer, Jr. (41), has over 5 years of direct private equity experience and over 17 years of operating experience. Prior to joining Forte, he was a managing director with Point West Partners from 1997 to 2000 in their San Francisco office. While at Point West, Palmer was responsible for deal origination, transaction execution, and portfolio company management, and focused on growth equity and buyout investments in the telecommunications, business-to-business services, industrial manufacturing, and auto sectors. Palmer led Point West investments in three competitive local exchange carriers (CLECs): Cobalt Telecommunications, MBCS Telecommunications, and Concept Telephone. He continues to represent Point West on the board of directors of both MBCS and Concept Telephone.

From 1995 to 1997 Palmer was a vice president in the Boston office of Advent International. While at Advent, he focused on industrial and technology investments and led Advent's investment in ISI, a financial and business information services provider. From 1986 to 1995 Palmer worked in various management and engineering positions for three startup companies, UltraVision Inc., Surglaze Inc., and DTech Corporation, which were all financed by private equity investors. During his startup career, Palmer was involved in the development and successful market introduction of 12 new products. In addition, Palmer held engineering positions with Borg Warner Corporation from 1984 to 1986 and with the diesel division of a major automotive firm from 1983 to 1984.

Palmer sits on the board of JT Technologies, a minority-owned firm that develops battery and ultra-capacitor technology. He also sits on the board of the Cooper Enterprise Fund, a minority-focused fund based in New York; the Community Preparatory School, a private inner-city school focused on preparing middle school students for college preparatory high schools; and the Zell Laurie Entrepreneurial Institute at the University of Michigan Business School.

Palmer holds a BSME from the Automotive Institute and an MBA cum laude from Babson College and was awarded a Kauffman Fellowship, graduating with the program's inaugural class.

Ray S. Turner
Ray S. Turner (61) has had a long and distinguished career as an operating executive at Fortune 50 companies. From October 1998 to March 2000 he was group vice president, North America Sales, Service, and Marketing for a multinational heavy-industry manufacturer. From 1990 to 1998 Turner also served as vice president and general manager for North America Sales and Manufacturing at that company.

From 1988 to 1990 he served as vice president for manufacturing operations. From 1977 to 1988 Turner served in senior manufacturing management and plant manager roles for a number of assembly and manufacturing operations for the company. Prior to his career at that corporation, Turner spent several years serving in a variety of positions in engineering, materials management, manufacturing, sales, personnel, and labor relations.

Turner serves on the board of directors of two Fortune 100 corporations.

Turner received a bachelor's degree in business administration from Western Michigan University. He also completed the Executive Development Program at Harvard Business School and an Advanced International General Management Program in Switzerland.

Clark T. Pierce   Clark T. Pierce (38) has over 7 years of mezzanine and private equity experience and over 4 years of corporate finance experience. Most recently he was a principal with Ninos Capital, a publicly traded mezzanine investment fund. While at Ninos he was responsible for leading all aspects of the investment process, including deal origination and evaluation, due diligence, deal execution, and portfolio company management. Pierce has closed numerous transactions in various industries, including business services, distribution, manufacturing, and financial services.

From 1993 to 1995 Pierce managed Ninos Capital's Specialized Small Business Investment Company ("SSBIC"). This SSBIC was a $45 million investment vehicle directed toward minority-owned and controlled companies. Prior to Ninos Capital, Pierce spent 1 year with Freeman Securities as a vice president in the Corporate Finance Group, where he advised bondholders and companies involved in the restructuring process. From 1989 to 1991 Pierce was an associate with Chase Manhattan Bank, N.A., in the Corporate Finance Group.

Pierce served on the board of directors of Sidewalks, Inc., a social services organization for troubled teenagers, and The Orphan Foundation of America, a nonprofit agency focusing on adoption of older children.

Pierce received a BA from Morehouse College, a JD from George Washington University, and an MBA from the Wharton Business School at the University of Pennsylvania.

Andrew L. Simon   Andrew L. Simon (30) has 4 years of direct private equity experience, as well as 3 years of strategy consulting experience. During his career Simon has worked on private equity investments in numerous industry sectors, including contract manufacturing, industrial products, health care, financial services, and direct marketing. Most recently he was a senior associate in the New York office at McCown De Leeuw & Co., Inc. ("MDC"), where he focused on growth and leveraged equity investments, including recapitalization and buy-and-build acquisitions. While at MDC, Simon played a lead role in identifying potential investments, negotiating with sellers, and structuring and arranging debt financing, as well as supervising the legal documentation and closing of transactions. Post acquisition he played an active role in the financing and strategic direction of MDC portfolio companies and participated at board meetings.

From 1995 to 1997 Simon was an associate in the Boston office of Trident Partners ("Trident"). At Trident Simon was responsible for evaluating, prioritizing, and analyzing potential new acquisition opportunities, as well as supporting deal teams with business and analytical due diligence. From 1992 to 1995 Simon was a senior analyst at Marakon Associates, where he was responsible for valuation analysis, industry research, and strategy development. In addition, Simon has worked for Littlejohn & Co., an LBO firm focused on restructuring; Physicians Quality Care, a venture-backed health care services company; and Lotus Development.

Simon earned an AB degree from Princeton University's Woodrow Wilson School and earned his MBA, with honors, from Harvard Business School, where he was a Toigo Fellow.

Vice President

Fidel A. Cardenas   Most recently Fidel A. Cardenas (31) was a managing director with MTG Ventures from 1999 to 2000. At MTG, a private equity firm focused on acquiring and operating manufacturing and service companies, Cardenas was responsible for deal origination, transaction execution, and portfolio company management. Prior to his role at MTG Ventures, Cardenas was a principal with MTG Advisors from 1992 to 1997, where he focused on strategy consulting and executive coaching. Concurrent with MTG Advisors, Cardenas was elected to two terms as mayor of Sunny Park, California, becoming, at 23, the mayor of that city. He has also served as assistant deputy mayor for public safety for the City of Los Angeles and as an analyst for McKinsey and Company.

Cardenas received a BA in political science from Harvard, cum laude, and his MBA from Harvard Business School.

VI. Summary of Principal Terms

The following is a Summary of Terms relating to the formation of Forte Ventures, L.P. (the "Partnership"), a Delaware limited partnership. This Summary of Terms is by its nature incomplete and subject to the terms and conditions contained in the definitive limited partnership agreement of the Partnership (the "Partnership Agreement") and certain other documents. In the event that the description of terms in this Summary of Terms or elsewhere in this Memorandum is inconsistent with or contrary to the description in, or terms of, the Partnership Agreement or related documents, the terms of the Partnership Agreement and the related documents shall control.

Purpose

The principal purpose of the Partnership is to produce long-term capital appreciation for its partners through equity and equity-related investments in companies that are owned or managed by ethnic minorities or serve or operate in the minority marketplace.

Partnership Capital

The Partnership will have a target size of $200 million (together with the General Partner Commitment) of capital commitments. Commitments in excess of this amount may be accepted at the discretion of the General Partner.

General Partner

The general partner (the "General Partner") of the Partnership will be Forte Ventures, LLC, a Delaware limited liability company formed under the laws of the State of Delaware. Maclean E. Palmer, Jr., Clark T. Pierce, Ray S. Turner, and Andrew L. Simon will be the initial members of the General Partner. The General Partner will control the business and affairs of the Partnership.

Management Company

The management company (the "Management Company") will be Forte Equity Investors, LLC, a Delaware limited liability company. The Management Company will act as investment advisor to the Partnership pursuant to the terms of the Management Agreement.

The Management Company will be responsible for identifying investment opportunities, structuring and negotiating the terms and conditions of each acquisition, arranging for all necessary financing, and, after consummation, monitoring the progress of, and arranging for the disposition of, its interest in each portfolio company. The Management Company may, at its discretion, retain other professionals, including but not limited to accountants, lawyers, and consultants, to assist in rendering any services described herein. In addition, the Management Company may provide services directly to portfolio companies.

General Partner's Capital Contribution

The General Partner shall contribute an amount equal to the greater of $2 million or 1 percent of the total contributions of the Partners, at the same time and in the same manner as the Limited Partners.

Partnership Term

The Partnership term shall be 10 years from the First Closing unless extended by the General Partner for up to a maximum of three additional 1-year periods to provide for the orderly liquidation of the Partnership.

Investment Period

The General Partner will generally not be permitted to make any capital calls for the purpose of making investments after the termination of the period (the "Investment Period") commencing on the First Closing and ending on the fifth anniversary thereof, other than commitments to make investments that were committed to prior to such fifth anniversary, and Follow-On Investments (occurring after the Investment Period) that will not exceed 15 percent of the committed capital of the Partnership.

Side Fund

The General Partner may establish an investment fund (the "Side Fund") for individual investors who will be assisting and/or advising the Management Company in connection with originating investment opportunities, recruiting senior management candidates, conducting due diligence, and analyzing selective industry opportunities. The aggregate capital commitments of the Side Fund shall not exceed $5 million. The Side Fund will have terms similar to the Partnership, *provided however* that the individual investors in the Side Fund will only be required to pay a nominal management fee, and the profits from investments made by the Side Fund will not be subject to a Carried interest. The Side Fund will invest alongside the Partnership in each Investment of the Partnership on a pro rata basis. A percentage of each Investment equal to the Capital Commitments of the Side Fund divided by the total Capital Commitments of the Side Fund, the Partnership, or any Parallel Regulatory Vehicle shall be reserved for co-investment by the Side Fund.

Investment Limits

The Partnership will not make investments (excluding Bridge Financings as noted next) in any single or group of related portfolio companies that exceed 25 percent of committed capital, or 35 percent of committed capital when combined with Bridge Financings, of such portfolio companies. With the consent of the Limited Partners, such investment limits may be increased by up to 10 percent with respect to one portfolio company or group of related companies.

Without the approval of the Limited Partners, the investments shall not include:

i. any investment in an entity that provides for "Carried interests" or management fees to any persons other than the management of a portfolio company or the General Partner or the Management Company unless the General Partner waives its right to receive "Carried interest" distributions with respect to such investment or the General Partner makes a good faith determination that such investment is expected to (a) yield returns on investments within the range of returns expected to be provided by the equity and equity-related securities in which the Partnership was organized to invest (taking into account any management fee or Carried interest relating thereto), and (b) foster a strategic relationship with a potential source of deal flow for the Partnership, *provided however* that such investments shall not exceed 15 percent of the committed capital of the Partnership;

ii. acquisition of control of businesses through a tender offer (or similar means) if such acquisition is opposed by a majority of the members of such business's board of directors or similar governing body;

iii. any investment in an entity the principal business of which is the exploration for or development of oil and gas or development of real property;

iv. investments in uncovered hedges or derivative securities; or

v. any investment in marketable securities unless immediately after giving effect to such investment the total amount of the Partnership's investments in marketable securities does not exceed 15 percent of aggregate capital commitments of all Partners (other than an investment in marketable securities of an issuer which the General Partner intends to engage in a going private transaction on the date of such investment or in which the General Partner expects to obtain management rights).

The Partnership will not invest more than 20 percent of its committed capital in businesses that have their principal place of business outside of the United States. The Partnership will not invest in securities of entities formed outside of the United States unless it has first obtained comfort that Limited Partners of the Partnership will be subject to limited liability in such jurisdiction that is no less favorable than the limited liability they are entitled to under the laws of Delaware. The Partnership will use its reasonable efforts to ensure that Limited Partners are not subject to taxation in such jurisdiction(s) other than with respect to the income of the Partnership. The Partnership will not guarantee the obligations of the portfolio companies in an amount in excess of 10 percent of capital commitments to the Partnership at any time. The Partnership may borrow money only to pay reasonable expenses of the Partnership or to provide interim financings to the extent necessary to consummate the purchase of a portfolio company prior to receipt of capital contributions.

Bridge Financings

The Partnership may provide temporary financings with respect to any portfolio company ("Bridge Financings"). Any Bridge Financing repaid within 18 months will be restored to unpaid capital commitments.

Any Bridge Financing that is not repaid within 18 months shall no longer constitute Bridge Financing and will be a permanent investment in the portfolio company in accordance with the terms of the Partnership. Bridge Financings may not be incurred if, after giving *pro forma* effect to such incurrence, the aggregate principal amount of Bridge Financings outstanding is in excess of 10 percent (or up to 20 percent with the approval of the Limited Partners) of the Partnership's aggregate capital commitments.

Distributions

Distributions from the Partnership may be made at any time as determined by the General Partner. All distributions of current income from investments, proceeds from the disposition of investments (other than Bridge Financings and proceeds permitted to be reinvested), and any other income from assets of the Partnership (the "Investment Proceeds") from or with respect to each investment initially shall be apportioned among each partner (including the General Partner) in accordance with such Partner's Percentage Interest in respect of such investment. Notwithstanding the previous sentence, each Limited Partner's share of such distribution of Investment Proceeds shall be allocated between such Limited Partner, on the one hand, and the General Partner, on the other hand, and distributed as follows:

i. *Return of Capital and Partnership Expenses:* First, 100 percent to such Limited Partner until such Limited Partner has received distributions equal to (a) such Limited Partner's capital contributions for all Realized Investments and such Limited Partner's pro rata share of any unrealized losses on writedowns (net of write-ups) of the Partnership's other portfolio company investments and (b) such Limited Partner's capital contributions for all Organizational Expenses and Partnership Expenses allocated to Realized Investments and write-downs of the Partnership's other portfolio company investments (the amounts discussed in clauses (a) and (b) are referred to collectively as the "Realized Capital Costs");

ii. *Eight Percent Preferred Return:* 100 percent to such Limited Partner until cumulative distributions to such Limited Partner from Realized Investments represent an 8 percent compound annual rate of return on such Limited Partner's Realized Capital Costs;

iii. *General Partner Catch-Up to 20 Percent:* 100 percent to the General Partner until cumulative distributions of Investment Proceeds under this clause (iii) equal 20 percent of the total amounts distributed pursuant to clauses (ii) and (iii); and

iv. *80/20 Split:* Thereafter, 80 percent to such Limited Partner and 20 percent to the General Partner (the distributions to the General Partner pursuant to this clause (iv) and clause (iii) above are referred to collectively as the "Carried Interest Distributions").

The rate of return regarding each distribution relating to an investment shall be calculated from the date the capital contributions relating to such investment were used to make such investment to the date that the funds or the property being distributed to each Limited Partner have been received by the Partnership. Proceeds from cash equivalent investments will be distributed to the Partners in proportion to their respective interests in Partnership assets producing such proceeds, as determined by the General Partner. Proceeds of Bridge Financings will be distributed in accordance with contributions to such Bridge Financings.

Subject, in each case, to the availability of cash after paying Partnership Expenses, as defined below, and setting aside appropriate reserves for reasonably anticipated liabilities, obligations, and commitments of the Partnership, current income earned (net of operating expenses) will be distributed at least annually, and the net proceeds from the disposition of securities of portfolio companies, other than proceeds permitted to be reinvested, shall be distributed as soon as practicable.

The General Partner may make distributions from the Partnership, as cash advances against regular distributions, to the Partners to the extent of available cash in amounts necessary to satisfy their tax liability (or the tax liability of the partners of the General Partner) with respect to their proportion of the Partnership taxable net income.

The Partnership will use its best efforts not to distribute securities in kind unless they are marketable securities or such distribution is in connection with the liquidation of the Partnership. If the receipt of such securities by a Limited Partner will violate law or if a Limited Partner does not wish to receive distributions in kind, the General Partner will make alternative arrangements with respect to such distribution.

Allocations of Profits and Losses

Profits and losses of the Partnership will be allocated among Partners in a manner consistent with the foregoing distribution provisions and the requirements of the Internal Revenue Code.

Clawback

If, following the dissolution of the Partnership, the General Partner shall have received Carried Interest Distributions with respect to a Limited Partner greater than 20 percent of the cumulative net profits (calculated as if all the profits and losses realized by the Partnership with respect to such Limited Partner had occurred simultaneously), then the General Partner shall pay over to such Limited Partner the lesser of (i) the amount of such excess or (ii) the amount of distributions received by the General Partner with respect to such Limited Partner reduced by the taxes payable by the General Partner with respect to such excess and increased by the amount of any tax benefits utilized by the General Partner as a result of such payment in the year of payment.

Management Fees

The Partnership will pay to the Management Company an annual management fee (the "Management Fee") equal to, during the Investment Period, 2 percent of the Partners' total capital committed to the Partnership and, during the period thereafter, 2 percent of the total capital contributions that were used to fund the cost of, and remain invested in, investments, which amount shall be increased quarterly by any capital contributions made during such period and decreased quarterly by amounts distributed to partners as a return of capital. The Management Fee will be payable in advance on a semiannual basis, with the first payment being made on the First Closing Date and each semiannual payment thereafter occurring on the first business day of each calendar semiannual period.

Management Fees may be paid out of monies otherwise available for distribution or out of capital calls. The payments by Additional Limited Partners with respect to the Management Fee and interest thereon will be paid to the Management Company.

Other Fees

The General Partner, the Management Company, and their affiliates may from time to time receive monitoring fees, directors' fees, and transaction fees from portfolio companies or proposed portfolio companies. All such fees will be first applied to reimburse the Partnership for all expenses incurred in connection with Broken Deal Expenses (as defined below) and 50 percent of any excess of such fees will be applied to reduce the Management Fees payable to the Management Company by the Partnership.

"Break-Up Fees" shall mean any fees received by the General Partner, Management Company, or their affiliates in connection with such proposed investment in a portfolio company that is not consummated, reduced by all out-of-pocket expenses incurred by the Partnership, the General Partner, the Management Company, or their affiliates in connection with such proposed investment in the portfolio company.

Partnership Expenses

The Partnership will be responsible for all Organizational Expenses and Operational Expenses (collectively, the "Partnership Expenses").

"Organizational Expenses" shall mean third-party and out-of-pocket expenses, including, without limitation, attorneys' fees, auditors' fees, capital raising, consulting and structuring fees, and other startup expenses incurred by either of the Partnership, the General Partner, or Management Company, or any affiliates thereof in connection with the organization of the Partnership.

"Operational Expenses" shall mean with respect to the Partnership, to the extent not reimbursed by a prospective or actual portfolio company, if any, all expenses of operation of the Partnership, including, without limitation, legal, consulting, and accounting expenses (including expenses associated with the preparation of Partnership financial statements, tax returns, and K-Is); Management Fees; any taxes imposed on the Partnership; commitment fees payable in connection with credit facilities, accounting fees, third-party fees and expenses, attorney's fees, due diligence, and any other costs or fees related to the acquisition or disposition of securities or investment, whether or not the transaction is consummated; expenses associated with the Limited Partners and other advisory councils and investment committees of the Partnership; insurance and the costs and expenses of any litigation involving the Partnership; and the amount of any judgments or settlements paid in connection therewith.

"Broken Deal Expenses" mean with respect to each investment, to the extent not reimbursed by a prospective or actual portfolio company, all third-party expenses incurred in connection with a proposed investment that is not ultimately made or a proposed disposition of an investment which is not actually consummated, including, without limitation, (i) commitment fees that become payable in connection with a proposed investment that is not ultimately made; (ii) legal, consulting, and accounting fees and expenses; (iii) printing expenses; and (iv) expenses incurred in connection with the completion of due diligence concerning the prospective portfolio company.

Limited Partner Advisory Committee

The General Partner shall establish a Limited Partner Advisory Committee (the "Advisory Committee") that will consist of between three and nine representatives of the Limited Partners selected by the General Partner.

VII. Risk Factors

An investment in Forte Ventures involves a high degree of risk. There can be no assurance that Forte Ventures' investment objectives will be achieved, or that a Limited Partner will receive a return of its capital. In addition, there will be occasions when the General Partner and its affiliates may encounter potential conflicts of interest in connection with Forte Ventures. The following considerations should be carefully evaluated before making an investment in Forte Ventures. Risk factors include

- Illiquid and long-term investments.

- General portfolio company risk.

- Reliance on the principals.

- Past performance not being indicative of future investment results.

- Lack of operating history.

- Lack of transferability of the limited partnership interests.

- Potential of contingent liabilities on dispositions of portfolio company investments.

- No separate counsel for limited partners.

- Uncertain nature of investments.

- Use of leverage increasing exposure to adverse economic factors.

Chapter Fourteen

The Deal: Valuation, Structure, and Negotiation

LEARNING OUTCOMES: After reading this chapter, you should be able to understand:

14-1 The art and craft of valuation

14-2 The theory and reality of company pricing

14-3 Valuation methods

14-4 Tar pits facing entrepreneurs

14-5 The term sheet

14-6 Sand traps

The Art and Craft of Valuation

Private markets where startups are financed are very different from public markets where companies are priced in well-established market-based exchanges. Valuations of private companies have no standard methodologies to determine value, so a general valuation is determined using a series of rough calculations with the final number based on negotiations between the financing source and the entrepreneur, with the financing source having all the leverage in this process. This is because of a multitude of factors all tied to the risk inherent in a new company. Once a company has overcome these risk factors by establishing a stable track record, risk is greatly reduced, and it is able to trade on the public markets providing both liquidity and a market-driven valuation.

Determinants of Value

A private company's value is determined by its risk in relationship to the potential return. For similar companies, the lower the risk, the higher the valuation. The risk factors include revenue, expense and earnings performance, cash flow, amount of available capital on the balance sheet, quality of customers, revenue growth rate, and a myriad of other factors that can differ based on the industry.

A Theoretical Perspective

Establishing Boundaries and Ranges Rather than Calculating a Number Valuation for a private company has no established methodology. There are dozens of theoretical methods that can be applied, but in the case of a private company raising money, the only valuation that matters is the price at which investors are willing to invest. Frequently approximations can be made by looking at publicly traded equivalents by industry. For example, software companies are typically traded at a multiple of revenue, reflecting the fact that revenue growth is more important than profitability. Alternatively, manufacturing companies are typically priced as a multiple of EBITDA, which essentially strips out depreciation and values the deal on its cash flow. These are appropriate methods to establish the price boundaries in a private deal.

Rate of Return (ROR)

Various investors will require a different rate of return (ROR) for investments in different stages of development and reflected in the investment expect holding period. The earlier the investment, the longer until the company establishes a stable financial track record, the more return an investor requires to compensate for the risk. Exhibit 14.1

EXHIBIT 14.1

Rate of Return Sought by Venture Capital Investors

Stage	Annual ROR (%)	Typical Expected Holding Period (Years)
Seed and startup	50–100% or more	More than 10
First stage	40–60	5–10
Second stage	30–40	4–7
Expansion	20–30	3–5
Bridge and mezzanine	20–30	1–3
LBOs	30–50	3–5
Turnarounds	50+	3–5

EXHIBIT 14.2

Investor's Required Share of Ownership under Various ROR Objectives

Assumptions:

Amount of initial startup investment = $1 million   Year 5 after-tax profit = $1 million

Holding period = 5 years   Year 5 price/earnings ratio = 15

Required rate of return = 50% $\dfrac{\text{FV of investment}}{\text{FV of company}}$ = % ownership required

Calculating the required share of ownership:

Price/Earnings Ratio	Investor's Return Objective (Percent/Year Compounded)			
	30%	40%	50%	60%
10×	37%	54%	76%	106%
15×	25	36	51	70
20×	19	27	38	52
25×	15	22	30	42

summarizes the annual rates of return that venture capital investors seek on investments by stage of development and holding period.

Investor's Required Share of Ownership

The ROR required by the investor can affect the investor's required share of the ownership, as Exhibit 14.2 illustrates. The future value of a $1 million investment at 50 percent compounded is $1 million $\times (1.5)^5$ = $1 million $\times$ 7.59 = $7.59 million. The future value of the company in Year 5 is profit after tax $\times$ price/earnings ratio + $1 million $\times$ 15 = $15 million. Thus the share of ownership required in Year 5 is

$$\frac{\text{Future value of the investment} = \$7.59 \text{ million}}{\text{Future value of the company} = \$15.00 \text{ million}} = 15\%$$

We can readily see that changing any of the key variables will change the results accordingly.

If the venture capitalists require the RORs mentioned earlier, the ownership they also require is: in the startup stage, 25 to 75 percent for investing all

of the required funds; beyond the startup stage, 10 to 40 percent, depending on the amount invested, maturity, and track record of the venture; in a seasoned venture in the later rounds of investment, 10 to 30 percent to supply the additional funds needed to sustain its growth.

The Theory of Company Pricing

In Chapter 13, we introduced the concept of the capital markets food chain, which we have included here as Exhibit 14.3. This chart depicts the evolution of a company from its idea stage through an initial public offering (IPO). The appetite of the various sources of capital–from family, friends, and angels, to venture capitalists, strategic partners, and the public markets–varies by company size, stage, and amount of money invested. The Theory of Company Pricing is shown in Exhibit 14.4. In the ideal scenario, a venture capital investor envisions two to three rounds, starting at a $1.00 per share, then a three to five times markup to Series B,

EXHIBIT 14.3

The Capital Markets Food Chain for Entrepreneurial Ventures

	Stage of Venture			
	R&D	**Seed**	**Launch**	**High Growth**
Company Enterprise Value at Stage	Less than $1 million	$1million–$5 million	$1 million–$50 million-plus	More than $100 million
Sources	Founders High net worth individuals FFF[a] SBIR	FFF[a] Angel funds Seed funds SBIR	Venture capital series A, B, C . . .[b] Strategic partners Very high net worth individuals Private equity	IPOs Strategic acquirers Private equity
Amount of Capital Invested	Less than $50,000–$200,000	$10,000–$500,000	$500,000–$20 million	$10 million–$50 million-plus
% Company Owned at IPO	10–25%	5–15%	40–60% by prior investors	15–25% by public
Share Price and Number[c]	$.01–$.50 1–5 million	$.50–$1.00 1–3 million	$1.00–$8.00 1/2 +/− 5–10 million	$12–$18 + 3–5 million

[a]Friends, families, and fools.

[b]Venture capital series A, B, C, . . .(average size of round)

Round $\begin{cases} \text{"A" @ \$3–\$5 million: startup} \\ \text{"B" @ \$5–\$10 million: product development} \\ \text{"C"+ @ \$10 million: shipping product} \end{cases}$

Valuations vary markedly by industry.

Valuations vary by region and VC cycle.

[c]At post–IPO.

EXHIBIT 14.4

Theory of Company Pricing

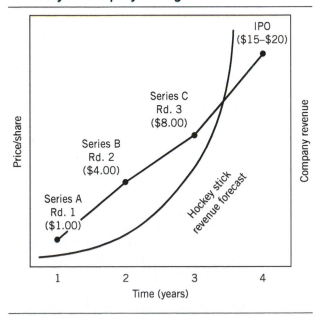

followed by a double markup to Series C, and then doubling that to $8.00 at an IPO. This should be considered a generic pattern to characterize a deal making it to an IPO.

The Reality

The past 25 years have seen the venture capital industry explode from investing only $50 million to $100 million per year to nearly $100 billion at the turn of the century. Exhibit 14.5 shows how the many realities of the capital marketplace are at work, and how current market conditions, deal flow, and relative bargaining power influence the actual deal struck. Exhibit 14.6 shows how the dot-com explosion and the plummeting of the capital markets led to much lower values for private companies. The NASDAQ index fell from over 5,000 to less than 2,000, a 63 percent collapse in about 9 months by year-end 2000. By 2005, the NASDAQ was barely above 2,000, and by the fall of 2007 it had exceeded 2,600.

The Down Round or Cram-Down circa 2003

In this environment, which also existed after the October 1987 stock market crash, entrepreneurs face rude shocks in the second or third round of financing. Instead of a substantial four or even five times increase in the valuation from Series A to B, or B to C, they are jolted with what is called a "cram-down" round: The price can be one-fourth

EXHIBIT 14.5

The Reality

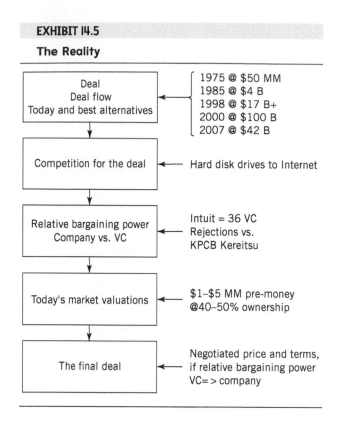

Deal Deal flow Today and best alternatives	1975 @ $50 MM 1985 @ $4 B 1998 @ $17 B+ 2000 @ $100 B 2007 @ $42 B
Competition for the deal	Hard disk drives to Internet
Relative bargaining power Company vs. VC	Intuit = 36 VC Rejections vs. KPCB Kereitsu
Today's market valuations	$1–$5 MM pre-money @40–50% ownership
The final deal	Negotiated price and terms, if relative bargaining power VC= > company

EXHIBIT 14.6

The Reality: The Down Round

#1: 3–4M shares @ $1–$1.50 $3–$5 M round
#2: 6–10M shares @ $.25–$.50 $2–$3 M round

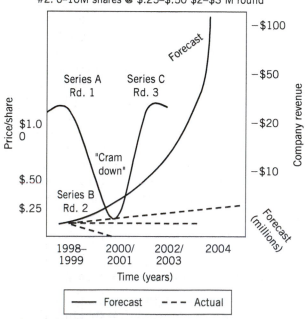

NASDAQ: peaked above 5,000 in March 2000.
Dropped 63 percent by 12/31/2000.

to two-thirds of the last round, as shown in Exhibit 14.6. This severely dilutes the founders' ownership, as investors are normally protected against dilution. Founder dilution as a result of failing to perform is one thing, but dilution because the NASDAQ and IPO markets collapsed seems unfair, but is part of the reality of valuation.

We can sense just how vulnerable and volatile the valuation of a company can be in these imperfect markets when external events, such as the collapse of the NASDAQ, trigger a downward spiral. We also gain a new perspective on how critically important timing is and how much external factors affect a market.

Improved Valuations by 2008

As we saw in the previous chapter, both the flows of venture capital and the IPO market continued their strong rebound in 2007. IPOs establish the high-water mark for valuations, and that affected valuations throughout the capital markets food chain. For entrepreneurs, higher valuations were a refreshing contrast to the post-Internet bubble bashing. Overall, looking ahead to 2014 and beyond, the capital markets and valuations were showing signs of recovery.

Valuation Methods

The Venture Capital Method[1]

This method is appropriate for investments in a company with negative cash flows at the time of the investment, but has the potential to generate significant earnings. As discussed in Chapter 13, venture capitalists are the most likely professional investors to make this type of investment. The steps involved in this method are as follows:

1. Estimate the company's *net income* in a number of years, at which time the investor plans on harvesting. This estimate will be based on sales and margin projections presented by the entrepreneur in his or her business plan.

2. Determine the appropriate *price-to-earnings ratio*, or P/E ratio, by studying current multiples for companies with similar economic characteristics.

---

[1]The venture capital method of valuation is adapted from W. A. Sahlman, "A Method for Valuing High-Risk, Long-Term Investment: The 'Venture Capital Method,'" Note 9-288-006, Harvard Business School, 1988, pp. 2–4. Copyright © 1988 by the President and Fellows of Harvard College.

3. Calculate the projected *terminal value* by multiplying net income and the P/E ratio.

4. The terminal value can then be discounted to find the *present value* of the investment, with venture capitalists using discount rates ranging from 35 to 80 percent based on the risk of this type of investment.

5. To determine the investors' *required percentage of ownership*, based on their initial investment, the initial investment is divided by the estimated present value.

To summarize these steps, the following formula can be used:

$$\text{Final ownership required} = \frac{\text{Required future value (investment)}}{\text{Total terminal value}}$$

$$= \frac{(1 + IRR)^{years} \text{ (investment)}}{\text{P/E ratio (terminal net income)}}$$

6. Finally, the number of shares and the share price must be calculated with the following formula:

$$\text{New shares} = \frac{\text{Percentage of ownership required by the investor}}{1 - \text{Percentage ownership required by the investor} \times \text{old shares}}$$

By definition, the share price equals the price paid divided by the number of shares.

The Fundamental Method

This method is simply the present value of the future earnings stream, shown in Exhibit 14.7.

The First Chicago Method[2]

Another alternative valuation method, developed at First Chicago Corporation's venture capital group, employs a lower discount rate but applies it to an *expected* cash flow. That expected cash flow is the average of three possible scenarios, with each scenario weighted according to its perceived probability. The equation to determine the investor's required final ownership is this:

$$\text{Required final ownership} = \frac{\text{Future value of investment} - \dfrac{\text{Future value of non-IPO cash flow}}{\text{Probability (success)}}}{\text{(Forecast terminal value)}}$$

This formula[3] differs from the original basic venture capital formula in two ways: (1) The basic formula assumes there are no cash flows between the investment and the harvest in Year 5; the future value of the immediate cash flows is subtracted from the future value of the investment because the difference between them is what must be made up for out of the terminal value; and (2) the basic formula does not distinguish between the *forecast* terminal

EXHIBIT 14.7

Example of the Fundamental Method

			Hitech, Inc.			
Year	Percentage Growth of Revenue	Revenue (millions)	After Tax Margin	After Tax Profit (millions)	Present Value Factor	PV of Each Year's Earnings ($ millions)
1	50%	$3.00	–0–	–0–	1.400	–0–
2	50	4.50	4.0%	$ 0.18	1.960	$0.09
3	50	6.75	7.0	0.47	2.744	0.17
4	50	10.13	9.0	0.91	3.842	0.24
5	50	15.19	11.0	1.67	5.378	0.31
6	40	21.26	11.5	2.45	7.530	0.33
7	30	27.64	12.0	3.32	10.541	0.32
8	20	33.17	12.0	3.98	14.758	0.27
9	15	38.15	12.0	4.58	20.661	0.22
10	10	41.96	12.0	5.03	28.926	0.17
Total present value of earnings in the supergrowth period						2.12
Residual future value of earnings stream				$63.00	28.926	2.18
Total present value of company						4.30

[2]This paragraph is adapted from Sahlman, "A Method for Valuing High-Risk, Long-Term Investments," p. 56.
[3]Ibid., pp. 58–59.

EXHIBIT 14.8

Example of the First Chicago Method

	Success	Sideways Survival	Failure
1. Revenue growth rate (from base of $2 million)	60%	15%	0%
2. Revenue level after 3 years	$8.19 million	$3.04 million (liquidation)	$ 2 million
3. Revenue level after 5 years	$20.97 million (IPO)	$4.02 million	
4. Revenue level after 7 years		$5.32 million (acquisition)	
5. After-tax profit margin and earnings at liquidity	15%; $3.15 million	7%; $0.37 million	
6. Price/earnings ratio at liquidity	17	7	
7. Value of company liquidity	$53.55 million	$2.61 million	$0.69 million
8. Present value of company using discount rate of 40%	$9.96 million	$0.25 million	$0.25 million
9. Probability of each scenario	0.4	0.4	0.2
10. Expected present value of the company under each scenario	$3.98 million	$0.10 million	$0.05 million
11. Expected present value of the company		$4.13 million	
12. Percentage ownership required to invest $2.5 million		60.5%	

value and the *expected* terminal value. The traditional method uses the forecast terminal value, which is adjusted through the use of a high discount rate. The formula employs the expected value of the terminal value and Exhibit 14.8 is an example using this method.

Ownership Dilution[4]

The previous example is unrealistic because in most cases, several rounds of investments are necessary to finance a high-potential venture. For instance the pricing worksheet presented in Exhibit 14.9, shows three financing rounds expected. In addition to estimating the appropriate discount rate for the current round, the first-round venture capitalist must now estimate the discount rates that are most likely to be applied in the following rounds, which are projected for Years 2 and 4. Although a 50 percent rate is still appropriate for Year 0, it is estimated that investors in Hitech, Inc., will demand a 40 percent return in Year 2 and a 25 percent return in Year 4. The final ownership that each investor must be left with, given a terminal price/earnings ratio of 15, can be calculated using the basic valuation formula:

Round 1:

$$\frac{\text{Future value (investment)}}{\text{Terminal value (company)}} = \frac{1.50^5 \times \$1.5 \text{ million}}{15. \times \$2.5 \text{ million}} = \frac{30.4\%}{\text{ownership}}$$

Round 2:

$$(1.40^3 \times \$1 \text{ million})/(15 \times \$ 2.5 \text{ million}) = 7.3\%$$

Round 3:

$$(1.25^1 \times \$1 \text{ million})/(15 \times \$1.5 \text{ million}) = 3.3\%$$

Discounted Cash Flow

In a simple discounted cash flow method, three time periods are defined: (1) Years 1–5; (2) Years 6–10; and (3) Year 11 to infinity.[5] While using this method, we should also note relationships and trade-offs. With these assumptions, the discount rate can be applied to the weighted average cost of capital (WACC).[6] Then the value for free cash flow (Years 1–10) is added to the terminal value. This terminal value is the growth perpetuity.

Other Rule-of-Thumb Valuation Methods

Several other valuation methods are also employed to estimate the value of a company. Many of these are based on recent transactions of similar firms, established by a sale of the company or a recent investment. Such comparables may look at different multiples like earnings, free cash flow, revenue, EBIT, EBITDA, and book value. Knowledgeable investment bankers and venture capitalists make it their business to know pricing activity in the private capital markets.

---

[4]Ibid., p. 24.
[5]J.A. Timmons, "Valuation Methods and Raising Capital," lecture, Babson College, 2006.
[6]Note that it is WACC, not free cash flow, because of the tax factor.

EXHIBIT 14.9

Example of a Three-Stage Financing

Hitech, Inc. (000)						
	Year 0	Year 1	Year 2	Year 3	Year 4	Year 5
Revenues	500	1,250	2,500	5,000	81,000	12,800
New income	(250)	(62)	250	750	1,360	2,500
Working capital at 20%	100	250	500	1,000	1,600	2,560
Fixed assets at 40%	200	500	1,000	2,000	3,200	5,120
Free cash flow	(550)	(512)	(500)	(750)	(440)	(380)
Cumulative external financial need	500	1,653	1,543	2,313	2,753	3,133
Equity issues	1,500	0	1,000	0	1,000	0
Equity outstanding	1,500	1,500	2,500	2,500	3,500	3,500
Cash balance	950	436	938	188	748	368
Assume: long-term IRR required each round by investors	50%	45%	40%	30%	25%	20%

Source: From "A Method for Valuing High-Risk, Long-Term Investments," by W. A. Sahlman, Harvard Business School Note 9-288-006, p. 45. Reprinted by permission of Harvard Business School; all rights reserved. Revised and updated for 2008.

Tar Pits Facing Entrepreneurs

There are several inherent conflicts between entrepreneurs and investors.[7] While the entrepreneur wants all of the investment upfront, the investors want to supply capital just as the company needs the money, using staged capital commitments to manage their risk exposure over finer increments of investing.

Staged Capital Commitments[8]

Venture capitalists rarely, if ever, invest all the external capital that a company will require to accomplish its business plan; instead they invest in companies at distinct stages in their development. As a result, each company begins life knowing that it has only enough capital to reach the next stage, or value inflection point. By staging capital, venture capitalists maintain the right to abandon a project whose prospects look dim. The right to abandon is essential because an entrepreneur will almost never stop investing in a failing project as long as others are providing capital.

Staging the capital also provides incentives to the entrepreneurial team. Capital is a scarce and expensive resource for individual ventures. Misuse of capital is very costly to venture capitalists but not necessarily to management. To encourage managers to conserve capital, venture capital firms apply strong sanctions if it is misused, and these sanctions ordinarily take two basic forms. First, increased

capital requirements invariably dilute management's equity share at an increasingly punitive rate. Second, the staged investment process enables venture capital firms to shut down operations. The credible threat to abandon a venture, even when the firm might be economically viable, is the key to the relationship between the entrepreneur and the venture capitalists. By denying capital, the venture capitalist also signals other capital suppliers that the company is a bad investment risk.

Structuring the Deal

What Is a Deal?

Deals are defined as economic agreements between at least two parties. In the context of entrepreneurial finance, most deals involve the allocation of cash flow streams (with respect to both amount and timing), the allocation of risk, and hence the allocation of value between different groups.

A Way of Thinking about Deals over Time   To assess and to design long-lived deals, the authors suggest asking a series of questions of the stakeholders as a guide for deal makers in structuring and in understanding how deals evolve:

- Who are the stakeholders?
- How does each stakeholder group define value?
- What is the risk tolerance of each stakeholder group?

---

[7]J.A. Timmons, "Deals and Deal Structuring," lecture, Babson College, 2006.

[8]W.A. Sahlman, "Structure of Venture Capital Organizations," *Journal of Financial Economics* 27 (1990), pp. 506–507. Reprinted with the permission of Elsevier.

- How do the stakeholders see the nature of your opportunity?
- How much "skin in the game" does each stakeholder have?
- What is each stakeholder's ownership right?
- Do the stakeholders perceive their influence on the company as active or passive?
- What is the action orientation of each stakeholder group?
- What leverage over you do they have?

The Characteristics of Successful Deals

While deal making is ultimately a combination of art and science, it is possible to describe some of the characteristics of deals that have proven successful over time:

- They are simple.
- They are robust (they do not fall apart when there are minor deviations from projections).
- They are organic (they are not immutable).
- They take into account the incentives of each party to the deal under a variety of circumstances.
- They provide mechanisms for communications and interpretation.
- They are based primarily on trust rather than on legalese.
- They are not patently unfair.
- They do not make it too difficult to raise additional capital.
- They match the needs of the user of capital with the needs of the supplier.
- They reveal information about each party
- They allow for the arrival of new information before financing is required.
- They do not preserve discontinuities (e.g., boundary conditions that will evoke dysfunctional behavior on the part of the agents of principals).
- They consider the fact that it takes time to raise money.
- They improve the chances of success for the venture.

The Generic Elements of Deals   A number of terms govern value distribution, as well as basic definitions, assumptions, performance incentives, rights, and obligations. Representations and warranties, default clauses, remedial action and covenants are all parts of the deal structure.

Tools for Managing Risk/Reward   In a deal, the claims on cash and equity are prioritized by the players through tools like common stock, partnerships, preferred stock (dividend and liquidation preference), debt (secured, unsecured, personally guaranteed, or convertible), performance conditional pricing (ratchets), puts and calls, warrants, and cash. Some of the critical aspects of a deal can go beyond just the money[9]:

- Number, type, and mix of stocks and various features that may go with them that affect the investor's ROR.
- The amounts and timing of takedowns and conversions.
- Interest rates on debt or preferred shares.
- The number of seats and the players on the board of directors.
- Possible changes to the current management team and the board.
- Registration rights for investor's stock in the case of a registered public offering.
- Right of first refusal granted to the investor in subsequent private placements or an IPO.
- Employment, noncompete, and proprietary rights agreements.
- The payment of legal, accounting, consulting, or other fees connected with putting the deal together.
- Specific performance targets for revenues, expenses, market penetration, and the like by certain target dates.

Understanding the Bets

Deals, because they are based on cash, risk, and time, are subject to interpretation. The players' perceptions of each of these factors contribute to the overall valuation of the venture and the proposed deal. As was described earlier, there are a number of different ways to value a venture, and these various valuation methods contribute to the complexity of deals. Consider, for instance, the following term sheets[10]:

- A venture capital firm proposes to raise $150 million to $200 million to acquire and build RSA Cellular Phone Properties. The venture capital firm will commit between $15 million and $30 million in equity and will lead in raising senior and subordinated debt to buy licenses. Licensees will have to claim about

---

[9]Timmons, Spinelli, and Zacharakis, "How to Raise Capital," McGraw-Hill, 2004.
[10]Timmons, "Deals and Deal Structuring" lecture, Babson College, 2006.

30 percent of the future equity value in the new company; the venture capital firm will claim 60 percent (subordinated debt claim is estimated at 10 percent); and management will get 5 to 10 percent of the future equity, but only after all prior return targets have been achieved. The venture capital firm's worst-case scenario will result in 33 percent ROR to the firm, 9 percent ROR to licensees, and 0 percent for management. The noncompete agreements extend for 12 years, in addition to the vesting.

- An entrepreneur must decide between two deals:

> Deal A: A venture capital firm will lead a $3 million investment and requires management to invest $1 million. Future gains are to be split 50-50 after the venture capital firm has achieved a 25 percent ROR on the investment. Other common investment provisions also apply (vesting, employment agreements, etc.). The venture capital firm has the right of first refusal on all future rounds and other deals management may find.

> Deal B: Another venture capital firm will lead a $4 million investment. Management will invest nothing. The future gains are to be split 75 percent for the venture capital firm and 25 percent for management on a side-by-side basis. Until the venture achieves positive cash flow, this venture capital firm has the right of first refusal on future financing and deals management may find.

- A group of very talented money managers is given $40 million in capital to manage. The contract calls for the managers to receive 20 percent of the excess return on the portfolio over the Treasury bond return. The contract runs for 5 years. The managers cannot take out any of their share of the gains until the last day of the contracts except to pay taxes.

While reading and considering these deals, try to identify the underlying assumptions, motivations, and beliefs of the individuals proposing the deals. Following are some questions that may help in identifying the players' bets:

- What is the bet?
- Whom is it for?
- Who is taking the risk? Who receives the rewards?

- Who should be making these bets?
- What will happen if the entrepreneurs exceed the venture capitalists' expectations? What if they fall short?
- What are the incentives for the money managers? What are the consequences of their success or failure to perform?
- How will the money managers behave? What will be their investing strategy?

The Specific Issues Entrepreneurs Typically Face[11]

Whatever method you choose in your negotiations, the primary focus is likely to be on how much the entrepreneur's equity is worth and how much is to be purchased by the investor's investment. Even so, numerous other issues involving legal and financial control of the company and the rights and obligations of various investors and the entrepreneur in various situations may be as important as valuation and ownership share. Not the least of these is the value behind the money–such as contacts and helpful expertise, additional financing when and if required, and patience and interest in the long-term development of the company–that a particular investor can bring to the venture. The following are some of the most critical aspects of a deal that go beyond "just the money":

- Number, type, and mix of stocks (and perhaps of stock and debt) and various features that may go with them (such as puts) that affect the investor's ROR.
- The amounts and timing of takedowns, conversions, and the like.
- Interest rate in debt or preferred shares.
- The number of seats, and who actually will represent investors, on the board of directors.
- Possible changes in the management team and in the composition of the board of directors.
- Registration rights for investor's stock (in case of a registered public offering).
- Right of first refusal granted to the investor on subsequent private or initial public stock offerings.
- Stock vesting schedule and agreements.
- The payment of legal, accounting, consulting, or other fees connected with putting the deal together.

[11]Ibid.

Entrepreneurs may find some subtle but important terms need to be negotiated and if they, or their attorneys, are not familiar with these, they may be viewed as boilerplate when they have crucial future implications for the ownership, control, and financing of the business. Here are some issues that can be burdensome for entrepreneurs:

- *Co-sale provision.* This is a provision by which investors can tender their shares of stock before an IPO. It protects the first-round investors but can cause conflicts with investors in later rounds and can inhibit an entrepreneur's ability to cash out.

- *Ratchet anti-dilution protection.* This enables the lead investors to get free additional common stock if subsequent shares are ever sold at a price lower than originally paid. This protection allows first-round investors to prevent the company from raising additional necessary funds during a period of adversity for the company. While nice from the investor's perspective, it ignores the reality that in distress situations the last money calls the shots on price and deal structure.

- *Washout financing.* This is a strategy of last resort that wipes out all previously issued stock when existing preferred shareholders will not invest additional funds, thus diluting everyone.

- *Forced buyout.* Under this provision, if management does not find a buyer or cannot take the company public by a certain date, then the investors can find a buyer at terms they agree upon.

- *Demand registration rights.* Here investors can demand an IPO. In reality, such clauses are hard to invoke because the market for new public stock issues, not the terms of an agreement, ultimately governs the timing of such events.

- *Piggyback registration rights.* These grant to the investors rights to sell stock at the IPO. Because the underwriters usually make this decision, the clause normally is not enforceable.

- *Key-person insurance.* This requires the company to obtain life insurance on key people. The named beneficiary of the insurance can be either the company or the preferred shareholders.

The Term Sheet

Regardless of whether you secure capital from angels or venture capitalists, you will want to be informed and knowledgeable about the terms and conditions that govern the deal you sign. Many experienced entrepreneurs will argue that the terms and who your investor is are more important than the valuation. To illustrate this point, consider the choice among four common instruments: (1) fully participating preferred stock, (2) partially participating preferred stock (four times return), (3) common preference ($1.00/share to common), and (4) nonparticipating preferred stock. Then consider a $200 million harvest realized through either an IPO or an acquisition by another company. Why does any of this matter? Are not these details better left to the legal experts?

Consider the economic consequences of each of these deal instruments under the two harvest scenarios in Exhibit 14.10. The graph shows there can be up to a $24 million difference in the payout received, even though, in the example, there are equal numbers of shares of common stock, typically owned by the founders, and preferred stock, owned by investors. The acquisition exit is more favorable to investors, especially because periodically the IPO market is closed to new companies.

Sand Traps[12]

Strategic Circumference

Each fund-raising strategy sets in motion some actions and commitments by management that will eventually scribe a circumference around the company in terms of its current and future financing choices. These future choices will permit varying degrees of freedom as a result of the previous actions. Those who fail to think through the consequences of a fund-raising strategy and the effect on their degrees of freedom fall into this trap. For example, a company that plans to remain private or plans to maintain a 1.5 to 1.0 debt-to-equity ratio has intentionally created a strategic circumference.

Legal Circumference

Many people have an aversion to becoming involved in legal or accounting minutiae. Many believe that because they pay sizable professional fees, their advisors should and will pay attention to the details.

---

[12]Copyright © 1990 by Jeffry A. Timmons.

EXHIBIT 14.10

Considering the Economics: $200 Million IPO or Acquisition?

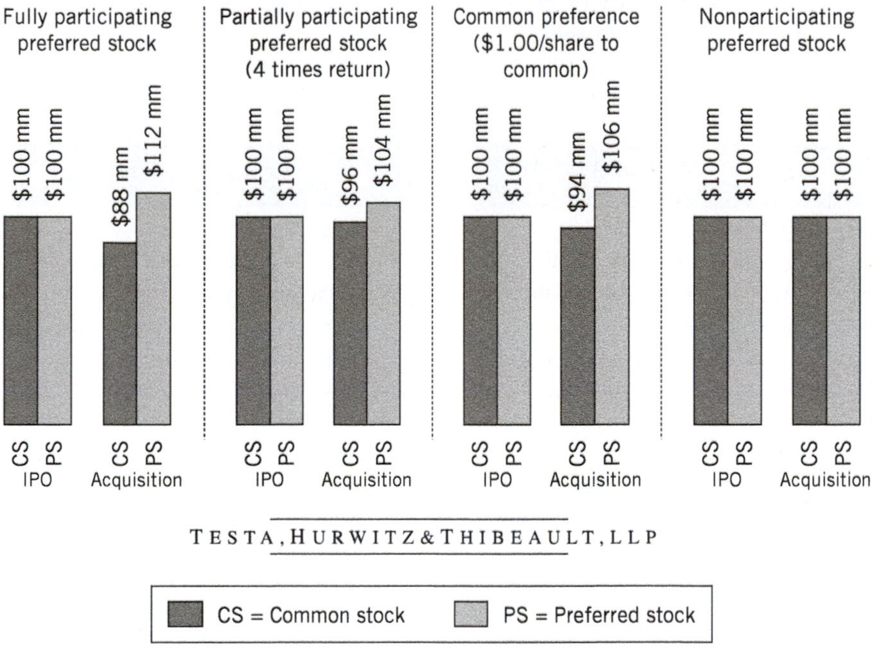

Fully participating preferred stock	Partially participating preferred stock (4 times return)	Common preference ($1.00/share to common)	Nonparticipating preferred stock
CS: $100 mm, PS: $100 mm (IPO); CS: $88 mm, PS: $112 mm (Acquisition)	CS: $100 mm, PS: $100 mm (IPO); CS: $96 mm, PS: $104 mm (Acquisition)	CS: $100 mm, PS: $100 mm (IPO); CS: $94 mm, PS: $106 mm (Acquisition)	CS: $100 mm, PS: $100 mm (IPO); CS: $100 mm, PS: $100 mm (Acquisition)

TESTA, HURWITZ & THIBEAULT, LLP

CS = Common stock   PS = Preferred stock

Source: Testa, Hurwitz & Thibeault, LLP, from a presentation by Heather M. Stone and Brian D. Goldstein at Babson College, October 3, 2001.

Legal documentation spells out the terms, conditions, responsibilities, and rights of the parties to a transaction. Because different sources have different ways of structuring deals, and because these legal and contractual details come at the *end* of the fund-raising process, an entrepreneur may arrive at a point of no return, facing some onerous conditions and covenants that not only are difficult to live with but also create tight limitations and constraints—legal circumference—on future choices that are potentially harmful. Entrepreneurs cannot rely exclusively on attorneys and advisors to protect them when negotiating these vital matters.

Unknown Territory

Venturing into unknown territory is another problem. Entrepreneurs need to know the terrain in sufficient detail, particularly the requirements and alternatives of various equity sources. If they do not, they may make critical blunders and waste time.

For example, a venture that is not a "mainstream venture capital deal" may be overvalued and directed to investors who are not a realistic match, rather than being realistically valued and directed to small and more specialized funds, private investors, or potential strategic partners.

Chapter Summary

- There is rarely a "fair fight" between users (entrepreneurs) and suppliers of capital (investors). Entrepreneurs need to be prepared by learning how the capital markets determine valuation risk.

- Several valuation methods are used to arrive at value for a company, the venture capital method being the most common.

- Investors prefer to stage their capital commitments, thereby managing and containing the risk and preserving their options to invest further or cease.

- Numerous potential conflicts exist between users and suppliers of capital, and these require appreciation and managing. The economic consequences can be worth millions to founders.

- Successful deals are characterized by careful thought and sensitive balance among a range of important issues.
- Deal structure can make or break an otherwise sound venture, and the devil is always in the details.

- Negotiating the deal is both art and science, and also can make or break the relationship.
- The entrepreneur encounters numerous strategic, legal, and other "sand traps" during the fund-raising cycle and needs awareness and skill in coping with them.

Study Questions

1. Why can there be such wide variations in the valuations investors and founders place on companies?
2. What are the determinants of value?
3. Define and explain why the following are important: long-term value creation, IRR, investor's required share of ownership, DCF, deal structure, and sand traps in fund-raising.
4. Explain five prevalent methods used in valuing a company and their strengths and weaknesses, given their underlying assumptions.
5. What is a staged capital commitment, and why is it important?
6. What is a company worth? Explain the theory and the reality of valuation.
7. What is a "cram-down" round?
8. What are some of the inherent conflicts between investors and entrepreneurs, and how and why can these affect a venture's odds for success?
9. What are the most important questions and issues to consider in structuring a deal? Why?
10. What issues can be negotiated in a venture investment, and why are these important?
11. What are the pitfalls and sand traps in fund-raising, and why do entrepreneurs sometimes fail to avoid them?

Internet Resources

http://www.valuationresources.com/ *Valuation Resources is a free resource guide to business valuation resources, industry and company information, economic data, and more.*

http://www.nacva.com/ *The National Association of Certified Valuation Analysts.*

Wiki–Google Search

Try these keywords and phrases:
valuation methods
deal structure
terms sheet

negotiating deals
venture capital
dilution

Case

Lightwave Technology, Inc.

Preparation Questions

1. In anticipation of an IPO, should Lightwave get another round of bridge financing? Why or why not?

2. How would you structure and price this round, and why?

3. What should Kinson and Weiss do to grow their company?

4. How should Lightwave decide whether to pursue an IPO? How does it plan and manage the IPO process?

> *The success of light-emitting diodes (LEDs) lies in their longevity (LEDs outlast incandescent lamps by a factor of 10), energy efficiency, durability, low maintenance cost, and compact size. Replacing conventional lamps with LEDs in the United States alone will bring energy benefits of up to $100 billion by 2025, saving up to 120 gigawatts of electricity annually.*
>
> Light-Emitting Diodes 2002;
> Strategic Summit for LEDs
> in Illumination

In summer 2003, seasoned entrepreneurs George Kinson and Dr. Schyler Weiss were again considering an initial public offering (IPO) for their illumination company, Lightwave Technology.

They first considered one in 2001, just before the Internet bubble burst. Instead, they had to implement a restructuring plan to reorganize Lightwave, which got the company back on track.

Because the IPO market was still soft, Kinson wondered whether Lightwave should remain private until it had better numbers and greater dominance in some key market segments. On the other hand, a successful IPO would provide capital and the high profile in the industry that could enable it to achieve those numbers and that dominance.

Traditional Illumination Products

Since the invention of the light bulb, several improvements had modified the lighting industry. Still, the standard screw-in light bulb remained its focus.

The lighting market had two segments: lamps (the bulbs and tubes) and fixtures (the plastic, metal, and glass housings for the lamps). In 2001,

the illumination industry had $79 billion in sales: $17 billion in lamps and $62 billion in fixtures.[1] More than one-third involved indoor lighting, with lamps and outdoor lighting being the next largest segments. The United States represented 26 percent of the world market.

The industry was dominated by a small group of multinationals, including General Electric Lighting, Philips Lighting, and OSRAM Sylvania, Inc., which together controlled at least 90 percent of the U.S. lamp market and 60 percent of the world lamp market in commercial lighting.[2] Each had a wide range of products for residential and commercial applications and was involved in the research and development of new products modified from existing lighting technology.

Solid-State Lighting

Light-emitting diodes (LEDs—small semiconductors encased in an epoxy material that give off light when electrically charged—had been around since the 1960s. By varying the structure of the semiconductor, or the band gap, the energy level of the LED changed to produce a colored light, typically either red or green (Exhibit A). The first applications of LEDs were clocks and indicators on appliances.

As solid-state lighting (SSL), LEDs exhibited theoretical quantum efficiencies (i.e., volume of light generated per unit of electrical input) of 60 to 70 percent. Incandescent and fluorescent lamps had topped out at 5 percent and 20 percent, respectively.[3] SSL was particularly efficient for colorized lighting. Unlike traditional fixtures, which used colored filters that could reduce standard lamps' luminous output by 70 to 80 percent. SSL emitted colors. Regular lights produced ultraviolet radiation that could damage or discolor many materials and cause skin and eye conditions. LEDs produced virtually no UV radiation. And rather than burn out like incandescent bulbs, SSL faded over time. Those attributes—in addition to long life, flexible form factors, and strong color contrast—made SSL appeal to a range of industrial, architectural, and retail businesses. For example, attracted by its low heat, fast turn-on time, and small size, automobile manufacturers were using SSL for brake, accent, and console lights.

This case was prepared by Carl Hedberg under the direction of Professor Jeffry A. Timmons. © Copyright Jeffry A. Timmons, 2005. All rights reserved.

[1]Freedonia Group, Inc., www.freedoniagroup.com.
[2]P. Thurk, "Solid State Lighting: The Case for Reinventing the Light Bulb," research paper in fulfillment of the requirements of a Kauffman Fellows Program grant, July 2002, p. 7.
[3]Ibid., pp. 4-5.

EXHIBIT A

How an LED Emits Colored Light

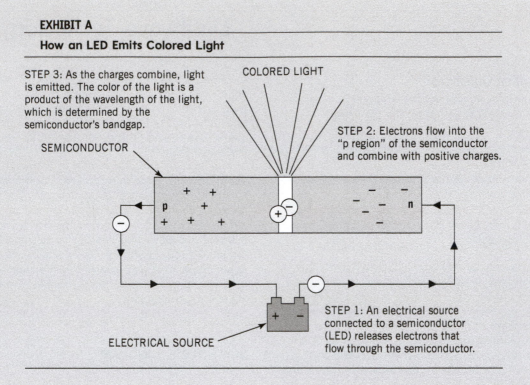

STEP 3: As the charges combine, light is emitted. The color of the light is a product of the wavelength of the light, which is determined by the semiconductor's bandgap.

COLORED LIGHT

STEP 2: Electrons flow into the "p region" of the semiconductor and combine with positive charges.

SEMICONDUCTOR

STEP 1: An electrical source connected to a semiconductor (LED) releases electrons that flow through the semiconductor.

ELECTRICAL SOURCE

Disruptive Ideas

Kinson and Weiss met at Carnegie Mellon University. Kinson was a research engineer in CMU's Field Robotics Center and attended its Graduate School of Industrial Administration. In 1993, he earned a degree in electrical and computer engineering, with a minor in fine art.

Weiss received his undergraduate, master's, and PhD degrees in electrical and computer engineering from Carnegie Mellon. His PhD thesis involved low-power digital circuitry. In the early 1990s, Weiss and Kinson tinkered with LEDs and concluded the technology was the future of illumination once someone invented a blue LED that could be digitally blended with existing red and green LEDs to create a full spectrum of colors.

By 1994, Kinson had co-founded a successful online securities portal, and Weiss had started up a software developer. Still, in 1996, when a Japanese group produced a blue LED, Kinson said they were ready to charge ahead:

> We had always figured that the development of a blue LED would change the way that people used LEDs. It just so happened that the one they created was a very bright blue LED, and that brought about tremendous change very quickly. We realized that this new, high-intensity technology was perfect for illumination, and we had done enough research on this boring, old, complacent industry to know how slowly they would react to any sort of disruptive

technology.[4] . . . Even though we felt we had a pretty big window of opportunity, we wanted to move fast.

The engineers began developing a digital color palette, pioneering a new industry—intelligent semiconductor illumination technologies—in the process. In spring 1997, Kinson left his company and, with Weiss's help, began developing their company's business model, business plan, and prototypes.

Lightwave Technology, Inc.

That summer, Kinson used his savings and credit cards to finance the company. After racking up $44,000 in credit card debt and shrinking his savings to $16, he incorporated Lightwave and filed for patent protection on its color mixer.

By linking red, green, and blue LEDs to a microprocessor, Lightwave could, with a very small device, tremendously expand the color-producing capabilities of lighting. Each string of LEDs linked to a microprocessor could generate up to 24-bit color (16.7 million colors) and such effects as color washing and strobe lighting.

---

[4]Disruptive technology was an idea developed by Clayton Christensen of the Harvard Business School. In his book, *The Innovator's Dilemma*, Christensen defined a disruptive technology as an innovation that disrupted performance trajectories and resulted in the failure of the industry's leading firms.

Believing their business would grow around the demands and imagination of clients in industries from architecture to entertainment, Kinson and Weiss decided to demonstrate its capabilities at the International Lighting Exposition in Las Vegas.

Affirmation

Kinson said the show demonstrated Lightwave could reinvent the illumination market:

> Schyler and I, accompanied by four MIT Sloan School students, flew out to this trade show with two backpacks full of prototypes. This was the first time we had shown these in public, and then we win Architectural Lighting Product of the Year—the top award. That's a pretty good statement from the industry that intelligent semiconductor illumination technology was a significant opportunity.

Lightwave's capabilities had immediate appeal—particularly in the retailing markets—because a tiny microprocessor system could replace lighting setups with numerous bulbs and large mechanical controls.

Lightwave's technology had functional—as well as aesthetic—benefits over conventional lighting technology. Its lower heat and lack of UV emissions meant SSL could be used where conventional lights could not, such as in retail displays, and near clothing and artwork. And since Lightwave products could be designed to complement existing technologies, they could be used alongside conventional lighting.

Lightwave's team also envisioned significant economic and environmental benefit from LED technologies. While conventional lighting products had an average life of hundreds or thousands of hours, the estimated life of LEDs was around 100,000 hours, or a little more than 11 years. Because lighting was a large energy user ($\sim$ 20 percent of the estimated $1 trillion spent annually on electricity[5]), SSL could produce significant savings. For general illumination for residences, hospitals, businesses, and the like, moving to SSL worldwide annually would save over $100 billion in electricity costs and reduce carbon emissions by 200 million tons. It also would alleviate the need for $50 billion in power plant construction.[6]

The technology's efficiency was attracting institutional users as well. California, for instance, was offering subsidies of up to 50 percent of the purchase price to municipalities that converted to SSL traffic signals. The state also offered subsidies of up to the entire purchase price for businesses that switched from neon to SSL signs.

Although SSL was a small portion of the overall illumination market, it had increased at a rate of 11 percent over the previous seven years to almost $2.3 billion in 1999. Signage lighting—which included full-color outdoor displays, highway signs, and traffic signals—was the largest market segment at 23 percent, or about $530 million. The market for full-color LED outdoor display sign lighting grew at almost 78 percent per year from 1995 to about $150 million in 1999.

Communications equipment displays were the second largest sector at 22 percent, followed by displays for computers and office equipment at 21 percent. The remainder of the market was divided among consumer applications (15 percent); automotive displays and lighting (11 percent); and industrial instrumentation (8 percent).[7] High-brightness LEDs—crucial to the illumination industry—had sales of $680 million in 1999 (up nearly 500 percent from $120 million in 1995). This was projected to reach almost $1.75 billion by 2004.[8]

Despite the progress, illumination industry experts were very slow to embrace LEDs. Kinson explained that while there were still hurdles to overcome, advances in SSL technology would eventually force lighting companies to change how they did business:

> Similar to other disruptive technologies, LEDs are hitting an incumbent market by surprise and therefore are frequently discredited due to the traditional metrics that apply to the old market—in our case, illumination intensity and price. But what's fascinating is that while traditional "brass, gas, and glass" technology is not seeing dramatic growth, Haitz's Law [Exhibit B] shows that LEDs are exhibiting dramatic increases in intensity and longevity while the cost of making them is rapidly decreasing. Sure, low price and brightness are still not there for the white light market, but that will come. So everybody who works with or uses lighting in their business needs to look at what is going on here; if they don't change, they're going to be left behind.

Pioneering

Following the success at the lighting convention, Kinson finished an $842,347 angel financing round. It wasn't easy, however. Kinson had spoken with over 150 prospective investors and called the head of a leading lighting manufacturer 35 times before getting a response.

[5]Bergh, Craford, Duggal, and Haitz, "The Promise and Challenge of Solid-State Lighting," *Physics Today*, December 2001, pp. 42–47.

[6]Tsao, Nelson, Haitz, Kish (Hewlett-Packard), "The Case for a National Research Program on Semiconductor Lighting," presented at the 1999 Optoelectronics Industry Development Association forum in Washington DC, October 6, 1999.

[7]Strategies Unlimited, *High-Brightness LED Market Overview and Forecast*, February 2000.

[8]Ibid.

EXHIBIT B

Haitz's Law: LED Light Output Increasing/Cost Decreasing

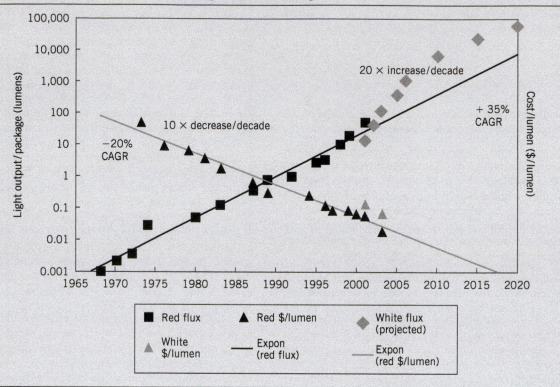

Source: Roland Haitz & Lumileds.

Lightwave rented space across the hall from Kinson's apartment. Bootstrapping every step of the way, Kinson built the company's first server on a desktop computer using a Linux platform. The mail server, Web site, domain name, and office network all ran through a single desktop computer—accessed through a dial-up connection. In January 1998, Lightwave hired its first outside employee, Daniel Murdock, as vice president of finance.

As a pioneer in full-spectrum SSL technology intent on gaining a sizable lead on established industry players, Lightwave aggressively patented its technology and applications. The partners believed their revolutionary technology and strong intellectual property portfolio had wide-ranging market and licensing opportunities in a number of markets (Exhibit C). Kinson commented on this aspect of their mission:

> One of our primary strategies is to file for all the intellectual property that we can, because we realize this will be a huge market in the future. We plan to have a war chest of patents to protect our interest in the market—and quite a few of those patents will be applicable in the emerging white light segment. Our intellectual property portfolio is probably going to be the strongest asset in our company.

Lightwave shipped its first order in September 1998. The company grew rapidly the next two years, moving to a large space in downtown Boston and expanding to over 75 employees. It continued developing products and applications at a frenetic pace.

In May 2000, Lightwave opened a European sales office. That December, it established a joint venture Japanese distributorship. The venture's channel partners included lighting product distributors, manufacturers' representatives, and original equipment manufacturers (OEMs). Marketing efforts involved industry analyst updates; appearances at industry conferences and trade shows; Web promotions; news articles; electronic newsletters; print ads; and speaking engagements. The marketing department also provided a variety of customer requirements, pricing, and positioning analysis for existing and new product offerings, and produced extensive material for distribution to potential customers.

Determined to stay flexible and lean, the company outsourced its manufacturing, developing supply agreements that allowed it to procure LEDs at favorable pricing with short lead times. Finished products and control systems were manufactured by companies in the United States and China, with the latter supplying the high-volume, low-priced items.

EXHIBIT C

Target Markets (Excerpted from the Lightwave Offering Memorandum)

The markets for our lighting systems include the traditional markets for color-changing lighting such as theater and entertainment venues. However, many applications for this technology exist in numerous additional markets. Our lighting systems have been installed in thousands of end-user sites worldwide, in applications such as the following:

Commercial and Civic Architecture. Our lighting systems are used to differentiate and accentuate architectural elements in a wide variety of corporate offices, public spaces, bridges, monuments, fountains, government facilities, churches, schools, universities, and hospitals.

Hospitality. Hotels, casinos, cruise ships, restaurants, bars, and nightclubs add entertainment elements to their properties to attract and retain patrons. Dynamic lighting is an effective tool because much of this industry's business comes alive in the evening hours.

Retail and Merchandising. Retailers competing for customer attention add entertainment value to the shopping experience by using dynamic lighting in their overall store design, in visual merchandising programs, and in store window displays.

Entertainment, Events, and Theatrical Production. Theaters, concert halls, amusement parks, themed environments, and producers of live performances and events make extensive use of dramatic theatrical lighting and appreciate the enhanced dynamic that lighting adds to set design, stage lighting, and themed displays.

TV Production. Studio-based television news programs, game shows, and talk shows use dynamic lighting to add excitement, glamour, and identity to show set designs and fill lighting.

Electronic Signage and Corporate Identity. Signage and point-of-purchase designers and fabricators use dynamic lighting in projects such as backlit and uplit displays, glass signs, interior or exterior signs, and channel letters.

Residential Architecture. Specialty and accent lighting are used in residential projects for applications such as cove, cabinet, undercounter, and landscape lighting, and home theaters.

Exhibits, Display, and Museums. Dynamic lighting is used in trade show booths and museum displays to highlight featured areas or to add impact and entertainment value to the overall display.

Kinson kept raising capital, and by early 2001 Lightwave had secured just over $31 million in four rounds of funding.[9]

Lightwave's success had not gone unnoticed. Since 1999, several ventures had been created between large traditional illumination companies and young, technologically advanced LED companies. Philips Lighting had joined up with Agilent Technologies to form an SSL venture called LumiLeds. Similarly, GE Lighting formed GELcore with the semiconductor company EMCORE, and OSRAM was working with LEDs in a subsidiary of Siemens in Germany. In addition, researchers from Agilent and Sandia National Laboratories in Albuquerque, New Mexico, were seeking federal funding for a $500 million, 10-year research program on semiconductor lighting.

In response, Kinson and his team felt an IPO was their best strategy. They thought going public would enhance their international exposure and provide them with enough capital to support rapid adoption of their products across a wide range of industries. They planned their public offering for summer 2001.

Pulling Back

The September 2001 terrorist attacks and Internet bust forced Lightwave to shelve its IPO plans. In the following months, the company saw a precipitous drop in orders and a recession-driven lack of interest by potential customers to pursue new and innovative projects. The company terminated 11 employees and abandoned a large portion of a noncancelable operating lease at its Boston facility.

Despite a nearly $3.9 million restructuring charge and dashed IPO hopes, Lightwave continued making progress in its core architecture and entertainment markets. By summer 2003, the company had stabilized and was poised to achieve cash flow breakeven in the coming year (Exhibits D–F).

A Pivotal Time

Kinson, Weiss, and their team seemed poised to influence the course of the entire lighting industry into the next century. The question was how best to position their company for the next big push.

[9]Series A—$842,347 for 1,020,285 shares; Series B—$4,354,994 for 3,956,208 shares; Series C—$13,020,880 for 3,355,897 shares; and Series D—$12,944,178 for 2,725,377 shares.

EXHIBIT D

Income Statements

	Internal Company Projections				
	2000	2001	2002	2003	2004
Revenues					
Lighting systems	15,080,547	18,037,552	26,197,034	34,435,012	47,040,012
OEM and licensing	1,485,653	2,128,806	2,651,466	5,714,988	5,714,988
Total Revenues	16,566,200	20,166,358	28,848,500	40,150,000	52,755,000
Cost of Revenues					
Lighting systems	10,556,540	11,224,786	13,285,688	16,777,212	23,012,000
OEM and licensing	1,013,804	1,448,029	1,489,807	3,072,788	3,138,000
Total Cost of Revenues	11,570,344	12,672,815	14,775,495	19,850,000	26,150,000
Gross Profit	4,995,856	7,493,543	14,073,005	20,300,000	26,605,000
Operating Expenses					
Selling and marketing	9,345,322	7,847,764	7,615,145	8,515,000	11,191,000
Research and development	2,810,842	2,826,032	2,465,599	3,510,000	3,510,000
General and administrative	3,706,739	4,494,364	4,607,946	6,750,000	6,750,000
Restructuring	3,887,865		161,413		
Total Operating Expenses	19,750,768	15,168,160	14,850,103	18,775,000	21,451,000
Operating income (loss)	(14,754,912)	(7,674,617)	(777,098)	1,525,000	5,154,000
Interest income (expense), net	48,283	124,922	46,782	518,000	680,000
Equity in earnings of joint venture (Japan)	24,415	85,232	3,350	300,000	395,000
Net income (loss)	(14,682,214)	(7,464,463)	(726,966)	2,343,000	6,229,000

EXHIBIT E

Cash Flow Statements

	2000	2001	2002
Cash Flows from Operating Activities			
Net loss	(14,682,214)	(7,464,463)	(726,966)
Adjustment to reconcile net loss to cash from operating activities:			
Depreciation and amortization	863,874	828,083	873,138
Stock-based compensation	150,000		76,449
Write-off of leasehold improvements in connection with restructuring	592,200		
Equity in earnings of joint venture (Japan)	(24,415)	(85,232)	(3,350)
Changes in current assets and liabilities			
Accounts receivable	329,027	443,049	(899,192)
Inventory	(1,588,379)	2,834,707	(1,502,304)
Prepaid expenses and other current assets	(44,526)	(62,983)	(113,144)
Restricted cash	480,848	(612,017)	676,436
Accounts payable	(675,949)	(475,901)	(41,502)
Accrued expenses	1,158,172	(757,473)	465,226
Deferred revenue	86,728	91,582	180,832
Accrued restructuring	1,956,152	(111,145)	(385,491)
Cash Flows from Operating Activities	(11,398,482)	(5,371,793)	(1,399,868)

(continued)

EXHIBIT E   (concluded)

Cash Flow Statements

	2000	2001	2002
Cash Flows from Investing Activities			
Investment in joint venture (Japan)	(165,260)		
Purchase of property and equipment	(1,085,427)	(467,181)	(519,197)
Cash Flows from Investing Activities	(1,250,687)	(467,181)	(519,197)
Cash Flows from Financing Activities			
Payments under equipment note payable and line of credit	(359,958)	(1,669,999)	(100,000)
Borrowings under line of credit	1,650,000		
Proceeds from the exercise of stock options	11,345	20,940	13,055
Proceeds from issuance of redeemable convertible preferred; net of issuance costs	17,095,382	6,883,266	
Cash Flows from Financing Activities	18,396,769	5,234,207	(86,945)
Effect of exchange rate changes on cash			3,719
Increase (Decrease) in Cash and Equivalents	5,747,600	(604,767)	(2,002,291)
Cash and equivalents: beginning of year	2,545,908	8,293,508	7,688,741
Cash and equivalents: end of year	8,293,508	7,688,741	5,686,450

EXHIBIT F

Balance Sheets

Assets	2001	2002
Current Assets		
Cash and equivalents	7,688,741	5,686,450
Restricted cash	1,055,748	479,312
Accounts receivable	3,450,919	4,284,529
Allowance for doubtful accounts	(469,000)	(270,000)
Accounts receivable from related parties	163,217	29,799
Inventory	3,522,002	5,024,306
Prepaid expenses and other current assets	315,304	428,448
Total Current Assets	15,726,931	15,662,844
Property and Equipment: at Cost		
Computer equipment	1,334,784	1,503,046
Furniture and fixtures	640,105	624,899
Tooling	541,899	873,961
Leasehold improvements	996,882	996,882
Less: accumulated depreciation and amortization	(2,094,333)	(2,933,392)
Property and Equipment: Net	1,419,337	1,065,396
Investment in joint venture	285,082	288,432
Restricted cash: long-term portion	1,200,000	1,100,000
Total Assets	18,631,350	18,116,672

(continued)

EXHIBIT F   (concluded)

Balance Sheets

Assets	2001	2002
Liabilities and Stockholders' Equity (Deficiency)		
Current Liabilities		
Current portion of equipment note payable	100,000	
Accounts payable	1,546,392	1,483,324
Accounts payable to related party		21,566
Accrued expenses	911,956	811,970
Accrued compensation	760,567	1,471,202
Accrued restructuring	434,135	425,692
Accrued warranty	549,014	403,591
Deferred revenue	205,831	386,663
Total Current Liabilities	4,507,895	5,004,008
Accrued restructuring	1,410,872	1,033,824
Redeemable convertible preferred stock	41,115,602	41,115,602
Stockholders' Equity (Deficiency)		
Common stock, $0.001 par value; authorized 34,000,000 shares; issued and outstanding 2,781,419 and 2,804,325 shares in 2001 and 2002, respectively (12,130,979 shares pro forma)	2,781	2,804
Additional paid-in capital	214,869	304,350
Accumulated other comprehensive income	10,177	13,896
Accumulated deficit	(28,630,846)	(29,357,812)
Total Stockholders' Equity (Deficiency)	(28,403,019)	(29,036,762)
Liabilities and Stockholders' Equity	18,631,350	18,116,672

Chapter Fifteen

Obtaining Debt Capital

LEARNING OUTCOMES: What this chapter covers:

15-1 Subprime loans and credit markets

15-2 The cyclical patterns of lending

15-3 Sources of debt capital

15-4 Leasing

15-5 Before the loan decision

15-6 Approaching and meeting the banker

15-7 The lending decision

2007: Subprime Loans Take Down Credit Markets

There was an unexpected story in the summer of 2007. The economy was experiencing the longest economic expansion in history without at least a 10 percent equity market correction for 71 months by October 2007, which was 12 months longer than the previous record in 1982 to 1987 of 64 months. The real estate boom of the post-2000 stock market meltdown and post 9/11 economic rebound was in its finale. Risky subprime loans had fueled a new version of "irrational exuberance" that drove lending and residential real estate prices to unsustainable levels. In a few short days in July the party was over, with major repercussions throughout the credit and banking system. A liquidity crisis ensued; banks simply did not have enough cash to meet their obligations. As it did in 1987, the Federal Reserve stepped in to lend money to the banking system in order to avert a deepening crisis. In September 2007 it lowered the Federal Reserve discount rate a surprising 50 basis points for the first time in over 4 years, and more reductions were expected by early 2008. The Fed's aim was to soften the housing recession and to prevent a wider economic recession in the United States.

The Cyclical Patterns of Lending: Shades of 1990 to 1993

Any time such a credit crisis occurs it takes a toll throughout the economy. Consumers, which represent 70% of the U.S. economy, reduce spending. Banks stop lending or when they do up their equity requirements significantly, from 10 to 25 percent in a typical case.

For entrepreneurs and their investors, the punishing credit crunch and stagnant equity markets of 1990 to 1993 gave way to the most robust capital markets in U.S. history as we approached the end of the millennium. Interest rates reached historical lows, and the credit environment was much friendlier, mimicking the heady days of pre-crash 1987. The availability of bank loans and competition among banks increased dramatically from the dormant days of the early 1990s.

A less severe credit crunch, even with extremely low interest rates, began in 2000 and increased into 2002. By 2004 banks had become more aggressive, and throughout 2006 and into 2007 the pace of lending for real estate and private equity deals was at an all-time high. The stage was thus set for the subprime collapse and subsequent collapse of lending. Even July's merger and acquisition activity dropped to a third of the April 2007 high. Many deals were postponed or canceled altogether.

A Word of Caution

History suggests a favorable credit environment can and will change sometimes suddenly. When a credit climate reverses itself, personal guarantees come back. Even the most creditworthy companies with enviable records for timely repayment of interest and principal could be asked to provide

The authors wish to thank Babson College colleague and long-time friend Mr. Leslie Charm for his significant contributions to the revisions on this chapter.

personal guarantees by the owners. As a credit crunch becomes more severe, banks face their own illiquidity and insolvency problems, which can result in so-called loans and the closure of banks. Pricing and terms become more onerous as the economy continues in a period of credit tightening.

The Lender's Perspective

Lenders have always been wary capital providers because banks may earn as little as a 1 percent net profit on total assets, making them especially sensitive to loss. If a bank writes off a $1 million loan to a small company it must then be repaid an incremental $100 million in profitable loans to recover that loss.

Yet lending institutions are businesses and seek to grow and improve profitability as well and historically loans with their associated points and fees have been a major contributor to bank profitability.

Sources of Debt Capital[1]

The principal sources of borrowed capital for new and young businesses are trade credit, commercial banks, finance companies, factors, and leasing companies.[2] Startups have more difficulty borrowing money because they do not have assets or a track record of profitability or positive cash flow. Nevertheless, startups managed by an entrepreneur with a track record and with equity investments can sometimes borrow money from one or more of these sources.

The advantages and disadvantages of these sources, summarized in Exhibit 15.1, are basically determined by such obvious dimensions as the

interest rate or cost of capital, the key terms, the conditions and covenants, and the fit with the owner's situation and the company's needs at the time.[3]

Exhibit 15.2 summarizes the term of financing available from these different sources. Note the difficulty in finding sources for more than 1 year of financing.

An entrepreneurial question is what does a bank consider collateral for a loan? How much money can I expect to borrow based on my balance sheet? Exhibit 15.3 summarizes some general guidelines. Because most loans and lines of credit are asset-based loans, knowing the lenders' guidelines is very important. The percentages of key balance sheet assets that are often allowable as collateral are only ranges and will vary from region to region, for different types of businesses, and for stages in the business cycle. For instance, nonperishable consumer goods versus technical products that may have considerable risk of obsolescence would be treated very differently in making a loan collateral computation. If the company already has significant debt and has pledged all its assets, there may not be anything available for the lender to collateralize.

Trade Credit[4]

Trade credit is a major source of short-term funds for small businesses and commonly represents 30 to 40 percent of the current liabilities of nonfinancial companies. It is reflected on the balance sheets as accounts payable or sales payable–trade.

If a small business is able to buy goods and services take 90 days to pay for them they essentially

---

EXHIBIT 15.1

Debt Financing Sources for Types of Business

Source	Startup Company	Existing Company
Trade credit	Yes	Yes
Finance companies	Occasionally with strong equity	Yes
Commercial banks	Rare (if assets are available)	Yes
Factors	Depends on nature of the customers	Yes
Leasing companies	Difficult, except for startups with venture capital	Yes
Mutual savings banks, savings, and loans	Depends on strength of personal guarantee	Real estate and asset-based companies
Insurance companies	Rare, except alongside venture capital	Yes, depending on size
Private investors	Yes	Sometimes

Source: J.A. Timmons, *Financing and Planning the New Venture* (Acton, MA: Brick House Publishing, 1990), p. 34.

---

[1]J.A. Timmons, *Financing and Planning the New Venture* (Acton, MA: Brick House Publishing, 1990).
[2]Ibid., p. 68.
[3]Ibid., p. 33.
[4]Ibid., pp. 68–80.

EXHIBIT 15.2

Debt Financing Sources by Term of Financing

Source	Term of Financing		
	Short	Medium	Long
Trade credit	Yes	Yes	Possible
Commercial banks	Most frequently	Yes (asset-based)	Rare (depends on cash flow predictability)
Factors	Most frequently	Rare	No
Leasing companies	No	Most frequently	Some
Mutual savings banks, savings, and loans	Yes	Yes	Real estate and other asset-based companies
Insurance companies	Rare	Rare	Most frequently
Private investors	Most frequently[a]	Yes	Rare

Source: J.A. Timmons, *Financing and Planning the New Venture* (Acton, MA: Brick House Publishing, 1990), p. 34.
[a]Usually as a convertible with equity or with warrants.

EXHIBIT 15.3

What Is Bankable? Specific Lending Criteria

Security	Credit Capacity
Accounts receivable	70–85% of those less than 90 days of acceptable receivables
Inventory	20–70% depending on obsolescence risk and salability
Equipment	70–80% of market value (less if specialized)
Chattel mortgage[a]	80% or more of auction appraisal value
Conditional sales contract	60–70% or more of purchase price
Plant improvement loan	60–80% of appraised value or cost

Source: J.A. Timmons, *Financing and Planning the New Venture* (Acton, MA: Brick House
Publishing, 1990), p. 33, table 1.
[a]A lien on assets other than real estate breaking a loan.

have a 90-day loan. Many small and new businesses are able to obtain such trade credit when no other form of debt financing is available to them. Suppliers offer trade credit as a way to get new customers and build the bad debt risk into their prices. In addition, channel partners who supply trade credit often do so with more industry-specific knowledge than can be obtained by commercial banks.[5]

A key to keeping trade credit open is to continually pay some amount, even if it is not the full amount. The effective interest rate for trade credit can be very high to cover the risks and the cost is seldom expressed as an annual amount, so it should be analyzed carefully.

Trade credit may take some of the following forms: extended credit terms; special or seasonal datings, where a supplier ships goods in advance of the purchaser's peak selling season and accepts payment 90 to 120 days later during the season; inventory on consignment, not requiring payment until sold; and loan or lease of equipment.

Commercial Bank Financing

Commercial banks prefer to lend to existing businesses that have a track record of sales, profits, loyal customers, and a current backlog. Since they are risk averse based on their thin profit margins, they look first to positive cash flow and then to collateral, and in new businesses are likely to require personal guarantees of the owners.

Notwithstanding these factors, certain banks occasionally make loans to startups with significant equity investments from institutional venture capitalists. This type of lending is called venture financing as is typically a percentage of the equity investment and uncollateralized.

Commercial banks primarily focus on existing businesses with long and substantial financial track records. Small business loans may be handled by a bank's small business loan department or through quantitative, objective credit scoring. Your personal credit history will impact this credit scoring

---

[5]N. Jain, "Monitoring Costs and Trade Credit," *Quarterly Review of Economics and Finance* 41 (2001), pp. 89–111.

matrix. Larger loans may require the approval of a loan committee. If a loan exceeds the limits of a local bank, part of the loan amount will be offered to "correspondent" banks to diversify the risk profile.

The most common loans by commercial banks are 1 year. Some of these loans are unsecured, whereas receivables, inventories, or other assets secure others. Commercial banks also do intermediate-term loans, also called or term loans, with a maturity ranging from 1 to 5 years. Most term loans are retired by systematic, but not necessarily equal, payments over the life of the loan. Apart from real estate mortgages and loans guaranteed by the SBA, commercial banks make few loans with maturities greater than 5 years.

There are now over 7,401 commercial banks in the United States—a 5 percent reduction in 3 years. A complete listing of banks can be found, arranged by states, in the *American Bank Directory* (McFadden Business Publications), published semiannually.

Line of Credit Loans

A line of credit is a loan specifying the maximum amount a bank will allow the borrower for a 1-year period. These are typically rolled forward annually by the company zeroing out the outstanding balance once a year.

Line of credit funds are used for seasonal purposes like inventory buildup and receivable financing, frequently the largest and most financeable items on a venture's balance sheet. It is general practice to repay these loans from the sales and reduction of short-term assets that they financed. Lines of credit can be unsecured, or the bank may require a pledge of inventory, receivables, equipment, or other acceptable assets.

For an established and financially sound company interest rates are frequently quoted using a public interest rate metric with an added premium. For example, the interest rate for a "prime risk" line of credit will be quoted at the prime rate or at a premium over LIBOR, the "London Interbank Offered Rate." Eurodollars—U.S. dollars held outside the United States are most actively traded here, and banks use Eurodollars as the "last" dollars to balance the funding of their loan portfolios, so LIBOR represents the marginal cost of funds for a bank.

Time-Sales Finance

Many dealers or manufacturers who offer installment payment terms to purchasers of their equipment cannot themselves finance installment or conditional sales contracts. In such situations, they sell and assign the installment contract to a bank or sales finance company. Some manufacturers do their own financing through captive finance companies as represented by car manufacturers like Ford Motor Company and Ford Credit. From the manufacturer's or dealer's point of view, time-sales finance is a way of obtaining short-term financing from long-term installment accounts receivable. From the purchaser's point of view, it is a way of financing the purchase of new equipment.

The purchase price of equipment under a sales financing arrangement includes a "time-sales price differential" to cover the discount rate taken by the financial institution. Payments of the installments may be made directly to the bank, the manufacturer, or the dealer.

Term Loans

Bank term loans are generally made for periods of 1 to 5 years, and may be unsecured or secured. Most of the basic features of bank term loans are the same for secured and unsecured loans.

Term loans provide needed growth capital to companies. They are also a substitute for a series of short-term loans made with the hope of renewal by the borrower. Banks make these generally on the basis of predictability of cash flow. Term loans have three distinguishing features: Banks make them for periods of up to 5 years; periodic repayment is required; and agreements are designed to fit the needs of the borrower, for example, payments that are smaller at the beginning of a loan and larger at the end.

Because term loans do not mature for a number of years, during which time the borrower's situation and fortunes could change significantly, the bank must carefully evaluate the prospects of the borrowing company. The protection by initially strong assets can be wiped out by several years of heavy losses, so term lenders scrutinize the managerial abilities of the borrowing company. The bank will also carefully consider such things as the long-range prospects of the company and its industry, its present and projected profitability, and its ability to generate the cash required to meet the loan payments.

To lessen the risks involved in term loans, a bank will require some restrictive covenants in the loan agreement. These covenants might prohibit additional borrowing, merger of the company, payment of dividends, sales of assets, increased salaries to the owners, and the like. Also, the bank will probably require financial covenants to provide early warning of deterioration of the business, like debt to equity and cash flow to interest coverage ratios.

Chattel Mortgages and Equipment Loans

A chattel is a common way of making secured term loans where the chattel is any machinery, equipment, or business property that is the collateral of a loan in the same way as a mortgage on real estate. The chattel remains with the borrower unless there is default, in which case the chattel goes to the bank to liquidate and pay off the remaining loan balance; so typically chattels are on new or highly serviceable and salable items.

Conditional Sales Contracts

Conditional sales contracts are used to finance a substantial portion of the new equipment purchased by businesses. Under a sales contract, the buyer agrees to purchase a piece of equipment, makes a nominal down payment, and pays the balance in installments over a period of 1 to 5 years. Until the payment is complete, the seller holds title to the equipment. Hence the borrower's final ownership is conditional upon completing the payments.

Plant Improvement Loans

Loans made to finance improvements to business properties and plants are called plant improvement loans. They can be intermediate or long-term and are generally secured by a first or second mortgage on the part of the property or plant that is being improved.

Commercial Finance Companies

The commercial bank is generally the lender of choice for a business. But when the bank says no, commercial finance companies, which aggressively seek borrowers, are a good option. They frequently lend money to companies that do not have positive cash flow, although commercial finance companies will not make loans to companies unless they consider them viable risks. In tighter credit economies, finance companies are generally more accepting of risk than are banks.

The primary factors in a bank's loan decision are the continuing successful operation of a business and its generation of more than enough cash to repay a loan. By contrast, commercial finance companies lend against the liquidation value of assets like receivables, inventory, and equipment, that it knows how and where to sell, and has sufficient liquidation value. Banks today own many of the leading finance companies and as a borrower gains financial strength and a track record, a transition to more attractively priced bank financing can be made easier.

In the case of inventories or equipment, liquidation value is the amount that could be realized from an auction or quick sale. Finance companies will generally not lend against receivables more than 90 days old, federal or state government agency receivables (difficult to get a lien and payment is slow), or any receivables whose collection is contingent on the performance of a delivered product.

Because of the liquidation criteria, finance companies prefer readily salable inventory items such as commodity electronic components or metal in such industry standard forms like billets. Equipment loans are made only by certain finance companies and against such standard equipment as lathes, milling machines, and the like. Finance companies have items with which they are more comfortable and therefore will extend more credit against certain kinds of collateral.

How much of the collateral value will a finance company lend? Generally 70 to 90 percent of acceptable receivables under 90 days old, 20 to 70 percent of the liquidation value of raw materials or finished goods inventory, and 60 to 80 percent of the liquidation value of equipment. Receivables and inventory loans are for 1 year, whereas equipment loans are for 3 to 7 years. All these loans have tough prepayment penalties as finance companies do not want to be immediately replaced by banks when a borrower has improved its credit rating.

The data required for a loan from a finance company includes all that would be provided to a bank. For inventory financing this includes details on the items in inventory, how long they have been there, and their rate of turnover. Requests for equipment loans should be accompanied by details on the date of purchase, cost of each equipment item, and appraisals.

The advantage of dealing with a commercial finance company is that it will make loans that banks will not and are more flexible in lending arrangements. The price a finance company exacts for this is an interest rate anywhere from 0 to 6 percent over that charged by a bank, and prepayment penalties.

Because of their greater risk taking and asset-based lending, finance companies usually place a larger reporting and monitoring burden on the borrowing firm to stay on top of the receivables and inventory serving as loan collateral. Personal guarantees will generally be required from the principals of the business. A finance company or bank will generally reserve the right to reduce the percentage of the value lent against receivables or inventory based on market conditions.

Factoring

Factoring is a form of accounts receivable financing. However, instead of borrowing and using receivables as collateral, the receivables are sold at a discounted value to a factor. Factoring is accomplished on a discounted value of the receivables pledged.

Factoring can make it possible for a company to secure a loan that it might not otherwise get and the loan can be increased as sales and receivables grow. However, factoring can have drawbacks as it can be expensive, and trade creditors sometimes regard factoring as evidence of a company with limited financial history and hence risky. In a standard factoring arrangement, the factor buys the client's receivables outright, without recourse, as soon as the client creates them by shipment of goods to customers.

Factoring fits some businesses better than others. For a business that has annual sales volume in excess of $300,000 and a net worth over $50,000 that sells on normal credit terms to a customer base that is 75 percent credit rated, factoring is a real option. Factoring has become almost traditional in such industries as textiles, furniture, clothing, toys, and plastics.

The same data required for a factor are the same as a bank. Because a factor is buying receivables with no recourse, it will analyze the quality and value of a prospective client's receivables. It will want a detailed aging of receivables plus historical data on bad debts, return, and allowances. It will also investigate the credit history of customers to whom its client sells and establish credit limits for each customer. The business client can receive factoring of customer receivables only up to the limits so set.

The cost of financing receivables through factoring is higher than that of borrowing from a bank or a finance company. The factor is assuming the credit risk, doing credit investigations and collections, and advancing funds. A factor generally charges up to 2 percent of the total sales factored as a service charge.

There is also an interest charge for money advanced to a business, usually 2 to 6 percent above prime. A larger, established business borrowing large sums would command a better interest rate than the small borrower with a one-time, short-term need. Finally, factors withhold a reserve of 5 to 10 percent of the receivables purchased.

Factoring is not the cheapest way to obtain capital, but it does quickly turn receivables into cash. Moreover, although more expensive than accounts receivable financing, factoring saves its users credit agency fees, salaries of credit and collection personnel, and maybe bad debt write-offs. Factoring also provides credit information on collection services that may be better than the borrower's.

Leasing Companies

The leasing industry has grown substantially in recent years, and lease financing has become an important source of medium-term financing for businesses. Many commercial banks and finance companies have leasing departments. Some leasing companies handle a wide variety of equipment, while others specialize in certain types.

Common and readily resalable items such as automobiles, trucks, typewriters, and office furniture can be leased by both new and existing businesses. However, the startup will find it difficult to lease other kinds of industrial, computer, or business equipment without providing a letter of credit or a certificate of deposit to secure the lease, or personal guarantees from the founders or from a wealthy third party.

Generally industrial equipment leases have a term of 3 to 5 years with lease renewal options. Leases are usually structured to return the entire cost of the leased equipment plus finance charges to the lessor, although some so-called operating leases do not produce revenues equal to or greater than the price of the leased equipment. Typically an up-front payment is required of about 10 percent of the value of the item being leased. The interest rate on equipment leasing may be more or less than other forms of financing, depending on the equipment leased, the credit of the lessee, and the time of year.

Leasing credit criteria are similar to the criteria used by commercial banks for equipment loans. Primary considerations are the value of the equipment leased, the justification of the lease, and the lessee's projected cash flow over the lease term.

Leasing provides the flexibility of returning equipment after the lease period if it is no longer needed or if it has become technologically obsolete. This can be a particular advantage to high-technology and life sciences companies.

Leasing may or may not improve a company's balance sheet because accounting practice currently requires that the value of the equipment acquired in a capital lease be reflected on the balance sheet. Operating leases, however, do not appear on the balance sheet. Generally this is an issue of economic ownership rather than legal ownership. If the economic risk is primarily with the lessee, it must be capitalized and it therefore goes on the balance sheet along with the corresponding debt. Depreciation also follows the risk, along with the corresponding tax benefits. Startups that do not need such tax relief should be able to acquire more favorable terms with an operating lease.

Before the Loan Decision

Much of the following discussion of lending practices and decisions applies to commercial finance company lenders as well as to banks. A good lender relationship can sometimes mean the difference between the life and death of a business during difficult times. There have been cases where one bank has called its loans to a struggling business, causing it to go under, and another bank has stayed with its loans and helped a business to survive and prosper.

Banks that will not make loans to startups and early-stage ventures generally cite the lack of an operating track record as the primary reason for turning down a loan. Lenders that make such loans usually do so for previously successful entrepreneurs of means or for firms backed by investors with whom they have had prior relationships and whose judgment they trust (e.g., established venture capital firms when they believe that the venture capital company will invest in the next round).

In centers of high technology and venture capital, the main officers of the major banks will have one or more high-technology lending officers who specialize in making loans to early-stage, high-technology ventures. Through much experience, these bankers have come to understand the market and operating idiosyncrasies, problems, and opportunities of such ventures. They generally have close ties to venture capital firms and will refer entrepreneurs to such firms for possible equity financing. The venture capital firms, in turn, will refer their portfolio ventures to the bankers for debt financing.

What should an entrepreneur consider in choosing a lender? What is important in a lending decision? How should entrepreneurs relate to their lenders on an ongoing basis? In many ways the lender's decision is similar to that of the venture capitalist. The goal is to make money for his or her company through interest earned on good loans; the lender fears losing money by making bad loans to companies that default on their loans. To this end, he or she avoids risk by building in every conceivable safeguard. The lender is concerned with the client company's loan coverage, its ability to repay, and the collateral it can offer. Finally, but

most important, he or she must judge the character and quality of the key managers of the company to whom the loan is being made.

Babson College Adjunct Professor Leslie Charm offers the following advice to entrepreneurs seeking to develop a constructive banking relationship:

Industry experience is critical. Choose a banker who understands your particular industry. He or she will have other clients in the same industry and may serve as a valuable resource for networking and service professionals with relevant experience. In addition, a bank that understands your industry will be more tolerant of problems and better able to help you exploit your opportunities. In the case of funding requests, bankers with industry knowledge are more apt to make a quick and reasoned determination.

Understand their business model. Every bank has different criteria with regard to working with new ventures, and their lending decisions are largely based on quantitative credit scoring metrics. The entrepreneur needs to understand how a particular bank works and determine whether that model is a fit with his or her venture.

Understand whom you are dealing with. Bankers are relationship managers whose job is to support their clients–including expediting the approval of loans and credit lines that fit with their bank's lending criteria. Like a lot of good vendors, the best of them have specialized knowledge and excellent contacts, and will take a genuine interest in your business.

Exhibit 15.4 outlines the key steps in obtaining a loan. Because of the importance of a banking relationship, an entrepreneur should shop around before making a choice. As Leslie Charm pointed out, the criteria for selecting a bank should be based on a lot more than just loan interest rates. Equally important, entrepreneurs should not wait until they have a dire need for funds to try to establish a banking relationship. When an entrepreneur faces a near-term financial crisis, the venture's financial statements are at their worst, and the banker has good cause to wonder about management's financial and planning skills–all to the detriment of the entrepreneur's chance of getting a loan.

G. B. Baty and J. M. Stancill describe some factors that are especially important to an entrepreneur in selecting a bank. First, the entrepreneur should consult accountants, attorneys, and other entrepreneurs who have had dealings with the bank.[6] The advice of entrepreneurs who have dealt with a bank through good and bad times can be especially useful. Second, the entrepreneur should meet with

---

[6]G.B. Baty, *Entrepreneurship: Playing to Win* (Reston, VA: Reston Publishing, 1974); and J.M. Stancill, "Getting the Most from Your Banking Relationship," *Harvard Business Review,* March–April 1980.

EXHIBIT 15.4

Key Steps in Obtaining a Loan

Before choosing and approaching a banker or other lender, the entrepreneur and his or her management team should prepare by taking the following steps:

- Decide how much growth they want, and how fast they want to grow, observing the dictum that financing follows strategy.
- Determine how much money they require, when they need it, and when they can pay it back. To this end, they must
  - —Develop a schedule of operating and asset needs.
  - —Prepare a real-time cash flow projection.
  - —Decide how much capital they need.
  - —Specify how they will use the funds they borrow.
- Revise and update the "corporate profile" in their business plan. This should consist of
  - —The core ingredients of the plan in the form of an executive summary.
  - —A history of the firm (as appropriate).
  - —Summaries of the financial results of the past 3 years.
  - —Succinct descriptions of their markets and products.
  - —A description of their operations.
  - —Statements of cash flow and financial requirements.
  - —Descriptions of the key managers, owners, and directors.
  - —A rundown of the key strategies, facts, and logic that guide them in growing the corporation.
- Identify potential sources for the type of debt they seek, and the amount, rate, terms, and conditions they seek.
- Select a bank or other lending institution, solicit interest, and prepare a presentation.
- Prepare a written loan request.
- Present their case, negotiate, and then close the deal.

After the loan is granted, borrowers should maintain an effective relationship with the lending officer.

Source: J.A. Timmons, *Financing and Planning the New Venture* (Acton, MA: Brick Housing Publishing, 1990), pp. 82–83.

loan officers at several banks and systematically explore their attitudes and approaches to their business borrowers. Who meets with you, for how long, and with how many interruptions can be useful measures of a bank's interest in your account. Finally, ask for small business references from their list of borrowers and talk to the entrepreneurs of those firms. Throughout all of these contacts and discussions, check out particular loan officers as well as the viability of the bank itself; they are a major determinant of how the bank will deal with you and your venture.

The bank selected should be big enough to service your venture's foreseeable loans but not so large as to be relatively indifferent to your business. Banks differ greatly in their desire and capacity to work with small firms. Some banks have special small business loan officers and regard new and early-stage ventures as the seeds of very large future accounts. Other banks see such new venture loans as merely bad risks. Does the bank tend to call or reduce its loans to small businesses that have problems? When it has less capital to lend, will it cut back on small business loans and favor older, more solid customers? Is the bank imaginative, creative, and helpful when

a venture has a problem or when things get tough? Or do they start looking in the small print for a quick exit? (See the accompanying box.) To quote Baty, "Do they just look at your balance sheet and faint, or do they try to suggest constructive financial alternatives?"

Approaching and Meeting the Banker

Obtaining a loan is, among other things, a sales job. Many borrowers tend to forget this. An entrepreneur with an early-stage venture must sell himself or herself as well as the viability and potential of the business to the banker. This is much the same situation that the early-stage entrepreneur faces with a venture capitalist.

The initial contact with a lender will likely be by telephone. The entrepreneur should be prepared to describe quickly the nature, age, and prospects of the venture; the amount of equity financing and who provided it; the prior financial performance of the business; the entrepreneur's experience and background; and the sort of bank financing desired. A referral from a venture capital firm, a lawyer or accountant, or other business associate who knows the banker can be very helpful.

Small Print, Big Problems

Matt Coffin, founder of LowerMyBills.com, was less than 2 years into his venture when the markets began to soften during the summer of 2001. Matt had just received a term sheet from a respected venture capitalist and a most unwelcome call from his bank:

- In the late 1990s we had established a million-dollar line through a big bank in Silicon Valley–which at the time was giving out credit lines like candy. We had drawn down that line and now our cash balance was $750,000–less than what we owed them.

- So they sent over what they call an *adverse change notice*. At the time I had signed the documents I didn't even know what that meant; yeah sure, just give me the million dollars.

- Now I realize that an adverse change notice is a small print clause that allows the bank to demand immediate repayment of the outstanding balance–pretty much at any time they felt like it. If you can't do that, they can take all the cash on hand and begin calling in assets. So now, instead of running my business and raising money, I was meeting with lawyers and fighting with my bank just to stay alive. Over time, it became clear that they were basically trying to squeeze me for more–that is, warrant coverage as a percentage of the loan.

Seeing how dire the situation was becoming at LowerMyBills.com–and how close the venture had been to turning the corner–original investors came forward to help out. Investor Brett Markinson said that they all understood that Matt was the type of individual to support in a down market:

> Everyone, including myself, had gotten sucked into the idea of raising as much money as you could and spending it on making noise. Matt had focused on raising as little as possible; he just kept his head down and concerned himself with driving value.
>
> Since Matt hadn't raised too much money and had maintained a lean infrastructure, he was in a good position to really take advantage of the circumstances. While everyone else was cutting back or going out of business, Matt was able to rent space at a great price and hire excellent talent at a great price.

With a couple of investors putting in their own money, LowerMyBills.com was able to payoff the bank and secure the round. In the last quarter of that year, LowerMyBills.com posted its first profit, and in May 2005 Matt harvested the company for $330 million.

Source: Adapted from the "Matt Coffin" teaching case, Babson College, 2005.

If the loan officer agrees to a meeting, he or she may ask that a summary loan proposal, description of the business, and financial statements be sent ahead of time. A well-prepared proposal and a request for a reasonable amount of equity financing should pique a banker's interest.

The first meeting with a loan officer will likely be at the venture's place of business. The banker will be interested in meeting the management team, seeing how team members relate to the entrepreneur, and getting a sense of the financial controls and reporting used and how well things seem to be run. The banker may also want to meet one or more of the venture's equity investors. Most of all, the banker is using this meeting to evaluate the integrity and business acumen of those who will ultimately be responsible for the repayment of the loan.

Throughout meetings with potential bankers, the entrepreneur must convey an air of self-confidence and knowledge. If the banker is favorably impressed by what has been seen and read, he or she will ask for further documents and references and begin to discuss the amount and timing of funds that the bank might lend to the business.

What the Banker Wants to Know[7]

You first need to describe the business and its industry. Exhibit 15.5 suggests how a banker "sees a company" from what the entrepreneur might say. What are you going to do with the money? Does the use of the loan make business sense? Should some or all of the money required be equity capital rather than debt? For new and young businesses, lenders do not like to see total debt-to-equity ratios greater than 1. The answers to these questions will also determine the type of loan (e.g., line of credit or term):

---

[7]This section is drawn from Timmons, *Financing and Planning the New Venture*, pp. 85–88.

EXHIBIT 15.5

How Your Banker Interprets the Income Statement

Sales	What do you sell?
	Whom do you sell to?
Cost of goods	How do you buy?
	What do you buy?
	Whom do you buy from?
Gross margin	Are you a supermarket or a boutique?
Selling	How do you sell and distribute the product?
G&A: general and administration	How much overhead and support are needed to operate?
R&D	How much is reinvested in the product?
Operating margins	Dollars available before financing costs?
Interest expense	How big is this fixed nut?
Profit before taxes	Do you make money?
Taxes	Corporation or LLC?
Profit after taxes	
Dividends/withdrawals	How much and to whom?
	How much money is left in the company?

Source: This exhibit was created by Kathie S. Stevens and Leslie Charm as part of a class discussion in the Entrepreneurial Finance course at Babson College, and is part of a presentation titled "Cash Is King, Assets Are Queen, and Everybody Is Looking for an Ace in the Hole." Ms. Stevens is former chief lending officer and member of the credit committee for a Boston bank.

1. How much do you need? You must be prepared to justify the amount requested and describe how the debt fits into an overall plan for financing and developing the business. Further, the amount of the loan should have enough cushion to allow for unexpected developments (Exhibit 15.6).

2. When and how will you pay it back? This is an important question. Short-term loans for seasonal inventory buildups or for financing receivables are easier to obtain than long-term loans, especially for early-stage businesses. How the loan will be repaid is the bottom-line question. Presumably you are borrowing money to finance activity that will generate enough cash to repay the loan. What is your contingency plan if things go wrong? Can you describe such risks and indicate how you will deal with them?

3. What is the secondary source of repayment? Are there assets or a guarantor of means?

4. When do you need the money? If you need the money tomorrow, forget it. You are a poor planner and manager. On the other hand, if you need the money next month or the month after, you have demonstrated an ability to plan ahead, and you have given the banker time to investigate and process a loan application. Typically it is difficult to get a lending decision in less than 3 weeks (some smaller banks still have once-a-month credit meetings).

One of the best ways for all entrepreneurs to answer these questions is from a well-prepared business plan. This plan should contain projections of cash flow, profit and loss, and balance sheets that will demonstrate the need for a loan and how it can be repaid. Particular attention will be given by the lender to the value of the assets and the cash flow of the business, and to such financial ratios as current assets to current liabilities, gross margins, net worth to debt, accounts receivable and payable periods, inventory turns, and net profit to sales. The ratios for the borrower's venture will be compared to averages for competing firms to see how the potential borrower measures up to them.

For an existing business, the lender will want to review financial statements from prior years prepared or audited by a CPA, a list of aged receivables and payables, the turnover of inventory, and lists of key customers and creditors. The lender will also want to know that all tax payments are current. Finally, he or she will need to know details of fixed assets and any liens on receivables, inventory, or fixed assets.

The entrepreneur-borrower should regard his or her contacts with the bank as a sales mission and provide required data promptly and in a form that can be readily understood. The better the material

EXHIBIT 15.6

Sample of a Summary Loan Proposal

Date of request:	May 30, 2008
Borrower:	Curtis-Palmer & Company, Inc.
Amount:	$4,200,000

Use of proceeds:		
	A/R, up to	$1,600,000
	Inventory, up to	824,000
	WIP, up to	525,000
	Marketing, up to	255,000
	Ski show specials	105,000
	Contingencies	50,000
	Officer loans due	841,000
		$4,200,000

Type of loan:	Seasonal revolving line of credit
Closing date:	June 15, 2008
Term:	1 year
Rate:	Prime plus ½ percent, no compensating balances, no points or origination fees
Takedown:	$500,000 at closing
	$1,500,000 on August 1, 2008
	$1,500,000 on October 1, 2008
	$700,000 on November 1, 2010
Collateral:	70 percent of acceptable A/R under 90 days
	50 percent of current inventory
Guarantees:	None
Repayment schedule:	$4,200,000 or balance on anniversary of note
Source of funds for repayment:	*a.* Excess cash from operations (see cash flow)
	b. Renewable and increase of line if growth is profitable
	c. Conversion to 3-year note
Contingency source:	*a.* Sale and leaseback of equipment
	b. Officer's loans (with a request for a personal guarantee)

Source: Updated and adapted from J.A. Timmons, *Financing and Planning the New Venture* (Acton, MA: Brick House Publishing, 1990), p. 86.

entrepreneurs can supply to demonstrate their business credibility, the easier and faster it will be to obtain a positive lending decision. The entrepreneur should also ask, early on, to meet with the banker's boss. This can go a long way to help obtain financing. Remember that you need to build a relationship with a bank–not just a banker.

The Lending Decision

One of the significant changes in today's lending environment is the centralized lending decision. Traditionally loan officers might have had up to several million dollars of lending authority and could make loans to small companies. Besides the company's creditworthiness as determined by analysis of its past results via the balance sheet, income statement, cash flow, and collateral, the lender's assessment of the character and reputation of the entrepreneur was central to the decision. Because

loan decisions are made increasingly by loan committees or credit scoring, this face-to-face part of the decision process has given way to deeper analysis of the company's business plan, cash flow drivers and dissipaters, competitive environment, and the cushion for loan recovery given the firm's game plan and financial structure.

The implication for entrepreneurs is a demanding one: You can no longer rely on your salesmanship and good relationship with your loan officer alone to continue to get favorable lending decisions. You, or the key team member, need to be able to prepare the necessary analysis and documentation to convince people (you may never meet) that the loan will be repaid. You also need to know the financial ratios and criteria used to compare your loan request with industry norms and to defend the analysis. Such a presentation can make it easier and faster to obtain approval of a loan because it gives your relationship manager the ammunition to defend your loan request.

Lending Criteria

First and foremost, as with equity investors, the quality and track record of the management team will be a major factor. Historical financial statements, which show 3 to 5 years of profitability, are also essential. Well-developed business projections that articulate the company's sales estimates, market niche, cash flow, profit projections, working capital, capital expenditure, uses of proceeds, and evidence of competent accounting and control systems are essential.

In its simplest form, what is needed is analysis of the available collateral, based on guidelines such as those shown in Exhibit 15.3, and of debt capacity determined by analysis of the coverage ratio once the new loan is in place. Interest coverage is calculated as earnings before interest and taxes divided by interest (EBIT/interest). A business with steady, predictable cash flow and earnings would require a lower coverage ratio (say, in the range of 2) than would a company with a volatile, unpredictable cash flow stream—for example, a high-technology company with risk of competition and obsolescence (which might require a coverage ratio of 5 or more). The bottom line, of course, is the ability of the company to repay both interest and principal on time.

Loan Restrictions[8]

A loan agreement defines the terms and conditions under which a lender provides capital. With it, lenders do two things: try to assure repayment of the loan as agreed and try to protect their position as creditor. Within the loan agreement (as in investment agreements) there are negative and positive covenants. Negative covenants are restrictions on the borrower: for example, no further additions to the borrower's total debt, no pledge to others of assets of the borrower, and no payment of dividends or limitation on owners' salaries.

Positive covenants define what the borrower must do. Some examples are maintenance of some minimum net worth or working capital, prompt payment of all federal and state taxes, adequate insurance on key people and property, repayment of the loan and interest according to the terms of the agreement, and provision to the lender of periodic financial statements and reports.

Some of these restrictions can hinder a company's growth, such as a flat restriction on further borrowing. Such a borrowing limit is often based on the borrower's assets at the time of the loan. However, rather than stipulating an initially fixed limit, the loan agreement should recognize that as a business grows and increases its total assets and net worth, it will need and be able to carry the additional debt required to sustain its growth; but banks (especially in tighter credit periods) will still put maximums after allowed credit because this gives them another opportunity to recheck the loan. Similarly, covenants that require certain minimums on working capital or current ratios may be difficult for a highly seasonal business, for example, to maintain at all times of the year. Only analysis of past financial monthly statements can indicate whether such a covenant can be met.

Covenants to Look For

Before borrowing money, an entrepreneur should decide what sorts of restrictions or covenants are acceptable. Attorneys and accountants of the company should be consulted before any loan papers are signed. Some covenants are negotiable (this changes with the overall credit economy), and an entrepreneur should negotiate to get terms that the venture can live with next year as well as today. Once loan terms are agreed upon and the loan is made, the entrepreneur and the venture will be bound by them. Beware if the bank says, "Yes, but . . . ."

- Wants to put constraints on your permissible financial ratios.
- Stops any new borrowing.
- Wants a veto on any new management.
- Disallows new products or new directions.
- Prevents acquiring or selling any assets.
- Forbids any new investment or new equipment.

What follow are some practical guidelines about personal guarantees: when to expect them, how to avoid them, and how to eliminate them.

Personal Guarantees and the Loan

Personal guarantees may be required of the lead entrepreneur or, more likely, shareholders of significance (more than 10 percent) who are also members of the senior management team. Also, personal guarantees are often "joint and severable"—meaning that each guarantor is liable for the total amount of the guarantee.

[8]Ibid., pp. 90–94.

When to Expect Them

- If you are undercollateralized.
- If there are shareholder loans or lots of "due to" and "due from" officer accounts.
- If you have had a poor or erratic performance.
- If you have management problems.
- If your relationship with your banker is strained.
- If you have a new loan officer.
- If there is turbulence in the credit markets.
- If there has been a wave of bad loans made by the lending institution, and a crackdown is in force.
- If there is less understanding of your market.

How to Avoid Them

- Good to spectacular performance.
- Conservative financial management.
- Positive cash flow over a sustained period.
- Adequate collateral.
- Careful management of the balance sheet.
- If they are required in the deal, negotiate elimination *upfront* when you have some bargaining chips, based on certain performance criteria.

How to Eliminate Them (If You Already Have Them)

- See "How to Avoid Them."
- Develop a financial plan with performance targets and a timetable.
- Stay active in the search for backup sources of funds.

Building a Relationship

After obtaining a loan, entrepreneurs should cultivate a close working relationship with their bankers. Too many businesspeople do not see their lending officers until they need a loan. The astute entrepreneur will take a much more active role in keeping a banker informed about the business, thereby improving the chances of obtaining larger loans for expansion and cooperation from the bank in troubled times.

Some of the things that should be done to build such a relationship are fairly simple.[9] In addition to monthly and annual financial statements, bankers should be sent product news releases and any trade articles about the business or its products. The entrepreneur should invite the banker to the venture's facility, review product development plans and the prospects for the business, and establish a personal relationship with him or her. If this is done, when a new loan is requested the lending officer will feel better about recommending its approval.

What about bad news? Never surprise a banker with bad news; make sure he or she sees it coming as soon as you do. Unpleasant surprises are a sign that an entrepreneur is not being candid with the banker or that management does not have the business under the proper control. Either conclusion by a banker is damaging to the relationship.

If a future loan payment cannot be met, entrepreneurs should not panic and avoid their bankers. On the contrary, they should visit their banks and explain why the loan payment cannot be made and say when it will be made. If this is done before the payment due date and the entrepreneur–banker relationship is good, the banker may go along. What else can he or she do? If an entrepreneur has convinced a banker of the viability and future growth of a business, the banker really does not want to call a loan and lose a customer to a competitor or cause bankruptcy. The real key to communicating with a banker is candidly to inform but not to scare. In other words, entrepreneurs must indicate that they are aware of adverse events and have a plan for dealing with them.

To build credibility with bankers further, entrepreneurs should borrow before they need to and then repay the loan. This will establish a track record of borrowing and reliable repayment. Entrepreneurs should also make every effort to meet the financial targets they set for themselves and have discussed with their banker. If this cannot be done, the credibility of the entrepreneur will erode, even if the business is growing.

Bankers have a right to expect an entrepreneur to continue to use them as the business grows and prospers, and not to go shopping for a better interest rate. In return, entrepreneurs have the right to expect that their bank will continue to provide them with needed loans, particularly during difficult times when a vacillating loan policy could be dangerous for business survival.

---

[9]Baty, *Entrepreneurship: Playing to Win.*

The TLC of a Banker or Other Lender

1. Your banker is your partner, not a difficult minority shareholder.
2. Be honest and straightforward in sharing information.
3. Invite the banker to see your business in operation.
4. Always avoid overdrafts, late payments, and late financial statements.
5. Answer questions frankly and honestly. *Tell the truth.* Lying is illegal and undoubtedly violates loan covenants.
6. Understand the business of banking.
7. Have an "ace in the hole."

What to Do When the Bank Says No

What do you do if the bank turns you down for a loan? Regroup, and review the following questions.

1. Does the company really need to borrow now? Can cash be generated elsewhere? Tighten the belt. Are some expenditures unnecessary? Sharpen the financial pencil: Be lean and mean.
2. What does the balance sheet say? Are you growing too fast? Compare yourself to published industry ratios to see if you are on target.
3. Does the bank have a clear and comprehensive understanding of your needs? Did you really get to know your loan officer? Did you do enough homework on the bank's criteria and its likes and dislikes? Was your loan officer too busy to give your borrowing package proper consideration? A loan officer may have 50 to as many as 200 accounts. Is your relationship with the bank on a proper track?
4. Was your written loan proposal realistic? Was it a normal request, or something that differed from the types of proposals the bank usually sees? Did you make a verbal request for a loan without presenting any written backup?
5. Do you need a new loan officer or a new bank? If your answers to the previous questions put you in the clear, and your written proposal was realistic, call the head of the commercial loan department and arrange a meeting. Sit down and discuss the history of your loan effort, the facts, and the bank's reasons for turning you down.
6. Who else might provide this financing (ask the banker who turned you down)?

You should be seeing multiple lenders at the same time so you do not run out of time or money.

Tar Pits: Entrepreneurs Beware

Modern corporate financial theory has preached the virtues of zero cash balances and the use of leverage to enhance return on equity (ROE). When applied to closely held companies whose dream is to last forever, such thinking can be extremely destructive. If you judge by the 1980s, the excessive leverage used by so many larger companies was apparently simply not worth the risk: Two-thirds of the LBOs done in the 1980s have ended up in serious trouble. The serious erosion of IBM began about the same time that the company acquired debt on its balance sheet for the very first time, in the early 1980s. This problem was manifest in the acquisition binges of the early 1990s and in the high-technology feeding frenzy of the late 1990s. Following the 2000 to 2003 downturn, LBOs once again emerged as a popular growth vehicle.

Beware of Leverage: The ROE Mirage

According to the theory, one can significantly improve ROE by utilizing debt. Thus the present value of a company would also increase significantly as the company went from a zero debt-to-equity ratio to 100 percent, as shown in Exhibit 15.7. On closer examination, however, such an increase in debt improves the present value, given the 2 to 8 percent growth rates shown, by only 17 to 26 percent. If the company gets into any trouble—and the odds of that happening sooner or later are very high—its options and flexibility become seriously constrained by the covenants of the senior lenders. Leverage creates an unforgiving capital structure, and the potential additional ROI often is not worth the risk. If the upside is worth risking the loss of the entire company should adversity strike, then go ahead. This is easier said than survived, however.

Ask any entrepreneur who has had to deal with the workout specialists in a bank and you will get a sobering, if not frightening, message: It is hell and you will not want to do it again.

IRS: Time Bomb for Personal Disaster

There is a much less known tar pit that entrepreneurs need to be aware of when considering leveraging their companies. Once the company gets into

EXHIBIT 15.7

Total Present Value

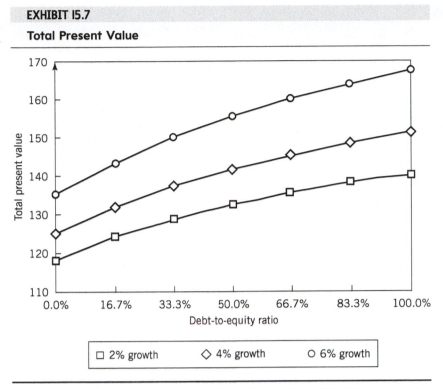

Source: W.A. Sahlman, "Note on Free Cash Flow Valuation Models," HBS Note 288-023, figure 5.

serious financial trouble, a subsequent restructuring of debt is often part of the survival and recovery plan. In such a restructuring, the problem becomes that the principal and interest due to lenders may be forgiven in exchange for warrants, direct equity, or other considerations. Such forgiven debt becomes *taxable income* for the entrepreneur who owns the company and who has personally had to guarantee the loans. *Beware:* In one restructuring of a Midwestern cable television company, the founder at one point faced a possible $12 million personal tax liability, which would have forced him into personal bankruptcy or possibly worse. In this case, fortunately, the creative deal restructuring enabled him to avoid such a calamitous outcome; but many other overleveraged entrepreneurs have not fared as well.

Neither a Lender nor a Borrower Be, But If You Must . . .

In Garrison Keillor's radio program *A Prairie Home Companion*, he describes the mythical town of Lake Wobegon, Minnesota. Inscribed in granite over the entrance to the Bank of Lake Wobegon is the motto

"Neither a Lender nor a Borrower Be," which is actually very good advice for early-stage entrepreneurs. Thus the following may serve as useful tips if you must borrow:

1. Borrow when you do not need it (which is the surest way to accomplish No. 2).
2. Avoid personal guarantees. Put caps and time limits on the amounts based on performance milestones, such as achieving certain cash flow, working capital, and equity levels. Also, don't be afraid in many markets to offer your guarantee and then negotiate ways to get it back in whole or in part!
3. The devil is in the details. Read each loan covenant and requirement carefully–only the owner can truly appreciate their consequences.
4. Try to avoid or modify so-called hair-trigger covenants, such as this: "If there is any change or event of any kind that can have any material adverse effect on the future of the company, the loan shall become due and payable."
5. Be conservative and prudent.

Chapter Summary

- Business cycles impact lending cycles, with more or less restrictive behavior.

- Startups are generally not candidates for bank credit, but numerous sources of debt capital are available once profitability and a decent balance sheet are established.

- Managing and orchestrating the banking relationship before and after the loan decision are key tasks for entrepreneurs.

- Knowing the key steps in obtaining a loan and selecting a banker—not a bank—who can add value can improve your odds.

- Loan covenants can have a profound impact on how you can and cannot run the business. The devil is in the details of the loan agreement.

- For the vast majority of small companies, leverage works only during the most favorable economic booms of credit availability. Leverage is a disaster if business turns sour.

- The IRS also places a time bomb for personal disaster with every entrepreneur who borrows money: If your bank debt is forgiven in a restructuring, it becomes taxable income to the borrower!

- When the bank says no to a loan request, several key questions need to be addressed in an effort to reverse the decision; or you need to seek sources of credit other than banks.

Study Questions

1. Define and explain the following and why they are important: sources of debt financing, trade credit, line of credit, accounts receivable financing, time-sales factoring, commercial finance company.

2. What security can be used for a loan, and what percentage of its value do banks typically lend?

3. What are the things to look for in evaluating a lender, and why are these important?

4. What does "value-added banker" mean, and how and why is this crucial?

5. What criteria do lenders use to evaluate a loan application, and what can be done before and after the loan decision to facilitate a loan request?

6. What restrictions and covenants might a lender require, and how and why should these be avoided whenever possible?

7. What issues need to be addressed to deal with a loan request rejection?

8. Why do entrepreneurs in smaller companies need to be especially wary of leverage?

9. Why is there an IRS time bomb anytime one borrows money?

10. When should a company borrow money?

Internet Resources

http://www.aba.com/default.htm *American Bankers Association.*

http://federalreserve.gov/ *Board of Governors of the Federal Reserve System.*

http://research.kauffman.org *The research portal of the Ewing Marion Kauffman Foundation.*

Wiki–Google Search

Try these keywords and phrases:
leverage
factoring
sources of debt: short-term, long-term
banking relationship

personal guarantee
lending decision
loan covenants
loan rejection
obtaining a loan

Case

Bank Documents: "The Devil Is in the Details"

Preparation Questions

1. Outline the transactions. Include the flow of funds among the individuals and corporations.

2. What specific risks was the bank trying to protect itself against? Which specific terms were intended to provide the protection?

3. What do "subordination" and "personal guarantee" mean to the respective parties?

4. What in the numbers indicates why the bank took the position it did?

The Parent Company ("TPC") had existed six to seven years under the control of a venture capital group. Although it was publicly traded, two-thirds of it were owned by the VCs and its operating manager. It made, under an overseas license, a product that was distributed throughout the United States. It had an annual sales of $3 million to $4 million, and substantially all its assets were secured under a loan agreement to Union Trust ("The Bank"). The company had a negative net worth and had not made a profit the last five years.

TPC determined it needed to expand by acquisition and went into a different industry to accomplish that. It found a chain of retail stores and while it was performing due diligence on The Retail Company ("TRC"), it opened discussions with the TRC's major supplier, The Distribution Company ("TDC"). TDC distributed products, all of which were manufactured by others, throughout the United States to 300 customers. It had two warehouses: one on the East Coast and one on the West Coast. The products were sold to retailers that did much of their business during the Christmas season.

TDC was the largest in its industry and was privately held with sales of approximately $25 million and an irregular earnings history (Exhibit A, TDC's audited financial statements, and Exhibit B, the bank's analysis of the financial statements).

In November 2000, TPC purchased TRC for $2.5 million in cash and $500,000 in a Noncompetition Agreement for the owner and chief operating officer, who left the business after the acquisition. TPC raised the money from its existing investors. TRC had locations in Massachusetts, New York, and Connecticut, revenues of approximately $6 million and pre-tax earnings of approximately $500,000.

In August 2001, TPC merged with TDC by giving the owners of TDC 20 percent of the stock of TPC. In addition, TPC raised approximately $3.2 million from its venture capitalists to infuse working capital into TDC.

In addition to receiving 20 percent of the stock of TPC, the owners of TDC received a consulting contract and a Noncompetition Agreement calling for monthly payments and continuing lease payments on certain equipment used by TDC. Both the consulting contract and the lease called for monthly payments that would be lowered if wholesale sales decreased by more than 10 percent or if certain specific extraordinary demands on TDC's cash flow occurred. In addition, the sellers had a secured note outstanding from TDC that was put on a full payout schedule. The owners and chief operating officer of TDC were not active in the business after the merger.

Because of the state of the financial markets, TPC needed to retain the bank that was lending money to TDC. The bank was asked to finance both TDC and TRC, and signed the Credit Facilities Modification Agreement (Exhibit C). The bank also required TPC and the selling shareholders to guarantee the line of credit. The bank also required the selling shareholders to pledge their 20 percent interest in TPC as additional security for the loan. In addition, the sellers' secured loan was subordinated to the bank.

This case was prepared by Babson Professor Leslie Charm. Funding provided by Ewing Marion Kauffman Foundation. © Copyright Babson College, 2002. All rights reserved.

EXHIBIT A

Consolidated Balance Sheets of The Distribution Company

	September 30, 1999, 1998, 1997		
	1999	1998	1997
Assets			
Current assets			
Cash and cash equivalents	$638,899	$1,149,730	$836,841
Accounts and notes receivable, net of allowance for doubtful accounts and notes (1994, $204,000; 1993, $510,000; 1992, $511,000)			
(Notes 2 and 7)[1]	5,081,489	3,279,823	2,674,876
Merchandise inventories			
(Notes 1 and 3)	3,831,577	3,969,947	4,180,428
Refundable income taxes	—	—	21,232
Other current assets			
(Notes 1 and 7)	82,251	306,775	757,031
Total current assets	9,634,216	8,706,275	8,470,408
Notes and receivable and other assets, noncurrent, net of allowance for doubtful notes (1994, $165,000; 1993, $640,000; 1992, $186,000) (Notes 1 and 2)	698,450	800,885	615,070
Investment in unconsolidated subsidiary, at cost, plus equity in undistributed earnings (Note 4)	669,652	641,521	601,512
Equipment and leasehold improvements at cost:			
Equipment	404,948	403,589	385,581
Leasehold improvements	123,040	213,978	192,530
	527,988	617,567	578,111
Less accumulated depreciation and amortization	(324,995)	(312,822)	(344,152)
	202,993	304,745	233,959
Total assets (Note 5)	$11,205,311	$10,453,426	$9,920,949
Liabilities and Shareholders' Equity			
Current liabilities			
Notes payable (Notes 5 and 7)[1]	$4,695,000	$3,251,000	$3,010,000
Current portion of long-term debt (Note 5)	345,595	349,344	353,156
Franchise deposits	75,835	49,000	67,000
Accounts payable and accrued expenses:			
Merchandise	1,723,836	2,397,287	2,723,878
Other (Note 7)	2,415,479	2,278,073	2,154,200
Income taxes payable	—	29,271	—
Deferred income taxes	356,537	265,083	282,448
Total current liabilities	9,612,282	8,619,058	8,590,682

[1]The accompanying notes are an integral part of the consolidated financial statements.

(continued)

EXHIBIT A   (concluded)

September 30, 1999, 1998, 1997			
	1999	1998	1997
Liabilities and Shareholders' Equity			
Long-term debt, net of current portion (Note 5)	646,534	1,116,524	776,573
Deferred income taxes	132,000	34,600	25,670
Commitments and contingencies (Notes 6 and 7)			
Shareholders' equity			
Common stock, $.01 par value; authorized 300,000 shares; issued and outstanding 4,275 shares	43	43	43
Additional paid-in capital	940,679	940,679	940,679
Accumulated deficit	(126,227)	(257,478)	(412,698)
Total shareholder's equity	814,495	683,244	528,024
Total liabilities and shareholders' equity (Note 5)	$11,205,311	$10,453,426	$9,920,949

Consolidated Statements of Operations of The Distribution Company

For the years ending September 30, 1999, 1998, 1997			
	1999	1998	1997
Revenues			
Merchandise sales	$19,172,938	$17,675,839	$16,050,887
Retail sales by company-owned stores	306,721	1,702,280	5,326,783
Franchise royalties and other income	5,818,428	5,356,993	4,691,235
Initial franchise and related fees	155,000	145,485	178,500
	25,453,087	24,880,597	26,247,405
Costs and expenses (Notes 6 and 7)[1]			
Cost of merchandise sold and distribution expenses	17,030,024	15,151,470	13,711,089
Cost of retail sales and direct operating expenses of company owned stores	317,345	1,721,405	4,972,098
Selling, general, and administrative expenses	7,915,565	7,915,053	7,360,408
Net (gain) loss from store sales	(48,391)	(244,394)	25,599
	25,214,543	24,543,534	26,069,194
Income from operations	238,544	337,063	178,211
Interest expense, net (Note 5)	425,293	176,043	149,956
Income (loss) before income taxes and cumulative effect of accounting change	(186,749)	161,020	28,255
Income tax expense (benefit) (Note 8)	(18,000)	5,800	19,000
Income (loss) before cumulative effect of accounting change	(168,749)	155,220	9,255
Cumulative effect to October 1, 1987, of change in method of accounting for inventory costs, net of tax (Note 1)	300,000	—	—
Net income	$131,251	$155,220	$9,255

[1]The accompanying notes are an integral part of the consolidated financial statements.

EXHIBIT B

Comparative Statement of Financial Condition of The Distribution Company Prepared by The Bank

The Distribution Company
COMPARATIVE STATEMENT OF FINANCIAL CONDITION
Business: Wholesale Supply
In: $000s   SIC Code: 5199

Date:	9/30/98 UNQUAL		9/30/99 UNQUAL		9/30/00 UNQUAL		8/10/01 UNQUAL	(7)	8/11/01 BEG. B.S.	(8)
1. Current assets	8,167		8,858		9,384		4,838		4,723	
2. Current liabilities	8,219		9,447		11,463		9,318		9,858	
3. Working capital	(52)		(589)		(2,079)		(4,480)		(5,135)	
4. Total long-term debt	1,552		1,241		321		1,744		4,157	
5. Tangible net worth	579		815		(473)		(3,600)		(3,590)	
6. Net sales	24,881		25,341		25,757		19,817		0	
7. Net profits	155		132		(1,288)		(3,127)		0	
8. Cash generation	280		174		(1,227)		(3,089)		0	
9. Cash	1,150	11%	678	5.9%	793	7%	5	0.1%	5	0.0%
10. Marketable securities										
11. Receivables—net	2,907	27.8%	4,266	37.1%	4,123	36.5%	1,524	20.4%	1,063	5.8%
12. Inventory (FIFO) (1)	3,970	38%	3,832	33.3%	4,324	38.2%	3,010	40.3%	3,356	18.4%
13.										
14.										
15.										
16. Other current assets	140	1.3%	82	0.7%	44	1.3%	299	4%	299	1.6%
17. Prepaid expenses										
18. Total current assets	8,167	78.1%	8,858	77%	9,384	83%	4,838	64.8%	4,723	25.9%
19.										
20. Net fixed assets	305	2.9%	203	1.8%	180	1.6%	174	2.3%	1,187	6.5%
21. Due from affiliates	58	.6%	25	.2%	45	.4%	75	1%	75	.4%
22. Other receivables	43	.4%	376	3.3%	295	2.6%	207	2.8%	512	2.8%
23.										
24. Notes receivable	1,073	10.3%	2,041	17.7%	1,407	12.4%	2,168	29.1%	1,789	9.8%
25. Stores held for resale	63	.6%								
26. Inv. in unconsol. subs	641	6.1%								
27. Noncompetitive agreement									1,564	8.6%
28. Option agreement									575	3.2%
29.										

374

Date:	9/30/98 UNQUAL		9/30/99 UNQUAL		9/30/00 UNQUAL		8/10/01 UNQUAL	(7)	8/11/01 BEG. B.S.	(8)
30. Intangibles (4)	104	1.0%							7,777	2.7%
31. Total Assets	10,454	100%	11,503	100%	11,311	100%	7,462	100%	18,202	100%
32. Notes payable	2,851	27.3%	3,645	31.7%	2,800	24.8%	2,236	30%	2,236	2.3%
33. Notes payable	166	1.6%	598	5.2%	598	5.3%	588	7.9%	588	3.2%
34. Accounts payable—trade	2,397	22.9%	1,724	15%	3,261	28.8%	2,939	39.4%	2,939	6.1%
35. Accruals and payables (other)	2,351	22.5%	2,231	19.4%	2,864	25.3%	3,427	45.9%	3,803	0.9%
36. Current maturities LTD	349	3.3%	390	3.4%	146	1.3%	75	1.0%	239	1.3%
37. Franchise deposits	49	.5%	76	.7%	61	.5%	52	.7%	52	.3%
38. A/P affiliate		2%	233	2%	383	3.4%	1	0%	1	0%
39. N/P affiliate	56	5%	550	4.8%	1,350	11.9%				
40.										
41.										
42. Total current liabilities	8,219	78.6%	9,447	82.1%	11,463	101.3%	9,318	124.9%	9,858	54.2%
43. LTD	442	4.2%	191	1.7%	71	.6%	155	2.1%	1,004	5.5%
44.										
45. Noncompetitive agreement									1,564	8.6%
46. Deferred items	35	.3%								
47. Subordinated LTD	1,075	10.3%	1,050	9.1%	250	2.2%	1,589	21.3%	1,589	8.7%
48. Total liability and reserves	9,771	93.5%	10,688	92.9%	11,784	104.2%	11,062	148.2%	14,015	77%
49. Preferred stock										
50. Common stock										
51. Capital surplus	941	9%	941	8.2%	941	8.3%	941	12.6%	4,187	23%
52. Earned surplus	(258)	-2.5%	(126)	-1.1%	(1,414)	-12.5%	(4,541)	-60.9%		
53. Treasury stock										
54. TOTAL NET WORTH	683	6.5%	815	7.1%	(473)	-4.2%	(3,600)	-48.3%	4,187	23%
55. TOTAL LIABIL AND NET WORTH	10,454	100%	11,503	100%	11,311	100%	7,462	100%	18,202	100%
56. Annual lease rental	2,413	9.7%	2,444	9.6%	2,501	9.7%	2,371	12%	2,371	0%
57. Contingent liabilities (5)	1,142	10.9%	1,174	10.2%	991	8.8%	579	7.8%	579	3.2%
58. Fin goods										
59. INVENTORY Work process										
60. Raw material										
61. Land										
62. Buildings										
63. Leaseholds	214	34.6%	123	23.3%	134	23.7%	146	24.4%	96	8.1%
64. Furn. and fixt										
65. FIXED ASSETS Mach. and equip	404	65.4%	405	76.7%	432	76.3%	452	75.6%	1,091	100%

(continued)

EXHIBIT B (continued)

Date:	9/30/98 UNQUAL		9/30/99 UNQUAL		9/30/00 UNQUAL		8/10/01 UNQUAL		(7)		8/11/01 BEG. B.S.	(8)
66. Gross F A	618	100%	528	100%	566	100%	598	100%			1,187	100%
67. Depreciation	313	50.6%	325	61.6%	386	68.2%	424	70.9%				100%
68. Spread done by:	MVD		CMS		CHV				CHV			
69. Date spread done by:	2/23/99		2/22/01		2/22/02				2/22/02			
70. Net sales	24,881	100%	25,341	100%	25,757	100%			19,817	100%		
71. Cost of merch sold/distr	15,152	60.9%	17,030	67.2%	17,779	69%			12,928	65.2%		
72. Cost of retail sales	1,721	6.9%	317	1.3%	0				14	.1%		
73. Gross profit	8,008	32.3%	7,994	31.5%	7,978	31%			6,875	34.7%		
74. General and admin expense	7,915	31.8%	7,838	30.9%	8,827	34.3%			9,750	49.2%		
75.												
76. Operating profit	93	.4%	156	.6%	(849)	-3.3%			(2,875)	-14.5%		
77. Other income												
78. Other expense												
79. Earnings pre int and tax	473	1.9%	357	1.4%	(690)	-2.7%			(2,640)	-13.3%		
80. Interest	312	1.3%	532	2.1%	598	2.3%			487	2.5%		
81. Profit before income tax	161	.6%	(175)	-.7%	(1,288)	-5%			(3,127)	-15.8%		
82. Income taxes	6	0%	(7)	0%								
83. Extraordinary items (7)			300	1.2%								
84. Net profit after tax	155	.6%	132	.5%	(1,288)	-5%			(3,127)	-15.8%		
85. BEGINNING NET WORTH	528		683		815				(427)			
86. Net income/loss	155		132		(1,288)				(3,127)			
87. New equity												
88.												
89.												
90.												
91. Dividends/withdrawals												
92. Inc treasury stock												
93. ENDING NET WORTH	683		815		(473)				(3,600)			
94. Change in net worth	155		132		(1,288)				(3,127)			
95. Officers salaries												
96. Net profit after taxes	155		132		(1,288)				(3,127)			
97. Depreciation	116		77		61				38			
98. Amortization												
99. Deferred items	9		(35)		0				0			
100. SUBTOTAL CASH GENERATION	280		174		(1,227)				(3,089)			
101. New long-term debt	0		0		0				84			

376

Date:	9/30/98 UNQUAL	9/30/99 UNQUAL	9/30/00 UNQUAL	8/10/01 UNQUAL	(7)	8/11/01 BEG. B.S.	(8)
102. New equity	0	0	0		0		
103. Decrease intangibles	96	104	0		0		
104. Due from affiliates	292	33	0		0		
105. Decrease other noncurren	0	0	715		0		
106. Inc in on—current liabs	0	0	0		0		
107. Inc subordinated debt	1,075	0	0		1,339		
108. Dec in fixed assets	0	25	0		0		
109.							
110. TOTAL SOURCES	1,743	336	(512)		(1,666)		
111.							
112.							
113.							
114. Repayment of LTD	335	251	120		0		
115. Capital expenditures	187	0	38		32		
116. Dividends/withdrawals	0	0	0		0		
117. Increase intangibles	0	0	0		0		
118. Due from affiliates	0	0	20		30		
119. Inc other noncurrent ass	139	597	0		673		
120. Dec subordinated debt	0	25	800		0		
121. Dec in noncurrent liabs	0	0	0		0		
122. Decrease in equity	0	0	0		0		
123.							
124.							
125.							
126. TOTAL APPLICATIONS	661	873	978		735		
127. CHANGE NET WORKING CAPITAL	1,082	(537)	(1,490)		(2,401)		
128. Current ratio	0.99	0.94	0.82		0.52	0.48	
129. Quick ratio	0.49	0.52	0.43		0.16	0.11	
130. Sales/receivables (days)	42	61	58		25		
131. Cost of sales/inven (days)	94	81	88		77		
132. Total debt/tang net worth	16.88	13.11	-24.91		-3.07	-3.9	
133. Unsub debt/tang cap funds	5.26	5.17	-51.72		-4.71	6.21	
134. Net profit as % net worth	22.69%	16.2%	272.3%		94.76%		
135. Sales/working capital	2478.48	243.02	-12.39		-4.83		
136. Sales/net worth	36.43	31.09	-54.45		6.01		
137. COGS/payables (days)	57	36	66		75		

(continued)

377

EXHIBIT B (concluded)

Cash Flow Summary of The Distribution Company Prepared by The Bank

Date:	9/30/98 UNQUAL	9/30/99 UNQUAL	9/30/00 UNQUAL	8/10/01 UNQUAL
GROSS CASH FLOW				
1. Net income (loss)	155	132	(1,288)	(3,127)
2. Depreciation	116	77	61	38
3. Amortization	0	0	0	0
4. Deferred items	9	(35)	0	0
5.				
6. TOTAL GROSS CASH FLOW	280	174	(1,227)	(3,089)
7. FLOWS FROM (FOR) WORKING ACCTS				
8. Receivables—net	(559)	(1,359)	143	2,599
9. Inventory (FIFO) (1)	210	138	(492)	1,314
10. Accounts payable—trade	(327)	(673)	1,537	(322)
11. Accruals and payables—other	790	(120)	633	563
12. Income taxes	0	0	0	0
13. Other current assets	(49)	58	(62)	(155)
14. Marketable securities	0	0	0	0
15. CASH GENER FROM OPER.	345	(1,782)	532	910
16. FLOWS FROM (FOR) NONCUR ACCTS				
17. Net fixed assets	(187)	25	(38)	(32)
18. Due from affiliates	292	33	(20)	(30)
19. Other noncurrent assets	(139)	(597)	715	(673)
20. Intangibles (4)	96	104	0	0
21. CASH AVAIL FOR EXT	407	(2,217)	1,189	175
22. REQUIRED PMTS AND RETIREMENTS				
23. Other cur liab	(837)	754	935	(1,741)
24. Other noncurrent liabs	0	0	0	0
25. Dividends/withdrawals	0	0	0	0
26. Current maturities LTD	(4)	41	(244)	(71)
27. INTERNAL CASH FLOW	(434)	(1,422)	1,880	(1,637)
28. FINANCING				
29. Notes payable—UST	(159)	794	(845)	(564)
30. Notes payable—bank fiveq	166	432	0	(10)

378

Date:	9/30/98 UNQUAL	9/30/99 UNQUAL	9/30/00 UNQUAL	8/10/01 UNQUAL
31. Long-term debt	(335)	(251)	(120)	84
32. Subordinated LTD	1,075	(25)	(800)	1,339
33. Equity financing	0	0	0	0
34. INCREASE/DECREASE IN CA	313	(472)	115	(788)

Footnotes:

1. As of 10/1/98, the company changed its method of accounting for inventory to include overhead costs, which had previously been charged to expense.
   As of 8/11/01, the company changed the method of inventory valuation from LIFO to FIFO.

2. Consolidation up to and including FYE '99 did not include the finance company subsidiary. FYE 2000 financials include this subsidiary as a wholly owned subsidiary.

3. Previous to 8/10/01, the company's auditors were Cooper's & Lybrand.

4. In FYE '98, intangibles consist of unrecognized costs.

At 8/11/97, intangibles consisted of goodwill, a noncompetition agreement, and an option agreement.

5. Contingent liabilities consist of the company's guarantee on obligations of some franchisees, letters of credit with the bank, and various lawsuits about normal business.

6. Extraordinary item at FYE 2000 is the cumulative effect of the change in the method of accounting for inventory costs, net of tax effects.

7. Deloitte & Touche feels that there is substantial doubt whether the company will continue as a going concern due to historical losses and a deficiency in capital.

8. On August 11, 2001, The Parent Company acquired all the outstanding shares of The Distribution Company. Accordingly, the company's historical balance sheet at August 10, 2001, has been revalued to fair market value on the opening balance sheet of the company as of August 11, 2001.

EXHIBIT C

Credit Facilities Modification Agreement

This is a Credit Facilities Modification Agreement made and entered into as of this 8th day of August 2001 by and among The Distribution Company, a Massachusetts corporation having a principal place of business at 385 Appleton Street, North Andover, Massachusetts ("TDC" "Borrower"); The Parent Company ("TPC"), a Delaware corporation with a principal place of business at 222 Benchley Avenue, Hartford, Connecticut; and The Retail Company ("TRC"), a Delaware corporation with principal place of business at 18 Holland Street, Hartford, Connecticut 06874; and the Bank ("Bank"), a Massachusetts banking corporation having an address at Boston, Massachusetts 02108.

Preamble

WHEREAS, on December 3, 1995, the Borrower entered into a $4,000,000.00 revolving loan facility with the Bank, as evidenced by two notes in the amounts of $1,500,000 and $2,500,000, respectively, secured by a security agreement covering all assets of the Borrower and further secured by an assignment of certain promissory notes payable to the Borrower (the Assignment); and

WHEREAS, on April 8, 1997, the Borrower executed a further "Security Agreement—Inventory, Accounts, Equipment and other Property" ("Security Agreement") securing all liabilities of the Borrower to the Bank (a true copy of which is attached hereto as Exhibit A-1); and

WHEREAS, on October 1, 1999, the Borrower executed a "Commercial Demand Note" in the amount of Three Million Five Hundred Thousand Dollars ($3,500,000.00), which Commercial Demand Note superseded the two notes dated as of December 3, 1995, and is secured by the Security Agreement (a true copy of which is attached hereto as Exhibit A-2); and

WHEREAS, on November 18, 1999, Sellers 1, 2, and 3 (S123) ("Individual Guarantors") each executed a "Limited Guaranty" of the liabilities of the Borrower (true copies of which are attached hereto as Exhibit A-3, A-4, and A-5); and

WHEREAS, on November 18, 1999, Seller, an affiliate of the Borrower, executed a Subordination Agreement in favor of the Bank in which certain notes of the Borrower held by Seller were subordinated to the Borrower's indebtedness to the Bank ("Subordination Agreement") (a true copy of which is attached hereto as Exhibit A-6); and

WHEREAS, the Individual Guarantors own all of the issued and outstanding common stock of the Borrower; and

WHEREAS, pursuant to an Agreement and Plan of Merger dated as of August 2001 ("Merger Agreement"), TDC has been merged into the Borrower so that the Borrower is now a wholly owned subsidiary of TPC and the Individual Guarantors have received Series E Preferred Stock of TPC in lieu of the common stock of the Borrower; and

WHEREAS, TRC is a wholly owned subsidiary of TPC which operates approximately nine TRCs in Massachusetts, Connecticut, and New York; and

WHEREAS, TPC, TRC, and the Borrower have requested that the existing credit facility from the Bank to the Borrower be continued and amended for the benefit of TPC and TRC, and in consideration thereof TPC and TRC have agreed to guaranty loans, the parties now wish to restate and amend the terms and conditions of the credit facility;

NOW, THEREFORE, for good and valuable consideration, the parties do hereby agree as follows:

Section I. Definitions

Section 1.1. Acceptable Inventory. Acceptable Inventory shall mean such of the Borrower's new, unopened salable inventory shelf for sale to others (but excluding raw materials, work in progress, and materials used or consumed in the Borrower's business) as the Bank in its sole discretion deems eligible for borrowing.

Section 1.2. Acceptable Accounts. Acceptable Accounts shall mean accounts under 60 days old measured from the date of the invoice, which arose from *bona fide* outright sales of merchandise to a Person which is not a subsidiary or affiliate of the Borrower, TPC, or TRC.

Section 1.3. Accounts. "Accounts" and "Accounts Receivable" include, without limitation, "accounts" as defined in the UCC, and also all accounts, accounts receivable, notes, drafts, acceptances, and other forms of obligations and receivables and rights to payment for credit extended and for goods sold or leased, or services rendered, whether or not yet earned by performance; all inventory which gave rise thereto, and all rights associated with such inventory, including the right of stoppage in transit; all reclaimed, returned, rejected, or repossessed inventory (if any) the sale of which gave rise to any Account.

Section 1.4. Bank. The Bank, a Massachusetts banking Corporation.

Section 1.5. Base Lending Rate. The rate of interest published internally and designated by the Bank from time to time, as its Base Lending Rate.

Section 1.6. Collateral. All assets of the Borrower, tangible and intangible, as described in the Security Agreement and in the Assignment, as amended herein.

Section 1.7. Corporate Guarantors. TPC and TRC.

Section 1.8. Credit Facilities Modification Agreement. This agreement and any and all subsequent amendments thereto.

EXHIBIT C   (continued)

Section 1.9. Credit Facility.   The Loans granted to or for the benefit of the Borrower pursuant to the Loan Documents.

Section 1.10. Event of Default.   Any event described in Section 8 hereto.

Section 1.11. Guarantors.   The Corporate Guarantors, the Individual Guarantors, and Sellers.

Section 1.12.   Individual Guarantors. Sellers 1, 2, 3.

Section 1.13. Loan Documents.   This term shall refer, collectively, to (i) the Commercial Demand Note, (ii) the Security Agreement, (iii) the Assignment, (iv) all UCC Financial Statements, (v) the Subordination Agreement, (vi) the Individual Guarantees, (vii) TPC Guaranty, (viii) TRC Guaranty, (ix) the Sellers Guaranty, (x) the Sellers Pledge and Security Agreement, (xi) TPC Pledge of Stock of Borrower and TRC, (xii) TPC Subordination Agreement, (xiii) the Individual Guarantor's Pledge of Preferred Stock of TPC, (xiv) TRC Security Agreement, (xv) this Credit Facilities Modification Agreement, and all amendments, modifications, and extensions thereof, and any other document or agreement pursuant to which the Bank is granted a lien or other interest as security for the Borrower's obligations to it.

Section 1.14. Loan(s).   Loans or advances by the Bank to the Borrower pursuant to the Loan Documents. The Loan shall consist of a Revolving Loan of up to $2,800,000 as provided for in Sections 2.1 through 2.5 hereof, including any letters of credit issued by the Bank for the account of the Borrower as provided in Section 2.4 hereof. The Borrower and the Lender acknowledge that as of August 2001, the outstanding balance of the Revolving Loans was $_____.

Section 1.15. Loan Review Date.   July 31, 2002, or such later date to which the Loan may be extended pursuant to Section 2.5 hereof.

Section 1.16. Note.   The $3,500,000.00 Commercial Demand Note dated October 1, 1999.

Section 1.17. Obligations.   Those obligations described in Section 2 hereof.

Section 1.18. Person.   A corporation, association, partnership, trust, organization, business, individual or government, or any governmental agency or political subdivision thereof.

Section 1.19. Sellers Debt.   All loans from Sellers to the Borrower whether now existing or hereafter arising.

Section 1.20. Revolving Loan or Revolving Credit.   The revolving working capital loan evidenced by the Commercial Demand Note as described in this Agreement.

Section 1.21. Subordinated Debt.   The Sellers Debt and TPC Debt.

Section 1.22. Subsidiary.   Means any entity that is directly or indirectly controlled by the Borrower or TPC.

Section 1.23.   Capitalized terms not otherwise defined herein shall have the meanings ascribed thereto in the Loan Documents.

Section 2. Loans, Revision of Terms, Confirmation of Security Documents; Additional Security

Section 2.1   (a) *Amount of Availability of Revolving Credit*. The Bank has established a discretionary revolving line of credit in the Borrower's favor in the amount of the Borrower's Availability (as defined below), as determined by the Bank from time to time hereafter. All loans made by the Bank under this Agreement, and all of the Borrower's other liabilities to the Bank under or pursuant to this Agreement, are payable ON DEMAND.

As used herein, the term "Availability" refers at any time to the lesser of (i) or (ii) below:

(i) up to (A) Two Million Eight Hundred Thousand Dollars ($2,800,000) (or such other amount as the Bank may set from time to time, in the Bank's discretion),

minus . . .

(B) the aggregate amounts then undrawn on all outstanding letters of credit issued by the Bank for the account of the Borrower.

(ii) up to (A) seventy percent (70%) (or such revised percentage as the Bank may set from time to time, in the Bank's discretion) of the face amount (determined by the Bank in the Bank's sole discretion) of each of the Acceptable Accounts,

Plus . . .

(B) thirty percent (30%) (or such revised percentage as the Bank may set from time to time, in the Bank's discretion) of the value of the Acceptable Inventory (Acceptable Inventory being valued at the lower cost or market after deducting all transportation, processing, handling charges, and all other costs and expenses affecting the value thereof, all as determined by the Bank in its sole discretion) but not to exceed $1,200,000.

minus . . .

(C) the aggregate amounts then undrawn on all outstanding letters of credit issued by the Bank for the account of the Borrower (the "Formula Amount").

The Revolving Credit is not a committed line of financing. The borrowing formula described in this Section 2.1 is intended solely for monitoring purposes.

(b) *Advances.*   Advances may consist of direct advances to the Borrower payable ON DEMAND, or letters of credit issued on behalf of the Borrower. The Borrower may borrow, repay, and re-borrow Revolving Loans under this Agreement by

---

EXHIBIT C   (continued)

---

written notice given to the Bank at least 2 business days prior to the date of the requested advance. Each request for an advance shall be in an integral multiple of $50,000 and shall be subject to approval by the Bank, which may be granted, denied, or granted conditionally in the Bank's sole discretion.

(c) *Mandatory Reduction.*   The Borrower shall reduce the outstanding balance of the Revolving Loan to $600,000 or less (exclusive of letters of credit) for a period of thirty (30) consecutive days between December 1, 2001 and January 31, 2002.

(d) *Availability—Overadvances.*   The Borrower's Availability shall not exceed the Formula Amount (as set forth in Section 2.1 (a) (ii)), provided that the Borrower may borrow $700,000 in excess of the Formula Amount prior to September 30, 2001 and $300,000 in excess of the Formula Amount between February 28, 2002 and July 31, 2002, provided further that in no event shall outstanding advances ever exceed $2,800,000.

(e) *Approval of Accounts and Inventory:*

(i) *Accounts.*   All account debtors shall be subject to the approval of the Bank in its sole discretion, and the Bank's eligibility determinations shall be final and conclusive. The determination by the Bank that a particular account from a particular account debtor is eligible for borrowing shall not obligate the Bank to deem subsequent accounts from the same account debtor to be eligible for borrowing, nor to continue to deem that account to be so eligible. All collateral not considered eligible for borrowing nevertheless secures the prompt, punctual, and faithful performance of the Borrower's Obligations. The determination that a given account of the Borrower is eligible for borrowing shall not be deemed a determination by the Bank relative to the actual value of the account in question. All risks concerning the creditworthiness of all accounts are and remain upon the Borrower.

(ii) *Inventory.*   The Bank's determinations that certain inventory is, or is not, eligible for borrowing shall be final and conclusive. No sale of inventory shall be on consignment, approval, or under any other circumstances such that such inventory may be returned to the Borrower without the consent of the Bank, except for transactions in the normal course of business. None of the inventory will be stored or processed with a bailee or other third party without the prior written consent of the Bank.

(f) *Borrowing Certificate.*   Each request for an advance shall be accomplished by a borrowing certificate, in form acceptable to the Bank, which shall be signed by such person whom the Bank reasonably believes to be authorized to act in this regard on behalf of the Borrower, and shall certify that as of the date of the subject certificate, (i) there has been no material adverse change in the Borrower's and Corporate Guarantors' respective financial conditions taken as a whole from the information previously furnished the Bank; (ii) the Borrower and TPC are in compliance with, and have not breached any of, the covenants contained herein; and (iii) no event has occurred or failed to occur which occurrence or failure is, or with the passage of time or giving of notice (or both) would constitute, an Event of Default (as described herein) whether or not the Bank has exercised any of its rights upon such occurrence.

(g) *Loan Account.*

(i) An account (hereinafter, the "Loan Account") has been opened on the books of the Bank in which account a record has been, and shall be, kept of all loans made by the Bank to the Borrower under or pursuant to this Loan and of all payments thereon.

(ii) The Bank may also keep a record (either in the Loan Account or elsewhere, as the Bank may from time to time elect) of all interest, service charges, costs, expenses, and other debits owed the Bank on account of the loan arrangement contemplated hereby and of all credits against such amounts so owed.

(iii) All credits against the Borrower's indebtedness indicated in the Loan Account shall be conditional upon final payment to the Bank of the items giving rise to such credits. The amount of any item credited against the Loan Account which is charged back against the Bank for any reason or is not so paid may be added to the Loan Account, or charged against any account maintained by the Borrower with the Bank (at the Bank's discretion and without notice, in each instance), and shall be Liability, in each instance whether or not the item so charged back or not so paid is returned.

(iv) Any statement rendered by the Bank to the Borrower shall be considered correct and accepted by the Borrower and shall be conclusively binding upon the Borrower unless the Borrower provides the Bank with written objection thereto within twenty (20) days from the mailing of such statement, which such written objection shall indicate with particularly the reason for such objection. The Loan Account and the Bank's books and records concerning the loan arrangement contemplated herein shall be prima facie evidence and proof of the items described therein.

Section 2.2. Note.   The Borrower has executed and delivered the Note to the Bank. The Note evidences each advance under the Loan. The Note is on a DEMAND basis and is payable as to interest in arrears on the first day of each calendar month. The Note may be prepaid at any time, in whole or in part, without penalty. Except as modified herein, the Borrower hereby ratifies and confirms the Note in every respect.

Section 2.3. Interest and Fees

(a) *Interest.*   The Loans (except the letters of credit) shall bear interest at a rate which, until the Loan may be due and payable, shall be the Base Lending Rate plus one percent (1%). The rate of interest shall vary from time to time as the Base Lending Rate varies, and any change in the rate of interest shall become effective on the date of the change in the

EXHIBIT C   (continued)

Base Lending Rate. Interest shall be computed and adjusted on a daily basis using a 360-day year. Overdue principal and interest shall bear interest at the rate of two percent (2%) per annum above the Base Lending Rate.

(b) *Balances.*   The Borrower shall maintain a balance (exclusive of balances necessary to cover service charges) at all times of at least ten percent (10%) of the outstanding balance of the Revolving Loan. For each day that the Borrower shall fail to maintain such balances, the Borrower shall pay to the Bank on the first day of the following month a fee to compensate the Bank for the lack of use of such funds during the previous month.

(c) *Alternative Pricing.*   At its election, the Bank may transfer the Revolving Credit from the commercial lending division to the asset-based lending division in which event the interest rate may be changed to the Base Lending Rate plus one and one-half percent (1 1/2%), with 2 business days' clearance. In addition, the Borrower shall provide such further reports and information as is customarily required of Borrowers serviced by such division.

Section 2.4. Letters of Credit.   From time to time, the Bank has made loans to the Borrower in the form of letters of credit, as evidenced by the Applications for Commercial Credit as attached hereto as Exhibit B. The borrower may request that the Bank make additional loans in the form of further letters of credit provided that the total amount of Documentary Letters of Credit outstanding at any time shall not exceed $550,000 and the total amount of Standby Letters of Credit outstanding at any time shall not exceed $72,000. Each such request for the issuance of a letter of credit shall be made at least five (5) business days in advance and shall be accompanied by the Bank's standard form of "Application for Commercial Credit" and "Commercial Letter of Credit Agreement" duly executed by the Borrower. The Bank shall have the right, at its option, to limit the term of any letter of credit to the Loan Review Date. In the event the Bank elects to issue a Standby Letter of Credit, the Borrower shall pay the Bank a fee of one percent (1%) per annum of the face amount of such Standby Letter of Credit, and one-half of one percent (.5%) of the face amount of a Documentary Letter of Credit or, if different, the then standard or customary fee for the type and amount of letter of credit requested, in lieu of the interest otherwise required on the Loan. All drafts drawn on a letter of credit shall be immediately repayable in full by the Borrower without need for notice or demand, together with interest thereon at the rate of three percent (3%) above the Base Rate for each day that such draft remains outstanding.

Section 2.5. Review of Loan.   Without derogating from the DEMAND nature of the Revolving Loan, the Revolving Credit facility will be subject to review on July 31, 2002. There is no obligation on the Bank to renew the Revolving Credit or to extend it beyond July 31, 2002.

Section 2.6. Subordination of Sellers Debt.   Sellers, a Massachusetts general partnership controlled by the Individual Guarantors, acknowledge that the Subordination Agreement remains in full force and effect, that the Loans constitute Senior Debt under the Subordination Agreement, and that the Sellers Debt in the amount of $1,800,000 as evidenced by a Term Promissory Note in said amount dated as of August 8, 2001, remains subject and subordinate to the Loans as provided in the Subordination Agreement. The Term Promissory Note evidencing the Sellers Debt has this day been delivered to the Bank duly endorsed.

Section 2.7. Assignment.   The Borrower hereby ratifies and confirms the Assignment, and acknowledges that the Assignment secures the Loans. A current Schedule A to the Assignment is attached hereto as Exhibit C. The notes secured by the Assignment have this day been delivered to the Bank duly endorsed. Upon payment in full of any of the assigned notes by the makers thereof and the deposit of such funds in the Borrower's account at the Bank, the Bank shall redeliver the paid note(s) to the Borrower. From time to time, the Borrower may renegotiate the terms of such notes with the makers thereof on commercially reasonable terms and conditions in the Borrower's reasonable judgment. All such amendments or renegotiated notes shall be delivered to the Bank against delivery to the Borrower of the original notes, if required by it, and shall be included in the Assignment.

Section 2.8. Guaranty; Security.   (a) *Individual Guarantors.* The Individual Guarantors hereby ratify and confirm their respective Limited Guarantees in all respects and further confirm that such Limited Guarantees apply to the Loan, including, without limitations to, the various letters of credit. To secure such guarantees, the Individual Guarantors have this day pledged to the Bank their Series E Preferred Stock of TPC as set forth in the respective Pledge Agreements attached hereto as Exhibit D. The Individual Guarantors may convert their Series E Preferred Stock into common stock of TPC, in which event all shares received as a result of such conversion shall be similarly pledged to the Bank as collateral for their respective Limited Guarantees.

(b) *Corporate Guarantors.* TPC and TRC have this day guaranteed all of the Borrower's obligations to the Bank by the execution of "TPC Guaranty" and "TRC Guaranty" attached hereto as Exhibit E and F, respectively. TPC has secured TPC Guaranty by pledging to the Bank all of the Borrower's and TRC shares as set forth in the Pledge Agreement attached hereto as Exhibit G. TRC has further secured TRC Guaranty by executing and delivering to the Bank a Security Agreement on all of its assets as set forth on Exhibit H attached hereto. TRC has deposited $250,000 in an account at the Bank which amount may be used by TRC for working capital purposes.

(c) *Seller Associates.* Seller has this day executed a limited guaranty of the Borrower's obligations to the Bank by the execution of the "Seller's Guaranty" attached hereto as Exhibit I. Seller has secured its guaranty by the execution and delivery to the Bank of a pledge and assignment of various payments due Seller from the Borrower under (i) the Consulting and Noncompetition Agreement, and (ii) the Seller's Debt, all as set forth in the "Seller's Pledge and Security Agreement" attached hereto as Exhibit J. Except as set forth in the Seller's Pledge and Security Agreement, all payments and proceeds

EXHIBIT C   (continued)

received by Seller pursuant to the Consulting and Noncompetition Agreement and the Seller Debt shall be immediately deposited in a separate account with the Bank and pledged to the Bank as further security for the Guarantee. Except as set forth in the Seller's Pledge and Security Agreement, no funds may be withdrawn from such account until Loan has been paid in full and the Bank has no further obligation to advance funds hereunder. In the event that the Bank shall apply any funds received by Seller under Sections 3(a), 3(c), and 3(d) of the Consulting and Noncompetition Agreement (but not the Seller debt) against the Loan, the Individual Guarantors shall receive credit against their respective Limited Guarantees for the amount so applied by the Bank.

Section 2.9. Security Agreement.   As the security for the prompt satisfaction of all its Obligations to the Bank, the Borrower has executed and delivered the Security Agreement. The Borrower hereby ratifies and confirms the Security Agreement and acknowledges that the Security Agreement remains in full force and effect and constitutes a first and exclusive lien on the Collateral. The Collateral, together with all other property of the Borrower of any kind held by the Bank, shall stand as one general continuing collateral security for all Obligations and may be retained by the Bank until all Obligations are paid in full.

Section 2.10. TPC Debt.   As of the date hereof, TPC has agreed to loan to the Borrower the sum of $2,750,000 ("TPC Loan") to be used as additional working capital. Of this sum, $575,000 will be advanced to Realty Trust to be applied toward the third mortgage on the property at 385 Appleton Street, North Andover, Massachusetts, and approximately $400,000 has been or will be advanced to pay (i) costs of a certain litigation settlement and (ii) accounting fees, legal fees, and closing costs incurred by the Borrower in connection with the Merger Agreement and this Loan. TPC has this day deposited the balance of TPC Loan, approximately $1,775,000, in an account to the Bank as security for the Loan as set forth in the "Pledge and Security Agreement—Cash Collateral Account" attached hereto as Exhibit K. At such time as TPC shall have restructured its loan with Union Bank & Trust as provided in Section 2.11 hereof (or otherwise restructured such debt in a manner reasonably satisfactory to the Bank), TPC may withdraw $250,000 from the Cash Collateral Account and may use such funds for its own corporate purposes. From time to time, and so long as there is not Event of Default hereunder, TPC may withdraw funds from the cash collateral account at the Bank and advance such funds to the Borrower by depositing such funds in the Borrower's account at the Bank for the purpose of implementing TPC Debt. At such time as TPC advances funds to the Borrower pursuant to TPC Debt, the Borrower shall execute one or more promissory notes to evidence TPC Debt and such note(s) shall be endorsed in favor of and delivered to the Bank. TPC Debt shall be fully subject and subordinate to the Loan, and the Bank and TPC have this day executed "TPC Subordination Agreement" in the form attached hereto as Exhibit L to evidence such subordination.

Section 2.11. Restructuring of Union Trust Debt.   TPC shall restructure its existing indebtedness with Union Trust Company as follows: (a) the line of credit shall not exceed $1,000,000; (b) the maturity date thereof shall be no earlier than July 31, 2002; and (c) Union Trust shall not have received any security interest in the assets of the Borrower or TPC Loan (or the proceeds thereof). TPC shall provide written evidence of such debt restructuring in form satisfactory to the Bank on or before August 30, 2001.

Section 2.12. Confirmation of Subsidiary Debt.   As of the date hereof, the Borrower shall provide written confirmation to the Bank, in form satisfactory to the Bank, that TDC debt to the Boston Five Cents Savings Bank has been extended on a term basis for not less than 1 year, that such debt does not exceed $598,000, that the Borrower has guaranteed the interest but not the principal thereof, and that the collateral securing the loan is set forth on a schedule submitted to and approved by the Bank.

Section 3. Use of Proceeds and Payments

Section 3.1. Use of Proceeds.   The Borrower has used and shall continue to use the proceeds of the Revolving Loan for its general working capital purposes.

Section 3.2. Payment.   All payments of commitment fees, fees for letters of credit, service fees, activity charges, and all payments and prepayments of principal and all payments of interest shall be made by the Borrower to the Bank in immediately available funds at the head office of the Bank in Boston, Massachusetts 02108. The Borrower hereby authorizes the Bank, without any further notice, to charge any account the Borrower maintains at the Bank for each payment due hereunder or under the Note (for interest, fees, service charges, activity charges, principal, or otherwise) on the due date thereof, provided that the Bank shall not charge any account in which the Borrower is acting as agent or trustee for any other person.

Section 3.3. Regular Activity Charges.   The Borrower shall pay to the Bank, on a monthly basis, the Bank's usual activity charges for banking services; such charges may be payable by maintaining adequate balances or by payment of a deficiency fee.

Section 4. Representations and Warranties of the Borrower

The Borrower represents and warrants the following.

Section 4.1. Corporate Authority.

(a) *Incorporation; Good Standing.* The Borrower is a corporation duly organized, validly existing, and in good standing under the laws of the Commonwealth of Massachusetts, and has all requisite corporate power to own its property and conduct its business as now conducted and as presently contemplated.

EXHIBIT C   (continued)

(b) *Authorization.* The execution, delivery, and performance of this Agreement, the Note, the Security Agreement, the Assignment, and the transactions contemplated hereby and thereby (i) are within the authority of the Borrower; (ii) have been authorized by the Board of Directors of the Borrower; and (iii) will not contravene any provision of law, or the Borrower's Articles of Organization, By-Laws, or any other agreement, instrument, or undertaking binding upon the Borrower.

Section 4.2. Governmental and Other Approvals.   The execution, delivery, and performance of this Agreement, the Note, the Security Agreement, the Assignment, and the transactions contemplated hereby and thereby by the Borrower (a) do not require any approval or consent of, or filing with, any governmental agency or authority in the United States of America or otherwise which has not been obtained and which is not in full force and effect as of the date hereof; and (b) do not require any approval or consent of any security holder of the Borrower.

Section 4.3. Title to Properties; Absence of Liens.   The Borrower has good and valid title to all of the Collateral free from all defects, liens, charges, and encumbrances.

Section 4.4. No Default.   The Borrower is not in default in any material respect under provision of its Articles of Organization, or any provisions of any material contract, agreement, or obligation, exclusive of leases (whether related to the Loans or otherwise), which default could result in a significant impairment of the ability of the Borrower to fulfill its obligations hereunder or under the Note or the Loan Documents or a significant impairment of the financial position or business of the Borrower.

Section 4.5. Margin Regulations.   The Borrower is not in the business of extending credit for the purpose of purchasing or carrying margin stock (within the meaning of Regulation G or Regulation U of the Board of Governors of the Federal Reserve System), and no portion of any Loan made to the Borrower hereunder has been or will be used, directly or indirectly, by the Borrower to purchase or carry or to extend credit to others for the purpose of purchasing or carrying any margin stock.

Section 4.6. Financial Statements.   The Borrower has furnished to the Bank an audited balance sheet and statement of income and changes in financial position of the Borrower for the period ended September 30, 2000 (the September 2000 Report), and an internally prepared income statement for the interim period ending May, 31, 2001 (May 2001 Report), which has been certified to be true, accurate, and complete by the chief financial officer of the Borrower. The balance sheets, income statements, and statements of changes in financial position set forth in the "September 2000 Report" and the "May 2001 Report" present fairly the financial position of the Borrower as at the date thereof.

Section 4.7. Changes.   To the best of the Borrower's knowledge, since the September 2000 Report and the May 2001 Report, there has been no material change in the assets, liabilities, financial condition, or business of the Borrower which taken together would have a material, adverse effect on the net worth therein reported.

Section 4.8. Taxes   Except as set forth in Schedule ____ of the Merger Agreement, the Borrower has filed all United States Federal and State income tax returns and all other state, federal, or local tax returns required to be filed, and the Borrower and its Subsidiaries have paid or made adequate provision for the payment of all taxes, assessments, and other governmental charges due. The Borrower knows of no basis for any material additional assessment with respect to any fiscal year for which adequate reserves have not been established.

Section 4.9. Litigation.   Except as set forth in Exhibit 3.18 of the Merger Agreement, there is no material litigation pending or, to the knowledge of its officers, threatened against the Borrower, or any of the Individual Guarantors.

Section 5. Representation and Warranties of TPC and TRC

Each of the Corporate Guarantors warrants and represents as to itself as follows:

Section 5.1. Corporate Authority.

(a) *Incorporation; Good Standing.*   Each corporation is a corporation duly organized, validly existing, and in good standing under the law of Delaware and has all requisite corporate power to own its property and conduct its business as now conducted and as presently contemplated.

(b) *Authorization.*   The execution, delivery, and performance of this Agreement, and the transactions contemplated hereby and thereby, (i) are within the authority of such corporation; (ii) have been authorized by the Board of such corporation; and (iii) will not contravene any provision of law, or Articles of Organization, By-Laws, or any other agreement, instrument, or undertaking binding upon such corporation.

Section 5.2. Governmental and Other Approvals.   The execution, delivery, and performance of this Agreement, and the transactions contemplated hereby and thereby by the Corporate Guarantors, (a) do not require any approval or consent of, or filing with, any governmental agency or authority in the United States of America or otherwise which has not been obtained and which is not in full force and effect as of the date hereof; and (b) do not require any approval or consent of any security holder of such corporations.

Section 5.3. Title to Properties; Absence of Liens.   TRC has good and valid title to all of the collateral described in the TRC Security Agreement free from all defects, liens, charges, and encumbrances. TPC has good and valid title to the shares of the Borrower described in the TPC Pledge of Stock Agreement.

EXHIBIT C   (continued)

Section 5.4. No Default. Such corporation is not in default in any material respect under any provision of its Articles of Organization, or any provisions of any material contract, agreement, or obligation (whether related to the Loans or otherwise), which default could result in a significant impairment of the ability of such corporation to fulfill its obligations hereunder or any of the Loan Documents or a significant impairment of the financial position or business of such corporation.

Section 5.5. Financial Statements. TPC has furnished to the Bank a copy of its audited Consolidated Balance Sheet and Consolidated Statement of Operations for the period ended December 31, 2000 (the December 2000 Report), and for the interim period ending March 31, 2001 (March 2001 Report), which have been certified to be true, accurate, and complete by the chief financial officer of the Borrower. The Consolidated Balance Sheets, and Consolidated Statement of Operations set forth in the December 2000 Report and the March 2002 Report, present fairly the financial position of TPC as at the dates thereof.

Section 5.6. Changes. Since the December 2000 Report and the March 2001 Report there has been no material change in the assets, liabilities, financial condition, or business of TPC which taken together would have a material, adverse effect on the net worth therein reported except as previously reported to the Bank in the May 31, 2001, interim Report.

Section 5.7. Taxes. TRC and its Subsidiaries have filed all United States Federal and State income tax returns and all other state, federal, or local tax returns required to be filed, and TPC and its Subsidiaries have paid or made adequate provision for the payment of all taxes, assessments, and other governmental charges due. TPC knows of no basis for any material additional assessment with respect to any fiscal year for which adequate reserves have not been established.

Section 5.8. Litigation. Except as set forth in TPC Form 10 K dated as of December 31, 2000, there is no material litigation pending or, to the knowledge of its officers, threatened against either of the Corporate Guarantors.

Section 6. Conditions Precedent to Loans

Section 6.1. Conditions Precedent to Each Advance. The obligation of the Bank to continue to make future Revolving Loan advances and to issue additional letters of credit shall be subject to the performance by the Borrower of all its agreements heretofore to be performed by it and to the satisfaction, prior to or at the time of making each such advances, of the following conditions ("Conditions Precedent"):

(a) *First Advance.* Prior to the Bank's making the first advance after the date hereof, the Borrower shall provide to the Bank and the Bank shall have approved (i) evidence of compliance with the provisions of Section 2.10 and 2.12 hereof; (ii) internally prepared financial statements of TPC and TRC as of May 31, 2001, certified as accurate by the chief financial officer of such corporation; (iii) copies of all documents executed in connection with the Merger Agreement, including all exhibits and schedules thereto; (iv) copies of all documents by which TPC has generated or raised the amount of TPC Debt; (v) fully executed Loan Documents; (vi) certified or original copies of all corporate votes, consents, and authorizations necessary to implement this Agreement; and (vii) such other documents, certificates, instruments, and opinions as the Bank may reasonably require.

(b) *Authorized Signatures.* The Borrower shall have certified to the Bank the name and a specimen signature of each officer of the Borrower, authorized to sign requests for loan advances, borrowing certificates, or applications for letters of credit. The Bank may rely conclusively on such certification until it receives notice in writing to the contrary from the Borrower.

(c) *Corporate Action.* The Bank shall have received duly certified copies of all votes passed or other corporate action taken by the Board of Directors of the Borrower with respect to the Loan.

(d) *No Adverse Development.* Neither the consolidated financial position nor the business as a whole of the Borrower or the Corporate Guarantors, nor any substantial portion of the properties and assets of the Borrower or the Corporate Guarantors, shall have been materially adversely affected between the date of application and the date of any advanced hereunder as a result of any legislative or regulatory change or of any fire, explosion, tidal wave, flood, windstorm, earthquake, landslide, accident, condemnation, or governmental intervention, order of any court or governmental agency or commission, invalidity or expiration of any patent or patent license, act of God or of the public enemy or of armed forces, rebellion, strike, labor disturbance or embargo, or otherwise, whether or not insured against, which might impair materially the ability of the Borrower or Corporate Guarantors to fulfill punctually their obligations under this Agreement, the Note, the Loan Documents, and the Guarantee executed in connection herewith.

(e) *Legality.* The making of such Loans shall not contravene any law or rule or regulations thereunder or any Presidential Executive Order binding on the Borrower.

(f) *Representatives True; No Default or Event of Default and Compliance with Covenants.* The representations and warranties in Section 4 and 5 hereof and all other representations in writing made by or on behalf of the Borrower or the Corporate Guarantors in connection with the transactions contemplated by this Agreement shall be true in all material respects as of the date on which they were made and shall also be true in all material respects at and as of the time of the making of such Loans with the same effect as if made at and as of the time of the making of such Loans; no Event of Default or condition which with notice or the passage of time or both would constitute an Event of Default shall exist; and each covenant set forth in this Agreement shall be fully compiled.

(g) *Fees and Expenses Paid.* Any expenses and other amounts due and payable in connection with the Loan prior to or on the date of such advance shall have been paid.

EXHIBIT C   (continued)

(h) *No Other Debt.*   Except for the Subordinated Debt and trade debt incurred in the normal course of business, the Borrower shall not have incurred any additional debt.

(i) *Delivery of Assigned Notes.*   All of the notes secured by the Assignment shall have been delivered to the Bank, duly endorsed, and the Borrower and the Bank shall not have been notified of any claims, offsets, or defenses to the enforceability of the notes asserted by the respective makers thereof.

(j) *Miscellaneous.*   The Borrower shall have submitted to the Bank such other agreements, documents, and certificates, in form and substance satisfactory to the Bank, as the Bank in its sole discretion deems appropriate or necessary.

Section 7. Covenants

The Borrower covenants and agrees that from the date hereof and as long as the Bank has any obligation to make Loans or any, indebtedness to the Bank is outstanding hereunder:

Section 7.I. Notices.   It will promptly notify the Bank in writing of the occurrence of any act, event, or condition which constitutes or which after notice or lapse of time, or both, would constitute a failure to satisfy any Condition Precedent set forth in Section 6 or a breach of any Warranty or Representation contained in Section 4 or 5.

Section 7.2. Accuracy of Accounts.   The amount of each Account shown on the books, records, and invoices of the Borrower represented as owing or to be owing by each account debtor is and will be the correct amount actually owing or to be owing by such Account Debtor. The Borrower has no knowledge of any impairment of the validity or collectibility of any of the Accounts and shall notify the Bank of any such fact immediately after the Borrower becomes aware of any such impairment.

Section 7.3. Receipt of Proceeds of Accounts

(a) All accounts receivable and all proceeds and collections therefrom received by the Borrower shall be held in trust by the Borrower for the Bank and shall not be commingled with any of the Borrower's other funds or deposited in any bank account of the Borrower other than the Loan Account.

(b) At such time as any advances made by the Bank pursuant hereto or any letters of credit are outstanding, the Borrower shall deliver to the Bank as and when received by the Borrower, and in the same form as so received, all checks, drafts, and other items which represent the Accounts and any proceeds and collections therefrom, each of which checks, drafts, and other items shall be endorsed to the Bank or as the Bank may otherwise specify from time to time and which shall be accompanied by remittance reports in form satisfactory to the Bank. In addition, the Borrower shall cause any wire or other electronic transfer of funds which constitutes the Accounts or proceeds therefrom to be directed to the Bank. The Bank may apply the proceeds thereof to the Obligations in such manner as the Bank may determine, in its direction.

(c) At the Bank's request, in the Bank's discretion, so long as any Loans are then outstanding, or so long as the Bank has any obligation to make future advances hereunder, the Borrower shall cause all checks, drafts, and other items which represent the Account and any proceeds and collections therefrom to be delivered by the Borrower's account debtors directly to a lockbox, blocked account, or similar recipient over which the Bank has sole access and control. The Bank may apply the proceeds and collections so delivered to the Obligations in such manner as the Bank may determine, in its discretion.

Section 7.4. Status and Reports with Respect to Accounts Receivable and Inventory.   At the Bank's request, either daily or weekly as determined by the Bank, the Borrower shall provide the Bank with a detailed report (in such form as the Bank may specify from time to time) of any of the following, and within business days prior to the date on which such report is so provided: (i) a listing of the name and amounts of all Accounts and the aging thereof; (ii) a schedule of all inventory and the location thereof; (iii) all allowances, adjustments, returns, and repossessions concerning the Accounts, account receivables, or inventory; (iv) any downgrading in the quality of any of the inventory or occurrence of any event which has an adverse effect upon such inventory's merchantability.

Section 7.5. Monthly Receivables and Inventory Reports.   Monthly, within fifteen (15) days following the end of the previous month (unless the Bank shall request such reports on a more frequent basis), the Borrower shall provide the Bank with:

(a) A listing and aging of the Borrower's Accounts as of the end of the subject month;

(b) A reconciliation of the Accounts with payments received as of the end of the month;

(c) A certificate listing the Borrower's inventory, in such form as the Bank may specify from time to time, as of the end of such month.

Section 7.6. Schedule of Collateral.   At such intervals as the Bank may indicate from time to time by written notice given the Borrower, the Borrower shall provide the Bank with a schedule (in such form as the Bank may specify from time to time) of all Collateral which has come into existence since the date of the last such schedule.

Section 7.7. Financial Statements.   It will furnish, or cause to be furnished, to the Bank:

(a) Within ninety (90) days after the end of each fiscal year, the consolidating balance sheet of the Borrower, TPC, and TRC as at the end of, and the related consolidated and consolidating statement of operations and consolidated and consolidating statement of changes in financial position for, such year certified by independent certified public accountants satisfactory to the Bank, together with a written statement by the accountants certifying such financial statements

EXHIBIT C   (continued)

to the effect that in the course of the audit upon which their certification of such financial statements was based, they obtained knowledge of no condition or event relating to financial matters which constitutes or which with notice or the passage of time, or both, would constitute an Event of Default under this Agreement, or, if such accountants shall have obtained in the course of such audit knowledge of any such condition or event, they shall disclose in such written statement the nature and period of existence thereof, provided that the consolidating statements need not be audited and may be internally prepared and certified as accurate by the chief financial officer of TPC.

(b) Within twenty (20) days after the end of each month, the balance sheet of the Borrower, TPC, and TRC as at the end of such month, and the related statements of operations for the portion of the Borrower's, TPC's, and TRC's fiscal years then elapsed, in each case certified by the principal financial officer of the Borrower, TPC, and TRC as constituting a fair presentation of the Borrower's, TPC's, and TRC's respective financial positions as of such date.

(c) By June 30th of each year, personal financial statements of the Individual Guarantors and Seller, prepared as of May 31st of such year, satisfactory to the Bank and certified as accurate by the Individual Guarantors and by a partner of Seller.

(d) Within a reasonable period of time, and from time to time, such other financial data and information (including accountant's management letters) as the Bank may reasonably request provided that the Borrower, TPC, and TRC shall not be required to furnish any further financial data in audited form unless such materials have been prepared in audited form apart from the Lender's request thereof.

The Bank shall use reasonable care to treat such information as being confidential, but the Bank shall have the unrestricted right to use such information in all ways in the enforcement of the Bank's rights against the Borrower or TPC.

The financial statements referred to above in this Section shall be prepared in accordance with generally accepted accounting principles in force at the time of the preparation thereof.

Section 7.8. Legal Existence; Maintenance of Properties; Ownership of Assets.   The Borrower and Corporate Guarantors will do or cause to be done all things necessary to preserve and keep in full force and effect their legal existence, rights, and franchises. The Borrower will cause all of its properties used or useful in the conduct of its business to be maintained and kept in good condition, repair, and working order and supplied with all necessary equipment and will cause to be made all necessary repairs, renewals, replacements, betterments, and improvements thereof, all as may be reasonably necessary so that the business carried on in connection therewith may be properly and advantageously conducted at all times.

Section 7.9. Conduct of Business Etc.   The Borrower will continue to engage solely in the businesses now conducted by it and in businesses directly related thereto.

Section 7.10. Use of Revolver.   Advances under the Revolving Loan shall be used for general working capital purposes of the Borrower, but in no event shall such advances be used to acquire Subsidiaries, to purchase new stores, or to open new company owned stores, it being expressly understood that any new stores shall be financed with additional equity; provided, however, that upon the prior written approval of the Bank which shall not be unreasonably withheld or delayed, the Borrower may use a portion of the Loan, not to exceed $25,000 per store, to purchase or repurchase existing TDC stores, up to a maximum of four stores.

Section 7.11. Deposit Account.   In order to perfect the Bank's security interest in the Borrower's assets, the Borrower shall maintain its principal depository and checking accounts at the Bank, including, without limitation, the account representing the proceeds of TPC Debt, when implemented.

Section 7.12. Compliance with Franchise Agreements.   The Borrower shall comply with all of the terms and conditions of its various franchise agreements.

Section 7.13. Books and Records.   The Borrower shall keep true records and books of account in which full, true, and correct entries will be made of all dealings or transactions in relation to its business and affairs in accordance with generally accepted accounting principals.

Section 7.14. Negative Covenants.   The Borrower does hereby covenant and agree with the Bank that, so long as any of the Obligations remain unsatisfied or any commitments hereunder remain outstanding, it will comply, and it will cause its Subsidiaries to comply, at all times with the following negative covenants, unless the Bank shall otherwise have agreed in writing:

(a) The Borrower will not change its name, enter into any merger, consolidation, reorganization, or recapitalization, or reclassify its capital stock, provided that nothing herein shall preclude the Borrower from changing the name of any of its product lines.

(b) The Borrower will not sell, transfer, lease, or otherwise dispose off all or (except in the ordinary course of business and except for obsolete or useless assets) any material part of its assets.

(c) The Borrower will not sell, lease, transfer, assign, or otherwise dispose off any of the Collateral except in the ordinary course of business (and except for obsolete or useless assets), provided that nothing herein shall preclude the Borrower from terminating unproductive or defaulting franchisees so long as the Borrower gives the Bank prior written notice of such intended action.

EXHIBIT C   (continued)

(d) The Borrower will not sell or otherwise dispose off, or for any reason cease operating, any of its divisions, franchises, or lines of business.

(e) The Borrower will not mortgage, pledge, grant, or permit to exist a security interest in, or a lien upon, any of its assets of any kind, now owned or hereafter acquired, except for those existing on the date hereof.

(f) The Borrower will not become liable, directly or indirectly, as guarantor or otherwise for any obligation of any other Person, except for the endorsement of commercial paper for deposit or collection in the ordinary course of business and except for guarantees of franchisees' leases in the normal course of business.

(g) The Borrower will not incur, create, assume, or permit to exist any Indebtedness except (1) the Loan; (2) the Subordinated Debt; (3) trade indebtedness incurred in the ordinary course of business (provided, however, that the Borrower may not acquire inventory other than for cash or on open account except as expressly approved in writing and in advance by the Bank).

(h) The Borrower will not declare or pay any dividends, or make any other payment or distribution on account of its capital stock, or make any assignment or transfer of accounts, or other than in the ordinary course of business or inventory.

(i) The Borrower will not form any subsidiary, make any investment in (including any assignment of inventory or other property), or make any loan in the nature of an investment to any Person, provided that nothing herein shall prohibit the Borrower from converting franchisees' accounts receivable into term notes, in which event such notes shall be endorsed in favor of and delivered to the Bank as additional Collateral hereunder.

(j) The Borrower will not make any loan or advance to any officer, shareholder, director, or employee of the Borrower, except for business travel and similar temporary advances in the ordinary course of business.

(k) The Borrower will not issue, redeem, purchase, or retire any of its capital stock or grant or issue, or purchase or retire for any consideration, any warrant, right, or option pertaining thereto or other security convertible into any of the foregoing, or permit any transfer, sale, redemption, retirement, or other change in the ownership of the outstanding capital stock of the Borrower.

(l) Except as permitted in the Subordination Agreement, the Borrower will not prepay any Subordinated Debt or indebtedness for borrowed money (except the Loan) or enter into or modify any agreement as a result of which the terms of payment of any of the foregoing Indebtedness are waived or modified.

(m) The Borrower will not acquire or agree to acquire any stock, in all or substantially all of the assets, of any Person.

(n) The Borrower will not amend its lease of the premises at 385 Appleton Street, North Andover, Massachusetts, in such a way as to increase the rent or other monetary obligations due thereunder.

(o) The Borrower will not furnish the Bank any certificate or other document that will contain any untrue statement of material fact or that will omit to state a material fact necessary to make it not misleading in light of the circumstances under which it was furnished.

Section 7.15. TPC Covenants.   So long as the Loan shall remain outstanding or Bank shall have any obligation to make future advances, TPC shall not (i) transfer, convey, sell, assign, hypothecate, grant a security interest in, or pledge any of the shares of the Borrower or all, or substantially all, of the assets of the Borrower; (ii) cause the Borrower to pay any dividends otherwise distribute cash or other assets to TPC, provided that TPC may cause the Borrower to distribute not more than $250,000 in the aggregate in any 12 month period by way of dividends, distributions, or salary to TPC and/or its officers and employees; or (iii) permit any transactions involving the stock of TPC which individually or in the aggregate shall cause a change of control or management of TPC.

Section 8. Events of Default

Without derogating from the DEMAND nature of the Note and the Credit Facility, if any of the following events shall occur:

Section 8.1.   If the Borrower shall fail to pay an installment of interest or of principal on the Note due hereunder on or before the due date thereof, if the Borrower shall fail to reduce the outstanding principal balance of the Loan as provided in Section 2.1 hereof, or if the full principal balance of the Note is not paid on the Loan Review Date (or such earlier date upon which such balance may become due and payable following an Event of Default) or on the making of demand by the Bank.

Section 8.2.   If the Borrower shall fail in any material respect to perform within ten (10) days following written notice from the Bank any term, covenant, or agreement contained in Section 7 hereof, provided, however, that if such default is susceptible of cure but may not be cured within 10 days, the Borrower shall commence to cure such default within 10 days after notice thereof and shall proceed continuously and diligently to complete such cure but in any event within thirty (30) days of the date of such notice.

Section 8.3.   If any representation or warranty of the Borrower in Section 4 or of the Corporate Guarantors in Section 5 hereof or in any certificate delivered hereunder shall prove to have been false in any material respect upon the date when made;

EXHIBIT C   (continued)

Section 8.4.   If the Borrower shall fail to perform any other term, covenant, or agreement herein contained or contained in any Loan Documents, as amended, for ten (10) days after written notice of such failure has been given to the Borrower by the Bank, provided, however, that if such default is susceptible of cure but may not be cured within ten (10) days, the Borrower shall commence to cure such default with ten (10) days after notice thereof and shall proceed continuously and diligently to complete such cure but in any event within thirty (30) days of the date of such notice.

Section 8.5.   If the Borrower, or any Guarantor, shall (i) apply for or consent to the appointment of, or the taking of possession by, a receiver, custodian, trustee, or liquidator of itself or of all or a substantial part of its property; (ii) admit in writing his or its inability, or generally unable, to pay his or its debts as such debts become due; (iii) make a general assignment for the benefit of its creditors; (iv) commence a voluntary case under the Federal Bankruptcy Code (as now or hereafter in effect); (v) file a petition seeking to take advantage of any other law relating to bankruptcy, insolvency, reorganization, winding-up, or composition or adjustment of debts; (vi) with respect to any Individual Guarantor, die, or become legally incompetent or incapacitated; (vii) with respect to any Corporate Guarantor dissolve or liquidate; (viii) fail to convert in a timely or appropriate manner, or acquiesce in writing to, any petition filed against the Borrower or any Corporate Guarantor in an involuntary case under such Bankruptcy Code; or (ix) take any corporate action for the purpose of effecting any of the foregoing.

Section 8.6.   If a proceeding or case shall be commenced without the application or consent of the Borrower in any court of competent jurisdiction seeking (i) the liquidation, reorganization, dissolution, winding-up, or composition or readjustment of debts, of the Borrower or any Corporate Guarantor; (ii) the appointment of a trustee, receiver, custodian, liquidator, or the like of the Borrower or any Corporate Guarantor or of all or any substantial part of its assets; (iii) similar relief in respect of the Borrower or any Corporate Guarantor under any law relating to bankruptcy, insolvency, reorganization, winding-up, or composition or adjustment of debts, and such proceeding or case shall continue undismissed, or an order, judgment, or decree approving or ordering any of the foregoing shall be entered or an order of relief against the Borrower or any Corporate Guarantor shall be entered in an involuntary case under such Bankruptcy Code;

Then, and in every such event (an "Event of Default"): the Commitments of the Banks hereunder (if then outstanding) shall forthwith terminate, and the principal of and interest on the Loans (if any are then outstanding) shall be and become forthwith due and payable in each case all without presentment or demand for payment, notice of nonpayment, protest, or further notice or demand of any kind, all of which are expressly waived by the Borrower. No remedy herein conferred upon the holder of the Note is intended to be exclusive of any other remedy, and each and every remedy shall be cumulative and shall be in addition to every other remedy given hereunder or under any other agreement or now or hereafter existing at law or in equity or by statute or any other provision of law.

Section 9. Miscellaneous

Section 9.1. Notices.   Any notice or other communication in connection with this Agreement shall be deemed to be delivered if in writing (or in the form of a telegram) addressed as provided below and if either (a) actually delivered at said address or (b) in the case of a letter, 3 business days shall have elapsed after the same shall have been deposited in the United States mails, postage prepaid and registered or certified, and in any case at such other address as the addressee shall have specified by written notice. All periods of notice shall be measured from the date of delivery thereof.

Section 9.2. Costs, Expenses, and Taxes.   The Borrower agrees to pay, whether or not any of the transactions contemplated hereby are consummated, the reasonable out-of-pocket costs and expenses of the Bank in connection with the preparation, execution, delivery, and enforcement of this Agreement, and any amendments, waivers, or consents with respect to any of the foregoing.

Section 9.3. Lien; Set-Off.   The Borrower grants to the Bank a direct and continuing lien and continuing security interest, as security for the performance of its obligations hereunder, in and upon all deposits, balances, and other sums credited by or due from the Bank to the Borrower. Regardless of the adequacy of any other collateral, if a demand has been made for the payment of the Note and has not been withdrawn, or if the Loan has otherwise become due and payable, any such deposits, balances, or other sums credited by or due from the Bank to the Borrower may at any time or from time to time, without notice to the Borrower or compliance with any other condition precedent now or hereafter imposed by statute, rule of law, or otherwise (all of which are hereafter expressly waived), be set off, appropriated, and applied by the Bank against any or all such obligation in such manner as the Bank in its discretion may determine; and, in addition, the Bank shall have the rights of a secured party under the Uniform Commercial Code with respect thereto.

Section 9.4. Cumulative Rights; Nonwaiver.   All of the rights of the Bank hereunder and under the Note, the Loan Documents, and each other agreement now or hereafter executed in connection herewith, therewith, or otherwise, shall be cumulative and may be exercised singly, together, or in such combination as the Bank may determine in its sole judgment. No waiver or condonation of a breach on any one occasion shall be deemed to be a waiver or condonation in other instance.

Section 9.5. Governing Law.   This Agreement and the rights and obligations of the parties hereunder and under the Loans shall be construed, interpreted, and determined in accordance with laws of the Commonwealth of Massachusetts.

EXHIBIT C   (concluded)

Section 9.6. Successors and Assigns.   This Agreement shall be binding upon the Borrower and its successors and assigns and shall be binding upon and inure to the benefit of the Bank and its successors and assigns; provided, however, that that Borrower may not assign any of its rights hereunder.

Section 9.7. Table of Contents; Title and Headings.   Any table of contents, the titles of the Articles, and the headings of the Sections are not parts of this Agreement and shall not be deemed to affect the meaning or construction of any of its provisions.

Section 9.8. Counterparts.   This Agreement may be executed in several counterparts, each of which when executed and delivered is an original, but all of which together shall constitute one instrument. In making proof of this Agreement, it shall not be necessary to produce or account for more than one such counterpart.

Section 9.9. Indemnification.   The Borrower hereby agrees to indemnify the Bank and hold it harmless against any and all liabilities, obligations, loans, damages, penalties, actions, judgments, costs, or expenses of any kind whatsoever (including without limitation, reasonable attorney fees and disbursements) that may be imposed on or incurred by or asserted against the Bank in any way relating to or arising out of or in connection with any of the transactions contemplated herein.

Section 9.10. Venue; Jury Trial.   The Borrower and the Guarantors hereby agree that any action or proceeding involving this Agreement or any other agreement or document referred to herein, including the Note, may be brought in, and hereby expressly submit to the jurisdiction of, all state courts located in the Commonwealth of Massachusetts. To the extent permitted by applicable law, the Borrower and the Guarantors hereby waive trial by jury in any action on or with respect to this Agreement, the Note, or any other agreement with the Bank.

Section 9.11. Conflicting Provisions.   In the event that any provision, term, and condition of any of the Loan Documents shall conflict with any of the provisions, terms, and conditions of this Agreement, the provisions, terms, and conditions set forth herein shall prevail.

IN WITNESS WHEREOF, the parties hereto have executed this Agreement as of August 8, 2001, by their respective officers hereunto duly authorized.

V

Startup and Beyond

Under conditions of rapid growth, entrepreneurs face unusual challenges as their companies grow and different management skills become critical to growth. They face mental, physical and emotional pressures during the rapid growth of their companies. Those who have a personal entrepreneurial strategy, are healthy, have their lives in order, and know what they are signing up for fare much better than those who do not.

Chapter Sixteen

Leading Rapid Growth, Crises, and Recovery

LEARNING OUTCOMES: After reading this chapter, you will be able to understand:

16-1 New organizational paradigms

16-2 Practices of high-growth companies

16-3 The causes of growth problems

16-4 Bankruptcy

16-5 Cultural and organizational climates

16-6 Entrepreneurial leadership for the 21st century

nature, entrepreneurial ventures abandoned the organizational practices and structures typical of the industrial giants from the World War II era to the 1990s. These organizations mapped well to the time period they thrived in, with organizational structure, hierarchy, and management techniques giving way in recent times to the need for organizational creativity, flexibility, and speed.

Inventing New Organizational Paradigms

At the beginning of this text we examined how nimble entrepreneurial firms can outmaneuver corporate giants by exploiting new market opportunities. Because of their innovative and competitive

Entrepreneurial Leaders Are Not Administrators or Managers

In the growing business, entrepreneurs focus on recognizing and choosing opportunities, allocating resources, motivating employees, and maintaining control while encouraging the innovative actions that cause a business to grow.

Traditional General Management	Entrepreneurial Leadership and Organization
▪ Pyramidal/hierarchical.	▪ Stepwise and disruptive change.
▪ Incremental improvement.	▪ Fearless, relentless experimentation.
▪ Risk avoidance/embrace stability.	▪ Specialize in new mistakes.
▪ Avoid and punish failure.	▪ Opportunity obsessed.
▪ Resource allocation, budget driven.	▪ Front-line, customer driven.
▪ Central command and control.	▪ Creativity 5 capital.
▪ Resource optimization.	▪ Resource frugality and parsimony.
▪ Cost oriented.	▪ Systems and nonlinear.
▪ Linear, sequential.	▪ Global perspective.
▪ Local focus.	▪ Create and share the wealth.
▪ Compensate and reward.	▪ People want to be led, not managed.
▪ Manage and control.	▪ Manage risk: reward and fit.
▪ Zero defects/error free.	

Special thanks to Ed Marram, entrepreneur, educator, and friend, for his lifelong commitment to studying and leading growing businesses and sharing his knowledge with the authors. Ed is past director of the Arthur M. Blank Center for Entrepreneurship at Babson College.

Leading Practices of High-Growth Companies[1]

In Chapter 3 we examined a summary of research conducted on fast-growth companies to determine the leading practices of these firms. As we examine each of these four practice areas—marketing, finance, management, and planning—we can see the practical side of how fast-growth entrepreneurs pursue opportunities; devise, manage, and orchestrate their financial strategies; build a team with collaborative decision making; and plan with vision, clarity, and flexibility.

Growing Up Big

Stages of Growth Revisited

Higher-potential ventures do not stay small for long and need to change how they operate after they have assessed the opportunity, formed the team, and assembled the resources in order to realize the potential.

Founders of high-potential ventures are frequently inexperienced in launching companies. Chapter 8 discussed the stages or phases companies experience during their growth. Recall that generally the first 3 years before startup are called the research and development stage; the first 3 years after launch, the startup stage; years 4 through 10, the early-growth stage; the 10th year through the 15th or so, maturity; and after the 15th year, the stability stage.

Various models, and our previous discussions, depicted the life cycle of a growing firm as a smooth curve with rapidly ascending sales and profits and a leveling off toward the peak and then dipping toward extended decline.

In truth, however, very few, if any, new and growing firms experience such smooth and linear phases of growth. If the actual growth curves of new companies are plotted over their first 10 years, the curves will look far more like the ups and downs of a roller-coaster ride than the smooth progressions usually depicted. Over the life of a typical growing firm, there are periods of jerks, bumps, and renewal interspersed with periods of steady growth. Sometimes there is continual upward progress and other times near collapse as shown in Exhibit 16.1.

Core Leadership Mode

As was noted earlier, changes in several critical variables determine just how frantic or easy transitions from one stage to the next will be. As a result,

EXHIBIT 16.1

Growth Stages

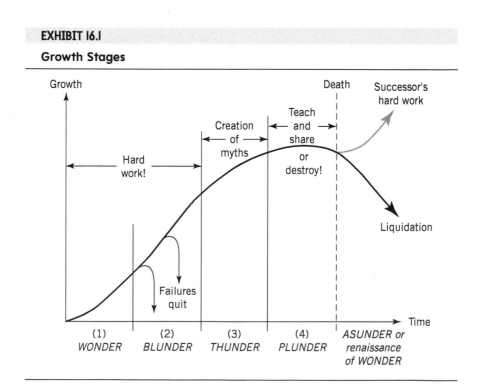

[1]Special appreciation is given to Ernst & Young LLP and the Kauffman Center for Entrepreneurial Leadership for permission to include the summary of their research here.

EXHIBIT 16.2

2007 Sales per Employee

Company	(005)
Genentech	1,089.0
Costco	943.7
Google	940.6
Netflix	907.7
Dell	715.6
Microsoft	684.4
Cisco	589.7
Nike	572.8
Biogen	560.0
Time Warner	504.0
Sony Corporation	490.7
Monsanto	485.1
Juniper Networks	462.8
Bristol-Myers Squibb	434.2
Sun Microsystems	406.4
Home Depot	359.2
Delta Airlines	333.7
Bank of America	330.8
Raytheon	300.2
IBM	262.4
Timberland	234.9
Wal-Mart	195.0
Yum Brands Restaurants	191.2
Blockbuster	162.8
Intercontinental Hotel Group	150.1
Sonesta International Hotels	77.4
McDonald's	49.8

Source: Yahoo! Finance.

it is possible to make some generalizations about the main leadership challenges and transitions that will be encountered as a company grows. Leadership modes are typically driven by industry sector, and further influenced by the size of the company as measured by employees or annual revenue.

As shown in Exhibit 8.1, until sales reach $5 million and employees number about 25, the core leadership mode is one of *doing*. Between $5 million and $15 million in sales and 25 to 75 employees, the leadership mode is *managing*. When sales exceed $10 million and employees number over 75, it becomes one of leading team leaders. The number of people is an indicator of the complexity of the leadership task and suggests a new wall to be scaled, rather than a precise point.

To illustrate how widely sales per employee (SPE) can vary among established firms, consider

Exhibit 16.2. Netflix, by virtue of an online model is generating over $907,000 in SPE, whereas a heavily retail-based comparable from the same industry, Blockbuster, was generating in the range of $163,000 in SPE.

SPE can illustrate how a company stacks up in its industry on a relative basis. Retailer Walmart with 2007 sales of $370.5 billion had SPE of $195,000, while biotechnology firm Genentech (2007 sales of $11.5 billion) was generating SPE of over $1 million. Interestingly another big-box retailer, Costco, with 2007 sales of $66 billion, is near the top of our list with SPE of just under $943,700.

During each growth stage of a firm there are hurdles that most firms will confront. Exhibit 16.3 and the following discussion look at these by stage.

The Problem in Rate of Growth

Difficulties in recognizing crisis signals and developing management approaches are compounded by rate of growth; the faster the rate the great and faster the complexity.

Growth rates affect all aspects of a business, as sales increase, more people are hired, inventory increases, and production scales. Facilities are expanded; systems and controls are put in place to manage growth. These developments and their capital investments are required to meet demand, and cash flow decreases even when a highly profitable business scales. This drives the working capital gap shown visually in Exhibit 16.4, necessitating investment to scale even the most profitable of companies.

Distinctive issues caused by rapid growth were considered at seminars at Babson College with the founders and presidents of rapidly growing companies—companies with sales of at least $1 million and growing in excess of 30 percent per year.[2] These founders and presidents pointed to the following:

- *Opportunity overload:* Rather than lacking enough sales or new market opportunities, a classic concern in mature companies, these firms faced an abundance of opportunities. Choosing from among these was a problem.
- *Abundance of capital:* Whereas most stable or established firms often have difficulties obtaining financing, most of the rapidly growing firms were not constrained by this, facing

Copyright © The McGraw-Hill Companies, Inc.

[2]These seminars were held at Babson College near Boston in 1985 and 1999. A good number of the firms represented had sales over $1 million, and many were growing at greater than 100 percent per year.

EXHIBIT 16.3

Crises and Symptoms

Pre–Startup (Years –3 to –0)

Entrepreneurs

- *Focus:* Is the founder really an entrepreneur, bent on building a company, or an inventor, technical dilettante, or the like?
- *Selling:* Does the team have the necessary selling and closing skills to bring in the business and make the plan—on time?
- *Management:* Does the team have the necessary management skills and relevant experience, or is it overloaded in one or two areas (e.g., the financial or technical areas)?
- *Ownership:* Have the critical decisions about ownership and equity splits been resolved, and are the members committed to these?

Opportunity

- *Focus:* Is the business really user-, customer-, and market-driven (by a need/pain point), or is it driven by an invention or a desire to create?
- *Customers:* Have customers been identified with specific names, addresses, and phone numbers, and have purchase levels been estimated, or is the business still only at the concept stage?
- *Supply:* Are costs, margins, and lead times to acquire supplies, components, and key people known?
- *Strategy:* Is the entry plan a shotgun and cherry-picking strategy, or is it a rifle shot at a well-focused niche?

Resources

- *Resources:* Have the required capital resources been identified?
- *Cash:* Are the founders already out of cash (OOC) and their own resources?
- *Business plan:* Is there a business plan, or is the team "hoofing it"?
- *Creativity-capital:* Are bootstrapping and sweat equity being used creatively? Is the brain trust being built?

Startup and Survival (Years 0 to 3)

Entrepreneurs

- *Leadership:* Has a top leader been accepted, or are founders vying for the decision role or insisting on equality in all decisions?
- *Goals:* Do the founders share and have compatible goals and work styles, or are these starting to conflict and diverge once the enterprise is under way and pressures mount?
- *Leadership:* Are the founders anticipating and preparing for a shift from doing to managing and letting go—of decisions and control—that will be required to make the plan on time?
- *Courage and ethics:* Can the founders stand the heat and maintain their integrity?

Opportunity

- *Economics:* Are the economic benefits and payback to the customer actually being achieved on time?
- *Strategy:* Is the company a one-product company with no encore in sight?
- *Competition:* Have previously unknown competitors or substitutes appeared in the marketplace? Are revenue targets met?
- *Distribution:* Are there surprises and difficulties in actually achieving planned channels of distribution on time?

Resources

- *Cash:* Is the company facing a cash crunch early as a result of not having a business plan (and a financial plan)? That is, is it facing a crunch because no one is asking, When will we run OOC? Are the owners' pocketbooks exhausted?
- *Schedule:* Is the company experiencing serious deviations from projections and time estimates in the business plan? Is the company able to marshall resources according to plan and on time?
- *Creativity-capital:* Is this practiced and rewarded?

Early Growth (Years 4 to 10)

Entrepreneurs

- *Doing or leading:* Are the founders still just *doing,* or are they building and leading the team for results by a plan? Have the founders begun to delegate and let go of critical decisions, or do they maintain veto power over all significant decisions?
- *Focus:* Is the mind-set of the founders operational only, or is serious strategic thinking going on as well?
- *E-culture:* Are the founders building an entrepreneurial organization?

Opportunity

- *Market:* Are repeat sales and sales to new customers being achieved on time, according to plan, and because of interaction with customers, or are these coming from the engineering, R&D, or planning group? Is the company shifting to a marketing orientation without losing its killer instinct for closing sales?
- *Competition:* Are price and quality being blamed for loss of customers or for an inability to achieve targets in the sales plan, while customer service is rarely mentioned?
- *Economics:* Are gross margins beginning to erode?

(continued)

EXHIBIT 16.3   (concluded)

Crises and Symptoms

Resources

- *Financial control:* Are accounting and information systems and control (purchasing orders, inventory, billing, collections, cost and profit analysis, cash management, etc.) keeping pace with growth and being there when they are needed?
- *Cash:* Is the company always out of cash or nearly OOC, and is no one asking when it will run out, or is sure why or what to do about it?
- *Contacts:* Has the company developed the outside networks (directors, contacts, etc.) it needs to continue growth?

Maturity (Years 10 to 15 plus)

Entrepreneurs

- *Goals:* Are the partners in conflict over control, goals, or underlying ethics or values?
- *Health:* Are there signs that the founders' marriages, health, or emotional stability are coming apart (i.e., are there extramarital affairs, drug and/or alcohol abuse, or fights and temper tantrums with partners or spouses)?
- *Teamwork:* Is there a sense of team building for a "greater purpose," with the founders now managing managers, or is there conflict over control of the company and disintegration?

Opportunity

- *Economics/competition:* Are the products and/or services that have gotten the company this far experiencing unforgiving economics as a result of perishability, competitor blind sides, new technology, or offshore competition, and is there a plan to respond?
- *Product encore:* Has a major new product introduction been a failure?
- *Strategy:* Has the company continued to cherry-pick in fast-growth markets, with a resulting lack of strategic definition (which opportunities to say no to)?

Resources

- *Cash:* Is the firm OOC again? Does it use cash rather than accrual budgeting?
- *Development/information:* Has growth gotten out of control, with systems, training, and development of new managers failing to keep pace?
- *Financial control:* Have systems continued to lag behind sales?

Harvest/Stability (Years 15 to 20 plus)

Entrepreneurs

- *Succession/ownership:* Are there mechanisms in place to provide for management succession and the handling of very tricky ownership issues (especially family)?
- *Goals:* Have the partners' personal and financial goals and priorities begun to conflict and diverge? Are any of the founders simply bored or burned out, and are they seeking a change of view and activities?
- *Entrepreneurial passion:* Has there been an erosion of the passion for creating value through the recognition and pursuit of opportunity, or are turf-building, acquiring status and power symbols, and gaining control favored?

Opportunity

- *Strategy:* Is there a spirit of innovation and renewal in the firm (e.g., a goal that half the company's sales come from products or services less than 5 years old), or has lethargy set in?
- *Economics:* Have the core economics and durability of the opportunity eroded so far that profitability and return on investment are nearly as low as that for the Fortune 500?

Resources

- *Cash:* Has OOC been solved by increasing bank debt and leverage because the founders do not want—or cannot agree—to give up equity?
- *Accounting:* Have accounting and legal issues, especially their relevance for wealth building and estate and tax planning, been anticipated and addressed? Has a harvest concept been part of the long-range planning process?

the problem of how to evaluate investors as partners and the terms of the deals with which they were presented.

- *Misalignment of cash burn and collection rates:* These firms all pointed to problems of cash burn rates racing ahead of collections. They needed effective accounting, inventory, purchasing, shipping, and invoicing systems to effectively manage cash flow.
- *Decision making:* Many of the firms succeeded because they executed functional day-to-day and week-to-week decisions, rather than strategizing. Many of the representatives of these firms argued that in conditions of rapid

EXHIBIT 16.4

Spend Rate/Orders/Collection Leads and Lags

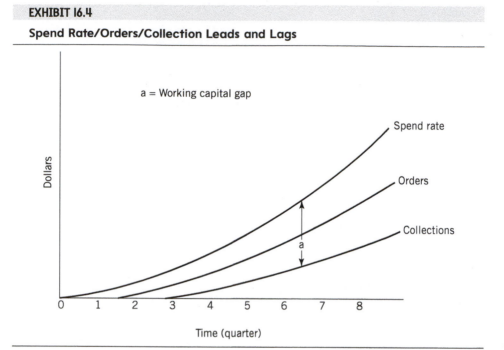

growth, strategy was only about 10 percent of the story.

- *Expanding facilities and space . . . and surprises:* Expansion of space or facilities is a problem and one of the most disrupting events during the early explosive growth of a company. Managers of many of these firms were not prepared for the surprises, delays, organizational difficulties, and system interruptions that came with expansion.

The Causes of Growth Problems

Trouble can be caused by external forces not under the control of management. Among the most frequently mentioned are recession, interest rate changes, changes in government policy, inflation, the entry of new competition, and industry or product obsolescence. Experts who manage turnarounds say that although such circumstances define the environment to which a troubled company needs to adjust, they are rarely the principal reason for a company failure. Most causes of failure can be found within company management, with the most frequently cited falling into three broad areas: inattention to strategic issues, general management problems, and poor financial and accounting systems and practices. There is striking similarity between these and the causes of failure for startups given in Chapter 3.

Strategic Issues

- *Misunderstood market niche:* The first of these issues is a failure to understand the company's market niche and to focus on growth without considering profitability. Instead of developing a strategy, these firms take on low-margin business and add capacity in an effort to grow, then run OOC.
- *Mismanaged relationships with suppliers and customers:* Related to the above is the failure to understand the economics of relationships with suppliers and customers. For example, some firms allow practices in the industry to dictate payment terms, when they may be in a position to dictate their own terms. In other cases, firms are slow to collect receivables for fear of offending new customers.
- *Diversification into an unrelated business area:* A common failing of cash-rich firms is using their cash position to expand to another market without understanding the financial implications.
- *Mousetrap myopia:* Related to the problem of starting a firm around an idea rather than an opportunity is the "great products" problem of looking for other markets to sell current products. This is done without strategically analyzing the firm's opportunities.
- *The big project:* The company gears up for a big project without looking at the cash flow

implications. Cash is expended by adding capacity and hiring personnel and when sales lag the forecast there is trouble.

- *Lack of contingency planning:* As has been stated over and over, the path to growth is not a smooth curve upward. Firms need to be geared to think about what happens if things go sour, sales fall, or collections slow.

Leadership Issues

- *Lack of leadership skills, experience, and know-how:* When companies grow founders need to change their leadership mode from doing to leading teams to leading team leaders.
- *Weak finance function:* Often, in a new company the finance function is a bookkeeper. One company was 5 years old, with $20 million in sales, before the founders hired a financial professional.
- *Turnover in key management personnel:* Although turnover of key management personnel can be difficult in any firm, it is a critical concern in businesses that deal in specialized or proprietary knowledge as their competitive advantage.
- *Big-company influence in accounting:* A mistake that some companies often make is to focus on accruals rather than cash. In the end, high growth companies need extreme focus on cash flow.

Poor Planning, Financial and Accounting Systems, Practices, and Controls

- *Poor pricing, overextension of credit, and excessive leverage:* Use of excess leverage can result from growth outstripping the company's internal financing capabilities.
- *Lack of cash management:* This is a most frequent cause of trouble as cash budgets and projections are often not done. In addition, lack of viability often stems from management failing to base their decisions on cash flow impact.
- *Poor management reporting:* While some firms have good financial reporting, they suffer from poor management reporting.
- *Lack of standard costing:* Poor management reporting extends to issues of costing, with many emerging businesses having no standard costs against which they can compare the actual costs of manufacturing products.

Getting Out of Trouble

The major protection against and the biggest help in getting out of these troubled waters is to have a set of advisors and directors who have been through this in the past. They possess skills that are not taught in school or in most corporate training programs. The speed of action has to be different; control systems have to be different; and the organization needs to move with a sense of urgency.

Predicting Trouble

Crises develop over time and typically result from an accumulation of fundamental errors. Can a crisis be predicted? The obvious benefit of being able to predict crisis is that the entrepreneur, employees, and outside constituents like investors, lenders, trade creditors, and customers can see trouble in time to take corrective actions.

There have been several attempts to develop predictive models and the two presented here use easily obtained financial data to help predict trouble. For public companies, these models can be used by all interested observers. With private companies, they are useful only to anyone who has access to the company's financials.

The most frequently used denominator in all these ratios is the figure for total assets. This figure often is distorted by creative accounting, with expenses occasionally improperly capitalized and carried on the balance sheet or by substantial differences between tangible book value and book value.

Net-Liquid-Balance-to-Total-Assets Ratio

The model shown in Exhibit 16.5 was developed by Joel Shulman, a Babson College professor, to predict loan defaults. Shulman found that his ratio can predict loan defaults with significant reliability as much as 2 years in advance.

Shulman's approach is noteworthy because it recognizes the importance of cash. Among current accounts, Shulman distinguishes between operating assets (such as inventory and accounts receivable) and financial assets (such as cash and marketable securities). The same distinction is made among liabilities, where notes payable and contractual obligations are financial liabilities and accounts payable are operating liabilities.

Shulman then subtracts financial liabilities from financial assets to obtain a figure known as the net liquid balance (NLB). NLB can be thought of as "uncommitted cash," cash the firm has available to meet contingencies. Because it is the short-term

EXHIBIT 16.5

Net-Liquid-Balance-to-Total-Assets Ratio

Net-liquid-balance-to-total-assets ratio = NLB/Total assets
where
NLB = (Cash + Marketable securities) − (Notes payable + Contractual obligations)

Source: J. Shulman, "Primary Rule for Detecting Bankruptcy: Watch the Cash," *Financial Analyst Journal*, September 1988.

margin for error should sales change, collections slow, or interest rates change, it is a true measure of liquidity. The NLB is then divided by total assets to form the predictive ratio.

Nonquantitative Signals

Earlier we discussed patterns and actions that could lead to trouble, indications of common trouble by growth stage, and critical variables that can be monitored.

Turnaround specialists also use some nonquantitative signals as indicators of possible trouble. As with the signals we outlined, the presence of a single one of these does not necessarily imply an immediate crisis. However, once any of these surfaces and if the others follow, then trouble is likely to mount:

- Inability to produce financial statements on time.
- Changes in behavior of the lead entrepreneur (such as avoiding phone calls or coming in later than usual).
- Change in management or advisors, such as directors, accountants, or other professional advisors.
- Accountant's opinion that is qualified and not certified.
- New competition.
- Launching of a big project.
- Lower research and development expenditures.
- Special write-offs of assets and/or addition of new liabilities.
- Reduction of credit line.

The Gestation Period of Crisis

In looking backward, the graph of a company's key statistics frequently indicates trouble. We can see things like sales growth have slowed considerably. This is followed by an increasing rise in expenses as

the company assumes that growth will continue; when the growth does not continue, the company still allows expenses to remain high so it can "get back on track."

The Bloom Is Off the Rose—Now What?

Generally when an organization is in trouble some tell-tale trends appear:

- Outside advice is ignored.
- The worst is yet to come.
- People have stopped making decisions and also have stopped answering the phone.
- Nobody in authority has talked to the employees.
- Rumors are flying.
- Inventory is out of balance. That is, it does not reflect historical trends.
- Accounts receivable aging is increasing.
- Customers are becoming afraid of new commitments.
- A general malaise has settled in while a still high-stressed environment exists (an unusual combination).

Decline in Organizational Morale

Among those who notice trouble developing are the employees, dealing with customer returns, calls from creditors, and the like, and they wonder why management does not respond. Despite troubled times, the lead entrepreneur talks and behaves optimistically or hides in the office declining to communicate with employees, customers, or vendors. Employees lose confidence in the formal communications of the company.

It is obvious there is a problem and that it is not being dealt with. Employees wonder what will happen, whether they will be laid off, and whether the firm will go into bankruptcy. With their security threatened, employees lapse into survival mode.

Crisis can force intervention. The occasion is usually forced by the board of directors, a lender, or a lawsuit. For example, the bank may call a loan, or the firm may be put on cash terms by its suppliers. Perhaps creditors try to put the firm into involuntary bankruptcy. Or something from the outside world fundamentally changes the business environment.

The Threat of Bankruptcy

Debtor control within the bankruptcy arena characterized the period of the 1970s through the early 1990s. During this time the courts gave the troubled company the flexibility to make disbursements to creditors for the benefit of the company. Having such control over cash often gave the debtor control over the outcome of the case.

Recently, however, there has been a dramatic shift to creditor-controlled proceedings. Debtors are now instructed that once they are in the vicinity of bankruptcy, they have to pay attention to all creditor groups. To further help control cash, lenders often demand that the company hire workout specialists to guide the debtor through the process.

In addition, the majority of bankruptcy cases today result in a change of ownership. Bidding for companies in bankruptcy has become a big business. This trend will likely continue because there are now well-capitalized groups that specialize in acquiring companies and technology in this fashion.

Voluntary Bankruptcy

When bankruptcy is granted to a business under bankruptcy law (often referred to as Chapter 10), the firm is given immediate protection from creditors. Payment of interest or principal is suspended, and creditors must wait for their money. Generally the current management (a debtor in possession) is allowed to run the company, but sometimes an outsider, a trustee, is named to operate the company, and creditor committees are formed to watch over the operations and to negotiate with the company.

The greatest benefit of Chapter 10 is that it buys time for the firm. The firm has 120 days to come up with a reorganization plan and 60 days to obtain acceptance of that plan by creditors. Under a reorganization plan, debt can be extended or restructured, interest rates can be changed, and convertible provisions can be introduced to compensate debt holders for any increase in their risk as a result of the restructuring. Creditors and debt holders may need to take part of their claims in the form of equity and partial payment. If liquidation is the result of the reorganization plan, partial payment is the rule, with the typical payment ranging from zero to 30 cents on the dollar depending on the priority of the claim.

In April 2005 President George Bush signed legislation making it more difficult for Americans with large credit card and medical bills to erase their obligations. The bill, representing the most significant change to the nation's bankruptcy laws in 25 years, makes it harder for individuals to file Chapter 6 bankruptcy, which eliminates most debts. Individuals whose earnings exceed their state's median income are required to file Chapter 12, which sets up a court-ordered repayment plan.

Involuntary Bankruptcy

In involuntary bankruptcy, creditors force a troubled company into bankruptcy. Although this is regarded as a rare occurrence, it is important for an entrepreneur to know the conditions under which creditors can force a firm into bankruptcy.

A firm can be forced into bankruptcy by any three creditors whose total claim exceeds the value of assets held as security by $5,000, and by any single creditor who meets this standard when the total number of creditors is less than 12.

Bargaining Power

For creditors, having a firm go into bankruptcy is not particularly attractive, making it a source of bargaining power for the troubled company. Bankruptcy is not attractive to creditors because once protection is granted to a firm, creditors must wait for their money and expect only a partial repayment, and they are no longer dealing with the company but with the judicial system and other creditors. Also the legal and administrative costs of bankruptcy must be paid before any payments are made to creditors.

Faced with these prospects, many creditors conclude that their interests are better served by negotiating with the firm. Because the law defines the priority of creditors' claims, an entrepreneur can use it to determine who might be willing to negotiate.

For example, because trade debt has the lowest claim, these creditors are often the most willing to negotiate. If the firm has negative net worth but is generating some cash flow, trade debt creditors should be willing to negotiate extended terms or partial payment, or both, unless there is no trust in current management.

However, secured creditors, with their higher priority claims, may be less willing to negotiate. Many factors affect the willingness of secured creditors to negotiate. Two of the most important are the strength of their collateral and their confidence in management. Bankruptcy is still something they wish to avoid for the reasons cited.

Bankruptcy can free a firm from obligations under executory contracts and has caused some firms to file for bankruptcy as a way out of union contracts. Because bankruptcy law in this case conflicts with the National Labor Relations Act, the law has been updated and a good-faith test has been added. The firm must be able to demonstrate that a contract prevents it from carrying on its business. It is also possible for the firm to initiate other executory contracts such as leases, executive contracts, and equipment leases. If a company has gradually added to its overhead in a noneconomic fashion, it may be able to this by using bankruptcy as a tool.

Intervention

A company in trouble usually will want to use the services of an outside advisor who specializes in turnarounds. The company is often technically insolvent or has negative net worth and may have been put on a cash basis by its suppliers. It may be in default on loans or in violation of loan covenants. Call provisions may be exercised on its loans. As the situation deteriorates more, creditors may be trying to force the company into bankruptcy.

Diagnosis

Diagnosis can be complicated by the mixture of strategic and financial errors. For example, in a company with large receivables, questions need to be answered about whether receivables are bloated because of poor credit policy or because the company is in a business where liberal credit terms are required to compete.

Diagnosis occurs in three areas: the appropriate strategic posture of the business, the analysis of management, and "the numbers."

Strategic Analysis   This analysis in a turnaround tries to identify the markets in which the company is capable of competing and decide on a competitive strategy. With small companies, turnaround experts state that most strategic errors relate to the involvement of firms in unprofitable product lines, customers, and geographic areas.

Analysis of Management   Analysis of management consists of interviewing members of the management team and coming to a subjective judgment of who belongs and who does not. Turnaround consultants can give no formula for how this is done except that it is the result of judgment that comes from experience.

The Numbers   Involved in "the numbers" is a detailed cash flow analysis, which will reveal areas for remedial action. The task is to identify and quantify the profitable core of the business.

- *Determine available cash:* The first task is to determine how much cash the firm has available in the near term. This is accomplished by looking at bank balances, receivables, and the confirmed order backlog.

- *Determine where money is going:* This is a more complex task than it appears to be. A common technique is called subaccount analysis, where every account that posts to cash is found and accounts are arranged in descending order of cash outlays. Accounts then are scrutinized for patterns. These patterns can indicate the functional areas where problems exist. For example, one company had its corporate-address on its bills, rather than the lockbox-address at which checks were processed, adding 2 days to its dollar days outstanding.

- *Calculate percentage-of-sales ratios for different areas of a business and then analyze trends in costs:* Typically several trends will show flex points where relative costs have changed.

- *Reconstruct the business:* After determining where the cash is coming from and where it is going, the next step is to compare the business as it should be to the business as it is. This involves reconstructing the business from the ground up. For example, a cash budgeting exercise can be undertaken and collections, payments, and so forth determined for a given sales volume. Or the problem can be approached by determining labor, materials, and other direct costs and the overhead required to drive a given sales volume. Essentially a cash flow business plan is created.

- *Determine differences:* Finally the cash flow business plan is tied into pro forma balance sheets and income statements. The ideal cash flow plan and financial statements are compared to the business's current financial statements. For example, the pro forma income statements can be compared to existing statements to see where expenses can be reduced. The differences between the projected and actual financial statements form the basis of the turnaround plan and remedial actions.

The most commonly found areas for potential cuts and improvements are: (1) working capital management, from order processing and billing to receivables, inventory control, and, of course, cash management; (2) payroll; and (3) overcapacity and underutilized assets. More than 80 percent of potential reduction in expenses can usually be found in workforce reduction.

The Turnaround Plan

The industry standard for turnarounds is the 13-week cash flow plan that is based on a longer-term cash flow model. In his practice as a turnaround expert, Carl Youngman requires the following:

- A 12-month cash flow model.
- A rolling 13-week cash flow plan, updated weekly.
- A rolling 30-day daily cash flow projection.

The turnaround plan not only defines remedial actions but, because it is a detailed set of projections, also provides a means to monitor and control turnaround activity. Further, if the assumptions about unit sales volume, prices, collections, and negotiating success are varied, it can provide a means by which worst-case scenarios–complete with contingency plans–can be constructed.

Because short-term measures may not solve the cash crunch, a turnaround plan gives a firm enough credibility to buy time to put other remedial actions in place. For example, one firm's consultant could approach its bank to buy time with the following: By reducing payroll and discounting receivables, we can improve cash flow to the point where the firm can be current in 5 months. If we are successful in negotiating extended terms with trade creditors, then the firm can be current in 3 months. If the firm can sell some underutilized assets at 50 percent off, it can become current immediately.

The turnaround plan helps address organizational issues. The plan replaces uncertainty with a clearly defined set of actions and responsibilities. Because it signals to the organization that action is being taken, it helps get employees out of their survival mode. An effective plan breaks tasks into the smallest achievable units, so successful completion of these simple tasks soon follows and the organization begins to experience success. Soon the downward spiral of organizational morale is broken.

Finally, the turnaround plan is an important source of bargaining power. By identifying problems and providing for remedial actions, the turnaround plan enables the firm's advisors to approach creditors and tell them in very detailed fashion how and when they will be paid. If the turnaround plan proves that creditors are better off working with the company as a going concern, rather than liquidating it, they will most likely be willing to negotiate their claims and terms of payment. Payment schedules can then be worked out that can keep the company afloat until the crisis is over.

Quick Cash   Ideally the turnaround plan establishes enough creditor confidence to buy the turnaround consultant time to raise additional capital and turn underutilized assets into cash. It is imperative, however, to raise cash quickly. The result of the actions described next should be an improvement in cash flow. The solution is far from complete, however, because suppliers need to be satisfied.

Accounts receivable is the most liquid noncash asset. Receivables can be factored, but negotiating such arrangements takes time, so the best route to cash is discounting receivables. A typical bank will lend up to 80 percent of the value of receivables that are under 90 days old and as receivables age past 90 days, the bank needs to be paid. Inventory is not as liquid as receivables but still can generate quick cash. An inventory "fire sale" gets mixed reviews from turnaround experts, with most common issue being excess inventory is often obsolete. The second issue is much inventory work in process, so it is not in salable form and requires money to put in salable form. The third is that discounting finished-goods inventory may generate cash but is liable to create customer resistance to restored margins after the company is turned around. The sale of raw materials inventory to competitors is generally considered the best route, with another option is to sell inventory at discounted prices to new channels of distribution where the discounted prices might not affect the next sale.

Also relevant to generating quick cash is current sales activity with the criteria to include increasing the total dollar value of margin, generating cash quickly, and keeping working capital in its most liquid form. Prices and discounts need to be increased and credit terms eased, with obvious care taken to maintain consistent policy.

Putting accounts payable on hold is the next option, acknowledging some arrangements to pay suppliers needs to be made, the most important uses of cash at this stage are meeting payroll and paying lenders as getting suppliers to ship is critical. It should be pointed out that suppliers are the least likely to force the company into bankruptcy because they have a low priority claim.

Dealing with Lenders   The next step in the turnaround is to negotiate with lenders. To continue to do business with the company, lenders need to be satisfied that there is a workable long-term solution.

However, at the point of intervention, the company is most likely in default on its payments. Or if payments are current, the financial situation has probably deteriorated to the point where the company is in violation of loan covenants. It also is likely that many of the firm's assets have been pledged as collateral. To make matters worse, it is likely that the troubled entrepreneur has been avoiding his or her lenders during the gestation period and has demonstrated that he or she is not in control of the situation and credibility has been lost.

There are two sources of bargaining power with lenders. The first is that bankruptcy is an unattractive event to a lender, despite its senior claims. A low-margin business cannot absorb large losses easily and recall that banks typically earn 0.5 to 1.0 percent total return on assets.

The second is credibility. The firm that, through its turnaround specialist, has diagnosed the problem and produced a detailed plan to prove to the lender that the company is capable of paying is in a better bargaining position.

Dealing with Trade Creditors   In dealing with trade creditors, the first step is to understand the strength of the company's bargaining position. Trade creditors have the lowest-priority claims should a company file for bankruptcy and are often the most willing to deal.

Another bargaining power boost with trade creditors is the existence of a turnaround plan. As long as a company demonstrates that it can offer a trade creditor a better result as a going concern than it can in bankruptcy, the trade creditor should be willing to negotiate. It is generally good to make sure that trade creditors are getting a little money on a frequent basis. Remember trade creditors have a higher gross margin than a bank, so their getting paid pays down their "risk" money faster. This is especially true if the creditor can ship new goods and gets paid for them.

The relative weakness in the position of trade creditors has allowed some turnaround consultants to negotiate impressive deals. For example, one

company got trade creditors to agree to a 24-month payment schedule for all outstanding accounts. In return, the firm pledged to keep all new payables current. The entrepreneur was able to keep the company from dealing on a cash basis with many of its creditors and to convert short-term payables into what amounted to long-term debt, so the effect on current cash flow was very favorable.

The second step is to prioritize trade creditors according to their importance to the turnaround. The company then needs to take care of those creditors that are most important.

The third step in dealing with trade creditors is to switch vendors if necessary. The lower-priority suppliers will put the company on cash terms or refuse to do business. The troubled company needs to be able to switch suppliers, and its relationship with its priority suppliers will help it to do this because they can give credit references. The fourth step in dealing with trade creditors is to communicate effectively. "Dealing with the trade is as simple as telling the truth," one consultant said. If a company is honest, at least a creditor can plan.

Workforce Reductions   With payroll typically being the major expense, layoffs are inevitable in a turnaround situation.

Turnaround specialists recommend that layoffs be announced and done as a one-time reduction and that they be accomplished as soon as possible. Also they should be deeper than necessary to compensate for other remedial actions that may be difficult to implement.

Longer-Term Remedial Actions

If the turnaround plan has created enough credibility and has bought the firm time, longer-term remedial actions can be implemented.

These actions will usually fall into three categories:

- *Systems and procedures:* Systems and procedures that contributed to the problem can be improved or eliminated, or new ones can be implemented.

- *Asset plays:* Assets that could not be liquidated in a shorter time frame can be liquidated. Many smaller companies, particularly older ones, carry real estate on their balance sheets at far below market value. This can be sold and leased back or can be borrowed against to generate cash.

- *Creative solutions:* Creative solutions need to be found. For example, one firm had a large amount of inventory that was useless in its current business; it found that if the inventory could be assembled into parts, there would be a market for it. The company shipped the inventory to Jamaica, where labor rates were low, and it was able to sell the entire inventory.

The Importance of Culture and Organizational Climate

Six Dimensions

The organizational culture and climate, either of a new venture or of an existing firm, are critical in how well the organization will deal with growth and crises. Studies of performance in large businesses that used the concept of organizational climate (i.e., the perceptions of people about the kind of place it is to work at) have led to two general conclusions.[3] First, the climate of an organization can have a significant impact on performance. Further, climate is created both by the expectations people bring to the organization and by the practices and attitudes of the key managers.

The climate notion has relevance for new ventures, as well as for entrepreneurial efforts in large organizations. An entrepreneur's style and priorities are well known by the people being managed and affect performance. Recall the entrepreneurial climate described by Roger Enrico of Pepsi, where the critical factors included setting high performance standards by developing short-run objectives that would not sacrifice long-run results, providing responsive personal leadership, encouraging individual initiative, helping others to succeed, developing individual networks for success, and so forth. Or listen to the tale of Gerald H. Langeler, the president of the systems group of Mentor Graphics Corporation, who explained what "the vision trap" was.[4] Langeler described the vision of his company's entrepreneurial climate as simply to "build something people will buy."[5] The culture of Mentor Graphics was definitely shaped by the founders' styles because "there were perhaps 15 of us at the time—we could not only share information very quickly, we could also create a sense of urgency and purpose without the help of an articulated vision."[6]

Evidence suggests that superior teams function differently than inferior teams in setting priorities, in resolving leadership issues, in what and how roles are performed by team members, in attitudes toward listening and participation, and in dealing with disagreements. Further, evidence suggests that specific approaches to management can affect the climate of a growing organization. For example, gains from motivation, commitment, and teamwork, which are anchored in a consensus approach to management, while not immediately apparent, are striking later. At that time, there is swiftness and decisiveness in action and in follow-through. Also, new disagreements that emerge generally do not bring progress to a halt, because there are both high clarity and broad acceptance of overall goals and underlying priorities. Without this consensus, each new problem or disagreement often necessitates a time-consuming and painful confrontation and renegotiation simply because this was not done initially.

Organizational climate can be described along six basic dimensions:

- *Clarity:* The degree of organizational clarity in terms of being well organized, concise, and efficient in the way that tasks, procedures, and -assignments are made and accomplished.
- *Standards:* The degree to which management expects and puts pressure on employees for high standards and excellent performance.
- *Commitment:* The extent to which employees feel committed to the goals and objectives of the organization.
- *Responsibility:* The extent to which members of the organization feel responsibility for accomplishing their goals without being constantly monitored and second-guessed.
- *Recognition:* The extent to which employees feel they are recognized and rewarded (non-monetarily) for a job well done, instead of only being punished for mistakes or errors.
- *Esprit de corps:* The extent to which employees feel a sense of cohesion and team spirit—of working well together.

E-Leadership

In achieving the Entrepreneurial culture and climate just described, certain approaches to management (also discussed in Chapter 8) are common

---

[3]See J. A. Timmons, "The Entrepreneurial Team: Formation and Development," paper presented at the Academy of Management annual meeting, Boston, August 1973.

[4]G.H. Langeler, "The Vision Trap," *Harvard Business Review*, March-April 1992, reprint 92204.

[5]Ibid., p. 4.

[6]Ibid., p. 5.

across core management modes. No single leadership pattern seems to characterize successful ventures. Leadership may be shared or informal, or a natural leader may guide a task. What is common, however, is a manager who defines and gains agreements on who has what responsibility and authority and who does what with and to whom. Roles, tasks, responsibilities, accountabilities, and appropriate approvals are defined.

There is no competition for leadership in these organizations, and leadership is based on expertise, not authority. Emphasis is placed on performing task-oriented roles, but someone invariably provides for "maintenance" and group cohesion by good humor and wit. Further, the leader does not force his or her own solution on the team or exclude the involvement of potential resources. Instead the leader understands the relationships among tasks and between the leader and his or her followers and is able to lead in those situations where it is appropriate, including managing actively the activities of others through directions, suggestions, and so forth.

This approach is in direct contrast to the commune approach, where two to four entrepreneurs, usually friends or work acquaintances, leave unanswered questions such as who is in charge, who makes the final decisions, and how real differences of opinion are resolved. While some overlapping of roles and a sharing in and negotiating of decisions are desirable in a new venture, too much looseness is debilitating.

This approach also contrasts with situations where a self-appointed leader takes over, where there is competition for leadership, or where one task takes precedence over other tasks.

Consensus Building   Leaders of most successful new ventures define authority and responsibility in a way that builds motivation and commitment to cross-departmental and corporate goals. Using a consensus approach to management requires managing and working with peers and with the subordinates of others (or with superiors) outside formal chains of command and balancing multiple viewpoints and demands.

In the consensus approach, the manager is seen as willing to relinquish his or her priorities and power in the interests of an overall goal, and the appropriate people are included in setting cross-functional or cross-departmental goals and in making decisions. Participation and listening are emphasized.

Communication   The most effective leaders share information and are willing to alter individual views. Listening and participation are facilitated by such methods as circular seating arrangements, few interruptions or side conversations, and calm discussion versus many interruptions, loud or separate conversations in meetings.

Encouragement   Successful leaders build confidence by encouraging innovation and calculated risk taking, rather than by punishing or criticizing what is less than perfect, and by expecting and encouraging others to find and correct their own errors and to solve their own problems. Their peers and others perceive them as accessible and willing to help when needed, and they provide the necessary resources to enable others to do the job. When it is appropriate, they go to bat for their peers and subordinates, even when they know they cannot always win. Further, differences are recognized and performance is rewarded.

Trust   The most effective leaders are perceived as trustworthy and straightforward. They do what they say they are going to do; they are not the corporate rumor carriers; they are more open and spontaneous, rather than guarded and cautious with each word; and they are perceived as being honest and direct. They have a reputation of getting results and become known as the creative problem solvers who have a knack for blending and balancing multiple views and demands.

Development   Effective leaders have a reputation for developing human capital; they groom and grow other effective managers by their example and their mentoring. As noted in Chapter 8, Bradford and Cohen distinguish between the heroic manager, whose need to be in control in many instances actually may stifle cooperation, and the postheroic manager, who actually brings about excellence in organizations by developing entrepreneurial middle management. If a company puts off developing middle management until price competition appears and its margins erode, the organization may come unraveled. Linking a plan to grow human capital at the middle management and the supervisory levels with the business strategy is an essential first step.

Entrepreneurial Leadership for the 21st Century: Three Breakthroughs

Three extraordinary companies have been built or revolutionized in the past two decades: Marion Labs, Inc., of Kansas City; Johnsonville Sausage of

Sheboygan Falls, Wisconsin; and Springfield Remanufacturing Corporation of Springfield, Missouri. Independently and unknown to each other, these companies created "high standard, perpetual learning cultures," which create and foster a "chain of greatness." The lessons from these three great companies provide a blueprint for entrepreneurial leadership in the 21st century. They set the standard and provide a tangible vision of what is possible. Not surprisingly, the most exciting, fast-growing, and profitable companies in America today have striking similarities to these firms.

Ewing Marion Kauffman and Marion Labs Marion Laboratories, founded in Ewing Marion Kauffman's garage in 1950, reached $2.5 billion in sales by the time it merged with Merrill Dow in 1989. Its market capitalization was $6.5 billion. Over 300 millionaires and 13 foundations, including the Ewing Marion Kauffman Foundation, were created from the builders of the company. In sharp contrast, RJR Nabisco, about 10 times larger than Marion Labs at the time of the KKR leveraged buyout, generated only 20 millionaires. Clearly these were very different companies. Central to Marion Labs' phenomenal success story was the combination of a high-potential opportunity with management execution based on core values and an entrepreneurial leadership philosophy ahead of its time. These principles are simple enough, but difficult to inculcate and sustain through good times and bad:

1. Treat everyone as you would want to be treated.
2. Share the wealth with those who have created it.
3. Pursue the highest standards of performance and ethics.

The company had no organizational chart, referred to all its people as associates, not employees, and had widespread profit-sharing and stock participation plans.

Jack Stack and Springfield Remanufacturing Corporation

Another example of entrepreneurial leadership is Jack Stack; his book, *The Great Game of Business*, should be read by all entrepreneurs. In 1983

Stack and a dozen colleagues acquired a tractor engine remanufacturing plant from the failing International Harvester Corporation. With an 89-to-1 debt-to-equity ratio and 21 percent interest, they acquired the company for 10 cents a share. In 1993 the company's shares were valued near $20 for the employee stock ownership plan, and the company had completely turned around with sales approaching $100 million. What happened?

Like Ewing Marion Kauffman, Jack Stack created and implemented some management approaches and values that changed the culture of the organization. At the heart of his leadership was creating a vision called *The Big Picture: Think and act like owners, be the best we can be, and be perpetual learners. Build teamwork as the key by learning from each other, open the books to everyone, and educate everyone so they can become responsible and accountable for the numbers, both short and long term.* Stack puts it this way:

> We try to take ignorance out of the workplace and force people to get involved, not with threats and intimidation but with education. In the process, we are trying to close the biggest gap in American business—the gap between workers and managers. We are developing a system that allows everyone to get together and work toward the same goals. To do that, you have to knock down the barriers that separate people, that keep people from coming together as a team.[7]

At Springfield Remanufacturing Corporation, everyone learns to read and interpret all the financial statements, including an income statement, balance sheet, and cash flow, and how his or her job affects each line item. This open-book leadership style is linked with pushing responsibility downward and outward, and to understanding both wealth creation and wealth sharing through short-term bonuses and long-term equity participation. Stack describes the value of this approach: "The payoff comes from getting the people who create the numbers to understand the numbers. When that happens, the communication between the bottom and the top of the organization is just phenomenal."[8] The results he achieved in 10 years are astounding. Even more amazing is that he has found the time to share this approach with others. More than 150 companies have participated in seminars that have enabled them to adopt this approach.

---

[7]J. Stack, *The Great Game of Business* (New York: Currency/Doubleday Books, 1991), p. 5.
[8]Ibid., p. 93.

Ralph Stayer and Johnsonville Sausage Company[9]

In 1975 Johnsonville Sausage was a small company with about $5 million in sales and a fairly traditional player in its industry. In just a few years Ralph Stayer, the owner's son, radically transformed the company through a leadership style whose values, culture, and philosophy are remarkably similar to the principles of Ewing Marion Kauffman and Jack Stack.

The results are astonishing: By 1980 the company had reached $15 million in sales; by 1985, $50 million; and by 1990, $150 million. At the heart of the changes he created was the concept of *a total learning culture: Everyone is a learner, seeking to improve constantly, finding better ways. High performance standards accompanied by an investment in training, and performance measures that made it possible to reward fairly both short- and long-term results were critical to the transition.* Responsibility and accountability were spread downward and outward. For example, instead of forwarding complaint letters to the marketing department, where they are filed and the standard response is sent, they go directly to the front-line sausage stuffer responsible for the product's taste. The sausage stuffers are the ones who respond to customer complaints now. Another example is the interviewing, hiring, and training process for new people. A newly hired woman pointed out numerous shortcomings with the existing process and proposed ways to improve it. As a result, the entire responsibility was shifted from the traditional human resources and personnel group to the front line, with superb results.

As one might guess, such radical changes do not come easily. Consider Stayer's insight:

> In 1980 I began looking for a recipe for change. I started by searching for a book that would tell me how to get people to care about their jobs and their company. Not surprisingly, the search was fruitless. No one could tell me how to wake up my own workforce; I would have to figure it out for myself... The most important question any manager can ask is, "In the best of all possible worlds what would I really want to happen?"[10]

Even having taken such a giant step, Stayer was ready to take the next, equally perilous steps:

> Acting on instinct, I ordered a change. "From now on," I announced to my management team, "you're all responsible for making your own decisions."... I went from authoritarian control to authoritarian abdication. No one had asked for more responsibility; I had forced it down their throats.[11]

Further insight into just how challenging it is to transform a company like Johnsonville Sausage is revealed in another Stayer quote:

> I spent those two years pursuing another mirage of well-detailed strategic and tactical plans that would realize my goals of Johnsonville as the world's greatest sausage maker. We tried to plan organizational structure two to three years before it would be needed... Later I realized that these structural changes had to grow from day-to-day working realities; no one could dictate them from above, and certainly not in advance.[12]

Exhibit 16.6 summarizes the key steps in the transformation of Johnsonville Sausage over several years. Such a picture undoubtedly oversimplifies the process and understates the extraordinary commitment and effort required to pull it off, but it does show how the central elements weave together.

The Chain of Greatness

As we reflect on these three great companies, we can see that there is clearly a pattern here, with some common denominators in both the ingredients and the process. This chain of greatness becomes reinforcing and perpetuating (Exhibit 16.7). A philosophy of perpetual learning throughout the organization accompanied by high standards of performance is key to the value-creating entrepreneurial cultures at these firms. A culture that teaches and rewards teamwork, improvement, and respect for each other provides the oil and glue to make things work. Finally, a fair and generous short- and long-term reward system, as well as the necessary education to make sure that everyone knows and can use the numbers, creates a mechanism for sharing the wealth with those who contributed to it. The results speak for themselves: extraordinary levels of personal, professional, and financial achievement.

---

[9]For an excellent discussion of this transformation, see "The Johnsonville Sausage Company," HBS case 387-103, rev. June 27, 1990. Copyright © 1990 by the President and Fellows of Harvard College. See also R. Stayer, "How I Learned to Let My Workers Lead," *Harvard Business Review*, November-December 1990. Copyright © 1990 by the President and Fellows of Harvard College.
[10]Stayer, "How I Learned to Let My Workers Lead," p. 1.
[11]Ibid., pp. 3–4.
[12]Ibid., p. 4.

EXHIBIT 16.6

Summary of the Johnsonville Sausage Company

The critical aspects of the transition:

1. Started at the top: Ralph Stayer recognized that he was the heart of the problem and recognized the need to change—the most difficult step.
2. Vision was anchored in human resource management and in a particular idea of the company's culture:
   - Continuous learning organization.
   - Team concept—change players.
   - New model of jobs (Ralph Stayer's role and decision making).
   - Performance- and results-based compensation and rewards.
3. Stayer decided to push responsibility and accountability downward to the front-line decision makers:
   - Front-liners are closest to the customer and the problem.
   - Define the whole task.
   - Invest in training and selection.
   - Job criteria and feedback development tool.
4. Controls and mechanisms make it work:
   - Measure performance, not behavior, activities, and the like.
   - Emphasize learning and development, not allocation of blame.
   - Customize to you and the company.
   - Decentralize and minimize staff.

EXHIBIT 16.7

The Chain of Greatness

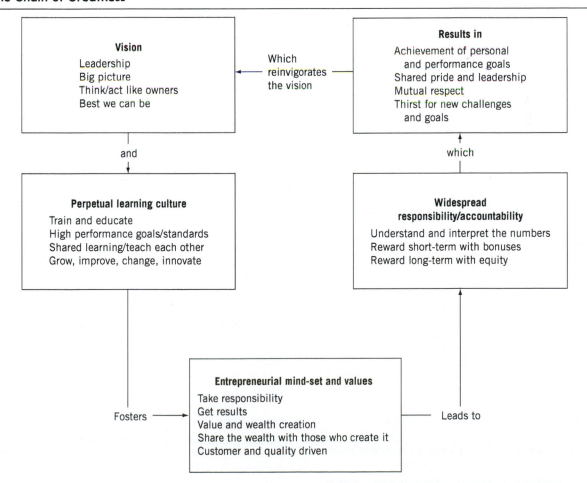

Chapter Summary

- The demands of rapid growth have led to the invention of new organizational and leadership paradigms by entrepreneurs.
- The entrepreneurial organization today is flatter, faster, and more flexible and responsive, and copes readily with ambiguity and change. It is the opposite of the hierarchy, layers of management, and more-is-better syndrome prevalent in brontosaurus capitalism.
- Entrepreneurs in high-growth firms distinguish themselves with leading entrepreneurial practices in marketing, finance, management, and planning.
- As high-potential firms "grow up big" they experience stages (Wonder, Blunder, Thunder, Plunder, and Asunder), each with its own special challenges and crises, which are compounded the faster the growth.

- Numerous signals of impending trouble–strategic issues, poor planning and financial controls, and running OOC–invariably point to a core cause: top management.
- Crises do not develop overnight. Both quantitative and qualitative signals can predict patterns and actions that could lead to trouble. Often it takes 18 months to 5 years before a company is sick enough to trigger a turnaround intervention.
- Turnaround specialists begin with a diagnosis of the numbers–cash, strategic market issues, and management–and develop a turnaround plan.
- Establishing a culture and climate conducive to entrepreneurship is a core task for the venture.
- A chain of greatness characterizes some breakthrough approaches to entrepreneurial leadership.

Study Questions

1. Why have old hierarchical management paradigms given way to new organizational paradigms?
2. What special problems and crises can new ventures expect as they grow? Why do these occur?
3. What role do the organizational culture and climate play in a rapidly growing venture?
4. Why is the rate of growth the central driver of the challenges a growing venture faces?
5. What do entrepreneurs need to know about how companies get into and out of trouble? Why?
6. Why do most turnaround specialists invariably discover that management is the root cause of trouble?
7. Why is it difficult for existing management to detect and to act early on signals of trouble?
8. What are some key predictors and signals that warn of impending trouble?
9. What diagnosis is done to detect problems, and why and how does cash play the central role?
10. What are the main components of a turnaround plan, and why are these so important?
11. What is the chain of greatness, and how can entrepreneurs benefit from this concept?

Internet Resources

Case
Telephony Translations, Inc. (A)

Preparation Questions

1. Evaluate Dave Santolli's entrepreneurial thinking and leadership at Faxtech and at TTI.

2. What are the most important lessons and insights to take from this case?

3. Evaluate TTI's progress and situation in 2006. What should it and its investors/directors do?

Dave Santolli's entrepreneurial career epitomized the notion that life is about the journey rather than the destination. At 42, he 'd experienced both success and failure in business. He 'd also found out his wife Terry was facing an uphill battle with cancer, and been relieved when she pulled through.

In early 2005, all that was beginning to seem like practice for his current challenges. He was facing an investor suit from his last venture and legal defense fees had left Dave and Terry without a safety net.

How does a young company with a global footprint, $50 million in revenue, 650 employees, and over $280 million in capitalization get forced into total liquidation via a Chapter 7 bankruptcy overnight?

Dave's new venture, Telephony Translations, Inc. (TTI), was still unprofitable after five years. Dave had told his investors to expect such losses, but they had replaced him as CEO anyway. While the business seemed to be on the right track, this was a critical time for it.

And yet here was Dave, informing his staff that he had cancer and would have to step away from the company for months. He told them he'd be back and the company would turn the corner soon. What else could he say?

A Passion for Enterprise

While majoring in industrial engineering at Cornell University, Dave Santolli developed a magazine for students living on campus. *Student Life* grew to a circulation of 1.2 million. In 1987, four years after graduating from Cornell, he sold it to Time, Inc., for nearly $1 million and moved to New York City to work for the publisher. Although he enjoyed his work, Dave was soon longing for the life he'd known as an entrepreneur.

The following year, Dave entered Harvard Business School (HBS), intent on having his next enterprise ready for launch by graduation. Dave was unconcerned that his search for a compelling opportunity would take him outside his immediate universe of understanding:

Conventional wisdom says you ought to start a venture in an industry where you have some previous experience, but given the fast pace of growth in information technologies, that's where I wanted to be. I had an engineering background, so I wasn't intimidated by technology. I was sure that I could start a successful venture in an area in which I had no experience—provided of course that I was willing to thoroughly research the industry and the idea.

Throughout his second year at HBS, Dave devised, reviewed, and ultimately rejected eight business concepts. He graduated in 1990 as an HBS Baker Scholar—a honor given to the top 5 percent of the graduating class—and received a lucrative offer from a prominent consulting firm.

I let them know that I would spend the summer trying to spot a viable opportunity, and if I hadn't found anything by September, I'd take the job.

In mid-July, a write-up in an AT&T technology journal caught his attention:

This article was describing the various types of information that people were sending over phone lines. The phone companies had no way of knowing whether an open line was being used for voice or data. It also said that data travels seven times more efficiently than voice, meaning a fax transmission was utilizing only one-seventh of the capacity of a given line.

I called the author of the article to confirm the fundamental viability of the idea that with the right equipment, a company could send many [more] times the volume of data than a basic fax machine transmitting over the switched-voice networks of companies like AT&T, Sprint, and MCI. I wasn't about to jump in without a lot more research, but I was pretty certain that this was the opportunity I'd been searching for.

Post-MBA Sweet Spot: Faxtech International

By the end of the summer of 1990, Dave had declined the consulting position to develop Faxtech International, which would offer vastly superior

This case was prepared by Carl Hedberg under the direction of Professor Jeffry Timmons. © Copyright Jeffry Timmons, 2007. All rights reserved.

facsimile transmission service between the United States and major international cities.

In February, 1991, he met John Tyler, a 52-year-old who had spent most of his adult life in either engineering project management or product development, including 16 years with two major telecom companies. John was doing well as an engineering management consultant. So well, in fact, that Dave had to give up more of the business than he had originally intended:

> John was pretty firm about what he needed to come on board, and this became a very difficult decision for me. I needed his expertise, we seemed to have a shared vision of what sort of company this could be, and I sensed that we would get along well. I concluded that it just doesn't pay to be greedy.

For his part, John recalled that his attraction to the opportunity went beyond what he saw in the plan for Faxtech:

> Virtually every company I consulted for had asked me to join them full-time. Dave's offer was the first one I even considered. My interest had to do with how I felt about Dave and his philosophy for treating people.... Dave and I saw eye-to-eye on the importance of treating and rewarding people fairly.

Faxtech took another six months to fill out its engineering team, find suitable headquarters, and begin developing its technology.

Clearing the Hurdles

The company thought the key to customer adoption would be a user-friendly, bug-free system that required little change in how faxes were transmitted. John's team designed a plug-in redialer that scanned every outgoing call.[1] The device would reroute fax transmissions destined for a foreign city. They would travel via regular phone lines to a Faxtech node in the states, where they would be bundled with other transmissions bound for the same foreign city. Once overseas, the faxes would reach their local destinations over regular phone lines.

Faxtech's system would provide customers with a 50 percent savings and generate gross margins of nearly 60 percent. Profitability, however, would require not only substantial margins but an enormous base of call volume, which meant Faxtech would need to establish centers all over the world.

Based on an analysis it conducted, Faxtech's initial objective was to establish a leadership position in the United States-to-Tokyo market, followed by a Tokyo-to-United States operation. Once that loop was secure, the company would set up operations in Paris and London.

Having saved most of the money he'd made from his magazine, Dave could fund Faxtech's initial IP development and early-stage operations. But he didn't want to use more than half his nest egg:

> It was important to raise money from outside sources because if I couldn't convince people to invest, then there was probably something wrong with the idea or how we were presenting it. At first I tried the approach I'd heard at HBS: Raise as much as you can up front. I soon discovered that venture capitalists who were willing to invest at this early stage insisted on taking a majority of the company. Private investors, on the other hand, were unwilling to take a risk at the idea stage.

He ultimately concluded that the best source of startup funding was his management team. Following an internal seed round of $335,000, Dave devised a milestone approach to attract outside investors:

> I decided to lay out our startup process as a series of distinct hurdles—such as a completed prototype or a government approval. As we moved forward and met our goals, the project gained credibility, and we were gradually able to find investors to share the risk.

In February 1992, the company brought total funding to $1 million with the close of a round with private investors. To cover a monthly burn rate of $175,000,[2] they closed a second $1 million round by late spring.

Its technology was testing well, and Faxtech planned to go live in March. In addition to its technology, Dave believed the company's success would depend on developing a responsive service department. To head it up, Dave hired Terry Carson, his wife:

> Terry had worked closely with me at Cornell on my first business. Not only did I find that she was extremely capable, but we didn't experience any of the problems that many couples seem to encounter

[1] A redialer was a simple device, smaller than a cigar box, that physically sat between a fax machine and the wall. Its sole purpose was to grab fax traffic before it reached the private branch exchange (PBX) switch or, at smaller organizations, the public switched telephone network (PSTN), then redirect it to a fax service bureau or ISP that would send the fax and bill the faxer. The Faxtech redialer was a highly sophisticated machine that could differentiate between all types of calls, block 900 numbers, and not reroute 800 numbers. The proprietary system, which was entirely and remotely programmable, recognized alternative fax numbers along with local holidays and business hours at the destination point, and, in the event of a busy signal, rerouted the documents and rescheduled delivery.

[2] The burn rate included salaries ($60 K), asset expenses ($16 K), office operating expenses ($15 K), expenses in Japan ($20 K), fixed communication expenses ($25 K), and miscellaneous startup expenses (lawyers, network installation, equipment, travel: $39 K).

in similar situations. With respect to Faxtech, I knew we might have to search months to find someone as qualified as she was for the position,[3] and even then it would take months more before that hire understood the business or our vision the way Terry already did.

Despite severe cash-flow challenges and sporadic, system-wide shutdowns, Faxtech's systems worked, and the company grew quickly. In late 1992, even though his U.S. operations were far from stable, Dave felt it was time to expand overseas.

Going Global before Globalization: Faxtech–Japan

Dave had always believed that one key to success would be opening up a two-way communications channel between the United States and Japan. Because that would utilize established Faxtech connections, it could carry traffic at a very low variable cost. Succeeding in Japan would also represent Faxtech's go-ahead to open offices around the world.

After evaluating alternatives,[4] Dave decided to work with Japanese companies as partners while maintaining a majority ownership. His first and most important contact was Sachio Moto, co-founder and senior vice president of a major Japanese telecommunications firm.

Moto agreed to help Faxtech enter the Japanese telecommunications market. As meetings got under way in 1993, he was pleased with Dave's drive and commitment:

Dave would spend whole days at the hotel analyzing changed conditions [from follow-up meetings]. He was patient and tremendously flexible. He'd come to Japan without specific return dates, which was very unusual for an American businessman. That way he had the slack to cope with last-moment changes in previously agreed-upon conditions. Dave also paid very good attention to each personal detail, like greeting others properly. Dave has the hearty collaboration and the personal, human touch that a good chief executive needs.

Throughout 1993, Dave struggled to secure commitments from Japanese businessmen. To make matters more difficult, Faxtech's efforts to break into Japan were destabilizing its U.S. operations. Dave recalled:

Faxtech was eating up more and more capital as our growth accelerated, and our breakeven was still out of reach and getting further away all the time.[5] I don't believe that we ever had more than two months of cash in the bank at any point in time that year. This might sound either impossible or extremely strange, but it was our reality. While I was trying to negotiate from strength in Japan, we were constantly involved in the process of raising money to keep the U.S. operations in business.

When Faxtech–Japan went live in late 1994, it ushered in the opportunity for global expansion Dave had envisioned. In 1995, however, the business became secondary to a far more critical challenge.

A Frightful Reality

By 1995, Terry was managing over 200 people. With Faxtech doing well, Dave and Terry decided to start a family. During a routine pregnancy examination, Terry's physician made a shocking discovery:

It was October of 1995, right when the company was really beginning to take off. Basically they told me I wasn't going to make it. It was a bad thing; they called it ALL—short for acute lymphocytic leukemia—*I had it ALL*—stage-four over my whole body. They were saying, "Even though you're only 30, it is very unlikely you'll be able to make it through this. But if you don't start treatment in a week, you'll be dead within a month."

Terry lost the baby but made it through the first month of treatment, and then the next. Unable to do much for his wife, Dave focused on their growing business. In addition to being CEO, he took over management of the service department.

Against all odds, Terry endured massive chemotherapy for two years and beat the cancer. But it left her unable to have children. Meanwhile, Faxtech achieved the critical mass it required to survive and prosper.

[3]Terry graduated from Cornell with a BS in mechanical engineering in 1986 and then entered the U.S. Air Force as an officer. Terry left the Air Force in 1991 as a captain and enrolled in graduate school at Harvard to pursue a master's degree in U.S. history. After completing all of her coursework at Harvard, in 1992 Terry made the difficult decision to put her thesis on hold to take the position of vice president of service at Faxtech International. After a 6-year diversion at Faxtech International, Terry finally returned to Harvard to complete her thesis and received her MS degree in 2001.

[4]Strategic possibilities for setting up FIJ included financing the startup through a franchise system, allowing a local partner to own a large part of the operation, and setting up Faxtech as a holding company for the Japanese operation.

[5]By mid-1993 their aggressive growth strategy in the United States had boosted the net monthly revenue of Faxtech to just under $350,000, but the negative cash flow rate had grown to $250,000/month. The monthly breakeven point grew at an equally aggressive pace of approximately $502,000.

Excellence and Execution

By 1997, Faxtech employed 650 people in 18 offices worldwide. Annual growth had averaged 180 percent since 1992, and in 1997 the company placed 20th on the *INC.* 500 list of fastest-growing private U.S. companies. By then, Faxtech had raised $105 million from a wide range of sources including friends, family, angels, and corporations like ORIX and Singapore Airlines.

Dave and his team felt the time was right to establish a dominant position in the marketplace with a massive effort that would include developing enhanced fax and delivery services and expanding Faxtech's international communications network to 27 countries. Well aware of the threat posed by the Internet, Faxtech was developing an online portal that would allow its customers to place service orders and track faxes.

Dave said Faxtech was preparing for another challenge:

Deregulation in our industry was a reality that we were preparing for. The world knew it was coming, and as a company we were investing in new products that anticipated that change. We said, "All right, given that those changes are clearly going to hurt our core value proposition, how do we transition and still make this happen?"

To support its push for market dominance, the company needed to raise an additional $175 million.[6] Instead of a public offering, it opted for an offering of high-yield (14 percent) debt securities—an equity preservation strategy made feasible by Faxtech's growing global reputation for excellence and execution.

[6]At the time of the closing, the company had less than $1 million on hand—and a monthly burn rate of over $3 million. Had the bond offering not closed in January 1997, Faxtech would have been forced to begin shutting down operations within weeks.

With the bond issue closed, total debt and equity funding stood at just over $260 million (Exhibit A). The company was approaching breakeven on annual sales of about $50 million; Faxtech had become a major force in the telecommunications sector.

Free Fall

In early 1997, the World Trade Organization (WTO) reached an agreement with over 200 countries to fully deregulate international communications. In less than a year, the average price per minute for international calls in every market where Faxtech was operating dropped from 75 to 25 cents per minute. Dave explained how this new environment stripped the wings off his company:

Our incremental cost per minute was about 15 cents. We entered 1997 charging 50 cents a minute on international fax calls—a cost savings to the customer of 33 percent over the average price of 80 cents a minute. By the end of the year we were forced to drop our price down to the new market price of 25 cents per minute...

The core model of our existing business was just totally broken. We realized that we had essentially gotten in at the tail end [of an industry cycle]; there was a huge market and tons of money sitting there. The downside, of course, was that the opportunity could disappear pretty quickly. The financial structure of the business has to be aligned with the duration of the opportunity, and with Faxtech, we had placed a long-term financial model on a short-term opportunity.

Having recently closed its debt round, Faxtech was flush with cash—enough, Dave felt, to fund a transition strategy his team had been conceptualizing for months. But the bondholders wanted out:

EXHIBIT A

Faxtech Capitalization

Timing	Round and Source	Debt @	Rate	Convertible Preferred @	Share Price	Total $ Raised
Fall 1990	Founder and seed financing	200,000	12%			300,000
Fall 1991	Series A: private investors @ $25,000 each	500,000	12%	500,000	$1.00	1,000,000
Fall 1992	Series B: several large angel investors			2,500,000	$1.00	2,500,000
Spring 1994	Faxtech–Japan financing; partners owned 49% of subsidiary					10,000,000
Spring 1994	Series C: several large international private equity funds			3,000,000	$3.50	3,000,000
Spring 1995	Malaysia Telecom investment	30,000,000	12%	40,000,000	$3.50	70,000,000
Spring 1997	Public high-yield debt offering	175,000,000	14%			175,000,000
	Total funding					**261,500,000**

Our current investors were telling us, "Look, we put the money in for the right reason, the world changed dramatically in a way you couldn't have anticipated, and so we need to shut the company down and return their money." They wanted to restructure by shutting it down; we wanted to restructure by bringing in new investors and by paying the bondholders some appropriate fee to bring them into an equity position. We had no legal obligation to return the funds, and we believed, of course, that we could produce a much bigger result if they let us finish the strategy. The early investors, whose money was already spent, were willing to let us try.

The debate over how best to move forward, the crashing market conditions, and having to let go hundreds of employees was straining Faxtech's management and board. By early 1998, Dave had replaced his CFO, COO, and vice president of development:

I asked the new COO and CFO to work together to drive a process of systematically reducing our sales staff by 50 percent in order to help conserve cash—without closing any of our international sales offices completely.[7] While my executive team focused on scaling back and completing the development of our new products, I shifted my full attention to finding a way to restructure and convert our high-interest bondholders to some form of partial equity.

In March 1998, all the outside directors resigned—ostensibly over a struggling branch office in France, but more as a vote of no confidence. Dave described another indicator of how fast Faxtech was falling:

At the end of 1997, I owned approximately 15 percent of the company. At the same time the directors were leaving, I was purchasing all of the stock owned by Malaysia Telecom in order to facilitate MalTel's exit from the business. MalTel originally invested $70 million ($30 million equity plus $40 million debt). In order to give MalTel a simple exit from their stock position, I agreed to purchase their shares for $10,000. At the end of this transaction I owned more than 50 percent of the... outstanding shares of the company, but obviously the stock wasn't worth anything at that point since we had a public high-yield debt overhang of $175 million.

Clark Thomas, the tax director in Faxtech's finance group, recalled that most employees remained hopeful:

We had a common goal as to where we were going as a company, and things seemed to have been going along very well. One of Dave's best attributes is being able to keep people moving forward and believing.

Clark added that although the customers were largely unaware of the turmoil at the company, the investors were very unhappy:

. . . There were some real, rational reasons in the industry why this was happening. Some investors were able to grasp that, and others were quite bitter about the prospect that the investment they made would not be returning something to them.

At the behest of an early investor, turnaround expert Steve Oldman came on the scene. He encountered a hopeless situation:

I met with Dave, [CFO] Tom Basinger, [tax director] Clark Thomas, and a couple of other key guys. I built a model and explained they'd be bankrupt in 90 days. The best I could do at that point was to make a series of recommendations and restructure their forecasts to give them nine to 10 months rather than 90 days.

. . . Faxtech had raised plenty of money, but they just hadn't anticipated how quickly institutional regulators were prepared to move in order to assert their authority over the system.

Steve added that Dave's state of mind was common for someone in that situation:

Dave is a very logical thinker. He wasn't emotional; he had the ability to convince people, through logic, that he was right. So he got great allegiance to his visions by the managers and the people around him. They wanted to follow that bright star.

When I got there, he was in deep trouble, and personally in denial: This couldn't happen to me, I've always been successful, I've always been right, the brightest, the best. It was an interesting time in his life—to discover that he could actually fail at something.

Clark noted that some loyal employees were struggling with reality as well:

The realization had now hit that we were not going to turn this thing around. There was still hope, and talk about some deals in the works to try to sell the company. There was certainly a core group that thought that might happen, that their jobs would still exist, and they could go on in some sort of buyout fashion.

The bondholders had grown angry. Knowing they couldn't force Dave to throw in the towel, they assured him that if he failed and lost their money, they would take legal action against him. Dave recalled that he didn't fully appreciate the situation:

I have to say that I didn't understand the risk posed by their threat to sue me if we failed. I'd been in business for a long time already; this was my second venture. I had a lot of experience, and we had a lot of sophisticated people around us. But nobody was able to articulate the downside of the risk I was taking.

---

[7] By the fall of 1998 Faxtech would cut its global staff from 750 to fewer than 400.

The team struggled for many more months to regain the footing Faxtech had lost; but by November they realized it was all over.

The bankruptcy court quickly initiated proceedings to force Faxtech into complete liquidation for less than 1 cent per dollar invested. Before the end of winter, the company would be closed forever.

Convergence of Opportunities

Back in the mid-1990s, Dave had spotted what he felt was going to be a fundamental disconnect in the telecom sector:

Faxtech was all about the early stage of bridging the telephone network—a circuit-switched network—with the Internet, which is a packet-switched network. A circuit switch is a physical communication system—like a tin can and a string—more sophisticated than that, but that's the idea. On the Internet, every bit of communication is broken down into little packets and routed through a general network—that's why router companies like Cisco have been pretty successful. There are no circuits anymore—just routes through a global electronic network.

That core transition from circuit-switched to packet-switched started in the telecom world in the early 1990s, and we were participating in it at Faxtech. I started to realize that when the transition really got going, a telephone number—the routable address in a circuit-switched network—would have no meaning on the Internet.

To many, this seemed like a nonissue; telephone numbers would simply become a thing of the past. Dave disagreed:

People who grow up [in the world of technology] almost always overstate their position; it's growing, it's exciting, it's new, it's the hip thing, it's the IN thing... They get confused into thinking that everything they're doing will make sense to everyone. But yet there were a good 50 years or so of pretty impressive work that went into building the global communications network that we know today.

I'm thinking that with 6 billion people on the planet—all trained over the years to dial telephone numbers—I'm thinking that the telephone number is going to survive—that this was going to be convergence, not a takeover. We filed a patent around the concept that giving meaning to telephone numbers in this new network was going to require a complex translation function inside that network.

At the time there was no standard, no names for what we were describing. So we made up our own phrasing to describe what we were doing, like this: The telephone number was going to have to be *queried* against the database to *discover* Internet

service addresses for different services associated with that number... The title of our core patent in this area explained the service as follows: *Method and apparatus for correlating a unique identifier, such as a PSTN telephone number, to an Internet address to enable communications over the Internet. . .*

With Faxtech headed for bankruptcy, Dave was spending more and more time looking at this convergent opportunity. It wasn't long before he got some pointed advice from back home:

My mother called me and said, "Just tell me you're not going to do that again; *get a job*." And that led to this real heart-to-heart with Terry about my career options. She asked about what I was willing to consider: Corporate work, consulting? I had the education and experience to do virtually anything. And we walked down the list: Would you consider this, that, this?

Ultimately it came down to deciding what I wanted to do with my life—independent of all the stuff that I couldn't control. That stuff is going to happen no matter what—I could only control how I was going to spend my life... The only thing I'm really interested in doing is starting a business that's going to have an objective of revolutionizing an industry—or participating in that revolutionizing process. The answer was obvious: I had to start this new venture, and Terry was totally supportive of that.

With regard to the looming lawsuit, Dave added,

There was no way to mitigate that personal risk. The reality was that if the creditors from Faxtech sued me and won, they could come after all my assets, including stock in a new business. But what am I going to do, not start?

The Phoenix Rises: Telephony Translations, Inc.

By the time proceedings to dispose of Faxtech's assets got under way in June 1999, Dave had walked turnaround specialist Steve Oldman through the details of the intellectual property (IP) that was going up for bid. Dave described the situation:

I laid out for Steve the Faxtech IP that I felt could become the foundation for a new company in the converged telephone number addressing space. My wife Terry and I decided to risk $26,000 to acquire that technology at the auction. That was pennies on the dollar of the actual value, and our assumption was that the bankruptcy trustee and the audience at the auction would not be aware of the years of work embodied in some key patent applications—and hence would be unwilling to bid up the price of those assets.

Steve knew how to approach, manage, and orchestrate a solution where Dave and Terry could execute the purchase legally and ethically:

Because Dave was explicitly excluded from participating in the auction process under direction from the bankruptcy trustee, we recruited his old friend John Tyler [the original vice president of engineering at Faxtech]. John Tyler agreed to join the auction and bid on the patents, with the understanding that he would then sell the patents back to Dave and Terry in return for a stock position in their new company.

Dave said it worked beautifully:

Although several people showed up to bid on the patent applications, John, who was armed with a briefcase full of cash, was successful in purchasing all of the patents we needed (see Exhibit B).

With his patents secured and a base of Faxtech employees ready for a new challenge, Dave's next enterprise rose seamlessly from the ashes of the previous one:

We hit the ground running with Telephony Translations (TTI). It was the benefit of having people from the original team, and this being my third time around; I mean, you do get better at this, right? It was so fast; six months from writing the first plan to having 20 people in an office writing code.

To fund the effort, Dave knew he needed to bring in new blood:

One of the real pains of Faxtech not making it was that I lost so many great financial contacts. I had raised money all over the world—the problem was I lost money all over the world.

Dave's father, a retired AT&T executive, found a friend who had a friend in the venture capital business: Bob Cooper of Signit Ventures. Bob recalled his first impressions:

Several things struck me at the time. Faxtech had clearly been a time-windowed opportunity that Dave hadn't understood. He had tried to grow it to the moon at a time when he should have been looking for a buyer. What I saw in Dave was a guy who was a brilliant thinker and strategist, but maybe not a skilled operator. He was also a guy that had the courage to stand up again even after the horrendous problems he went through.

Dave's best skill, as is the case with all of us, can also be a liability. He believes in himself so strongly, and he is so bright, he can go into a closet by himself

EXHIBIT B

TTI Intellectual Property

TTI's patents and pending applications include hundreds of claims covering processes and implementation concepts relating to the use of a shared directory in IP-based communications. Outlined below is a brief summary of TTI's three areas of patent activity.

Method and apparatus for correlating a unique identifier, such as a PSTN Telephone number, to an Internet address to enable communications over the Internet
This series of issued patents (U.S. Patent 6,539,077, U.S. Patent 6,748,057, European Patent 1142286) and pending applications initially filed in December 1999 describe the use of a shared "Directory Service" (DS) to convert a PSTN telephone number into Internet address information. Such information will allow the creation of a communication link over a data network between two unrelated communications platforms using only standard telephone numbers for addressing. The application contains claims specifically relating to the use of a shared directory to allow real-time voice, voice messaging, remote printing, and unified messaging applications over the Internet using standard telephone numbers for addressing.

Method and apparatus for identifying and replying to a caller
This set of issued patents (U.S. Patent 6,292,799, Chinese Patent ZL 99807952.9, Australian Patent 748758) initially filed in June 1998 apply a shared Internet directory to global voice messaging services. Specifically, the patent describes the use of a shared directory enabling end users to utilize an IP network to "reply for free" to voicemail messages. The directory converts a return telephone number into a reply address for any Internet-enabled voicemail, e-mail, or unified-messaging system. The patent was granted with multiple claims covering various aspects of Internet voice messaging and directory services.

Method and apparatus for accessing a network computer to establish a push-to-talk session
This patent application (continuation-in-part of U.S. 6,539,077, 6,748,057, 6,292,799) describes a communications architecture where a wireless phone user registered for push-to-talk (PTT) services desires a PTT session with a party on a network computer accessible via a public data network that is not registered with any PTT service. The wireless phone user initiates a session by entering a unique identifier as a destination address for the network computer. The wireless operator's PTT server queries a Directory Service, available on the public data network, to obtain a PTT address for the destination computer, thus enabling the PTT server to discover any number of PTT enabled PCs available on the public data network.

Source: www.TTI.com.

and think through the 40 zillion different combinations of the strategy and come out and say, "I know the answer and that's it." That process dredges out a better depth than anyone else, and once aligned to the right direction, Dave can contribute better on a new idea, and communicate it to a community and to the rest of the team in a way that they can build a product around it, better than any person I've ever seen.

The downside, of course, is that his certainty makes Dave as stubborn as he can be. That is the good and bad news about an entrepreneur: They rarely see the market not aligned with that strategy they have settled on.

I would also tell you that I saw Dave as the chief marketing officer and never anticipated that Dave would be the CEO of that company long-term. I shared with him that I would watch him for a while as CEO, but I would only do the deal if I had the choice as to when we needed to bring in a CEO to be his partner, not to replace him.

Dave was excited to have found a new supporter:

So I was hot on the heels of having lost many millions of dollars, and yet Bob and his group were willing to listen. Signit is to be credited for having the foresight and the willingness to accept that experience often comes with setbacks and failures.

Dave added that Signit was very intrigued by his vision that at some point in the future, the telecommunications industry was going to need a technical bridge to transition the old physical structures into the digital age:

Phone numbers are going to need to survive because that's how people are accustomed to placing a call, but they don't have any real meaning on the digital network. To bridge the two, there has to be a highly complex solution in the middle. When the big telcos realize they need this bridge, they are going to buy that solution from someone. As a new entrant, the only way to have any chance of participating is to build [the technology] when nobody wants it—so when they do want it, you've actually got it. Alternatively, if you're not there when they want it, they are going to contact proven names like Ericsson, Lucent, Siemens, or Nortel, and they are going to pay one of them to develop it.

Those big-name guys aren't building it right now because nobody's willing to pay them to do it. So we have to go spend venture money to build this technology, and it's going to take years. And I don't know when it's going to happen. But when it happens, it's going to be a great business for 30 years because people don't make these transitions very quickly. Customers need stability. The industry needs stability. But the problem is, how do you know when they're going to need it? I don't know. If it turns out they need it in six months, we're screwed because we can't build it in six months. If it turns out they

won't need it for 10 years, we're also screwed because we can't wait around that along.

Signit agreed to invest $10 million for 40 percent of the business (fully diluted)—in monthly allocations in order to mitigate the risk of the legal cloud that was hanging over Dave's head. In June 2000, just 3 days before the statute deadline, the cloud burst.

Trust—But Verify

A group of creditors led by the bankruptcy trustee filed an $80 million lawsuit against Factech's directors and officers. Dave and the other officers did not have sufficient assets to warrant the creditors' attention. Instead, the creditors wanted to use Faxtech lawsuit to gain access to the company's $10 million directors and officers (D&O) insurance policy. The entire board was named in the suit, but Dave would have to fight it. When Dave referred the action to his insurance carrier, he got bad news:

The first thing that happened is the insurance company says, "That's not a valid claim,[8] so we're not going to cover it." I'm trying to build TTI, and at the same time, I'm putting pressure on the insurance company—while I dig and scrape and sell assets to pay for my own defense. By the time the insurance company agreed to pick it up, I had already paid $140,000—after tax—in legal fees.

Dave recalled that the legal attack itself was far more painful than the money worries it caused:

The actual act of getting sued is so much worse than I had been prepared for. I didn't think I did anything wrong, but that didn't stop them from suing me, and it didn't stop them from writing really long papers that described me as absolute scum; he's bad for this reason, he's really bad for this reason, and just imagine how bad he must be for these other reasons. I had to say to the [TTI] board, "Look, I'm sorry, I'm being sued for $80 million for breach of fiduciary responsibility." That just sounds so bad: *breach of fiduciary responsibility!*

And of course that destabilizes the board. All of a sudden the board isn't sure about anything: Are you sure about this direction [for TTI]? Do you think we should do it this way? Maybe we should do it another way.

[8]Faxtech had maintained a $10 million directors and officers (D&O) insurance policy. From Dave's perspective, the policy covered the board members against all external claims. The policy, however, had an exclusion for claims brought by the company against its own members. This "insured vs. insured" exclusion was the clause the insurance cited when they refused to cover the directors against a lawsuit that was brought by the bankruptcy trustee on behalf of the company's creditors. The insurance company claimed that the bankruptcy trustee was acting "on behalf of the company" and hence this triggered the "insured vs. insured" exclusion.

Remember: These are really good people who bet on me for all the right reasons. Nonetheless, having that outside force sending thick documents that say I'm a terrible person and a crooked manager is an understandable cause for investor concern.

The board believed, as the insurance company did, that the lawsuit would be dismissed or settled before it reached a jury. Nevertheless, the affair had heightened investor concerns about Dave's role in their TTI investment. Dave recalled one particularly stressful meeting:

They said, "Look, you're the largest stockholder. You invented all the technology; you're the holder of all the patents; you've brought in the whole team; and that team is committed to you and would leave anytime you told them to. You raised all the money. You're the founder and the CEO, and you're the only one we can talk to. How do we know you're right? We're supposed to be the board, but what exactly would we say? How do we actually have a debate?"

Dave said the board was also concerned that even the technology plan (Exhibit C) had to be taken largely on faith:

EXHIBIT C

Multiapplication Addressing Architecture

The TITAN platform is a highly flexible, carrier-grade, multiprotocol, next-generation addressing infrastructure that service providers and interconnect carriers license to support multiple IP and SS7/C7 address resolution services. Addressing applications supported on TITAN include among others: Carrier-ENUM, Number-Portability, Calling-Name, SPID, and GTT.

Query protocols supported on the platform include ENUM, SIP, DNS, SOAP/XML, and multiple SS7/C7 protocols (AIN 0.2, PCS-1900, IS-41, GSM/MAP) via SIGTRAN or low-speed link.

This platform is licensed to carriers as a software package that can be configured or customized to support multiple address resolution services on a variety of high-performance, off-the-shelf hardware platforms and operating systems.

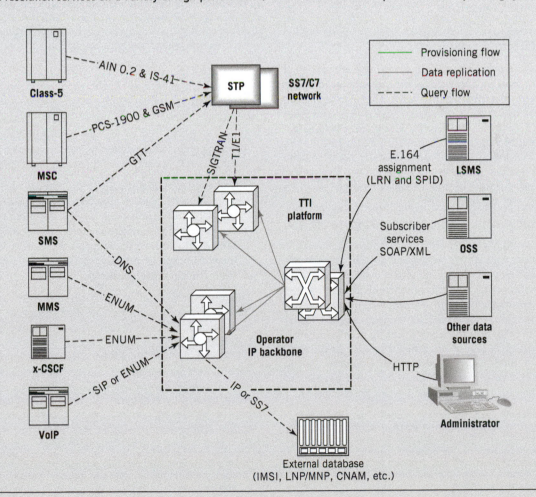

What we do is so geeky. I'm not kidding—there are not 50 people on the planet who understand what we do well enough to evaluate our potential. I don't even bother to explain it. Just trust me: Phone numbers don't work on the Internet, the world is going to demand phone numbers, so somehow you have to achieve that transition. Our technology solution is the special sauce that performs that function.

New CEO

Dave swallowed hard when the board presented what seemed like a harsh solution for mitigating their risk:

Their answer was, "Hire someone they know and trust to be CEO of TTI," and I just have to accept that. And then they'll have someone here who can assure them that I know what I'm doing, and that I can do what I say. So George Marsh will be coming in to *replace me (!)* as CEO.[9] His job will be to run the business side: pricing, sales, contracts, fulfillment. As the founder, I will be in charge of strategy and product development.

Bob Turner was not surprised that Dave thought a new CEO was not necessary:

This happened about a year into the process, so it didn't take that long. I say the same thing to all the entrepreneurs that I start with: That I will take you as far as I can, I'll surround you with all the skills that I think will make you better and be able to last as long as you can. If at some point in time I see the mix not being right, then we will quickly add the right people with the right skills. They are almost always shocked by the speed of change once we make that decision.

Bob explained his reasoning for making the change:

Dave's skill is his great ability to conceptualize a business that hasn't yet been formed where there are no rules. But to be successful, someone like that needs someone who can balance his strong intellect and brilliant mind with his absolute devotion to his brilliant mind. He needs someone to say no, to say no not now, and someone to argue points with him.

George is one of my senior guys, my best strategist, and one of my best business executors. He ran four or five of my businesses for me—from tens of

millions to billions. I trusted George implicitly, but I said to them both, "Neither can proceed unless you can both agree. I respect you both greatly, and this is an area that is going to take some judgment, some perceptualizing on how an industry might be formed, and a terrific bond to each other to make it happen."

Fortunately, Dave soon embraced the arrangement:

George was an excellent choice: smart and flexible. The two of us were thrown into this, and it's worked out really well. His ability to be CEO is totally dependent on his ability to maintain a tie with me, and my ability to continue being the entrepreneur and driver of this business is completely dependent on my ability to maintain a relationship with him.

You know, it takes two people to have a great relationship, and we both work at it every day. It's not like it's painful, it's like anything—you've got to keep working at it. I have total respect for his area, he has total respect for my area, and we spend plenty of time staying in synch with each other and with Sam Walker,[10] the head of our development team. And it works.

As the TTI team successfully adjusted to the new management dynamic, a European telco giant was realizing that its 21st-century digital network was going to require a complex software link to preserve the "meaningless" telephone number.

Success in Trying

By early 2000, Terry looked and felt recovered. Although she and Dave still wanted to start a family, Terry said no one believed that was possible:

The doctors were saying that after going through two years of intense chemotherapy, there was no way I could possibly have a baby. We went to fertility clinics that turned us away the moment they learned about my cancer treatments—they wouldn't even consider us because all we'd do is mess up their [success rate] statistics.

The couple refused to give up hope. In January 2001, Terry gave birth to their first daughter. A year and a half later they would be a family of four with two healthy little girls.

In April 2001, TTI formed a strategic partnership with Indica Software, a Los Angeles–based Internet infrastructure company, to "facilitate the deployment of wholly transparent, network access numbering technologies." In August, the venture closed a $15 million round with participation from a

---

[9] Prior to joining TTI, George was the chief executive officer, president, and cochair of a public video processing technology company. He was formerly president and CEO of a provider of wireless messaging services with 9 million subscribers. Earlier George served as vice chair of a leading worldwide provider of credit card transaction processing, health care claims processing, and document management/imaging services with revenues exceeding $3 billion.

[10] Sam was TTI's chief technical officer and vice president of development and operations. At Faxtech Sam had served as head of architecture and technology.

venture capital subsidiary of Science International Corp. and by VeriSign, an Internet security firm. A vice president from each company was given a seat on TTI's board of directors.

Dave recalled that the tragic events of 9/11 threw everything off schedule:

We are about a year into [the venture], and all of a sudden the world goes through this total telecom meltdown. Nobody was buying anything. Lucent let go 40,000 people! It was an unbelievable disaster... and it was happening all over the world. Fortunately our partnership with Indica enabled us to grab onto an existing niche and apply our technology to deliver that service more efficiently. That was just a better mousetrap, but it gave us some money while we waited for the industry to recover.

In early 2002, the team offered former Faxtech manager Clark Thomas the post of vice president of finance and administration. Clark, who had been building a successful practice as a tax and finance consultant to high-tech startups, took a hard look before saying yes:

I think Dave has a lot of skills to run a company and to rally people and focus people on a particular direction. He is a great dynamic leader, he is a very good visionary, but I thought there were some things he needed to learn from [the Faxtech] experience.

I thought a couple of things he was lacking at Faxtech were a real strong board of directors and some real strong dissenting opinions on his executive team. I saw that with TTI Dave recognized those weaknesses, and this time he is very open to taking advice from other people to make it work.

At around the same time, Dave began to have some interesting conversations about the future:

In February I flew out to meet with one of British Telecom's [BT] R&D groups outside London. I felt that I had achieved a real meeting of the minds with Ned Saxon, a young guy in the group. BT was still years away from needing the TTI solution, and we were still in the middle of building it, but I could see how it might all come together.

Ned did a great job of finding the right group within BT. This group was designing the "21st-Century Network"—a $20 billion project to make the transition away from circuit-switched technologies. Ned succeeded in getting me a meeting with the design group despite their reluctance to meet with a small company from Massachusetts. During the initial meeting, we reviewed the complete problem space and explored how our technology could solve their routing problems. I explained to them why the [big players] in the industry can't do this, and why what we are building is in fact the answer they will be looking for.

At the end of the meeting, they said, "That's an outstanding story, but we simply are not knowledgeable

enough to know whether it's right or wrong." The head of the group says, "I can tell you for sure it's an impressive story, but I can also tell you we don't buy things from 30-person organizations in Massachusetts."

Dave thanked them for their time. He was determined they'd meet again:

BT was the only tier-one carrier on the planet planning such a complete transition. I knew one thing: We had to win that contract. In fact, the whole reason we are here is to win that contract. And if we don't win it, we're not going to get the learning. And if we don't get it, that learning will go to someone named Siemens or Ericsson—firms with infinite resources. If we lose out to one of them, we're all done.

In early 2004 Dave had another meeting with the British Telecom group:

They seemed a bit exasperated. They said, "The way this is supposed to work is BT goes to a big company—like Ericsson—and Ericsson is supposed to find you. You don't come to us." Then they say that Ericsson has assured them that they have the technology. And I shake my head and say, "Okay, I understand that you guys can't possibly know whether I'm telling you the truth, or whether this is just a total story. I get that."

So I hand them my card and say, "In some amount of time in the future you're going to find out that Ericsson can't do this, and it's going to be painful, because they're going to stretch you out, and it's going to be at the last minute, and they're going to have to finally fess up that they can't do it. And when that happens, you call me."

As a confident group inside Ericsson got down to work to devise their version of this technology, TTI began fielding offers from other industry players interested in buying it. Dave and the team felt it was far too early to consider a harvest:

We won't be interested in selling until we feel that someone is way overvaluing the business, or the dynamics change and our real competitive advantage has been narrowed. We believe that even if [a competitor] is working really hard right now, they're still several years behind us. We'll eventually sell to someone who is planning to run with it for 30 years. But first we want to build value by getting our solution into the marketplace.

A Sudden Leave of Absence

In December 2004, with his company right in the middle of its most critical phase of development, Dave's world took a nasty turn:

They called it head and neck cancer, stage three. They believed it originated somewhere in my throat region—sinuses, tongue, throat, somewhere in there—and then it moved to my lymph system. But because they couldn't find the exact origin, the doctors were going to have to treat the cancer by applying maximum radiation to everything from my upper chest to the bridge of my nose.

... I was in for a horrible period of many months of radiation treatment and recovery, and I just knew I was going to have to disappear for a while.

The initial shock was followed by great sorrow the five-year survival rate for Dave's type of cancer was just 40 percent. Clark said the news was a huge blow to the company but that Dave handled it well:

He has that unique characteristic of being able to put a positive spin on almost anything. He was totally upfront about what he was facing. He had a meeting and explained in great detail what he was going to have to go through, and he explained his whole treatment process of aggressively attacking the cancer. His openness, and his willingness to let people know what he was facing, helped people to deal with it in the best way possible.

With the company still in the development phase and with revenues still an undetermined way out, the team needed to assess the impact of this terrible news and decide how best to move forward.

Chapter Seventeen

The Family as Entrepreneur

LEARNING OUTCOMES: After reading this chapter, you will be able to understand:

17-1 Building entrepreneurial family legacies

17-2 The mind-set and method for family enterprising

17-3 The six dimensions for family enterprising

17-4 The familiness advantage for family enterprising

Building Entrepreneurial Family Legacies[1]

The purpose of this chapter is to deepen our understanding of entrepreneurship in the family context and we will explore entrepreneurial commitments, capabilities, and contributions of families and their businesses. Consistent with earlier definitions of entrepreneurship, families who are enterprising generate new economic activity and build long-term value across generations; we refer to this outcome as *transgenerational entrepreneurship and wealth creation*. This chapter will provide families with three sets of assessment and strategy tools to assist them in building their family legacy.

Large Company Family Legacies

We must first begin by understanding the economic and entrepreneurial significance of family businesses. It is difficult to walk into a Marriott Hotel, see the father and son picture of J. Willard Marriott Jr. and Sr., and not think about entrepreneurial family legacies. From a small root beer concession stand, who would have expected the emergence of a $10 billion, 133,000-employee company? The Marriotts are now in their third generation of family leadership and are just one example of the many U.S. companies and branded products that are synonymous with family names and legacies.

Ford Motor Company celebrated 100 years of making cars in 2003. Henry Ford's original company is in its fifth generation with fourth-generation leader William (Bill) Clay Ford, Jr., as the chairman and CEO. The Ford family still controls about 40 percent of the voting shares in the $170 billion-plus company.

Walgreens began when Chicago pharmacist and entrepreneur Charles Walgreen borrowed $2,000 from his father for a down payment on his first drugstore in 1901. Today the company is in its fourth generation of Walgreen family involvement with Charles R. Walgreen III as the chairman emeritus of the board of directors and his son Kevin Walgreen as a vice president. It has grown through the generations to over 4,800 stores with $37.5 billion in annual revenue and has fewer stores than its rival CVS but still beats them in annual sales.

Cargill is the largest privately held corporation in the United States, generating more than $62 billion in annual revenues across a diversified group of food, agricultural, and risk management businesses around the globe. One hundred and forty years after its inception, the founding Cargill and MacMillan families still own 85 percent of the company.

The concepts and models presented in this chapter are based on the research and writing of Timothy Habbershon and colleagues, including T. G. Habbershon and M. L. Williams, "A Resource Based Framework for Assessing the Strategic Advantages of Family Firms," *Family Business Review* 12 (1999), pp. 1–25; T. G. Habbershon, M. Williams, and I. C. MacMillan, "A Unified Systems Perspective of Family Firm Performance," *Journal of Business Venturing* 18, no. 4 (2003), pp. 451–65; and T. G. Habbershon and J. Pistrui, "Enterprising Families Domain: Family-Influenced Ownership Groups in Pursuit of Transgenerational Wealth," *Family Business Review* 15, no. 1 (2002), pp. 223–37.
[1]Primary financial, performance, and ownership data from Hoovers Online.

Although it is often assumed that family companies cannot play in the technology and telecommunications arena, father and son team Ralph and Brian Roberts have grown the Comcast cable company into the largest in the United States. Even with a $54 billion takeover of AT&T Broadband in 2002, the Roberts family still maintains 33 percent of the voting shares and top leadership positions.[2]

Families also dominate many of the leading financial services and banking institutions worldwide. In Boston, Fidelity is owned by the Johnson family, controlling 49 percent of the largest mutual fund company in the world with more than $1 trillion under management. Ned Johnson continues to lead the company as CEO and chairman, while his daughter is president of the fastest-growing Retirement Services Unit.

Many of the popular branded product companies are controlled by families, including Tyson Foods, an Arkansas-based $26 billion company in which the family controls 80 percent, and the grandson of the founder is the current chairman and CEO. Mars is still 100 percent family owned, and the $20 billion company has multiple generations of family members at all levels of top leadership. Cosmetic, fragrance, and skin care products company Estee Lauder generates nearly $6 billion in revenues with the founding family controlling approximately 88 percent of its voting shares and six members in top management bearing the Lauder name. Wrigleys gum, a $3.6 billion company currently run by the founder's great-grandson, William Wrigley Jr., far outperforms its rivals with a 20.3 percent return on assets. Smucker's Jam—"With a name like Smucker's, it has to be good"—has sales of over $2 billion with brothers Tim and Richard continuing to grow the 100-year-old company.

Another interesting category of entrepreneurial family involvement is the investment-holding company. Warren Buffet may be one of the most famous examples. Buffet's company, Berkshire Hathaway, owns many recognizable companies such as GEICO Insurance, Fruit of the Loom, and Dairy Queen. For over 37 years, Buffet's investments in companies have provided an average annual return of 22.6 percent and have increased the value of Berkshire by over 195,000 percent since 1965. His 38 percent stake in the $74 billion Berkshire gives him an estimated net worth of $41 billion and makes him the second richest person in the world,

behind only Bill Gates.[3] Warren's son, Howard G. Buffet, is a director at several Berkshire subsidiaries and currently sits on the board at Berkshire. Although succession planning at Berkshire is highly secretive, it is anticipated that Howard Buffet will take over as chairman of the board.

Minnesota-based Carlson Companies is a less well-known company. In 1998 Marilyn Carlson Nelson took over as CEO of her family holding company. By 2007 she had grown the business nearly 70 percent to $37.1 billion in revenues. The 100 percent family-owned company is predominantly in hospitality and travel, owning companies such as the TGI Friday's restaurant chain, Radisson, Regent International Hotels, and Park Plaza Hotels & Resorts.

There are many smaller family investment-holding companies such as the Berwind Group in Philadelphia, Pennsylvania, that fly under the radar in our cities. The multibillion-dollar fifth-generation family company invested more than $900 million in acquisitions during their most recent 3-year planning cycle, including the acquisition of Elmer's Products.

In keeping with this picture of family legacy contributions, in 2006 over a third of Fortune 500 companies were controlled or managed by families. These family-influenced companies consistently outperform nonfamily businesses on annual shareholder return, return on assets, and both annual revenue and income growth.[4] But these large family companies only begin to tell the story of the entrepreneurial and economic contribution made by business families.

Smaller and Midsized Family Legacies

In many regards, the real heart and often overlooked segment of the U.S. economy and entrepreneurial activity is the smaller and midsize companies. This segment is substantively controlled by families, and they are not all your typical mom-and-pop operations.

Cardone Manufacturing in Philadelphia, Pennsylvania, is a prime example. Founded by a father and son team in 1970, it is the largest nongovernment employer in the city and the largest privately held remanufacturer of car parts in the United States. The founding son, Michael Cardone, and his third-generation children are continuing their entrepreneurial legacy by expanding the multi-hundred-million-dollar company into Europe and China, while moving into the new car parts arena.

[2]"A New Cable Giant," *BusinessWeek*, November 18, 2002, p. 108.
[3]"Forbes 400 List," September 24, 2004, *Forbes*, http://www.forbes.com/400richest/.
[4]J. Weber et al., "Family Inc.," *Business Week*, November 10, 2003.

Walmart: a Growth-Oriented Family Enterprise

Whether one loves or hates Walmart, the Walton family tops the list of family wealth creation legacies. The family still controls nearly 40 percent of the largest company in the world with $288 billion in annual revenue. The family fortune totals $100 billion–more than Bill Gates and Warren Buffet combined, or more than the GDP of Singapore. There are five Walton family members[5] in the top 10 of the list of richest Americans,[6] and they contributed more than $700 million in charitable giving with 80 percent of their donations to education since 1998. The visible link between the company and the family is Walmart Chairman Rob Walton, who is commended by *Fortune* magazine as one of "the most knowledgeable nonexecutive chairmen in American business." Rob's father, Sam Walton, had a vision to allow ordinary folks to buy what only rich people could once buy. This aspiration was translated into the company slogan "everyday low prices." Chairman Rob Walton makes clear that the Walton vision is alive and well, proclaiming that "Walmart is still a growth company."[7]

The largest privately held hair salon chain in the United States was founded by a husband and wife. The Ratner Company has a strong top leadership team and is training its second generation of family members. They outperform their larger public rival, Regis, and continue to act entrepreneurially. With nearly 1,000 company stores in their largest brand, Hair Cuttery, they are moving into franchising, expanding their upscale brands, and establishing strategic partnerships to continue their global expansion. Although cofounder Dennis Ratner could be resting on his accomplishments, he is committed to family enterprising, telling his children, "You either eat or get eaten."

Many family companies may not have brand names consumers recognize, but they are dominant in their industries because they play in the supply chains of large multinationals. Bloomer Chocolates in Chicago, Illinois, is known as the company that makes Chicago smell like chocolate. The third-generation multi-hundred-million-dollar company is the largest roaster of chocolate beans in the United States. They have taken a low-margin commodities business that large chocolate companies have outsourced and created a profitable niche. Many of the chocolate products from companies such as Hershey's and Nestlé are made from chocolate produced by Bloomer.

The list of these "everyday" family entrepreneurs is endless. In Boston, Gentle Giant is the largest regional moving company. The entrepreneurial vision of this $20 million company sets the standard for the moving industry, and they plan to replicate it in other cities. The largest distributor of IAMS pet food on the East Coast has a third generation of entrepreneurs at the helm. Having recently bought the business from their father, two brothers are next-generation entrepreneurs, growing Pet Food Experts and diversifying it to lessen the risk of being a dedicated distributor. In the ski industry, dominated by large public resort companies, Tim and Diane Mueller stand out as successful family entrepreneurs. Since 1982 they have grown the run-down Vermont ski resort they purchased to a $100 million company and have acquired a resort in Denver. CarSense is a new concept car dealership that has grown to $100 million in sales in 7 years after the second-generation entrepreneur sold the family's traditional car dealerships to innovate for the future. Majestic Athletic, a sports apparel company in eastern Pennsylvania, run by the Capobianco family, makes the uniforms for all of major league baseball. Many critics felt major league baseball was crazy to choose a small family-run company instead of a large apparel maker, but the hands-on quality approach of the family has been a big hit for the company and the league.

In this montage of families we have not even mentioned the nascent entrepreneurs and smaller companies that will become the next-generation Marriott, Smucker, or Ratner family companies. Nor have we considered the children in existing family firms who will become nascent entrepreneurs. In a recent undergraduate class on family entrepreneurship at Babson College, more than 80 percent of the students said that they wanted to start *their own company* as an extension of their family company.

The Family Contribution and Roles

It is clear from our descriptions of family companies that families still dominate the U.S. economy and even more fully the economies of other countries

---

[5]On June 27, 2005, John Walton, son of Sam Walton, tragically died in a crash of his ultralight plane near Jackson Hole, Wyoming. John was tied for fourth richest person according to *Forbes* with a net worth of $18 billion. It is still unsure what will be done with his remaining fortune.

[6]"Forbes 400 List," September 24, 2004, *Forbes*, http://www.forbes.com/400richest/.

[7]A. Serwer et al., "The Waltons: Inside America's Richest Family," *Fortune* 150, no. 10 (November 15, 2004), p. 86.

worldwide. The most recent economic impact study in the United States reported that 89 percent of all business tax returns and 60 percent of all public companies had family participation and strategic control, that is, more than 24 million businesses and represents nearly $6 trillion in gross domestic product (64 percent of GDP) and 82 million jobs (62 percent of the workforce).[8] Worldwide, the economic numbers are similar to those in countries like Italy, reporting that 93 percent of their businesses are family controlled, and Brazil, 90 percent[9] as outlined in Exhibit 17.1.

There was a day when "business" meant "family" because the family was understood to be foundational to all socioeconomic progress.[10] Today, however, we must more intentionally categorize the roles families play economically and entrepreneurially. Exhibit 17.2 presents five different roles families can play in the entrepreneurial process and distinguishes between a formal and informal application of these roles.

In this regard the categories are both descriptive and prescriptive. They describe what roles families play and how they play them, but also hint at a prescription for a more formal approach to entrepreneurship in the family context. By "formal" we mean establishing individual and organizational

disciplines and structure of the entrepreneurial process and not meaning "bureaucratic."

The first and dominant role families play is what we call *family-influenced startups*. Data from the GEM report indicated that there were 25 million "new family firms" started in 2002 worldwide.[11] Because families are driven by social forces of survival, wealth creation, and progeny, it is natural that startup businesses think family first. Family-influenced startups are new businesses where the family ownership vision and leadership influences the strategic intent, decision making, and financial goals of the company.

The *family corporate venturing* category occurs when an existing family company or group starts new businesses. Families are often, and quite naturally, portfolio entrepreneurs who build numerous businesses under a family umbrella. Although they may not always grow each of the businesses to their fullest potential, the new businesses are often synergistic, create jobs for a community, and grow the net worth of the family. Often they are started so that family members have their own businesses to run. The more formal approach to family corporate venturing makes the new business process part of an overall strategic plan for growing family wealth while leveraging the resources and capabilities of family members.

Family corporate renewal occurs where the family's entrepreneurial activity is focused on creating new streams of value within the business or group through innovation and transformational change activities. Companies that launch new products or services, enter new markets, or establish new business models are renewing their strategies for the future. This type of strategic or structural renewal is particularly prevalent during family generational transitions or when a family realizes their legacy business can no longer compete. A more formal approach to corporate renewal is proactive, continuous, and institutionalized versus waiting for transitions or competitive triggers to start the renewal processes.

One of the roles families play is to provide *investments* to family members starting a business. More than 63 percent of businesses in the planning stage and up to 85 percent of existing new ventures use family funding. Between 30 and 80 percent of all informal, nonventure capital, funding comes from family. In the United States this amounts to nearly 0.05 percent of GDP and as high as 3 percent of GDP in South Korea.[12] Most often the family cash is

EXHIBIT 17.1

Worldwide Highlights of Family Businesses

Country	Definition	FBs (%)	GNP (%)
Brazil	Middle	90	63
Chile	Broad	75	50–70
USA	Broad	96	40
Belgium	Narrow	70	55
Finland	Narrow	80	40–45
France	Broad	> 60	> 60
Germany	Middle	60	55
Italy	Broad	93	
Netherlands	Narrow	74	54
Poland	Broad	Up to	35
Portugal	Broad	70	60
Spain	Narrow	79	
UK	Middle	70	
Australia	Narrow	75	50
India	Broad		65

[8]J.H. Astrachan and M.C. Shanker, "Family Businesses' Contribution to the U.S. Economy: A Closer Look," *Family Business Review* 16, no. 3 (September 2003), p. 211.

[9]"IFERA: Family Businesses Dominate," *Family Business Review* 16, no. 4 (December 2003), p. 235.

[10]H.E. Aldrich and J.E. Cliff, "The Pervasive Effects of Family on Entrepreneurship: Toward a Family Embeddedness Perspective," *Journal of Business Venturing* 18, no. 5 (September 2003), p. 573.

[11]GEM 2002, Special Report on Family Sponsored New Ventures.

[12]Ibid.

EXHIBIT 17.2

Roles Families Play in the Entrepreneurial Process

	Family-Influenced Startups	Family Corporate Venturing	Family Corporate Renewal	Family Private Cash	Family Investment Funds
Formal	An entrepreneur with no legacy assets/existing business, but who formally launches a new business with family and/or intending to involve family.	Family holding companies or businesses that have formal new venture creation and/or acquisition strategies, plans, departments, or capabilities.	Family-controlled companies with a formal strategic growth plan for creating new streams of value through change in business strategy, model, or structure.	Startup money from family member or business with a formal written agreement for market-based ROI and or repayment.	Stand-alone professional private equity or venture capital fund controlled by family and/or using family-generated capital.
Informal	An entrepreneur with no legacy assets/existing business who happens to start a new business out of necessity and it begins to involve family members.	Family holding companies or businesses that grow through more informal, intuitive, and opportunistic business startup and acquisitions.	Intuitive growth initiatives that result in a change in business strategy, model, or structure and new streams of value for the family company.	Startup money or gift from family member or business with no agreement or conversation about ROI or repayment.	Internal capital and/or funds used by family owners to invest in real estate or passive partnerships or seed new businesses.

given based on altruistic family sentiments rather than having more formal investment criteria. While providing seed capital, whether formal or informal, is clearly a significant role in the entrepreneurial process, having some formal investment criteria can avoid future confusion or conflict among family members. It also creates more discipline and accountability for family entrepreneurs (see Exhibit 17.3).

Family investment funds are pools of family capital that families use for entrepreneurial activities. These family funds, both formal and informal, are becoming increasingly more common as families find themselves flush with cash. Most often the formal family investment funds are created after a family has liquidated all or part of their family group. These funds are generally formed in conjunction with a family office. Informal family investment

funds are pools of money, generally from cash flows, that family leaders invest in entrepreneurial activities as a way to diversify their family portfolios and/or have fun. They often invest within their network of peers, and the investments are usually nonoperating investments in businesses or real estate deals. These investments are often significant portions of their total wealth.

When we catalog the wide range of informal and formal roles families can play in the entrepreneurial process, we see the contribution they are capable of making to the entrepreneurial economy. We believe business families who are interested in transgenerational entrepreneurship and wealth creation must cultivate the more formal approach to entrepreneurship. The remainder of this chapter assists families in formalizing their entrepreneurship roles. We present three strategy frames that are based on the Timmons Model introduced in Chapter 3. The frames focus on the controllable components of the entrepreneurial processes that can be assessed, influenced, and altered.

EXHIBIT 17.3

Distribution of Businesses with Family Venture Backing

	Planning Stage Startups	New Firms	Established Firms
Number of Cases	1,425	1,594	3,743
Family-Sponsored Ventures	63%	76%	85%

Source: *Family Sponsored Ventures*. J. H. Astrachan, S. A. Zahra, and P. Sharma. Publication for The Entrepreneurial Advantage of Nationals: First Annual Global Entrepreneurship Symposium, United Nations Headquarters. April 29, 2003; based on findings from the Global Entrepreneurship Monitor 2002 sponsored by Babson College, London Business School and the Kauffman -Foundation.

Frame One: The Mind-Set and Method for Family Enterprising

Enterprising families understand that today's dynamic and hypercompetitive marketplace requires families to act entrepreneurially; they must generate new economic activity if they intend to survive and prosper over long periods of time. The Timmons Model shows us that at the heart of the entrepreneurial process is the opportunity. Consistent with this focus, enterprising is seen as the decision that leaders and organizations make to investigate opportunity and seek growth "when expansion is neither pressing nor particularly obvious."[13] The enterprising decision to search for opportunity precedes the economic decision to capture the opportunity. It is when families are faced with a decision to continue along their existing path, versus to expend effort and commit resources to investigate whether there are higher-potential opportunities that are not yet obvious, that the "spirit of enterprising" is evidenced. We thus define enterprising as the proactive and continuous search for opportunistic growth.

Enterprising families institutionalize the opportunity-seeking processes in the mind-set and methods of both their family ownership group and their business organizations. Those families who simply try to maintain their local advantage, safeguard their brands, assets, and customers, or hone their operational efficiencies put themselves at a competitive risk in the shorter run. In the longer run, if their strategic planning is mainly focused on how to pass their business from one generation to the next, rather than developing people and strategies for creating new streams of value, their future may be limited.

Enterprising Mind-Set and Methods

The first assessment and strategy frame for family enterprising is the mind-set and methods model (Exhibit 17.4) that shows family enterprising is the combination of a financial ownership mind-set and entrepreneurial strategic methods. The purpose of the model is to ensure that families talk about both the ownership *and* management requirements for carrying out the entrepreneurial process in their family and business. The mind-set and methods assessment instruments[14] at the back of this chapter will enable families to determine their level of congruence on the two dimensions. It will also allow them to have a strategic conversation about where they currently are and how they might need to change in order to become more enterprising.

Twelve Challenges to Family Enterprising

Like the gravitational pull that keeps us bound to the earth, families face a number of inherent challenges that may keep them bound to past strategies rather than pursuing new opportunities.

1. Families assume that their past success will guarantee their future success.
2. Family members attribute "legacy value" to their businesses or assets, but that value does not translate into a market value or advantage.
3. Families want a "legacy pass" in the market—"We are 50 years old and we deserve another 50 years since we have been such good citizens."
4. Leaders try to balance the risk profile (risk and reward expectations) of their shareholders with the risk and investment demands of the marketplace.
5. Senior and successor generations have different risk profiles and goals for how the business should grow in the future.
6. Families find it hard to pass the entrepreneurial commitments and capabilities from the senior generation to a less "hungry" successor generation.
7. Families build their first-generation businesses on the founder's intuition, but the business never establishes more intentional entrepreneurial processes to keep the entrepreneurial contributions alive.
8. Families will not use many of the financial strategies that entrepreneurs use to grow businesses: debt, equity capital, strategic alliances, and partnerships.
9. Families do not shed unproductive assets and underperforming businesses to reallocate resources to more productive places.
10. Successor generation family members feel entitled to get a business rather than seek next-generation entrepreneurial opportunity.
11. Senior leaders communicate to the next generation that business planning and entrepreneurial analysis are a waste of time.
12. Family members are given a business to run as part of their legacy, and that is viewed as entrepreneurship in the family.

---

[13]J.E. Penrose, *The Theory of the Growth of the Firm*. 3rd ed. (New York: Oxford University Press, 1995).

[14]The content and questions from the mind-set and methods inventories are based on the following literature:

J.G. Covin and D.P. Slevin, "Strategic Management in Small Firms in Hostile and Benign Environments," *Strategic Management Journal* 10, no. 1 (1989), pp. 75-87.

R.G. McGrath and I. MacMillan, *The Entrepreneurial Mindset: Strategies for Continuously Creating Opportunity in an Age of Uncertainty* (Boston, MA: Harvard Business School Press, 2000).

D.L. Mconaughy, C.H. Matthews, and A.S. Fialko, "Founding Family Controlled Firms: Performance, Risk, and Value," *Journal of Small Business Management* 39, no. 1 (January 2001), p. 31.

D. Miller, "The Correlates of Entrepreneurship in Three Types of Firms," *Management Science* 29, no. 7 (1983), p. 770.

D. Miller and P.H. Friesen, "Innovation in Conservative and Entrepreneurial Firms: Two Models of Strategic Momentum," *Strategic Management Journal* 3, no. 1 (January-March 1982), p. 1.

S. Zahra, "Entrepreneurial Risk Taking in Family Firms," *Family Business Review* 18, no. 1 (March 2005), p. 23.

EXHIBIT 17.4

Mind-Set and Methods Enterprising Model

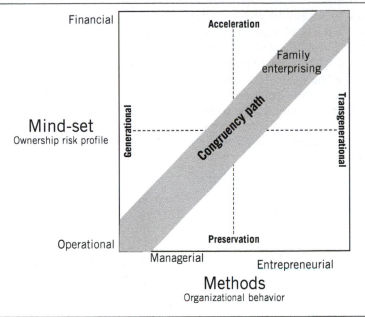

The *mind-set continuum* is primarily a measure of the financial risk profile of the family owners-shareholders. In general, it reflects the financial premise that entrepreneurial leaders gain strategic advantage and find above-normal returns by deploying their resources to points of highest return and by developing strategies that exploit new opportunity. Family leaders who have an operational mind-set predominantly focus on management strategies, operational efficiencies, and the perpetuity of a *particular* business. A financial mind-set moves beyond the operational focus to an investor focus with a view toward the overall capital strategy of the family, creating new streams of value and finding a return on the *totality* of assets. While the operational mind-set is a requirement for running an efficient business, the financial focus is a requirement for transgenerational entrepreneurship and wealth creation.

The financial mind-set for enterprising includes the following characteristics:[15]

- A proclivity for higher risk and above-normal returns.
- A willingness to sell and redeploy assets to seek higher returns.
- A desire to grow by creating new revenue streams with higher returns.
- A commitment to generating next-generation entrepreneurship.

- A willingness to continuously revisit the existing business model.
- An assumption that a percentage of the business will become obsolete.
- A willingness to leverage the business to grow and find higher returns.
- A desire to reinvest versus distribute capital.
- A willingness to enter into partnerships and alliances to grow.
- A strategy to manage the family's wealth for a total return.
- A commitment to innovation in business strategies and structures.
- A belief that bold, wide-ranging acts are necessary to achieve investment objectives in today's environment.

The *methods continuum* is a measure of the entrepreneurial orientation and actions in business organizations. It assumes that enterprising organizations are taking bold, innovative, market-leading actions to seek a competitive advantage and generate new streams of value. It also reflects the premise that to be enterprising organizations must have a collection of individuals who act like an entrepreneur and not just a single leader or small group of family leaders. A single leader acting entrepreneurially might generate entrepreneurial actions in the business

[15]J. G. Covin and D. P. Slevin, "Strategic Management in Small Firms in Hostile and Benign Environments," *Strategic Management Journal* 10, no. 1 (1989), p. 75.

during his or her generation but will not create a transgenerational family business or group. Enterprising organizations move beyond managerial methods that focus on maintaining the existing and implementing incremental change. They are seeking and creating and establishing entrepreneurial-renewal processes. Although entrepreneurial methods do not replace the need for managerial actions, managerial actions are not sufficient conditions for enterprising and transgenerational wealth creation.

The entrepreneurial methods for enterprising include the following characteristics:[16]

- Allocating disproportionate resources to new business opportunities.
- Systematically searching for and capturing new investment opportunities.
- Seeking new opportunities beyond the core (legacy) business.
- Creating a core competency in innovation at the business unit level.
- Making significant changes in products, services, markets, and customers.
- Initiating competitive change to lead the market.
- Investing early to develop or adopt new technology and processes.
- Typically adopting an "undo the competitor" market posture.
- Having institutionalized the entrepreneurial process in the organization.
- Having formal routines for gathering and disseminating market intelligence.
- Having people at every level in the organization think like competitors.
- Typically adopting a bold, aggressive posture to maximize the probability of exploiting potential investment opportunities.

Creating the Dialogue for Congruence

The mind-set and methods model helps families fulfill key process conditions for family enterprising and transgenerational wealth creation:

- Creating a healthy *dialogue* in the family ownership group and organization around the mind-set and methods issues.
- Establishing *congruence* between the mind-set of the owner–shareholder group and the methods of the business organization(s).

What Enterprising is Not

It is often useful in defining a concept to understand *what it is not*. Judith Penrose takes this approach by contrasting the concept of enterprising with three categories of firms that are not necessarily enterprising.*

"Just grew firms": The "just grew" category are firms in the right place at the right time. They were on the wave of an expanding market, and they had to expand to keep up with demand. The decision to grow was automatic, and because they were able to capitalize on the circumstances, they grew. The situation may continue for a long time, but because markets do not expand indefinitely and competitors fill the opportunity gap, firm growth and the firm will come to an end.

"Comfort firms": This category is often referred to as lifestyle firms. There are firms who refrain from taking full advantage of opportunities for expansion because it would increase their effort and risk. Firms that are comfortable with their income and position have no incentive to grow beyond their acceptable level of profits. These are firms where the goals of the owners to be comfortable are closely aligned with the goals of the firm. Like "just grew firms," comfort firms may continue for decades, but in the end meeting the comfort needs of the owners is not a driver for advantage or renewal.

"Competently managed firms": Many firms are competently managed and consequently are able to find normal returns for relatively long periods by maintaining their operational efficiencies. Competently managed firms are often striving to sustain the entrepreneurial efforts of a founder. They may be competing in more traditional, less dynamic circumstances, have a distinctive market niche, or maintain a regional advantage as a favored business. Although these are exploitable strategies, they are not inherently sustainable and may quickly disappear.

* J. E. Penrose, *The Theory of the Growth of the Firm*, 3rd ed. (New York: Oxford University Press, 1995).

One of the major differences between family enterprising and entrepreneurship is that by definition the team includes the family. Family entrepreneurs are either currently working with family members or planning to work with family members; they either are multigenerational teams or hope to be a multigenerational team; they either have multiple family member shareholders and stakeholders or will have them as they go through time. This inherent familial condition requires

[16]Ibid.

families to cultivate effective communication skills to build relationship capital for family enterprising. Sabine Veit, founder of Backerhaus Veit in Toronto, Canada, realized the importance of dialogue and congruence when her son came home from college toting a business plan for aggressive growth. She had built her artisan bread manufacturing company into a $20 million (U.S.) force in the industry. When her son Toby won Babson's business planning competition she was definitely proud, but she also knew she was in trouble. The plan was to grow *her* business. Sabine loved the thought of working with Toby, and he definitely shared her passion for artisan breads. In fact, during college Toby took every class with the artisan bread industry in mind. How could a parent hope for anything more?

But Toby did not want to just run her company someday. He wanted to move the business beyond manufacturing and wholesaling into branded products and retailing, and he wanted to do it now. On the mind-set and methods model (Exhibit 17.5), Backerhaus Veit was on the congruency path as an operationally focused, managerially sound business. Sabine had a self-defined lifestyle firm that was competitive in her niche with a clear harvest strategy. But Toby was committed to family enterprising and wanted to be a growth firm. This meant

moving beyond their current niche and lifestyle expectations. Clearly Toby had a mind-set for much higher risk than Sabine.

On the methods continuum, Backerhaus Veit did not have the entrepreneurial methods to exploit Toby's plan. Sabine individually had the capabilities and Toby believed he did, but the entrepreneurial team and organization would have to be built. There was clearly significant incongruence as a family and business. The challenge for Sabine and Toby was to establish a plan and process for aligning their mind-set and methods if they wanted to capture the new opportunity and become an enterprising family.

There are a number of things Toby and Sabine needed to do to ensure they were an enterprising family. First, they needed to develop communication skills to have an effective dialogue. Most families assume they are able to carry on a dialogue simply because they are a family. In actuality the familiarity of a family can make it very difficult to challenge assumptions and talk about differing views. Often families need a facilitator to help them develop communication skill and have a dialogue.

Second, they needed to make sure their views of the future were the same. Families often have a vague notion of "working together," and they assume that they will figure the details out over

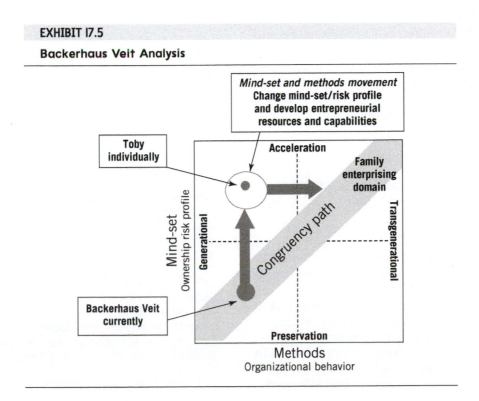

EXHIBIT 17.5

Backerhaus Veit Analysis

time. This is a clear formula for future discontent and conflict. In reality, Toby and Sabine had very different visions for their futures. Sabine's vision was to enjoy her passion for breads while balancing growth with her lifestyle interests. Toby's vision was to exploit his passion for breads by building new businesses on the family's reputation and skills.

Third, Toby and Sabine had very different risk profiles. What Sabine was willing to risk for future returns was very different from what Toby was willing to risk and the returns he desired. It is not surprising that the successor generation is willing to risk more than the senior generation. The key is to keep talking until you understand each other's perspective. Once you understand each other you can create a business model and structures that accommodate the risk profiles of both generations. Locking into one generational perspective or the other undermines the collective strengths of a multigenerational team.

Fourth, remember that timing is everything. Usually for the successors the time is *now* and for the seniors the time is *someday*. Chances are that both generations will end up out of their comfort zones a little. Toby and Sabine realized that timing was really a strategy question of how they would proceed, not just if or when they would proceed.

Fifth, get creative. You can be sure that the final outcome will not look exactly as either of you envisioned. Through dialogue it became clear to Toby and Sabine that the range of options was fairly extensive. We often tell family members to "remember their algebra" when it comes to dialogue. Just because "a equals b" it does not mean that "a" might not equal "c, d, or even e, f, and g." The point is that once you start a true dialogue, you may find many more options than you originally envisioned.

Frame Two: The Six Dimensions for Family Enterprising

The second assessment and strategy frame for family enterprising addresses the team component of the Timmons Model. In family enterprising "team" is a much broader and complex concept. It encompasses the family ownership group and the family and nonfamily entrepreneurial capabilities. The entrepreneurial process cannot occur unless there is alignment in the team's ownership mind-set and entrepreneurial methods as just described. When the

entrepreneurial leader is a family member, there is potentially another layer of team complexity around issues such as parent-child relationships, altruistic versus entrepreneurial decision making, nepotism and competency, family versus personal equity and compensation, and success measures. In essence, the family as team can create more perfect balance in the Timmons Model or can cause imbalance. One key is to stay focused on the opportunity and stress that the team is in support of exploiting that opportunity.

The six dimensions for family enterprising provide family teams with six areas that they can address to assist them in aligning their mind-set and methods and moving up the congruency path toward the enterprising domain. The six dimensions and the corresponding strategic questions apply key entrepreneurial considerations to the family context. As family owners and leaders answer the questions, they are creating unity within the team for entrepreneurial action. The six dimensions are as follows:

- Leadership
- Relationship
- Vision
- Strategy
- Governance
- Performance

Successful Next-Generation Entrepreneurship

The challenge for multigenerational family teams like Toby and Sabine is to "keep it in dialogue" rather than letting it turn into a debate or disconnect. Debates become personal, and disconnect cuts off opportunity. When family members turn the situation into right and wrong, good and bad, winning or losing, there is very little listening, give-and-take, or changing one's position. In contrast, the word *dialogue* actually means "talking through" an issue. It assumes the ability to challenge each other's assumptions, to keep an open mind, and to test different options. It looks at the big picture, considers the long-term perspective, and discusses the process for getting there. Most important, dialogue does not follow hierarchical roles like parent-child, boss-employee, or the one who owns the business versus the one who does not. The goal of dialogue is to find solutions that are not constrained by the boundaries of either of the original positions.

Leadership Dimension: Does Your Leadership Create a Sense of Shared Urgency for Enterprising and Transgenerational Wealth Creation?

Entrepreneurial leaders create a sense of shared urgency in the organization. The goal is to have everyone, from the owners to those carrying out tasks, thinking and acting like competitors.[17] Families are traditionally and systemically hierarchical in nature—parent-child, older-younger siblings, male-female—and their family organizations often embody these hierarchies in their leadership models. A transgenerational commitment requires families to move beyond the "great leader" model to the "great group."[18] Family leaders who strive to turn their families into a team based on the great group philosophy overcome many of the negative caricatures often associated with family business leadership and empower the family and organization to be enterprising.

Leadership Dimension Diagnostic Questions

- Do family leaders understand the requirements to be transgenerational?
- Do they develop next-generation leadership?
- Do they move the family beyond the "great leader" model?
- Do they promote a sense of openness and mutuality?
- Do they encourage participation by family members at all levels in the family and organization?
- Do they lead others to think and act like entrepreneurs?
- Do they help the family grow beyond a hierarchical model of leadership to become the "great group"?

Relationship Dimension: Does Your Family Have the Relationship Capital to Sustain Their Transgenerational Commitments?

Effective teams are built on healthy relationships. We describe healthy relationships as those that build relationship capital and allow efficient interpersonal interactions in the team. Relationship capital is the reserve of attributes such as trust, loyalty, positive feelings, benefit of the doubt, goodwill, forgiveness, commitment, and altruistic motives.

Relationship capital is a necessary condition for long-lasting teams and transgenerational families. Now here are two opposite but simultaneously true statements: Families have the natural potential to build relationship capital better than other social groups *and* families have the natural potential to destroy relationship capital more ruthlessly than any other social group. Is this good news or bad news for family enterprising? It depends. Those families who intentionally gain the skills and strive to build relationship capital leverage the natural advantage of family teams. But those families who assume they will always have relationship capital or take their relationships for granted open themselves up to potentially destructive tendencies of families. Families who have relationship capital reserves are more likely to create the dialogue that moves them up the congruence path to the family enterprising domain.

Relationship Dimension Diagnostic Questions

- Is your family intentionally building relationship capital?
- Are you investing in the communication and relationship building skills you need to build relationship capital?
- Are there healthy relationships among family siblings and branches and across generations?
- Does your family have formal family meetings to discuss family ownership and relationship issues?
- Do you experience synergy in your family relationships?
- Do you have a positive vision for working together as a family?
- Do family members see relationship health as part of their competitive advantage?

Vision Dimension: Does Your Family Have a Compelling Multigenerational Vision That Energizes People at Every Level?

A compelling vision is what creates the shared urgency for family enterprising and mobilizes people to carry out the vision. By "compelling" we mean that it makes sense to people in light of tomorrow's marketplace realities. Often a vision might make sense for the moment, but it does not make sense for the future. For enterprising families,

---

[17]R.G. McGrath and I. MacMillan, *The Entrepreneurial Mindset: Strategies for Continuously Creating Opportunity in an Age of Uncertainty* (Boston, MA: Harvard Business School Press, 2000).

[18]D.R. Ireland and M.A. Hitt, "Achieving and Maintaining Strategic Competitiveness in the 21st Century: The Role of Strategic Leadership," *The Academy of Management Executive* 13, no. 1 (February 1999), p. 43.

the vision must describe how the family will collectively create new streams of wealth that allow them to be transgenerational. It also has to be multigenerational. It is easy for the different generations to craft their personal visions for the future. Transgenerational families must craft a vision that is compelling to all generations and in a sense transcends generational perspectives. This multigenerational necessity also underscores the importance of establishing participatory leadership and building relationship capital.

Vision Dimension Diagnostic Questions

- Does your family have a vision that makes sense for tomorrow's marketplace?
- Would all generations describe the vision as compelling?
- Was the vision developed by everyone in the family?
- Does the vision have relevance for your decision making and lives?
- Does your family regularly review and test the vision as an ownership group?
- Is the vision transgenerational?
- Is the vision larger than the personal interests of the family?
- Does the vision mobilize others to create new streams of value?
- Do all family members share in the rewards from the vision?

Strategy Dimension: Does Your Family Have an Intentional Strategy for Finding Their Competitive Advantage as a Family?

We have already said that there is a more intentional and formal application of the entrepreneurial process within the family context. Part of that formal approach is developing strategies for both cultivating and capturing new business opportunities. But for families it means much more. The family's strategic thinking and planning should be based on determining how to exploit their unique family-based resources and capabilities to find advantages in enterprising. Although we will address this more specifically in the next section, it includes things like finding synergies with current assets, leveraging networks of personal relationships, cultivating next-generation entrepreneurs, and extending the power of the family reputation. Because families tend to take their family-influenced resources and capabilities for granted, they often fail to see the opportunities they represent for providing them with a long-term advantage for enterprising.

Strategy Dimension Diagnostic Questions

- How does your family provide you with an advantage in entrepreneurial wealth creation?
- What resources and capabilities are unique to your family?
- Does your family have a formal planning process to direct their enterprising?
- Does your organization have formal systems for cultivating and capturing new opportunities?
- Does your family mentor next-generation family members to become entrepreneurs?
- Do your strategic thinking and planning empower your family to fulfill their transgenerational vision?
- What role does your family play in the strategy process?

Governance Dimension: Does Your Family Have Structures and Policies That Stimulate Change and Growth in the Family and Organization?

Few family leaders would consider that governance structures and policies could actually stimulate growth and change. Most would equate the word *governance* with bureaucracies and, at best, acknowledge that structures and policies are a necessary evil to be tolerated and minimized. But we offer two different perspectives. First, the lack of effective governance structures and policies creates significant ambiguity in families and constrains enterprising. Second, when entrepreneurial processes are institutionalized through the governance structures and policies, this promotes growth and change activities. For example, when ownership, equity, or value realization is unclear or cannot be discussed, it discourages family entrepreneurs. But when financial conversations are part of the professional culture and there are transparent ownership structures, family entrepreneurs are clear on the rules of the game. Governance structures are thus critical to transgenerational entrepreneurship and wealth creation.

Governance Dimension Diagnostic Questions

- Does your family view governance as a positive part of their family and business lives?
- Are your governance structures static or fluid?
- Do your structures and policies promote family unity?
- Do your governance structures and policies give an appropriate voice to family members?

- Do your governance structures and policies assist you in finding your family advantage?
- Do you have formal processes that institutionalize the entrepreneurial process in your family and businesses?
- Do your governance structures and policies promote next-generation involvement and entrepreneurship?

Performance Dimension: Does Your Performance Meet the Requirements for Transgenerational Entrepreneurship and Wealth Creation?

The performance dimension is where families clarify whether or not they are really committed to family enterprising. Families who are enterprising are market driven and seek to accelerate their wealth creation through their opportunistic entrepreneurial actions. They have clear financial benchmarks and information for assessing their performance against the market. Lifestyle firms often assume that they are performing well because they are sustaining their lifestyles. Enterprising also implies a process of matching the organization's core competencies with external opportunities in order to create new streams of value. Enterprising families do not rely on past performance as an indicator that they will perform well in the future; nor do they define success by the preservation of an asset. Their success measures are their abilities to fulfill their transgenerational vision for social and economic wealth creation.

Performance Dimension Diagnostic Questions

- Does your family talk openly about financial performance issues, or are finances secretive?
- Are you in lifestyle or enterprising mode?
- Are your strategies driven by a clear market orientation?

- Do family owners agree on their risk and return expectations?
- Are performance expectations clear to next-generation entrepreneurs?
- Are there clear transparency and accountability structures in relation to meeting performance expectations?
- Is there family dialogue about performance expectations–growth, dividends, reinvestment, ROE?

Frame Three: The Familiness Advantage for Family Enterprising

All entrepreneurial success and the opportunity to capture above-average returns are premised upon finding an advantage over your competitors. Correspondingly, the potential for finding an advantage is rooted in the distinctive resources and capabilities that an organization possesses. The "resources" aspect of the Timmons Model is where enterprising can get exciting for families. Because every family is unique, they can generate very idiosyncratic bundles of resources and capabilities that can give them an advantage in the entrepreneurial process if they know how to identify and leverage them. We refer to this idiosyncratic bundle of resources and capabilities as their *familiness*.

When these familiness resources and capabilities lead to a competitive advantage for the family, we refer to them as "distinctive familiness" or an "f+" as shown in Exhibit 17.6. When they constrain the competitive enterprising ability of the family, we refer to them as "constrictive familiness" or "f−." Exhibit 17.6 allows families to place their resources and capabilities on an assessment continuum. The job of families who desire to be enterprising is to determine how to generate and exploit their distinctive familiness and to minimize or shed their constrictive

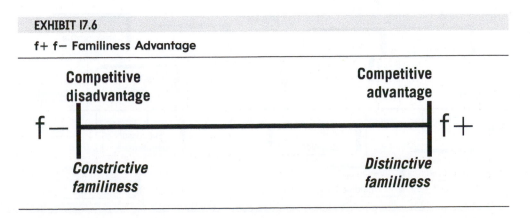

EXHIBIT 17.6

f+ f− Familiness Advantage

familiness. When families begin assessing and planning based on their distinctive and constrictive familiness, they move from an intuitive and informal to the intentional and formal mode of family enterprising.

To better understand familiness, let us return to the family enterprising decision that Toby and Sabine have to make in regard to Backerhaus Veit (BV). If we analyze the distinctive (f+) and constrictive (f−) familiness in their situation, we can bring significant focus to the dialogue and move them along the mindset and methods congruence path.

Exhibit 17.7 is their familiness resource and capabilities continuum as it relates to the new venture opportunity. When you see the f+ f− assessment, it is a comprehensive and revealing picture of their individual and organizational contribution to the new venture. But it is not only the final picture that is useful to families. The conversation to identify the resources and capabilities and to determine where they should be placed is the real learning outcome.

First, you will notice that there are clear resources and capabilities specifically associated with the senior and successor generations and others that are mixed. While Toby's successor drive is an f+, his business capabilities and lack of experience are an f−. Sabine readily admits that without Toby's drive she would never consider this opportunity. But Sabine's advisors are concerned that Toby may overestimate his capabilities and contribution. This discussion is very natural in next-generation entrepreneurship, and families should "normalize" it and not allow it to become personal. Conversely, Sabine's senior capabilities, business networks, and reputation are an f+ for Toby's new venture. Toby readily admits that Sabine's role makes his business plan a much higher-potential venture. On the other hand, Sabine's risk profile

and lifestyle goals are a significant f− and constraint to enterprising. But we need to remember that they fit very well for her current strategy.

Second, there are resources and capabilities associated with BV. Toby's business plan calls for BV to provide valuable shared resources such as wholesale bread supply, bookkeeping, used equipment, repair services, and the like. This opportunity creates a very significant resource advantage that we would call "plan$_{f+}$" because only family members with existing businesses could incorporate these into their plan. The existing management team capabilities are also an f+, but because the existing team is not entrepreneurial (in fact, they see the new venture as a drain on the existing business), we have to give an f− to entrepreneurial team.

Third, certain resources are associated with both Sabine and Toby. Most important is the f+ for tacit bread knowledge. They both know bread making, but the particularly interesting point is to see how advanced Toby is as a young person because he grew up in the bread industry. Correspondingly, the f− for retailing is significant. While Sabine grew up in the retail bread industry (her family has 70 retail bakeries in Germany), she does not know the casual dining bread industry (like Panera Bread Company), and this is the target for Toby's plan. While decision making is an f+, family communication is an f−. The family has great relationships, but in the business setting, they sometimes communicate like mother and son rather than business peers.

The f+ f− continuum makes Toby's and Sabine's "prelaunch" work very clear. Managing the f+ and f− continuum is how families build their resources and capabilities bundle as part of formalizing the entrepreneurial process. It is a critical step in getting the odds more in their favor. Toby and Sabine

EXHIBIT 17.7

Backerhaus Veit f+ f− Analysis

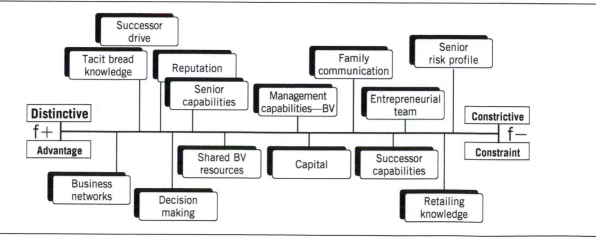

now need to create a work plan for each of the constraining resources in order to move them to a point of neutrality or advantage.

An additional realization from this analysis is to see the potential synergy between the successor and senior generations for family enterprising. Four things are immediately clear from the analysis. First, as we already noted, Sabine would never explore or capture this opportunity if it were not for Toby driving the process. Second, Toby does not have the synergistic familiness resources and capabilities if he tries to do the business on his own. Third, while there are positive reasons to do it together, there are also constraints that must be addressed. Fourth, family enterprising will occur when they decide to do it together as a family, rather than not doing it, or Toby doing it on his own. That is not to say that one way is right or wrong, but simply that doing it together is a family enterprising approach.

We will provide a final assessment of Sabine and Toby using the Timmons Model to discuss fit and balance. Clearly the opportunity for Backerhaus Veit to move into the retail fast-casual-eating market is very large and growing. In fact, the opportunity is probably greater than the current resources and capabilities of BV, Toby, and Sabine to meet them without outside resources. Currently the weakest link in the model is the team. While Toby and Sabine have great bread knowledge, they do not have the entrepreneurial team for the retailing initiative. Further, the BV leaders and advisors are strongly committed to managing their current assets rather than launching an entrepreneurial business. Exhibit 17.8 shows that the model is "out of balance" and reaffirms the conclusions from our

previous assessment that there is significant pre-launch work to be done to ensure a fit. If they do this prelaunch work and can get the Timmons Model into balance, however, they have a great high-potential venture for the family.

Conclusion

For business families who would like to act more entrepreneurially and become intentional enterprising families that have multiple generations seeking higher-potential opportunities, we suggest that four strategic shifts may need to occur:

- From a lifestyle firm that has the goal of personal comfort to an enterprising family committed to transgenerational entrepreneurship and wealth creation.
- From an intuitive family business that "kicks around" (as one family entrepreneur described it) to see what new opportunities turn up to an intentional entrepreneurial process that seeks to generate and capture new opportunities.
- From a senior-generation entrepreneur who does it to a successor-generation entrepreneurial process and team that create opportunities for others to do it.
- From a low-potential entrepreneurial family that creates one-off businesses as they can to a higher-potential entrepreneurial family that mobilizes resources to create transgenerational wealth.

EXHIBIT 17.8

Timmons Model for Backerhaus Veit

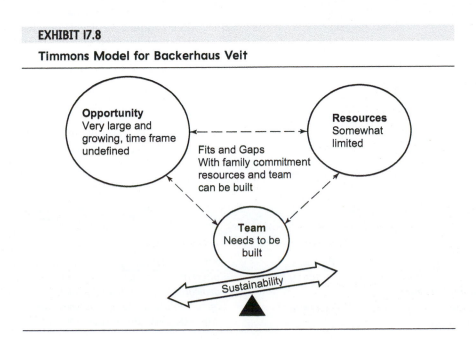

Chapter Summary

- We began by demonstrating the significant contributions families make to the economy and entrepreneurial process. It is often overlooked that the majority of the businesses worldwide are controlled and managed by families, including many of the very largest businesses that we normally do not associate with family.

- Families play a diverse number of formal and informal roles in the entrepreneurial process. We described them as (a) the family-influenced startup, (b) family corporate venturing, (c) family corporate renewal, (d) family private cash, and (e) family investment funds.

- Family enterprising was defined as the proactive and continuous search for opportunistic growth when expansion is neither pressing nor particularly obvious. The outcome of family enterprising is transgenerational entrepreneurship and wealth creation through balance in the Timmons Model.

- The mind-set continuum assesses the family's risk profile, and those interested in enterprising move from an operational to a financial investor strategy. The methods continuum assesses the organizational behavior of leaders and organizations and requires a move from managerial to entrepreneurial strategies for enterprising.

- There are six dimensions for family enterprising that were described as antecedents from the entrepreneurship literature: leadership, relationship, vision, strategy, governance, and performance. The chapter presented key questions for each dimension to assist families in becoming more enterprising.

- We defined the familiness of an organization as the unique bundle of resources and capabilities that result from the interaction of the family and individual family members with the business entities. Families can have positive and negative family influence, which we described as an f+ or f−.

Study Questions

1. What are the entrepreneurial implications of not appreciating or understanding the role of families in, and contributions of families to, the economies of our communities and countries?

2. Describe the advantages of a more formal approach for each role families play in the entrepreneurial process. Give a few contrasting examples from a family firm you know.

3. Define family enterprising, familiness, and relationship capital and relate each of them to the Timmons Model of the entrepreneurial process.

4. Choose a family firm you know and plot it on the mind-set and methods model. Describe the firm in light of the mind-set and method definition. Name six ways it could become more enterprising.

5. How do the six dimensions for family enterprising relate to one another? How do they enhance family enterprising? How can they be used to stimulate positive family dialogue.

6. How can the familiness assessment approach help a family trying to find its competitive advantage? How is the familiness approach a more formal application of the entrepreneurial process? How can the familiness approach change the family dialogue?

7. Given the familiness assessment of Backerhaus Veit in the chapter, describe why Sabine should or should not partner with Toby to implement his business plan. Describe the familiness action steps they should take if you say they should launch the business. Describe the familiness reasons for why they possibly should not launch the business.

8. Assess a family firm with which you are familiar on the familiness resource and capabilities continuum. Describe the action steps it should take to enhance its competitive advantage as a family organization.

Internet Resources

www.fbn-i.org/ *The International Family Business Network is a nonprofit international network run by family businesses for family businesses.*

http://familybusinessmagazine.com/ *The website of Family Business magazine.*

http://www.ffi.org/ *The Family Firm Institute (FFI) is an international professional membership organization dedicated to providing education and networking opportunities for family business and family wealth advisors, consultants, educators, and researchers.*

Exercises

Determine your family's location on the mind-set and methods continuum and what familiness advantage it might have for enterprising. Fill out the assessment surveys, plot your family group on the family enterprising model, and fill out the resources and capabilities continuum.

Mind-Set Continuum

The mind-set continuum establishes the family's financial risk and return expectations and its competitive posture in relation to the marketplace. The assessment is meant to reveal family members' beliefs and get them talking.

Have the current and future family shareholders fill in the mind-set continuum by circling the number between the two statements that best reflects the strength of their belief about the family as a shareholder group. Total scores are between 12 and 84, reflecting views from the most traditional to the most enterprising.

In general, family member shareholders...

Have a strong proclivity for low-risk businesses and investment opportunities (with normal and certain returns).	1 2 3 4 5 6 7	Have a strong proclivity for high-risk business and investment opportunities (with chances for high -returns).
Would sacrifice a higher return to preserve the family's legacy business.	1 2 3 4 5 6 7	Are willing to sell and redeploy assets to find a higher return in the market.
Tend to think about cultivating our current businesses for current returns.	1 2 3 4 5 6 7	Desire to grow by creating new revenue streams with higher possibilities for returns.
Have a commitment to operating the business and providing job opportunities for family.	1 2 3 4 5 6 7	Have a commitment to mentoring next-generation entrepreneurs to create new streams of value.
Feel we have a good business model that will take us into the future.	1 2 3 4 5 6 7	Feel we should continuously revisit the assumptions of our business model.
Feel that our current businesses and products will serve us well in the future.	1 2 3 4 5 6 7	Assume that a significant percentage of our businesses will become obsolete.
Desire to avoid debt and grow with internally generated cash as we can.	1 2 3 4 5 6 7	Are willing to leverage the businesses to grow and find higher returns in the market.
Desire to increase our financial ability to provide distributions and/or liquidity.	1 2 3 4 5 6 7	Desire to reinvest more aggressively for faster growth and higher returns.
Desire to grow within our current financial and equity structures in order to ensure control over our destiny.	1 2 3 4 5 6 7	Are willing to use alliances and partnerships, share equity, or dilute share positions in order to grow.
Would describe ourselves more as a conservative company meeting our family's financial and personal goals.	1 2 3 4 5 6 7	Would describe ourselves as a risk-taking group seeking higher total returns for the family as investment group.
Would describe our business models and strategy as making us steady rather than opportunistic.	1 2 3 4 5 6 7	Are willing to be innovative in our business models and structures in order to be opportunistic.
Believe that a steady and consistent approach will allow us to fulfill our family's vision and goals for the future.	1 2 3 4 5 6 7	Believe that bold, wide-ranging acts are necessary to achieve our family investment objectives in today's environment.

Total:

Methods Continuum

The methods continuum establishes the organization's entrepreneurial orientation and actions. It reflects the beliefs of the shareholders and stakeholders on how the leaders incite entrepreneurship in the organization.

Using the assessment continua, have the family member shareholders and future shareholders answer the questions on the methods continuum listed here. Circle the number between the two statements that best reflects the strength of your belief about the family as a shareholder group. Total scores are between 12 and 84, reflecting views from the most traditional to the most enterprising.

In general, senior leaders in our family organization(s)...

Spend their time nurturing the existing businesses.	1 2 3 4 5 6 7	Pay a disproportionate amount of attention to new business opportunities.
Place a strong emphasis on pursuing returns by reinvesting in tried and true businesses.	1 2 3 4 5 6 7	Place a strong emphasis on searching for and capturing new business investment opportunities.
Have pursued no new investment opportunities outside of our core operating arena (in the last 5 years).	1 2 3 4 5 6 7	Have pursued many new investment opportunities beyond our core operating arena (in the last 5 years).
Believe our core competency is in managing efficient businesses.	1 2 3 4 5 6 7	Believe our core competency is in innovating for opportunistic growth.
Have made minor changes in our businesses, products, services, markets, or business units during the current generation of leaders.	1 2 3 4 5 6 7	Have made significant changes in our products, services, markets, or business units as the market required it.
Typically respond to actions that competitors or the market initiates.	1 2 3 4 5 6 7	Typically initiate actions and competitive change to lead the market and competitors.
Are generally moderate to slow in adopting new technologies and technological processes in our industry.	1 2 3 4 5 6 7	Are often early in investing to develop or adopt new technologies and technological processes in our industry.
Tend to avoid competitive clashes, preferring friendly "live and let live" competition.	1 2 3 4 5 6 7	Typically adopt a competitive "undo-the-competitor" posture when making investment decisions.
Are more intuitive and informal in how the organization thinks about seeking or capturing new opportunities.	1 2 3 4 5 6 7	Have established formal structures and policies to institutionalize the entrepreneurial process in the organization.
Rely on family leaders to know the markets and customers and get the information to the organization.	1 2 3 4 5 6 7	Have more formal plans and approaches to how they gather and disseminate market intelligence.
Rely on family leaders to set the tone and ensure that the organization is competitive through time.	1 2 3 4 5 6 7	Encourage and empower people at every level of the organization to think and act like competitors.
Typically adopt a cautious "wait and see" posture to minimize the probability of making costly investment decisions.	1 2 3 4 5 6 7	Typically adopt a bold, aggressive posture to maximize the probability of exploiting potential investment opportunities.

Total

Family Enterprising Model

Plot your score totals from the mind-set and methods assessment surveys. The lowest possible score is a 12 and the highest possible score is an 84. Plotting the

scores provides you with a visual basis for your family dialogue. Does the plotted score rightly describe your family? Is your family on the "congruence path"? Does everyone agree on where your family is on the model? Develop strategies to move your family on the model if necessary.

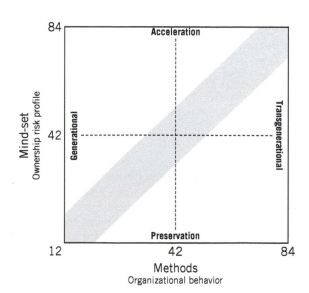

Familiness f+ f− Continuum

Identify where the family influences on your resources and capabilities are part of a competitive advantage (f+) and a competitive constraint (f−). You can conduct this analysis on many levels. The "meta" analysis would be of the larger family group as a whole, while the "micro" analysis would be of a particular business unit, or in relation to a specific innovation or new venture (such as the Backerhaus Veit example in the chapter). Identify the unit of analysis you are assessing and list the f+ and f− resources and capabilities.

Identify Unit of Analysis	
Resources and Capabilities (f+)	**Resources and Capabilities (f−)**

Plot the f+ and f− resources and capabilities from the chart on the following continuum. Place them in position relative to one another so that you see a picture of how the resources and capabilities are related.

Here is a list of potential resources and capabilities to choose from:

Successor leadership	Experienced leadership	Entrepreneurial processes	Team
Land	Treatment of employees	Firm-specific knowledge	Patient capital
Location	Conflict resolution	Firm-specific skills	Debt structure
Cash	Effective communication	Leadership development	Strategic alliances
Access to capital	Decision making	Managerial talent	Compensation
Distribution systems	Learning environment	Employee productivity	Strategy making and planning
Intellectual property	Openness to ideas	Network of relationships	Information flow
Raw materials	Cross-functional communication	Employee commitment	Organizational culture
Contracts/alliances	Reputation of company	Personal values	Unified beliefs and goals
Manufacturing processes	Market intelligence gathering	Flexible work practices	Time horizons
Innovation processes	Reporting structures	Trustworthiness	Brand name
Reputation of company	Coordination and control	Training	Governance structure

Case
Indulgence Spa Products

Preparation Questions

1. Are this family and case about "family business" or "family enterprising"? What are the differences? Why does this distinction matter for understanding the case?

2. Assess the Dawson business/family using the mind-set and methods model for family enterprising.

3. How well is Jimella prepared to grow Indulgence Spa? What are her strengths and weaknesses? Identify the resources and capabilities she brings to the family group and to her startup.

4. What are the differences between Indulgence's target market and Dawson Products' target market? How will these differences affect Indulgence's business model? Does the different target market change the business's resource and capabilities requirements?

5. Give Jimella a series of recommendations to help her grow her entrepreneurial business while advancing a family enterprising strategy. Are the two mutually exclusive? How do your recommendations address the succession and family legacy issues in the case?

Jimella, the younger of the Dawson children, smiled as she peeked into her mother's office.

"Good morning, Mom! Do you have a minute?"

"Sure, come in. I'm just preparing for a meeting.."

Jimella, age 32, liked to work hard. She had learned every aspect of the family personal care products business—from filling and capping containers to working with markets, spas, and salons—and had started selling products door-to-door at 11. After earning an undergraduate degree from Wharton and an MBA from Duke, Jimella became Dawson's chief marketing officer. Soon after, she cleaned house in the department—transferring a well-liked 45-year-old worker and firing employees she considered lazy and unproductive. The company had developed a reputation for being a nurturing, family-oriented place where workers—even unproductive ones—could feel confident of long-term employment. Jimella's initiative sent a wake-up call to marginal employees, cut the marketing budget by a third and doubled profits—just as she had predicted.

Ulissa had come to expect this type of performance from her daughters (Angela, 39, was Dawson's COO). Since her husband and cofounder, Robert Dawson, had begun spending much of his time speaking about the need for African Americans to become economically self-sufficient, Jimella and Angela had become key figures in their

family enterprise. And now her younger daughter looked ready to take another bold step. Ulissa was intrigued.

"What's on your mind, Jimella?"

"I'm going in some new directions with my plans for Indulgence Spa Products, and I'd like your opinion."

"Sure."

"First of all, I'm changing my marketing strategy. My target market will be all women—not just women of color. These products are outstanding, and Indulgence is limiting its growth by not positioning itself as a company that creates luxury spa products for all women."

"Sounds interesting, Jimella. But how do you plan to do this?"

"My main marketing method will be direct sales—the same basic strategy that we have recently begun using at Dawson's Cosmetics. I'm going to build a national team of independent beauty advisors who will sell primarily through home calls and Indulgence house parties."

"And?"

"And to do that right, I'll need to make Indulgence a separate company from Dawson Products.

"Mom," Jimella added as gently as she could, "I've decided to go off on my own."

A Family Enterprise

In 1959, Robert Dawson bought a Fuller Products sales kit and began selling personal care products door-to-door in Brooklyn. In 1962, he met Ulissa Moser, who was selling Fuller Products to earn money for college. They married in 1963 and a few years later opened a Fuller Products distributorship in Chicago that quickly became Fuller's top producer. In 1971, when their mentor S. B. Fuller was hit hard by a national boycott (see Appendix A), the Dawsons quickly established their own manufacturing capabilities—initially in their kitchen. They packaged their products in used containers from local hairdressers, as well as old jelly and mayonnaise jars.

By 1978, the company had expanded to include the Dawson Beauty School and a Midwest chain of beauty supply stores. Robert served as president,

This case was prepared by Sandra Sowell-Scott. © Copyright Babson College, 2005.

and Ulissa assumed a significant role in administration and manufacturing. From an early age, their two girls had participated in the company and learned door-to-door sales by developing their own businesses with products such as popcorn, baked goods, fruit, and even panty hose.

Robert and Ulissa wanted their children and employees to understand that building and running a business was about hard work and discipline. They regularly brought Angela and Jimella to the office and gave the girls specific tasks to perform. This helped instill a powerful work ethic and provided a common mission that brought the family together.

In 1988, the Dawsons opened a 37,000-square-foot corporate headquarters and manufacturing facility south of Chicago. The children continued to learn all aspects of the business from sales and marketing to manufacturing. In 1991, they opened the Dawson Cosmetology Center (DCC) at the site. The DCC became an important facility for training employees interested in working for the Dawson Beauty Schools. In 1997, Dawson's corporate and manufacturing divisions moved nearby into an 80,000-square-foot state-of-the-art facility.

By 2000, the company manufactured and marketed over 400 professional and retail hair and personal care products for African Americans.[1] The Dawson campus included a travel agency, hotel, and convention center. The Dawsons' overall goal continued to be to empower people and provide opportunities for self-sufficiency and economic development. In 2004, revenues were just over $32 million, and Dawson employed nearly 500 people, mostly as outside sales representatives.

The Cosmetics Division

In 1993, after completing Harvard Law School, Jimella's older sister Angela joined the business as legal counsel. A year later, the company acquired a cosmetics manufacturing firm to build a Dawson Cosmetics line. Angela developed it and became its president and Dawson's chief operating officer. Like all Dawson products, the cosmetics were not sold in retail stores, but to salons that sold them to customers. This enabled salon owners to make money on a proprietary brand product. Although Dawson sales representatives occasionally sold door-to-door, this represented a very small portion of total sales.

Jimella came on board as marketing director in 1998. Her reorganization initiatives caused a stir among rank-and-file employees, but the resounding support from her parents quelled those rumblings. In 2000, she launched a new product line within the cosmetics division. This line of luxury spa products—named Indulgence—was initially sold alongside other Dawson products. As demand for the line grew,[2] however, Jimella began planning to more effectively capitalize on its popularity.

In the spring of 2003, Jimella drastically altered the cosmetology division's work and compensation structure. Instead of using salaried sales representatives, Dawson Cosmetics moved to a multilevel marketing model. Sales representatives were independent distributors who sold products and recruited and mentored new representatives.[3] Companies such as Mary Kay, The Pampered Chef, and Tupperware had used this method successfully. Jimella felt it supported Dawson's mission of promoting economic self-sufficiency within the African American community.

Parental Support

Until that morning, Ulissa had been assuming that Jimella would follow in her sister's path and become a director of Dawson Products. She also had assumed that the new Indulgence line would remain in the division. Ulissa got up and walked to the window. From her office, she had an excellent view of the Dawson complex—now the city's third largest employer. She looked out at the "Dawson University Inn" and the Manors Convention Center and Dawson Cosmetology University. She thought about how hard they had worked to create this enterprise. Like a proud mother, Ulissa had loved watching this special child develop and grow. Although she and her husband were not ready to relinquish control, this move of Jimella's would upset a succession plan that they had been taking for granted.

[1] Many African American hair products were specially formulated. For example, Caucasian hair products took oil out, while African American products put oil in. Dawson offered different products based on hair texture and style. (Examples of styles were Naturals, Dreads, Straight styles, and all of the preceding including color.)

[2] There was an explosion of personal care/spa products in the United States. Many consumers who had difficulty justifying spa treatments were instead turning to comparable products that they could self-administer in the home. In fact, as quality personal care products continued to proliferate, spas were having an increasingly difficult task creating a significantly value-added experience. (Source: *The ISPA 2004 Consumer Trends Report*—Executive Summary.)

[3] The multilevel compensation plan paid representatives/distributors based not only on their personal production but on the product sales of their "downline"—the people they had brought into the business. In turn, as those downline representatives established their own network, a portion of their commissions would flow back up to the original sponsor. This multitiered commission structure was most appropriate with proprietary, premium-priced, consumable products. In 2003 there were approximately 13.3 million people involved in direct selling—90 percent operated their business part-time. Products were sold primarily through in-home product demonstrations, parties, and one-on-one selling. The Direct Selling Association (www.dsa.org) estimated that more than 55 percent of the American public had purchased goods or services through direct selling.

"With a dad like Robert Dawson," she mused to herself, "the world's greatest salesman and entrepreneur—we've raised them to dream big and not take the easy path." It seemed that instilling their daughters with that entrepreneurial spirit and drive had led to this situation. So how could she not support Jimella?

Jimella walked in. Ulissa turned to face her younger child.

"Jimella, are you sure this is what you want? Running a business is tough, you know."

"Yes, I'm confident that I can make it work—you and Dad prepared me for challenges like this. I'm used to working long hours, and I can make tough choices. When we were growing up and working in the business, you taught us to expect at least one problem a week. Learning to anticipate challenges and planning for the unexpected has helped me tremendously. I guess I just have good genes. I know I'm ready."

"How do you plan to finance this move?"

"I've been saving for several years and I have enough to make a reasonable start."

"That's good."

Ulissa smiled. Jimella had always been frugal. By the time she was ready to attend undergraduate school, she had saved $25,000 to put toward her first-year tuition.

"However, I am going to need some additional working capital."

Ulissa was not surprised. She knew her daughter.

"I could go to a bank," Jimella continued, "but before I do that I wanted to discuss this with you and Dad. I'd like to see if we could make an arrangement to have Dawson Products help fund Indulgence."

"That sounds reasonable to me, and I'm sure your father will be willing to listen."

Jimella sensed her mom was not excited about the idea. Her parents had raised her and her sister to run the family business, not go out on their own. Jimella did not want to hurt them or Dawson Products, but she needed her independence. She knew that as long as she was at Dawson, her parents would continue to make all the important decisions for her. Jimella realized that although her parents were past retirement age, they were not even close to being ready to slow down.

"Thanks, Mom. I've got to run. I have a staff meeting. I'll speak with you and Dad together later this week when he gets back."

Jimella's "Indulgence"

It took three weeks to develop a plan that provided Jimella with capital support and independence without straining the parent company. Jimella would continue to work at Dawson and handle special projects. In return, Dawson would lend Indulgence Spa Products $250,000 and allow Jimella to use the Dawson business infrastructure to support it and manufacture most of its products.

Jimella's responsibilities included managing Dawson Hotel. Realizing that continued support for Indulgence would depend on her performance at Dawson, she increased the hotel's profitability by raising prices (they were well below market) and increasing outside events there.

Jimella tried to use every resource to assist her with Indulgence. She became active with the Direct Selling Association,[4] taking advantage of its educational programs and using it to develop helpful contacts. She met the leaders of Mary Kay, Avon, and other companies with door-to-door operations.

She began creating competitive marketing strategies. She determined that her major direct competitor was The Body Shop at Home—a new division of The Body Shop. She believed her other direct competitor was Warm Spirits, a new venture owned by a white male chemist and a black female. She didn't think other large health and beauty care companies were competitors because they didn't specialize in spa products.

Jimella designed a product guide that featured women of all races using the spa products. The guide stated that "the company was founded on the belief that women can be better friends, mothers, and wives when they take a moment to refresh and rejuvenate their inner spirit." She also expanded the product line to include luxury linens and a monthly flower club.

Jimella presented her products at numerous holiday bazaars, trade shows, and other events. Some prospective distributors and customers openly questioned her age, while others politely moved on when they learned she owned the company.

By advertising in national publications, she slowly developed a national group of independent beauty advisors. Laura Michaels—a top producer—responded to an ad and joined the company. A middle-aged white woman with experience in direct sales, Laura represented the demographic that Jimella was certain Indulgence needed to appeal to. Still, despite Laura's success in building a base of white clients, most Indulgence recruits were African American.

Jimella set aggressive growth goals. She planned to attract 100 beauty advisors, have $100,000 in

[4]The Direct Selling Association (DSA) was the national trade association of the leading firms that manufactured and distributed goods and services sold directly to consumers. In the early 2000s more than 150 companies were members of the association, including many well-known brand names. DSA provided educational opportunities for direct selling professionals and worked with Congress, numerous government agencies, consumer protection organizations, and others on behalf of its member companies.

EXHIBIT A

Pro Forma Profit and Loss, FY 2005–2009

	2005	2006	2007	2008	2009
Sales	$585,271	$869,755	$1,561,976	$2,829,716	$5,158,227
Direct costs of goods	$169,831	$195,417	$340,731	$603,346	$1,081,017
Fulfillment payroll	$0	$12,500	$12,500	$75,000	$100,000
Fulfillment	$18,729	$27,832	$49,983	$90,551	$165,063
Cost of goods sold	$188,560	$235,749	$403,214	$768,897	$1,346,080
Gross margin	$396,712	$634,006	$1,158,762	$2,060,819	$3,812,147
Operating expenses					
Sales and marketing expenses:					
Sales and marketing payroll	$52,000	$75,000	$165,000	$240,000	$280,000
Advertising/promotion	$15,000	$26,093	$62,479	$141,486	$257,911
National trade shows and distributor rallies	$50,000	$75,000	$100,000	$125,000	$150,000
Total sales and marketing expenses	$117,000	$176,093	$327,479	$506,486	$687,911
General and administrative expenses					
General and administrative payroll	$73,000	$90,000	$120,000	$152,500	$180,000
Commissions and overrides	$92,000	$156,556	$281,156	$622,538	$392,721
Depreciation	$24,123	$36,720	$45,580	$63,328	$79,992
Rent	$7,500	$12,000	$25,000	$35,000	$50,000
Utilities	$3,000	$3,600	$3,600	$3,600	$5,000
Insurance	$16,749	$21,756	$27,599	$44,039	$58,075
Payroll taxes	$21,900	$26,625	$44,625	$70,125	$84,000
Legal fees	$8,000	$14,000	$35,000	$50,000	$75,000
Total general and administrative expenses	$246,272	$361,256	$582,560	$1,041,130	$1,924,788
Purchase of Indulgence assets	$75,000	$0	$0	$0	$0
Total operating expenses	$438,272	$537,349	$910,039	$1,547,616	$2,612,699
Profit before interest and taxes	($41,560)	$96,657	$248,723	$513,204	$1,199,447
Interest expense	$12,924	$12,373	$10,392	$8,288	$6,054
Taxes incurred	$0	$31,185	$88,183	$186,819	$441,556
Net profit	($54,484)	$53,099	$150,149	$318,097	$751,838
Net profit/sales	−9.31%	6.11%	9.61%	11.24%	14.58%

monthly sales, and be profitable by the end of fiscal year 2006 (Exhibit A). She was off to a good start. After just 7 weeks in business, she had 28 beauty consultants and $15,000 in monthly sales.

Parent Company Concerns

By the spring of 2005, Ulissa noted that Jimella seemed quite satisfied with the arrangement with Dawson Products and with Indulgence's progress. Still, Ulissa felt pulled in two directions: She truly wanted Jimella to succeed, but she also wanted Dawson Products to remain a successful, growing family business. Earlier that week, she had confided to a close friend:

What makes Dawson Products so successful is not the bottles or jars that contain our products. It's not even the products themselves because many of our competitors have similar things. It's our spirit that makes us number one. We have always known how to take what we've got and make what we want of it.

In time Robert and I will start focusing on leaving this business to our daughters, but now we might have to re-craft our succession strategy. If Jimella leaves and Angela is in charge, we'll certainly have to hire an executive support staff. Even if most of those hires come from within the company, I wonder whether or not the employees would have the same loyalty to Angela as they have had toward us all these years. Would old-timers be constantly questioning new ideas and procedures?

Robert and I feel strongly that Dawson products must always remain a family business. We treat all of our employees like family. Many have several children and family members that work for Dawson.

We will always try to take care of them—they believe in us and our mission.

Ulissa and Robert had another reason for wanting to keep the company private. Dawson was one of a very few African American personal care businesses that had managed to avoid being bought by white-controlled multinationals (see Appendix B). One particularly painful sale had involved their close friends, the Johnsons.

Johnson Products had been a premier African American-owned hair care company. In the early 1990s, George and Joan Johnson had divorced after 35 years of marriage. To avoid a messy court battle, George transferred his stock to his wife. Their son, Eric, became president and boosted profits 50 percent. But he deeply offended his sister Joanie by offering her a position in the company that she felt was beneath her. Joanie retaliated and convinced her mother, who chaired the company's board, to oust Eric. He resigned in 1993 and the company was sold to IVAC, a majority-owned Florida-based generic drug company, for $61 million.[5]

Ulissa understood why the Johnson saga had caused such a controversy within the African American community. Although she and her husband had been approached to sell, they had always refused. They were dedicated to keeping Dawson Products an African American family-owned business—a role model for the community and a driving force in helping African Americans become "job makers" instead of "job takers."

Ulissa looked at her watch. Curiously, Jimella was late for their usual lunch date.

[5]K. Springer and L. Reibstein, "So Much for Family Ties," *Newsweek* 119, no. 12 (March 23, 1992), p. 49.

A Hard Truth

Indulgence's fiscal 2005 sales had fallen short of expectations (Exhibit B). Jimella realized she would have to increase sales dramatically in the coming weeks to keep the company on track (Exhibits C and D).

Just as Jimella rose from her desk to head over for lunch with her mom, she got a phone call from Laura Michaels.

"Jimella, I don't understand what happened."

"Laura, what are you talking about?"

"My cousin Patricia was ready to sign up, and then she called back and told me she had changed her mind. I had been so excited about her potential—she has a lot of friends who would love these products. She would have been an excellent distributor—with a lucrative down line in the white market."

Jimella knew building a white customer base would be tough, but not this tough. She had been warned. When she presented her business idea at a local university, the graduate students questioned whether a black female could be successful in a white-dominated, competitive market. And white bias wasn't the only problem. Jimella knew that many blacks, including Dawson Products' employees, resented the fact that she was using the Spa Indulgence line to "cross over" into the white market.

"It will be okay; things like this always happen in direct sales," Jimella said

Laura caught her faltering tone.

"You know, I'm usually really good at spotting potential distributors. I hate to say it, Jimella, but my cousin's attitude changed when I told her that a young black female owned the company. Lately, I'm sensing that kind of attitude more and more. I really don't understand it. How can people be so narrow-minded?"

"I don't know, Laura. Or maybe it's just that I don't want to know."

EXHIBIT B

Actuals, FY 2005

	Jun	Jul	Aug	Sep	Oct	Nov	Dec	Jan	Feb	Mar	Apr	May	2005
	$5,500	$6,750	$10,000	$15,000	$25,000	$50,000	$60,000	$70,000	$75,000	$80,000	$90,000	$100,000	$587,250
Sales	$5,500	$6,750	$9,813	$14,961	$24,665	$46,020	$34,199	$36,172	$46,195	$55,330	$62,293	$67,383	$409,281
Direct costs of goods	$1,670	$2,055	$2,836	$4,359	$6,999	$12,398	$9,807	$10,459	$13,441	$16,084	$18,431	$20,223	$118,763
Fulfillment payroll	$0	$0	$0	$0	$0	$0	$0	$0	$0	$0	$0	$0	$0
Fulfillment	$176	$216	$314	$479	$789	$1,473	$1,094	$1,158	$1,478	$1,771	$1,993	$2,156	$13,097
Cost of goods sold	$1,846	$2,271	$3,150	$4,837	$7,788	$13,870	$10,902	$11,617	$14,920	$17,854	$20,425	$22,380	$131,860
Gross margin	$3,654	$4,479	$6,662	$10,124	$16,877	$32,150	$23,297	$24,556	$31,276	$37,475	$41,868	$45,003	$277,421
Operating expenses:													
Sales and marketing expenses:													
Sales and marketing payroll	$3,500	$3,500	$3,500	$3,500	$3,500	$3,500	$3,500	$5,000	$5,000	$5,000	$5,000	$5,000	$49,500
Advertising/promotion	$165	$230	$294	$449	$740	$1,381	$1,026	$1,085	$1,386	$1,660	$1,869	$2,021	$12,278
National trade shows	$0	$0	$15,000	$10,000	$0	$0	$0	$15,000	$0	$0	$3,500	$3,500	$47,000
Total sales and marketing expenses	$3,665	$3,703	$18,794	$13,949	$4,240	$4,881	$4,526	$21,085	$6,386	$6,660	$10,369	$10,521	$108,778
General and administrative expenses:													
General and administrative payroll	$5,666	$5,666	$5,666	$5,666	$5,666	$5,666	$5,666	$5,666	$5,666	$5,666	$5,666	$5,670	$67,996
Commissions and overrides	$990	$1,215	$1,766	$2,693	$4,440	$8,284	$6,156	$6,511	$8,315	$9,959	$11,213	$12,129	$73,671
Depreciation	$1,271	$1,271	$1,271	$1,757	$1,757	$1,757	$2,507	$2,507	$2,507	$2,507	$2,507	$2,507	$24,123
Rent	$0	$0	$750	$750	$750	$750	$750	$750	$750	$750	$750	$750	$7,500
Utilities	$0	$0	$300	$300	$300	$300	$300	$300	$300	$300	$300	$300	$3,000
Insurance	$642	$645	$1,550	$1,259	$690	$729	$708	$1,701	$819	$1,797	$2,560	$3,649	$16,749
Payroll taxes	$1,375	$1,375	$1,375	$1,375	$1,375	$1,375	$1,375	$1,600	$1,600	$1,600	$1,600	$1,601	$17,624
Legal fees	$0	$2,500	$2,500	$0	$0	$0	$0	$1,000	$0	$1,000	$0	$1,000	$8,000
Total general and administrative expenses	$9,945	$12,672	$15,180	$13,801	$14,978	$18,860	$17,461	$20,035	$19,957	$23,579	$24,595	$27,605	$218,664
Purchase of Indulgence assets	$0	$75,000	$0	$0	$0	$0	$0	$0	$0	$0	$0	$0	$75,000
Total other expenses	$9,944	$12,671	$15,178	$13,800	$14,978	$18,860	$17,461	$20,035	$19,957	$23,579	$24,595	$27,605	$218,664
Total operating expenses	$13,609	$91,374	$33,972	$27,749	$19,218	$23,741	$21,987	$44,120	$26,343	$30,239	$34,964	$38,127	$402,442
Profit before interest and taxes	($9,955)	($86,895)	($27,310)	($17,625)	($2,341)	$8,409	$1,310	($16,564)	$4,933	$7,236	$6,905	$6,876	($125,021)
Interest expense	$0	$1,238	$1,225	$1,213	$1,200	$1,188	$1,175	$1,163	$1,150	$1,137	$1,124	$1,111	$12,924
Taxes incurred	$0	$0	$0	$0	$0	$0	$0	$0	$0	$0	$0	$0	$0
Net profit	($9,955)	($88,132)	($28,535)	($18,838)	($3,540)	$7,221	$135	($17,727)	$3,783	$6,099	$5,781	$5,765	($137,945)
Net profit/sales	181.01%	1305.67%	290.81%	125.91%	14.36%	15.69%	0.39%	49.01%	8.19%	11.02%	9.28%	8.56%	33.20%

EXHIBIT C

Indulgence Actual and Projected Cash Flows

			Actual Fiscal Year		
Cash Received	2005	2006	2007	2008	2009
Cash from operations:					
Cash sales	$409,281	$869,755	$1,561,976	$2,829,716	$5,158,227
Cash from receivables	$0	$0	$0	$0	$0
Subtotal cash from operations	$409,281	$869,755	$1,561,976	$2,829,716	$5,158,227
Additional cash received					
Sales tax, VAT, HST/GST received	$30,696	$65,232	$117,148	$212,229	$386,867
Dawson loan proceeds	$250,000	$0	$0	$0	$0
Sales of long-term assets	$689,977	$934,987	$1,679,124	$3,041,945	$5,545,094
Subtotal cash received					
Expenditures	2005	2006	2007	2008	2009
Expenditures from operations:					
Cash spending	$117,496	$177,500	$297,500	$467,500	$560,000
Payment of accounts payable	$336,763	$547,641	$973,793	$1,836,107	$3,462,894
Subtotal spent on operations	$454,260	$725,141	$1,271,293	$2,303,607	$4,022,894
Additional cash spent					
Sales tax, VAT, HST/GST paid out	$25,905	$65,232	$117,148	$212,229	$386,867
Principal repayment of Dawson loan	$27,776	$32,027	$34,008	$36,112	$38,346
Purchase long-term assets	$40,950	$75,000	$85,000	$125,000	$150,000
Subtotal cash spent	$548,891	$897,400	$1,507,450	$2,676,948	$4,598,107
Net cash flow	$141,086	$37,586	$171,674	$364,997	$946,987
Cash balance	$161,086	$198,672	$370,346	$735,344	$1,682,331

EXHIBIT D

Indulgence Actual and Projected Balance Sheets

	Actual Fiscal Year				
Assets	2005	2006	2007	2008	2009
Current assets					
Cash	$161,086	$198,672	$370,346	$735,344	$1,682,331
Accounts receivable	$0	$0	$0	$0	$0
Inventory	$75,000	$100,000	$125,000	$200,000	$300,000
Other current assets	$0	$0	$0	$0	$0
Total current assets	$236,086	$298,672	$495,346	$935,344	$1,982,331
Long-term assets					
Long-term assets	$65,950	$140,950	$225,950	$350,950	$500,950
Accumulated depreciation	$0	$60,843	$106,423	$169,751	$249,743
Total long-term assets	$65,950	$80,107	$119,527	$181,199	$251,207
Total assets	$302,036	$378,779	$614,873	$1,116,542	$2,233,538
Liabilities and Capital	2005	2006	2007	2008	2009
Accounts payable	$70,924	$150,718	$270,672	$490,356	$893,860
Dawson loan balance	$222,224	$190,196	$156,188	$120,076	$81,730
Other current liabilities	$4,791	$4,791	$4,791	$4,791	$4,791
Subtotal current liabilities	$297,938	$345,706	$431,651	$615,223	$980,381
Long-term liabilities	$0	$0	$0	$0	$0
Total liabilities	$297,938	$345,706	$431,651	$615,223	$980,381
Paid-in capital	$0	$0	$0	$0	$0
Retained earnings	$138,000	$55	$53,154	$203,303	$521,400
Earnings	($119,404)	$53,099	$150,149	$318,097	$751,838
Total capital	$18,596	$53,154	$203,303	$521,400	$1,273,238
Total liabilities and capital	$316,534	$398,860	$634,954	$1,136,624	$2,253,619
Net worth	$4,097	$33,073	$183,222	$501,319	$1,253,157

Appendix A

S. B. FULLER (1905–1988)

It is contrary to the laws of nature for man to stand still; he must move forward, or the eternal march of progress will force him backward. This the Negro has failed to understand; he believes that the lack of civil rights legislation, and the lack of integration have kept him back. But this is not true. . . .

S. B. Fuller

Samuel B. Fuller was one of the wealthiest and most successful black entrepreneurs in mid-20th-century America. His Chicago-based business empire included Fuller Products, which manufactured health and beauty aids and cleaning products; $3 million in real estate; the South Center (later changed to Fuller) Department Store and Office Building; a New York real estate trust; the largest black newspaper chain; the Fuller Philco Home Appliance Center; and farm and livestock operations.

Fuller was born into rural poverty in Ouachita Parish, Louisiana, in 1905. Early on, he gained a reputation for reliability and resourcefulness. After coming to Chicago in 1920, he worked menial jobs, eventually becoming manager of a coal yard. Despite having a secure job during the Depression, he struck out on his own and founded Fuller Products with $25 in 1934.

In 1960, at the height of its success, the Fuller Products Company had sales of $10 million and 85 branches in 38 states. His employees, black and white, included 5,000 salespeople and 600 office and factory workers who produced and sold Fuller's 300 different products. In 1947, Fuller secretly purchased Boyer International Laboratories, a white cosmetic manufacturer that sold to southern Whites. Fuller also held interest in the Patricia Stevens Cosmetic Company and J. C. McBrady and Company.

Fuller Products trained many future entrepreneurs. Publisher John H. Johnson and hair products manufacturers George Johnson and Robert Dawson, all black millionaires, considered Fuller their role model. He had little patience for race baiters, black or white. "It doesn't make any difference," he declared, "about the color of an individual's skin. No one cares whether a cow is black, red, yellow, or brown. They want to know how much milk it can produce."

Fuller was a leading black Republican, although he always had an independent streak. He promoted civil rights and briefly headed the Chicago South Side NAACP. Along with black Birmingham businessman A. G. Gaston, he tried to organize a cooperative effort to purchase the segregated bus company during the Montgomery bus boycott. He told Martin Luther King, Jr., "The bus company is losing money and is willing to sell. We should buy it." King was skeptical of the idea, and not enough blacks came forward to raise the money. Despite his belief in civil rights, however, Fuller always emphasized the need for blacks to go into business. In 1958 he blasted the federal government for undermining free enterprise and fostering socialism.

In the early 1960s, Fuller's financial empire collapsed. Southern whites discovered his ownership in Boyer International Laboratories and boycotted it. Then, black leaders called for a boycott of Fuller Products after Fuller said in a 1963 speech to the National Association of Manufacturers that too many blacks were using their lack of civil rights as an excuse for failure.

Fuller's attempts to raise money by selling stock in Fuller Products failed and in 1964 the Securities and Exchange Commission charged him with sale of unregistered securities. He was forced to pay $1.5 million to his creditors and sold off various enterprises to meet his debts.

After bankruptcy, but with six-figure financial support in gifts and loans from leading Chicago black business people, Fuller Products was reorganized in 1972 but never recovered as a major black business. Fuller continued manufacturing a line of cleaning products and cosmetics, with sales through distributorship franchises. In 1975, Fuller showed sales of almost $1 million. S. B. Fuller died in 1988.

Source: J. E. K. Walker and S. B. Fuller, *Encyclopedia of African American Business History* (Westport, CT: Greenwood Press, 1999).

Appendix B

THE ETHNIC HEALTH AND BEAUTY CARE INDUSTRY

Overview

The ethnic health and beauty care industry (HBC) consisted of hair and skin products and cosmetics, designed for and sold to minority groups. The three largest minority groups in the United States were African Americans, Hispanics, and Asians. Since African Americans were by far the biggest purchasers of ethnic HBC products, most ethnic HBC products were aimed at them. The industry was once the domain of African American companies, but when major manufacturers realized its potential, they rapidly took it over.

In 2004, the market for ethnic hair care, color cosmetics, and skin care products was $1.6 billion and was estimated to grow to $1.9 billion by 2006. The largest HBC category was hair care, 72 percent of the total at $1.124 billion, then cosmetics at $327 million (20 percent), and skin care at $110 million (7 percent). Products not sold through traditional retail chains (such as products used by professional stylists, Indulgence Spa and Dawson Products) are not reflected in these figures.

African Americans Are the Largest Consumers of HBC Products

Research indicated that African Americans spent three to five times more on HBC products than the general population. According to AHBAI (American Health and Beauty Aids Institute), a trade group of African American hair care manufacturers, African Americans buy 19 percent of all health and beauty aids and 34 percent of all hair care products while accounting for 12 percent of the overall population. In 2005, African Americans' purchasing power exceeded $688 billion.

The Growth and Development of the Ethnic Health and Beauty Care Industry

African Americans founded and built the ethnic health and beauty care industry. The founding pioneers, Madame

C. J. Walker, S. B. Fuller, and George E. Johnson, were among the first to see the great potential in catering to the hair and skin care needs of African American men and women.

During their time, there were virtually no hair and skin care products designed for African Americans. Up until the late 19th century, the ethnic market consisted mainly of products manufactured by African Americans for African Americans.

Madame C. J. Walker, America's first black self-made female millionaire, set the pace with the development, manufacturing, and selling of hair care products she created herself. She also developed innovations to the pressing comb, which gave rise to an entire industry. Following in her footsteps was S. B. Fuller (see Appendix A). One of Fuller's many disciples, George E. Johnson, pioneered the modern ethnic health and beauty care industry. From their legacy came Dawson Products, Bronner Brothers, Pro-Line, Soft Sheen, Luster, and many others.

The Role African American Hair Companies Played in the African American Community

The few African American health and beauty care companies existing during Madame C. J. Walker's time grew to nearly 20 over the next three decades. As the industry developed, it created thousands of jobs within the African American community.

During segregation, many African Americans felt that developing strong businesses in their community was the only way to achieve freedom, justice, and equality. For that reason, African American entrepreneurs were hailed as heroes, leaders, and examples in their communities.

Following desegregation, many black-owned businesses began losing market share to white companies. Black-owned banks, hotels, and corner stores soon disappeared. The only black businesses making big profits serving blacks were black hair care companies, and by the 1970s they began to face serious challenges from mainstream corporations.

The Movement of Non–African American Companies into the Ethnic Health and Beauty Care Industry

In the early 1970s, mainstream companies began to see abundant opportunities in the ethnic market. Prior to that, the handful of African American hair companies were growing and thriving. In the late 1970s, the ethnic market received a tremendous boost with the enormous popularity of the Jheri Curl—one of the hottest styles of the time. Many companies experienced skyrocketing profits—some exceeding 40 percent.

The Jheri Curl was a product of the International Playtex Corporation—a white-owned company. Customer demand for Jheri Curls was fueled when celebrities like Michael Jackson began sporting them. Ample products were needed to achieve and maintain the Jheri Curl look, and many African American hair care companies profited from it. According to a 1986 *Newsweek* article, the Jheri Curl "spurred industry growth at a 32 percent rate."

The success of African American hair care companies caused corporate giants like Alberto-Culver and Revlon to enter the market followed by Gillette, which bought Lustrasilk in the middle 1980s.

How the Changes in Ownership Affected African Americans' Companies

Many African American health and beauty care companies, unable to compete with these behemoths, sold, merged, or went bankrupt. The survivors lost significant market share.

The shake-up shifted the balance of power to non-African American companies. For example, Johnson Products controlled 80 percent of the relaxer market in 1976. In 1977 the Federal Trade Commission ordered Johnson Products to put warning labels on its lye-based relaxer, hurting the company's image, and costing it customers. Revlon avoided a similar FTC ruling for almost 2 years, only complying after it had captured a significant portion of the relaxer market. Carson Products cornered the market in the late 1970s when it introduced its no-lye relaxer product. Atlanta-based M&M, Inc sold over $47 million of products in 1983 but was out of business by 1990. Johnson Products later acquired its assets.

By the 1980s, African American health and beauty care companies were in serious trouble, their market share having gone from 80 percent to below 50 percent.

The Founding of the American Health and Beauty Aids Institute

In response, the American Health and Beauty Aids Institute (AHBAI) was formed in 1981. AHBAI is a national nonprofit organization of black-owned companies that produce hair care and cosmetic products for black consumers. AHBAI created the "Proud Lady" logo (a black woman in silhouette featuring three layers of hair), which was stamped on its members' products and packing and promotional materials. AHBAI's mission was to make consumers aware of products that were manufactured by African American–owned companies.

The Revlon Pronouncement

While African American hair care companies were facing dwindling revenues and threats of corporate acquisitions, mergers, and takeovers, Irving Bottner, a high-ranking Revlon official, was quoted in the October 1986 *Newsweek* magazine as having said, "In the next couple of years, the black-owned businesses will disappear. They'll all be sold to the white companies."

Bottner went on to criticize AHBAI, saying its campaign to encourage black consumers to buy from black companies was unfair to white business: "They're making a social issue out of a business issue. When you produce what the consumer wants, loyalties disappear."

Bottner also stated that black companies tend to offer "poorer grade" products: "We are accused of taking business away from the black companies, but black consumers buy quality products—too often their black brothers didn't do them any good." In response, Jesse Jackson launched a boycott against Revlon, demanding that Revlon divest its South African operations, hire more black managers, and use more black suppliers. Black publications such as *Essence, Ebony*, and *Jet* temporarily stopped carrying Revlon advertisements. In response, Revlon sponsored a $3 million advertising campaign, announcing that money spent with black businesses supports the black community.

The situation escalated in the 1990s. Company by company, mergers and acquisitions dismantled black-owned health and beauty care businesses. In 1993 majority-owned IVAX, a Florida-based generic drug company, acquired Johnson Products Co., the maker of Afro-Sheen and Ultra-Sheen. IVAX also purchased Flori Roberts Cosmetics, a majority-owned line of cosmetics for women of color. In 1998 L'Oreal bought Soft Sheen. Ownership of Johnson Products changed hands that same year from IVAX to Carson Inc., a mainstream company based in Savannah, Georgia. In March 2000, Alberto-Culver bought Pro-Line, the third largest black-owned manufacturer, for an undisclosed amount.

In 2000 L'Oreal acquired Carson. As a result, the top two black-owned hair care companies (Johnson Products and Soft Sheen) were joined under the L'Oreal umbrella. Based in France, L'Oreal was now the world's dominant manufacturer of ethnic health and beauty care products.

Lafayette Jones, president and CEO of Segmented Marketing Services, estimated that the 2004 sales of L'Oreal's ethnic market divisions were in the range of $1 billion, and those of Alberto-Culver were around $100 million.

For a better understanding of the impact of the sales of many prominent African American–owned HBC product manufacturers, see "Bad Hair Days" in *Black Enterprise Magazine* (November 2000).

Chapter Eighteen

The Harvest and Beyond

LEARNING OUTCOMES: After reading this chapter, you will be able to understand:

18-1   Harvesting as a journey, not a destination

18-2   Wealth in families

18-3   The journey can be addictive

18-4   The harvest goal of value realization

18-5   Wealth building vehicles

18-6   Devising a personal entrepreneurial strategy

A Journey, Not a Destination

A common sentiment among successful entrepreneurs is that the challenge and exhilaration of the journey give them the greatest energy and fulfillment. Perhaps Walt Disney said it best: "I don't make movies to make money. I make money to make movies." It is the thrill of the chase that counts.

These entrepreneurs also talk of the venture's insatiable appetite for not only cash but also time, attention, and energy to the point some say it is an addiction. Most say it is far more demanding and difficult than they ever imagined and would do it again.

For the vast majority of entrepreneurs, it takes 10, 15, even 20 years or more to build significant net worth. According to the popular press and government statistics, there are more millionaires than ever in the United States, and in 2007 there were nearly 10 million millionaires in the world.

Wealth in Families

This is the title of a wonderful book by Charles W. Collier, senior philanthropic advisor at Harvard University. The book is a must-read: full of wisdom, lessons, and practical advice on the delicate, contradictory, and often perplexing subject of handling wealth in families. In nearly every culture there is an equivalent version of the proverb "Shirtsleeves to shirtsleeves in three generations." In China, for example, it is "Rice paddy to rice paddy in three generations." Around the world the global entrepreneurial revolution is creating unprecedented family wealth. As the proverbs reveal, this wealth can become a curse or a vehicle for renewal.

Collier's book shares many stories of how wealthy families handle wealth–how they teach the next generation a deeper meaning of wealth, instill a passion for work, and express their financial well-being through philanthropy, not just consumption. These case studies illustrate how families use wealth for personal renewal, to create a sense of social responsibility among the next generation, and to create a legacy of societal renewal through giving back. Time and again this philanthropy is a shared family activity that expresses deep family and personal values and creates significant family legacies. *Wealth in Families* is also an excellent resource book with a rich bibliography of Web sites and sources of information.

The Journey Can Be Addictive

The immersion, workload, the many sacrifices of a family, and the burnout often experienced by an entrepreneur are real. Maintaining the energy, enthusiasm, and drive to get across the finish line, to achieve a harvest, may be exceptionally difficult. For instance, one entrepreneur in the computer software business, after working alone for several years, developed highly sophisticated software. Yet he insisted he could not stand the computer business for another day. Imagine trying to position a company for sale effectively and to negotiate a deal for a premium price after such a long battle.

First Build a Great Company

One of the simplest but most difficult principles for nonentrepreneurs to grasp is that wealth and liquidity are the results, not causes, of building a great company. They fail to recognize the difference between making money and spending money. Most successful entrepreneurs possess a clear understanding of this distinction; they get their kicks from growing the company. They know the payoff will take care of itself if they concentrate on proving and building a sustainable venture for the founders, the investors, and other stakeholders.

Create Harvest Options and Capture the Value

Innumerable examples exist whereby entrepreneurs sold or merged their companies and then went on to acquire or start another company and pursued new dreams:

- Robin Wolaner founded *Parenting* magazine in the mid-1980s and sold it to Time-Life.[1] Wolaner then joined Time and built a highly successful career there, and in July 1992 she became the head of Time's Sunset Publishing Corporation.[2]
- Right after graduate school, brothers George and Gary Mueller launched a company George had started as an MBA student. That company grew rapidly and was sold in early 2000 for more than $50 million. About 3 years into the startup, younger brother Gary decided he would pursue his own startup. He left Securities Online on the best of terms and created ColorKinetics, Inc., in Boston. That company, by early 2003, had raised over $48 million of venture capital and would soon exceed $30 million in sales as the leading firm in LED lighting technology. We predict these will not be either George's or Gary's last startups.

- Craig Benson founded Cabletron in the 1980s, which became a highly successful company. Eventually he brought in a new CEO and became involved as a trustee of Babson College, and then began teaching entrepreneurship classes with a focus on information technology and the Internet. He later served as governor of New Hampshire as another way of giving back to society and to pursue his new dreams.
- While in his early 20s, Steve Spinelli was recruited by his former college football coach, Jim Hindman (see the Jiffy Lube case series), to help start and build Jiffy Lube International. As a captain of the team, Steve had exhibited the qualities of leadership, tenacity, and competitive will to win that Hindman knew were needed to create a new company. Steve later built the largest franchise in America, and after selling his 49 stores to Pennzoil in 1993, he returned to his MBA alma mater to teach. So invigorated by this new challenge, he even went back to earn his doctorate. Steve then became director of the Arthur M. Blank Center for Entrepreneurship at Babson, first division chair of the very first full-fledged entrepreneurship department at any American university, and then vice provost. Steve is now president of Philadelphia University.
- After creating and building the ninth largest pharmaceutical company in the United States, Marion Laboratories, Ewing Marion Kauffman led an extraordinary life as a philanthropist and sportsman. His Kauffman Foundation and its Center for Entrepreneurial Leadership became the first and premier foundation in the nation dedicated to accelerating entrepreneurship. He brought the Kansas City Royals baseball team to that city and made sure it would stay there by giving the team to the city with the stipulation that it stay there when the team was sold. The $75 million proceeds of the sale were also donated to charitable causes in Kansas City.
- Jeff Parker built and sold two companies, including Technical Data Corporation,[3] by the time he was 40. His substantial gain from these ventures has led to a new career as a private investor who works closely with young entrepreneurs to help them build their companies.

---

[1]This example is drawn from "Parenting Magazine," Harvard Business School case 291-015.
[2]L.M. Fisher, "The Entrepreneur Employee," *New York Times*, August 2, 1992, p. 10.
[3]For TDC's business plan, see "Technical Data Corporation Business Plan," Harvard Business School case 283-973. Revised November 1987. For more about TDC's progress and harvest strategy, see "Technical Data Corporation," Harvard Business School case 283-072. Revised December 1987.

- In mid-1987 George Knight, founder and president of Knight Publications,[4] was actively pursuing acquisitions to grow his company into a major force. Stunned by what he believed to be exceptionally high valuations for small companies in the industry, he concluded that this was the time to be a seller rather than a buyer. Therefore, in 1988 he sold Knight Publications to a larger firm, within which he could realize his ambition of contributing as a chief executive officer to the growth of a major company. Having turned around the troubled divisions of this major company, he is currently seeking a small company to acquire and to grow into a large company.

A Harvest Goal: Value Realization

Having a harvest goal and crafting a strategy to achieve it are what separate successful entrepreneurs from the rest of the pack. Many entrepreneurs seek only to create a job and a living for themselves. It is quite different to grow a business that creates a living for many others, including employees and investors, by creating value that can result in a capital gain.

Setting a harvest goal achieves many purposes, not the least of which is helping an entrepreneur get after-tax cash out of an enterprise and enhancing substantially his or her net worth. Such a goal can also create high standards and a serious commitment to excellence over the course of developing the business. It can provide, in addition, a motivating force and a strategic focus that does not sacrifice customers, employees, and value-added products and services just to maximize quarterly earnings.

There are other good reasons to set a harvest goal. The workload demanded by a harvest-oriented venture versus one in a venture that cannot achieve a harvest may actually be less and is probably no greater. Such a business may be less stressful than managing a business that is not oriented to harvest.

Crafting a Harvest Strategy: Timing Is Vital

Consistently, entrepreneurs avoid thinking about harvest issues. In a survey of the computer software industry between 1983 and 1986, Steven Holmberg found that 80 percent of the 100 companies surveyed had only an informal plan for harvesting. The rest of the sample confirmed the avoidance of harvest plans by entrepreneurs—only 15 percent of the companies had a formal written strategy for harvest in their business plans, and the remaining 5 percent had a formal harvest plan written after the business plan.[5] When a company is launched, then struggles for survival, and finally begins its ascent, the furthest thing from its founder's mind usually is selling out. Selling is often viewed by the entrepreneur as the equivalent of complete abandonment of his or her very own "baby."

Too often a founder does not consider selling until terror, in the form of the possibility of losing the whole company, is experienced. Usually this possibility comes unexpectedly: new technology threatens to leapfrog the current product line, a large competitor suddenly appears in a small market, or a major account is lost. A sense of panic then grips the founders and shareholders of the closely held firm, and the company is suddenly for sale—at the wrong time, for the wrong reasons, and thus for the wrong price. Selling at the right time, willingly, involves hitting one of the many strategic windows that entrepreneurs face.

Entrepreneurs find that harvesting is a nonissue until something begins to sprout, and again there is a vast distance between creating an existing revenue stream of an ongoing business and ground zero. Most entrepreneurs agree that securing customers and generating continuing sales revenue are much harder and take much longer than they could have imagined. Further, the ease with which those revenue estimates can be cast and manipulated on a spreadsheet belies the time and effort necessary to turn those projections into cash.

Shaping a harvest strategy is an enormously complicated and difficult task. Thus crafting such a strategy cannot begin too early. In 1989–1991 banking policies that curtailed credit and lending severely exacerbated the downturn following the October 1987 stock market crash. One casualty of this was a company we will call Cable TV. The value of the company in early 1989 exceeded $200 million and by mid-1990 this had dropped to below zero. The heavy debt overwhelmed the company. It took over 5 years of sweat, blood, tears, and rapid aging of the founder to eventually sell the company. The price: about one-quarter of the peak value of 1989.

This same pattern was common again in 2001 and 2002 as major companies declared bankruptcy

---

[4]For a detailed description of this process, see Harvard Business School case 289-027, revised February 1989.
[5]S.R. Holmberg, "Value Creation and Capture: Entrepreneurship Harvest and IPO Strategies." In *Frontiers of Entrepreneurship Research: 1991*, ed. N. Churchill et al. (Babson Park, MA: Babson College, 1991), pp. 191-205.

in the wake of the dot-com and stock market crash, including luminaries such an Enron, Kmart, Global Crossing, and dozens of lesser known but larger telecommunications and networking-related companies. This is one history lesson that seems to repeat itself. While building a company is the ultimate goal, failure to preserve the harvest option, and utilize it when it is available, can be deadly.

In shaping a harvest strategy, some guidelines and cautions can help:

- *Patience:* As has been shown, several years are required to launch and build most successful companies; therefore patience can be valuable. A harvest strategy is more sensible if it allows for a time frame of at least 3 to 5 years and as long as 7 to 10 years. The other side of the patience coin is not to panic as a result of sudden events. Selling under duress is usually the worst of all worlds.

- *Realistic valuation:* If impatience is the enemy of an attractive harvest, then greed is its executioner.

- *Outside advice:* It is difficult but worthwhile to find an advisor who can help craft a harvest strategy while the business is growing and, at the same time, maintain objectivity about its value and have the patience and skill to maximize it. A major problem seems to be that people who sell businesses, such as investment bankers or business brokers, are performing the same economic role and function as real estate brokers; in essence, their incentive is their commission during a short time frame, usually a matter of months. However, an advisor who works with a lead entrepreneur for 5 years or more can help shape and implement a strategy for the whole business so that it is positioned to spot and respond to harvest opportunities when they appear.

Harvest Options

There are seven principal avenues by which a company can realize a harvest from the value it has created covered in the next pages. Coverage is brief as entire books have been written about each.

Capital Cow

A "capital cow" is to the entrepreneur what a "cash cow" is to a large corporation. In essence, the venture (the cow) throws off more cash for personal use (the milk) than most entrepreneurs can spend. The result is a capital and cash-rich company with capacity for debt and reinvestment. Take, for instance, a health care–related venture that was started in the early 1970s that realized early success and went public. Several years later the founders decided to buy the company back from the public shareholders and to return it to its closely held status. Today the company has sales in excess of $100 million and generates capital of several million dollars each year. This capital cow has enabled its entrepreneurs to form entities to invest in several other higher-potential ventures, which included participation in the leveraged buyout of a $150 million sales division of a larger firm and in some venture capital deals. Sometimes the creation of a capital cow results in substantial real estate holdings by the entrepreneur, off the books of the original firm. This allows for greater flexibility in the distribution of cash flow and the later allocation of the wealth.

Employee Stock Ownership Plan

Employee stock ownership plans have become very popular among closely held companies as a valuation mechanism for stock for which there is no formal market. They are also vehicles through which founders can realize some liquidity from their stock by sales to the plan and other employees. And because an ESOP usually creates widespread ownership of stock among employees, it is viewed as a positive motivational device as well.

Management Buyout

Another avenue, called a management buyout (MBO), is one in which a founder can gain liquidity by selling it to existing partners or to other key managers in the business. If the business has both assets and cash flow, the financing can be arranged via banks, insurance companies, and financial institutions that do leveraged buyouts (LBOs) and MBOs. Even if assets are thin, cash flow that can service the debt to fund the purchase price can convince lenders to do the MBO.

Usually the problem is that the managers buying out the owners and running the company do not have the capital. MBOs typically require the seller to take a limited amount of cash up front and a note for the balance of the purchase price over several years. If the purchase price is linked to the future profitability of the business, the seller is totally dependent on the ability of the buyer to run the business successfully.

Merger, Acquisition, and Strategic Alliance

Merging with a firm is still another way for a founder to realize a gain. For example, two founders who had developed high-quality training programs for the rapidly emerging personal computer industry merged with another company. These entrepreneurs had computer backgrounds and lacked marketing or general management experience. This showed in the results of the company's first 5 years where sales were under $500,000, and the company's inability to attract venture capital. The firm with which they merged was a $15 million company with an excellent reputation for its management training programs and a Fortune 1000 customer base. The buyer obtained 80 percent of the shares of the smaller firm to consolidate the revenues and earnings from the merged company into its own financial statements, and the two founders of the smaller firm retained a 20 percent ownership in their firm. The two founders also obtained employment contracts, and the buyer provided nearly $1.5 million of capital advances during the first year of the new business. Under a put arrangement, the founders will be able to realize a gain on their 20 percent of the company, depending on performance of the venture over the next few years.[6] The two founders now are reporting to the president of the parent firm, and one founder of the parent firm has taken a key executive position with the smaller company, an approach common for mergers between closely held firms.

In a strategic alliance, founders can attract badly needed capital from a large company interested in their technologies. Such arrangements often can lead to complete buyouts of the founders downstream.

Outright Sale

Most advisors view outright sale as the ideal route to go because up-front cash is preferred over most stock, even though the latter can result in a tax-free exchange.[7] In a stock-for-stock exchange, the problem is the volatility and unpredictability of the stock price of the purchasing company. Many entrepreneurs have been left with a fraction of the original purchase price when the stock price of the buyer's company declined steadily. Often the acquiring company wants to lock key management into employment contracts for several years.

Public Offering

The most attractive option of all in terms of value is taking the company public.[8] For many would-be entrepreneurs, this aspiration is enormously appealing, yet taking a company public is a rare event.

After the stock market crash of October 1987, the market for new issues of stock shrank to a fraction of the robust IPO market of 1986 and a fraction of those of 1983 and 1985, as well. The number of new issues and the volume of IPOs did not rebound; instead they declined between 1988 and 1991. Then in 1992 and into the beginning of 1993 the IPO window opened again. During this IPO frenzy, "small companies with total assets under $500,000 issued more than 68 percent of all IPOs."[9] Previously small companies had not been as active in the IPO market. (Companies such as Lotus, Compaq, and Apple Computer do get unprecedented attention and fanfare, but these firms were truly exceptions.)[10] The SEC tried "to reduce issuing costs and registration and reporting burdens on small companies, and began by simplifying the registration process by adopting Form S-18, which applies to offerings of less than $7,500,000, and reduced disclosure requirements."[11] Similarly, Regulation D created exemptions from registration of up to $500,000 over a 12-month period.[12]

This cyclical pattern repeated itself again during the mid-1990s into 2002. As the dot-com, telecommunications, and networking explosion accelerated from 1995 to 2000, the IPO markets exploded as well. In June 1996, for instance, nearly 200 small companies had initial public offerings, and the pace remained very strong through 1999, even into the first 2 months of 2000. Once the NASDAQ began its collapse in March 2000, the IPO window virtually shut. In 2001 there were months when not a

---

[6]This is an arrangement whereby the two founders can force (the put) the acquirer to purchase their 20 percent at a predetermined and negotiated price.

[7]See several relevant articles on selling a company in *Growing Concerns*, ed. D.E. Gumpert (New York, NY: John Wiley & Sons, 1984), pp. 332-98.

[8]The Big Five accounting firms, such as Ernst & Young, publish information on deciding to take a firm public, as does NASDAQ. See also R. Salomon, "Second Thoughts on Going Live with Wall Street," *Harvard Business Review*, reprint no. 91309.

[9]S. Jones, M.B. Cohen, and V.V. Coppola, "Going Public." In *The Entrepreneurial Venture*, ed. W.A. Sahlman and H.H. Stevenson (Boston, MA: Harvard Business School Publishing, 1992), p. 394.

[10]For an updated discussion of these issues, see C. Bagley and C. Dauchy, "Going Public." In *The Entrepreneurial Venture*. 2nd ed., ed. W.A. Sahlman and H.H. Stevenson (Boston, MA: Harvard Business School Publishing, 1999), pp. 404-40.

[11]Jones et al., "Going Public," p. 395.

[12]Ibid.

EXHIBIT 18.1

Number of Recent IPOs

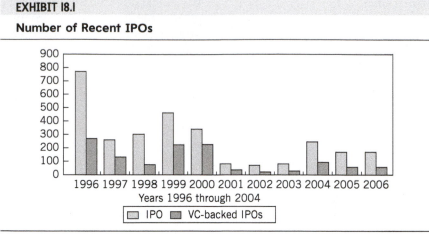

Source: Thomson Venture Economics/NVCA. Used by permission.

EXHIBIT 18.2

Recent IPOs ($millions)

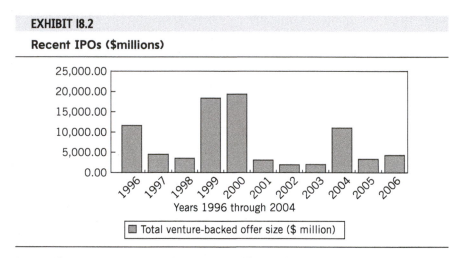

Source: Thomson Venture Economics/NVCA. Used by permission.

single IPO occurred, and for the year it was well under 100! Few signs of recovery were evident in 2002. The lesson is clear: Depending on the IPO market for a harvest is a highly cyclical strategy, which can cause both great joy and disappointment. Such is the reality of the stock markets. Exhibits 18.1 and 18.2 show this pattern vividly.

There are several advantages to going public, many of which relate to the ability of the company to fund its rapid growth. Public equity markets provide access to long-term capital while also meeting subsequent capital needs. Companies may use the proceeds of an IPO to expand the business in the existing market or to move into a related market. The founders and initial investors might be seeking liquidity, but SEC restrictions limiting the timing and the amount of stock that the officers, directors,

and insiders can dispose off in the public market are increasingly severe. As a result, it can take several years after an IPO before a liquid gain is possible. In addition, as Jim Hindman (of Jiffy Lube) believed, a public offering not only increases public awareness of the company but also contributes to the marketability of the products, including franchises.

However, there are disadvantages to being a public company. For example, 50 percent of the computer software companies surveyed by Holmberg agreed that the focus on short-term profits and performance results was a negative attribute of being a public company.[13] Also, because of the disclosure requirements, public companies lose some of their operating confidentiality, not to mention having to support the ongoing costs of public disclosure, audits, and tax filings. With public shareholders, the

---

[13]Holmberg, "Value Creation and Capture," p. 203.

management of the company has to be careful about the flow of information because of the risk of insider trading. Thus it is easy to see why companies need to think about the positive and negative attributes of being a public company.

Wealth-Building Vehicles

The 1986 Tax Reform Act severely limited the generous options previously available to build wealth within a private company through large deductible contributions to a retirement plan. To make matters worse, the administrative costs and paperwork necessary to comply with federal laws have become a nightmare. Nonetheless, there are still mechanisms that can enable an owner to contribute up to 25 percent of his or her salary to a retirement plan each year, an amount that is deductible to the company and grows tax free. Entrepreneurs who can contribute such amounts for just a short time will build significant wealth.

The Road Ahead: Devise a Personal Entrepreneurial Strategy

Goals Matter—A Lot!

Of all the anchors one can think of in the entrepreneurial process, three loom above all the rest:

1. A passion for achieving goals.
2. A relentless competitive spirit and desire to win.
3. A high standard of personal ethics and integrity.

Chapter Summary

- Entrepreneurs thrive on the challenges and satisfactions of the game: It is a journey, not a destination.
- First and foremost, successful entrepreneurs strive to build a great company: wealth follows that process.
- Harvest options mean more than simply selling the company, and these options are an important part of the entrepreneur's know-how.

- Entrepreneurs know that to perpetuate the system for future generations, they must give back to their communities and invest time and capital in the next entrepreneurial generation.

Study Questions

1. Why did Walt Disney say, "I don't make movies to make money. I make money to make movies"?
2. Why is it essential to focus first on building a great company, rather than on just getting rich?
3. Why is a harvest goal so crucial for entrepreneurs and the economy?
4. Define the principal harvest options, the pros and cons of each, and why each is valuable.
5. Beyond the harvest, what do entrepreneurs do to give back, and why is this so important to their communities and the nation?

Internet Resources

http://www.main-usa.com *Minority Angel Investor Network (MAIN) is a network of accredited investors with an interest and commitment to invest in high-growth, minority-owned, or minority-led companies.*

http://www.investopedia.com *Articles, resources, and definitions for investors.*

http://www.philanthropyroundtable.org *The Philanthropy Roundtable is a national association of individual donors, foundation trustees and staff, and corporate giving officers.*

Exercise

"Wisdom from the Harvest"
An Interview with a Harvested Entrepreneur

"Success is getting what you want. Happiness is wanting what you get!"
Dorothy Stevenson

At the beginning of the book we asked you to interview an entrepreneur who had built a company in the past 10 years or so into sales of $10 million or more. Now, in the spirit of Dorothy Stevenson's wisdom here, we suggest there is much to learn from engaging an entrepreneur at the other end of the life cycle of value creation and realization.

Tim Russert, the famed national journalist, in his recent book *Wisdom of Our Fathers*, captured wonderfully insightful and heartrending stories about relationships between children and their fathers. The book is based on tens of thousands of letters he received from these kids—now in their 30s to 50s—after they read his book *Big Russ and Me*, a chronicle about the love and wisdom gained from his own father. A third must-read book is Charlie Collier's *Wealth in Families*, noted earlier in this chapter. We highly recommend these books in general, and they will provide an excellent foundation for this exercise and interview as well.

Find a founder, aged 45 to 60!, who has a very substantial net worth realized from building and harvesting his or her company. As a guideline, if the company exceeded $50 million to $100 million in revenue, the odds are the firm would have been valued for a similar amount or more. Further, determine whether this entrepreneur has any intention of retiring; in all likelihood, he or she is involved in another venture, or even two or three, as a founder, cofounder, or angel investor who also serves as an advisor or director.

We find this pattern the rule rather than the exception. Take, for example, John Connolly. He founded Course Technology in Boston in the early 1990s. His company later achieved an IPO and became one of the first very successful learning technology companies. Then, in his mid-40s John acquired another company, MainSpring, for about $20 million; he turned it around, built it up, and sold it for over $600 million. Now 54 years old and financially able to retire and never work again, he made it clear in a recent conversation that this is the furthest thing from his mind. He put it this way: "I love building and starting companies and being a CEO. I don't think I'll ever retire!"

There are precious insights and lessons to gain from spending an hour or more over a cup of coffee or lunch with harvested entrepreneurs like John. Here are some questions to guide your conversation and for sharing what you have learned with classmates, friends, and family.

We urge you to pursue many such interviews along your own entrepreneurial journey.

1. Tell me about your company, your decision to sell/merge or take it public, and what you have been doing since, and why.

2. What were the most difficult conflicts, ethical dilemmas, and decisions you had to make along the way and in deciding to harvest?

3. What were the most challenging and rewarding aspects of balancing your marriage, family life, and the welfare of your associates and investors?

4. Were there any experiences and tribulations along the way that you were glad you did not know about in advance, or you might never have tried to start a company? How might that advice translate for me?

5. Some very ambitious entrepreneurs (perhaps blindly) are so consumed by winning and financial success that they abandon their personal integrity and reputation for ethical dealing. They seem to be able to rationalize their behavior, believing all the way to prison or the grave that they did nothing wrong—as we saw with Koslowski at Tyco and with Skilling and Delay at Enron. What advice and insights do you have from your observations of entrepreneurs who have maintained their reputation for integrity—and those who did not?

6. When you became very successful financially, how old were your children? How aware were they of your family's elite financial status? Did you talk about your family's wealth, family values, and philanthropy? What impact did this have on their beliefs and values, their expectations (cars, vacations, material things, etc.), and their motivation to work hard?

7. Were there any specific things you said or did with your children in their formative years to enable them to remain grounded, to give them a sense of frugality and a work ethic, and to leave them a legacy of ambition and giving back?

8. What have you seen as the best and the worst in how other successful entrepreneurs have handled these issues with their kids, and the outcomes?

What did they—and you—want to preserve besides financial assets?

9. Tell me about the most inspiring and the most depressing wealthy families you know of (you do not have to reveal any names) in dealing with the visibility, peer pressures, and circumstances the family faced growing up. What does each consider to be the family's true assets?

10. For someone like me who aspires to have my own venture(s) and become very successful, what are the most important advice, insights, and lessons you have for me?

11. Some entrepreneurs seem to achieve balance in their lives, have meaningful marriages, contribute to the community, and have children who are valuable additions to the family and the community. Others tell horror stories about wealthy entrepreneurs that include alcoholism and drug abuse (by the parents and eventually the children), affairs leading to failed marriages, little community involvement, and other sad tales that seem to negate most sensible notions of success. What have you seen in this regard, and what, in your experience, is the difference between these outcomes? What can a young entrepreneur do to emulate the former rather than the latter?

12. What made you decide *not* to retire and to continue to pursue more ventures? Tell me about the personal and psychological rewards this entails for you.

13. How wealthy do you want your kids and grand-children to be, and why?

14. Are there any other things you would like to share with me in the way of observations and advice that we have not talked about?

Finally, add any other questions you would like here.

_____

_____

_____

_____

Summation and Sharing

Put together a one- to two-page summary of what you have found, the lessons and insights that you believe are most important, and any way you feel this will change your own goals and thinking. Share your results with classmates.

You will likely want to revisit these topics along the way in your own entrepreneurial career.

A Final Thought: What If the Money Is Gone?

What will your legacy be? What do you want to preserve besides financial assets? How do you want to be able to answer these questions when you are 50 or so, and what do you need to do about that now and in the future? (*Tip:* Read *Wealth in Families.*)

Case

Optitech

Preparation Questions

1.   What strategy should Jim Harris choose? Why?

2.   Discuss the process and methods for valuing a privately held company.

3.   Discuss the dilemmas and decisions Harris faces.

4.   Evaluate the analysis presented by Shields and Company in Exhibits A–G. What criteria would you use to select an investment banker?

January 2008. Heading back to Denver, Jim Harris taxied his Lear 35 onto the small, dusty airstrip east of Tucson. As he waited for clearance, Harris thought about Optitech, which he'd been building for nearly 14 years—and which had enabled him to pursue his love of flying. He was in talks to sell it and he wanted to be sure that his life would be as enjoyable post-harvest as it was now.

Competitive Urges

Jim Harris attended the University of Colorado at Boulder, fairly close to his Denver home. His father Bill, an accomplished businessman, was a bit concerned about his son's grade point average but not his long-term prospects:

Jim has always been super-competitive, and athletics were a major factor in his background . . . It was pretty clear that whatever he got into he was going to give it 110 percent.

After graduating in 1993 with a history and political science degree, Harris followed his girlfriend Karen to San Diego to try to make a living as professional triathlete. He ran out of money and moved back to Denver but stayed in touch with Karen.

Harris found work in sales with a supplier of remanufactured laser jet toner cartridges.[1] After 3 months, the New York–based company closed its Denver office and Harris struck out on his own:

I was living at home, with few bills other than my car and gas. My parents lent me $8,500, and I started selling remanufactured toner cartridges out of my car.

This case was prepared by Carl Hedberg under the direction of Professor Jeffry Timmons. © Copyright Jeffry Timmons, 2008. All rights reserved.

[1]An early method of remanufacturing involved refilling units through a hole drilled in the side. These "drill and fill" operations could turn around units quickly, but their products often failed when low-grade toner mixed with shards of plastic left from the drilling.

Getting in the Game

In 1994, the $2.2 billion aftermarket for printer cartridges was dominated by nearly 6,000 small sales and fulfillment operations. Harris sourced ready-for-sale inventory and set up shop in his garage. To find customers, he applied a telemarketing formula:

I was targeting area businesses that were likely to have a high print volume, like hospitals and legal and accounting firms. These were not huge companies, and at the time there was not a lot of competition for their business. From working at the other company I knew this was a numbers game; if I set 15 appointments a week, I could expect to sell one out of three of those. It took a lot of discipline and hundreds of calls just to get started. I was on the phone several hours a day, five days a week—mostly 7 days.

One of the main challenges in this industry that never goes away is that most big companies bundle their office supply purchases and order everything from one vendor. Trying to convince purchasing managers that it is worth it to pull the toner out of that one-stop-shop order is often a tough sell...

I will say that all the rejection was awful, and I tried to use my discipline from triathlons to block that negativity out of my mind. I also felt that when some of the better prospects didn't actually say no, that represented a light at the end of the tunnel. If I could just get one or two of those accounts to come on board, I knew it was going to get a lot easier.

To build a sustainable revenue base, Harris needed a few large accounts. Organizations like that could take years to make a decision—and required big account references Harris would not have until he landed a few. Fortunately, due to margins ranging from 25 to 30 percent, Harris turned a small profit almost from day one. By the summer, Harris' monthly revenues were around $12,000. Still, he knew he'd have to do a lot better to grow out of his parents' garage.

Just when he'd begun to explore the idea of factoring his meager receivables as a way to free up some additional capital, he scored:

I had been talking to a VA hospital here in Denver for a long time. Hospitals place large orders at the end of every fiscal year, and in September they gave me a purchase order for $118,000. That was huge in two ways. It gave me a base of working capital, and that sale got me a foot in the door to the health care industry.

Relentless Dissatisfaction

In late 1995, Harris set up his own remanufacturing operation using empty cartridges (blanks) sourced from third parties.[2] Over the next couple of years, Optitech built up a wide range of clients and began earning a reputation for quality products and good customer service.

Harris maintained a flat, simple structure as his business grew. His accountant worked out of his home; the Optitech plant was no-frills and low-rent. But he didn't skimp on his most important asset:

> By running a lean operation, we are able to treat our employees very well. Their pay and benefit packages have always been among the best in the industry. That has given us a very low turnover and a culture that goes the extra mile to service our customers.

In 1996, Karen moved back from California. The following spring, she and Jim were married.

By the late 1990s, Optitech's monthly sales were $800,000. Jim's father, who had continued to offer advice and encouragement from the sidelines, commented on Jim's path to profits:

> One of the things that helped Jim out a lot was that he concentrated on selling to end users. All of Optitech's biggest competitors are wholesalers because, in many ways, selling and managing retail accounts as Jim does is a more difficult business to build and operate. But that high-service business has given Jim an extra layer of margin to work with relative to the competition.
>
> I thought it was great that he was building a lean and profitable organization, but I was starting to feel that the company could use a bit more structure.

Big Win

By the early 2000s, office supply superstores had begun stocking remanufactured toner cartridges. In February 2004, Harris learned that All Office Supply (AOS), a national superstore, was taking bids from toner remanufacturers. He approached with caution:

> Wholesale is a low-margin, volume business, which is completely different than what we were doing. But one thing led to another, and we ended up being one of 12 companies that AOS decided to consider.

With annual sales of $15 million, Optitech was by far the smallest company in the running. After AOS executives toured the modest but well-run plant in Denver, Harris learned Optitech had made the final cut and his competitive nature kicked in:

> Nobody was going to offer consignment because the slim margins didn't allow any room for error. So I took a chance by offering that on a few models. It wasn't a very good deal for us at all. I was just trying to get our foot in the door—and after that I would figure out how to maneuver where we could make money at it.

After 15 months, Optitech won a five-year contract with a 3-year renewal option. In May 2005, Optitech purchased a 55,000-square-foot wholesale facility in Tucson, Arizona, where Harris and Karen had a vacation home.[3] The new operation had a manager and eight employees who, like Harris, were willing to do whatever it took to keep and build the AOS account. Harris said it was even more difficult than he had imagined it would be:

> We had made a good deal of money going into this deal, so I thought we'd have a pretty good buffer. Equipment-wise we put in about $2.5 million, which was a lot for us. We were used to getting paid in 20 days. When we started shipping product [in November 2005] AOS was stretching us to 140 days. By early 2006 we were holding over $12 million in receivables out for AOS alone.
>
> It was a huge and risky undertaking, and there were times when we were in bad shape. We had to pull a line of credit out of Merrill Lynch, and we put all of the cash we were making from the retail side into supporting this deal. Two years earlier we wouldn't have had enough money to pull it off, and as it was, there were at least 6 months where it was really uncertain whether we would continue to do it. Building the retail side was a piece of cake compared to this, and that was a lot of hard work. It's been the best learning experience I've ever had in my life.

Optitech persevered, and by early summer AOS was paying in the standard 70 days and accepting

---

[2] Remanufacturers generally considered empties management to be a noncore and nondifferentiating activity. Therefore, many large-scale remanufacturing companies relied on vendors to collect, inspect, sort, and store their empty cartridges, buying only those cartridges required for production demand.

[3] As an experienced pilot and owner of a pair of Learjets for both business and pleasure, Harris almost never used commercial airlines when traveling within the continental United States. Harris discussed the economics: "I paid $1.8 million for the first plane and put $300 K into it, and I have about $3.5 million into the second jet. Using a charter service, I generate $80,000 a month in revenue, plus a 20 percent depreciation write-off on the $5.7 million for both planes. So now I can fly about 20 hours a month at no cost because the charter program and write-off are covering those expenses. Not only is it working out as a good investment, but I can get to a bunch of locations quickly. For example, on Tuesday I'm going on a 2-day trip to visit current and potential customers in Birmingham (AL), Dallas, Oakland, Los Angeles, Las Vegas, and Tucson. Can you imagine trying to do that using commercial airlines?"

product without consignment.[4] Within a year, the Optitech plant in Tucson was operating at full capacity with 40 employees. Seeing an area where he could help his son, Bill Harris joined Optitech to help source Asian suppliers:

> Going to China for parts and finished product requires substantial volume to get the kind of prices that they can offer. We knew the AOS deal would give us the means to attract some highly credible suppliers, but we were also aware of some of the horror stories about getting into China, including quality that was nothing like the level of the samples they would send, complicated paperwork, delivered inventory counts that were way off, and shipments often delayed for weeks...
>
> We knew we had to have somebody on site in China who could check on quality and shipments. We didn't have anybody in mind, but my brother-in-law suggested a gentleman in Taiwan whom he'd done business with off and on for 25 years. His name is Vincent Ma: very honest and hardworking—sleeps maybe three or four hours a night...

Vincent accompanied the Optitech team to a trade show in Taiwan. After he was satisfied with five suppliers, the team toured their plants and, with his help, negotiated contracts with the owners. For a 1.42 percent commission on all the products Optitech ordered from China, Vincent handled the export documentation and inspected every shipment. Although this complex supply chain wasn't perfect, Bill Harris said going offshore had been a significant win:

> The quality has been excellent. Most of the owners of these plants are young and entrepreneurial—in their middle to late 40s. We have been bowled over by how good and responsive they are. When we've had a problem, they've jumped on it right away. Right now we are dealing with shipping delays of as much as 3 weeks, but that is being addressed. The key is having an honest and intelligent and hardworking individual in Taiwan who is there for us.
>
> This has helped us tremendously with AOS, and the cost advantages have spilled over to the retail side of the business. Big-box stores are getting more and more powerful, so we are planning retail stores that will help us continue to go direct to big end users . . . If we don't, eventually we will get cut out of that business.

By mid-2006, annual sales to AOS were approaching $30 million.[5] Optitech was well-positioned with industry-leading levels of profitability. It had 200 employees, production facilities in Tucson and Denver, and regional sales offices in Denver, Kansas City, and Los Angeles. Although Optitech could have closed its original operation in Denver, Harris was not about to do that:

> The Denver factory is pieced together and not very well laid out. It should all be in Tucson. I could shut it down and literally save $300,000 a year. At the end of the day, it's about being loyal to the people who have taken care of me over the years.

OEMs on the Offense

As the industry matured, original equipment manufacturers (OEMs) began to look for ways to interrupt the flow of their branded empties to "profiteering" remanufacturers. One tactic involved the use of smart chips. Touted as an end user feature that tracked printer functions and prints remaining, chip-enabled cartridges were useless as blanks because the imbedded chips couldn't be reset. For a while, this made life difficult for consumers who refilled their own cartridges and posed a significant challenge for recyclers and remanufacturers. Although compatible replacement chips were soon widely available in the remanufacturing sector, these added to the cost of the finished product.

Seeking a more sustainable pushback, OEMs, including Canon, Epson, HP, Lexmark, Ricoh, and Xerox, began suing remanufacturers for patent infringement.[6] Harris said this was the beginning of what could become a major struggle:

> These big players have a lot of money, and they are making billions of dollars a year from this product as a consumable. The aftermarket business accounts for 20 to 25 percent market share...That's a ton of money in what is now an $80 billion industry.
>
> Epson just got a ruling for a general exclusion for products in violation of their patents. That's pretty much all of the compatible Epsons that we sell. It's not a huge percentage of our sales—less than $2 million of $45 million, but it is a profitable part of our business.
>
> The ruling does not cover older-model blanks, and we already have an inside line with a major broker in the United States to tie up and ship 150,000 Epson empties to China for remanufacturing. Dozens of third-party supplier firms have been named in infringement suits like this; so far we've been under the radar.

Harris and his team took some comfort in the idea that because Epson did a significant volume of sales with AOS, it might not push too hard—even if Optitech did appear on its radar. George Arnold, Harris's

---

[4]By mid-2006 Optitech had worked out a deal with a bank in Denver that effectively cut the AOS payment terms to 25 days, minus a small discount.

[5]Remanufactured toner cartridges were a $120 million category for All Office Supply. A second supplier made up the difference.

[6]Intellectual property (IP) cases were being heard in high-level courts around the world. The U.S. Supreme Court ruled against Independent Ink; an IP case reached the High Court, Japan; and Epson and HP fielded complaints with the U.S. International Trade Commission as well as in U.S. federal courts.

long-time broker at Merrill Lynch, said OEMs weren't the only challenge Optitech was facing:

> Things have changed a lot since Jim started, and in many ways it's a lot tougher space to be in. In the last couple of years, 30 percent of the competition has gone out of business because they weren't doing the quantities to stay price competitive.
>
> Staples is now into remanufacturing, and Cartridge World is offering a refill program.[7] All of this is pushing prices down further, increasing the competition for blanks, and giving Optitech's best retail clients more options.

Because Harris very much enjoyed the business he was building, and the people he had hired to grow with him, it took a few calls from Arnold to convince Harris to hire an investment banking firm.

Assessing the Possibilities

Founded in 1991, Boston-based Shields and Company provided investment banking services to private and public companies.[8] Harris's broker thought it was a good match for Optitech. It had worked extensively with entrepreneurs and closely held ventures and its managing director, Timothy White, had worked in the technology group of Barclays Global Investors banking division, where he had been involved in IBM's spinoff of Lexmark.

In early 2007, White and two associates met with Harris in Denver.[9] They toured the Optitech facility and collected additional data to help them size up the company. They offered their assessment of the industry (Exhibit A) and worked up a financial snapshot that included an estimated fiscal 2007 EBITDA of $8.3 million on sales of $50 million (Exhibits B and C). Although the Shields team was very impressed with Optitech's performance and profitability, White noted that Harris's rather loose approach to building Optitech had created some issues:

> Jim has built a great enterprise, but it lacks structure. They've got to hire a national sales manager and a quality engineer to manage and develop documentation on that side of the operation. Our biggest frustration was with the finance and accounting; they were going to have to get a better handle on the numbers.

[7]Harris said it was unlikely that All Office Supply would be going direct anytime soon: Four years ago AOS tried to do business in China and fell flat on its face. It is not easy to do if you are a big company. You need to be fairly quick on your feet, and it takes some learning.

[8]Investment banking services included exclusive sale and acquisition assignments; debt and equity capital raising; recapitalizations and other financial transactions; fairness opinions; and business, intangible assets, and securities valuations.

[9]Engaging the services of investment bankers began with meetings and due diligence to determine whether there was a mutual interest in moving forward. The investment banker would produce a prospectus outlining the nature of the challenges and opportunities facing the client, as well as scenarios and valuations based on a range of methodologies. In this case, Shields and Company would charge a retainer fee of $84,000, paid monthly. That fee was absorbed by their fee upon sale: 2 percent up to $50 million plus 1 percent of anything over $50 million.

EXHIBIT A

Industry Overview

The industry has been in a constant state of change for the past several years.
- Market is mature and increasingly aware of remanufacturing as an option.
- Educated end users continue to change the marketplace.
- Trends toward global sourcing are continuing.
- Uncertainty of availability of supplies (blanks) is a continuing issue.
- Increasingly complex links and quality demands.
- Cartridge World and retailers offering refill programs are a concern.

Larger, vertically integrated OEMs are getting increasingly aggressive.
- Xerox selling drums and bulk toner.
- Pitney Bowes penetrating the market through acquisition.
- Most OEMs have been involved in one or more lawsuits.

New OEM strategies, tactics, and trends are emerging.
- Smart chips (examples: Canon's *war chip* and Lexmark's *killer chip*).
- Mechanical vs. chemical solutions.
- Licensing remanufactures: Is this the future?

The investment community is showing more aggressive interest in the consumables market.
- PE friendly business model; low CapEx, scalable, fragmented.
- Public markets have been less favorable, due in part to weaker performance of several players, such as Adsero, American Toner Serve, and Danka.
- Global Imaging Systems has been rewarded by the markets for its consolidation strategy.

Source: Shields and Company, Boston, Massachusetts.

EXHIBIT B

Income Statement and Forecast

($ in thousands)	Fiscal Year Ended December 31,				Shields Forecast Fiscal
	2003	2004	2005	2006	2007
Revenue	$11,960	$13,816	$20,471	$33,699	$50,000
Cost of sales	8,248	9,582	15,066	25,173	37,500
Gross profit	3,712	4,234	5,405	8,526	12,500
Officers' compensation	195	219	200	200	200
Operating expense	1,874	1,394	1,788	2,958	4,000
Depreciation	3	—	—	—	—
Operating income	$1,640	$2,621	$3,417	$5,368	$8,300
Calculation of EBITDA:					
Operating income	$1,640	$2,621	$3,417	$5,368	$8,300
Plus: Depreciation and amortization	3	—	—	—	—
EBITDA	$1,643	$2,621	$3,417	$5,368	$8,300
Sales growth	NA	15.5%	48.2%	NA	144.2%
As a percentage of revenue:					
Gross profit	31.0%	30.6%	26.4%	25.3%	25.0%
Operating expense	15.7%	10.1%	8.7%	8.8%	8.0%
EBITDA	13.7%	19.0%	16.7%	15.9%	16.6%

Source: Optitech management and Shields and Company.

EXHIBIT C

Balance Sheet: June 2007

($ in thousands)	As of June 30, 2007		
Assets		**Liabilities and Stockholder's Equity**	
Current assets:		Current liabilities:	
Cash and cash equivalents	$ 191	Line of credit	$ 655
Accounts receivable, net	9,768	Accounts payable—trade	7,311
Inventory	730	Accounts payable—other	8
Deposits	2	*Total current liabilities*	7,974
Total current assets	10,691	Long-term liabilities	—
Fixed assets, net	641	*Total liabilities*	7,974
Other assets	—	Stockholder's equity	3,358
Total assets	$11,332	**Total liabilities and stockholder's equity**	$11,332

Source: Optitech management.

Our other major concern was their heavy dependence on AOS, especially because there are three or four good-sized competitors that would love to get that business. They are constantly knocking on All Office Supply's door, and Optitech is doing somersaults to keep AOS happy.

Two weeks after a follow-up visit to the Tucson plant, the Shields team presented their assessment of the opportunity, including strengths and risks (Exhibit D), and a discussion of the strategic alternatives they saw for Optitech: status quo, acquisitions, strategic sale (Exhibit E). Harris felt two of the alternatives were worth pursuing:

Status quo wasn't going to work because in this industry if you're not growing you're shrinking. We didn't have much interest in going public or bringing in minority interests for an equity recapitalization. That was a way to get some money off the table, but I was already making plenty of money, and I didn't really want additional shareholders.

EXHIBIT D

Preliminary Discussion of Investment Considerations

Positive Factors	Risks That Need to Be Mitigated
Remarkable revenue growth trend.	Industry is becoming increasingly competitive. Hardware OEMs are litigious, and imports are a threat. How will Optitech drive continued growth at current levels?
Industry-leading levels of profitability.	Growth in big-box channel and imports create pressure on margins. Higher-margin customer programs need to be protected.
Strong balance sheet with capacity to support organic or external growth.	Growth with All Office Supply and larger entities will place pressure on working capital. Need to understand and position management's ability to operate in a leveraged environment
Young but experienced management.	Lean organization supported by Harris's energy and experience. Could current infrastructure support the company under a range of future scenarios?
Opportunities for continued organic or external expansion.	Organic growth will require investment in sales and marketing infrastructure. Growth through acquisition will require investment in management and financial infrastructure.
Favorable trends in consumables usage.	Although more cartridges are being used, the current lawsuits will be a negative factor with banks and/or investors. Need to watch pending rulings with Lexmark carefully.
Consistent investment in R&D and technology.	Although it is clear that Optitech has made substantial investments in capacity, "smart chip" technologies appear to be here to stay, and technology spending will only be increasing.
Excellent customer reputation.	Increased retail competition (Cartridge World, Staples) could disrupt relationships. More educated consumers help remanufactures but create more price sensitivity.
Low capital requirements.	Ongoing growth can be supported through imports from Asia requiring little capital expenditure; but this also lowers competitive barriers to entry.

Source: Shields and Company.

Based on their valuation methods (Exhibit F) and comparables (Exhibit G), Shields and Company came up with a potential value of around $60 million. That was a big surprise, and it got me thinking a lot about the other two options they talked about—especially using our profitable base to grow by acquisition.

Such a strategy was in line with Harris's goal to aggressively build up the retail side of the business to balance out the wholesale account with AOS. He explained how he would do that:

> I've talked with Shields and Company about maybe doing some B2B [business to business] acquisitions of remanufacturers with retail sales of around $5 million—not nearly enough volume to buy direct from China. If we rolled four or five of those up into our business, we could build a $150 million business and increase our overall margin a good 20 percent. We think we'd get our money back [from those investments] in 18 to 24 months and have a very profitable and balanced company.

In the midst of planning to take the company in this direction, Shields and Company suddenly came up with a new possibility.

The Exit Option

Harris and his team had been in contact with Shields and Company for about 7 months when the investment banker came across a $2 billion private equity firm in St. Louis that was showing interest in the toner industry. In the previous year, Talcott Equity Partners had done some acquisitions in that space, and Shields spotted an opportunity. Harris was intrigued:

> Andrew Fields is a guy who used to work for the largest aftermarket supply company in the world, which is where we bought all of our toner drums. So we had a good relationship with them for a long time, and Andrew was real familiar with us. Andrew's job [at Talcott] was to go out and find companies to buy [in the industry].

Andrew Fields explained what he had in mind:

> We are looking at building a business to $400 million revenue from about four to five acquisitions: a roll-up strategy to an IPO that will max out the value. Optitech is a strategic buy because they are selling B2B retail as well as to superstores. The All

EXHIBIT E

Strategic Alternatives

Key Scenario Considerations

- Liquidity goals and risk/return profiles of shareholders.
- Projected company performance and corresponding business risk associated with projections.
- Ongoing roles and involvement of current management.
- Transaction due diligence consideration, including litigation, environmental, management.
- Market timing: current M&A and capital market conditions and corresponding market risk in future periods.
- Size and growth potential of toner cartridge manufacturing industry.

Option A: Status Quo—Maintain Private Company Structure

Benefits	Disadvantages
Maintain control of operations.	Lack of significant liquidity for shareholders.
Continuity for management.	Increased liability exposure for officers.
Ability to dividend funds to shareholders.	Competition from large growing companies.
Pursue continued growth strategy.	Potential capital constraints for growth.
	Management succession issues.

Option B: Growth through Acquisition Strategy

Benefits	Disadvantages
Provides immediate growth.	Integration risk.
Increased market share.	Realization of synergies.
Greater purchasing power and other synergies.	Finding the right target(s) at the right price.
Could generate substantial future value.	Managing additional leverage. More eggs in the
same basket.	

Option C: Strategic Sale of the Company

Benefits	Disadvantages
Significant liquidity to all shareholders.	Few large industry players.
Potentially partnering with larger entity.	Lack of control to manage and run company.
Capitalizing on current strength in the M&A and capital markets.	Management and employees may or may not stay on following the transaction.
Potential synergies may increase sale value.	Exposure to industry competition from sharing confidential information. Limited ability to benefit from future growth in the business.

Source: Shields and Company.

Office Supply percentage of their business is fine with us because the roll-up will dilute that dependence. They've also got some minor issues like outmoded facilities, especially in Denver, and some challenges on the accounting end.

Harris discussed the conversation:

In the roll-up, everything we have in the way of accounting and financial reports will have to comply with Sarbanes-Oxley.[10] We've had a firm working on that for the last 4 months. And it is pretty accurate from what they are telling us.

[10]Due to the requirements of the Sarbanes-Oxley Act, companies required more control of what they were outsourcing, and senior management had to be more closely and directly involved in making sure their company conformed to expected standards of care and good practices, many of which had been codified in industry or regulatory papers.

Talcott would definitely shut down the Denver facility and put it all into one. There would be a lot of job loss. I have some key people in this company, and it has to be a good deal for everyone involved. There are people who really helped me get to this point, and I obviously want to make sure they are taken care of. It sounds like a good fit, though.

They're talking between $40 million and $50 million, but because we'd have no control over the stock, we're going to push for at least 75 percent up front in cash. There are not a lot of companies out there our size making this kind of money, so I think we are in a good [bargaining] position for that.

As the early-stage talks progressed, Talcott indicated that they would present two separate deal structures based on whether Harris would be willing to stay at the helm of his acquired company—and

EXHIBIT F

Methodologies and Valuation

Methodology	Description
Guideline company analysis	Publicly traded guideline companies whose operations are similar to those of the subject company demonstrate relative minority interest positions being accorded by the investing public to earnings, book values, and revenues of such businesses.
Precedent transaction analysis	Publicly disclosed data from arm's-length transactions involving similar companies demonstrate relationships or value measures between the price paid for target company and the underlying financial performance of that company.
Specific company accretion/dilution analysis	Maximum value that a specifically identified buyer can pay for a target without having the acquisition be dilutive to its unadjusted pro forma earnings per share.
Discounted cash flow/leveraged buyout analysis	The fair market value of the subject company is derived by assuming returns on invested equity based on Optitech's future cash flows and the availability of debt capital.

Preliminary Valuation Analysis

	Median Multiples	Optitech Estimated Financials	Implied Enterprise Value	Less: Debt Net of Cash	Implied Equity Value
Comparable company analysis					
Enterprise value/2006 net sales	0.8×	$50,000	$40,000	—	$40,000
Enterprise value/2006 EBITDA	8.7×	$8,300	$72,210	—	$72,210
Recent M&A transaction analysis					
Enterprise value/2006 net sales	1.0×	$50,000	$50,000	—	$50,000
Enterprise value/2006 EBITDA	7.5×	$8,300	$62,250	—	$62,250
Shields and Company recent private equity recapitalizations					
Enterprise value/2006 EBITDA	8.0×	$8,300	$66,400	—	$66,400

Source: Based on Shields and Company financial estimates and recapitalization processes.

for how long. Harris, realizing he'd never worked for anyone before, had a lot to consider.

Life Choices

As he dipped one wing of his sleek jet toward the desert below in a graceful arc that set him on course for the Rocky Mountains, Harris recalled what he'd told his parents last week:

> If I sell the company, I'll have the money to do whatever I want to do; but what would I do? I've been enjoying this for 13 years. Part of me would love

to keep it all together and grow by acquisition; but then I think, how much energy do I really have to get this to $150 million in sales?

At 36, Harris was at a fork in the road. With a recession looming in the wake of the subprime mortgage mess, he knew it would be difficult to grow his business exponentially. Still, Harris had spent all but a few months since college building Optitech, the success of which he attributed to family support and his loyal and hardworking employees. As the deal with the private equity firm moved into the go/no go phase, Harris knew he had to make some major life decisions.

EXHIBIT G

Valuation Multiples

($ in millions)

Consumables Industry Participants	Ticker Symbol	Total Enterprise Value	Revenue	Gross Profit	EBITDA	EBIT	LTM Revenue	LTM EBITDA	Book Value	Net Income
			Latest 12 Months as of March 21, 2007				*Total Enterprise Value*		*Market Cap*	
Adsero Corp.	OTCPK: ADSO	$19.9	$27.3	$4.1	($4.6)	($6.7)	0.7×	NM*	NM	NM
American TonerServ Corp.	OTCBB: SSVP	$9.6	$0.4	$0.2	($0.4)	($0.4)	23.8×	NM	NM	NM
Astro-Med Inc.	NasdaqNM: A LOT	$58.3	$64.0	$26.6	$5.2	$3.9	0.9×	11.2×	1.8×	13.0×
Color Imaging Inc.	OTCPK: CHG	$9.1	$20.9	$6.0	$1.0	$0.4	0.4×	8.7×	0.6×	30.9×
Danka Business Systems plc	NasdaqSC: DANK.Y	$638.8	$1,017.4	$323.0	$2.2	($1.8)	0.6×	28.8×	5.5×	NM
Global Imaging Systems Inc.	NasdaqNM: GISX	$1,182.0	$1,096.8	$429.2	$142.1	$123.6	1.1×	8.3×	1.9×	14.7×
Ingram Micro Inc.	NYSE: IM	$3,477.2	$31,357.5	$1,685.3	$510.8	$449.6	0.1×	6.8×	1.1×	12.4×
Jadi Imaging Holdings Bhd	KLSE: JADI	$42.1	$15.5	$5.7	$5.1	$4.1	2.7×	8.2×	2.4×	13.9×
Media Sciences International	NasdaqSC: MSII	$56.5	$23.1	$13.2	$4.8	$3.9	2.4×	11.9×	5.0×	24.4×
Turbon AG	Duse: Tur	$58.6	$160.3	$30.1	$6.7	$4.1	0.4×	8.7×	0.9×	NM
						Median	0.8×	8.7×	1.8×	14.3×
						Mean	3.3×	11.6×	2.4×	18.2×
						High	23.8×	28.8×	5.5×	30.9×
						Low	0.1×	6.8×	0.6×	12.4×
Industry Giants										
Hewlett-Packard Co.	NYSE: HPQ	$102,798.4	$93,748.0	$23,060.0	$10,161.0	$7,728.0	1.1×	10.1×	2.8×	16.5×
Lexmark International	NYSE: LXK	$5,293.1	$5,108.1	$1,694.1	$811.8	$610.9	1.0×	6.5×	5.5×	16.8×
Pitney Bowes Inc.	NYSE: PBI	$14,592.7	$5,004.9	$3,093.5	$1,541.5	$1,187.4	2.9×	9.5×	14.5×	96.3×
Xerox Corp.	NYSE: XRX	$22,434.6	$15,055.0	$6,459.0	$2,279.0	$1,643.0	1.5×	9.8×	2.3×	13.4×
						Median	1.3×	9.7×	4.2×	16.7×

Source: Capital IQ c/o Shields and Company.

*Not meaningful.

INDEX

Page numbers followed by n indicate source notes and footnotes; *italicized* page numbers indicate material in exhibits.